ISBN 978-1-330-37650-8
PIBN 10044249

This book is a reproduction of an important historical work. Forgotten Books uses
state-of-the-art technology to digitally reconstruct the work, preserving the original format
whilst repairing imperfections present in the aged copy. In rare cases, an imperfection in
the original, such as a blemish or missing page, may be replicated in our edition. We do,
however, repair the vast majority of imperfections successfully; any imperfections that
remain are intentionally left to preserve the state of such historical works.

1 MONTH OF
FREE
READING

at

www.ForgottenBooks.com

By purchasing this book you are eligible for one month membership to ForgottenBooks.com, giving you unlimited access to our entire collection of over 700,000 titles via our web site and mobile apps.

To claim your free month visit:

www.forgottenbooks.com/free44249

A HISTORY OF FORMAL LOGIC · BOCHEŃSKI

A HISTORY
OF FORMAL LOGIC

BY

I. M. BOCHEŃSKI

TRANSLATED AND EDITED BY

IVO THOMAS

UNIVERSITY OF NOTRE DAME PRESS · 1961

A HISTORY OF FORMAL LOGIC

is a revised translation by Ivo Thomas of the German edition, *Formale Logik*,
by J. M. Bocheński, published and copyrighted by Verlag Karl Alber,
Freiburg/München, in 1956

PREFACE TO THE GERMAN EDITION

This history of the problems of formal logic, which we believe to be the first comprehensive one, has grown only in small part from the author's own researches. Its writing has been made possible by a small group of logicians and historians of logic, those above all of the schools of Warsaw and Münster. It is the result of their labours that the work chiefly presents, and the author offers them his thanks, especially to the founders Jan Łukasiewicz and Heinrich Scholz.

A whole series of scholars has been exceptionally obliging in giving help with the compilation. Professors E. W. Beth (Amsterdam), Ph. Boehner O.F.M. (St. Bonaventure, N.Y.), A. Church (Princeton), O. Gigon (Bern), D. Ingalls (Harvard), J. Łukasiewicz (Dublin), B. Mates (Berkeley, California), E. Moody (Columbia University, New York), M. Morard O.P. (Fribourg), C. Regamey (Fribourg/Lausanne) and I. Thomas O.P. (Blackfriars, Oxford) have been kind enough to read various parts of the manuscript and communicate to me many valuable remarks, corrections and additions. Thanks to them I have been able to remove various inexactitudes and significantly improve the content. Of course they bear no responsibility for the text in its final state.

The author is further indebted for important references and information to Mlle. M. T. d'Alverny, Reader of the Department of Manuscripts of the Bibliothèque Nationale in Paris, Dr. J. Vajda of the Centre National de la Recherche Scientifique in Paris, Professors L. Minio-Paluello (Oxford), S. Hulsewé (Leiden), H. Hermes and H. Scholz (Münster i. W.), R. Feys (Louvain) and A. Badawi (Fuad University, Cairo). Dr. A. Menne has been kind enough to read the proofs and make a number of suggestions.

My assistant, Dr. Thomas Räber, has proved a real collaborator throughout. In particular, I could probably not have achieved the translation of the texts into German without his help. He has also been especially helpful in the compilation of the Bibliography and the preparation of the manuscript for press.

In the course of my researches I have enjoyed the help of several European libraries. I should like to name here those in Amsterdam (University Library), Basel (University Library), Göttingen (Niedersächsische Landes- und Universitätsbibliothek), Kolmar (Stadtbibliothek), London (British Museum and India Office Library), Munich (Bayerische Staatsbibliothek), Oxford (Bodleian Library) and Paris (Bibliothèque Nationale); above all the Kern-Institut in Leiden and the institutes for mathematical logic in Louvain and Münster which showed me notable hospitality. Finally, last but not least, the Cantonal and University Library of Fribourg, where the staff has made really extraordinary efforts on my behalf.

The completion of my inquiries and the composition of this book was made materially possible by a generous grant from the Swiss national fund for the advancement of scientific research. This enabled me to employ an assistant and defray the costs of several journeys, of microfilms etc. My best thanks are due to the administrators of the fund, as to all who have helped me in the work.

Since the manuscript was completed, Fr. Ph. Boehner O.F.M. and Dr Richard Brodführer, editor of the series 'Orbis Academicus', have died. Both are to be remembered with gratitude.

I. M. BOCHEŃSKI

PREFACE TO THE ENGLISH EDITION

A. GENERAL

In this edition of the most considerable history of formal logic yet published, the opportunity has of course been taken to make some adjustments seen to be necessary in the original, with the author's full concurrence. Only in § 36, however, has the numeration of cited passages been altered owing to the introduction of new matter. Those changes are as follows:

German edition	English edition
36.13	**36.17**
36.14	**36.18**
36.15—17	**36.21—23**

Other alterations that may be noted are: the closing paragraphs of § 15 have been more accurately suited to the group of syllogisms which they concern; **16.17** appears here as a principle rejected, not accepted, by Aristotle; **27.28** has been re-interpreted and the lengthy citation dropped; a new sub-section, on the beginnings of combinatory logic, has been added to § 49. A few further items have been added to the Bibliography. On grounds of economy this last has been reproduced photographically; probably such German remarks and abbreviations as it contains will not much inconvenience its users.

A word needs to be said about § 5 A, 'Technical Expressions', which has naturally had to be largely re-written. In the orginal, the author expressed his intention of using 'Aussage' as a name for sentential *expressions*, and so for certain dispositions of black ink, or bundles of sound-waves. So understood, the word could be treated as generally synonymous with the Scholastic *'propositio'* and the English 'sentence' when used in an equally technical sense, and was deemed a tolerable translation of Russell's 'proposition' the reference of which is often ambiguous. But these equations evidently cannot be maintained here; for one thing, they would warrant the change of 'proposition' to 'sentence' throughout quotations from

Russell; secondly we prefer, with A. Church (**1.01**), to speak of 'propositional logic' rather than 'sentential logic'; and thirdly, one risks actual falsification of one's material by imposing on it a grid of sharp distinctions which for the most part belongs to a later period than anything here treated. As noted in the body of the work, the Stoics and Frege were alone in making the distinction between sign and significate as sharply as is now customary. So we have normally used 'proposition' where the author used 'Aussage' – always, indeed, when the Scholastic '*propositio*' needs translation. In Part V usage is of course largely conditioned by the fact that so many citations now appear in their original language.

B. ABÉLARD

As to the contents, an evident lacuna is the absence of any texts from the 12th century A.D., and the author himself has suggested that **30.03** is quite insufficient reference to Peter Abelard, described in an epitaph as 'the Aristotle of our time, the equal or superior of all logicians there have been' (**1.02**), and in similar words by John of Salisbury (**1.03**). We propose only to elaborate that single reference, by way of giving a taste of this twelfth century logic, closely based on Boethius in its past, growing in an atmosphere of keen discussion in its present, evidently holding the seeds of later Scholastic developments as exemplified in this book.

Abelard's consequences are certainly not fully emancipated from the logic of terms (cf. **30.03**) yet he realizes that *propositions* are always involved. His explanation of '*consequentia*' may first be noted:

1.04 A hypothetical proposition is called a 'consequence' after its consequent, and a 'conditional' after its condition.

Speaking later of a form of the laws of transposition (**43.33**) he says:

1.05 My opinion is that while the force of the inference lies in the terms, yet the whole proposition is to be denied. . . . Rightly the whole sequent and antecedent proposition is to be denied, since the inference lies between the entire propositions, though the force of the inference depends on the terms. . . . So that the hypothetical proposition is rightly said not to be composed of simple terms, but to be conjoined from several propositions, inasmuch as it propounds that what the sequent proposition manifests, follows from what the precedent (manifests). So that the denial is not to be effected according to the terms alone, but according to the entire propositions between which the relation of consequence is propounded.

Consequences themselves are distinguished from their metalogical formulations (cf. the commentary preceding **31.14**), the latter being called '*maximae propositiones*' and defined thus:

1.06 That proposition which contains the sense of many consequences and manifests the manner of proof common to their determining features (*differentiae*) according to the force of their relationship, is called a 'maximal proposition'. E.g. along with these consequences: 'if it is man, it is animal', 'if it is pearl, it is stone', 'if it is rose, it is flower', 'if it is redness, it is colour' etc., in which species precede genera, a maximal proposition such as the following is adduced: of whatever the species is predicated, the genus too (is predicated). . . . This maximal proposition contains and expresses the sense of all such consequences and manifests the way of yielding inference common to the antecedents.

There is a rich store of maxims in Abelard, but it is not always easy to see whether they belong to the logic of terms or propositions. This ambiguity has been noted with reference to Kilwardby (cf. § 31, B) where one might be tempted to think that it was unconscious. But the terminology is not subject to direct attention in Kilwardby; in Abelard it is, and the ambiguity is noted and accepted. The following passage may need apology for its length, but not for its great interest in respect of terminology, semantic considerations (on which we cannot here delay), maxims both of validity and invalidity, and the reduction of some of them to others, **1.06** and **1.07** are enough to establish the basis and essentials of § 31 firmly in the 12th century.

1.07 'Antecedent' and 'consequent' are sometimes used to designate complete enunciations as when in the consequence: if Socrates is man, Socrates is animal, we say that the first categorical is antecedent to the second; sometimes in the designation of simple terms (*dictio*) or what they signify, as when we say in regard to the same consequence that the species is antecedent to the genus, i.e. 'man' to 'animal', the nature or relationship provides inferential force. . . . But whether we take 'antecedent' and 'consequent' for simple terms or complete enunciations, we can call them the parts of hypothetical enunciations, i.e. the parts of which the consequences are composed and of which they consist, not parts of which they treat. For we cannot accept as true this consequence: if he is man, he is animal, if it treats of utterances (*vocibus*) be they terms or propositions. For it is false that if the utterance 'man' exists, there should also be the utterance 'animal'; and similarly in the case of enunciations or their concepts (*intellectibus*). For it is not necessary that he who has a concept generated by the precedent proposition should also have one generated from the consequent. For no diverse concepts are so akin that one must be possessed along with the other; indeed everyone's own experience will convince him that his soul does not retain diverse concepts and will find that it is totally occupied with each single concept while he has it. But if someone were to grant that the essences of concepts follow on one another like the essences of the things from which the concepts are gained, he would have to concede that every knower has an infinity of concepts since every proposition has innumerable consequences. Further, whether we treat of enunciations or of their concepts, we have to use their names in a consequence; but if 'man' or 'animal' are taken as names either of enunciations or concepts, 'if there is man there is animal' cannot at all be a consequence, being composed entirely of terms, as much as to say: 'if man animal'; indeed as a statement it is quite imperfect. To keep, therefore, a genuine relation of consequence we must concede that it is things which are being treated of, and accept the rules of antecedent and consequent as given in the nature of things. These rules are as follows:

(1) on the antecedent being posited, the consequent is posited;
(2) on the consequent being destroyed, the antecedent is destroyed, thus:
'if there is man there is animal', 'if there is not animal there is not man';
(3) neither if the antecedent is posited, is the consequent destroyed,
(4) nor if the antecedent is destroyed need the consequent be destroyed
(5) or posited, just as
(6) neither if the consequent is destroyed is the antecedent posited,
(7) nor if the same (the consequent) is posited is it (the antecedent) either posited
(8) or removed.

Since the last ((6)–(8)) are equivalent to the former ((3)–(5)) as also their affirmatives are mutually equivalent, the two sets must be simultaneously true or false. The two first rules

ABELARD

are also in complete mutual agreement and can be derived from one another, e.g. if it is conceded: if there is man there is animal, it must also be conceded: 'if there is not animal there is not man, and conversely.

When the first is true, the second will be proved true as follows, by inducing an impossibility. Let us posit this as true: if there is man there is animal, and doubt about this: if there is not animal there is not man, i.e. whether 'animal' negated negates 'man'. We shall confirm this in the following way. Either 'animal' negated negates 'man' or negated it admits 'man', so that it may* happen that when 'animal' is denied of something man may exist in that thing. Suppose it be conceded that when 'animal' is denied, man may persist; yet it was formerly conceded that 'man' necessarily requires 'animal', viz. in the consequence: if there is man there is animal. And so it is contingent that what is not animal, be animal; for what the antecedent admits, the consequent admits. . . . But this is impossible. . . .

Quite definitely propositional are the rules:

1.08 Whatever follows from the consequent (follows) also from the antecedent;

Whatever implies the antecedent (implies) also the consequent;

used in the derivation of categorical syllogisms.

While it is clear that the primary source of all this doctrine of consequence is the *De Differentiis Topicis* of Boethius, we can also see the germ of later developments in Abelard's realization that some are deducible from others (**1.07**, **1.09**), and his examinations of some that he finds doubtful (**1.10**).

It is noteworthy that categorical syllogisms are presented entirely by means of concrete instances and metalogical rules (*regulae*) — which are not reckoned as maxims since the inferential (or implicative) 'force' of the premisses is derived entirely from the disposition of the terms, is, in Abelard's terminology, 'complexional', a term preserved in Kilwardby. Variables of the object-language are nowhere used. Indeed, except in expositions of the Boethian hypothetical syllogisms, the only place we find variables in Abelard is a passage where he introduces a simple lettered diagram to help the intuition in an original argument:

1.11 If a genus was always to be divided into proximate species or proximate differences, every division of a genus

* Emending De Rijk's *possint* to *possit*

xi

would be dichotomous – which was Boethius's view. . . . But I remember having an objection to this on the score of (the predicament of) relation. . . . This will be more easily seen if we designate the members of the predicament by letters and distinguish its arrangement by a figure like this.

Relation

If now C and D were mutually related on the one hand, B and C on the other, since B is prior to its species D, while D is together with (*simul*) its relative C, B would precede C; so that B would precede both its species and its relative; hence also itself.

There follow two more arguments to show that the system suppos-ed figured stands or falls entire with any one of its parts.

There is no suggestion in Abelard that syncategorematica, important for later theory of consequences, are a primary concern of logic, the purpose of which he states as follows:

1.12 Logic is not a science of using or composing arguments, but of discerning and estimating them rightly, why some are valid, others invalid.

But he is puzzled about the signification, if any, of syncategore-matica, and refers to various contemporary views:

1.13 Conjunctions and prepositions ought to have some signification of their own. . . . What concepts are designated by expressions of this kind, it is not easy to say. . . . Some think that such expressions have sense but no reference (*solos intellectus generare, nullamque rem subiectam habere*) as they grant also to be the case with propositions. . . . There are also some who make out that logicians have quite removed such expressions from the class of significant ones. . . . The opinion I favour is that of the grammarians who make contributions to logic, that we should admit them as significant, but should say that their significance lies in their determining certain properties of the references (*res*) of the words governed by the prepositions. . . . Conjunctions too, as indicating conjunction of things, determine a property in their regard, e.g. when I say: 'a man and a horse runs', by the conjunction 'and' I unite them in runing, and at the same time indicate that by the 'and'.

The emergence of a logic of propositions from one of terms is exemplified in the rather sophisticated, and disputed, distinction between propositional and term connectives:

1.14 It is to be remarked that while disjunctive connectives are applied to the terms both of categorical and hypothetical propositions, they seem to have a different sense in each. . . . But some allow no difference . . . saying that there is the same proposition when it is said: 'Socrates is healthy or (*vel*) sick' and when it is said: 'Either Socrates is healthy or (*aut*) he is sick', reckoning every disjunctive as hypothetical.

Again of temporal propositions, compounded by means of 'when', which Abelard treats as conjunctives, he says:

1.15 It is evident in temporals that we should not estimate the relation of consequence according to any force in the relationship of terms, . . . but only in the mutual accompaniment (of the components).

And again, with the addition of truth-conditions:

1.16 In these (temporals) in which the relation of consequence is to be reckoned nothing else than coincidence in time . . . provided the members are true, people concede that the consequence is true, and otherwise false.

Some 'rules' follow for the construction of consequences on this basis. Among them the following deserves special notice:

1.17 Of whatever (hypotheticals) the antecedents are concomitant, the consequents too (are concomitant), thus: if when he is a man he is a doctor, when he is an animal he is an artificer.

This is Leibniz's *praeclarum theorema* (cf. **43.37**) in essentials, though it seems impossible to say whether Abelard envisaged it in its Leibnizian classical or its Russellian propositional form. He explains it indeed by saying that 'as "man" is necessarily antecedent to "animal", so "doctor" is to "artificer"', yet he clearly thinks of it as compounded of propositions. The fact is that the two kinds of logic were not yet perfectly clearly distinguished. A further indication that the full generality of propositional logic had not yet been achieved, though, as we have seen, it was already in the making, is that while Abelard gives us as a consequence: if he is man and stone, he is animal, he does not rise to: if he is man and stone, he is man.

There is evidently a vast deal more to be said both about the prowess and the limitations of this logician, both on this and other subjects, but we already exceed the limits of discussion proper to this history. It is, however, certain that the serious beginnings of Scholastic logic must be looked for in the 12th century.

IVO THOMAS

ACKNOWLEDGEMENTS

Grateful acknowledgements are due to Bertrand Russell for permission to quote from his *The Principles of Mathematics* (London, 1903), and to the respective publishers for permission to use passages from: *The Dialogues of Plato*, translated in English by B. Jowett (Oxford University Press); *The Works of Aristotle*, translated into English under the editorship of J. A. Smith and W. D. Ross (Oxford University Press); *Principia Mathematica*, by A. N. Whitehead and Bertrand Russell (Cambridge University Press, 1925–27); *Tractatus Logico-Philosophicus*, by L. Wittgenstein (Routledge and Kegan Paul, 1922); *Translations from the Philosophical Writings of Gottlob Frege*, by Peter Geach and Max Black (Basil Blackwell, Oxford, 1952); to The Belknap Press of Harvard University Press, for quotations from *The Collected Papers of Charles Sanders Peirce*, edited by Charles Hartshorne and Paul Weiss (copyright 1933 by the President and Fellows of Harvard University).

CONTENTS

PART I

Introduction

PART II

The Greek Variety of Logic

CONTENTS

I. The precursors

II. Aristotle

CONTENTS

CONTENTS

PART III

The Scholastic Variety of Logic

CONTENTS

CONTENTS

CONTENTS

CONTENTS

xxii

PART I

Introduction

§1. THE CONCEPT OF FORMAL LOGIC

Preliminary definition of the subject matter of the history of logic is hard to come by. For apart from 'philosophy' there is perhaps no name of a branch of knowledge that has been given so many meanings as 'logic'. Sometimes the whole of philosophy, and even knowledge in general, has been thus named, from metaphysics on the one hand, cf. Hegel, to aesthetics ('logic of beauty') on the other, with psychology, epistemology, mathematics etc. in between. With such a wide choice it is quite impossible to include in a history of logical problems all that has been termed 'logic' in the course of western thought. To do so would practically involve writing a general history of philosophy.

But it does not follow that the use of the name 'logic' must be quite arbitrary, for history provides several clues to guide a choice between its many meanings. This choice can be arrived at by the following stages.

1. First let us discard whatever most authors either expressly ascribe to some other discipline, or call 'logic' with the addition of an adjective, as for example epistemology, transcendental logic, ontology etc.

2. When we examine what remains, we find that there is one thinker who so distinctly marked out the basic problems of this residual domain that all later western inquirers trace their descent from him: Aristotle. Admittedly, in the course of centuries very many of these inquirers – among them even his principal pupil and successor Theophrastus – have altered Aristotelian *positions* and replaced them with others. But the essential *problematic* of their work was, so far as we know, in constant dependence in one way or another on that of Aristotle's *Organon*. Consequently we shall denote as 'logic' primarily those problems which have developed from that problematic.

3. When we come to the post-Aristotelian history of logic, we can easily see that one part of the *Organon* has exercised the most decisive influence, namely the *Prior Analytics*. At some periods other parts too, such as the *Topics* or the *Posterior Analytics*, have indeed been keenly investigated and developed. But it is generally true of all periods marked by an active interest in the *Organon* that the problems mainly discussed are of the kind already to hand in the *Prior Analytics*. So the third step brings us to the point of describing as 'logic' in the stricter sense that kind of problematic presented in the *Prior Analytics*.

4. The *Prior Analytics* treats of the so-called syllogism, this being defined as a λόγος in which if something is posited, something else necessarily follows. Moreover such λόγοι are there treated as formulas which exhibit variables in place of words with constant

meaning; an example is '*B* belongs to all *A*'. The problem evidently, though not explicitly, presented by Aristotle in this epoch-making work, could be formulated as follows. What formulas of the prescribed type, when their variables are replaced by constants, yield conditional statements such that when the antecedent is accepted, the consequent must be admitted? Such formulas are called 'logical sentences'. We shall accordingly treat sentences of this kind as a principal subject of logic.

5. Some logicians have limited themselves to the discovery, examination and systematic ordering of logical theorems, e.g. many scholastic and mathematical logicians, as also Aristotle himself in the *Prior Analytics*. But logic so understood seems too narrowly conceived. For two kinds of problem naturally arise out of the theorems. First those about their nature – are they linguistic expressions, word-structures, psychical forms or functions, objective complexes? What does a logical law *mean*, what does a statement mean? These are problems which nowadays are dealt with in semiotics. Second, problems relevant to the question how logical laws can be correctly applied to practical scientific thought. These were dealt with by Aristotle himself, principally in the *Posterior Analytics*, and nowadays are the concern of general methodology. So semiotic and methodological problems are closely connected with logic; in practice they are always based on semiotics and completed in methodology. What remains over and above these two disciplines we shall call *formal logic*.

6. A complete history of the problems of logic must then have formal logic at its centre, but treat also of the development of problems of semiotics and methodology. Before all else it must put the question: what problems were in the past posited with reference to the formulation, assessment and systematization of the laws of formal logic? Beyond that it must look for the sense in which these problems were understood by the various logicians of the past, and also attempt to answer the question of the application of these laws in scientific practice. We have now delimited our subject, and done so, as we think, in accordance with historical evidence.

But such a program has proved to be beyond accomplishment. Not only is our present knowledge of semiotic and methodological questions in the most important periods too fragmentary, but even where the material is sufficiently available, a thorough treatment would lead too far afield. Accordingly we have resolved to limit ourselves in the main to matters of purely formal logic, giving only incidental consideration to points from the other domains.

Thus the subject of this work is constituted by those problems which are relevant to the structure, interconnection and truth of sentences of formal logic (similar to the Aristotelian syllogism). Does it or does it not follow? And, why? How can one prove the

validity of this or that sentence of formal logic? How define one
or another logical constant, e.g. 'or', 'and', 'if--then', 'every' etc.
Those are the questions of which the history will here be considered.

§ 2. ON THE HISTORY OF THE HISTORY OF LOGIC

A. THE BEGINNINGS

The first efforts to write a history of logic are to be found among
the humanists, and perhaps Petrus Ramus may here be counted as
the first historian. In his *Scholarum dialecticarum libri XX* we find
some thirty long colums allotted to this history. To be sure, Ramus's
imagination far outruns his logic: he speaks of a *logica Patrum*
in which Noah and Prometheus figure as the first logicians,
then of a *logica mathematicorum* which alludes to the Pythagoreans.
There follow a *logica physicorum* (Zeno of Elea, Hippocrates, Demo-
critus etc.), the *logica Socratis, Pyrrhonis et Epicretici (sic!)*, the
logica Antistheniorum et Stoicorum (here the Megarians too are
named, among others Diodorus Cronus) and the *logica Academiorum*.
Only then comes the *logica Peripateticorum* where Ramus mentions
what he calls the *Aristotelis bibliotheca* i.e. the *Organon* (which
according to him, as in our own time according to P. Zürcher. S.J., is
not by Aristotle), and finally the *logica Aristoteleorum interpretum et
praecipue Galeni* (**2.01**).

This book was written in the middle of the 16th century. Some
fifty years later we find a less comprehensive but more scientific
attempt by B. Keckermann. His work (**2.02**) is still valuable, particularly for a large collection of accurately dated titles. It remains an
important foundation for the study of 16th century logic. But its
judgments are not much more reliable than those of Ramus. Keckermann seems to have given only a cursory reading to most of the
logicians he cites, Hospinianus (**2.03**) for example. The book is
indeed more of a bibliography than a history of logic.

B. PREJUDICES

For all his faults, Ramus was a logician; Keckermann too had
some knowledge of the subject. The same can seldom be said of their
successors until Bolzano, Peirce and Peano. Most historians of logic
in the 17th, 18th and 19th centuries treat of ontological, epistemological and psychological problems rather than of logical ones. Furthermore, everything in this period, with few exceptions, is so conditioned by the then prevailing prejudices that we may count the
whole period as part of the pre-history of our science.

These prejudices are essentially three:

1. First, everyone was convinced that formalism has very little to do with genuine logic. Hence investigations of formal logic either passed unnoticed or were contemptuously treated as quite subsidiary.

2. Second, and in part because of the prejudice already mentioned, the scholastic period was treated as a *media tempestas*, a 'dark middle age' altogether lacking in science. But as the Scholastics were in possession of a highly developed formal logic, people sought in history either for quite different 'logics' from that of Aristotle (not only those of Noe and Epictetus, as Ramus had done, but even, after his time, that of Ramus himself), or at least for a supposedly better interpretation of him, which put the whole investigation on the wrong track.

3. Finally, of equal influence was a strange belief in the linear development of every science, logic included. Hence there was a permanent inclination to rank inferior 'modern' books higher than works of genius from older classical writers.

1. Thomas Reid

As an example of how history was written then, we shall cite one man who had the good will at least to read Aristotle, and who succeeded in doing so for most parts of the *Organon*, though he failed for just the most important treatises. Here are his own words on the subject:

2.04 In attempting to give some account of the Analytics and of the Topics of Aristotle, ingenuity requires me to confess, that though I have often purposed to read the whole with care, and to understand what is intelligible, yet my courage and patience always failed before I had done. Why should I throw away so much time and painful attention upon a thing of so little real use? If I had lived in those ages when the knowledge of Aristotle's Organon entitled a man to the highest rank in philosophy, ambition might have induced me to employ upon it some years' painful study; and less, I conceive, would not be sufficient. Such reflections as these, always got the better of my resolution, when the first ardour began to cool. All I can say is, that I have read some parts of the different books with care, some slightly, and some perhaps not at all. . . . Of all reading it is the most dry and the most painful, employing an infinite labour of demonstration, about things of the most abstract nature, delivered in a laconic style, and often, I think, with affected obscurity; and all to prove general propositions, which when applied to particular instances appear self-evident.

5

In the first place this is a really touching avowal that Reid lectured on the teaching of a logician whom he had not once read closely, and, what is much more important, that for this Scottish philosopher formal logic was useless, incomprehensible and tedious. But beyond that, the texts that seemed to him most unintelligible and useless are just those that every logician counts among the most exquisite and historically fruitful.

Nearly all philosophers of the so-called modern period, from the humanists to the rise of mathematical logic, held similar views. In such circumstances there could be no scientific history of logic, for that presupposes some understanding of the science of logic.

The attitude towards formal logic just described will be further illustrated in the chapter on 'classical' logic. Here we shall delay only on Kant, who expressed opinions directly relevant to the history of logic.

2. Kant

Kant did not fall a victim to the first and third of the prejudices just mentioned. He had the insight to state that the logic of his time — he knew no other — was no better than that of Aristotle, and went on to draw the conclusion that logic had made no progress since him.

2.05 That *Logic* has advanced in this sure course, even from the earliest times, is apparent from the fact that since Aristotle, it has been unable to advance a step, and thus to all appearance has reached its completion. For if some of the moderns have thought to enlarge its domain by introducing *psychological* discussions ... *metaphysical* ... or *anthropological* discussions ... this attempt, on the part of these authors, only shows their ignorance of the peculiar nature of logical science. We do not enlarge, but disfigure the sciences when we lose sight of their respective limits, and allow them to run into one another. Now logic is enclosed within limits which admit of perfectly clear definition; it is a science which has for its object nothing but the exposition and proof of the *formal* laws of all thought, whether it be *a priori* or empirical. . . .

3. Prantl

It is a remarkable fact, unique perhaps in the writing of history, that Carl Prantl, the first to write a comprehensive history of western logic (**2.06**), on which task he spent a lifetime, did it precisely to prove that Kant was right, i.e. that formal logic has no history at all.

His great work contains a collection of texts, often arranged from a wrong standpoint, and no longer sufficient but still indispensable. He is the first to take and discuss seriously all the ancient and scholastic logicians to whom he had access, though mostly in a polemical and mistaken spirit. Hence one can say that he founded the history of logic and bequeathed to us a work of the highest utility.

Yet at the same time nearly all his comments on these logicians are so conditioned by the prejudices we have enumerated, are written too with such ignorance of the problems of logic, that he cannot be credited with any scientific value. Prantl starts from Kant's assertion, believing as he does that whatever came after Aristotle was only a corruption of Aristotle's thought. To be formal in logic, is in his view to be unscientific. Further, his interpretations, even of Aristotle, instead of being based on the texts, rely only on the standpoint of the decadent 'modern' logic. Accordingly, for example, Aristotelian syllogisms are misinterpreted in the sense of Ockham, every formula of propositional logic is explained in the logic of terms, investigation of objects other than syllogistic characterized as 'rank luxuriance', and so of course *not one* genuine problem of formal logic is mentioned.

While this attitude by itself makes the work wholly unscientific and, except as a collection of texts, worthless, these characteristics are aggravated by a real hatred of all that Prantl, owing to his logical bias, considers incorrect. And this hatred is extended from the teachings to the teachers. Conspicuous among its victims are the thinkers of the Megarian, Stoic and Scholastic traditions. Ridicule, and even common abuse, is heaped on them by reason of just those passages where they develop manifestly important and fruitful doctrines of formal logic.

We shall illustrate this with some passages from his *Geschichte der Logik*, few in number when compared with the many available.

Chrysippus, one of the greatest Stoic logicians, 'really accomplished nothing new in logic, since he only repeats what the Peripatetics had already made available and the peculiarities introduced by the Megarians. His importance consists in his sinking to handle the material with a deplorable degree of platitude, triviality and scholastic niggling', Chrysippus 'is a prototype of all pedantic narrow-mindedness' (**2.07**). Stoic logic is in general a 'corruption' of that previously attained (**2.08**), a 'boundless stupidity', since 'Even he who merely copies other people's work, thereby runs the risk of bringing to view only his own blunders' (**2.09**). The Stoic laws are 'proofs of poverty of intellect' (**2.10**). And the Stoics were not only stupid; they were also morally bad men, because they were subtle: their attitude has 'not only no logical worth, but in the realm of ethics manifests a moment deficient in morality' (**2.11**). — Of Scholasticism Prantl says: 'A feeling of pity steals over us when we see how even such partialities as are possible within an extremely limited field of view are exploited with plodding industry even to the point of exhaustion, or when centuries are wasted in their fruitless efforts to systematize nonsense' (**2.12**). Consequently 'so far as concerns the progress of every science that can properly be termed philosophy, the Middle Ages must be considered as a lost millennium' (**2.13**).

In the 13th century and later, things are no better. 'Between the countless authors who without a single exception subsist only on the goods of others, there is but one distinction to be made. There are the imbeciles such as e.g. Albertus Magnus and Thomas Aquinas, who hastily collect ill-assorted portions of other people's wealth in a thoughtless passion for authority; and those others, such as e.g. Duns Scotus, Occam and Marsilius, who at least understand with more discernment how to exploit the material at hand' (**2.14**). 'Albertus Magnus too . . . was a muddle-head' (**2.15**). To take Thomas Aquinas 'for a thinker in his own right' would be 'a great mistake' (**2.16**). His pretended philosophy is only 'his unintelligent confusion of two essentially different standpoints; since only a muddled mind can . . .' etc. (**2.17**).

Similar judgment is passed on later scholastic logic; a chapter on the subject is headed 'Rankest Luxuriance' (**2.18**). Prantl regrets having to recount the views of these logicians, 'since the only alternative interpretation of the facts, which would consist simply in saying that this whole logic is a mindless urge, would be blameworthy in a historian, and without sufficient proof would not gain credence' (**2.19**).

To refute Prantl in detail would be a huge and hardly profitable task. It is better to disregard him entirely. He must, unhappily, be treated as non-existent by a modern historian of logic. Refutation is in any case effected by the total results of subsequent research as recapitulated in this book.

4. After Prantl

Prantl exercised a decisive influence on the writing of history of logic in the 19th and to some extent also in the 20th century. Till the rise of the new investigations deriving from circles acquainted with mathematical logic, Prantl's interpretations and evaluations were uncritically accepted almost entire. For the most part, too, the later historians of logic carried still further than Prantl the mingling of non-logical with logical questions. This can be seen in the practice of giving a great deal of space in their histories to thinkers who were not logicians, and leaving logicians more and more out of account.

Some examples follow. F. Ueberweg, himself no mean logician, (he could, e.g. distinguish propositional from term-logic, a rare gift in the 19th century), devoted four pages of his survey of the history of logic (**2.20**) to Aristotle, two to 'the Epicureans, Stoics and

Sceptics', two to the whole of Scholasticism – but fifty-five to the utterly barren period stretching from Descartes to his own day. Therein Schleiermacher, for instance, gets more space than the Stoics, and Descartes as much as all Scholasticism. R. Adamson (**2.21**) allots no less that sixteen pages to Kant, but only five to the whole period between the death of Aristotle and Bacon, comprising the Megarians, Stoics, Commentators and Scholastics. A few years ago Max Polenz gave barely a dozen pages to Stoic logic in his big book on this school (**22.2**).

Along with this basic attitude went a misunderstanding of ancient logical teaching. It was consistently treated as though exhibiting nothing what corresponded with the content of 'classical' logic; all else either went quite unnoticed or was interpreted in the sense of the 'classical' syllogistic, or again, written off as mere subtlety. It is impossible to discuss the details of these misinterpretations, but at least they should be illustrated by some examples.

The Aristotelian assertoric syllogistic is distortedly present in 'classical' i.e. Ockhamist style (**34.01**) as a rule of inference with the immortal 'Socrates' brought into the minor premiss, whereas for Aristotle the syllogism is a conditional propositional form (§13) without any singular terms. Stoic logic was throughout absurdly treated as a term logic (**2.23**), whereas it was quite plainly a propositional logic (§20). Aristotelian modal logic (§15) was so little understood that when A. Becker gave the correct interpretation of its teaching in 1934 (**2.24**), his view was generally thought to be revolutionary, though in essence this interpretation is quite elementary and was known to Albert the Great (**33.03**). Aristotle and Thomas Aquinas were both credited with the Theophrastan analysis of modal propositions and modal syllogisms, which they never advocated (**2.25**).

No wonder then that with the rise of mathematical logic theorems belonging to the elementary wealth of past epochs were saddled with the names of De Morgan, Peirce and others; there was as yet no scientific history of formal logic.

C. RESEARCH IN THE 20th CENTURY

Scientific history of formal logic, free from the prejudices we have mentioned and based on a thorough study of texts, first developed in the 20th century. The most important researches in the various fields are referred to in the relevant parts of our survey. Here we shall only notice the following points.

The rise of modern history of logic concerning all periods save the mathematical was made possible by the work of historians of philosophy and philologists in the 19th century. These published for the first time a series of correct texts edited with reference to their context in the history of literature. But the majority of ancient

9

philologists, medievalists and Sanskrit scholars had only slight understanding of and little interest in formal logic. History of logic could not be established on the sole basis of their great and laborious work.

For its appearance we have to thank the fact that formal logic took on a new lease of life and was re-born as mathematical. *Nearly all* the more recent researches in this history were carried out by mathematical logicians or by historians trained in mathematical logic. We mention only three here: Charles Sanders Peirce, the forerunner of modern research, versed in ancient and scholastic logic; Heinrich Scholz and Jan Łukasiewicz, with their publications of 1931 and 1935 (**2.26, 2.27**), both exercising a decisive influence on many parts of the history of logic, thanks to whom there have appeared serious studies of ancient, medieval and Indian logic.

But still we have only made a start. Though we are already in possession of basic insights into the nature of the different historical varieties of formal logic, our knowledge is still mostly fragmentary. This is markedly the case for Scholastic and Indian logic. But as the history of logic is now being systematically attended to by a small group of researchers it can be foreseen that this state of affairs will be improved in the coming decades.

§3. THE EVOLUTION OF FORMAL LOGIC

As an introduction to the present state of research and to justify the arrangement of this book, a summary presentation of results is now needed. The view we present is a new one of the growth of formal logic, stated here for the first time. It is a view which markedly diverges not only from all previous conceptions of the history of logic, but also from opinions that are still widespread about the general history of thought. But it is no 'synthetic *a priori* judgment', rather is it a position adopted in accordance with empirical findings and based on the total results of the present book. Its significance seems not to be confined within the boundaries of the history of logic: the view might be taken as a contribution to the general history of human thought and hence to the sociology of knowledge.

A. CONCERNING THE GEOGRAPHY AND CHRONOLOGY OF LOGIC

Formal logic, so far as we know, originated in two and only two cultural regions: in the west and in India. Elsewhere, e.g. in China, we do occasionally find a method of discussion and a sophistic (**3.01**), but no formal logic in the sense of Aristotle or Dignāga was developed there.

Both these logics later spread far beyond the frontiers of their native region. We are not now speaking merely of the extension of

European logic to America, Australia and other countries settled from Europe; North America, for instance, which from the time of Peirce has been one of the most important centres of logical research, can be treated as belonging to the western cultural region. Rather it is a matter of western logic having conquered the Arabian world in the high Middle Age, and penetrated Armenian culture through missionaries.* Other examples could be adduced. The same holds for Indian logic, which penetrated to Tibet, China, Japan and elsewhere. Geographically, then, we are concerned with two vital centres of evolution for logic, whose influence eventually spread far abroad.

On the subject of the chronology of logic and its division into periods there is this to be said: this history begins in Europe in the 4th century B.C., in India about the 1st century A.D. Previously there is in Greece, India and China, perhaps also in other places, something like a pre-history of logic; but it is a complete mistake to speak of a 'logic of the Upanishads' or a 'logic of the Pythagoreans'. Thinkers of these schools did indeed establish chains of inference, but logic consists in studying inference, not in inferring. No such study can be detected with certainty before Plato and the Nyāga; at best we find some customary, fixed and canonical rules of discussion, but any complete critical appreciation and analysis of these rules are missing.

The history of western logic can be divided into five periods: 1. the ancient period (to the 6th century A.D.); 2. the high Middle Age (7th to 11th centuries); 3. the Scholastic period (11th to 15th centuries); 4. the older period of modern 'classical' logic (16th to 19th centuries); 5. mathematical logic (from the middle of the 19th century). Two of those are not creative periods — the high Middle Age and the time of 'classical' logic, so that they can be left almost unnoticed in a history of problems. The hypothesis that there was no creative logical investigation between the ancient and Scholastic periods might very probably be destroyed by a knowledge of Arabian logic, but so far little work has been done on this, and as the results of what research has been undertaken are only to be found in Arabic, they are unfortunately not available to us.

Indian logic cannot so far be divided into periods with comparable exactness. It only seems safe to say that we must accept at least two great periods, the older Nyāya and Buddhism up to the 10th century of our era, and the Navya (new) Nyāya from the 12th century onwards.

* I am grateful to Prof. M. van den Oudenrijn for having drawn my attention to this fact.

B. HOW LOGIC EVOLVED

Logic shows no linear continuity of evolution. Its history resembles rather a broken line. From modest beginnings it usually raises itself to a notable height very quickly — within about a century — but then the decline follows as fast. Former gains are forgotten, the problems are no longer found interesting, or the very possibility of carrying on the study is destroyed by political and cultural events. Then, after centuries, the search begins anew. Nothing of the old wealth remains but a few fragments; building on those, logic rises again.

We might therefore suppose that the evolution of logic could be presented as a sine-curve; a long decline following on short periods of elevation. But such a picture would not be exact. The 'new' logic which follows on a period of barbarism is not a simple expansion of the old; it has for the most part different presuppositions and points of view, uses a different technique and evolves aspects of the problematic that previously received little notice. It takes on a different shape from the logic of the past.

That holds in the temporal dimension for western and, with some limitations, for Indian logic. Perhaps it also holds in the spatial dimension for the relation between the two considered as wholes. We can indeed aptly compare Indian logic with ancient and Scholastic logic in Europe, as lacking the notion of calculation; but beyond that there is hardly any resemblance. They are *different* varieties of logic. It is difficult to fit the Indian achievements into a scheme of evolution in the west.

The essential feature of the whole history of logic seems then to be the appearance of different varieties of this science separated both in time and space.

C. THE VARIETIES OF LOGIC

There are in essence, so far as we can determine, four such forms:

1. *The Ancient Variety of Logic.* In this period logical theorems are mostly formulated in the object-language, and semantics is in being, though undeveloped. The logical formulae consist of words of ordinary language with addition of variables. But this ordinary language is as it were simplified, in that the chief words in it occur only in their immediate semantic function. The basis of this logic is the thought as expressed in natural language, and the syntactical laws of the language are presupposed. It is from this material that the ancient logicians abstract their formal laws and rules.

2. *The Scholastic Variety of Logic.* The Scholastics began by linking themselves to antiquity, and thus far simply took over and developed what was old. But from the end of the 12th century they started to construct something entirely new. This logic which is properly

12

their own is almost all formulated metalogically. It is based on and accompanied by an accurate and well-developed semantics. Formulae consist of words from ordinary language, with very few or no variables, but there results no narrowing of the semantic functions as in antiquity. Scholastic logic is accordingly a thorough-going attempt to grasp formal laws expressed in natural language (Latin) with plentifully differentiated syntactical rules and semantic functions. As in ancient logic, so here too we have to do with abstraction from ordinary language.

3. *The Mathematical Variety of Logic.* Here we find a certain regress to the ancient variety. Till a fairly late date (about 1930) mathematical logic is formulated purely in the object-language, with rich use of variables; the words and signs used have narrowly limited semantic functions; semantics remains almost unnoticed and plays not nearly so marked a role as in the Middle Ages and after its resurgence since about 1930. Mathematical logic introduces two novelties; first, the use of an artifical language; second, and more important, the constructive development of logic. This last means that the system is first developed formalistically and only afterwards interpreted, at least in principle.

Common to the three western varieties of logic is a far-reaching formalism and preponderantly extensional treatment of logical laws.

4. *The Indian Variety of Logic.* This differs from the western in both the characteristics just mentioned. Indian logic succeeds is stating certain formal laws, but formalism is little developed and is obviously considered to be subsidiary. Again the standpoint is preponderantly intensional in so far as the Indian logicians of the last period knew how to formulate a highly developed logic of terms without employing quantifiers.

The fore-going arrangement is schematic and oversimplified, especially in regard to ancient and Indian logic. One could ask, for instance, whether Megarian-Stoic logic really belongs to the same variety as Aristotelian, or whether it is on the contrary mainly new, having regard to its markedly semantic attitude.

Still more justified would perhaps be the division of Indian logic into different forms. One could find, for example, considerable justification for saying that Buddhist logic differs notably from the strict Nyāya tradition not only in its philosophical basis, nor only in details, but with this big difference that the Buddhists show a manifestly extensional tendency in contrast to the Nyāya commentators. Again, evidence is not lacking that the Navya Nyāya does not properly exhibit a quite new type of logic, since in some doctrines, as in the matter of *Vyāpti*, it takes over Buddhist modes of expression, in others it follows the Nyāya tradition, in others again it develops a new set of problems and takes up a fresh standpoint.

However the difference between Aristotle and the Megarian-Stoic school seems hardly significant enough to justify speaking of two different forms of logic. As to Indian logic our knowledge is so incomplete that it would be rash to draft a division and characterization of its different forms.

A further problem that belongs here is that of the so-called 'classical' logic. One *could* understand it as a distinct variety, since while it consists of fragments of scholastic logic (taking over for example the mnemonic *Barbara, Celarent* etc., yet these fragments are interpreted quite unscholastically, in an ancient rather than scholastic way. But the content of this logic is so poor, it is loaded with so many utter misunderstandings, and its creative power is so extremely weak, that one can hardly risk calling something so decadent a distinct variety of logic and so setting it on a level with ancient, scholastic, mathematical and Indian logic.

D. THE UNITY OF LOGIC

We said above that every new variety of logic contains new logical problems. It is easy to find examples of that: in Scholasticism there are the magnificent semiotic investigations about the *proprietates terminorum*, then the analysis of propositions containing time-variables, investigations about quantifiers, etc; in mathematical logic the problems of multiple quantification, description, logical paradoxes, and so on. It is evident that quite different systems of formal logic are developed as a result. To be sure, that also sometimes happens within the framework of a single form of logic, as when we single out Theophrastan modal logic as different from Aristotle's. The class of alternative systems of formal logic has increased greatly especially since *Principia Mathematica*.

One might therefore get the impression that the history of logic evidences a relativism in logical doctrine, i.e. that we see the rise of different *logics*. But we have spoken not of different logics, rather of different *varieties* of *one* logic. This way of speaking has been chosen for speculative reasons, viz. that the existence of many *systems* of logic provides no proof that logic is relative. There is, further, an empirical basis for speaking of one logic. For history shows us not only the emergence of new problems and laws but also, and perhaps much more strikingly, the persistent recurrence of the same set of logical problems.

The following examples may serve to support this thesis:

1. *The problem of implication.* Posed by the Megarians and Stoics (**20.05** ff.), it was resumed by the Scholastics (**30.09** ff.), and again by the mathematical logicians (**41.11** ff.). Closely connected with it, so it seems, was what the Indians called *vyāpti* (**53.20**, **54.07** f.). Perhaps more remarkable is the fact that the same results were

reached quite independently in different periods. Thus material implication is defined in just the same way by Philo (**20.07**), Burleigh (**30.14**) and Peirce (**41.12** f.), in each case by means of truth-values. Another definition is also first found among the Megarians (**20.10**), again, and this time as their main concept of implication, among the Scholastics (**30.11** f.), and is re-introduced by Lewis in 1918 (**49.04**).

2. The *semantic paradoxes* serve as a second example. Already posed in the time of Aristotle (**23.18**), discussed by the Stoics (**23.20**), the problem of these is found again in the Scholastics (**35.05** ff.), and forms one of the main themes in mathematical logic (§ 48). Re-discovery of the same solutions is again in evidence here, e.g. Russell's *vicious-circle principle* was already known to Paul of Venice.

3. A third group of problems common to western logic is that of questions about *modal logic*. Posed by Aristotle (§ 15), these questions were thoroughly gone into by the Scholastics (§ 33) and have taken on a new lease of life in the latest phase of mathematical logic (**49.03**).

4. We may refer again to the *analysis of quantifiers*: the results of Albert of Saxony and Peirce are based on the same understanding of the problem and run exactly parallel.

5. Similar correspondences can be noticed between Indian and western logic. D. H. H. Ingalls has recently discovered a long series of problems and solutions common to the two regions. Most remarkable is the fact that Indian logic, evolving in quite different conditions from western, and independently of it, eventually discovered *precisely* the scholastic syllogism, and, as did western logic, made its central problem the question of 'necessary connection'.

Still further examples could be adduced in this connection; it seems as though there is in the history of logic a set of basic problems, taken up again and again in spite of all differences of standpoint, and, still more important, similarly solved again and again.

It is not too easy to express exactly, but every reader who is a logician will see unmistakeably the community of *mind*, by which we mean the recurrent interest in certain matters, the way and style of treating them, among all inquirers in the field of what we comprehend within the different forms of formal logic. Read in conjunction our texts **16.19**, **22.16** ff., **31.22**, **33.20**, **41.11** ff. There can be no doubt that the same attitude and spirit is expressed in them all.

E. THE PROBLEM OF PROGRESS

Closely connected with the question of the unity of logic is the difficult problem of its progress. One thing is certain: that this problem cannot be solved *a priori* by blind belief in the continuous growth to perfection of human knowledge, but only on the basis of a thoroughly empirical inquiry into detail. We can only learn whether logic has progressed in the course of its history from that history itself. We cannot discover it by means of a philosophic dogma.

But the problem is not easily solvable with our present historical knowledge. One question which it involves seems indeed to be safely answerable, but the requisites for dealing with others are still lacking.

We can safely state the following:

1. The history of logic shows, as has already been remarked, no linear ascending development. Consequently in the case of an advance, it can only take place *firstly*, within a given period and form of logic, and *secondly*, so as to raise the later forms to a higher level than the earlier.

2. Some advance within single periods and forms of logic is readily perceivable. We can see it best in Indian, but also in Scholastic and mathematical logic. Every particular of these periods affords a safe criterion of progress; each of them has its essential problems, and by comparing their formulation and solution in different logicians of the same period we can easily see that the later writers pose the questions more sharply, apply better method to their solution, know more laws and rules.

3. If the history of logic is considered as a whole, here too a certain advance can be established with safety. This consists in the fact that new problems are forthcoming in the later forms of logic. Thus for example the highly wrought semiotic problematic of the Scholastics is quite new in comparison with that of antiquity, and therefore also more complete; the logical paradoxes (not the semantic ones) of the mathematical logicians are new; so too Albert of Saxony's problem of defining quantifiers is new. These are again only some examples from the many possible ones.

On the other hand, the following question seems to be still undecidable in the present state of knowledge: taking logic *as a whole*, is every later form superior to all earlier ones?

Too often this question is answered affirmatively with an eye on mathematical logic, particularly because people compare it with its immediate predecessor, 'classical' logic, and are struck by the mass of laws and rules which calculation makes available in the new form.

But 'classical' logic is by no means to be equated with the whole of older logic; it is rather a decadent form of our science, a 'dead period' in its evolution. Calculation, again, is certainly a useful tool for logic, but only as facilitating new insights into logical interconnection. It is undeniable that such insights, e.g. in the logic of relations, have been reached by its means, and the convenience and accuracy of this instrument are so great that no serious logician can now dispense with it. But we would not go so far as to say that calculation has *at every point* allowed mathematical logic to surpass the older forms. Think for example of two-valued propositional logic: the essentially new features introduced by *Principia Mathematica* are quite unimportant when we compare the scholastic treatment.

Once again the matter reduces to our insufficient knowledge of the earlier forms of logic. For years people spoke of a supposed great discovery by De Morgan; then Łukasiewicz showed that his famous law was part of the elementary doctrine of Scholasticism. The discovery of truth-matrices was ascribed to Peirce, or even Wittgenstein; Peirce himself found it in the Megarians. D. Ingalls found Frege's classical definition of number in the Indian Mathurānātha (17th century). And then we are all too well aware that we know, as has been said, only fragments of Scholastic and Indian logic, while much more awaits us in manuscripts and even in unread printed works. The Megarian-Stoic logic, too, is lost, except for a few poor fragments transmitted by its opponents.

Also highly relevant to the question of the continual progress of logic throughout its history is the fact that the earlier varieties are not simply predecessors of contemporary logic, but deal in part with the same or similar problems though from a different standpoint and by different methods. Now it is hard for a logician trained in the contemporary variety of logic to think himself into another. In other words, it is hard for him to find a criterion of comparison. He is constantly tempted to consider valuable only what fits into the categories of his own logic. Impressed by our technique, which is not by itself properly logic, having only superficial knowledge of past forms, judging from a particular standpoint, we too often risk misunderstanding and under-rating other forms.

Even in the present state of knowledge we can be sure that various points about the older forms still escape our comprehension. One example is the Scholastic doctrine of supposition, which is evidently richer in important insights and rules than the semiotic so far developed by mathematical logic. Another is perhaps the treatment of implication (*vyāpti*) by the thinkers of the Navya Nyāya. Still further examples could be given.

Again, when an unprejudiced logician reads some late-Scholastic texts, or it may be some Stoic fragments, he cannot resist the impression that their general logical level, their freedom of movement in a very abstract domain, their exactness of formulation, while they are equalled in our time, have by no means been excelled. The modern mathematical logician certainly has a strong support in his calculus, but all too frequently that same calculus leads him to dispense with thought just where it may be most required. A conspicuous example of this danger is provided by statements made for long years by mathematical logicians concerning the problem of the null class.

These considerations tell against the thesis that logic has progressed as a whole, i.e. from variety to variety; it looks as though we have insufficient grounds for holding it. But of course it does not at all follow that another thesis, viz. of a purely cyclic development of formal logic with continual recurrence of the same culminating points, is sufficiently established.

The historian can only say; we do not know whether there is an over-all progress in the history of logic.

§4. METHOD AND PLAN

A. HISTORY OF PROBLEMS, AND DOCUMENTATION

Conformably to the directions of the series *Orbis Academicus* this work will present a *documented* history of *problems*.

We are not, therefore, presenting a material history of logic dealing with *everything* that has any historical importance, but a delineation of the history of the *problematic* together with the complex of essential ideas and methods that are closely connected with it. We only take into account those periods which have made an essential contribution to the problematic, and among logicians those who seem to us to rank as specially good representatives of their period. In this connection some thinkers of outstanding importance, Aristotle above all, Frege too, will receive much fuller treatment than would be permissible in a material history.

The story will be told with the help of texts, and those originally written in a foreign language have been translated into English. This procedure, unusual in a scientific work, is justified by the consideration that only a few readers could understand *all* the texts if they were adduced in their original language. For even those readers with some competence in Greek are not automatically able to understand with ease a text of formal logic in that tongue. But the specialist logician will easiliy be able to find the original text by reference to the sources.

The passages quoted will be fairly thoroughly commented where this seems useful, for without some commentary many of them would not be readily intelligible.

B. PLAN OF THE WORK

In itself such a history admits of being arranged according to problems. One could consider first questions of semiotics, then propositional ones, then those of predicate logic etc., so as to pursue the whole history of each class of problems. E.g. the chapter on propositional logic could begin with Aristotle, go on to the Megarian-

Stoic theory of λόγος, then to the scholastic *consequentiae*, to the propositional interpretation of the Boolean calculus, to McColl, Peirce and Frege, to chapters 2—5 of the *Principia*, finally to Lukasiewicz.

Such a method of treatment is, however, forbidden by the non-linear evolution of logic, and above all by the fact that it takes on a different form in every epoch. For every particular group of problems within one variety is closely connected with other complexes of problems in the same variety. Torn from its context and ranged with the cognate problems in another variety, it would be, not just unintelligible, but quite misunderstood. The problem of implication provides a good example: the Scholastics put it in the context of their theory of meaning, and their theory is not to be understood apart from that. Every problem considered in a given variety of logic needs viewing in the context of the total problematic of that variety.

It is necessary, therefore, to arrange the whole history according to the varieties of logic. Within each we have tried to show the connection of the various groups of problems. This has, however, not proved to be the best course everywhere. In the discussion of antiquity a grouping of the material according to the chronology of logicians and schools has seemed preferable, especially because one logician, Aristotle, has an incomparably great importance.

C. CHARACTER OF THE CONTENTS

As our knowledge of many domains is still very fragmentary, we cannot aim at completeness. One period that is probably fairly important, the Arabian, cannot be noticed at all. Citations from Scholasticism are certainly only fragments. Even our knowledge of ancient and mathematical logic is far from satisfactory. Consequently this work serves rather as a survey of *some* aspects of the history of logical problems than as a compilation of all that is essential to it.

What is rather aimed at is a general orientation in whatever *kind* of problems, methods and notions is proper to each variety of logic, and by that means some presentation of the general course of the history of logic and its laws. The emphasis will be put on this course of the problematic as a whole.

Hence we have also decided to risk a short account of Indian logic, in spite of subjective and objective reasons to the contrary. For this logic seems to be of great interest precisely with reference to the laws of the whole development. At the same time it is the only form which has developed *quite independently* of the others. The chapter on Indian logic must, however, be managed differently from the rest, not only because our knowledge of the subject is even less sufficient than of Scholastic logic, but also because we have to rely on translations. This chapter will be treated as a kind of appendix.

§5. TERMINOLOGY

In order to establish a comparison between the problems and theorems which have been formulated in different epochs and languages, we have had to use a unified terminology in our comments. For the most part we have taken this from the vocabulary of contemporary formal logic. But as this vocabulary is not at all familiar to the majority of readers, we shall here explain the most important technical expressions.

A. TECHNICAL EXPRESSIONS

By 'expression', 'formula', 'word', 'symbol' etc. we here intend what Morris calls the *sign-vehicle*, and so the material component of the sign; i.e. a certain quantity of ink, or bundle of sound waves. A specially important class of expression is that of *sentences*, i.e. expressions which can be characterized as true or false. It must be stressed that a sentence, so understood, is an expression, a material sign, and not what that signs stands for. The word 'proposition' has been variously used, as synonymous with 'sentence' in the sense just explained (cf. **26.03**), more normally for a sentence precisely as meaningful (Scholastics generally), sometimes with various psychological and subjective connotations (cf. the 'judgment' of the 'classical' logicians), nowadays commonly as the objective content of a meaningful sentence (cf. the Stoic ἀξίωμα). In our commentaries we keep 'sentence' for the material expression, as above and use 'proposition' in the sense appropriate to the historical context and as indicated by normal usage, which seems frequently to approximate to that of the Scholastics.

We divide expressions into *atomic* and *molecular* (the thought is Aristotelian, cf. **10.14** and **10.24**), the former being without parts that are themselves expressions of the given language, the latter containing such parts. Molecular expressions are analysed sometimes into *subject* and *predicate* in accordance with the tradition of Aristotle and the Scholastics, sometimes into *functor* and *argument*. The functor is the determining element, the argument the one determined; this is also true of predicate and subject respectively, but the other pair of terms is more general in applicability. 'And', 'not', names of relations, are thought of as functors.

We distinguish between constant and variable expressions (again with Aristotle, cf. **13.04**), called *constants* and *variables* for short. The former have a determinate sense, the latter only serve to mark void places in which constants can be substituted. Thus, for example, in 'x smokes', 'x' is a variable and 'smokes' a constant. With Frege (**42.02**) we call a molecular expression which exhibits a variable a *function*. Thus we speak of *propositional functions*, that is to say of expressions which, if the variables that occur in them are properly replaced by constants, become sentences (or propositions in the Scholastic sense). '*x* smokes' is such a propositional function.

Among propositional functions we often mention the *logical sum* or *inclusive disjunction* of two propositions or terms, the *logical product* or *conjunction*, *implication* and *equivalence*. *Quantifiers* (cf. **44.01**), 'all', 'some', 'for every *x*', 'there is a *y* such that', are sometimes counted as functors.

Variables which can only be meaningfully replaced by propositions we call *propositional variables;* such as can only be meaningfully replaced by terms we call *term-variables.* Correspondingly we speak of laws of propositional logic and term-logic. Term-logic is divided into predicate-, class- (or classial), and relation-logic. Predicate-logic treats of intensions, class-logic of extensions; relation-logic is the theory of those special formal properties which belong to relations, e.g. symmetry (if *R* holds between *a* and *b*, then it also holds between *b* and *a*), transitivity (if *R* holds between *a* and *b* and between *b* and *c*, then it also holds between *a* and *c*) etc.

The general doctrine of signs we call, with W. Morris (**5.01**), *semiotic.* This is divided into *syntax* (theory of the relationships between signs), *semantics* (theory of the relationships between signs and their significates), and *pragmatics* (theory of the relationships between signs and those who use them). Correspondingly we speak of syntactical, semantic and pragmatic laws and theories. In the field of semantics we distinguish between the denotation and the meaning or sense of a sign — which denotes the object of which it is a sign (its reference), and means its content. (In translating Scholastic texts we use 'signifies' for '*significat*' and leave further determination to be judged, where possible, by the context.) Thus for example, the word 'horse' denotes a horse, but means what makes a horse a horse, what we might call 'horseness'. We distinguish further between *object-language* in which the signs denote objects that are not part of the language, and the corresponding *meta-language* in which the signs denote those of the object-language. In accordance with this terminology the word 'cat' in the sentence 'a cat is an animal' belongs to the object-language since it denotes a non-linguistic object, but in the sentence ' "cat" is a substantive' it belongs to the meta-language, since it denotes the word 'cat' and not a cat itself. When an expression is used as the name of another expression that has the same form, we follow the prescription of Frege (**39.03**) and write it between quotation-marks.

Finally we distinguish between logical *laws* and *rules*, as did the Stoics (§ 22, A and B) and Scholastics (cf. the commentary on **31.13**). Laws state what is the case, rules authorize one to proceed in such and such a way.

B. CONCERNING MATHEMATICO-LOGICAL SYMBOLISM

In divergence from the widespread practice, which is that of the author himself, all use of mathematico-logical symbolism has been avoided in the commentaries on texts not of this character. In many cases this symbolism affords easy abbreviation, and laws formulated by its means are much easier for the specialist to read than verbally expressed propositional functions or propositions. But two reasons militate against its use:

1. First, objectively, it introduces an appreciable risk of misunderstanding the text. Such a risk is present in every case of translation, but it is particularly great when one uses a terminology with so narrowly defined a sense as that of mathematical logic. Take, for example, signs of implication. Those at our disposal essentially reduce to two: '⊃' and 'F'. Which of them are we to use to express Diodorean implication? Certainly not the first, for that means Philonian implication; but not the second either, for that would mean that one was sure that Diodorus defined implication just like Lewis or Buridan, which is by no means certain. Another example is the Peano-Russellian paraphrase of Aristotelian syllogistic as it occurs in the *Principia* (**5.02**). It is undoubtedly a misinterpretation of Aristotle's thought, for it falsifies many laws of the syllogistic which on another interpretation (that of Łukasiewicz) can be seen to be correct (**5.03**).

Some notions not deriving from mathematical logic could indeed be expressed in its symbolism, e.g. the Philonian implication or that of Buridan; but to single out these for such interpretation and to make use of verbal formulation in other cases would be to cause a complication that is better avoided.

But of course that is not to say that no such symbolism ought to be employed for any form of logic. For particular logicians, or a particular form, the use of an artificial symbolism is not only possible, but to be desired. But then every case requires a *special* symbolism. What we cannot do is to create a unique symbolism suitable for all the ideas that have been developed in the different varieties of logic.

2. A subjective reason is provided by the limits of the work, which aims to make allowance for the reader who is formed in the humanities but innocent of mathematics. For such, and they are obviously the majority, mathematico-logical symbolism would not clarify his reading, but cloud it unnecessarily.

In these circumstances we have been at pains to use such texts as exhibit no artificial symbolism, even in the chapter on mathematical logic, so far as that is possible. Symbolic texts are of course cited as well, and in such a way that one who wishes to acquire the symbolic language of mathematical logic can learn the essentials from this work. But the texts which treat of the basic problems of logic have been chosen in such a way that they are as far as possible intelligible without a knowledge of this symbolism.

C. TYPOGRAPHICAL CONVENTIONS

All texts are numbered decimally, the integral part giving the paragraph in which the citation occurs, the decimals referring to a consecutive numbering within the paragraph.

Texts are set in larger type than the commentaries, except for formulas due to the author, which are also in larger type.

Added words are enclosed in round parentheses. Expressions in square parentheses occur thus in the text itself. Formulas are an exception to this: *all* parentheses occurring in them, together with their contents, occur so in the original texts.

Quotation marks and italics in ancient and scholastic texts are due to the author.

Remarks concerning textual criticism are presented in starred footnotes.

Special points concerning the chapter on Indian logic are stated in § 50, D.

PART II

The Greek Variety of Logic

§6. INTRODUCTION TO GREEK LOGIC

A. LOGICIANS IN CHRONOLOGICAL ORDER

Aristotle, the first historian of philosophy, calls Zeno of Elea the 'founder of dialectic' (**6.01**), but the first two men, so far as we know, to reflect seriously on logical problems were Plato and Euclid of Megara, both pupils of Socrates. And as Aristotle himself ascribes to Socrates important services in the domain of logic (**6.02**), or rather of methodology from which logic later developed, perhaps Socrates should be considered to be the father of Greek logic.

Aristotle was a pupil of Plato, and his logic undoubtedly grew out of the practice of the Platonic Academy. Aristotle's chief pupil and long-time collaborator, Theophrastus, provides the link between the logical thought of his master and that of the Stoa. For contemporaneously and parallel with Aristotelian logic there developed that derived from Euclid, of which the first important representatives were Megarians, Diodorus Cronus, Philo of Megara and others; later came the Stoics, who were closely connected with the Megarians, having Chrysippus as their most important thinker.

After the death of Chrysippus, disputes arose between the Peripatetic and Megarian-Stoic schools, the latter now represented by the Stoics alone, and syncretism became prominent. Even then logicians were not lacking, the more important among them being apparently the commentators on Aristotle's logical works (Alexander, Philoponus), many Sceptics (especially Sextus Empiricus), these in the 3rd century B.C., and finally Boethius (5th–6th century A.D.).

The following table shows the chronological and doctrinal connection down to Chrysippus:

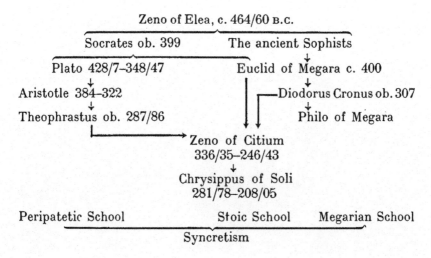

26

B. PERIODS

The problematic of formal logic by and large began with Aristotle. He was undoubtedly the most fertile logician there has ever been, in the sense that a great many logical problems were raised for the first time in his works. Close to him in the history of ancient logic is a group of thinkers who are nearly as important, the Megarian-Stoic school. Aristotle lived in the 4th century B.C.; the essential development of the Megarian-Stoic school can be thought of as ending with the death of Chrysippus of Soli at the end of the 3rd century B.C. Hence in Greek antiquity there is a relatively short period to be considered, from the second half of the 4th to the end of the 3rd century B.C.

But that does not mean that there was no logical problematic outside those 150 years. Even before Aristotle, a problematic emerged in the form of the pre-Socratic and Platonic dialectic, admittedly without ever developing into a logical theory. Again, long after the death of Chrysippus, and right on to the end of antiquity, i.e. to the death of Boethius (6th century A.D.), many reflections on logical problems are to be found in the so-called Commentators. This last period is not comparable in fruitfulness with that of Aristotle and the Stoics, but we are indebted to it for various insights worth remark.

Accordingly, from our point of view, antiquity is divided into three main periods:

1. the preparatory period, to the time when Aristotle began to edit his *Topics*.

2. the Aristotelian-Megarian-Stoic period, occupying the second half of the 4th to the end of the 3rd century B.C.

3. the period of the Commentators, from about 200 B.C. to the death of Boethius at the beginning of the 6th. century A.D.

The second of these periods is so outstandingly important that it is appropriate to divide it into two sections covering respectively Aristotle and the Megarian-Stoic school. We have then four temporally distinct sections: 1. pre-Aristotelians, 2. Aristotle and his immediate pupils, 3. the Megarian-Stoic school, 4. Commentators.

C. STATE OF RESEARCH

The history of Greek logic is the relatively best-known period in the development of formal logic. By contrast with the Middle Ages and after, and to some extent with logistic too, nearly all the surviving texts of the logicians of this age are readily available in good modern editions, together with a whole series of scientific treatises on their contents. In this connection there are two classes of works:

a) On the one hand the philologists have been busy for more than a century with solving numerous and often difficult problems of literary history relevant to ancient logic. Yet great as is the debt of gratitude owed by logicians to this immense work, one cannot pass over the fact that most philologists lack training in formal logic and so too often overlook just the most interesting of the ancient texts. Mostly, too, their interest centres on ontological, metaphysical, epistemological and psychological questions, so that logic comes to be almost always neglected. To quote only one example: logic is allotted few pages in Polenz's two big volumes on the Stoa. Then again editions made without a thorough logical training are often insufficient: Kochalsky's edition of Stoic fragments may serve as an instance.

b) On the other hand logicians too, especially since the pioneer work of G. Vailati (1904) and A. Rüstow (1908), have considered a fair number of problems arising from these texts. Epoch-making in this field is the article *Zur Geschichte der Aussagenlogik* (1935) by J. Łukasiewicz. The same scholar has given us books on the principle of contradiction in Aristotle and the Aristotelian (assertoric) syllogistic. Important too are the researches of H. Scholz whose *Geschichte der Logik* appeared in 1931 and who has written a number of other studies. Each of these has formed a small school. J. Salamucha investigated the concept of deduction in Aristotle (1930). I. M. Bocheński wrote a monograph on Theophrastus (1939); his pupils J. Stakelum (1940) and R. van den Driessche (1948) published studies on the period of the Commentators, the former dealing with Galen, the latter with Boethius. Boethius has also been dealt with by K. Dürr (1952). A. Becker, a pupil of Scholz, produced an important work on Aristotle's modal syllogisms (1933). B. Mates, influenced by Łukasiewicz, has made a thorough study of Stoic logic (1953).

The state of inquiry up to now may be characterized thus: Aristotelian studies are well opened up, though much is still missing, e.g. discussion of the *Topics;* good editions of the text are also available. We also have a very fair knowledge of Megarian-Stoic logic, though fresh editions of the texts are desirable. Very little work has been done on the period of the Commentators, but good editions are mostly to hand. The pre-Aristotelian period is also very insufficiently explored, notwithstanding the valuable studies by A. Krokiewicz, a philologist with logical training. Especially desirable is a thorough-going treatment of the beginnings of logic in Plato, though admittedly such a work would meet with considerable difficulties.

More exact information about the literature will be found in the Bibliography.

I. THE PRECURSORS

§ 7. THE BEGINNINGS

When Aristotle brought to a close the earliest part of his logical work, i.e. the *Topics* and *De Sophisticis Elenchis*, he could proudly write:

7.01 In the case of all discoveries the results of previous labours that have been handed down from others have been advanced bit by bit by those who have taken them on, whereas the original discoveries generally make an advance that is small at first though much more useful than the development which later springs out of them. For it may be that in everything, as the saying is, 'the first start is the main part': and for this reason also it is the most difficult; . . .

Of this inquiry, on the other hand, it was not the case that part of the work had been thoroughly done before, while part had not. Nothing existed at all.

A. TEXTS

What Aristotle says of 'this inquiry' of his seems still to hold good; we know of no logic, i.e. an elaborated *doctrine* of rules or laws, earlier than the *Topics*. Certain rules of inference, however, appear to have been consciously applied long before Aristotle by many Greeks, without being reflectively formulated, much less axiomatized. Aristotle himself says elsewhere that Zeno of Elea was the 'founder of dialectic' (**6.01**), and it is in fact hardly possible that Zeno formulated his famous paradoxes without being aware of the rules he was applying. The texts ascribed to him are only to be found in late commentators, including, however, Simplicius who was a serious investigator; criticism casts no doubt on their authenticity. We give some examples of his dialectic:

7.02 In the case that they (beings) are many, they must be as many as they are, neither more nor less. But if they are as many as they are, then they are limited (determinate). If (however) beings are many, then they are unlimited (indeterminate): since there are yet other beings between the beings and others again between those. And thus beings are unlimited (indeterminate).

7.03 If beings are, every one must have magnitude and volume, and one part of it must be distinct from another . . . And so, if they are many they must be at once small and great; small, since they have no magnitude, and great since they are un-limited (indeterminate).

7.04 If there is a place, it is in something; for every being is in something; but what is in something is also in a place. Hence the place will itself be in a place, and so on without end; hence there is no place.

G. Vailati stressed a text from Plato in which a similar process of inference is used:

7.05 *Socrates:* And the best of the joke is, that he acknow-ledges the truth of their opinion who believe his own opinion to be false; for he admits that the opinions of all men are true.

Theodorus: Certainly.

Socrates: And does he not allow that his own opinion is false, if he admits that the opinion of those who think him false is true?

Theodorus: Of course.

Socrates: Whereas the other side do not admit that they speak falsely?

Theodorus: They do not.

Socrates: And he, as may be inferred from his writings, agrees that this opinion is also true.

Theodorus: Clearly.

Socrates: Then all mankind, beginning with Protagoras, will contend, or rather, I should say that he will allow, when he concedes that his adversary has a true opinion, Protagoras, I say, will himself allow that neither a dog nor any ordinary man is the measure of anything which he has not learned – am I not right?

Theodorus: Yes.

The big fragment of Gorgias (**7.06**) also contains something similar, but this is so evidently composed in the technical terminology of the Stoics and betrays so highly developed a technique of logical thought that we cannot ascribe it to the Sophists, nor even to Aristotle. It is, however, possible that the young Aristotle did indeed formulate the famous proof of the necessity of philosophy in the way which it ascribed to him. This proof is transmitted to us in the following three passages among others:

7.07 There are cases in which, whatever view we adopt, we can refute on that ground a proposition under consideration. So for instance, if someone was to say that it is needless to philosophize: since the enquiry whether one needs to philosophize or not involves philosophizing, as he (Aristotle) has himself said in the *Protrepticus*, and since the exercise of a philosophical pursuit is itself to philosophize. In showing that both positions characterize the man in every case, we shall refute the thesis propounded. In this case one can rest one's proof on both views.

7.08 Or as Aristotle says in the work entitled *Protrepticus* in which he encourages the young to philosophize. For he says: if one must philosophize, then one must philosophize; if one does not have to philosophize, one must still philosophize. So in any case one has to philosophize.

7.09 Of the same kind is the Aristotelian dictum in the *Protrepticus*: whether one has to philosophize or not, one must philosophize. But either one must philosophize or not; hence one must in any case philosophize.

B. SIGNIFICANCE

All the texts adduced above spring from the milieu of 'dialectic'. This word that is later given so many meanings and is so mis-used originally had the same meaning as our 'discussion'. It is a matter of disputation between two speakers or writers. That is probably the reason why most of the rules of inference used here – termed, as it seems, 'logoi' – lead to negative conclusions: the purpose was to refute something, to show that the assertion propounded by the opponent is false.

This suggests the conjecture that these logoi belong to the field of propositional logic, that is to say that it is here a matter of logical relations between propositions as wholes without any analysis of their structure. And in fact the pre-Aristotelian logoi were often so understood. However, this interpretation seems untenable: Aristotle himself was aware of the very abstract laws of propositional logic only exceptionally and at the end of his scientific career; so much the less ought we to ascribe this – Megarian-Stoic – manner of thought to the pre-Aristotelians. We have rather to do with certain specifications of general rules of propositional logic. Thus these dialecticians were not thinking of, for example, the abstract scheme of propositional logic corresponding to *modus ponendo ponens:*

7.101 If p, then q; but p; therefore q:

but rather of the more special law

7.102 If A belongs to x, then B also belongs to x; but A belongs to x; therefore B also belongs to x.

We purposely omit quantifiers here, since while such were necessarily present to the thought obscurely, at this level there can be no question of a conscious acceptance of such logical apparatus.

We note further, that at the level of pre-Aristotelian dialectic, it is always a matter of rules not of laws; they are principles stating how one should proceed, not laws, which describe an objective state of affairs. That does not mean of course that the dialecticians were in any way conscious of the distinction between the two; but from our point of view, what they used were rules.

This said, we can interpret as follows the several logoi previously adduced. For each we give the *logical* sentence corresponding to the rule of inference which it employs.

Zeno quoted by Simplicius (**7.02, 03, 04**):

7.021 If A belongs to x then B and C also belong to x; but B and C do not belong to x; therefore neither does A belong to x.

7.022 Suppose that if A belongs to x, B also belongs to x and if B belongs to x, C also belongs to x, then if A belongs to x, C also belongs to x.

Plato in the *Theaetetus* (**7.05**):

7.051 If A belongs to x then A does not belong to x; therefore A does not belong to x.

Closer examination of that last item shows that it is much more complex and belongs to the realm of metalogic. Plato's thought proceeds after this fashion: the proposition propounded by Protagoras means: for every x, if x says 'p', then p. Let us abbreviate that by 'S'. Now there is some (at least one) x who says that S is not the case. Therefore S is not the case. Therefore if S, then not S. From which it follows in accordance with **7.051**, that S is not the case. While Plato certainly did not expressly draw this conclusion, he evidently intended it.

Aristotle quoted by Alexander (**7.07**):

7.071 Suppose that if A belongs to x, A belongs to x, and if A does not belong to x, A belongs to x, then A belongs to x.

The anonymous scholiast has a fuller formula (**7.09**):

7.091 If A belongs to x, then A belongs to x; if A does not belong to x, then A belongs to x; either A belongs to x or A does not belong to x; therefore A belongs to x,
but whether it actually occurred in Aristotle may be doubted. Possibly the *Protrepticus* contained merely the simple formula, transmitted by Lactantius:

7.092 If A does not belong to x, then A belongs to x; therefore A belongs to x.

A series of similar formulae underlie the processes to be found in the great Gorgias-fragment (**7.06**), but these appear to be so markedly interpreted in the light of Stoic logic that we have no guarantee of anything genuinely due to the sophist himself.

§ 8. PLATO

While Plato, in respect of many rules used in his dialectic, belongs to the same period as Zeno (as too does the youthful Aristotle), he begins something essentially new in our field, and that from several points of view.

A. CONCEPT OF LOGIC

In the first place Plato rendered the immortal service of being the first to grasp and formulate a clear idea of logic. The relevant text occurs in the *Timaeus* and runs:

8.01 God invented and gave us sight to the end that we might behold the courses of intelligence in the heaven, and apply them to the courses of our own intelligence which are akin to them, the unperturbed to the perturbed; and that we, learning them and partaking of the natural truth of reason, might imitate the absolutely unerring courses of God and regulate our own vagaries.

Such a conception of logic was, however, only possible for Plato, because he was, as it seems, the originator of another quite original idea, namely that of universally necessary laws (granting that he depended in this on the logos-doctrine of Heracleitus and other earlier thinkers). The concept of such laws is closely connected with Plato's theory of ideas, which itself developed through reflection on Geometry as it then existed. The whole post-Platonic western tradition is so penetrated with these ideas, that it is not easy for a westerner to grasp their enormous significance. Evidently no formal logic was possible without the notion of universally valid law. From this point of view the importance of Plato for the history of logic can best be seen when we consider the development of the science in India, i.e. in a culture which had to create logic without a Plato. One can see in the history of Indian logic that it took hundreds of years to accomplish what was done in Greece in a generation thanks to the élan of Plato's genius, namely to rise to the standpoint of universal validity.

We cannot here expound Plato's doctrine of ideas, as it belongs to ontology and metaphysics, and is further beset with difficult problems of literary history.

B. APPROACHES TO LOGICAL FORMULAE

Plato tried throughout his life to realize the ideal of a logic as laid down above, but without success. The following extracts from his dialectic, in which he makes a laboured approach to quite simple laws, show how difficult he found it to solve logical questions that seem elementary to us.

8.02 *Socrates:* Then I shall proceed to add, that if the temperate soul is the good soul, the soul which is in the opposite condition, that is, the foolish and intemperate, is the bad soul. – Very true. – And will not the temperate man do what is proper, both in relation to the gods and to men; – for he would not be temperate if he did not? – Certainly he will do what is proper.

8.03 *Socrates:* Tell me, then, – Is not that which is pious necessarily just?

Euthyphro: Yes.

Socrates: And is, then, all which is just pious? or, is that which is pious all just, but that which is just, only in part and not all, pious?

Euthyphro: I do not understand you, Socrates.

8.04 When you asked me, I certainly did say that the courageous are the confident; but I was never asked whether the confident are the courageous; if you had asked me, I should have answered 'Not all of them:' and what I did answer you have not proved to be false, although you proceeded to show that those who have knowledge are more courageous than they were before they had knowledge, and more courageous than others who have no knowledge, and were then led on to think that courage is the same as wisdom. But in this way of arguing you might come to imagine that strength is wisdom. You might begin by asking whether the strong are able, and I should say 'Yes'; and then whether those who know how to wrestle are not more able to wrestle than those who do not know how to wrestle, and more able after than before they had learned, and I should assent. And when I had admitted this, you might use my admissions in such a way as to prove that upon my view wisdom is strength; whereas in that case I should not have admitted, any more than in the other, that the able are strong, although I have admitted that the strong are able. For there is a difference between ability and strength; the former is given by knowledge as well as by madness or rage, but strength comes from nature and a healthy state of the body. And in like manner I say of confidence and courage, that they are not the same; and I argue that the courageous are confident, but not all the confident courageous. For confidence may be given to men by art, and also, like ability, by madness and rage; but courage comes to them from nature and the healthy state of the soul.

In the first of these texts is involved the (false) thesis: Suppose, if A belongs to x, B also belongs to x, then: if A does not belong to x, then B does not belong to x. The second shows the difficulties found concerning the convertibility of universal affirmative sentences: viz. whether 'all B is A' follows from 'all A is B'. The third text shows still more clearly how hard Plato felt these questions to be; it further has the great interest that, to show the invalidity of the foregoing rule of conversion, he betakes himself to complicated extra-logical discussions – about bodily strength, for instance.

C. DIAERESIS

Yet Plato's approximations were not without fruit. He seems to have been the first to progress from a negative dialectic to the concept of positive proof; for him the aim of dialectic is not to refute the opinions of opponents but positive 'definition of the essence'. In this he definitely directed attention to the logic of predicates, which is probably the cause of Aristotelian logic taking the form it did. The chief goal which Plato set himself was to discover essences, i.e. to find statements which between them define what an object is. For this he found a special method – the first logical, consciously elaborated inferential procedure known to us – namely his famous 'hunt' for the definition by division (διαίρεσις). How thoroughly conscious he was of not only using such a method but of endeavouring to give it the clearest possible formulation, we see in the celebrated text of the *Sophist* in which the method, before being practised, is applied in an easy example:

8.05 *Stranger:* Meanwhile you and I will begin together and enquire into the nature of the Sophist, first of the three: I should like you to make out what he is and bring him to light in a discussion; for at present we are only agreed about the name, but of the thing to which we both apply the name possibly you have one notion and I another; whereas we ought always to come to an understanding about the thing itself in terms of a definition, and not merely about the name minus the definition. Now the tribe of Sophists which we are investigation is not easily caught or defined; and the world has long ago agreed, that if great subjects are to be adequately treated, they must be studied in the lesser and easier instances of them before we proceed to the greatest of all. And as I know that the tribe of Sophists is troublesome and hard to be caught, I should recommend that we practise beforehand the method which is to be applied to him on some simple and smaller thing, unless you can suggest a better way.

Theaetetus: Indeed I cannot.

Stranger: Then suppose that we work out some lesser example which will be a pattern of the greater?

Theaetetus: Good.

Stranger: What is there which is well known and not great, and is yet as susceptible of definition as any larger thing? Shall I say an angler? He is familiar to all of us, and not a very interesting or important person.

Theaetetus: He is not.

Stranger: Yet I suspect that he will furnish us with the sort of definition and line of enquiry which we want.

Theaetetus: Very good.

Stranger: Let us begin by asking whether he is a man having art or not having art, but some other power.

Theaetetus: He is clearly a man of art.

Stranger: And of arts there are two kinds?

. . . .

Stranger: Seeing, then, that all arts are either acquisitive or creative, in which class shall we place the art of the angler?

Theaetetus: Clearly in the acquisitive class.

Stranger: And the acquisitive may be subdivided into two parts: there is exchange, which is voluntary and is effected by gifts, hire, purchase; and the other part of acquisitive, which takes by force of word or deed, may be termed conquest?

Theaetetus: That is implied in what has been said.

Stranger: And may not conquest be again subdivided?

Theaetetus: How?

Stranger: Open force may be called fighting, and secret force may have the general name of hunting?

Theaetetus: Yes.

Stranger: And there is no reason why the art of hunting should not be further divided.

Theaetetus: How would you make the division?

Stranger: Into the hunting of living and of lifeless prey.

Theaetetus: Yes, if both kinds exist.

Stranger: Of course they exist; but the hunting after lifeless things having no special name, except some sorts of diving, and other small matters, may be omitted; the hunting after living things may be called animal hunting.

Theaetetus: Yes.

Stranger: And animal hunting may be truly said to have two divisions, land-animal hunting, which has many kinds and names, and water-animal hunting, or the hunting after animals who swim?

Theaetetus: True.

Stranger: And of swimming animals, one class lives on the wing and the other in the water?

Theaetetus: Certainly.

Stranger: Fowling is the general term under which the hunting of all birds is included.

Theaetetus: True.

Stranger: The hunting of animals who live in the water has the general name of fishing.

Theaetetus: Yes.

Stranger: And this sort of hunting may be further divided also into two principal kinds?

Theaetetus: What are they?

Stranger: There is one kind which takes them in nets, another which takes them by a blow.

Theaetetus: What do you mean, and how do you distinguish them?

Stranger: As to the first kind – all that surrounds and encloses anything to prevent egress, may be rightly called an enclosure.

Theaetetus: Very true.

Stranger: For which reason twig baskets, casting-nets, nooses, creels, and the like may all be termed 'enclosures'?

Theaetetus: True.

Stranger: And therefore this first kind of capture may be called by us capture with enclosures, or something of that sort?

Theaetetus: Yes.

Stranger: The other kind, which is practised by a blow with hooks and three-pronged spears, when summed up under one name, may be called striking, unless you, Theaetetus, can find some better name?

Theaetetus: Never mind the name – what you suggest will do very well.

Stranger: There is one mode of striking, which is done at night, and by the light of a fire, and is by the hunters themselves called firing, or spearing by firelight.

Theaetetus: True.

Stranger: And the fishing by day is called by the general name of barbing, because the spears, too, are barbed at the point.

Theaetetus: Yes, that is the term.

Stranger: Of this barb-fishing, that which strikes the fish who is below from above is called spearing, because this is the way in which the three-pronged spears are mostly used.

Theaetetus: Yes, it is often called so.

Stranger: Then now there is only one kind remaining.

Theaetetus: What is that ?

Stranger: When a hook is used, and the fish is not struck in any chance part of his body, as he is with the spear, but only about the head and mouth, and is then drawn out from below upwards with reeds and rods: – What is the right name of that mode of fishing, Theaetetus?

Theaetetus: I suspect that we have now discovered the object of our search.

Stranger: Then now you and I have come to an understanding not only about the name of the angler's art, but about the definition of the thing itself. One half of all art was acquisitive – half of the acquisitive art was conquest or taking by force, half of this was hunting, and half of hunting was hunting animals, half of this was hunting water animals – of this again, the under half was fishing, half of fishing was striking; a part of striking was fishing with a barb, and one half of this again, being the kind which strikes with a hook and draws the fish from below upwards, is the art which we have been seeking, and which from the nature of the operation is denoted angling or drawing up.

Theaetetus: The result has been quite satisfactorily brought out.

The process is evidently not conclusive: as Aristotle has forcibly shown (**8.06**), it involves a succession of assertions, not a proof; it may be helpful as a method, but it is not formal logic.

Formal logic is reserved for Aristotle. But a close examination of the contents of his logical works assures us that everything contained in the *Organon* is conditioned in one way or another by the practice of Platonism. The *Topics* is probably only a conscious elaboration of the numerous logoi current in the Academy; even the *Analytics*, invention of Aristotle's own as it was, is evidently based on 'division', which it improved and raised to the level of a genuine logical process. That is the second great service which Plato rendered to formal logic: his thought made possible the emergence of the science with Aristotle.

II. ARISTOTLE

§9. THE WORK OF ARISTOTLE AND THE PROBLEMS OF ITS LITERARY HISTORY

The surviving logical works of Aristotle set many difficult problems of literary history which as yet are only partly solved. They are of outstanding importance for the history of the problems of logic, since within the short span of Aristotle's life formal logic seems to have made more progress than in any other epoch. It is no exaggeration to say that Aristotle has a unique place in the history of logic in that 1. he was the first formal logician, 2. he developed formal logic in at least *two* (perhaps three) different forms, 3. he consciously elaborated some parts of it in a remarkably complete way. Furthermore, he exercised a decisive influence on the history of logic for more than two thousand years, and even today much of the doctrine is traceable back to him. It follows that an adequate understanding of the development of his logical thought is of extreme importance for an appreciation of the history of logical problems in general, and particularly of course for western logic.

A. WORKS

The surviving works of the Stagirite were set in order and edited by Andronicus of Rhodes in the first century B.C. The resulting *Corpus Aristotelicum* contains, as to logical works, first and foremost what was later called the *Organon*, comprising:
1. The *Categories*,
2. About Propositions (properly: *About Interpretation;* we shall use the title *Hermeneia*),
3. The *Prior Analytics*, two books: A and B,
4. The *Posterior Analytics*, two books: A and B,
5. The *Topics*, eight books: A, B, Γ, Δ, E, Z, H, Θ,
6. The *Sophistic Refutations*, one book.

Besides these, the whole fourth book (Γ) of the so-called *Metaphysics* is concerned with logical problems, while other works, e.g. the *Rhetoric* and *Poetics* contain occasional points of logic.

B. PROBLEMS

The most important problems concerning the *Organon* are the following:

1. Authenticity

In the past the genuineness of all Aristotle's logical writings has often been doubted. Today, apart from isolated passages and perhaps individual chapters, the *Categories* alone is seriously considered to be spurious. The doubt about the genuineness of the

40

Hermeneia seems not convincing. The remaining works rank by and large as genuine. *

2. Character

Should we view the logical works of Aristotle as methodically constructed and systematic treatises? Researches made hitherto allow us to suppose this only for some parts of the *Organon*. The *Hermeneia* and *Topics* enjoy the relatively greatest unity. The *Prior Analytics* are evidently composed of several strata, while the *Posterior Analytics* are mainly rather a collection of notes for lectures than a systematic work. But even in those parts of the *Organon* that are systematically constructed later additions are to be found here and there.

3. Chronology

The *Organon*, arranged as we have it, is constructed on a systematic principle: the *Categories* treats of terms, the *Hermeneia* of propositions, the remaining works of inference: thus the *Prior Analytics* treats of syllogisms in general, the three other works successively of apodeictic (scientific), dialectical and sophistical syllogisms. For this systematization Andronicus found support in the very text of the *Organon*; e.g. at the beginning of the *Prior Analytics* it is said (**9.02**) that the syllogism consists of propositions (πρότασις), these of terms (ὅρος). In the *Topics* (**9.03**) and also in the *Prior Analytics* (**9.04**) the syllogism is analysed in just that way. At the end of the *Sophistic Refutations* occurs the sentence already cited (**7.01**), which appears to indicate that this work is the latest of Aristotle's logical works.

It is also not impossible that at the end of his life Aristotle himself drafted an arrangement of his logic and accordingly ordered his notes and treatises somewhat as follows. But of course this late systematization has, to our present knowledge, little to do with the actual development of this logic.

We have no extrinsic criteria to help us establish the chronological sequence of the different parts of the *Organon*. On the other hand their content affords some assistance, as will now be briefly explained. **

---

* The thesis of Josef Zürcher (**9.01**) that nearly all the formal logic in the *Organon* is due not to Aristotle but to his pupil Theophrastus, is not worth serious consideration.

** Chr. Brandis opened up the great matter of the literary problems of the *Organon* in his paper *Über die Reihenfolge des aristotelischen Organons* (**9.05**); the well-known work of W. Jäger (**9.06**) contributed important insights; its basic pre-suppositions were applied to the *Organon* by F. Solmsen (**9.07**). Solmsen's opinions were submitted to a thorough criticism by Sir W. D. Ross (**9.08**) with an adverse result in some cases. Important contributions to the chronology of the *Organon* are to be found in A. Becker (**9.09**) and J. Lukasiewicz (**9.10**).

a. Chronological criteria

aa) A first criterion to determine the relative date of origin is afforded by the fact that the syllogism in the sense of the *Prior Analytics* (we shall call it the 'analytical syllogism') is completely absent from several parts of the *Organon*. But it is one of the most important discoveries, and it can hardly be imagined that Aristotle would have failed to make use of it, once he had made it. We conclude that works in which there are no analytic syllogisms are earlier than those in which they occur.

bb) In some parts of the *Organon* we find variables (viz. the letters A, B, Γ, etc.), in others not. But variables are another epoch-making discovery in the domain of logic, and the degree to which it impressed Aristotle can be seen in the places where he uses and abuses them to the point of tediousness. Now there are some works where variables would be very useful but where they do not occur. We suppose that these works are earlier than those where they do occur.

cc) The third criterion – afforded by the technical level of the thought – cannot, unlike the first two, be formulated simply, but is apparent to every experienced logician at his first perusal of a text. From this point of view there are big differences between the various passages of the *Organon*: in some we find ourselves at a still very primitive level, reminiscent of pre-Socratic logic, while in others Aristotle shows himself to be the master of a strictly formal and very pure logical technique. One aspect of this progress appears in the constantly developing analysis of statements: at first this is accomplished by means of the simple subject-predicate schema $(S - P)$, then quantifiers occur ('P belongs [does not belong] to all, to none, to some S'), finally we meet a subtle formula that reminds us of the modern formal implication: 'All that belongs to S, belongs also to P'. This criterion can be formulated as follows: the higher and more formal the technique of analysis and proof, so much the later is the work.

dd) Modal logic corresponds much better with Aristotle's own philosophy (which contains the doctrine of act and potency as an essential feature) than does purely assertoric logic in which the distinction between act and potency obtains no expression. Assertoric logic fits much better with the Platonism to which Aristotle subscribed in his youth. Accordingly we may view those writings and chapters containing modal logic as having been composed later.

ee) Some of these criteria can be further sharpened. Thus we can trace some development in the theory of analytic syllogism. Again, Aristotle seems to have used letters at first as mere abbreviations for words and only later as genuine variables. Finally one can detect a not insignificant progress in the structure of modal logic.

It may certainly be doubted whether any one of these criteria is

of value by itself for establishing the chronology. But when all, or
at least several of them point in the same direction, the resulting
sequence seems to enjoy as high a degree of probability as is ever
possible in the historical sciences.

b. Chronological list

The application of these criteria enable us to draw up the following
chronological list of Aristotle's logical writings:

aa) The *Topics* (together with the *Categories* if this is to be accepted as genuine) undoubtedly comes at the start. There is to be found
in it no trace of the analytic syllogism, no variables, no modal logic,
and the technical level of the thought is relatively low. While the
Sophistic Refutations simply forms the last book of the *Topics*, it
appears to have been composed a little later. Book Γ of the *Metaphysics* probably belongs to the same period. The *Topics* and the
Refutations together contain Aristotle's *first logic*. The remark at
the end of the *Sophistic Refutations* about the 'whole' of logic
refers to *that* elaboration.

bb) The *Hermeneia* and – perhaps – book B of the *Posterior
Analytics* form a kind of transitional stage: the syllogistic can be
seen emerging. In the *Hermeneia* we hear nothing of syllogism and
there are no variables. Both, but evidently only in an early stage
of development, occur in *Posterior Analytics* book B. The technical
level of thought is much higher than in the *Topics*. The *Hermeneia*
also contains a doctrine of modality, which is, however, quite
primitive compared with that in the *Prior Analytics*.

cc) Book A of the *Prior Analytics*, with the exception of chapters
8–22, contains Aristotle's *second logic*, a fully developed assertoric
syllogistic. He is by now in possession of a clear idea of analytic
syllogism, uses variables with sureness, and moves freely at a relatively high technical level. The analysis of propositions has been
deepened. Missing, as yet, are modal logic, and reflective consideration of the syllogistic system. Perhaps book A of the *Posterior
Analytics* may be ascribed to the same period. Solmsen made this
the first of all the analytic books, but W. D. Ross's arguments
against this seem convincing. (The latter holds that book B of the
Posterior Analytics is also later than the *Prior*.)

dd) Finally we may ascribe to a still later period chapters 8–22 of
book A, which contains the modal syllogistic logic, and book B of
the *Prior Analytics*. These can be said to contain Aristotle's *third
logic*, which differs less from the second than does the second from
the first. We find here a developed modal logic, marred admittedly
by many incompletenesses and evidently not finished, and also
penetrating remarks, partly metalogical, about the system of

syllogistic. In them Aristótle offers us insights into formal logic of remarkable subtlety and acuteness. He states too some theorems of propositional logic with the aid of propositional variables.

Of course there can be no question of absolute certainty in answering the chronological questions, especially as the text is corrupt in many places or sprinkled with bits from other periods. It is only *certain* that the *Topics* and *Sophistic Refutations* contain a different and earlier logic than the *Analytics*, and that the *Hermeneia* exhibits an intermediate stage. For the rest we have well-founded hypotheses which can lay claim at least to great probability.

In accordance with these hypotheses we shall speak of three logics of Aristotle.

§ 10. CONCEPT OF LOGIC. SEMIOTIC

A. NAME AND PLACE OF LOGIC

Aristotle has no special technical name for logic: what we now call 'logical' he calls 'analytic' (ἀναλυτικός: **10.01**) or 'following from the premisses' (ἐκ τῶν κειμένων: **10.02**), while the expression 'logical' (λογικός) means the same as our 'probable' (**10.03**) or again 'epistemological'.

10.04 Of propositions and problems there are – to comprehend the matter in outline – three divisions: for some are ethical propositions, some are on natural philosophy, while some are logical. . . such as this are logical, e.g. 'Is the knowledge of opposites the same or not?'

The question whether logic is a part of philosophy or its instrument (ὄργανον) – and hence an art – is nowhere raised by Aristotle in the extant works.

B. THE SUBJECT-MATTER OF LOGIC

Yet Aristotle knew well enough what he demanded of logic. That appears from the model statements of the subject-matter of his logical treatises. For instance he says in the *Topics:*

10.05 First then we must say what reasoning is, and what its varieties are, in order to grasp dialectical reasoning: for this is the object of our search in the treatise before us. Now reasoning is an argument in which, certain things being laid down, something other than these necessarily comes about through them. It is a 'demonstration' when the premisses from which the reasoning starts are true and primary . . .

44

reasoning, on the other hand, is 'dialectical', if it reasons from opinions that are generally accepted. . . . Again, reasoning is 'contentious' if it starts from opinions that seem to be generally accepted, but are not really such, or again if it merely seems to reason from opinions that are or seem to be generally accepted.

Compare the following text from the *Prior Analytics:*

10.06 After these distinctions we now state by what means, when, and how every syllogism is produced; subsequently we must speak of demonstration. Syllogism should be discussed before demonstration, because syllogism is the more general: demonstration is a sort of syllogism, but not every syllogism is a demonstration.

The thought is perfectly clear: Aristotle is looking for relations of dependence which authorize necessary inference, and in that connection makes a sharp distinction between the validity of this relation and the kind of premisses, or their truth. The text contains what is historically the first formulation of the concept of a *formal* logic, universally valid and independent of subject-matter.

Accordingly it is syllogism which is the subject of logic. This is a form of speech (λόγος) consisting of premisses (προτάσεις) themselves composed of terms (ὅροι). 'Premiss' and 'term' are thus defined by Aristotle:

10.07 A premiss is a form of speech which affirms or denies something of something. . . . A term I call that into which the premiss is resolved, that is to say what is predicated and that of which it is predicated by means of the addition of being or not being.

What emerges from that text is the complete neutrality of the technical expressions 'term', 'premiss', 'syllogism', relative to any philosophical interpretation. For the premiss consists of terms, the syllogism of premisses, and premisses are *logoi*, which can equally well mean utterances or thoughts or objective contents, so that the way is open to a formalist, psychological or objectivist interpretation. All these interpretations are permissible in regard to Aristotelian logic; the purely logical system excludes none of them. Guided by his original intuition the founder of formal logic so chose his terminology as to rise above the clash of interpretations to the level of pure logic.

However if one considers Aristotelian logic in its entirety, it is easy to see that this neutrality is not the result of a lack of interest in problems of interpretation, but is on the contrary an abstraction from a complex semiotic doctrine. In some places Aristotle seems to plead for a psychological type of theory, as when, for example, he says:

10.08 All syllogism and therefore *a fortiori* demonstration, is addressed not to outward speech but to that within the soul.

At the same time it must be said that he attaches great importance to the 'outward speech', since he elaborates a well-developed theory of logical syntax and many points of semantic interest. All this teaching, which is next to be considered, warrants the conclusion that the practice of Aristotelian logic was undoubtedly to regard *meaningful words* as its subject-matter.

C. SYNTAX

Aristotle is the founder of logical syntax, following here some hints of the Sophists and Plato. He sketched the first attempt known to us at a system of syntactical categories. For we find in the *Hermeneia* an explicit division of the parts of speech into atomic (nouns and verbs) and molecular (sentences).

10.09 By a noun we mean a sound significant by convention, which has no reference to time, and of which no part is significant apart from the rest.

10.10 A verb is that which, in addition to its proper meaning, carries with it the notion of time. No part of it has any independent meaning, and it is a sign of something said of something else.

This theory is further supplemented by discussions of cases and inflexions of words, and by considerations about negated nouns and verbs.

10.11 A sentence is a significant portion of speech, some parts of which have an independent meaning, that is to say, as an utterance (φάσις), though not as the expression of any positive judgement (κατάφασις).

10.12 The first unified declarative sentence is the affirmation; the next, the denial. All other sentences are unified by combination.

Anticipating the further explanations, we may summarize the whole scheme of syntactical categories as presented in the *Hermeneia*, after this fashion:

ARISTOTLE

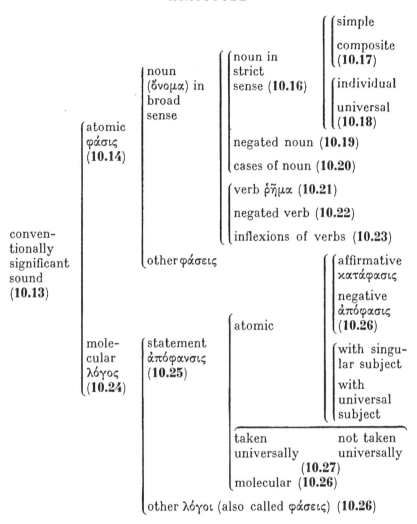

This schema underlies the whole development of logical syntax, and semantics too, until the rise of mathematical logic. Only this last will introduce anything essentially new: the attempt to treat syntactical categories by means of an *artificial* language. Aristotle on the other hand, and with him the Stoic and scholastic traditions, sought to grasp the syntactical structure of ordinary language.

D. SEMANTICS

The texts previously cited already contain points belonging to the domain of semantics. The general principle is thus formulated by Aristotle:

47

10.28 Spoken words are the symbols of mental experience and written words are the symbols of spoken words.

It follows that thoughts are themselves symbols of things. Aristotle lays great stress on the parallelism between things, thoughts and symbols, and correspondingly develops two important semiotic theories:

10.29 Things are said to be named 'equivocally' when, though they have a common name, the definitions corresponding with the name differs for each. Thus a real man and a figure in a picture can both lay claim to the name 'animal'. . . .

Things are said to be named 'univocally' which have both the name and the definition answering to the name in common. A man and an ox are both 'animal' . . . .

Things are said to be named 'derivatively', which derive their name from some other name, but differ from it in termination. Thus the grammarian derives his name from the word 'grammar' and the courageous man from the word 'courage'.

Equivocity must be excluded from demonstrations, since it leads to fallacies (**10.30**). Elsewhere Aristotle distinguishes various kinds of equivocity.

10.31 The good, therefore, is not some common element answering to one Idea. But what then do we mean by the good? It is surely not like the things that only chance to have the same name. Are goods one, then, by being derived from one good or by all contributing to one good, or are they rather one by analogy? Certainly as sight is in the body, so is reason in the soul, and so on in other cases.

This division can be presented schematically as follows:

equivocal expressions
- in strict sense ἀπὸ τύχης (accidentally equivocal)
- in broad sense (systematically equivocal)
  - from one (ἀφ' ἑνός)
  - to one (πρὸς ἕν)
  - by proportion (κατ' ἀναλογίαν)

In the *Metaphysics* and *Hermeneia* we find a clear semiotic theory of truth:

10.32 For falsity and truth are not in things – it is not as if the good were true and the bad were in itself false – but in thought.

10.33 As there are in the mind thoughts which do not involve truth or falsity, and also those which must be either true or false, so it is in speech. For truth and falsity imply combination and separation. Nouns and verbs, provided nothing is added, are like thoughts without combination or separation.

10.34 Yet not every sentence states something, but only those in which there is truth or falsity, and not all are of that kind. Thus a prayer is a sentence, but is neither true nor false . . . the present theory is concerned with such sentences as are statements (ἀποφαντικὸς λόγος).

Aristotle also constructs a definition of truth by means of equivalences:

10.35 If it is true to say that a thing is white, it must necessarily be white; if the reverse proposition is true, it will of necessity not be white. Again, if it is white, the proposition stating that it is white was true; if it is not white, the proposition to the opposite effect was true. And if it is not white, the man who states that it is is making a false statement; and if the man who states that it is white is making a false statement, it follows that it is not white.

§ 11. THE TOPICS

A. SUBJECT AND PURPOSE

The *Topics* contains Aristotle's first logic, and so the first attempt at a systematic presentation of our science. We cannot here do more than glance over the mass of rules contained in this work, giving only its purpose, a discussion of the analysis of statements as made by Aristotle in this early work, and a brief review of his teaching about fallacies. The most important of the formal rules and laws of inference occurring here, continued, as it seems, to be recognized as valid in the later works, and they will therefore be considered in the section on the non-analytical formulae (§ 16).

11.01 Next in order after the foregoing, we must say for how many and for what purposes the treatise is useful. They are three – intellectual training, casual encounters, and the philosophical sciences. That it is useful as a training is obvious on the face of it. The possession of a plan of inquiry will enable us more easily to argue about the subject proposed. For purposes of casual encounters, it is useful because when we have counted up the opinions held by most people, we shall meet them on the ground not of other people's convictions but of their own, while we shift the ground of any argument that they appear to us to state unsoundly. For the study of the philosophical sciences it is useful, because the ability to raise searching difficulties on both sides of a subject will make us detect more easily the truth and arror about the several points that arise. It has a further use in relation to the ultimate bases of the principles used in the several sciences. For it is impossible to discuss them at all from the principles proper to the particular science in hand, seeing that the principles are the *prius* of everything else: it is through the opinions generally held on the particular points that these have to be discussed, and this task belongs properly, or most appropriately, to dialectic: for dialectic is a process of criticism wherein lies the path to the principles of all inquiries.

The logic thus delineated treats of propositions and problems, described as follows:

11.02 The materials with which arguments start are equal in number, and are identical, with the subjects on which reasonings take place. For arguments start with 'propositions', while the subjects on which reasonings take place are 'problems'.

11.03 The difference between a problem and a proposition is a difference in the turn of the phrase. For if it be put in this way, ' "An animal that walks on two feet" is the definition of man, is it not?' or ' "Animal" is the genus of man, is it not?' the result is a proposition: but if thus, 'Is "an animal that walks on two feet" a definition of man or no?' the result is a problem. Similarly too in other cases. Naturally, then, problems and propositions are equal in number: for out of every proposition you will make a problem if you change the turn of the phrase.

Of epoch-making importance is the classification of methods of proof given in the same connection:

11.04 Having drawn these definitions, we must distinguish how many species there are of dialectical arguments. There is on the one hand Induction, on the other Syllogism. Now what a syllogism is has been said before: induction is a passage from individuals to universals, e.g. the argument that supposing the skilled pilot is the most effective, and likewise the skilled charioteer, then in general the skilled man is the best at his particular task. Induction is the more convincing and clear: it is more readily learnt by the use of the senses, and is applicable generally to the mass of men, though syllogism is more forcible and effective against contradictious people.

The subject of the Topics are essentially the so-called *loci* (τόποι). Aristotle never defined them, and so far no-one has succeeded in saying briefly and clearly what they are. In any case it is a matter of certain very general prescriptions for shaping arguments.

An example:

11.05 Now one commonplace rule (τόπος) is to look and see if a man has ascribed as an accident what belongs in some other way. This mistake is most commonly made in regard to the genera of things, e.g. if one were to say that white happens to be a colour – for being a colour does not happen by accident to white, but colour is its genus.

B. PREDICABLES

As an introduction to these *loci* Aristotle in the first book of the *Topics* developed two different doctrines of the structure of statements, both of which obtained considerable historical importance and still remain of interest: namely the doctrines of the so-called predicables and of the categories.

11.06 Every proposition and every problem indicates either a genus or a peculiarity or an accident – for the differentia too, applying as it does to a class (or genus), should be ranked together with the genus. Since, however, of what is peculiar to anything part signifies its essence, while part does not, let us divide the 'peculiar' into both the aforesaid parts, and call that part which indicates the essence a 'definition', while of the remainder let us adopt the terminology which is generally current about these things, and speak of it as a 'property'.

11.07 We must now say what are 'definition', 'property', 'genus', and 'accident'. A 'definition' is a phrase signifying a thing's essence. It is rendered in the form either of a phrase in lieu of a term, or of a phrase in lieu of another phrase; for it is sometimes possible to define the meaning of a phrase as well.

11.08 A 'property' (ἴδιον) is a predicate which does not indicate the essence of a thing, but yet belongs to that thing alone, and is predicated convertibly of it. Thus it is a property of man to be capable of learning grammar: for if A be a man, then he is capable of learning grammar, and if he be capable of learning grammar, he is a man.

11.09 A 'genus' is what is predicated in the category of essence of a number of things exhibiting differences in kind.

11.10 An 'accident' is (1) something which though it is none of the foregoing – i.e. neither a definition nor a property nor a genus – yet belongs to the thing: (2) something which may possibly either belong or not belong to any one and the self-same thing, as (e.g.) the 'sitting posture' may belong or not belong to some self-same thing.

The logical significance of this division of the 'predicables' consists in the fact that it is an attempt to analyse propositions, with reference moreover to the relation between subject and predicate. This analysis is effected in terms of the matter rather than the form, yet contains echoes of purely structural considerations, as for instance in the distinction between genus and specific difference or property, where the genus is evidently symbolized by a name, properties by a functor.

As a kind of pendent to the doctrine of the predicables, Aristotle presents a theory of identity:

11.11 Sameness would be generally regarded as falling, roughly speaking, into three divisions. We generally apply the term numerically or specifically or generically – numerically in cases where there is more than one name but only one thing, e.g. 'doublet' and 'cloak'; specifically, where there is more than one thing, but they present no differences in respect of their species, as one man and another, or one horse and another: for things like this that fall under the same species are said to be 'specifically the same'. Similarly, too, those things are called generically the same which fall under the same genus, such as a horse and a man.

C. CATEGORIES

Another analysis of propositions is contained in the theory of the categories. This seems to be a systematic development of hints in Plato. Only in one place (apart from the Categories: **11.12**) do we find an enumeration of ten categories (the only one usually ascribed to Aristotle):

11.13 Next, then, we must distinguish the classes of predicates in which the four orders in question **(11.06—11.10)** are found. These are ten in number: Essence, Quantity, Quality, Relation, Place, Time, Position, State, Activity, Passivity. For the accident and genus and property and definition of anything will always be in one of these categories: for all the propositions found through these signify either something's essence or its quality or quantity or some one of the other types of predicate. It is clear, too, on the face of it that the man who signifies something's essence signifies sometimes a substance, sometimes a quality, sometimes some one of the other types of predicate. For when a man is set before him and he says that what is set there is 'a man' or 'an animal', he states its essence and signifies a substance; but when a white colour is set before him and he says that what is set there is 'white' or is 'a colour', he states its essence and signifies a quality. Likewise, also, if a magnitude of a cubit be set before him and he says that what is set there is a magnitude of a cubit, he will be describing its essence and signifying a quantity. Likewise also in the other cases.

This text contains an ambiguity: 'essence' (τί ἐστι) means first a particular category – that of substance (οὐσία) as we see from a parallel text of the *Categories* (**11.14**) – secondly that essence or intrinsic nature which is found in every category, not only in that of substance. The thought becomes clear if 'substance' is put in the list of the ten categories in place of 'essence'.

Here the doctrine of the categories is treated as a division of sentences and problems for practical purposes. But beyond this Aristotle regarded it as involving two more important problems. In the *Prior Analytics* we read:

11.15 The expressions 'this belongs to that' and 'this holds true of that' must be understood in as many ways as there are different categories.

That means that the so-called copula of the sentence has as many meanings as there are categories. That is the first reason why the theory of the categories is logically so important. The second is that while this theory constitutes an attempt at classifying objects according to the ways in which they are predicable, it put in Aristotle's path the problem of the univeral class. He solved it with brilliant intuition, though, as we now know, with the help of a faulty proof. The relevant passage occurs in the third book of the *Metaphysics:*

11.16 It is not possible that either unity or being should be a single genus of things; for the differentiae of any genus must each of them both have being and be one, but it is not possible for the genus taken apart from its species (any more than for the species of the genus) to be predicated of its proper differentiae; so that if unity or being is a genus, no differentia will either have being or be one.

The line of thought which Aristotle expresses in this very compressed formula is as follows:
1. For all A: if A is a genus, then there is (at least) one B, which is the specific difference of A;
2. for all A and B: if B is the specific difference of A, then not: B is A. Suppose now
3. there is an all-inclusive genus V: of this it would be true that
4. for every B: B is V.
As V is a genus, it must have a difference (by 1.); call it D. Of this D it would be true on the one hand that D is V (by 4.), and on the other that D is not V (by 2.). Thus a contradiction results, and at least one of the premisses must be false (cf. **16.33**). As Aristotle holds 1. and 2. to be true, he must therefore reject the supposition that there is an all-inclusive genus (3.): there is no *summum genus*. We have here the basis of the scholastic doctrine of analogy (**28.19**) and the first germ of a theory of types (cf. § 47).

The proof is faulty: for 'D is V' is not false but meaningless (**48.24**). But beyond all doubt the thought confronting us deserves to be styled a brilliant intuition.

D. SOPHISTIC

The last book of the *Topics*, known as the *Sophistic Refutations*, contains an extensive doctrine of fallacious inferences. Like most other parts of the *Topics* this one too belongs to the first form of Aristotelian logic, not yet formal, but guided by the practical interests of every-day discussion. There is a second doctrine of fallacious inference, in the *Prior Analytics* (**11.17**), much briefer than the first but incomparably more formal; all fallacious inferences are there reduced to breaches of syllogistic laws. However neither Aristotle himself, nor anyone after him, really succeeded in replacing the doctrine of the *Sophistic Refutations*, primitive though it is from the formal point of view. Knowledge of it is also indispensable for the understanding of scholastic logic. For all of which reasons we shall cite a few passages from it here.

11.18 Refutation is reasoning involving the contradictory of the given conclusion. Now some of them do not really achieve this, though they seem to do so for a number of reasons; and of these the most prolific and usual domain is the argument that turns upon names only. It is impossible in a discussion to bring in the actual things discussed: we use their names as symbols instead of them; and therefore we suppose that what follows in the names, follows in the things as well, just as people who calculate suppose in regard to their counters. But the two cases (names and things) are not alike. For names are finite and so is the sum-total of formulae, while things are infinite in number. Inevitably, then, the same formulae, and a single name, have a number of meanings.

Historically, a very important text: in it Aristotle rejects formalism, rightly so for the purposes of ordinary language. For without preliminary distinction of the various functioning of signs correct laws cannot be formulated in such a language. The text just cited underlies the vast growth of medieval doctrine about supposition, appellation and analogy (§§ 27 and 28). So far as concerns Aristotle and the other ancient logicians, it appears that they got round the difficulty mentioned by applying rules by which ordinary language was turned into an artificial language with a single function for every verbal form.

11.19 There are two styles of refutation: for some depend on the language used, while some are independent of language. Those ways of producing the false appearance of an argument which depend on language are six in number: they are ambiguity, amphiboly, combination, division of words, accent, form of expression.

11.20 Arguments such as the following depend upon ambiguity. 'Those learn who know: for it is those who know their letters who learn the letters dictated to them.' For 'to learn' is ambiguous; it signifies both 'to understand' by the use of knowledge, and also 'to acquire knowledge'.

11.21 Examples such as the following depend upon amphiboly: . . . 'Speaking of the silent is possible': for 'speaking of the silent' also has a double meaning: it may mean that the speaker is silent or that the things of which he speaks are so.

11.22 Upon the combination of words there depend instances such as the following: 'A man can walk while sitting, and can write while not writing'. For the meaning is not the same if one divides the words and if one combines them in saying that 'it is possible to walk-while-sitting . . .'. The same applies to the latter phrase, too, if one combines the words 'to write-while-not-writing': for then it means that he has the power to write and not to write at once; whereas if one does not combine them, it means that when he is not writing he has the power to write.

11.23 Upon division depend the propositions that 5 is 2 and 3, and even and odd, and that the greater is equal: for it is that amount and more besides.

11.24 Of fallacies, on the other hand, that are independent of language there are seven kinds:

(1) that which depends upon Accident:

(2) the use of an expression absolutely or not absolutely but with some qualification of respect, or place, or time, or relation:

(3) that which depends upon ignorance of what 'refutation' is:

(4) that which depends upon the consequent:

(5) that which depends upon assuming the original conclusion:

(6) stating as cause what is not the cause:

(7) the making of more than one question into one.

And example of (1) is: 'If Coriscus is different from a man he is different from himself' (**11.25**); of (2): 'Suppose an Indian to be black all over, but white in respect of his teeth; then he is both white and not white' (**11.26**); (3) consists in proving something other than what is to be proved (**11.27**); (5) consists in presupposing what is to be proved (**11.28**). (4) alone involves a formal fallacy, namely concluding from the consequent to the antecedent of a conditional sentence (**11.29**).

§ 12. THEORY OF OPPOSITION; PRINCIPLE OF CONTRADICTION; PRINCIPLE OF TERTIUM EXCLUSUM

A. THEORY OF OPPOSITION

Aristotle developed two different theories of opposition. The first, contained in the *Topics* (**12.01**) and belonging to the earlier period of his development, is most clearly summarized in the pseudo-aristotelian *Categories:*

12.02 There are four senses in which one thing is said to be opposed to another: as correlatives, or as contraries, or as privation and habit (ἕξις), or as affirmation and denial. To give a general outline of these oppositions: the double is correlative to the half, evil is contrary to good, blindness is a privation and sight a habit, 'he sits' is an affirmation, 'he does not sit' a denial.

Two points are worth remark: the division presupposes a material standpoint, and even in the last case, contradictory opposition, concerns relationships between terms, not sentences.

It is quite otherwise in the later period. The second doctrine presupposes the Aristotelian theory of quantification, which is later than the *Topics:*

12.03 Some things are universal, others individual. By the term 'universal' I mean that which is of such a nature as to be predicated of many subjects, by 'individual' that which is not thus predicated. Thus 'man' is a universal, 'Callias' an individual. ... If, then, a man states a positive and a negative proposition of universal character with regard to a universal, these two propositions are 'contrary'. By the expression 'a proposition of universal character with regard to a universal', such propositions as 'every man is white', 'no man is white' are meant. When, on the other hand, the positive and negative propositions, though they have regard to a universal, are yet not of universal character, they will not be contrary, albeit the meaning intended is sometimes contrary. As instances of propositions made with regard to a universal, but not of universal character, we may take the propositions 'man is white', 'man is not white'. 'Man 'is a universal, but the proposition is not made as of universal character; for the word 'every' does not make the subject a universal, but rather gives the proposition a universal character. If, however, both predicate and subject are distributed, the proposition thus constituted is contrary to truth; no affirmation will, under such circumstances, be true. The proposition 'every man is every animal' is an example of this type.

This text contains the following points of doctrine: 1. distinction between general and singular sentences, according to the kind of subject; 2. divison of general sentences into universal and particular according to the extension of the subject; 3. rejection of quantification of the predicate. The whole doctrine is now purely formal, and is explicitly concerned with sentences.

Another division is to be found at the beginning of the *Prior Analytics:*

12.04 A premiss then is a sentence affirming or denying one thing of another. This is either universal or particular or indefinite. By universal I mean the statement that something belongs to all or none of something else; by particular that it belongs to some or not to some or not to all; by indefinite that it does or does not belong, without any mark to show whether it is universal or particular.

Here Aristotle enumerates three kinds of sentence: universal, particular and indefinite. It is striking that no mention is made of singular sentences. This is due to the fact that every term in the syllogistic must be available both as subject and predicate, but according to Aristotle singular terms cannot be predicated (**12.05**). In the particular sentence 'some' means 'at least one, not excluding all'. Whereas, as Sugihara has recently shewn (**12.06**), an indefinite sentence should probably be interpreted in the sense: 'at least one *A* is *B* and at least one *A* is not *B*'. However cases in which the formal properties of particular and indefinite sentences differ are rare in the syllogistic, so that Aristotle himself often states the equivalence of these sentences (**12.07**). Later, even in Alexander of Aphrodisias (**12.08**), these cases are dropped altogether.

12.09 Verbally four kinds of opposition are possible, viz. universal affirmative to universal negative, universal affirmative to particular negative, particular affirmative to universal negative, and particular affirmative to particular negative: but really there are only three: for the particular affirmative is only verbally opposed to the particular negative. Of the genuine opposites I call those which are universal *contraries*, the universal affirmative and the universal negative, e.g. 'all science is good', 'no science is good'; the others I call *contradictories*.

Here we have the 'logical square' later to become classical, which can be set out schematically thus:

12.091

to belong to all   *contrary*   to belong to none

to belong to some   *only verbal*   not to belong to all

The logical relationships here intended are shown in the following passages:

12.10 Of such corresponding positive and negative propositions as refer to universals and have a universal character, one must be true and the other false.

12.11 It is evident also that the denial corresponding to a single affirmation is itself single; . . . for instance, the affirmation 'Socrates is white' has its proper denial in the proposition 'Socrates is not white' . . . The denial proper to the affirmation 'every man is white' is 'not every man is white'; that proper to the affirmation 'some man is white' is 'no man is white'.

In the later tradition the so-called laws of subalternation also came to be included in the 'logical square'. They run:
If *A* belongs to all *B*, then it belongs to some *B* (**12.12**).
If *A* belongs to no *B*, then to some *B* it does not belong (**12.13**).

B. OBVERSION

In Aristotle's logic negation normally occurs only as a functor determining a sentence, but there are a number of places in the *Organon* where formulae are considered which contain a negation determining a name. Thus we read in the *Hermeneia:*

12.14 The proposition 'no man is just' follows from the proposition 'every man is not-just' and the proposition 'not every man is not-just', which is the contradictory of 'every man is not-just', follows from the proposition 'some man is just'; for if this be true, there must be some just man.

These laws were evidently discovered with great labour and after experimenting with various false formulae (12.15). Aristotle has similar ones for sentences with individual subjects in the *Hermeneia* (12.16).

In the *Prior Analytics* Aristotle develops a similar doctrine in more systematic form and with variables:

12.17 Let A stand for 'to be good', B for 'not to be good', let C stand for 'to be not-good', and be placed under B, and let D stand for 'not to be not-good' and be placed under A. Then either A or B will belong to everything, but they will never belong to the same thing; and either C or D will belong to everything, but they will never belong to the same thing. And B must belong to everything to which C belongs. For if it is true to say 'it is not-white', it is true also to say 'it is not white': for it is impossible that a thing should simultaneously be white and be not-white, or be a not-white log and be a white log; consequently if the affirmation does not belong, the denial must belong. But C does not always belong to B: for what is not a log at all, cannot be a not-white log either. On the other hand D belongs to everything to which A belongs. For either C or D belongs to everything to which A belongs. But since a thing cannot be simultaneously not-white and white, D must belong to everything to which A belongs. For of that which is white it is true to say that it is not not-white. But A is not true of all D. For of that which is not a log at all it is not true to say A, viz. that it is a white log. Consequently D is true, but A is not true, i.e. that it is a white log. It is clear also that A and C cannot together belong to the same thing, and that B and D may possibly belong to the same thing.

C. THE PRINCIPLE OF CONTRADICTION

While Aristotle was well acquainted with the principle of identity, so much discussed later, he only mentions it in passing (12.18). But to the principle of contradiction he devoted the whole of Book Γ of the *Metaphysics*. This book is evidently a youthful work, and was perhaps written in a state of excitement, since it contains logical errors; nevertheless it is concerned with an intuition of fundamental importance for logic.

The following are the most important formulations of the principle of contradiction:

12.19 The same attribute cannot at the same time belong and not belong to the same subject and in the same respect.

12.20 Let A stand for 'to be good', B for 'not to be good'.... Then either A or B will belong to everything, but they will never belong to the same thing. ·

12.21 It is impossible that contradictories should be at the same time true of the same thing.

12.22 It is impossible to affirm and deny truly at the same time.

The first two of these formulae are in the object language, the last two in a metalanguage, and the author evidently understands the difference.

In the *Topics* and *Hermeneia* Aristotle has a stronger law:

12.23 It is impossible that contrary predicates should belong at the same time to the same thing.

12.24 Propositions are opposed as contraries when both the affirmation and the denial are universal . . . in a pair of this sort both propositions cannot be true.

This last statement is quite understandable if one remembers that when Aristotle was young proofs principally consisted of refutations. But when Aristotle had developed his syllogistic, in which refutation has only a subordinate part to play, he not only found that the principle of contradiction would not do at all as the first axiom, but also that violence may be done to it in a correct syllogism.

The first in modern times to advert to this Aristotelian doctrine was I. Husic in 1906 (**12.27**). It may seem so astonishing to readers accustomed to the 'classical' interpretation of Aristotelian logic, that it is worth while shewing not merely its absolute necessity but also the context from which our logician's thought clearly emerges.

12.28 The law that it is impossible to affirm and deny simultaneously the same predicate of the same subject is not expressly posited by any demonstration except when the conclusion also has to be expressed in that form; in which case the proof lays down as its major premiss that the major is truly affirmed of the middle but falsely denied. It makes no difference, however, if we add to the middle, or again to the minor term, the corresponding negative. For grant a minor term of which it is true to predicate man – even if it be also true to predicate not-man of it – still grant simply that man is animal and not not-animal, and the conclusion follows: for it will still be true to say that Callias – even if it be also true to say that not-Callias – is animal and not not-animal.

The syllogism here employed has then, omitting quantifiers, the following form:

12.281 If M is P and not not-P, and S is M, then S is P and not not-P.

So the principle of contradiction is no axiom, and does not need to be presupposed, except in syllogisms of the fore-going kind. The text quoted is also remarkable in that the middle term in **12.281** is a product (cf. the commentary on **15.151**), and that in the minor term an individual name is substituted (cf. § 13, C, 5) – in each case contrary to normal syllogistic practice. However the text comes from the *Posterior Analytics* and must belong to a relatively early period.

Aristotle goes still further and states that the principle of contradiction can be completely violated in a conclusive syllogism:

12.29 In the middle (i.e. second: cf. **13.07**) figure a syllogism can be made both of contradictories and contraries. Let 'A' stand for 'good', let 'B' and 'C' stand for 'science'. If then one assumes that every science is good, and no science is good, A belongs to all B and to no C, so that B belongs to no C: no science is then a science.

This syllogism has the following form:

12.291 If all M is P and no M is P, then no M is M.

D. THE PRINCIPLE OF TERTIUM EXCLUSUM

One formulation of this principle has already been quoted (**12.20**). Others are:

12.30 In the case of that which is, or which has taken place, propositions, whether positive or negative, must be true or false. Again, in the case of a pair of contradictories, either when the subject is universal and the propositions are of a universal character, or when it is individual, as has been said, one of the two must be true and the other false.

12.31 One side of the contradiction must be true. Again, if it is necessary with regard to everything either to assert or to deny it, it is impossible that both should be false.

Aristotle's normal practice was to presuppose the correctness of these theses, and he devoted a notable chapter of the fourth book of the Metaphysics (Γ 8) to the defence of the principle of *tertium exclusum* (or *tertium non datur*). At least once, however, he called it into question: in the ninth chapter of the *Hermeneia* he will not allow it to be valid for future contingent events. He bases his argument thus:

12.32 If it is true to say that a thing is white, it must necessarily be white; if the reverse proposition is true, it will of necessity not be white .... It may therefore be argued that it is necessary that affirmations or denials must be either true or false. Now if this be so, nothing is or takes place fortuitously, either in the present or in the future, and there are no real alternatives; everthing takes place of necessity and is fixed. ... It is therefore plain that it is not necessary that of an affirmation and a denial one should be true and the other false. For in the case of that which exists potentially, but not actually, the rule which applies to that which exists actually does not hold good.

These considerations had no influence on Aristotle's logical system, as has already been said, but they came to have great historical importance in the Middle Ages.

The doubt about the validity of the principle of *tertium exclusum* arose from an intuition of the difficult problems which it sets. The debate is not closed even today.

§ 13. ASSERTORIC SYLLOGISTIC

We give here a page of the *Prior Analytics* in as literal a translation as possible, and comment on it afterwards. It contains the essentials of what later came to be called Aristotle's assertoric syllogistic. It is a leading text, in which no less than three great discoveries are applied for the first time in history: variables, purely formal treatment, and an axiomatic system. It constitutes the beginning of formal logic. Short as it is, it formed the basis of logical speculation for more than two thousand years – and yet has been only too often much misunderstood. It deserves to be read attentively.

A. TEXT

Aristotle begins by stating the laws of conversion of sentences. These are cited below, **14.10** ff., among the bases of the systematic development. He goes on:

13.01 When then three terms are so related one to another that the last is in the middle (as in a) whole and the middle is or is not in the first as in a whole, then there must be a perfect syllogism of the two extremes.

13.02 Since if A (is predicated) of all B, and B of all C, A must be predicated of all C.

13.03 Similarly too if A (is predicated) of no B, and B of all A, it is necessary that A will belong to no C.

13.04 But if the first follows on all the middle whereas the middle belongs to none of the last, there is no syllogism of the extremes; for nothing necessary results from these; for the first may belong to all and to none of the last; so that neither a particular nor a universal is necessary; and since there is nothing necessary these produce no syllogism. Terms for belonging to all: animal, man, horse; for belonging to none: animal, man, stone.

13.05 But if one of the terms is related wholly, one partially, to the remaining one; when the wholly related one is posited either affirmatively or negatively to the major extreme, and the partially related one affirmatively to the minor extreme, there must be a perfect syllogism . . . for let A belong to all B and B to some C, then if being predicated of all is what has been said, A must belong to some C.

13.06 And if A belongs to no B and B to some C, to some C A must not belong . . . and similarly if the BC (premiss) is indefinite and affirmative.

13.07 But when the some belongs to all of one, to none of the other; such a figure I call the second.

13.08 For let M be predicated of no N and of all X; since then the negative converts, N will belong to no M; but M was assumed (to belong) to all X; so that N (will belong) to no X; for this has been shewn above.

13.09 Again, if M (belongs) to all N and to no X, X too will belong to no N; for if M (belongs) to no X, X too (belongs) to no M; but M belonged to all N; therefore X will belong to no N, for the first figure has arisen again; but since the negative converts, N too will belong to no X, so that it will be the same syllogism. It is possible to shew this by bringing to impossibility.

13.10 If M belongs to no N and to some X, then to some X N must not belong. For since the negative converts, N will belong to no M, but M has been supposed to belong to some X; so that to some X N will not belong; for a syllogism arises in the first figure.

13.11 Again, if M belongs to all N and to some X not, to some N X must not belong. For if it belongs to all, and $\acute{M}$ is predicated of all $\dot{N}$, M must belong to all X; but to some it has been supposed not to belong.

13.12 If to the same, one belongs to all, the other to none, or both to all or to none, such a figure I call third.

13.13 When both P and R belong to all S, of necessity P will belong to some R; for since the affirmative converts, S will belong to some R, so that when P (belongs) to all S, and S to some R, P must belong to some R; for a syllogism arises in the first figure. One can make the proof also by (bringing to) the impossible and by setting out (terms); for if both belong to all S, if some of the (things which are) S be taken, say N, to this both P and R will belong, so that to some R P will belong.

13.14 And if R belongs to all S, and P to none, there will be a syllogism that to some R P necessarily will not belong. For there is the same manner of proof, with the RS premiss converted. It could also be shewn by the impossible as in the previous cases.

13.15 If R (belongs) to all S and P to some, P must belong to some R. For since the affirmative converts, S will belong to some P, so that when R (belongs) to all S, and S to some P, R too will belong to some P; so that P (will belong) to some R.

13.16 Again, if R belongs to some S and P to all, P must belong to some R; for there is the same manner of proof. One can also prove it by the impossible and by setting out, as in the previous cases.

13.17 If R belongs to all S, and to some (S) P does not, then to some R P must not belong. For if to all, and R (belongs) to all S, P will also belong to all S; but it did not belong. It is also proved with reduction (to the impossible) if some of what is S be taken to which P does not belong.

13.18 If P belongs to no S, and R to some S, to some R P will not belong; for again there will be the first figure when the RS premiss is converted.

B. INTERPRETATION

This passage is composed in such compressed language that most readers find it very hard to understand. Indeed the very style is of the greatest significance for the history of logic; for here we have the manner of thought and writing of all genuine formal logicians, be they Stoics or Scholastics, be their name Leibniz or Frege. Hence we have given a literal version, but shall now interpret it with the aid of paraphrase and commentary:

on **13.01**: Aristotle defines the first figure. This may serve as an example: Gainful art is contained in art in general as in a whole; the art of pursuit (e.g. hunting) is contained in gainful art as in a whole; therefore the art of pursuit is contained in art in general as in a whole. The example is taken from Plato's division (**8.05**), from which the Aristotelian syllogism seems to have developed.

We shall explain what a perfect syllogism is in § 14.

on **13.02**: This mood later (with Peter of Spain) came to be called '*Barbara*'. Hereafter we refer to all moods by the mnemonic names originating with Peter of Spain (cf. **32.04** ff.).

We obtain an example by substitution:

> If animal belongs to all man
> and man belongs to all Greek,
> then animal belongs to all Greek.

on **13.03**: *Celarent:* If stone belongs to no man
> and man belongs to all Greek,
> then stone belongs to no Greek.

on **13.04**: Names are here given for two substitutions by which it can be shewn that a further mood is invalid. Probably the following are intended:

Mood	*Substitution*
If A to all B	1. If animal belongs to all man
and B to no C,	and man belongs to no horse,
then A to no C,	then animal belongs to no horse.
	2. If animal belongs to all man
	and man belongs to no stone,
	then animal belongs to no stone.

In each case the premisses are true, but the conclusion is once true, once false. Therefore the mood is invalid.

on **13.05**: *Darii:* If Greek belongs to all Athenian
> and Athenian belongs to some logician,
> then Greek belongs to some logician.

It is to be noticed that here and subsequently 'some' must have the sense of 'at least one'.

on **13.06**: *Ferio:* If Egyptian belongs to no Greek
> and Greek belongs to some logician,
> then to some logician Egyptian does not belong.

on **13.07**: Aristotle defines the second figure, in which the middle term is predicate in both premisses. He considers three cases: 1. one premiss is universal and affirmative, the other universal and negative, 2. both premisses are universal and affirmative, 3. both premisses are negative. Only in the first case there are valid syllogisms.

on **13.08**: *Cesare:* If man belongs to no stone
and man belongs to all Greek,
then stone belongs to no Greek.

This is reduced to Celarent (**13.03**) by conversion of the major (first) premiss: If stone belongs to no man
and man belongs to all Greek,
then stone belongs to no Greek.

on **13.09**: *Camestres:* If (1) animal belongs to all man
and (2) animal belongs to no stone,
then (3) man belongs to no stone.

The proof proceeds by reduction to *Celarent* (**13.03**). First the minor premiss (2) is converted:

(4) stone belongs to no animal;

then comes the other premiss:

(1) animal belongs to all man.

(4) and (1) are the premisses of *Celarent*, from which follows the conclusion,

(5) stone belongs to no man. This is converted, and so the desired conclusion is obtained.

It is important to notice that this conclusion is first stated by Aristotle at the end of the process of proof.

on **13.10**: *Festino:* The proof of this mood is by reduction to *Ferio* (**13.06**), the major premiss being converted as in Cesare (**13.08**).

on **13.11**: *Baroco:* If (1) Greek belongs to all Athenian
and (2) to some logician Greek does not belong,
then (3) to some logician Athenian does not belong.

The proof proceeds by first hypothesizing the conclusion as false, i.e. its contradictory opposite is supposed:

(4) Athenian belongs to all logician.

Now comes the first (major) premiss:

(5) Greek belongs to all Athenian.

From these one obtains a syllogism in *Barbara* (**13.02**):

If (5) Greek belongs to all Athenian
and (4) Athenian belongs to all logician,
then (6) Greek belongs to all logician.

But the conclusion (6) of this syllogism is contradictorily opposed to the minor premiss of *Baroco*, (2), and as this is accepted, the former must be rejected. So one of the premisses (4) and (5) must be rejected: as (5) is accepted, (4) must be rejected; and so we obtain the contradictory opposite of (4), namely (3).

on **13.12**: Aristotle defines the third figure, in which the middle term is subject in both premisses. He considers the same three cases as in **13.07**.

on **13.13**: *Darapti:* If Greek belongs to all Athenian
and man belongs to all Athenian,
then Greek belongs to some man.

This syllogism is first reduced to *Darii* (**13.05**) by conversion of the minor premiss – just as *Cesare* (**13.08**) is reduced to *Celarent* (**13.03**). But Aristotle then develops two further methods of proof: a process – as with *Baroco* (**13.11**) – 'through the impossible', and the 'setting out of terms'. This last consists in singling out a part, perhaps an individual (but this is debated in the literature), from the Athenians, say Socrates. It results that as Greek as well as man belongs to all Athenian, Socrates must be Greek as well as man. Therefore this is a Greek who is man. Accordingly Greek belongs to (at least) one man.

on **3.14**: *Felapton:* If Egyptian belongs to no Athenian
and man belongs to all Athenian,
then to some man Egyptian does not belong.

The proof proceeds by conversion of the minor (second) premiss, resulting in Ferio (**13.06**).

on **3.15**: *Disamis:* If Athenian belongs to all Greek
and logician belongs to some Greek,
then logician belongs to some Athenian.

The first thing to be noticed is that Aristotle here writes the minor premiss first, as also in **13.16** and **13.17**. The proof is by reduction to *Darii* (**13.05**), just as Camestres (**13.09**) was reduced to Celarent (**13.03**).

on **13.16**: *Datisi:* If logician belongs to some Greek
and Athenian belongs to all Greek,
then Athenian belongs to some logician.

The proof proceeds by reduction to *Darii* (**13.05**), the minor premiss (here the first!) being converted.

on **13.17**: *Bocardo:* If Greek belongs to all Athenian
and to some Athenian logician does not belong,
then to some Greek logician does not belong.

The premisses are again in reversed order, the minor coming first. The proof proceeds by reduction to the impossible, with use of *Barbara* (**13.02**) as in the case of *Baroco* (**13.11**). A proof by setting out of terms is also recommended, but not carried through.

on **13.18**: *Ferio:* If Egyptian belongs to no Greek
and logician belongs to some Greek,
then to some logician Egyptian does not belong.

Aristotle reduces this syllogism to *Ferio* (**13.06**), by conversion of the minor (second) premiss.

This paraphrase with comments is, be it noted, a concession to the modern reader. For in his *Analytics* Aristotle never argued by means of substitutions, as we have been doing, except in proofs of invalidity. However, in view of the contemporary state of logical awareness, it seems necessary to elucidate the text in this more elementary way.

C STRUCTURE OF THE SYLLOGISM

If we consider the passages on which we have just commented, the first thing we notice is that the definition which Aristotle gives of the syllogism (**10.05**), does indeed contain it, but is much too wide: the *analytic syllogism* as we call the class of formulae considered in chapters 4–6 of the first book of the *Prior Analytics*, can be described as follows:

1. It is a conditional sentence, the antecedent of which is a conjunction of two premisses. Its general form is: ' If p and q, then r', in which propositional forms are to be substituted for 'p', 'q' and 'r'. So the Aristotelian syllogism has *not* the later form: '$p; q;$ therefore r', which is a *rule*. The Aristotelian syllogism is not a rule but a *proposition*.

2. The three propositional forms whose inter-connection produces a syllogism, are always of one of these four kinds: 'A belongs to all B', 'A belongs to no B', 'A belongs to (at least) some B', ' (at least) to some B A does not belong'. Instead of this last formula, there sometimes occurs the (equivalent) one: 'A belongs not to all B'. The word 'necessary' or 'must' is often used: evidently that only means here that the conclusion in question follows logically from the premisses.

3. Where we have been speaking not of propositions but of forms, seeing that Aristotelian syllogisms always contain letters ('A', 'B', 'Γ' etc.) in place of words, which are evidently to be interpreted as variables, Aristotle himself gives examples of how substitutions can be made in them. That is indeed the only kind of substitution for variables known to him: he has, for example, no thought of substituting variables for variables. Nevertheless this is an immense discovery: the use of letters instead of constant words gave birth to formal logic.

4. In every syllogism we find six such letters, called 'terms' (ὅροι, 'boundaries'), equiform in pairs. Aristotle uses the following terminology: the term which is predicate in the conclusion and the term equiform to it in one of the premisses, are called 'major', evidently because in the first figure – but there only – this has the greatest extension. The term which is subject in the conclusion, and the term equiform to it in one of the premisses, he calls a 'minor' or 'last' term (ἔλαττον, ἔσχατον) for the same reason. Finally the two equiform terms that occur only in the premisses are called 'middle' terms. By contrast the two others are called 'extremes' (ἄκρα).

Admittedly the terms are not so defined in the text of Aristotle: he gives complicated definitions based on the meaning of the terms; but his customary syllogistic practice keeps to the foregoing definitions. – Sometimes the premiss containing the major term is called 'the major', the other 'the minor'.

5. The letters (variables) can, in the system, only be substituted by universal terms; they are term-variables for universal terms. But it would not be right to call them class-variables, for that would be to ascribe to Aristotle a distinction between intension and extension which is out of place. One may ask why the founder of logic, whose philosophical development proceeded steadily away from Platonism towards a recognition of the importance of the individual, completely omitted singular terms in what (by contrast to the *Hermeneia*) is his most mature work. The reason probably lies in his assumption that such terms are not suitable as predicates (**13.19**), whereas syllogistic technique requires every extreme term to occur at least once as predicate.

6. It is usually said that a further limitation is required, namely that void terms must not be substituted for the variables. But this is only true in the context of certain interpretations of the syllogistic; on other interpretations this limitation is not required.

To sum up: we have in the syllogistic a formal system of term-logic, with variables, limited to universal terms, and consisting of propositions, not rules.

This system is also axiomatized. Hence we have here together three of the greatest discoveries of our science: formal treatment, variables, and axiomatization. What makes this last achievement the more remarkable is the fact that the system almost achieves completeness (there is lacking only an exact elaboration of the moods of the fourth figure). This is something rare for the first formulation of a quite original logical discovery.

D. THE FIGURES AND FURTHER SYLLOGISMS

The syllogisms are divided into three classes (σχήματα), 'figures' as this was later translated, according to the position of the middle term. According to Aristotle there are only three such figures:

13.20 So we must take something midway between the two, which will connect the predications, if we are to have a syllogism relating this to that. If then we must take something common in relation to both, and this is possible in three ways (either by predicating A of C, and C of B, or C of both, or both of C), and these are the figures of which we have spoken, it is clear that every syllogism must be made in one or other of these figures.

But evidently this is so far from being the case that Aristotle himself was well aware of a fourth figure. He treats its syllogisms as arguments obtainable from those already gained in the first figure:

13.21 It is evident also that in all the figures, whenever a proper syllogism does not result, if both the terms are affirmative or negative nothing necessary follows at all, but if one is affirmative, the other negative, and if the negative is stated universally, a syllogism always results relating the minor to the major term, e.g. if A belongs to all or some B, and B belongs to no C: for if the premisses are converted it is necessary that C does not belong to some A. Similarly also in the other figures.

The case under consideration is this: the premisses are (1) 'A belongs to all B', (2) 'B belongs to no C'. They are both converted and their order is reversed (an operation that is irrelevant for Aristotle), so that we get: 'C belongs to no B' and 'B belongs to some A'. But those are the premisses of the fourth mood of the first figure (*Ferio*, **13.06**), which has as conclusion 'to some A C does not belong'. Now if 'major term' and 'minor term' are defined as has been done above (§ 13, C 4) in accordance with the practice of Albalag and the moderns, then evidently C is the major term, A the minor, and so (2) is the major premiss, (1) the minor premiss. From that it follows that the middle term is predicate in the major premiss, subject in the minor, just the reverse of the situation in the first figure. We have here therefore a fourth figure. That Aristotle refuses to recognize any such, is due to his not giving a theoretical definition of the terms according to their place in the conclusion, but according to their extension, and so not a formal definition but one dependent on their meaning. – The syllogism just investigated later came to be called *Fresison*.

Aristotle explicitly stated two syllogism of this figure, *Fresison* already cited, and in the same passage (**13.31**) *Fesapo;* he hints only at three more (**13.32**): *Dimaris, Bamalip* and *Camenes.*

The same text (**13.22**) would permit us to gain still other syllogisms from two of the second figure *Cesare:* **13.08** and *Camestres:* **13.09**) and from three of the third (*Darapti:* **13.13**, *Disamis:* **13.15** and *Datisi:* **13.16**). It is worth remarking that these hints do not occur in the text of the proper presentation of the syllogistic; apparently Aristotle only made these discoveries when his system was already in being.

Consequently the following passage seems to be a later addition. It is at the origin of what later came to be called the 'subalternate syllogisms', *Barbari, Celaront, Cesaro, Camestrop* and *Calemop.*

13.23 It is possible to give another reason concerning those (syllogisms) which are universal. For all the things that are subordinate to the middle term or to the conclusion may be proved by the same syllogism, if the former are placed in the middle, the latter in the conclusion; e.g. if the conclusion AB is proved through C, whatever is subordinate to B or C must accept the predicate A: for if D is included in B as in a whole, and B is included in A, then D will be included in A. Again if E is included in C as in a whole, and C is included in A, then E will be included in A. Similarly if the syllogism is negative. In the second figure it will be possible to infer only that which is subordinate to the conclusion, e.g. if A belongs to no B and to all C; we conclude that B belongs to no C. If then D is subordinate to C, clearly B does not belong to it. But that B does not belong to what is subordinate to A, is not clear by means of the syllogism.

These syllogisms, however, are not developed.

If we want to summarize the content of the texts we have adduced, we see that Aristotle in fact expressly formulated the conditions required for a system of twenty-four syllogistic moods, six in each figure. Of these twenty-four he only developed nineteen himself, only fourteen of them thoroughly. The remaining ten fall into three classes: (1) exactly formulated (*Fesapo, Fresison*: **13.21**): (2) not formulated, but clearly indicated (*Dimaris, Bamalip, Camenes*: **13.22**); (3) only indirectly indicated: the five 'subalternate' moods (**13.23**).

That explains how historically sometimes fourteen, sometimes nineteen and again at other times twenty-four moods are spoken of. The last figure is obviously the only correct one. For evidently no systematic principle can be derived from the fact that the author of the syllogistic did not precisely develop certain moods.

§ 14. AXIOMATIZATION OF THE SYLLOGISTIC FURTHER LAWS

A. AXIOMATIC THEORY OF THE SYSTEM

Aristotle axiomatized the syllogistic, and in more than one way. In this connection we shall first cite the most important passages in which he presents his theory of the system as axiomatized, and then give the axiomatization itself. For this theory is the first of its kind known to us, and notwithstanding its weaknesses, must be considered as yet another quite original contribution made to logic by

Aristotle. The point is a methodological one of course, not a matter of formal logic, and that Aristotle was himself aware of:

14.01 We now state by what means, when, and how every syllogism is produced; subsequently we must speak of demonstration. Syllogism should be discussed before demonstration, because syllogism is the more general: demonstration is a sort of syllogism, but not every syllogism is a demonstration.

Aristotle's doctrine of demonstration is precisely his methodology. But as the methodology of deduction is closely connected with formal logic, we must go into at least a few details.

14.02 We suppose ourselves to possess unqualified scientific knowledge of a thing, as opposed to knowing it in the accidental way in which the sophist knows, when we think that we know the cause on which the fact depends, as the cause of that fact and of no other, and, further, that the fact could not be other than it is . . . There may be another manner of knowing as well – that will be discussed later. What I now assert is that at all events we do know by demonstration. By demonstration I mean a syllogism productive of scientific knowledge, a syllogism, that is, the grasp of which is *eo ipso* such knowledge. Assuming then that my thesis as to the nature of scientific knowing is correct, the premisses of demonstrated knowledge must be true, primary, immediate, better known than and prior to the conclusion, which is further related to them as effect to cause. Unless these conditions are satisfied, the basic truths will not be 'appropriate' to the conclusion. Syllogism there may indeed be without these conditions, but such syllogism, not being productive of scientific knowledge, will not be demonstration.

14.03 There are three elements in demonstration: (1) what is proved, the conclusion – an attribute inhering essentially in a genus; (2) the axioms, i.e. the starting points of proof; (3) the subject-genus whose attributes, i.e. essential properties, are revealed by the demonstration.

It emerges clearly from this text that for Aristotle a demonstration (1) is a syllogism, (2) with specially constructed premisses, and (3) with a conclusion in which a property (**11.08**) is predicated of a genus. That, however, can only be achieved by means of a syllogism in the first figure:

14.04 Of all figures the most scientific is the first. Thus, it is the vehicle of the demonstrations of all the mathematical sciences, such as arithmetic, geometry, and optics, and practically of all sciences that investigate causes . . . a second proof that this figure is the most scientific; for grasp of a reasoned conclusion is the primary condition of knowledge. Thirdly, the first is the only figure which enables us to pursue knowledge of the essence of a thing. . . . Finally, the first figure has no need of the others, while it is by means of the first that the other two figures are developed, and have their intervals close-packed until immediate premises are reached. Clearly, therefore, the first figure is the primary condition of knowledge.

This doctrine is only of historical importance, though that is considerable: on the other hand the essential of Aristotle's views on the structure of an axiomatic system has remained a part of every methodology of deduction right to our own day:

14.05 Our own doctrine is that not all knowledge is demonstrative: on the contrary, knowledge of the immediate premises is independent of demonstration. (The necessity of this is obvious; for since we must know the prior premises from which the demonstration is drawn, and since the regress must end in immediate truths, those truths must be indemonstrable.) . . Now demonstration must be based on premises prior to and better known than the conclusion; and the same things cannot simultaneously be both prior and posterior to one another: so circular demonstration is clearly not possible in the unqualified sense of 'demonstration', but only possible if 'demonstration' be extended to include that other method of argument which rests on a distinction between truths prior to us and truths without qualification prior, i.e. the method by which induction produces knowledge. . . . The advocates of circular demonstration are not only faced with the difficulty we have just stated: in addition their theory reduces to the mere statement that if a thing exists, then it does exist – an easy way of proving anything. That this is so can be clearly shown by taking three terms, for to constitute the circle it makes no difference whether many terms or few or even only two are taken. Thus by direct proof, if A is, B must be; if B is, C must be; therefore if A is, C must be. Since then – by the circular proof – if A is, B must be, and if B is, A must be, A may be substituted for C above. Then 'if B is, A

74

must be' = 'if *B* is, *C* must be', which above gave the conclusion 'if *A* is, *C* must be', but *C* and *A* have been identified.

This is, be it said at once, far the clearest passage about our problem, which evidently faced Aristotle with enormous difficulties. Two elements are to be distinguished: on the one hand it is a matter of *epistemological* doctrine, according to which all scientific knowledge must finally be reduced to evident and necessary premisses; on the other hand is a *logical* theory of deduction, which states that one cannot demonstrate all sentences in a system, but must leave off somewhere; for neither a *processus in infinitum* nor a circular demonstration is possible. In other words: there must be axioms in every system.

B. SYSTEMS OF SYLLOGISTIC

This doctrine was now applied by Aristotle to formal logic itself, i.e. to the syllogistic; yes, the syllogistic is the first known axiomatic system, or more precisely the first class of such systems: for Aristotle axiomatized it in several ways. One can distinguish in his work the following systems: 1) with the four syllogisms of the first figure (together with other laws) as axioms, 2) with the first two syllogisms of the same figure, 3) with syllogisms of any figure as axioms, in which among other features the syllogisms of the first figure are reduced to those of the second and third. These three systems are presented in an object-language; there is further to be found in Aristotle a sketch for the axiomatization of the syllogistic in a metalanguage.

We take first the second system, the first having been fully presented above in § 13.

14.06 It is possible also to reduce all syllogisms to the universal syllogisms in the first figure. Those in the second figure are clearly made perfect by these, though not all in the same way; the universal syllogisms are made perfect by converting the negative premiss, each of the particular syllogisms by reductio *ad impossibile*. In the first figure particular syllogisms are indeed made perfect by themselves, but it is possible also to prove them by means of the second figure, reducing them *ad impossibile*, e.g. if *A* belongs to all *B*, and *B* to some *C*, it follows that *A* belongs to some *C*. For if it belonged to no *C*, and belongs to all *B*, then *B* will belong to no *C*: this we know by means of the second figure.

It is here shewn that *Darii* (**13.05**) can be reduced to *Camestres* (**13.09**); the proof of *Ferio* (**13.06**) is similarly effected, and it is then

75

shewn that the syllogisms of the third figure can also be easily deduced.

In these operations the syllogisms of the first figure always play. the part of axioms, for the reason that they are to be 'perfect' (τέλειοι) syllogisms (**14.08**). This expression is explained thus:

14.09 I call that a perfect syllogism which needs nothing other than what has been stated to make plain what necessarily follows; a syllogism is imperfect, if it needs either one or more propositions, which are indeed the necessary consequences of the terms set down, but have not been expressly stated as premisses.

But this can only mean that perfect syllogisms are intuitively evident.

C. DIRECT PROOF

To be able to deduce his syllogisms Aristotle makes use of three procedures, and in each of another class of formulae, not named as axioms and in part tacitly presented. The procedures are direct proof (δεικτιῶς ἀνάγειν), reduction to the impossible (εἰς τὸ ἀδύνατον ἀνάγειν) and ecthesis (setting out of terms, ἔκθεσις).

In direct proof the laws of conversion of sentences are explicitly presupposed; they are three:

14.10 If A belongs to no B, neither will B belong to any A. For if to some, say to C, it will not be true that A belongs to no B; for C is one of the things (which are) B.

14.11 If A belongs to all B, B also will belong to some A; for if to none, then neither will A belong to any B; but by hypothesis it belonged to all.

14.12 If A belongs to some B, B also must belong to some A; for if to none, then neither will A belong to any B.

Aristotle prefaces the syllogistic proper with these laws and their justification, clearly conscious that he needs them for the 'direct procedure' .They are the laws of conversion of affirmative (universal and particular), and universal negative propositions. (The conversion of particular negatives is expressly recognized as invalid: **14.13**.)

It is noteworthy that Aristotle tries to axiomatize these laws too: the first is proved by ecthesis and serves as axiom for the two others.

Besides these explicit presuppositions of the syllogistic, some rules of inference are also used, without Aristotle having consciously reflected on them. They are these:

14.141 Should 'If p and q, then r' and 'If s, then p' be valid, then also 'If s and q, then r' is valid.

14.142 Should 'If p and q, then r' and 'If s, then q' be valid, then also 'If p and s, then r' is valid.

14.151 Should 'If p and q, then r' be valid, then also 'If q and p, then r' is valid.

14.161 Should 'If p, then q' and 'If q, then r' be valid, then also 'If p, then r' is valid.

Some of these rules also used – without being explicitly appealed to – for constructing formulae that later came to be called 'polysyllogisms, or 'soriteses':

14.17 It is clear too that every demonstration will proceed through three terms and no more, unless the same conclusion is established by different pairs of propositions; . . . Or again when each of the propositions A and B is obtained by syllogistic inference, e.g. A by means of D and E, and again B by means of F and G. . . . But thus also the syllogisms are many; for the conclusions are many, e.g. A and B and C.

Also to be noted in this text is Aristotle's evident use of propositional variables.

D. INDIRECT PROOF

Aristotle has two different procedures for reduction to the impossible, the first being invalid and clearly earlier. In both, the laws of opposition are presupposed. By contrast to the laws of conversion these are neither systematically introduced nor axiomatized; they occur as the occassion of the deduction requires. The reason for their not being systematized or axiomatized may be that the essential points about them have been stated already in the *Hermeneia*. The main features have been summarized above (**12.10, 12,11**).

The procedures are as follows:

First procedure

It is used to reduce *Baroco* (**13.11**) and *Bocardo* (**13.17**), and takes the course outlined above (in the commentary on **13.11**). As Łukasiewicz (**14.18**) has shown, it is not conclusive. This can be made evident by the following substitution: we put 'bird' for 'M', 'beast' for 'N' and 'owl' for 'X' in *Baroco* (**13.11**). We obtain:

> If (1) bird belongs to all beast
> and (2) to some owl bird does not belong,
> then (3) to some owl beast does not belong.

The syllogism is correct, being a substitution in *Baroco;* but all its three component sentences are manifestly false. Now if we apply the procedure described above (commentary on **13.11**), we must form the contradictory opposite to (3):

(4) Beast belongs to all owl.

This produces with (1) a syllogism in Barbara (**13.02**), having as conclusion

(5) Bird belongs to all owl, which so far from being false, is evidently true. Hence the procedure fails to give the required conclusion and must be deemed incorrect.

It would certainly be correct if Aristotle had not expressed the syllogism as a conditional sentence (in which the antecedent does not need to be asserted), but in the scholastic manner as a rule (**31.11**) in which one starts from asserted premisses.

Second procedure

We do not know whether Aristotle saw the incorrectness of the first procedure; in any case in book B of the *Prior Analytics* he several times uses another which is logically correct.

It is to be found in the place where he treats of the so-called 'conversion' (ἀντιστροφή) of syllogisms, a matter of replacing one premiss by the (contradictory) opposite of the conclusion.

14.19 Suppose that *A* belongs to no *B*, and to some *C:* the conclusion is *BC*. . . . If the conclusion is converted into its contradictory, both premisses can be refuted. For if *B* belongs to all *C*, and *A* to no *B*, *A* will belong to no *C:* but it was assumed to belong to some *C*.

The following scheme reproduces the thought:

Original syllogism (*Festino*)	Converted syllogism (*Celarent*)
If *A* belongs to no *B* and *A* belongs to some *C*, then to some *C B* does not belong.	If *A* belongs to no *B* and *B* belongs to all *C*, then *A* belongs to no *C*

The rule presupposed, of which Aristotle was conscious (cf. **16.33**) – he often used it, – is this:

14.201 Should 'If *p* and *q*, then *r*' be valid then also 'If not-*r* and *q*, then not-*p*' is valid.

A similar rule, also often used, is:

14.202 Should 'If *p* and *q*, then *r*' be valid, then also 'If *p* and not-*r*, then not-*q*' is valid.

By the use of these rules with the laws of opposition and some of the rules given above (**14.151**, **14.161**), any syllogism can in fact be reduced to another.

Applications

By varying this second procedure Aristotle was able to construct a third axiomatization – or rather a class of further axiomatizations – of his syllogistic: Syllogisms of either the first, second or third figure are taken, and the others proved from them by reduction to the impossible. The result is summarized thus:

14.21 It is clear that in the first figure the syllogisms are formed through the middle and the last figures . . . in the second through the first and the last figures . . . in the third through the first and the middle figures.

We shall not go into the practical details (**14.22**), but only note that Aristotle replaces premisses not only by their contradictory, but also by their contrary opposites, and that he investigates all syllogisms.

The results of replacing premisses by the contradictory opposite of the conclusion can be clearly presented in the following way:

From a syllogism of figure	1	2	3
there results by substitution of the negation of the conclusion a syllogism of figure:			
substitution for the major premiss	3	3	1
substitution for the minor premiss	2	1	2

E. DICTUM DE OMNI ET NULLO

A word must now be said about the *'dictum de omni et nullo'* that later became so famous. It concerns the following sentence:

14.23 That one thing should be in the whole of another and should be predicated of all of another is the same. We say that there is predication of all when it is impossible to take anything of which the other will not be predicated; and similarly predication of none.

It is not clear whether Aristotle really intended here to establish an axiom for his system, as has often been supposed. One is rather led to suppose that he is simply describing the first and second moods of the first figure (**13.02, 13.03**). However, the *dictum can* be understood as an axiom if it is considered as a summary of the first four moods of the first figure, which is not in itself impossible.

In this connection we quote a historically and systematically more important passage in which Aristotle deals with a problem of the theory of the three figures (**13.20**). In it he makes an essential advance in analyzing propositions and gives expression to thoughts that are not without significance for the theory of quantification.

14.24 It is not the same, either in fact or in speech, that *A* belongs to all of that to which *B* belongs, and that *A* belongs to all of that to all of which *B* belongs: for nothing prevents *B* from belonging to *C*, though not to all *C:* e.g. let *B* stand for 'beautiful' and *C* for 'white'. If beauty belongs to something white, it is true to say that beauty belongs to that which is white: but not perhaps to everything that is white.

Here an analysis of the sentence *A* belongs to all *B* 'is presented, which could be interpreted in this way: 'For all *x:* if *B* belongs to *x*, then *A* belongs to *x*'; it would then be a matter of the modern formal implication. That Aristotle thought of such an analysis – at least during his later period – seems guaranteed by the fact that he explicitly applied it to modal logic (cf. **15.13**). The Scholastics, as we shall see, treated these thoughts as an elucidation of the *dictum*.

F. BEGINNINGS OF A METALOGICAL SYSTEM

Aristotle also described his syllogisms metalogically in such a way that a new, metalogical system could easily be established:

14.25 In every syllogism one of the premisses must be affirmative, an universality must be present.

14.26 It is clear that every demonstration will proceed through three terms and no more, unless the same conclusion is established by different pairs of propositions.

14.27 This being evident, it is clear that a syllogistic conclusion follows from two premisses and not from more than two.

14.28 And it is clear also that in every syllogism either both or one of the premisses must be like the conclusion. I mean not only in being affirmative or negative, but also in being necessary, assertoric or contingent.

Aristotle does not carry out this application to modal logic; possibly this is an interpolation by another hand.

In developing the several figures Aristotle established similar rules for each. **13.05** contains an example. Taken all together these rules form an almost complete metalogical description of the syllogistic, which one would like to develop.

G. THE INVENTIO MEDII

Here we want to allude briefly to a doctrine of the *Prior Analytics* which is not essentially a matter of formal logic but rather of methodology, and that is the discussions about what was later called the *inventio medii*. In connection with axiomatization one can ask two different basic questions: (1) What follows given premisses? (2) From what premisses can a given sentence (conclusion) be deduced? Aristotle primarily considered the first question, but in the following text and its continuation he poses also the second, and tries to show the premisses of a syllogism must be constructed in order to yield a given conclusion. At the same time he gives practical advice on the forming of syllogisms:

14.29 The manner in which every syllogism is produced, the number of the terms and premisses through which it proceeds, the relation of the premisses to one another, the character of the problem proved in each figure, and the number of the figures appropriate to each problem, all these matters are clear from what has been said. We must now state how we may ourselves always have a supply of syllogisms in reference to the problem proposed and by what road we may reach the principles relative to the problem: for perhaps we ought not only to investigate the construction of syllogisms, but also to have the power of making them.

We do not need to pursue the details of this theory here. It only interests us as the starting-point of the scholastic *pons asinorum*.

§ 15. MODAL LOGIC*

A. MODALITIES

Aristotle distinguishes three principal classes of premisses:

15.01 Every premiss is either about belonging to, or necessarily belonging to, or possibly belonging to.

The expressions 'necessary' (ἐξ ἀνάγκης) and 'possible' (can belong to, ἐνδέχεται, δύναται) have several meanings.

1. In respect of the functor 'necessary' (or 'must') we have already remarked (§ 13, C, 2) that it often only expresses logical consequence.

---

* The Aristotelian (as also the Theophrastan) modal logic is here interpreted in the way that was customary among the Scholastics, rediscovered by A. Becker in 1934, and served as a basis for my ideas in works on the history of modal logic, on Theophrastus and on ancient logic.

However, while I was writing this work, Prof. J. Lukasiewicz communicated his being in possession of a quite different interpretation, showing the Aristotelian system to have contained mistakes which were rectified by Theophrastus. This new interpretation has now been published (*Aristotle's Syllogistic*, 2nd ed., Oxford, 1957).

That this is so, can be clearly seen where for instance Aristotle says 'It is necessary that *A* necessarily belongs to *B*' (**15.02**), or again 'It is necessary that *A* possibly belongs to B' (**15.03**). The first 'necessary' evidently means logical (ἁπλῶς) and hypothetical (τούτων ὄντων) necessity (**15.04**). The necessity that something is when it is (ὅταν ᾖ) obviously belongs to the second of these classes (**15.05**).

2. Even the simple, unqualified (assertoric) 'belonging to', which Aristotle often calls 'mere belonging to', is divided into an absolute (ἁπλῶς) and temporally qualified (κατὰ χρόνον) kind, with different logical properties (**15.06**).

3. As to possibility, Aristotle distinguishes at first two kinds: the one-sided and the two-sided.

This distinction emerges from a searching discussion which Aristotle conducts in the *Hermeneia*. The passage is of great importance for the understanding of the whole doctrine of modalities, and so we give it in full:

15.07 When it is necessary that a thing should be, it is possible that it should be. (For if not, the opposite follows, since one or the other must follow; so, if it is not possible, it is impossible, and it is thus impossible that a thing should be which must necessarily be; which is absurd.) Yet from the proposition 'it may be' it follows that it is not impossible, and from that it follows that it is not necessary; it comes about therefore that the thing which must necessarily be need not be; which is absurd. But again, the proposition 'it is necessary that it should be' does not follow from the proposition 'it may be', nor does the proposition 'it is necessary that it should not be'. . . . For if a thing may be, it may also not be, but if it is necessary that it should be or that it should not be, one of the two alternatives will be excluded. It remains, therefore, that the proposition 'it is not necessary that it should not be' follows from the proposition 'it may be'. For this is true also of that which must necessarily be.

The sequence of thought here is, in summary form: If something is necessary, then it is also possible; but what is possible, can also not be (it is not impossible that it should not be); but from that it follows that it is not necessary, and so a contradiction results. The solution consists in distinguishing the two meanings of being 'possible':

15.071 One-sided possibility: that is possible which not necessarily is not (which is not impossible).

15.072 Two-sided possibility: that is possible which neither necessarily is nor necessarily is not (nor impossibly is).

This second, two-sided possibility is the one intended in the syllogistic, and Aristotle only uses the first kind when forced to it. He defines two-sided possibility in the *Prior Analytics* thus:

15.08 I use the terms 'to be possible' and 'the possible' of that which is not necessary but, being assumed, results in nothing impossible.

It coincides, as can be seen, with the definition just given above; we find a similar one in the *Metaphysics* (**15.09**).

In two texts – but both extremely unclear and so hard to reconcile with the teaching as a whole as to constitute an unsolved problem (**15.10**) – Aristotle subdivides two-sided possibility. In the first passage he speaks of a possibility in the sense of 'in most cases' (ὡς ἐπὶ τὸ πολύ) and of another besides (**15.11**); in the second passage he distinguishes between a 'natural' (τὸ πεφυκὸς ὑπάρχειν) and an indeterminate (τὸ ἀόριστον) or 'contingent' (τὸ ἀπὸ τύχης) possibility which, so he says, is no concern of science. Both passages are probably interpolations.

B. STRUCTURE OF MODAL SENTENCES

The normal use of 'possible' in the sense of two-sided possibility is a distinguishing characteristic of Aristotle's modal logic. Another, of no less importance, is his view of the structure of modal sentences. He only gives explicit expression to this view in one place, but it lies at the base of the whole modal syllogistic and exercises a most remarkable influence.

15.13 The expression 'it is possible for this to belong to that' may be understood in two senses: either as 'to the thing to which that belongs' or as 'to the thing to which that can belong'; for 'to that of which *B* (is predicated) *A* can (belong)' means one of the two: 'to that of which *B* is predicated' or 'to that of which (*B* as) possibly (belonging) is predicated'.

This contains two points:

First a sentence of the form '*A* belongs to *B*' is paraphrased by the formula 'to that to which *B* belongs (of which *B* is predicated) *A* also belongs': implying a very subtle analysis of the sentence, reminiscent of the modern formal implication, which we find elsewhere in the Analytics (cf. **14.24**).

Secondly it can be gathered from this text that the modal functor does not determine the sentence as a whole, but part of it. So that for Aristotle a modal sentence is not to be conceived in such a sense as: 'It is possible that: A belongs to B'. The modal functor does not precede the whole sentence but one of its arguments. This distinction quickly becomes still clearer, for the distinction is three times made between two possible cases:

1. to that to which B belongs, A also can belong,
2. to that to which B can belong, A also can belong. In the first case the modal functor determines only the consequent, in the second case it determines the antecedent too.

This analysis is not expressly extended to necessity, but that extension must be supposed: for otherwise many syllogisms would be invalid.

C. NEGATION AND CONVERSION

In the *Hermeneia* Aristotle establishes a 'logical' square for sentences with modal functors, in which the two expressions for 'possible' (δυνατόν and ἐνδεχόμενον) mean one-sided possibility. This square can be compressed into the following scheme, in which all expressions in any one row are equivalent:

possible	not impossible	not necessary not
not possible	impossible	necessary not
possible not	not impossible not	not necessary
not possible not	impossible not	necessary (**15.14**)

More complicated is the doctrine of the negation of sentences containing the functor of two-sided possibility. Since this has been defined by a conjunction of two sentences, Aristotle rightly deduces, on the basis of the so-called de Morgan law (not to be found in him):

15.15 If anyone then should claim that because it is not possible for C to belong to all D, it necessarily does not belong to some D, he would make a false assumption: for it does belong to all D, but because in some cases it belongs necessarily, therefore we say that it is not *possible* for it to belong to all. Hence both the propositions 'A necessarily belongs to some B' and 'A necessarily does not belong to some B' are opposed to the proposition 'A may belong to all B'.

The passage is not quite clear; but the author's intention can be formulated:

15.151 p is not possible, if and only if, one of the two, p and not-p, is necessary.

From this it results that the negation of such a sentence issues as an alternation, such as is in no case permissible as a premiss in an Aristotelian syllogism. This prevents Aristotle from using reduction to the impossible in certain cases.

Another result which Aristotle subtly deduces from his suppositions is his doctrine of the equivalence of affirmative and negative sentences when they contain the functor under consideration:

15.16 It results that all premisses in the mode of possibility are convertible into one another. I mean not that the affirmative are convertible into the negative, but that those which are affirmative in form admit of conversion by opposition, e.g. 'it is possible to belong' may be converted into 'it is possible not to belong'; 'it is possible to belong to all' into 'it is possible to belong to none' and 'not to all'; 'it is possible to belong to some' into 'to some it is possible not to belong'. And similarly in other cases.

Take the three modal sentences:
  (a) '*A* possibly belongs to *B*',
  (b) '*A* does not possibly belong to *B*',
  (c) '*A* possibly does not belong to *B*'.
(b) is the proper denial of (a), (c) is no denial of (a) but it is 'negative in form'. Then it is stated that sentences such as (a) imply those such as (c), and are even equivalent to them. So we have following laws:

15.161 *p* is possible if and only if *p* is not possible.

15.162 It is possible that *A* belongs to all *B*, if and only if, it is possible that *A* belongs to no *B*.

15.163 It is possible that *A* belongs to some *B*, if and only if, it is possible that to some *B A* does not belong.

Laws analogous to those for ordinary conversion (**14.10**) hold for sentences containing the functors of necessity and one-sided possibility (**15.17**), just parallel to the corresponding laws in assertoric logic (**15.18**).
By contrast, the laws of conversion for sentences with the two-sided functor are different: the universal negative cannot be converted (**15.19**), but the particular negative can (**15.20**). The affirmative sentences are converted like assertoric ones (**15.21**).

D. SYLLOGISMS

On this basis and with the aid of the same procedures developed for the assertoric syllogistic, Aristotle now builds the vast structure of his system of syllogisms with modal premisses. Vast it is even in the number of formulae explicitly considered, they are not fewer than one hundred and thirty seven. But it appears much vaster – in spite of many points where it is incomplete – in view of the subtlety with which the original master-logician operates in so difficult a field. *De modalibus non gustabit asinus* was a medieval proverb; but one does not need to be a donkey to get lost in this maze of abstract laws: Theophrastus quite misunderstood the system, and nearly all the moderns, until 1934.

The syllogisms which it comprises can be arranged in eight groups. If we write '*N*' for a premiss with the functor 'necessary', '*M*' for one with the functor 'possible' and '*A*' for an assertoric premiss (that is, one which predicates mere belonging to), these groups can be shown as follows:

Group	1	2	3	4	5	6	7	8
Major premiss	*N*	*N*	*A*	*M*	*M*	*A*	*M*	*N*
Minor premiss	*N*	*A*	*N*	*M*	*A*	*M*	*N*	*M*
*An.Pr.*A, chap.	8	9–11	9–11	14/17/20	15/18/21		16/19/22	

A striking characteristic of this syllogistic is that in very many syllogisms the conclusion (contrary to **14.28**) has a stronger modality than the premisses, necessity being reckoned as stronger that mere belonging to and this as stronger than possibility.

15.22 It happens sometimes also that when *one* premiss is necessary the conclusion is necessary, not however, when either premiss is necessary, but only when the major is, e.g. if *A* is taken as necessarily belonging or not belonging to *B*, but *B* is taken as simply belonging to *C:* for if the premisses are taken in this way, *A* will necessarily belong or not belong to *C*. For since *A* necessarily belongs, or does not belong, to every *B*, and since *C* is one of the *B*s, it is clear that for *C* also the positive or the negative relation to *A* will hold necessarily.

And of course that is the case, if one presupposes the structure of the modal sentences as given above. For then the syllogism here described (an analogue of *Barbara*) will be interpreted as follows:·
    If to all to which *B* belongs, *A* necessarily belongs,
    and to that to which *C* belongs, *B* belongs,
    then to all to which *C* belongs, *A* necessarily belongs,
which is clearly correct.

Hence it is quite wrong to extend the validity of the principle 'the conclusion follows the weaker premiss' (cf. **14.28** and **17.17**) to Aristotle's modal syllogistic.

Another striking fact is that there are numerous valid modal syllogisms whose analogues in the assertoric syllogistic are invalid, as for instance those two negative premisses (in opposition to **14.25**); this is especially the case when the modal syllogism has a premiss with the functor of possibility where the assertoric analogue has an affirmative. For, as has been said, affirmative and negative possible premisses are equivalent and can replace one another. We take as an example a passage where Aristotle, after giving an analogue of *Barbara*, in the fourth group, to which he refers by such phrases as 'previously', 'the same syllogism', 'as before', then proceeds:

15.23 Whenever A may belong to all B, and B may belong to no C, then indeed no syllogism results from the premisses assumed, but if the premiss BC is converted after the manner of problematic propositions, the same syllogism results as before. For since it is possible that B should belong to no C, it is possible also that it should belong to all C. This has been stated above. Consequently if B is possible for all C, and A is possible for all B, the same syllogism again results. Similarly if in both the premisses the negative is joined with 'it is possible': e.g. if A may belong to none of the Bs, and B to none of the Cs. No syllogism results from the assumed premisses, but if they are converted we shall have the same syllogism as before.

This syllogistic is, like the assertoric, axiomatized. There serve as axioms the syllogisms of the first figure in all groups, except the sixth and eighth, together with the laws of conversion and, when assertoric premisses occur, principles of the assertoric syllogistic. The other syllogisms are reduced to those axioms, mostly by conversion of premisses (direct procedure). Reduction to the impossible serves to prove syllogisms of the first figure in the eighth group and the analogue of *Bocardo* in the fifth. The analogues of *Baroco* and *Bocardo* in the first group are proved only by ecthesis, while the same analogues in the second and third groups remain unproved, though it should not be hard to prove them.

The hardest problem for Aristotle are the syllogisms of the sixth group. The first figure ones among them rightly do not rank as intuitively evident; e.g. the analogue of *Barbara* would be:

    If to all to which B belongs A belongs,
    and to all to which C belongs, B may belong,
    then to all to which C belongs, A belongs.

For this to be evident one would have to see the rightness of the sentence 'To all to which B may belong, B belongs'; but according to the definition of possibility, that is false. The details of Aristotle's complicated attempts to validate this syllogism are matter of conjecture and dispute, but the fact that he has to replace the problematic minor premiss with an assertoric one is a sufficient indication of its essential weakness (**15.24**). However, the passage which contains this 'proof' is one of the few where Aristotle rises to the use of propositional variables, and for that reason remains of the greatest logical interest (15.25).

This abortive proof is moreover not the only inconsistency in the Aristotelian modal logic. There are for instance essential difficulties in connection with the conversion of premisses with the functor of necessity, and consequently in the proving of many syllogisms which contain such premisses. In general one gets the impression that this modal logic, by contrast to the assertoric syllogistic, is still only in a preliminary and incomplete stage of development.

§ 16. NON-ANALYTIC LAWS AND RULES

For those reasons there is no possible doubt that the theory of what Aristotle would have called 'analytic' syllogisms is his chief accomplishment in the field of formal logic. And so great an accomplishment is it from the historical and systematic points of view, that later, 'classical' logicians have mostly overlooked all else in his work. Yet the *Organon* contains a profusion of laws and rules of other kinds. Aristotle himself recognized some of them as autonomous formulae, irreducible to his syllogistic. In other words: he saw that a 'reduction' of these laws and rules to the syllogistic is impossible – a thing which all too many after him did not see.

From the historical standpoint these formulae are to be divided into three classes: first we have the formulae which are to be attributed to a period in which Aristotle had not yet discovered his analytic syllogisms. These are to be found in the *Topics* (and in the *Rhetoric*). Some of them were later re-edited with the help of variables, and recognized as valid also in the period of the *Analytics*. Secondly there are the formulae which Aristotle indeed considered but mistakenly, as analytic, the *syllogismi obliqui* as they were later called. Finally, in reviewing the completed system of his syllogistic he discovered the 'hypothetical' procedure and in some cases attained to full consciousness of propositional formulae.

But all these formulae are contained only in asides, and were never systematically develop ed as was the syllogistic. Furthermore, Aristotle thought, quite rightly in view of his methodological standpoint, that only the analytic formulae were genuinely 'scientific', i.e. usable in demonstration.

We give first the passages which, as it seems, introduce us to Aristotle's last thoughts on this question, then the actual non-analytic formulae divided into five classes: those belonging to the logic of classes, to the theory of identity, to the 'hypothetical' syllogistic, to the theory of relations, and to propositional logic.

A. TWO KINDS OF INFERENCE

16.01 In some arguments it is easy to see what is wanting, but some escape us, and appear to be syllogisms, because something necessary results from what has been laid down, e.g. if the assumptions were made that substance is not annihilated by the annihilation of what is not substance, and that if the elements out of which a thing is made are annihilated, then that which is made out of them is destroyed: these propositions being laid down, it is necessary that any part of substance is substance; this has not, however, been drawn by syllogism from the propositions assumed, but premisses are wanting. Again if it is necessary that animal should exist, if man does, and that substance should exist if man does: but as yet the conclusion has not been drawn syllogistically: for the premisses are not in the shape we required. We are deceived in such cases because something necessary results from what is assumed, since the syllogism also is necessary. But that which is necessary is wider than the syllogism: for every syllogism is necessary, but not everything which is necessary is a syllogism.

We must pass over the first example, about parts of substance, as its elucidation would take up too much space. But the second is clear; it concerns a law, not of propositional, but of predicate logic:

16.011 If, when x is A then it is B, and when x is B then it is C, then, when x is A then it is C.

This is a correct logical formula, and Aristotle is quite right in saying that it permits necessary inference. Hence he also realized that it falls under his definition of syllogism (**10.05**). But he refuses to admit it as syllogism. That means that his conception of syllogism had developed between the time when he penned the definition and that when he penned this passage. The definition applies to all correct logical formulae (and substitutions in them), but only a sub-class retains the name 'syllogism'. We know what this sub-class is that of the 'analytic' syllogisms. All other formulae may indeed be logically necessary, but are not genuine syllogisms.

This distinction is not merely a matter of terminology. That becomes evident in the passages where Aristotle deals with the 'hypothetical' syllogisms.

16.02 We must not try to reduce hypothetical syllogisms; for with the given premisses it is not possible to reduce them. For they have not been proved by syllogism, but assented to by agreement. For instance if a man should suppose that unless there is one faculty of contraries, there cannot be one science, and should then argue that there is no* (one) faculty of contraries, e.g. of what is healthy and what is sickly: for the same thing will then be at the same time healthy and sickly. He has shown that there is not one faculty of all contraries, but he has not proved that there is not a science. And yet one must agree. But the agreement does not come from a syllogism, but from an hypothesis. This argument cannot be reduced: but the proof that there is not a single faculty can.

Evidently a substitution is there being made in the law:

If (1) when not *p* then not *q*, and (2) not *p*, then (3) not *q*. (2) is proved by an *analytic* syllogism, but as (1) is merely supposed and not proved, the conclusion (3) also counts as not proved. That may be so, but Aristotle has not noticed that the assumed formula is no mere supposition but a correct logical *law*. The matter is still worse in the next text, an immediate continuation of the last:

16.03 The same holds good of arguments which are brought to a conclusion *per impossibile*. These cannot be analyzed either; but the reduction to what is impossible can be analyzed since it is proved by syllogism, though the rest of the argument cannot, because the conclusion is reached from an hypothesis. But these differ from previous arguments: for in the former a preliminary agreement must be reached if one is to accept the conclusion; e.g. an agreement that if there is proved to be one faculty of contraries, then contraries fall under the same science; whereas in the latter, even if no preliminary agreement has been made, men still accept the reasoning, because the falsity is patent, e.g. the falsity of what follows from the assumption that the diagonal is commensurate, viz. that then odd numbers are equal to evens.

So in reduction to the impossible too, Aristotle regards the inference as not 'demonstrated', though he has to recognize that no agreement needs to be presupposed to warrant inference.

One could express this doctrine as follows: the class of correct formulae contains two sub-classes: that of the 'better' and that of the 'less good' in relation to 'scientific demonstration'. The less good

---

* Reading μία with the manuscript tradition $A^2B^2C^2\Gamma$, against the (better) tradition $ABCnAl$, Waitz and Ross. For πᾶσα, read by the latter, would mean a logical mistake in Aristotle which seems to me unlikely in this connection. For the critical apparatus vid. Ross ad loc.

are precisely our non-analytic formulae, for which we have chosen this name because according to Aristotle they are not reducible to the classical syllogistic, 'not analyzable into the figures'. (In this he is evidently right, by contrast to a certain tradition.) That does not mean that these formulae are worthless for him; on the contrary he views them with a lively interest.

16.04 These points will be made clearer by the sequel, when we discuss the reduction to impossibility. . . . In the other hypothetical syllogisms, I mean those which proceed by substitution, or positing a certain quality, the inquiry will be directed to the terms of the problem to be proved – not the terms of the original problem, but the new terms introduced; and the method of the inquiry will be the same as before. But we must consider and determine in how many ways hypothetical syllogisms are possible.

16.05 Many other arguments are brought to a conclusion by the help of an hypothesis; these we ought to consider and mark out clearly. We shall describe in the sequel differences, and the various ways in which hypothetical arguments are formed: but at present this much must be clear, that it is not possible to resolve such arguments into the figures. And we have explained the reason.

On that Alexander of Aphrodisias remarks:

16.06 He says that many others (syllogisms) besides are formed from hypotheses, and promises to treat thoroughly of them later. But no writing of his on this subject is extant.

B. LAWS OF CLASS- AND PREDICATE-LOGIC

16.07 If man (is) an animal, what is not-animal is not man.
16.08 If the pleasant (is) good, the not-good (is) not pleasant.

Notice that quantifiers are here lacking: so it is not a question of contraposition in the ordinary sense of the word.
Aristotle was well aware that conversion of such sentences is invalid:

16.09 For animal follows on man, but not-animal does not (follow) on not-man; the reverse is the case.

Here there belong perhaps some rules which otherwise interpreted could be counted in with those of the 'logical square':

16.10 When we have shown that a predicate belongs in every case, we shall also have shown that it belongs in some cases. Likewise, also, if we show that it does not belong in any case, we shall also have shown that it does not belong in every case.

It is to be noted here that these formulae are not laws but, as is mostly the case in the *Topics*, rules.

A series of similar laws is concerned with contrariety (in the sense of the earlier notion: **12.02**):

16.11 Health follows upon vigour, but disease does not follow upon debility; rather debility follows upon disease.

16.12 Public opinion grants alike the claim that if all pleasure be good, then also all pain is evil, and the claim that if some pleasure be good, then also some pain is evil. Moreover, if some form of sensation be not a capacity, then also some form of failure of sensation is not a failure of capacity. . . . Again, if what is unjust be in some cases good, then also what is just is in some cases evil; and if what happens justly is in some cases evil, then also what happens unjustly is in some cases good.

It may be doubted whether Aristotle continued to recognize these laws as valid. But they are not without historical and even systematic interest.

C. THEORY OF IDENTITY

As already noted (**11.11**) Aristotle distinguishes three kinds of identity. Concerning the first, numerical identity, he developed the outline of a theory; its discovery is often falsely attributed to Leibniz.

16.13 Again, look and see if, supposing the one to be the same as something, the other also is the same as it: for if they be not both the same as the same thing, clearly neither are they the same as one another. Moreover, examine them in the light of their accidents or of the things of which they are accidents: for any accident belonging to the one must belong also to the other, and if the one belongs to anything as an accident, so must the other also. If in any of these respects there is a discrepancy, clearly they are not the same.

We have here in very compressed form a rather highly developed doctrine of identity; indeed this text contains a greater number of fundamental laws of identity than the corresponding chapter of *Principia Mathematica* (*13), and moreover Aristotle was the first to call to mind identity, in the passage mentioned above (**12.18**). The laws here sketched, can be formulated as follows with the help of variables:

16.131 If B is identical with A, and C is not identical with A, then B and C are not identical.

16.132 If A and B are identical, then (for all C): if C belongs to A, then it belongs also to B.

16.133 If A and B are identical, then (for all C): if A belongs to C, then it belongs also to B.

16.134 If there is a C which belongs to A but not to B, then A and B are not identical.

16.135 If there is a C to which A belongs but B does not, then A and B are not identical.

Admittedly the last two laws are only hinted at. In another passage we find:

16.14 For only to things that are indistinguishable and one in essence is it generally agreed that all the same attributes belong.

This is almost the Leibnizian *principium indiscernibilium* in so many words, originating as we see with Aristotle. It is remarkable that we do not find the simple principle:

16.141 If A is identical with B, and B with C, then A is identical with C.

D. SYLLOGISMS FROM HYPOTHESES

Aristotle did not know the expression 'hypothetical syllogism', but he often speaks of syllogisms *from* hypotheses (ἐξ ὑποθέσεως). We have shown above (in the commentary on citations **16.02** and **16.03**) that in general these need not be hypotheses; usually it is a matter only of logical laws or rules, similar to syllogisms in certain respects but not reducible to them. We have already seen some examples of such formulae. Here are some more which Aristotle would probably class with them.

16.15 The refutation which depends upon the consequent arises because people suppose that the relation of consequence is convertible. For whenever, if this is, that necessarily is, they suppose that also when that is, this is.

16.16 When two things are so related to one another, that if the one is, the other necessarily is, then if the latter is not, the former will not be either, but if the latter is, it is not necessary that the former should be.

16.17 If this follows that, it is claimed that the opposite of this will follow the opposite of that.... But that is not so; for the sequence is vice versa.

16.18 In regard to subjects which must have one and one only of two predicates, as (e.g.) a man must have either disease or health, supposing we are well supplied as regards the one for arguing its presence or absence, we shall be well equipped as regards the remaining one as well. This rule is convertible for both purposes: for when we have shown that the one attribute belongs, we shall have shown that the remaining one does not belong; while if we show that the one does not belong, we shall have shown that the remaining one does belong.

We have there, evidently, the exclusive alternative (negation of equivalence).

16.19 In general whenever *A* and *B* are such that they cannot belong at the same time to the same thing, and one of the two necessarily belongs to everything, and again *C* and *D* are related in the same way, and *A* follows *C* but the relation cannot be reversed, then *D* must follow *B* and the relation cannot be reversed. And *A* and *D* may belong to the same thing, but *B* and *C* cannot. First it is clear from the following consideration that *D* follows *B*. For since either *C* or *D* necessarily belongs to everything; and since *C* cannot belong to that to which *B* belongs, because it carries *A* along with it and *A* and *B* cannot belong to the same thing; it is clear that *D* must follow *B*. Again since *C* does not reciprocate with *A*, but *C* or *D* belongs to everything, it is possible that *A* and *D* should belong to the same thing. But *B* and *C* cannot belong to the same thing, because *A* follows *C;* and so something impossible results. It is clear then that *B* does not reciprocate with *D* either, since it is possible that *D* and *A* should belong at the same time to the same thing.

This text is one of the peaks of Aristotelian logic: the founder of our science conducts himself with the same sureness and freedom as in the best parts of his syllogistic, though here dealing with a new field, that of non-analytic formulae. The run of this text can be formulated thus:

(1) For all X: A or B (and not both) belongs to X, and
(2) for all X: C or D (and not both) belongs to X, and
(3) for all X: if C belongs to X, then it belongs also to A.

From these hypotheses there follows on the one hand:

(4) for all X: if B belongs to X, then it belongs also to D,

and on the other:

(5) for all X: not both B and C belong to X.

These consequences are quite correct. The thing to notice is that there are three different binary propositional functors ('or', 'and', 'if ... then'). In his proof Aristotle uses, among others, the following three laws, apparently with full consciousness:

16.191 For all X: if not both A and B belong to X, and B belongs to X, then A does not belong to it.

16,192 For all X: if, when A belongs to X B also belongs to X, but B does not belong to X, then A also does not belong to X.

16.193 For all X: if either A or B belongs to X, and A does not belong to it, then B does belong to it.

E. LAWS OF THE LOGIC OF RELATIONS

16.20 If knowledge be a conceiving, then also the object of knowledge is an object of conception.

16.21 If the object of conception is in some cases an object of knowledge, then also some form of conceiving is knowledge.

16.22 If pleasure is good, then too a greater pleasure is a greater good; and if injustice is bad, then too a greater injustice is a greater evil.

In this connection the following piece of history deserves to go on record. De Morgan stated that the whole Aristotelian logic was unable to prove that if the horse is an animal, then the head of the horse is head of an animal. The reproach is evidently unjustified, since the law stated in **16.20** is just what is needed for this proof. Further, Whitehead and Russell (**16.23**) remark that the supposed lack of this law is really a good point about Aristotelian logic, since it is invalid without an additional existential postulate. This may be right in relation to De Morgan's problem, i.e. if he understood 'horse' as an individual name; but the law in which **16.20** is a substitution is correct – since it concerns not an individual but a class name ('knowledge').

Aristotle gives three further laws of the logic of relations in the chapter about those syllogisms which later came to be called '*obliqui*':

16.24 That the first term belongs to the middle, and the middle to the extreme, must not be understood in the sense that they can always be predicated of one another. . . . But we must suppose the verb 'to belong' to have as many meanings as the senses in which the verb 'to be' is used, and in which the assertion that a thing 'is' may be said to be true. Take for example the statement that there is a single science of contraries. Let *A* stand for 'there being a single science', and *B* for things which are contrary to one another. Then *A* belongs to *B*, not in the sense that contraries are the fact of there being a single science of them, but in the sense that it is true to say of the contraries that there is a single science of them.

16.25 It happens sometimes that the first term is stated of the middle, but the middle is not stated of the third term, e.g. if wisdom is knowledge, and wisdom is of the good, the conclusion is that there is knowledge of the good. The good then is not knowledge, though wisdom is knowledge.

16.26 Sometimes the middle term is stated of the third, but the first is not stated of the middle, e.g. if there is a science of everything that has a quality, or is a contrary, and the good both is a contrary and has a quality, the conclusion is that there is a science of the good, but the good is not science, nor is that which has a quality or is a contrary, though the good is both of these.

16.27 Sometimes neither the first term is stated of the middle, nor the middle of the third, while the first is sometimes stated of the third, and sometimes not: e.g. if there is a genus of that of which there is a science, and if there is a science of the good, we conclude that there is a genus of the good. But nothing is (there) predicated of anything. And if that of which there is a science is a genus, and if there is a science of the good, we conclude that the good is a genus. The first term then is predicated of the extreme, but in the premisses one thing is not stated of another.

We have here four more relational laws; of greater importance is the introductory remark that the so-called 'copula' need not be 'is' but can be replaced by some other relation. A further interesting fact is that Aristotle presupposes *inter alia* the following law from the logic of classes (in **16.26**):

16.261 For all x: if x is A and B, then x is A or B.

The introductory remark admittedly only reveals an intuition that is undeveloped. Nor did Aristotle link it up with his own penetrating thesis of the manifold structure of the sentence according to the diversity of the categories (**11.15**), so rising to a higher systematic unity. Nevertheless the text cited does contain the beginnings of a logic of relations.

Finally we can collect from at least six places in the *Topics* a group of rules, totalling eighteen altogether, which perhaps are to be interpreted as belonging to the logic of relations. We give three of them, again concerned with 'more':

16.28 Moreover, argue from greater and less degrees. In regard to greater degrees there are four commonplace rules. One is: See whether a greater degree of the predicate follows a greater degree of the subject: e.g. if pleasure be good, see whether also a greater pleasure be a greater good. ... Another rule is: If one predicate be attributed to two subjects; then supposing it does not belong to the subject to which it is the more likely to belong, neither does it belong where it is less likely to belong; while if it does belong where it is less likely to belong, then it belongs as well where it is more likely. ... Moreover: If two predicates be attributed to two subjects, then if the one which is more usually thought to belong to the one subject does not belong, neither does the remaining predicate belong to the remaining subject; or, if the one which is less usually thought to belong to the one subject does belong, so too does the remaining predicate to the remaining subject.

F. PROPOSITIONAL RULES AND LAWS

Finally we find in Aristotle four formulae belonging to the most abstract part of logic, namely, propositional logic. Two of them even contain propositional variables:

16.29 If when A is, B must be, (then) when B is not, A cannot be.

That these are propositional variables, Aristotle says expressly:

16.30 A is posited as one thing, being two premisses taken together.

16.31 If, when A is, B must be, (then) also when A is possible, B must be possible.

It is to be noted that these propositional variables permit substitution only of quite determinate expressions, namely conjunctions of premisses suitable for an analytic syllogism.

16.32 From true premisses it is not possible to draw a false conclusion, but a true conclusion may follow from false premisses, true, however, only in respect to the fact, not to the reason.

That is not yet the scholastic principle *ex falso sequitur quodlibet*, but only the assertion that one can form syllogisms in which one or both premisses are false, the conclusion true.

16.33 If the conclusion is false, the premisses of the argument (λόγος) must be false, either all or some of them.

This rule underlies the indirect proof of syllogisms (cf. **14.201–202**). Note that it is a rule, not a law, and formulated quite generally, without being limited to two premisses.

SUMMARY

Reviewing the logical doctrines of Aristotle as presented, we can state:

1. Aristotle created *formal logic*. For the first time in history we find in him: (a) a clear idea of universally valid logic law, though he never gave a definition of it, (b) the use of variables, (c) sentential forms which besides variables contain only logical constants.

2. Aristotle constructed the first *system of formal logic* that we know. This consists exclusively of logical laws, and was developed axiomatically, even in more than one way.

3. Aristotle's masterpiece in formal logic is his *syllogistic*. This is a system of term-logic consisting of laws, not rules. In spite of certain weaknesses it constitutes a faultlessly constructed system.

4. Besides the syllogistic, Aristotle constructed other portions of term-logic, including an extremely complex modal logic, as well as a number of laws and rules which overstep the bounds of the syllogistic.

5. At the end of his life Aristotle, in a few texts, succeeded in formulating even *propositional formulae;* but these, like the non-analytic formulae of term-logic, he did not develop systematically.

6. Aristotelian logic, though formal, is not *formalistic*. It is lacking also in understanding of the difference between rules and laws, and the semantics remain rudimentary, in spite of the many works which Aristotle devoted to the subject.

It is no exaggeration to say that nothing comparable has been seen in the whole history of formal logic. Not only is Aristotle's logic, according to all our information, a completely new creation, but it has been brought even by him to a high degree of completeness. Since moreover Aristotle's most important writings – most important because they were the only complete logical works – survived the cultural catastrophe of Greece, it is no wonder that the huge body of doctrine they contain should have continued to fascinate nearly all logicians for more than two thousand years, and that the whole history of logic has developed along the lines traced out in advance by Aristotle's thought.

That has not been harmless for the development of our science. Even in antiquity there was a school of logicians which introduced a new set of problems different from those posed by the logic of Aristotle. We have only fragments of their work, and the authority of the founder of logic was so great that the achievements of this school were not at all understood during the long period from the time of the Renaissance up to and including the nineteenth century. We must now concern ourselves with them, but first a brief word must be said about Aristotle's first disciple, Theophrastus.

§17. THEOPHRASTUS

Theophrastus of Eresos, Aristotle's chief disciple and leader of the Peripatetic school after the founder's death, has, in company with his less significant colleague Eudemus, an important place in the history of logic, and that in three respects. First, he developed various of his master's doctrines in such a way as to prepare the ground for the later 'classical' logic; secondly, he set his own quite different system in opposition to the Aristotelian modal logic; thirdly, he developed a doctrine of hypothetical arguments which was a preparation for Megarian-Stoic logic.

His very numerous works (**17.01**) have all perished save for some one hundred fragments. These, however, are enough to tell us that he commented on the most important of Aristotle's logical works (**17.02**), and they give us some insight into his own logical thought.

A. DEVELOPMENT AND ALTERATION OF VARIOUS DOCTRINES

17.03 Speech having a twofold relation – as the philosopher Theophrastus has shown – one to the hearers, to whom it signifies something, the other to the things about which it informs the hearers, there arise in respect of the relation to the hearers poetics and rhetoric, ... in respect of that to the things, it will be primarily the philosopher's business, as he refutes falsehood and demonstrates truth.

We can see that this is a new semiotic, with stress on what is now called the 'pragmatic' dimension of signs.

17.04 Theophrastus rightly calls the singular sentence determined, the particular undetermined.

17.05 Alexander opines that 'not belonging to all' and 'to some not belonging' differ only in the expression, whereas Theophrastus's view is that they differ also in meaning: for 'not belonging to all' shows that (something) belongs to several, 'to some not belonging' that (not belonging) to one.

A more important thought is the following:

17.06 Consequently Theophrastus says that in some cases, if the determination (of quantity) προσδιορισμός) does not also stand with the predicate, opposites, contradictories, will be true, e.g. he says that 'Phanias possesses knowledge', 'Phanias does not possess knowledge', can both be true.

This is not a matter, as Theophrastus mistakenly supposed, of quantification of the predicate, which Aristotle had rejected (**12.03**), but of a quantification of both parts of a subject when there is a two-place functor (cf. **44.22** ff.). This structure was only later treated in detail (cf. **28.15** ff., **42.06**, **42.22**). We have here the first beginnings of it.

17.07 In those premisses which potentially contain three terms, viz. those . . . which Theophrastus called κατὰ προσλήψιν (for these have three terms in a sense; since in (the premiss) 'to all of that to all of which *B* belongs, *A* also belongs' in the two terms *A* and *B* which are explicit there is somehow comprised the third of which *B* is predicated . . .): (these premisses) . . . seem to differ from categorical ones only in expression, as Theophrastus showed in his *On Affirmation*.

17.08 But Theophrastus in *On Affirmation* treats 'to that to which *B* (belongs, there belongs also) *A*' as equivalent (ἴσον δυναμένην) to 'to all of that to all of which *B* belongs, *A* (also belongs) (cf. **14.24**).

17.09 But Theophrastus and Eudemus have given a simpler proof that universal negative premisses can be converted. . . . They conduct the proof so: *A* belongs to no *B*. If it belongs to none, *A* must be disjoined (ἀπεζεύκται) and separated (κεχώρισται) from B. But what is disjoined is disjoined from something disjoined. Therefore B too is quite disjoined from A. And if this is so, it belongs to no A.

This shows that Theophrastus takes a purely extensional view of the terms (cf. § 36, E) – so much so that one is led by this text (as by **17.13**) to think of a diagrammatic scheme such as Leibniz used (**36.14**).

17.10 To these four (Aristotelian syllogisms of the first figure) Theophrastus added five others, which are neither perfect nor indemonstrable.

We no longer have the relevant text. Alexander's explanations (**17.11**) show that these are the five:

17.111 If A belongs to all B and B to all C, then too C belongs to some A *(Baralipton)*.

17.112 If A belongs to no B, and B to all C, then too C belongs to no A *(Celantes)*.

17.113 If A b longs to all B and B to some C, then too C belongs to some A *(Dabitis)*.

17.114 If A belongs to all C and B to no C, then to some A C does not belong *(Fapesmo)*.

17.115 If A belongs to some B and B to no C, then too to some A C does not belong *(Frisemomorum)*.

These are what were later called the 'indirect' syllogisms of the first figure, deduced by means of the Aristotelian rules (cf. § 13, D).

B. MODAL LOGIC

All the texts so far quoted contain developments of or – often questionable – improvements on the Aristotelian logic. The Theophrastan theory of modal syllogisms, on the other hand, is an entirely new system, set in fundamental oppositions, as it appears, to that of Aristotle.

17.12 Hence Aristotle says that universal negative possible premisses are not convertible. But Theophrastus says that these too, like the other negatives, can be converted.

17.13 But Theophrastus and Eudemus, as we have already explained at the beginning, say that universal negative (possible premisses) can be converted, like universal negative assertoric and necessary ones. Their convertibility they prove thus: if A possibly does not belong to all B, B also possibly does not (belong) to all A; for if A possibly does not belong to all B . . ., then A can be disjoined from all B; but if this is so, B also can be disjoined from A; and in that case B also possibly does not belong to all A.

17.14 It is (according to Aristotle) a property of the possible to convert, i.e. the affirmations and negations concerning it follow on each other . . . but it should be known that this conversion of premisses is not valid in the school of Theophrastus, and they do not use it. For there is the same reason (1) for saying that the universal negative possible (premiss) is convertible, like the assertoric and necessary, and (2) (for saying) that affirmative possibles are not convertible into negatives.

In brief: according to Theophrastus all laws of conversion for problematic sentences are exactly analogous to those for assertoric sentences; and the 'reason' of which Alexander speaks, can only be, so it would seem, that the modal doctrine of Theophrastus is based on *one-sided* possibility, while Aristotle's is based on two-sided.

Similarly the second fundamental thesis of the Aristotelian system is also rejected: for Theophrastus the functor of modality must be thought of as determining the whole sentence, not just one or both of its arguments, i.e. it must be thought of as standing at the beginning of the sentence (cf. commentary on **15.13**).

17.15 But his companions who are with Theophrastus and Eudemus, deny this, and say that all formulae consisting of a necessary and an assertoric premiss, so constituted as to be suitable for syllogistic inference, yield an assertoric conclusion. They take that from the (principle according to which) in all (syllogistic) combinations the conclusion is similar to the last and weaker premiss.

17.16 But Theophrastus, (in order to prove) that in this combination (συμπλοκή) the conclusion yielded is not necessary, proceeds thus: 'For if B necessarily (belongs) to C and A does not necessarily belong to B, if one disjoins the not necessary, evidently, as B is disjoined (from A), C too will be disjoined from A: hence does not necessarily belong to it in virtue of the premisses.

17.17 They prove that this is so by material means (= by substitutions) also. For they take a necessary universal affirmative or negative as major (premiss), an assertoric universal affirmative as minor, and show that these yield an assertoric conclusion. Suppose that animal (belongs) to all man necessarily, but man belongs (simply) to all in motion: (then) animal will not necessarily belong to all in motion.

Now the basis for Aristotle's permitting the drawing of a necessary conclusion from one necessary and one assertoric premiss, was precisely his idea of the structure of modal sentences. Theophrastus certainly does not reject this idea in his extant fragments, and perhaps was not fully aware of it. But in any case all that we have of his modal logic gives evidence of a system presupposing the rejection of the Aristotelian structure of modal sentences.

C. HYPOTHETICAL SYLLOGISMS

We have no text of Theophrastus that contains anything of his theory of hypothetical propositions. He seems to have treated of them, for he distinguished the meaning of εἰ and ἐπεί (**17.18**). Possibly too it was he who introduced the terminology for these propositions which Galen ascribes to the 'old Peripatetics' (**17.19**). However, we know that he developed hypothetical syllogisms:

17.20 He (Aristotle) says that many syllogisms are formed on hypotheses. . . . Theophrastus mentions them in his *Analytics*, as do Eudemus and some others of his companions.

According to Philoponus, both of them 'and also the Stoics' wrote 'many-lined' treatises about these syllogisms (**17.21**). In fact, however, the treatment of only one kind of these syllogisms is expressly attributed to Theophrastus, that namely which consists of 'thoroughly (δι' ὅλων) hypothetical' syllogisms.

17.22 However, the thoroughly hypotheticals are reduced to the three figures in another way, as Theophrastus has proved in the first book of the *Prior Analytics*. A thoroughly hypothetical syllogism is of this kind: If A, then B; if B, then C; if therefore A, then C. In these the conclusion too is hypothetical; e.g. if man is, animal is; if animal is, then substance is: if therefore man is, substance is. Now since in these too there must be a middle term in which the premisses convene (for otherwise here also there cannot be a conclusive link), this middle will be positioned in three ways. For if one premiss ends with it and the other begins with it, there will be the first figure; it will be in fact as though it was predicated of one extreme, subjected to the other. . . . In this way of linking one

can take also the converse of the conclusion, in such a way that
(*C*) is not the consequent (ἑπόμενον) but the antecedent
(ἡγούμενον), not indeed simply, but with opposition, since
when a conclusion 'if *A*, then *C*' has been gained, there is
gained a conclusion 'if not *C*, then not *A*'.

If the premisses begin differently and end similarly, the
figure will be the second, like the second (in the system) of
categorical (syllogisms). . . . e.g. If man, then animal; if
stone, then not animal; therefore if man, then not stone. . . .

If the premisses begin similarly and end differently, the
figure will be like the third . . . e.g. if *A*, then *B;* if not *A*, then
C; it will follow: therefore, if not *B*, then *C*, or, if not *C*, then *B*.

The formulae contained in this text are presented in such a way
that from them alone it is impossible to tell whether their variables
are term- or propositional variables. However, the substitutions
show that the former is the case. Hence we have no reason to ascribe
any law of propositional logic to Theophrastus. Yet it is most
probable that in developing Aristotle's hints about 'syllogisms from
hypotheses' he prepared the way for the Megarian-Stoic doctrine.

The formulae in the text just cited are worded as rules; but we
do not know whether this wording is due to Theophrastus himself,
or to Alexander and so mediately to the Stoics.

III. THE MEGARIAN-STOIC SCHOOL

§ 18. HISTORICAL SURVEY

18.01 Euclid originated from Megara on the Isthmus. . . . He occupied himself with the writings of Parmenides; his pupils and successors were called 'Megarians', also 'Eristics' and later 'Dialecticians'.

18.02 The Milesian Eubulides also belongs among the successors of Euclid; he solved many dialectical subtleties, such as The Liar.

18.03 Eubulides was also hostile to Aristotle and made many objections to him. Among the successors belonged Alexinus of Elis, a most contentious man, whence he gained the name 'Elenxinus' ('Refuter').

18.04 Among (the pupils) of Eubulides was Apollonius, surnamed Cronus, whose pupil Diodorus, the son of Ameinias of Iasus, was also called Cronus . . . . He too was a dialectician. . . . During his stay with Ptolemy Soter he was challenged by Stilpo to solve some dialectical problems; but as he could not do this immediately . . ., he left the table, wrote a treatise on the problems propounded, and died of despondency.

18.05 Stilpo, from the Greek Megara, studied under some pupils of Euclid; others say that he studied under Euclid himself, and also under Thrasymachus of Corinth, the friend of Icthyas. He surpassed the rest in inventiveness of argument and dialectical art to such an extent that well-nigh all Greece had their eyes on him and was fain to follow the Megarian school.

18.06 He caught in his net Crates and very many more. Among them he captured Zeno the Phoenician.

18.07 Zeno, the son of Mnaseas or Demeas, was born at Citium, a small Greek town on the island of Cyprus, where Phoenicians had settled.

18.08 He was . . . a pupil of Crates; some say that he also studied under Stilpo.

18.09 He was assiduous in discussion with the dialectician Philo and studied with him; so that Philo came to be admired by the more youthful Zeno no less than his master Diodorus.

18.10 He also spent some time under Diodorus, . . . studying hard at dialectics.

18.11 Kleanthes the son of Phanias was born at Assus . . . joined Zeno . . . and remained true to his teaching.

18.12 Chrysippus the son of Apollonius from Soli or Tarsus . . ., was a pupil of Cleanthes.

18.13 He became so famous as a dialectician, that it was generally said that if the gods were to use dialectic, it would be none other than that of Chrysippus.

It was necessary to cite these extracts from the *Lives and Opinions of Famous Philosophers* of Diogenes Laertius, in order to counter a widespread error to the effect that there was a Stoic, but no Megarian logic. From the passages quoted it appears unmistakably that (a) the Megarian school antedated the Stoic, (b) the founders of the Stoa, Zeno and Chrysippus, learned their logic from the Megarians, Diodorus, Stilpo and Philo. And again (c) we know at least three Megarian thinkers of importance in the history of logic – Eubulides, Diodorus, and Philo – while only one can be named from the Stoa, viz. Chrysippus who can lay claim to practically no basically original doctrine, whereas each of the three Megarians conceived a definitely original idea.

Admittedly the Megarian school seems to have died out by the close of the 3rd century B.C., whereas the Stoa continued to flourish. Also the adherents of the latter disseminated logic in many excellent handbooks with the result that people, as in Galen's time, spoke only of Stoic logic. The least that can justly be required of us is to speak of a Megarian-Stoic logic. Possibly the basic ideas should be attributed to the Megarians, their technical elaboration to the Stoics, but this is mere conjecture.

The names and doctrinal influences recorded by Diogenes can be conveniently summarized in the following table:

Euclid of Megara, pupil of Socrates,
founder of the Megarian or 'dialectical' school
(ca. 400 B.C.)

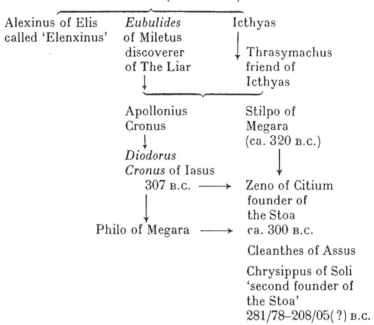

Alexinus of Elis   *Eubulides*   Icthyas
called 'Elenxinus'   of Miletus
       discoverer   Thrasymachus
       of The Liar   friend of
                      Icthyas

Apollonius   Stilpo of
Cronus   Megara
                  (ca. 320 B.C.)
Diodorus
Cronus of Iasus
     307 B.C. ⟶   Zeno of Citium
                      founder of
                      the Stoa
Philo of Megara ⟶   ca. 300 B.C.

Cleanthes of Assus

Chrysippus of Soli
'second founder of
the Stoa'
281/78–208/05(?) B.C.

B. PROBLEMS OF LITERARY HISTORY

The conditions for investigation of the Megarian-Stoic logic are much less favourable than those for that of the logic of Aristotle or even Theophrastus. We have the essential works of Aristotle entire, and in the case of Theophrastus are in possession at least of fragments quoted by competent experts who are not absolutely hostile to the author they cite. But for Megarian-Stoic teaching we have to rely essentially on the refutations of Sextus Empiricus, an inveterate opponent. As B. Mates rightly says, it is as though we had to rely for a knowledge of R. Carnap's logic only on existentialist accounts of it. Fortunately Sextus, though no friend to the Stoics, was (in contrast to most existentialists) well acquainted with formal logic, which he opposed from his sceptical point of view. We can moreover control at least some of his reports by means of other texts.

But still we have nothing but fragments. We can hardly doubt that the material to hand suffers from many gaps: for instance term-logic is almost completely missing, and it seems hardly likely that it was wholly unconsidered in the Stoa.

107

Another problem concerns the interpretation. Even in antiquity Stoic texts were often 'aristotelized', propositional variables taken for term-variables etc. A similar defect characterizes all modern historians of logic, Prantl most of all, who completely mistook the significance of this logic. Peirce was the first to see that it was a propositional logic, and J. Łukasiewicz did a lasting service in giving the correct interpretation. Now there is available a scientific monograph – a rarity in history of logic – by B. Mates. So in the present state of research it can be stated with some certainty that we are again in a position to understand this extremely interesting logic.

C. ORIGIN AND NATURE

In reading the Megarian-Stoic fragments one's first impression is that here is something different from Aristotelian logic: terminology, laws, the very range of problems, all are different. In addition we are confronted with a new technique of logic. The most striking differences are that the Megarian-Stoic logic is firstly not a logic of terms but of propositions, and secondly that it consists exclusively of rules, not of laws – as does the *Prior Analytics*. The question at once arises, what was the origin of this logic.

The answer is complex. First of all one cannot doubt that the Megarians and Stoics, who as we have seen (cf. **18.03**) found an only too frequent delight in refutation, had a tendency to do everything differently from Aristotle. Thus for example they introduce quite new expressions even where Aristotle has developed an excellent terminology.

Yet it should not be said that their logical thought could have developed uninfluenced by Aristotle. On the contrary, they appear to have developed just those ideas which are last to appear in the *Organon*. We find, for instance, a more exact formulation of the rules which Aristotle used in axiomatizing the syllogistic, and himself partially formulated. Nor can it be denied that they developed his theory of 'syllogisms from hypotheses', chiefly on the basis of the preparatory work of Theophrastus. And generally speaking they everywhere show traces of the same spirit as Aristotle's, only in a much sharper form, that spirit being the spirit of *formalized* logic.

And that is not yet all. In many of his non-analytical formulae Aristotle depends directly on pre-Platonic and Platonic discussions, and this dependence is still greater in the oase of the Megarian-Stoic thinkers. It often happens that they transmute these discussions from the language of term-logic into that of propositional logic, and one can understand how they, rather than Aristotle, came to do this on such a scale. Aristotle always remained at heart a pupil of Plato's, looking for essences, and accordingly asking himself the question: 'Does A belong to B?' But the Megarians start from the pre-Platonic question: 'How can the statement p be refuted?' Alexinus was called 'Refuter', and all these thinkers continued to be fundamentally refuters in their logic. Which means that their basic problems were concerned with complete propositions, whereas Aristotle had his attention fixed on terms. The thorough empiricism too, to which the Stoics gave their allegiance, contributed to this difference.

As to details, propositional logic originated with the Megarians and Stoics, the second great contribution made by the Greeks to logic, and just what was almost entirely missing from Aristotelian logic. Then, as already stated, they understood formal treatment in a formalistic way, and laid the foundations of an exact semantics and syntax. Misunderstood for centuries, this logic deserves recognition as a very great achievement of thought.

Unfortunately no means is available for us to pursue the historical development of Megarian-Stoic investigations; we can only consider what we find at the *end* of this development, which seems to have already come with Chrysippus. Within a hundred and fifty years Greek logic rose with unbelievable speed to the very heights of formalism. We now have to view these heights as already attained. Our presentation cannot be historical; it can only proceed systematically.

§ 19. CONCEPT OF LOGIC. SEMIOTICS. MODALITIES

A. LOGIC

19.01 They (the Stoics) say there is a threefold division of philosophical speech: one (part) is the physical, another the ethical, the third the logical.

19.02 They compare philosophy to an animal, the logical part corresponding to the bones and sinews, the ethical to the fleshy parts, the physical to the soul. Or again to an egg, the logical (part) being the outside (=the shell). . . . Or again to a fertile field. The fence then corresponds to the logical.

19.03 According to some the logical part is divided into two sciences, rhetoric and dialectic. . . . They explain rhetoric as the science of speaking well . . . and dialectic as the science of right discussion in speech, by question and answer. Hence the following definition: it is the science of the true, the false, and of what is neither of the two.

That of course does not mean that the Stoics knew of a three-valued logic (cf. **49.08**); they refer only to sentences (which are true or false) and their parts (which are neither). – The text cited expresses the attitude of the Stoics to the problem of the place of logic among the sciences: for them it is quite unmistakably a *part* of the system. What more is said seems to concern a methodology of discussion rather in the manner of the Aristotelian *Topics* (**11.01**). But as we know from other fragments, it is only a consequence of the Stoic doctrine of the principal subject-matter of logic which consists in *lecta* (λεκτά). This important notion requires immediate clarification.

B. LECTA

19.04 The Stoics say that these three are connected: the significate (σημαινόμενον), the sign (σημαῖνον) and the thing (τυγχάνον). The sign is the sound itself, e.g. the (sound) 'Dion', the significate is the entity manifested by (this sign) and which we apprehend as co-existing with our thought, (but) which foreigners do not comprehend, although they hear the sound; the thing is the external existent, e.g. Dion himself. Of these, two are bodies, viz. the sound and the thing, and one immaterial, viz. the entity signified, the *lecton*, which (further) is true or false.

19.05 They say that the lecton is what subsists according to a rational presentation (κατὰ φαντασίαν λογικήν).

19.06 Some, and above all those of the Stoa, think that truth is distinguished in three ways from what is true, . . . truth is a body, but what is true is immaterial; and this is shown, they say, by the fact that what is true is a proposition (ἀξίωμα), while a proposition is a *lecton*, and *lecta* are immaterial.

We have refrained from translating the Greek expression λεκτόν which derives from λέγειν and literally means 'what is said', i.e. what one means when one speaks meaningfully. The text last cited, about truth and what is true, is to be specially noted. The former is something psychic, and for the Stoics all such, every thought in particular, is material. But the *lecton* is not a quality of the mind, or in scholastic terminology a *conceptus subjectivus*. To use Frege's language it is the sense (*Sinn*) of an expression, scholastically the *conceptus objectivus*, what is objectively meant. In the (pseudo-) Aristotelian *Categories* there is a passage (**10.29**) about the λόγος τοῦ πράγματος, which corresponds to the Stoic *lecton*. Only in the Stoa the *lecton* has become the chief subject-matter of logic and indeed the unique subject of formal logic. That certainly jettisons the Aristotelian neutrality of logic and supposes a definite philosophical standpoint. But the original philosophical intuition involved is to be the more noticed in that very many philosophers and logicians, up to the most recent times, have confused the *lecton* with psychic images and occurrences (cf. **26.07**, **36.08**). That the Stoic logic is a science of *lecta* is made plain by their division:

19.07 Dialectic is divided, they say, into the topic of significates and (the topic) of the sound. That of significates is divided into the topic of conceptions, and that of the *lecta* which co-exist with them: propositions, independents (*lecta*), predicates, and so on . . ., arguments and moods and syllogisms, and fallacies other than those arising from the sound and the things. . . . A topic proper to dialectic is also that already mentioned about the sound itself.

C. SYNTAX

19.08 The elements of speech are the twenty-four letters. But 'letter' can have three meanings: the letter (itself), the (written) sign (χαρακτήρ) of the letter, and its name, e.g. 'alpha'. . . . Utterance (φωνή) is distinguished from locution (λέξις) in that a mere sound is utterance, but only articulated sound is locution. Locution is distinguished from speech in that speech is always meaningful, while what has no meaning can be locution, e.g. 'blityri' – which is not speech.

19.09 There are five parts of speech, as Diogenes, in his (treatise) *On Utterance*, and Chrysippus say: proper names (ὄνομα), general names (προσηγορία), verbs (ῥῆμα), connections (σύνδεσμος), articles. . . .

19.10 A general name is according to Diogenes a part of speech which signifies a common quality, e.g. 'man', 'horse'. But a proper name is a part of speech which manifests a quality proper to one, e.g. 'Diogenes', 'Socrates'. A verb is according to Diogenes a part of speech, which signifies an incomposite predicate (κατηγόρημα), or as others (define it), an indeclinable part of speech which signifies something co-ordinated with one or more, e g. 'I write', 'I speak'. A conjunction is an indeclinable part of speech which connects its parts.

Accounts of the division of *lecta* contradict one another, and are obscure. The following scheme composed by B. Mates (**19.11**) may best correspond to the original Stoic teaching:

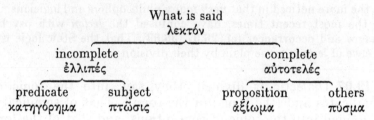

But the division of propositions is clearly and fully transmitted.

19.12 A proposition is what is true or false, or a complete entity (πρᾶγμα) assertoric by itself, e.g. 'It is day', 'Dion walks about'. It is called 'axiom' (ἀξίωμα) from being approved (ἀξιοῦσθαι) or disapproved. For he who says 'it is day' seems to admit that it is day; and when it is day, the foregoing axiom is true; but when it is not (day), false. Different from one another are axiom, question, inquiry, command, oath, wish, exhortation, address, entity similar to an axiom.

19.13 Of axioms, some are simple, some not simple, as is said in the schools of Chrysippus, Archedemus, Athenodorus, Antipater and Crinis. Simple are those which consist of an axiom not repeated (μὴ διαφορουμένου), e.g. 'it is day'. Ones not simple are those consisting of a repeated axiom or of more than one axiom. An example of the former is: 'if it is day, it is day'; of the latter: 'if it is day, it is light'.

19.14 Of simple axioms some are definite (ὡρισμένα), others indefinite, others again intermediate (μέσα). Definite are those which are referentially expressed, e.g. 'this man walks about', 'this man sits': (for they refer to an individual man). Indefinite are those in which an indefinite particle holds the chief place (κυριεύει), e.g. 'someone sits'. Intermediate are those such as: ' a man sits' or 'Socrates walks about'. . . .

19.15 Among axioms not simple is the compound (συνημμένον = conditional), as Chrysippus in the *Dialectic* and Diogenes in the *Dialectic Art* say, which is compounded by means of the implicative connective 'if'; this connective tells one that the second follows from the first, e.g. 'if it is day, it is light'. An inferential axiom (παρασυνημμένον) is, as Crinis says in the *Dialectic Art*, one which begins and ends with an axiom and is compounded παρασυνῆπται) by means of the connective 'since' (ἐπεί), e.g. 'since it is day, it is light'. This connective tells one that the second follows from the first and that the first is the case. Conjunctive (συμπεπλεγμένον) is the axiom compounded by means of a conjunctive connective, e.g. 'it is day and it is light'. Disjunctive (διεζευγμένον) is the axiom compounded by means of the separative connective 'or', e.g. 'it is day or it is night'. This connective tells one that one of the axioms is false. Causal (αἰτιῶδες) is the axiom compounded by means of the connective 'because', e.g. 'because it is day, it is light'. For it is here to be understood that the first is the cause of the second. An axiom showing what is rather the case is one compounded by means of the connective 'rather than' which shows this and stands in the middle of the axiom, e.g. 'it is night rather than day'.

Note in these texts that *lecta*, not words or psychic events are the subject-matter throughout. Hence most translations (those e.g. of Apelt, **19.16**, and Hicks) are misleading, since they talk of connective '*words*' and 'judgements'.

D. DOCTRINE OF CATEGORIES

19.17 The common genus 'what is' has nothing over it. It is the beginning of things and everything is inferior to it. The Stoics wanted to put another, still more principal genus above it.

19.18 To some Stoics 'what' seems to be the prime genus; and I will say why. In nature, they say, some things exist, others do not. Even those which do not exist are contained in nature, those which occur in the soul, like centaurs, giants and anything else which acquires an image when falsely framed in thought, though having no substance.

So according to these Stoics there *is* a *summum genus*. This is a regression in comparison with Aristotle's subtle anticipation of a theory of types (**11.16**).

19.19 But the Stoics think that the prime genera are more limited in number (than the Aristotelian). . . . For they introduce a fourfold division into subjects (ὑποκείμενα), qualia (ποιά), things that are in a determinate way (πῶς ἔχοντα), and things that are somehow related to something (πρὸς τί πως ἔχοντα).

113

These four categories are *not* to be understood as supreme genera (under the 'what'): That is, it is not the case that one being is a subject, another a relation, but *all* the categories belong to *every* being, and every category presupposes the preceding ones (**19.20**). This doctrine has no great significance for logic.

E. TRUTH

Apart from the distinction already mentioned between what is true and truth (**19.06**), the Stoics seem to have used the word 'true' in at least five senses. On this Sextus says:

19.21 Some of them have located the true and the false in the significates (=*lecta*), others in the sound, others again in the operation of the mind.

As regards the truth of *lecta*, a further threefold distinction can be made between:
1. truth of propositions.
2. truth of propositional forms (i.e. what it is that sentential functions refer to). That the Megarians and Stoics attributed truth and falsity to such propositional forms is seen in their teaching about functors (vide infra).
3. truth of arguments (vid. **21.07**).
Those are all *lecta*, but Sextus refers to two further kinds of truth:
4. truth of ideas (**19.22**).
5. truth of sentences.
According to all our information the first kind of truth was fundamental, as presupposed in all the others. Thus for instance the Stoics defined the truth of propositional forms by its means, with the help of time-variables; the truth of arguments in terms of the truth of the corresponding conditional propositions; while the truth of ideas and sentences is similarly reducible to that of *lecta*, according to what we know of the relation between them.

F. MODALITIES

Only fragments have come down to us of the very interesting Megarian doctrine of modalities. It seems to be an attempt to reduce necessity and possibility to simple existence by means of time-variables, a proceeding wholly consonant with the empirical stand-point of these thinkers. We give only the two most important passages on the subject:

19.23 'Possible' can also be predicated of what is possible in a 'Diodorean' sense, that is to say of what is or will be. For he

(Diodorus) deemed possible only what either is or will be. Since according to him it is possible that I am in Corinth, if I am or ever shall be there; and if I were not going to be there, it would not be possible. And it is possible that a child should be a grammarian, if he will ever be one. To prove this, Diodorus devised the master-argument (κυριεύων). Philo took a similar view.

19.24 The (problem of) the master-argument seems probably to have originated from the following considerations. As the following three (propositions) are incompatible: (1) Whatever is true about the past is necessary, (2) the impossible does not follow from the possible which neither is nor will be true – Diodorus, comparing this incompatibility with the greater plausibility of the first two, inferred that nothing is possible which neither is nor will be true.

Unfortunately that is the only really explicit text about the celebrated master-argument of Diodorus. It fails to enable us to survey the whole problem, because we do not know why the three propositions should be incompatible. One thing seems clear: that possibility was defined in the following way:

19.241 p is (now) possible if and only if p is now true or will be true at some future time.

From a rather vague text of Boethius (**19.25**) we further learn that the definitions of the other possibility-functors must be more or less as follows:

19.242 p is (now) impossible if and only if p is not true and never will be true.

19.243 p is (now) necessary if and only if p is true and always will be true.

19.244 p is (now) not necessary if and only if p is not true or will not be true at some future time.

§ 20. PROPOSITIONAL FUNCTORS

To the credit of the Megarian-Stoic school are some very subtle researches into the most important propositional functors. The thinkers of the school even succeeded in stating quite correct truth-matrices.

A. NEGATION

20.01 Negative are said to be only those propositions to which the negative particle is prefixed.

This text shows something to which many passages bear witness, that the Stoics constructed their logic not merely formally, but quite formalistically. This was blamed by Apuleius (**20.02**) and Galen (**20.03**), who said that the Stoics were only interested in linguistic form. But this reproach – if indeed it is one – cannot be sustained in view of what we know of the subject-matter of Stoic logic; Stoic formalism is concerned with words only as signs of *lecta*.

20.04 Among simple axioms are the negative (ἀποφατικόν), the denying (ἀρνητικόν), the privative (στερητικόν). . . . An example of the negative is: 'it is not day'. A species of this is the super-negative (ὑπεραποφατικόν). The super-negative is the negation of the negative. e.g. 'not – it is not day'. This posits 'it is day'. A denying (axiom) is one which consists of a negative particle and a predicate, e.g. 'No-one walks about'. Privative is one which consists of a privative particle and what has the force of an axiom, e.g. 'this man is unfriendly to man'.

The extant fragments do not contain a table of truth-values for negation, but the text cited evidently contains the law of double negation:

20.041 not-not *p* if and only if *p* (cf. **24.26**).

B. IMPLICATION

The definition of implication was a matter much debated among the Megarians and Stoics:

20.05 All dialecticians say that a connected (proposition) is sound (ὑγιές) when its consequent follows from (ἀκολουθεῖ) its antecedent – but they dispute about when and how it follows, and propound rival criteria.

Even so Callimachus, librarian at Alexandria in the 2nd century B.C., said:

20.06 The very crows on the roofs croak about what implications are sound.

1. Philonian implication

20.07 Philo said that the connected (proposition) is true when it is not the case that it begins with the true and ends with the false. So according to him there are three ways in which a true connected (proposition) is obtained, only one in which a false. For (1) if it begins with true and ends with true, it is true, e.g. 'if it is day, it is light'; (2) when it begins with false and ends with false, it is true, e.g. 'if the earth flies, the earth has wings'; (3) similarly too that which begins with false and ends with true, e.g. 'if the earth flies, the earth exists'. It is false only when beginning with true, it ends with false, e.g. 'if it is day, it is night'; since when it is day, the (proposition) 'it is day' is true – which was the antecedent; and the (proposition) 'it is night' is false, which was the consequent.

Here some terminological explanations are required. The Stoics called the antecedent ἡγούμενον, the consequent λῆγον, and moreover had the corresponding verbs: ἡγεῖται, λήγει, untranslatable in their technical use. Hence we have simply translated these words according to their ordinary sense, by 'begins' and 'ends'. The term too for the sentences themselves (or the propositions to which they refer) has been translated according to its everyday sense by 'connected', the word 'conditional' having been avoided because apparently the idea of condition was foreign to Megarian-Stoic thought.

As to the content of the passage, it gives us a perfect truth-matrix, which can be set out in tabular form thus:

20.071	Antecedent	Consequent	Connected proposition
	true	true	true
	false	false	true
	false	true	true
	true	false	false

It is, as we can see, the truth-value matrix for material implication, ordered otherwise than is usual nowadays (**41.12**; but **42.27**). The latter therefore deserves to be called 'Philonian'.

2. Diodorean implication

20.08 Diodorus says that the connected (proposition) is true when it begins with true and neither could nor can end with false. This runs counter to the Philonian position. For the connected (proposition) 'if it is day, I converse' is true according to Philo, in case it is day and I converse, since it begins with the true (proposition) 'it is day' and ends with the true (proposition) 'I converse'. But according to Diodorus (it is) false. For at a given time it can begin with the true (proposition) 'it is day' and end with the false (proposition) 'I converse', suppose I should fall silent . . . (and) before I began to converse it began with a true (proposition) and ended with the false one 'I converse'. Further, the (proposition) 'if it is night, I converse' is true according to Philo in case it is day and I am silent; for it (then) begins with false and ends with false. But according to Diodorus (it is) false; for it can begin with true and end with false, in case the night is past and I am not conversing. And also the (proposition) 'if it is night, it is day' is according to Philo true in case it is day, because, while it begins with the false (proposition) 'it is night', it ends with the true (proposition) 'it is day'. But according to Diodorus it is false because, while it can begin – when night is come – with the true (proposition) 'it is night', it can end with the false (proposition) 'it is day'.

So we can fix Diodorean implication by the following definition:

20.081 If *p*, then *q*, if and only if, for every time *t* it is not the case that *p* is true at *t* and *q* is false at *t*.

3. 'Connexive' implication

20.09 (According to Diodorus) this (proposition) is true: 'if there are no atomic elements of things, then there are atomic elements of things' . . . but those who introduce connection (συνάρτησιν) say that the connected (proposition) is sound when the contradictory (ἀντικείμενον) of its consequent is incompatible (μάχηται) with its antecedent. So according to them the aforesaid connected (propositions) (**20.07**) are bad (μοχθηρά), but the following is true (ἀληθές): 'if it is day, it is day'.

20.10 A connected (proposition) is true in which the opposite of the consequent is incompatible with the antecedent, e.g. 'if it is day, it is light'. This is true, since 'it is not light', the opposite of the consequent, is incompatible with 'it is day'. A connected (proposition) is false in which the opposite of the consequent is not incompatible with the antecedent, e.g. 'if it is day, Dion walks about'; for 'Dion is not walking about' is not incompatible with 'it is day'.

This definition is often ascribed to Chrysippus (**20.11**), but that it originated with him may be doubted (**20.12**). It is not clear how it is to be understood. Perhaps we have here an ancient form of *strict implication* (**49.04 31.13**).

4. 'Inclusive' implication

20.13 Those who judge (implication) by what is implicit (ἐμφάσει κρίνοντες) say that the connected (proposition) is true when its consequent is potentially (δυνάμει) contained in the antecedent. According to them the (proposition) 'if it is day, it is day' and every repetitive connected (proposition) is probably false, since nothing can be contained in itself.

This definition too is not now fully intelligible. It seems to concern a relation of subordination something like that which holds between a statement about all elements of a class and one about the elements of one of its sub-classes. No further reference to this definition is to be found in our sources; perhaps it was only adopted by isolated logicians of the school.

C. DISJUNCTION

We know much less about disjunction than about implication. Apparently it formed the subject of the same sort of dispute that there was about the definition of implication. But our texts are few and obscure. It is only certain that two kinds of disjunction were recognized: the complete (exclusive) and the incomplete (not exclusive), of which the first is well exemplified.

1. Complete disjunction

20.14 The disjunctive (proposition) consists of (contradictorily) opposed (propositions), e.g. of those to the effect that there are proofs and that there are not proofs. . . . For as every disjunctive is true if (and only if) it contains a true (proposition) and since one of (two contradictorily) opposed (propositions) is evidently always true, it must certainly be said that the (proposition) so formed is true.

20.15 There is also another (proposition) which the Greeks call διεζευγμένον ἀξίωμα and we call *disjunctum*. This is of the kind: 'pleasure is either good or bad, or neither good nor bad'. Now all (propositions) which are disjoined (*disjuncta*) (within one such proposition) are mutually incompatible, and their opposites, which the Greeks call ἀντικείμενα must also be mutually opposed (*contraria*). Of all (propositions) which are disjoined, one will be true, the others false. But when none of them at all are true, or all, or more than one are true, or when the disjoined (propositions) are not incompatible, or when their opposites are not mutually opposed, then the disjunctive (proposition) will be false. They call it παραδιεζευγμένον.

20.16 The true disjunctive (proposition) tells us that one of its propositions is true, the other or others false and incompatible.

These texts offer a difficulty, in the supposition that a statement can be contradictory to more than one other. However, the practice of the school concerning the disjunction here defined is clear: in the sense envisaged '*p* or *q*' is understood as the negation of equivalence (vide infra **22.07**), i.e. in such a way that just one of the two arguments is true and just one false.

2. Incomplete disjunction

The surviving information about this is very vague. The best is given by Galen, but raises the question how much of it is Megarian-Stoic doctrine and how much Galen's own speculation:

20.17 This state of things exhibits a complete incompatibility (τέλειαν μάχην), the other an incomplete (ἐλλιπήν) according to which we say for example: 'if Dion is at Athens, Dion is not at the Isthmus'. For this is characteristic of incompatibility, that incompatibles cannot both be the case; but they differ in that according to the one the incompatibles can neither both be true nor both false, but according to the other this last may occur. If then only inability to be true together characterizes them, the incompatibility is incomplete, but if also inability to be false together, it is complete.

20.18 There is no reason why we should not call the proposition involving complete incompatibility 'disjunctive' and that involving incomplete incompatibility 'quasi-disjunctive'. . . . But in some propositions not only one, but more or all components can be true, and one must be. Some call such 'sub-disjunctive' (παραδιεζευγμένα); these contain only one true (proposition) among those disjoined, independently of whether they are composed of two or more simple propositions.

Evidently this is a matter of two different kinds of disjunctive propositions, and so of disjunction. The first is called 'quasi-disjunction' and seems to be equivalent to the denial of conjunction:

20.181 *p* or *q* if and only if, not: *p* and *q*.

Then the intended functor would be that of Sheffer (**43.43**).

The second kind is called 'sub-disjunctive' and could be defined by the following equivalence:

20.182 p or (also) q if and only if: if not p, then q.

This is the modern functor of the logical sum (cf. **14.10** ff.).

Neither of these two functors was used by the Stoics in practice, at least so far as we can ascertain from the extant sources.

D. CONJUNCTION

20.19 What the Greeks call συμπεπλεγμένον we call *conjunctum* or *copulatum*. It is as follows: 'Publius Scipio, son of Paulus, was twice consul and had a triumph and was censor and was colleague of Lucius Mummius in the censorship.' In every conjunctive the whole is said to be false if one (component) is false, even if the others are true. For if I were to add to all that I have truly said about that Scipio: 'and overcame Hannibal in Africa', which is false, then the whole conjunctive which includes that would be false: because that is a false addition, and the whole is stated together.

E. EQUIVALENCE

20.20 Syllogisms which have hypothetical premisses are formed by transition from one thing to another, because of consequence (ἀκολουθία) or incompatibility, each of which may be either complete or incomplete.

20.21 The (exclusive) disjunctive premiss (διαιρετική) is equivalent to the following: 'if it is not day, it is night'.

This last cited text, in which quite certainly complete disjunction is intended (**20.14** ff.) can only be understood as referring to 'complete consequence' (**20.20**) – and then we have equivalence. In this case we have the following definition, in which 'or' is to be understood in the exclusive sense:

20.211 q completely follows from p if and only if, not: p or q.

We owe the discovery of these facts to Stakelum (**20.22**). Boethius, probably drawing on a Stoic source, understands 'if $A - B$' in just this sense **20.23**). So it can be taken as likely that the functor of equivalence was known to the Stoics as 'complete consequence'.

F. OTHER FUNCTORS

We also have definitions of the inferential proposition (cf. **19.15**). This consists of a combination of conjunction with Diodorean (certainly not Philonian) implication. Other kinds of compound propositions are the causal and the relative; their functors are not definable by truth-matrices. Possibly there are further functors of similar nature.

§ 21. ARGUMENTS
AND SCHEMES OF INFERENCE

A. CONCLUSIVE, TRUE, AND DEMONSTRATIVE ARGUMENTS

21.01 An argument (λόγος) is a system of premisses and conclusion. Premisses are propositions agreed upon for the proof of the conclusion, the conclusion is the proposition proved from the premisses. E.g. in the following (argument): 'if it is day, it is light; it is day; therefore it is light', 'it is light' is the conclusion, the other propositions are premisses.

21.02 Some arguments are conclusive (συνακτικοί), others not conclusive. They are conclusive when a connected proposition, beginning with the conjunction of the premisses of the argument and ending with the conclusion, is true. E.g. the argument mentioned above is conclusive, since from the conjunction of its premisses 'if it is day, it is light' and 'it is day' there follows 'it is light' in this connected proposition: 'if: it is day and if it is day, it is light: then it is light.' * Not conclusive are arguments not so constructed.

This is a very important text, showing how accurately the Stoic distinguished between a conditional proposition and implication on the one hand, and an argument or inferential scheme and the consequence-relation on the other. For an argument is conclusive (συνακτικός) when the corresponding conditional proposition is true (ὑγιές).

The Stoics had a set terminology for the components of an argument. In the simplest case it has two premisses, λήμματα (in the wider sense); the first is also called λῆμμα (the narrower sense), in contrast to the second which is called πρόσληψις **21.04**); when the first premiss is connected, it is also called τροπικόν (**21.05**).

21.06 Of arguments, some are not conclusive (ἀπέραντοι), others conclusive (περαντικοί). Not conclusive are those in which the contradictory opposite of the conclusion is not

---

* Reading εἴπερ εἰ ἡμέρα ἐστί, καὶ ἡμέρα ἐστί, φῶς ἐστίν. This reading was called a 'monstrosity' by Heintz, whereas it is evidently the only correct one (**21.03**).

incompatible with the conjunction of the premisses, e.g. such as: 'if it is day, it is light; it is day; therefore Dion walks about'.

It seems to follow that the conditional sentence corresponding to an argument must contain the functor of connexive implication for an argument to be conclusive (cf. **20.09** f. and the commentary).

21.07 Of conclusive arguments some are true, others false. They are true when besides the connected proposition, which consists of the conjunction of the premisses and the conclusion, being true, the conjunction of the premisses is also* true, i.e. that which forms the antecedent in the connected proposition.

Again a text of the utmost importance, expressing a clear distinction between formal validity and truth. This distinction was admittedly known to Aristotle (**10.05** f.), but this is the first explicit accurate formulation.

21.09 Of true arguments some are demonstrative (ἀποδεικτικοί) others not demonstrative. Demonstrative are those concluding to the not evident from the evident, not demonstrative are those not of that kind. E.g. the argument: 'if it is day, it is light; it is day; therefore it is light' is not demonstrative, for that it is light (which is evident) is its conclusion. On the other hand, this is demonstrative: 'if the sweat flows through the surface, there are intelligible (νοητοί) pores; the sweat flows through the surface; therefore there are intelligible pores', for it has a non-evident conclusion, viz. 'therefore there are intelligible pores'.

'Intelligible' here means 'only to be known by the mind'; the pores are not visible.
The division of arguments comprised in this last series of texts is logically irrelevant, but of great methodological interest. It can be presented thus:

			demonstrative
		true	not demonstrative
arguments	conclusive	not true	
	not conclusive		

---

* Omitting with Mates (**21.08**): καὶ τὸ συμπέρασμα.

123

B. NON-SYLLOGISTIC ARGUMENTS

A further interesting division shows how accurately the Stoics distinguished between language and meta-language:

21.10 Of conclusive arguments, some are called by the name of the genus, 'conclusive' (περαντικοί), others are called 'syllogistic'. Syllogistic are those which are either indemonstrable (ἀναπόδεικτοι) or are reduced to the indemonstrable by means of one or more rules (τῶν θεμάτων), e.g. 'if Dion walks about, Dion is in motion; Dion walks about; therefore Dion is in motion'. Conclusive in the specific sense are those which do not conclude syllogistically, those of e.g. the following kind: 'it is false that it is day and it is night; it is day; therefore it is not night'. Non-syllogistic, on the other hand, are arguments which appear to resemble syllogistic ones, but do not conclude, e.g. 'if Dion is a horse, Dion is an animal; Dion is not a horse; therefore Dion is not an animal'.

21.11 . . . but the moderns, who follow the linguistic expression, not what it stands for, . . . say that if the expression is formulated thus: 'if *A*, then *B; A*; therefore *B*,' the argument is syllogistic, but '*B* follows on *A; A;* therefore *B*' is not syllogistic, though it is conclusive.

21.12 . . . The kind of argument which is called 'unmethodically concluding' (ἀμεθόδως περαίνοντες) is e.g. this: 'it is day; but you say that it is day; therefore you say true'.

21.13 (Those which the moderns call 'unmethodically concluding' . . .) are such as the following: 'Dion says that it is day; Dion says true; therefore it is day'.

21.14 . . . like the unmethodically concluding arguments among the Stoics. When e.g. someone says: 'the first (is) greater than the second, the second than the third, therefore the first (is) greater than the third'.

C. FURTHER KINDS OF ARGUMENT

21.15 Those arguments too which they call 'duplicated' (διαφορούμενοι) are not syllogistic, e.g. this: 'if it is day, it is day; therefore it is day'.

21.16 The argument): 'if it is day, it is light; it is day; therefore it is day', and in general those which the moderns call 'not diversely concluding' (ἀδιαφόρως περαίνοντες). . . .

21.17 Antipater, one of the most celebrated men of the Stoic sect, used to say that arguments with a single premiss can also be formed (μονολήμματοι).

21.18 From one premiss there results no (conclusive) combination (*collectio*), though the consequence (*conclusio*) 'you see, therefore you live' seemed complete to Antipater the Stoic, against the doctrine of all (others) – for it is complete (only) in the following way; 'if you see, then you live; you see; therefore you live'.

21.19 Such an argument as that which says: 'it is day; not: it is not day; therefore it is light' has potentially a single premiss.

Further, apparently numberless, divisions of arguments are obscure in our sources. Diogenes speaks of 'possible, impossible, necessary and not necessary' arguments (**21.20**). Sextus has a division into demonstrable and indemonstrable arguments, the last-named being either simple or compound, and the compound being reducible to the simple (which makes them demonstrable), (**21.21**). The whole account is so vague that we are not in a position to grasp the meaning of this division. But in Diogenes we find a consistent doctrine of these same 'indemonstrable' arguments; they are simply the axioms of the Stoic propositional logic, and we consider them in the next chapter.

D. SCHEMES OF INFERENCE

The Stoics made clear distinction between a logical rule and an instance of it, i.e. between the moods (τρόποι) of an argument and the argument itself – a distinction which Aristotle applied in practice, but without a theoretic knowledge of it.

21.22 These are some of the arguments. But their moods or schemata (σχήματα) in which they are formed are as follows: of the first indemonstrable: 'if the first, then (the) second; the first; therefore the second'; of the second: 'if the first, (then) the second; not the second; therefore not the first'; of the third: 'not: the first and the second; the first; therefore not the second'.

We have similar schemata for other arguments as well (**21.23**), even for some of the not indemonstrable (cf. **22.17**). It is striking that only numerical words occur in them as variables. One might conjecture that this was so in Aristotle too, since in Greek the letters of the alphabet could function as numerals; but the fact that Aristotle did not only use the early letters of the alphabet, but often Π, P, and Σ as well, seems to exclude this.

Along with these homogeneous formulae the Stoics also had 'mixed' half-arguments, half-schemata. They were called 'argument-schemata' (λογότροποι).

21.24 An argument-schema consists of both, e.g. 'if Plato lives, Plato breathes; the first; therefore the second'. The argument-schema was introduced in order not to have to have a long sub-premiss in long formulae, so as to gain the conclusion, but as short as possible: 'the first; therefore the second'.

Another example is this:

21.25 If the sweat flows through the surface, there are intelligible pores; the first; therefore the second.

§ 22. AXIOMATIZATION. COMPOUND ARGUMENTS

The Stoic propositional logic seems to have been thoroughly axiomatized, distinction even being made between axioms and rules of inference.

A. THE INDEMONSTRABLES

The tradition is obscure about the axioms (**22.01**; et vid. supra **21.21**). We here give the *definition* of the indemonstrables according to Diogenes, their description, with examples, from Sextus.

22.02 There are also some indemonstrables (ἀναπόδεικτοι) which need no demonstration, by means of which every (other) argument is woven; they are five in number according to Chrysippus, though other according to others. They are assumed in conclusives, syllogisms and hypotheticals (τροπικῶν)

22.03 The indemonstrables are those of which the Stoics say that they need no proof to be maintained. . . . They envisage many indemonstrables, but especially five, from which it seems all others can be deduced.

This is no less than an assertion of the completeness of the system: whether it is correct we cannot tell, since we do not know the metatheorems and have only a few of the derivative arguments.

22.04 The first (indemonstrable) from a connected (proposition) and its antecedent yields its consequent, e.g. 'if it is day, it is light; it is day; therefore it is light';

22.05 the second from a connected (proposition) and the contradictory opposite (ἀντικειμένου) of its consequent yields the contradictory opposite of its antecedent, e.g. 'if it is day, it is light; it is not light; therefore it is not day';

22.06 the third from the negation (ἀποφατικοῦ) of a conjunction together with one of its components, yields the contradictory opposite of the other, e.g. 'not: it is day and it is night; it is day; therefore it is not night';

22.07 the fourth, from a (complete) disjunctive (proposition) together with one of the (propositions) disjoined (ἐπεζευγμένων) in it, yields the contradictory opposite of the other, e.g. 'either it is day or it is night; it is day; therefore it is not night';

22.08 the fifth from a (complete) disjunctive (proposition) together with the contradictory opposite of one of the disjoined (propositions) yields the other, e.g. 'either it is day or it is night; it is not night; therefore it is day'.

Other less reliable sources speak of two further indemonstrables, the sixth and seventh (**22.09**).

B. METATHEOREMS

The reduction of demonstrable arguments to indemonstrable, was effected in Stoic logic by means of certain metalogical rules. One name for such was θέμα, but it seems that the expression θεώρημα was also used (**22.10**). We shall call them 'metatheorems', in accordance with modern usage. A text of Galen shows that there were at least four of them (**22.11**), but only the first and third are stated explicitly.

22.12 There is also another proof common to all syllogisms, even the indemonstrable, called '(reduction) to the impossible' and by the Stoics termed 'first metatheorem' (*constitutio*) or 'first exposition' (*expositum*). It is formulated thus: 'If some third is deduced from two, one of the two together with the opposite of the conclusion yields the opposite of the other.'

This is the rule for reduction to the impossible (**16.33**), already stated by Aristotle in another form.

22.13 The essentials of the so-called third metatheorem (θέματος) look like this: if some third is deduced from two and

127

one (of the two) can be deduced syllogistically from others, the third is yielded by the rest and those others.

This metatheorem is what in fact underlies the aristotelian 'direct reduction' of syllogisms, and can be formulated:

22.131 If *r* follows from *p* and *q*, and *p* from *s*, then *r* follows from *q* and *s* (cf. **14.141**).

The following is given by Alexander as the 'synthetic theorem' (συνθετικὸν θεώρημα):

22.14 If some (third) is deduced from some (premisses), and if the deduced (third) together with one or more (fourth) yields some (fifth), then this (fifth) is deduced also from those (premisses) from which this (third) is deduced.

The rule being stated is this:

22.141 If *r* follows from *p* and *q*, and *t* from *r* and *s*, then *t* follows from *p*, *q* and *s;*

or, if one represents the premisses with a single variable:

22.142 If *q* follows from *p*, and *s* from *q* and *r*, then *s* follows also from *p* and *r*.

Sextus cites a similar but seemingly different metatheorem:

22.15 It should be known that the following dialectical theorem (θεώρημα) has been handed down for the analysis of syllogisms: 'if we have premisses to yield a conclusion, then we have this conclusion too potentially among these (premisses), even if it is not explicitly (κατ' ἐκφοράν) stated.

We have two detailed examples of the apllication of this metatheorem, which belong to the highest development of Stoic logic.

C. DERIVATION OF COMPOUND ARGUMENTS

22.16 Of the not-simple (arguments) some consist of homogeneous, others of not homogeneous (arguments). Of not homogeneous, those which are compounded of two first indemonstrables (**22.04**), or of two second (**22.05**). Of not homogeneous, those which (are compounded) of second and third* (**22.06**), or in general of such (dissimilars). An example of

---

* Reading καὶ τρίτου in the lacuna with Kochalsky.

those consisting of homogeneous (arguments) is the following: 'if it is day*, then if it is day it is light; it is day; therefore it is light'. . . . For we have here two premisses, (1) the connected proposition: 'if it is day**, then if it is day it is light', which begins with the simple proposition 'it is day' and ends with the not simple, connected proposition 'if it is day it is light'; and (2) the antecedent in this (first premiss:) 'it is day'. If by means of the first indemonstrable we infer from those the consequent of the connected (proposition, viz.) 'if it is day it is light', then we have this inferred (proposition) potentially in the argument, even though not explicitly stated. Putting this now together with the minor premiss of the main argument, viz. 'it is day', we infer by means of the first indemonstrable: 'it is light', which was the conclusion of the main argument.

22.17 That is what the arguments are like which are compounded from homogeneous (indemonstrables). Among the not homogeneous is that propounded by Ainesidemus about the sign, which runs thus: 'if all phenomena appear similarly to those who are similarly disposed, and signs are phenomena, then signs appear similarly to all those who are similarly disposed; signs do not appear similarly to all those who are similarly disposed; phenomena appear similarly to all those who are similarly disposed; therefore signs are not phenomena'. This argument is compounded of second and third indemonstrables, as we can find out by analysis. This will be clearer if we put the process in the form of the schema of inference: 'if the first and second, then the third; not the third; the first; therefore not the second'. For we have here a connected (proposition) in which the conjunction of the first and second forms the antecedent, and the third the consequent, together with the contradictory opposite of the consequent, viz. 'not the third'. Hence we infer by means of the second indemonstrable the contradictory opposite of the antecedent, viz. 'therefore not: the first and the second'. But this is potentially contained in the argument, as we have it in the premisses which yield it, though not verbally expressed. Putting it*** together with the other premiss, the first, we infer the conclusion (of the main argument), 'not the second', by means of the third indemonstrable.

* Adding with Kochalsky: εἰ ἡμέρα ἐστίν.
** Completing the text as before.
*** reading ὅπερ instead of ἄπερ, with Kochalsky.

D. FURTHER DERIVED ARGUMENTS

According to Cicero (**22.18**) the Stoics derived 'innumerable' arguments in similar ways.

22.19 The said (Chrysippus) says that it (the dog) often*
applies the fifth indemonstrable, when on coming to the
meeting of three roads it sniffs at two down which the game
has not gone and immediately rushes down the third without
sniffing at it. The sage says in fact that it virtually infers:
the game has gone down this, or this, or that; neither this nor
this; therefore that.

22.21 If two connected (propositions) end in contradictorily
opposed (consequents) – this theorem is called (the theorem)
'from two connecteds' (τροπικῶν) – the (common) antecedent
of the two is refuted .... This argument is formed according to
the schema of inference: 'if the first, the second; if the first**,
not the second; therefore not the first'. The Stoics give it
material expression (i.e. by a substitution) when they say
that from the (proposition) 'if you know that you are dead
(you are dead if you know that you are dead) you are not dead'
there follows this other: 'therefore you do not know that you
are dead'.

22.22 Some argue in this way: 'if there are signs, there are
signs; if there are not signs, there are signs; there are either no
signs or there are signs; therefore there are signs'.

§ 23. THE LIAR

The Stoics and above all the Megarians devoted much attention
to fallacies. Some of the ones they considered derive from the problem
of the continuum and belong to mathematics in the narrower sense
of that word; the rest are mostly rather trifles than serious logical
problems (**23.01**). But one of their fallacies, 'the Liar' (ψευδόμενος)
has very considerable logical interest and has been deeply studied
by logicians for centuries, in antiquity, the middle ages, and the
20th century. The Liar is the first genuine semantic fallacy known to
us.

---

* διὰ πλειόνων: this could also mean 'the (argument) from the more'; but I
follow Mates (**22.20**) since (1) we know of no such indemonstrable, and (2) the
argument is reducible to the simple fifth indemonstrable.
** omitting οὐ with Koetschau.

A. HISTORY

In St. Paul is to be found the following notable text:

23.02 One of themselves, a spokesman of their own, has told us: The men of Crete were ever liars, venomous creatures, all hungry belly.

According to various sources (**23.03**) this spokesman was Epimenides, a Greek sage living at the beginning of the 6th century B.C. Hence the Liar is often called after him, but wrongly, for Epimenides was clearly not worrying about a logical paradox. Plato, too, who considered similar problems in the *Euthydemus* (ca. 387 B.C.; **23.04**) did not know the Liar. But Aristotle has it in the *Sophistic Refutations*, about 330 B.C. (**23.05**). Now that is just the period when Eubulides was flourishing, to whom Diogenes Laertius explicitly ascribes the discovery of the Liar (**18.02**). After that, Theophrastus wrote three books on the subject (**23.06**), Chrysippus many more, perhaps twenty-eight (**23.07**). How much people took the problem to heart at that time can be seen from the fact that one logician, Philetas of Cos (ca. 340–285 B.C.), died because of it:

23.08 Traveller, I am Philetas; the argument called the Liar and deep cogitations by night, brought me to death.

B. FORMULATION

In spite of this interest and the extensive literature about the Liar, we no longer possess Eubulides's formulation of the antinomy, and the versions that have come down to us are so various that it is impossible to determine whether a single formula underlies them all, and which of the surviving ones has been considered by competent logicians. Here we can only give a simple list of the most important, collected by A. Rüstow (**23.09**). They seem to fall into four groups.

I.

23.10 If you say that you lie, and in this say true, do you lie or speak the truth?

23.11 If I lie and say that I lie, do I lie or speak the truth?

II

23.12 If you say that you lie, and say true, you lie; but you say that you lie, and you speak the truth; therefore you lie.

23.13 If you lie and in that say true, you lie.

III.

23.14 I say that I lie, and (in so saying) lie; therefore I speak the truth.

23.15 Lying, I utter the true speech, that I lie.

IV.

23.16 If it is true, it is false; if it is false, it is true.

23.17 Whoso says 'I lie', lies and speaks the truth at the same time.

The relation of the four groups to one another is as follows: the texts of the first group simply posit the question: is the Liar true or false? Those of the second conclude that it is true, of the third that it is false. The texts of the fourth group draw both conclusions together; the proposition is both true and false.

C. EFFORTS AT SOLUTION

Aristotle deals with the Liar summarily in that part of his *Sophistic Refutations* in which he discusses fallacies dependent on what is said 'absolutely and in a particular respect':

23.18 The argument is similar, also, as regards the problem whether the same man can at the same time say what is both false and true: but it appears to be a troublesome question because it is not easy to see in which of the two connections the word 'absolutely' is to be rendered – with 'true' or with 'false'. There is, however, nothing to prevent it from being false absolutely, though true in some particular respect (πῇ) or relation (τινός), i.e. being true in some things though not true absolutely.

It has been said (**23.19**) that the difficulty is here 'quite unresolved, and indeed unnoticed', and indeed Aristotle has not solved our antinomy nor understood its import. Yet, as is so often the case with this pastmaster, he reveals a penetrating insight into the principle of the medieval and modern solutions – the necessity of distinguishing different aspects, levels as we now say, in the Liar. Worth noting too, is Aristotle's standpoint of firm conviction that a solution is discoverable. This conviction has remained the motive power of logic in this difficult field.

The solution of Chrysippus has reached us in a very fragmentary papyrus, written moreover in difficult language. Its essential, and most legible, part is as follows*:

---

* Thanks are due to Prof O. Gigon for help with this text.

23.20 The (fallacy) about the truth-speaker and similar ones are to be ... (solved in a similar way). One should not say that they say true and (also) false; nor should one conjecture in another way, that the same (statement) is expressive of true and false simultaneously, but that they have no meaning at all. And he rejects the afore-mentioned proposition and also the proposition that one can say true and false simultaneously and that in all such (matters) the sentence is sometimes simple, sometimes expressive of more.

The most important words in this text are σημαινομένου τέλεως ἀποπλανῶνται, translated '(that) they have no meaning at all'. The Greek phrase is ambiguous as between (1) that whoever states the Liar attributes a false assertion to the proposition, and (2) that he says something which has no meaning at all. The fragmentary context *seems* to indicate the second interpretation as the correct one, but it is impossible to be certain of this. If it is correct, Chrysippus's solution is that the Liar is no proposition but a senseless utterance, which would be a view of the highest importance. The Aristotelian attempt to solve it is definitely rejected in this text.

IV. THE CLOSE OF ANTIQUITY

§ 24. PERIOD OF COMMENTARIES
AND HANDBOOKS*

A. CHARACTERISTICS AND HISTORICAL SURVEY

With the end of the old Stoa there begins a period into which hardly any research has been done. However, on the basis of the few details known to us we may suppose with great probability that the formal logic of this period was of the following kind:

1. The period is not a creative one. No new problems or original methods such as those developed by Aristotle and the Megarian-Stoic school are to be found.

2. Yet, apparently right up to the fall of the Roman empire, individual scholarly works appeared. Some earlier methods were improved, the material was systematized and sometimes developed. There were even not wanting genuinely gifted logicians, among the best of whom was Alexander of Aphrodisias.

3. The logical literature consisted chiefly of two kinds of work: big commentaries, mainly on Aristotle, and handbooks.

4. As to their content, we discern mostly a syncretizing tendency in the sense that Aristotelian and Stoic-Megarian elements are mingled, Stoic methods and formulations being applied to Aristotelian ideas.

Lack of monographs makes it impossible to survey the state of the logical problematic during the period, and we limit ourselves to the choice of some particular doctrines so far found in the mass of commentaries and handbooks. But first some of the most important thinkers must be named.

The first well-known logicians of this period are Galen and the less notable Apuleius of Madaura whose handbooks have survived; the former is the subject of the only monograph on the period (24.01). In the 3rd century A.D. we find Alexander of Aphrodisias, already mentioned, one of the best commentators on the whole Aristotelian logic, and unlike Galen and Apuleius a fairly pure Aristotelian. Porphyry of Tyre lived about the same time, and composed an *Introduction* (εἰσαγωγή) to the Aristotelian categories. In it he systematized the doctrine of the predicables (11.06 ff.), giving a five-fold enumeration: genus, specific difference, species, property and accident (24.02). This work was to be basic in the Middle Ages. Later logicians include Iamblichus of Chalcis, not to be taken very seriously, Themistius (both these in the 4th century A.D.), Ammonius Hermeae (5th century), Martianus Capella, author

of a handbook which formed an important link between ancient
and later logic (5th century), Ammonius the Peripatetic, Simplicius
(6th century), who was another of the better commentators on
Aristotle, and finally Philoponus (7th century), but these have
little importance so far as we can judge. On the other hand the last
Roman logician, Boethius (ca. 480–524) is of fairly considerable
importance both because his works became a prime source for the
Scholastics and also because he transmits doctrines and methods
not mentioned elsewhere, though he himself was only a moderate
logician. With his execution the West enters on a long period without
any logic worth speaking of.

B. THE TREE OF PORPHYRY

Of the commentators' discoveries the 'tree of Porphyry' has
certainly achieved the greatest fame. While it can be regarded as
only a compendium of Aristotelian doctrines it has great importance
as comprising (1) a system of classification, which was not to the
fore in Aristotle's thought (**11.13**), and (2) an extensional view of
terms. First we give the text:

24.03 Let what is said in one category now be explained.
Substance (οὐσία) is itself a genus, under this is body, and under
body is living (ἔμψυχον) body, under which is animal. Under
animal is rational (λογικόν) animal, under which is man. Under
man are Socrates and Plato and individual (κατὰ μέρος) men.
But of these, substance is the most generic and that which is
genus alone; man is the most specific and that which is species
alone. Body is a species of substance, a genus of living body.

The following text shows how thoroughly extensional a view is
being taken:

24.04 (Genus and species) differ in that genus contains
(περιέχει) its species, the species are contained in but do not
contain their genus. For the genus is predicated of more things
than the species.

This conception is carried so far that one can here properly speak
of a beginning of calculus of classes. At the same time Porphyry
makes a distinction which corresponds fairly closely to the modern
distinction between extension and intension (**36.10, 45.03**) – or,
again, between simple and personal supposition (**27.15**). For among
a number of definitions of the predicables, he has:

24.05 The philosophers ... define, saying that genus is what is predicated essentially (ἐν τῷ τί ἐστι) of several things differing in species.

24.06 The genus differs from the difference and the common accidents in that, while the difference and the common accidents are predicated of several things differing in species, they are not predicated essentially but as qualifying (ἐν τῷ ὁποῖόν τι ἐστιν). For when we ask what it is of which these are predicated, we answer with the genus; but we do not answer with the differences or accidents. For they are not predicated essentially of the subject but rather as qualifying it. For on being asked of what quality man is, we say that he is rational, and to the question of what quality crow is, we answer that it is black. But *rational* is a difference, and *black* an accident. But when we are asked *what* man is, we answer that he is animal, *animal* being a genus of man.

C. EXTENSION OF LOGICAL TECHNIQUE

Among the most important achievements of this period are two devices which so far as we know were unknown to Aristotle and the Stoics, viz. (1) identification of variables, (2) substitution of sentential forms for variables.

1. Alexander of Aphrodisias

The first is to be found in Alexander in a new proof of the convertibility of universal negative sentences:

24.07 If someone were to say that the universal negative (premiss) does not convert, (suppose) A belongs to no B; if (this premiss) does not convert, B belongs to some A; there results in the first figure (the conclusion that) to some A A does not belong, which is absurd.

Alexander here makes use of the fourth syllogism of the first figure (*Ferio:* (**13.06**)), which in Aristotle's presentation runs: 'if A belongs to no B, but B to some C, then to some C A cannot belong'. He identifies C with A – i.e. substitutes one variable for the other, and obtains: 'if A belongs to no B, but B to some A, then to some A A does not belong'. That is the novelty of the process.

This is consonant with Alexander's clear insight into the nature of laws of formal logic. He seems to have been the first to make explicit the distinction between form and matter, and at the same time to have come close to an explicit determination of the notion of a variable.

24.08 He (Aristotle) introduces the use of letters in order to show us that the conclusions are not produced in virtue of the matter but in virtue of such and such a form (σχῆμα) and composition and the mood of the premisses; the syllogism concludes ... not because of the matter, but because the formula (συζυγία) is as it is. The letters show that the conclusion is of such a kind universally and always and for every choice (of material).

2. Boethius

A further development of the technique of formal logic is to be found in Boethius. He is evidently aiming at the formulation of a rule of substitution for propositional variables; this is not given in the form of such a rule, but in a description of the structure of formulae. Again we have a fairly clear distinction between form and matter in a proposition, a distinction which was to play a great part in later history:

24.09 We shall now show the likenesses and differences between simple propositions and compound hypothetical ones. For when the (hypothetical propositions) which consist of simple ones are compared with those which are compounded of two hypotheticals, (one sees that) the sequence (in both cases) is the same and the relation (of the parts to one another) remains, only the terms are doubled. Since the places which are occupied by simple propositions in those hypotheticals consisting of simple propositions, are occupied in hypotheticals consisting of hypotheticals by those conditions in virtue of which those (component) propositions are said to be joined and linked together. For in the proposition which says: 'if A is, B is', and in that which says: 'if, if A is, B is, (then) if C is, D is' the place occupied in that consisting of two simple propositions by that which is first: 'if A is', in the proposition consisting of two hypotheticals is occupied by that which (there) is first: 'if, if A is, B is'.

If we remember the Stoic distinction between argument and mood (**21.22**) the last two texts do not seem very original; but they are the first in which an explicit statement of the distinction is found.

D. FRESH DIVISION OF IMPLICATION

It is Boethius again who gives a fresh division of implication:

24.10 Every hypothetical proposition is formed either by connection (*connexionem*) . . . or by disjunction. . . . But since it has been said that the same thing is signified by the connectives (*conjunctione*) 'si' and 'cum' when they are put in hypothetical sentences, conditionals can be formed in two ways: accidentally, or so as to have some natural consequence. Accidentally in this way, as when we say: 'when fire is hot, the sky is round'. For the sky is round not because fire is hot, but the sentence means that at what time fire is hot, the sky is round. But there are others which have within them a natural consequence, . . . e.g. we might say: 'when man is, animal is'.

There is here, as often elsewhere, a certain obscurity in Boethius's thought (**24.11**). Apart from that, his division of implication is something of a backward step in comparison with the Stoic discussions of the subject (vide supra **20.05** ff.). Yet the text just cited is important for our history, being an evident starting-point for scholastic speculations about implication.

Hence also we mention the following details of Boethius's doctrine about propositional functors. He often seems to use '*si*' (**24.12**) as a symbol of equivalence (cf. **20.20** ff.). The sense of the expression '*aut*' is ambiguous. On the one hand, we find – and for the first time – a definition in the sense of non-exclusive alternation (logical sum: cf. **20.17, 30.18, 40.11, 41.18**):

24.13 The disjunctive proposition which says (*proponit*): 'either *A* is not or *B* is not' is true (*fit*) of those things which can in no way co-exist, since it is also not necessary that either one of them should exist; it is equivalent to that compound proposition in which it is said: 'if *A* is, *B* is not'. . . . In this proposition only two combinations yield (valid) syllogisms. For, if *A* is, *B* will not be, and if *B* is, *A* will not be. . . . For if it is said: 'either *A* is not or *B* is not', it is said: 'if *A* is, *B* will not be', and 'if *B* is, *A* will not be'.

First we have here Sheffer's functor ('not *p* or not *q*', **43.43**); secondly this text contains an exact definition of the logical sum. The essential idea can be formulated:

24.131 Not *p* or not *q* if and only if: if *p* then not *q*.

Putting therein 'not-*p*' for '*p*' and 'not-*q*' for '*q*', we get by the principle of double negation:

24.132 *p* or *q* if and only if: if not-*p* then *q*.

On the other hand, Boethius defines in analogous fashion his '*si*' in the sense of equivalence by means of the same '*aut*' – which therefore and in this case has the sense of negated equivalence (*p* or *q* but not both, and necessarily one of the two) (**24.14**).

It is also worth remarking that Boethius regularly uses the principle of double negation and a law analogous to **24.21**.

E. BOETHIUS'S HYPOTHETICAL SYLLOGISMS

We here give the list of Boethius's hypothetical syllogisms. They seem to be the final result of Stoic logic, if understood as laws of the logic of propositions. Our supposition that Boethius aspired to a rule of substitution for propositional variables (cf. **24.09**), requires them to be so understood. They would be the final result of Stoic logic in the sense that they are practically the only part of this logic that was preserved by Boethius for the Middle Ages.

24.15 If *A* is, *B* is; but *A* is; therefore *B* is.

24.16 If *A* is, *B* is; but *B* is not; therefore *A* is not.

24.17 If *A* is, *B* is, and if *B* is, *C* must be; but then: if *A* is, *C* must be.

24.18 If *A* is, *B* is, and if *B* is, *C* too must be; but *C* is not; therefore *A* is not.

24.19 If *A* is, *B* is; but if *A* is not, *C* is; I say therefore that if *B* is not, *C* is.

24.20 If *A* is, *B* is not; if *A* is not, *C* is not; I say therefore that if *B* is, *C* is not.

24.21 If *B* is, *A* is; if *C* is not, *A* is not; on this supposition I say that if *B* is, it is necessary that *C* is not.

24.22 If *B* is, *A* is; if *C* is not, *A* is not; I say therefore: if *B* is is, *C* will be.

24.23 If one says: 'either *A* is or *B* is', (then) if *A* is, *B* will not be; and if *A* is not, *B* will be; and if *B* is not, *A* will be; and if *B** is, *A* will not be.

24.25 The (proposition) that says: 'either *A* is not or *B* is not', certainly means this, that if *A* is, *B* cannot be.

Boethius developes these syllogisms by substituting a conditional proposition for one or both variables (cf. **24.09**); in so doing he treats the negation of a conditional as the conjunction of the antecedent with the negation of the consequent, according to the law, which is not expressly formulated:

24.251 Not: if *p*, then *q*, if and only if: *p* and not-*q*.

---

* omitting *non* with van den Driessche (**24.24**).

Finally he applies the law of double negation (cf. **20.041**), thus gaining eighteen more syllogisms (**24.26**).

F. ALTERATIONS AND DEVELOPMENT OF THE CATEGORICAL SYLLOGISTIC

24.27 But Ariston the Alexandrian and some of the later Peripatetics further introduce five more moods (formed from those) with a universal conclusion: three in the first figure, two in the second figure, which yield particular conclusions. (But) it is extremely foolish to conclude to less from that to which more is due.

This text is not very clear. But its difficulty is somewhat lessened if we suppose that a combination of two Aristotelian rules is envisaged: (1) that allowing a universal conclusion to be weakened to the corresponding particular (**13.23**), (2) that yielding a further conclusion by conversion of the one first obtained. Then the following would be the moods intended:

24.271 A to all B; B to all C; therefore A to some C (*Barbari*).

24.272 A to no B; B to all C; therefore to some C, A not (*Celaront*).

24.273 A to all B; B to some C; therefore C to some A (*Dabitis*).

24.274 B to no A; B to all C; therefore to some C, A not (*Cesaro*).

24.275 B to all A; B to no C; therefore to some C, A not (*Camestrop*).

Beyond these, Galen transmits a further mood of this kind in the third figure (**24.28**):

24.281 A to all B; C to all B; therefore C to some A (*Daraptis*).

These formulae all have a Stoic rather than an Aristotelian form. In fact from Apuleius on, such alteration of the old laws into rules is more or less standard practice, especially in Boethius.

A further precision given to the Aristotelian syllogistic is in the famous logical square. This figure is first found in Apuleius again. It looks like this:

24.29

Contrariae		vel		incongruae	
Subalternae	universal affirmative			universal negative	*Subalternae*
	all pleasure is good			no pleasure is good	
		Alterutrae			
	some pleasure is good			some pleasure is not good	
	particular affirmative			particular negative	
Subcontrariae		vel		subpares	

G. THE SUPPOSEDLY FOURTH FIGURE

In an anonymous fragment, belonging possibly to the 6th century, we read:

24.30 Theophrastus and Eudemus also added other formulae to those of Aristotle in the first figure . . . many moderns have thought to form the fourth figure therefrom, citing Galen as the author of this intention.

But this allegedly 'Galenic' figure is not to be found in him. On the contrary he plainly states that there are only three figures:

24.31 These syllogisms are called, as I have said, categorical; they cannot be formed in more than the three figures mentioned, nor in another number in each (of these figures); this has been shown in the treatises *On Demonstration*.

J. Łukasiewicz was able to explain by means of another anonymous fragment how nevertheless the discovery of the fourth figure could be credited to Galen (**24.32**). This fragment is not without historical interest even apart from this question:

24.33 Of the categorical (syllogism) there are two kinds; the simple and the compound. Of the simple syllogism there are three kinds: the first, the second, and the third figure. Of the compound syllogism there are four kinds: the first, the second, the third, and the fourth figure. For Aristotle says that there are only three figures, because he looks at the simple syllogisms, consisting of three terms. Galen, however, says in his *Apodeictic* that there are four figures, because he looks at the compound syllogisms consisting of four terms, as he has found many such syllogisms in Plato's dialogues.

24.34   The categorical syllogism

simple, as (in) Aristotle   compound, as (in) Galen
        Figure 1, 2 , 3

Compound figure
1 to 1, 1 to 2, 1 to 3, 2 to 2, 2 to 1, 2 to 3, 3 to 3, 3 to 1, 3 to 2.

Compound figure
syllogistic:

1 to 1	1 to 2	1 to 3	2 to 3
1	2	3	4

unsyllogistic:

2 to 2   3 to 3   2 to 1   3 to 1   3 to 2
since no syllogism   2   3   4
arises from two
negatives or two
particulars.

1 to 1, as in the *Alcibiades*

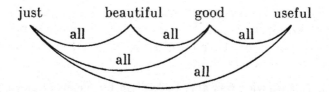

just   beautiful   good   useful
        all   all   all
              all
                    all

The numerals denote the successive figures, and the author
means that a valid compound syllogism can be formed in four
different ways, viz. when of the two simple syllogisms from which it
is composed
(1) both are in the first figure,
(2) the first is in the first, the second in the second figure.
(3) the first is in the first, the second in the third,
(4) the first is in the second, the second in the third.
Those are the four figures. So there is no question of a fourth figure of
simple syllogism, which was only ascribed to Galen by a misunderstanding. Yet the unknown scholiast (**24.30**), in falling a victim to
this misunderstanding at least made the principle of the fourth
figure another interpretation of the indirect moods of Theophrastus
(**17.10**).

H. PONS ASINORUM

Here we should introduce a scheme which was to become famous in the Middle Ages as the *pons asinorum* or 'asses' bridge' (**32.33** ff.). It is to be found in Philoponus*, and is an elaboration of the Aristotelian doctrine of the *inventio medii* (**14.29**). Although it belongs to methodology rather than logic, it is relevant to the latter also. The scheme seems typical of the way in which the commentators developed the syllogistic. In Philiponus the lines are captioned in the figure itself. For graphical reasons we put these comments afterwards and refer to them by numbers.

24.35*

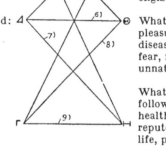

GOOD
A

What follows on the good: helpful, eligible, to be pursued, suitable, desirable, profitable, expedient.

What is alien to the good: imperfect, to be fled from, harmful, bad, ruinous, alien, unprofitable.

What the good follows upon: happiness, natural well-being, final cause, perfect, virtuous life.

PLEASURE
E

What follows on pleasure: movement, natural activity, unimpeded life, object of natural desire, undisturbed, eligible.

What is alien to pleasure: disease, labour, fear, need, unnatural movement.

What pleasure follows upon: health, good repute, virtuous life, plenty, good children, freedom from pain, comfort.

1) Unsyllogistic, because of concluding in the second figure from two universal affirmative (premisses).

2) Universal negative (conclusion) in the first and second (figures) by two conversions.

3) Particular affirmative (conclusion in the first and third) figures by conversion of the conclusion.

4) Universal negative (conclusion) in the first and second figure.

---

* Thanks are due to Prof. L. Minio-Paluello for pointing out this passage.
** For typographical reason the words in the figure are set in small type, though they belong to the quotation.

5) Universal affirmative (conclusion) in the first figure.
6) Unsyllogistic, from two universal negatives.
7) Particular negative (conclusion) in the third and first (figure) through conversion of the minor (premiss).
8) Unsyllogistic, since the particular does not convert, and in the first (figure) because (the syllogism) has a negative minor (premiss).
9) Particular affirmative (conclusion) in the third and first figures by conversion of the minor premiss.

I. ANTICIPATION OF THE LOGIC OF RELATIONS

Finally we shall speak of a detail which had no influence on the later development of logic, but which yet may be reckoned an ingenious anticipation of the logic of relations. Galen, dividing syllogisms in his *Introduction*, distinguishes first between categorical and hypothetical syllogisms, thus separating term- and class-logic; he then adds a further class:

24.36 There is still a further, third class of syllogisms, useful for demonstration, which I characterize as based on relation. Aristotelians claim that they are counted as categoricals. They are not a little in use among the Sceptics, Arithmeticians and experts in calculation in certain arguments of this kind: 'Theon possesses twice what Dion possesses; but Philo too possesses twice what Theon possesses; therefore Philo possesses four times what Dion possesses.'

This is in fact a substitution in a law of the logic of relations, and it is remarkable that Galen divides his logic just as Whitehead and Russell were to do in the 20th century. The content of his logic of relations is of course very poor, and he thinks that such laws are reducible to categorical syllogisms (**24.37**), which is a regress from the position of Aristotle.

SUMMARY

To summarize the results of post-Aristotelian antiquity we can say:
1. Propositional logic was then created. Some theorems of this kind were already known to Aristotle, sometimes even stated with propositional variables: but these were rather *obiter dicta* than systematically presented. In the Stoics on the other hand we meet systematic theory developed for its own sake.
2. This system is based on a fairly well worked out semantics, and it was expressly stated in the Stoic school that it was concerned

neither with words nor psychic images, but with objective meanings, the *lecta*. We have therefore to thank them for a fundamental thesis which was to play a great part in the history of logic.

3. Megarian-Stoic logic contained an astonishingly exact *analysis of proposition-forming functors:* we find correctly formed truth-tables and a more intricate discussion of the meaning of implication than we seem yet to have attained in the 20th century.

4. In this period the method is formalistic. Unambiguous correlation of verbal forms to *lecta* being presupposed, attention is exclusively directed to the syntactical structure of expressions. The application of this method and the logical subtlety shown by the Stoics must be deemed quite exemplary.

5. This formalism is accompanied by a significant *extension of logical technique*, shown in the clear distinction between propositional functions and propositions themselves, the method of identification of variables, and the application of the rule permitting substitution of propositional functions for propositional variables.

6. Propositional logic is axiomatized, and a clear *distinction drawn between laws and metatheorems*.

7. Finally we have to thank the Megarian school for propounding the first important logical *antinomy* – the Liar – which for centuries remained one of the chief problems of formal logic, and is so even today. So without exaggeration one can say that the achievements of this period make up antiquity's second basic contribution to formal logic.

PART III

The Scholastic Variety of Logic

§ 25. INTRODUCTION TO SCHOLASTIC LOGIC

A. STATE OF RESEARCH

At the present time much less is known about the history of scholastic than of ancient logic. The reason is that when Scholasticism ceased to be disparaged at the end of the nineteenth century, there was at first little revival of interest in its formal logic. This lack of interest is shown in the fact that of more than ten thousand titles of recent literature on Thomas Aquinas (up to 1953), very few concern his formal logic. There are indeed earlier works treating of questions of the literary history of scholastic logic – Grabmann having done most to find and publish texts –, but the investigation of their logical content only began with Łukasiewicz's paper of 1934 (**25.01**), pioneering in this field too. Under his influence some notable medievalists, e.g. besides Grabmann, K. Michalski, applied themselves to logical problems, and from his school there came the first work, well and systematically prepared, on medieval logic, the paper on the propositional logic of Ockham by J. Salamucha (1935) (**25.02**). A number of texts and treatises followed, those of Ph. Boehner O.F.M. and E. Moody in the forefront. Today there is quite a group at work, though as yet a small one.

But we are still at the beginning. Arabian and Jewish logic has hardly been touched; texts and treatises are alike lacking. In the western domain some texts of Abelard have been published for the 12th century; for the 14th and 15th centuries we have hardly anything, either new editions of texts or works on them; the 13th century is almost completely inaccessible and unknown. For this last, besides the (fairly) reliable older editions of the works of Thomas Aquinas and (some works) of Duns Scotus, Peter of Spain and William of Shyreswood are available only in provisional editions. For the 14th century there is an edition of the first book of Ockham's Summa, and one of a small work ascribed to Burleigh.*

Altogether we must say that the present state of research permits no general survey of the sources, growth and details of scholastic logic.

B. PROVISIONAL PERIODS

However, on the basis of the works of Ph. Boehner, E. Moody, L. Minio-Paluello, and of the ever-growing number of general studies of medieval philosophy, the history of medieval logic can be provisionally divided into the following periods:

---

* The late Fr. Ph. Boehner was working on a critical edition of another work of Burleigh's and of the *Perutilis Logica* of Albert of Saxony.

1. transitional period: up to Abelard. So far as we know this is not remarkable for any logical novelties, and acquaintance even with earlier achievements was very limited.

2. creative period: beginning seemingly after Abelard, about 1150, and lasting to the end of the 13th century. Former achievements now became known in the West, partly through the Arabs, partly (as L. Minio-Paluello has shown*) directly from Byzantium. At the same time work began on new problems, such as the *proprietates terminorum*, properties of terms. By about 1260 the essentials of scholastic logic seem to have taken shape and been made widely known in text-books. The best known book of this kind, and the most authoritative for the whole of Scholasticism – though by no means the first or the only one – is the *Summulae Logicales* of Peter of Spain.

3. period of elaboration: beginning approximately with William of Ockham (ob. 1349/50)** and lasting till the close of the Middle Ages. No essentially new problems were posed, but the old were discussed very thoroughly and very subtly, which resulted in an extremely comprehensive logic and semiotic.

So little is known of the whole development that we are unable even to name only the most important logicians. We can only say with certainty that the following among others exercised great influence:

in the 12th century:. Peter Abelard (1079–1142);
in the 13th century: Albert the Great (1193–1280);
Robert Kilwardby (ob. 1279),
William of Shyreswood (ob. 1249),
Peter of Spain (ob 1277);
in the 14th century: William of Ockham (ob. 1349/50),
John Buridan*** (ob. soon after 1358),
Walter Burleigh (ob. after 1343),
Albert of Saxony (1316–1390),
Ralph Strode (ca. 1370);
in the 15th century: Paul of Venice (ob. 1429),
Peter Tarteret (wrote between 1480 and 1490),
Stephanus de Monte

Appearance in this list comports no judgment of worth, especially as we hardly ever know whether a logician was original or only a copyist.

* Verbal communication from Prof. L. Minio-Paluello to whom the author is obliged for much information about the 12th and beginning of the 13th century.
** Ockham's productive period in logic was wholly prior to 1328/29 (**25.03**).
*** Ph. Boehner states that John of Cornubia (Pseudo-Scotus) may belong to the same period.

C. THE PROBLEM OF SOURCES

Even the question of the literary sources for Scholasticism's new logical problems is not yet satisfactorily answered. The works of Aristotle provide some starting-points for the semiotic, especially the first five chapters of the *Hermeneia* and the *Sophistic Refutations*. Recent research shows that the latter had a decisive influence on the scholastic range of problems*. But even the early scholastic theory of the 'properties of terms' is so much richer and more many-sided than the Aristotelian semiotic, that other influences must be supposed. Grammar was certainly an important one: so far as we can tell, that was the basis on which the main semiotic problems were developed without much outside influence − e.g. the whole doctrine of supposition, the growth of which can be traced with some continuity.

We have no more certain knowledge about the origin of the 'consequences'. Boethius's teaching about hypothetical sentences (rather than about hypothetical syllogisms) was undoubtedly very influential.** I. Thomas's recent inquiries (cf. footnote on **30.04**) point to the *Topics* as a principal source; the Stoic fragments do not seem to have been operative, at least directly, although the *Outlines of Pyrrhonism* of Sextus Empiricus were already translated into Latin in the 14th century (**25.04**). We do find doctrines here and there which are recognizably Stoic, but in scholastic logical literature as a whole Stoic logic seems to have been known only in the (obscure) form of Boethius's syllogisms. But these do not underlie the consequences, since even in fairly late works the two are treated in distinction. Probably scholastic propositional logic is a rediscovery, starting from hints in the *Topics* and perhaps also the *Hermeneia*, rather than a continuation of Stoic logic.

Arabian logicians certainly exercised some influence, though perhaps less than has commonly been supposed. But hardly any research has been done on this subject.***

D. LOGIC AND THE SCHOOLS

The opinion has often been expressed in writings on the history of scholastic logic that it can be divided *firstly* according to schools, as it might be into nominalist and realist logic, *secondly* according to faculties, and so into an 'artistic' and a 'theological' logic. But these divisions are little relevant to formal logic as such. More

---

* Verbal communication from Prof. Minio-Paluello.
** Prof. E. Moody has remarked on this to me.
*** I. Madkour's *L'Organon d'Aristote dans le monde Arabe* (**25.05**) is quite inadequate. Prof. A. Badawi in Cairo has published and discussed a series of Arabic logical texts but unfortunately only in Arabic. Communications received from him indicate the presence of many interesting doctrines.

modern research has shown that a number of logicians belonging
to sharply opposed philosophical schools, treated of just the same
range of problems and gave the same answers. Thus in every case
we have met there is but one doctrine of supposition, and differences
are either to be ascribed to personal idiosyncrasy rather than
philosophical presupposition, or else are more epistemological than
logical. Any contrast between artistic and theological logic is hardly
more in place. In the middle ages logic was always part of the
curriculum of the faculty of arts, but no-one was admitted to the
study of theology without having become *Baccalaureus artium.*
Hence the chief theological works of this period presuppose and use
the full range of 'artistic' logic. We should maintain only two
distinctions relevant to this double division of logic: (1) the theolo-
gians were not primarily interested in logic; (2) some of them
elaborated logical doctrines of special importance for theology; an
example is the doctrine of analogy of Thomas Aquinas.

Thus in the Middle Ages we find essentially only *one* logic.
Exceptions only occur where epistemological or ontological problems
exert an influence, as in the determination of the notion of logic
itself, and in the assigning of denotations. Everywhere else we find a
unified logic, developing organically. The very multiplicity of medieval views about extra-logical matters supports the thesis that
formal logic is independent of any special philosophical position on
the part of individual logicians.

E. METHOD

Our insufficient knowledge of the period makes it impossible to
write a history of the evolution of its logic. A historical presentation
would be possible for a few problems only, and even for those only
for isolated spaces of time. The justification of this chapter in a
work on the history of logical problems lies in the fact that, while
un-historical in itself, it does to some extent exhibit one stage in
the general development of logic.

Two questions are raised by the choice of problems for discussion.
The present state of research makes it likely that we are not acquainted with them all. In order not to miss at least the essentials,
we have made great use of the *Logica Magna* of Paul of Venice, which
expressly refers to all contemporary discussions and may rank as a
veritable *Summa* of 14th century logic. Paul's range of problems
has been enlarged by some further questions from other authors.

The second difficulty is posed by those logical problems which
overlap epistemology and methodology. Aristotle and the thinkers
of the Megarian-Stoic school envisage them in a fairly simple way,
but scholastic conceptions and solutions are much more complicated.
In order not to overstep our limits too far, these matters will be
touched on only very superficially.

F. CHARACTERISTICS

A survey of the logical problems dealt with by the Scholastics clearly shows that they fall into two classes: on the one hand there are the ancient ones, Aristotelian or Megarian-Stoic, concerning e.g. categorical and modal syllogistic, hypothetical syllogisms (i.e. Stoic arguments) etc. The rest, on the other hand, are either quite new, or else presented in so new a guise as no longer to remind one of the Greeks. Conspicuous in this class are the doctrines of 'properties of terms', of supposition, copulation, appellation and ampliation, then too the doctrine of consequences which while dependent on Aristotle's *Topics* and the Stoics, generalizes the older teaching and puts it in a new perspective. The same must be said about the insolubles (§ 35) which treat of the Liar and such-like but by new methods and in a much more general way.

Generally speaking, whatever the Scholastics discuss, even the problems of antiquity, is approached from a new direction and by new means. This is more and more the case as the Middle Ages progress. There is firstly the metalogical method of treatment. Metalogical items are indeed to be found in Aristotle (**14.25 ff.**), but in Scholasticism, at least in the later period, there is nothing but metalogic, i.e. formulae are not exhibited but described, so that in many works, e.g. in the *De puritate artis logicae* of Burleigh not a single variable of the object language is to be found. Even purely Aristotelian matters such as the categorical syllogism are dealt with from the new points of view, semiotic and other. In early Scholasticism a double line of development is detectable, problems inherited from antiquity being treated in the spirit of the ancient logicians, as in the commentaries of Albert the Great, and the new doctrine being developed in the very same work. Later the latter becomes more and more prominent, so that, as has been said, even genuinely Aristotelian problems are presented metalogically, in terms of the doctrine of supposition etc.

In addition, scholastic logic, even by the end of the 13th century, is very rich, very formalistic and exact in its statement. Some treatises undoubtedly rank higher than the *Organon* and perhaps than the Megarian-Stoic fragments too. The title of Burleigh's work – '*De puritate artis logicae*' – suits the content, for here is a genuinely *pure* formal logic.

I. SEMIOTIC FOUNDATIONS

§ 26. SUBJECT-MATTER OF LOGIC

To be able to understand what the Scholastics thought logic was about, one must be acquainted with the elements of their semiotic. Hence we give first two texts from Peter of Spain followed by one from Ockham, about sounds and terms.

A. BASIC NOTIONS OF SEMIOTICS

26.01 A sound is whatever is properly perceived by hearing; for though a man or a bell may be heard, this is only by means of sound. Of sounds, one is voice, another not voice. Sound-voice is the same as voice; so voice is sound produced from the mouth of an animal, formed by the natural organs. . . . Of voices, one is literate, another not literate. Literate voice is that which can be written, e.g. 'man'; not literate is that which cannot be written. Of literate voices one is significant, another not significant. Significant voice is that which represents something to the hearing, e.g. 'man' or the groans of the sick which signify pain. Not significant voice is that which represents nothing to the hearing, e.g. 'bu', 'ba'. Of significant voices one signifies naturally, another conventionally. Conventionally significant voice is that which represents something at the will of one who originates it, e.g. 'man'. Naturally significant voice is that which represents the same thing to all, e.g. the groans of the sick, the bark of dogs. Of conventionally significant voices one is simple or not complex, e.g. a noun or a verb, another composite or complex, e.g. a speech (*oratio*). . . .

And it should be known that logicians (*dialecticus*) posit only two parts of speech, viz. noun and verb, calling the others 'syncategoremata'.

26.02 Of things which are said, some are said with complexity, e.g. 'a man runs', 'white man'. Others without complexity, e.g. 'man' by itself, a term that is not complex. . . . A term, as here understood, is a voice signifying a universal or particular, e.g. 'man' or 'Socrates'.

These texts contain doctrine generally accepted in Scholasticism. Another, no less widely recognized, is excellently summarized by Ockham, who uses the expression '*terminus conceptus*' ('conceived term') instead of the usual '*terminus mentalis*' ('thought term').

26.03 It is to be known that according to Boethius . . . speech is threefold, viz. written, spoken and conceived, this last having being only in the intellect, so (too) the term is threefold, viz. written, spoken and conceived. A written term is part of a proposition written down on some body which is seen or can be seen by a bodily eye. A spoken term is part of a proposition spoken by the mouth and apt to be heard with a corporeal ear. A conceived term is an intention or affection of the soul, naturally signifying something or con-signifying, apt to be part of a proposition in thought. . . .

Those are the most important presuppositions for what follows.

B. LOGIC AS A THEORY OF SECOND INTENTIONS

Many early Scholastics give explicit definitions of logic. Disregarding these, we shall proceed to descriptions of the subject-matter of logic, of which we know two kinds. According to the first it consists in so-called second intentions. Three series of texts will illustrate the matter, taken from Thomas Aquinas (13th century), Ockham and Albert of Saxony (early and late 14th century respectively).

26.04 Being is two-fold, being in thought (*ens rationis*) and being in nature. Being in thought is properly said of those intentions which reason produces (*adinvenit*) in things it considers, e.g. the intention of genus, species and the like, which are not found among natural objects, but are consequent on reason's consideration. This kind, viz. being in thought, is the proper subject-matter of logic.

26.05 The relation which is denoted (*importatur*) by this name 'the same' is merely a being in thought, if what is the same without qualification is meant: for such a relation can only consist in an ordering by the reason of something to itself, according to some two considerations of it.

26.06 Because relation has the weakest being of all the categories, some have thought that it belongs to second intentions (*intellectibus*). For the first things understood are the things outside the soul, to which the intellect is primarily directed, to understand them. But those intentions (*intentiones*) which are consequent on the manner of understanding are said to be secondarily understood. . . . So according to this thesis (*positio*) it would follow that relation is not among the things outside the soul but merely in the intellect, like the intention of genus and species and second (i.e. universal) substances.

Thus according to Thomas the subject-matter of logic is such 'secondarily understood things' or 'second intentions', belonging to the domain of being in thought, and so *lecta*. Not all *lecta*, however, but a special kind, such as those corresponding to the meaning of logical constants. It is to be stressed that according to Thomas, as for the Stoics, the subject-matter of logic is nothing psychical, but something objective, which yet exists only in the soul.

The nature of second intentions war much debated among Scholastics, and we know of many different opinions. Ockham says:

26.07 It should first be known that that is called an 'intention of the soul' which is something in the soul apt to signify something else. . . . But what is it in the soul which is such a sign? It must be said that on that point (*articulum*) there are various opinions. Some say that it is only something fashioned by the soul. Others that it is a quality subjectively existing in the soul, distinct from the act of understanding. Others say that it is the act of understanding. . . . These opinions will be examined later. For the present it is enough to say that an intention is something in the soul which is a sign naturally signifying something for which it can stand (*supponere*) or which can be part of a mental proposition.

Such a sign is twofold. One which is a sign of something which is not such a sign, . . . and that is called a 'first intention' such as is that intention of the soul which is predicable of all men, and similarly the intention predicable of all whitenesses, and blacknesses, and so on. . . . But a second intention is that which is a sign of such first intentions, such as are the intentions 'genus', 'species' and such-like. For as one intention common to all men is predicated of all men when one says: 'this man is a man', 'that man is a man', and so on of each one, similarly one intention common to those intentions which signify and stand for things is predicated of them when one says: . . . 'stone is a species', 'animal is a species, 'colour is a species' etc.

The same doctrine is further developed by Albert of Saxony:

26.08 'Term of first intention' is the name given to that mental term which is significative of things not from the point of view of their being signs. Thus this mental term 'man', or this mental term 'being', or this mental term 'quality', or this mental term 'voice'. Hence this mental term 'man' signifies Socrates or Plato, and not insofar as Socrates or Plato are signs for other things. . . . But a mental term which is naturally significative of things insofar as they are signs is called a 'term of second intention', and if they ceased to be signs it would not signify them. Of this kind are the mental terms 'genus', 'species', 'noun', 'verb', 'case of a noun' etc.

In the last two texts the conception is other than that of Thomas. Second intentions are there conceived in a purely semantic way; they are signs of signs, and for Albert signs of signs *as such*.

Whether Ockham and Albert thought of logic as in any sense a science of second intentions remains open to question. One might perhaps give expression to both their views by saying that logic is a science constructed throughout in a meta-language,* remarking at the same time that the Scholastics included under 'signs' mental as well as exterior (written or spoken) signs.

However, one common feature underlies all these fundamental differences; logic is sharply distinguished from ontology in the whole scholastic tradition. This is so for Thomas, since its object is not real things, but second intentions; and for his successors, since it is expressed not in an object- but in a meta-language.

It should also be noted that in fact the *entire* practice of medieval logic corresponds to the Thomist conception of the object of logic, even though this conception was not the only one. For scholastic logic essentially consists of two parts: the doctrine of the properties of terms, and the doctrine of consequences. The properties of terms are evidently second intentions in the Thomist sense; and one must think of consequences in the same light, since the logical relationships they exhibit (e.g. between antecedent and consequent) are not real things.

C. FORMAL LOGIC AS A THEORY OF SYNCATEGOREMATIC EXPRESSIONS

There is a difficulty in adopting the view that we have hypothetically ascribed to Ockham about the subject matter of logic, in that it does not achieve a definition of logic as a distinct science, since every science can be formulated in a meta-language. But we find, though not explicitly, logic limited to concern with *logical* form, which leads to an exact definition of formal logic when this form is equated with the syncategoremata. Scholastic practice is wholly in accord with this definition in its cultivation of the corresponding

---

* I am particularly obliged to Prof. E. Moody for valuable assistance with these questions.

theory of logical form. Three texts about syncategoremata follow, one from William of Shyreswood (13th century), one from Ockham (beginning of 14th) and one from Buridan* (end of 14th).

26.09 To understand propositions one must know their parts. Their parts are twofold, primary and secondary. Primary parts are substantival names and verbs; these are necessary for an understanding of propositions. Secondary parts are adjectival names, adverbs, conjunctions and prepositions; these are not essential to the constitution of propositions.

Some secondary parts are determinations of primary ones with reference to (*ratione*) their things (i.e. to which they refer), and such are not syncategoremata; e.g. when I say 'white man' 'white' signifies that one of its things, a man, is white. Others are determinations of primary parts insofar as these are subjects or predicates; e.g. when I say 'every man runs', the 'every', which is a universal sign, does not mean that one of its things, namely a man, is universal, but that 'man' is a universal subject. Such are called 'syncategoremata' and will be treated (here), as offering considerable difficulties in discourse.

Ockham affords a development of the same thought:

26.10 Categorematic terms have a definite and certain signification, e.g. this name 'man' signifies all men, and this name 'animal' all animals, and this name 'whiteness' all whitenesses. But syncategorematic terms, such as are 'all', 'no', 'some', 'whole', 'besides', 'only', 'insofar as' and suchlike, do not have a definite and certain signification, nor do they signify anything distinct from what is signified by the categoremata. Rather, just as in arabic numeration a zero (*cifra*) by itself signifies nothing, but attached to another figure makes that signify, so a syncategorema properly speaking signifies nothing, but when attached to something else makes that signify something or stand for some one or more things in a determinate way, or exercises some other function about a categorema. Hence this syncategorema 'all' has no definite significate, but when attached to 'man' makes it

---

* It is taken from the *Consequentiae* which is ascribed to Buridan in the early printed editions, though a letter from Fr. Ph. Boehner informs us that no MS of this work has yet been found.

stand or suppose for all men . . . , and attached to 'stone' makes it stand for all stones, and attached to 'whiteness' makes it stand for all whitenesses. And the same is to be held proportionately for the others, as for that syncategorema 'all', though distinct functions are exercised by distinct syncategoremata, as will later be shown for some of them.

Evidently, the syncategoremata are our logical constants. That they determine logical form is expressly and consciously propounded by Buridan (whose text was later adopted almost word for word by Albert of Saxony: **26.11**).

26.12 When form and matter are here spoken of, by the matter of a proposition or consequence is understood merely the categorematic terms, i.e. the subject and predicate, to the exclusion of the syncategorematic* ones attached to them, by which they are restricted, negated, or divided and given (*trahuntur*) a determinate kind of supposition. All else, we say, belongs to the form. Hence we say that the copula, both of the categorical and of the hypothetical proposition belongs to the form of the proposition, as also negations, signs, the number both of propositions and terms, as well as the mutual ordering of all the aforesaid, and the interconnections of relative terms and the ways of signifying (*modos significandi*) which relate to the quantity of the proposition, such as discreteness**, universality etc. . . .

E.g. . . Since modals have subordinate copulas and so differ from assertoric propositions, these differ in form; and by reason of the negations and signs *(signa)* affirmatives are of another form than negatives, and universals than particulars; and by reason of the universality and discreteness*** of their terms singular propositions are of another form than indefinites; by reason of the number of terms the following propositions are of different forms: 'man is man' and 'man is ass', as are the following consequences or hypothetical propositions: 'every man runs, therefore some man runs' and 'every man runs, therefore some ass walks about'. Similarly by reason of the order the following are of different forms: 'every man is animal', 'animal is every man', and likewise the following

* Reading *syncategorematicis* for *categoricis*.
** Reading *discretio* for *descriptio*.
*** See last note.

consequences: 'every B is A, therefore some B is A' and 'every B is A, therefore some A is B' etc. Similarly by reason of the relationship and connection . . . 'the man runs, the man does not run' is of another form than this: 'the man runs and the same does not run': since its form makes the second impossible, but it is not so with the first.

It is easy to establish that scholastic logic has for its object precisely form so conceived. The doctrine of the properties of terms treats of supposition, appellation, ampliation and such-like relationships, all of which are determined in the proposition by syncategorematic terms; while the second part of scholastic logic, comprising the doctrine of the syllogism, consequences etc., treats of formal consequence, which holds in virtue of the form as described.

Expressed in modern terms, the difference between the two conceptions of logic that have been exemplified, is that the first is semantic, the second syntactical: for the first uses the idea of reference, the second determines logical form in a purely structural way. According to the second the *logical constants* are the subject-matter of logic, while on the view of Thomas this object is their *sense*. On either view Scholasticism achieved a very clear idea of logical form and so of logic itself.

D. CONTENT OF THE WORKS

Two kinds of logical works can be distinguished in Scholasticism, commentaries on Aristotle and independent treatises or manuals. To begin with, the composition of works even of the second kind is strongly influenced by the Aristotelian range of problems, at least in the sense that newer problems are incorporated into the framework of the *Organon*. It is only gradually that the ever growing importance of the new problems finds expression in the very construction of the works. We shall show this in some examples collected for the most part by Ph. Boehner (**26.13**).

Albert the Great has no independent arrangement; his logic consists of commentaries on the writings of Aristotle and Boethius.

The chief logical work of Peter of Spain falls into two parts; the first is markedly Aristotelian and contains the following treatises:

On Propositions (= *Hermeneia*),
On the Predicables (= *Porphyry*),
On the Categories (= *Categories*),
On Syllogisms (= *Prior Analytics*),
On Loci (= *Topics*),
Suppositions,
On Fallacies (= *Sophistic Refutations*).

159

In the second part is to be found nothing but the new problematic, for it is divided into treatises on

Relatives,
Ampliations,
Appellations,
Restrictions,
Distributions.

Two points are notable: that propositions are discussed at the start (and not in the third place as in Porphyry and the *Categories*), and that the doctrine of supposition is inserted before the treatise on fallacies. That shows how the new problematic began to influence the older one.

Ockham's *Summa* is divided in another way:

I. Terms:
  1. In general.
  2. Predicables.
  3. Categories.
  4. Supposition.

II. Propositions:
  1. Categorical and modal propositions.
  2. Conversion.
  3. Hypothetical propositions.

III. Arguments:
  1. Syllogisms:
    a) assertoric,
    b) modal,
    c) mixed (from the first two kinds),
    d) 'exponibilia',
    e) hypothetical.

  2. Demonstration (in the sense of the *Posterior Analytics*).

  3. Further rules:
    a) Consequences.
    b) Topics.
    c) Obligations.
    d) Insolubles.

  4. Sophistics.

The general framework here is still Aristotelian, more so even than with Peter, but the new problematic has penetrated into the subdivisions. An Aristotelian title often conceals strange material, as when the chapter on the categories deals with typically scholastic problems about intentions etc.

Walter Burleigh's *De puritate artis logicae* is divided thus:
I. On terms:
1. Supposition.
2. Appellation.
3. Copulation.

II. (Without title):
1. Hypothetical propositions.
2. Conditional syllogisms.
3. Other hypothetical syllogisms.

Even this small sample shows how the scholastic range of problems is to the fore.

Albert of Saxony divides his logic in this way:
1. Terms (in general).
2. Properties of terms (supposition, ampliation, appellation).
3. Propositions.
4. Consequences:
   a) in general.
   b) Propositional consequences.
   c) Syllogistic consequences.
   d) Hypothetical syllogisms.
   e) Modal syllogisms.
   f) Topics.
5. Sophistics.
6. Antinomies and obligations.

Here the whole of Aristotelian and Stoic formal logic has been built into the scholastic doctrine of consequences, while this last is introduced by discussion of another typically scholastic matter, the properties of terms.

Finally we consider the division of the *Logica Magna* of Paul Nicollet of Venice (ob. 1429), which is probably the greatest systematic work on formal logic produced in the Middle Ages. It falls into two parts, the first designed to treat of terms, the second of propositions, though in fact the first contains much about propositions, and the second includes also the doctrine of consequences and syllogisms.

Part I:
1. Terms.
2. Supposition.
3. Particles that cause difficulty.
4. Exclusive particles.
5. Rules of exclusive propositions.
6. Exceptive particles.
7. Rules of exceptive propositions.
8. Adversative particles.

9. 'How'.
10. Comparatives.
11. Superlatives.
12. Objections and counter-arguments.
13. Categorematic 'whole' (*totus*).
14. 'Always' and 'ever'.
15. 'Infinite'.
16. 'Immediate'.
17. 'Begins' and 'ceases'.
18. Exponible propositions.
19. *Propositio officiabilis*.
20. Composite and divided sense.
21. Knowing and doubting.
22. Necessity and contingence of future events.

Part II:
1. Propositions (in general).
2.-3. Categorical propositions.
4. Quantity of propositions.
5. Logical square.
6. Equivalences.
7. Nature of the proposition in the square.
8. Conversion.
9. Hypothetical propositions.
10. Truth and falsity of propositions.
11. Signification of propositions.
12. Possibility, impossibility.
13. Syllogisms.
14. Obligations.
15. Insolubles.

Here the treatise on consequences has disappeared, having been incorporated into that on hypothetical propositions. *

§ 27. SUPPOSITION

We begin our presentation of scholastic logic with the doctrine of supposition. This is one of the most original creations of Scholasticism, unknown to ancient and modern logic, but playing a

---

* The following figures will give an idea of the scope of this work. The *Logica Magna* occupies 199 folios of four columns each containing some 4600 printed signs, so that the whole work comprises about 3,650,000 signs. This corresponds to at least 1660 normal octavo pages, four to five volumes. But the *Logica Magna* is only one of four works by Paul on formal logic, the others together being even more voluminous. None of it is merely literary work, but a pure logic, written in terse and economical language.

central role here. Unpublished research of L. Minio Paluello enables us to trace its origin to the second half of the 12th century. By the middle of the 13th all available sources witness to its being everywhere accepted. Later there appear some developments of detail, but no essentially new fundamental ideas.

We shall first illustrate the notion of supposition in general, then proceed to the theory of material and simple supposition, and finally mention other kinds.

A. CONCEPT OF SUPPOSITION

The notion of supposition is already well defined in Shyreswood, and distinguished by him from similar 'properties of terms':

27.01 Terms have four properties, which we shall now distinguish. . . . These properties are signification, supposition, copulation and appellation. Signification is the presentation of a form to the reason. Supposition is the ordering of one concept (*intellectus*) under another. Copulation is the ordering of one concept over another. It is to be noted that supposition and copulation, like many words of this kind, are proffered (*dicuntur*) in two senses, according as they are supposed to be actual or habitual. Their definitions belong to them according as they are supposed to be actual. But insofar as they are supposed to be habitual, 'supposition' is the name given to the signification of something as subsisting; for what subsists is naturally apt to be ordered under another. And 'copulation' is the name given to the signification of something as adjacent, for what is adjacent is naturally apt to be ordered over another. But appellation is the present attribution of a term, i.e. the property by which what a term signifies can be predicated of something by means of the verb 'is'.

It follows that signification is present in every part of speech, supposition only in substantives, pronouns or substantival particles; for these (alone) signify the thing as subsistent and of such a kind as to be able to be set in order under another. Copulation is in all adjectives, participles and verbs, appellation in all substantives, adjectives and participles, but not in pronouns since these signify substance only, not form. Nor is it in verbs. . . . None of these three, supposition, copulation and appellation is present in the indeclinable parts (of speech), since no indeclinable part signifies substance or anything in substance.

Thomas Aquinas speaks in similar fashion:

27.02 The proper sense (*ratio*) of a name is the one which the name signifies; . . . But that to which the name is attributed if it be taken directly under the thing signified by the name, as determinate under indeterminate, is said to be supposed by the name; but if it be not directly taken under the thing of the name, it is said to be copulated by the name; as this name 'animal' signifies sensible animate substance, and 'white' signifies colour disruptive of sight, while 'man' is taken directly under the sense of 'animal' as determinate under indeterminate. For man is sensible animate substance with a particular kind of soul, viz. a rational one. But it is not directly taken under white, which is extrinsic to its essence.

27.03 The difference between substantives and adjectives consists in this, that substantives refer to (*ferunt*) their suppositum, adjectives do not, but posit in the substance* that which they signify. Hence the logicians (*sophistae*) say that substantives suppose, adjectives do not suppose but copulate.

The doctrine implicit in these texts was later expressly formulated by Ockham:

27.04 (Supposition) is a property belonging to terms, but only as (they occur) in a proposition.

B. MATERIAL AND FORMAL SUPPOSITION

Shyreswood writes:

27.05 Supposition is sometimes material, sometimes formal. It is called material when an expression (*dictio*) stands either for an utterance (*vox*) by itself, or for the expression which is composed of an utterance and (its) significance, e.g. if we were to say: 'homo' consists of two syllables, 'homo' is a name. It is formal when an expression stands for what it signifies.

27.06 The first division of supposition is disputed. For it seems that kinds not of supposition but of signification are there distinguished. For signification is the presentation of a form to the reason. So that where there is different presenta-

---

* Reading *substantiam* for *substantivum*.

164

tion there is different signification. Now when an expression supposes materially it presents either itself or its utterance; but when formally, it presents what it signifies; therefore it presents something different (in each case); therefore it signifies something different. But that is not true, since expressions by themselves always present what they signify, and if they present their utterance they do not do this of themselves but through being combined with a predicate. For some predicates naturally refer to the mere utterance or to the expression, while others refer to what is signified. But this effects no difference in the signification. For the expression as such, before ever being incorporated in a sentence, already has a significance which does not arise from its being co-ordinated with another.

On this question Thomas Aquinas remarks:

27.07 One could object to this (teaching of ours) also, that verbs in other moods (than the infinitive) seem to be put as subjects, e.g. if one says: 'I run is a verb'. But it must be said that the verb 'I run' is not taken formally in this statement (*locutio*), (i.e.) with its signification referred to a thing, but as materially signifying the word itself which is taken as a thing.

The expressions '*suppositio materialis*' and '*suppositio formalis*' have also another meaning for Thomas. He sometimes uses the first for *suppositio personalis* (cf. **27.23** ff.) and the second for *suppositio simplex* (cf. **27.17** f.):

27.08 A term put as subject holds (*tenetur*) materially, i.e. (stands) for the suppositum; but put as predicate it holds formally, i.e. (stands) for the nature signified.

Perhaps this ambiguity accounts for the expression 'formal supposition', that we have found in Shyreswood and Thomas, later disappearing, so far as we know, outside the Thomist school.* Even by Ockham's time supposition is divided immediately into three kinds:

27.09 Supposition is first divided into personal, simple and material.

---

*Fr. Ph. Boehner is to be thanked for the information that this expression occurs in Chr. Javellus (ob. 1538).

The two first of those are sub-species of the formal supposition of
Shyreswood and Thomas, which Ockham no longer refers to. His
division is subsequently the usual one, except among the Thomists.

In **27.05** we read of an 'utterance by itself' and an 'expression
which is composed of an utterance and (its) significance'. This
distinction is developed at the end of the 15th century by Peter
Tarteret:

27.10 Material supposition is the acceptance of a term for
its non-ultimate significate, or its non- ultimate significates....
In which it is to be noticed that significates are two-fold,
ultimate and non-ultimate. The ultimate significate is that
which is ultimately signified by a term signifying conventionally, and ultimately or naturally and properly. But the
non-ultimate significate is the term itself, or one vocally or
graphically similar, or one mentally equivalent. From which
it follows that a vocal or written term is said to signify
conventionally in two ways, either ultimately or non-ultimately. Ultimately it signifies what it is set to signify; but
a vocal term is said to signify conventionally and non-ultimately a synonymous written term; and a written term
is said to signify non-ultimately an utterance synonymous
with it. . . .

From the modern point of view this doctrine reflects our distinction of language and meta-language, except that in place of two
languages, symbols of one language exercise a two-fold supposition.
Furthermore, the two last-cited texts exhibit the important distinction between the name of an individual symbol and the name of a
class of equiform symbols. We do not find this in the logistic period
till after 1940.

This distinction first occurs, so far as we know, in St. Vincent
Ferrer* (14th century), as a division of material supposition:

27.11 Material supposition is divided as is formal. One
(kind of material supposition) is common, the other discrete.

---

* Vincent Ferrer was the greatest preacher of his time. We would add that
Savonarola was also an important logician. A similar link between deep religious
life and a talented interest in formal logic is also to be observed in Indian culture
especially among the Buddhists. This would seem to be a little known and as yet
unexplained phenomenon. The authenticity of Vincent Ferrer's philosophical
opuscules *De Suppositionibus* and *De unitate universalis* has been challenged so
far as we know only by S. Brettle (vid. Additions to Bibliography **3.98**). To his
p. 105 note 3 should be added a, here relevant, reference to p. 33 note 10. M. G.
Miralles (vid. Additions) summarizes the arguments for and against, and
concludes with M. Gorce (vid. Additions): 'L'authenticité des deux écrits n'a été
jamais mise en doute. Le témoignage du contemporain Ranzzano suffit à la
prouver.'

It is discrete if the term or utterance stands determinately for a suppositum of its material significate. And thus discrete material* suppositum occurs in three ways. In one way through the utterance or term itself, as when one asks: 'What is it you want to say?' and the other answers: 'I say "buf"' and '"baf" is said by me', (then) the subject of this proposition supposes materially and discretely since it stands for the very utterance numerically identical (with it) (cf. **11.11**). This becomes more evident if names are assigned to the individual terms in such a way that as this name 'man'** signifies this individual man so this name 'A' signifies that individual word 'buf' and 'B' the other ('baf'). And then if it is said: 'A is an utterance' or 'A is said by me', the subject supposes materially and discretely, as in the proposition 'Socrates runs' the subject supposes formally and discretely.

27.12 It occurs secondly through a demonstrative name (*nomen*) demonstrating an utterance or singular term, as when the utterance of the term 'man' is written somewhere and one says, with reference to this utterance: 'That is a name'. Then the subject of the proposition supposes materially for that which it demonstrates.

It occurs in a third way through a term. . . ., which is determined by a demonstrative pronoun, as when it is said of the written utterance 'man': 'this "man" is a name' or 'this utterance is a name'.

And each of these ways . . . can be varied by natural, personal or simple supposition, as was said about singular formal supposition.

Common (*communis*) material supposition is when the utterance or term stands indeterminately for its material signification, as when it is said: '"people" is written' the subject of this proposition stands indeterminately for this term 'people', or (in another example) for some other (term). I do not say that in the proposition '"people" is written' or in some other such that the supposition is indeterminate, but that the subject is indeterminate and is taken indeterminately

Material common supposition is divided into natural, personal and simple supposition, like common formal supposi-

---

* Reading *materialis* for *formalis*.
** Reading *homo* for *primo*.

tion. .... An example of personal: '"man" is heard', '"man" is written', '"man" is answered'. An example of simple (supposition): '"man" is a species of utterance', '"man" is conceived', '"man" is said by this man'; and so on in many other cases as everyone can see for himself.

So material supposition is divided just as is formal. These texts exhibit scholastic semantics at its best. This accuracy of analysis is the more astonishing when one remembers that the distinction mentioned in the introduction to **27.11** remained unknown, not only to the decadent 'classical' logicians, but also to mathematical ones for nearly a century.

It should also be noticed that in the text of Tarteret just cited, a distinction occurs which cannot be expressed in contemporary terms. The Scholastics distinguished, as has already be said above (**26.03**) three inter-related kinds of sign: graphical, vocal and psychic, and a materially supposing graphical sign can stand either for itself (or its equiforms) or for the corresponding vocal or psychic sign.

Burleigh has another division, parallel to that between material and formal supposition:

27.13 The tenth rule is: that on every act that is accomplished there follows the act that is signified, and conversely. For it follows: 'man is an animal, therefore "animal" is predicated of "man"', for the verb 'is' accomplishes predication, and this verb 'is predicated' signifies predication, and syncategorematic particles accomplish acts, and adjectival verbs signify such acts. E.g. the sign 'all' accomplishes distribution, and the verb 'to distribute' signifies distributions; the particle 'if' exercises consequence, and this verb 'it follows' signifies consequence.

It was said above that this distinction runs parallel with that between formal and material supposition, for it could easily be translated into it. But Burleigh would not seem to be thinking of these suppositions here; by 'the act signified' he means not words, but their significates. For in his example, the *word* 'animal' is not predicated of the *word* 'man', but what the first signifies is predicated of that for which the second supposes.

C. SIMPLE SUPPOSITION

Along with the idea of material supposition, that of simple (*simplex*) supposition is an interesting scholastic novelty. On this subject we can limit ourselves to the 13th century, and mainly to

168

Peter of Spain. First we shall give some of his general divisions of formal supposition:

27.14 One kind of supposition is common, another discrete. Common supposition is effected by a common term such as 'man'. Again of common suppositions one kind is natural, another accidental. Natural supposition is the taking of a common term for everything of which it is naturally apt to be predicated, as 'man' taken by itself naturally possesses supposition for all men who are and who have been and who will be. Accidental supposition is the taking of a common term for everything for which its adjunct requires (it to be taken). E.g. 'A man exists'; the term 'man' here supposes for present men. But when it is said: 'a man was', it supposes for past men. And when it is said: 'a man will be', it supposes for future ones, and so has different suppositions according to the diversity of its adjuncts.

Later on we also meet with an 'improper' (**27.15**) and a 'mixed' (**27.16**) supposition. The first simply consists in the metaphorical use of a term. The second was introduced to elucidate the function of terms of which one part supposed in one way, another in another. From the logical point of view these are not very important ideas. Of greater importance is Peter's continuation:

27.17 Of accidental suppositions one is simple, another personal. Simple supposition is the taking of a common term for the universal thing symbolized (*figurata*) by it, as when it is said: 'man is a species' or 'animal is a genus', the term 'man' supposes for man in general and not for any of its inferiors, and similarly in the case of any common term, as 'risible is a proprium', 'rational is a difference'.

27.18 Of simple suppositions one belongs to a common term set as subject, as 'man is a species'; another belongs to a common term set as an affirmative predicate, as 'every man is an animal'; the term 'animal' set as a predicate has simple supposition because it only supposes for the generic nature; yet another belongs to a common term put after an exceptive form of speech, as 'every animal apart from man is irrational'. The term 'man' has simple supposition. Hence it does not follow: 'every animal apart from man is irrational, therefore every animal apart from this man (is irrational)', for there is there the fallacy of the form of speech (cf. **11.19**), when passage is made from simple to personal supposition. Similarly here: 'man is a species, therefore some man (is a species)'. In all such cases passage is made from simple to personal supposition.

27.19 But that a common term put as predicate is to be taken with simple supposition is clear when it is said: 'of all contraries there is one and the same science', for unless the term 'science' had simple supposition there would be a fallacy. For no particular science is concerned with all contraries; medicine is not concerned with all contraries but only with what is healthy and what is sick, and grammar with what is congruous and incongruous, and so on.

This is to be compared with the text of Thomas cited above (**27.08**). The following text from him from a theological context expresses the matter clearly:

27.20 The proposition *homo factus est Deus* . . . can be understood as though *factus* determines the composition, so that the sense would be: 'a man is in fact God', i.e. it is a fact that a man is God. And in this sense both are true, *homo factus est Deus* and *Deus factus est homo*. But this is not the proper sense of these propositions (*locutionum*), unless they were to be so understood that 'man' would have not personal but simple supposition. For although this (concrete) man did not become God, since the suppositum of this, the person of the Son of God, was God from eternity, yet man, speaking universally, was not always God.

This text has the further importance that it may suggest the reason why the Scholastics spoke of 'personal' supposition, this being the function exercised by a term in standing for individuals or an individual (*suppositum*). For this recalls to the mind of a Scholastic the famous theological problem of the person of Christ, as in **27.20**.

The essentials of the scholastic doctrine of simple supposition may be summed up thus: in the proposition '*A* is *B*', the subject '*A*' has of itself personal supposition, i.e. it stands for the individuals, but the predicate '*B*' has simple supposition, i.e. it stands either for a property or a class. But one can also frame propositions in which something is predicated of such a property or class, and then the subject must have simple supposition. It can be seen that this doctrine deals with no less a subject than the distinction between two logical types, the first and second (cf. **48.21**).

These simple but historically important facts are complicated by the scholastic development of two other problems along with this doctrine. They are (1) the problem of analysing propositions, whether they should be understood in a purely extensional fashion, or with extensional subject and intensional predicate. Thomas and Peter, in the texts cited, adopt the second position. We shall treat this problem a little more explicitly in a chapter on the analysis of propositions (**29.02–04**). Then (2) there is the problem of the semantic correlate of a term having simple supposition. This is a very difficult philosophical problem, and the Scholastics were of varying opinions about its solution. In **27.18** Peter seems to think that a term with simple supposition stands for the essence (nature) of the object. On the other hand Ockham and his school hold that the semantic correlate of such a term is simple, 'the intention of the soul':

27.21 A term cannot have simple or material supposition in every proposition but only when . . . it is linked with another extreme which concerns an intention of the soul or an utterance or something written. E.g. in the proposition 'a man is running' the 'man' cannot have simple or material supposition, since 'running' does not concern either an intention of the soul, nor an utterance nor something written. But in the proposition 'man is a species' it can have simple supposition because 'species' signifies an intention of the soul.

In this and similar texts (**27.22**) it is of logical interest that Ockham and his followers were apparently trying to give an extensional interpretation even to terms having simple supposition; their correlates would be (concrete) intentions.

After Buridan there were in the Middle Ages, as at the beginning of the 20th century, some logicians who equated simple and material supposition. Paul of Venice gives that information:

27.23 Simple supposition is distinct from material and personal; some say otherwise, and make no distinction between simple and material supposition. But (*unde*) it is evident that the subject does not suppose materially when it is said: 'the divine essence is inwardly communicable'.

D. PERSONAL SUPPOSITION

The most usual supposition of a term is personal. As Ockham says:

27.24 It is also to be noticed that in whatever proposition it be put, a term can always have personal supposition, unless it be restricted to some other by the will of those who use it.

We give the definition and divisions of this kind of supposition according to Peter of Spain, whose text contains the essentials of the doctrine that remained standard till the end of the scholastic period.

27.25 Personal supposition is the taking of a common term for its inferiors, as when it is said 'a man runs', the term 'man' supposes for its inferiors, viz. for Socrates and for Plato and so on.

27.26 Of personal suppositions one kind is determinate, another confused. Determinate supposition is the taking of a common term put indefinitely or with the sign of particularity, as 'a man runs' or 'some man runs', and both are called 'determinate' because although in both the term 'man' supposes for every man, whether running or not, yet they are true only for one man running. For it is one thing to suppose (for things), and another to render the proposition true for one of them*. But as has been said, the term 'man' supposes for all whether running or not, yet renders the propositions true only for one who is running. But it is clear that the supposition is determinate in both (propositions), because when it is said: 'An animal is Socrates, an animal is Plato, and so on, therefore every animal is every man', this is the fallacy of the form of speech (proceeding) from a number of determinates to one (cf. **11.19** and **27.18**). And so a common term put indefinitely has determinate supposition, and similarly if it has the sign of particularity.

27.27 But confused supposition is the taking of a common term for a number of things by means of the sign of universality, as when it is said: 'every man is an animal', the term 'man' is taken for a number by means of the sign of universality, being taken for each of its individuals.

Subsequent division of confused supposition into that which is confused by the requirements of the sign (*necessitate signi*) and that which is confused by the requirements of the thing (*rei*) (**27.28**) is shortly after rejected by Peter. He gives a further division of personal supposition:

27.29 Of personal supposition one kind is restricted, another extended (*ampliata*).

---

* Reading *praedictis* for *praedicatis*.

If we ask how the expression 'supposition' is to be rendered in modern terms, we have to admit that it cannot be. 'Supposition' covers numerous semiotic functions for which we now have no common name. Some kinds of supposition quite clearly belong to semantics, as in the case of both material suppositions, and personal; others again, such as simple supposition and those into which personal supposition is subdivided, are as Moody has acutely remarked (**27.30**), not semantical but purely syntactical functions.

The most notable difference between the doctrine of supposition and the corresponding modern theories lies in the fact that while contemporary logic as far as possible has one sign for one function, e.g. a sign for a word, another for the word's name, one for the word in personal, another for it in simple supposition, the Scholastics took equiform signs and determine their functions by establishing their supposition. And this brings us back to the fundamental difference already remarked on between the two forms of formal logic; scholastic logic dealt with ordinary language, contemporary logic develops an artificial one.

§ 28. AMPLIATION, APPELLATION, ANALOGY

Among the other properties of terms three that seem to be of particular interest for formal logic will be illustrated with some texts, viz. ampliation, appellation and analogy.

Peter of Spain writes:

28.01 Restriction is the narrowing of a common term from a wider (*maiore*) supposition to a narrower, as when it is said 'a white man runs' the adjective 'white' restricts 'man' to supposing for white ones. Ampliation is the extension (*extensio*) of a common term from a narrower supposition to a wider, as when it is said 'a man can be Antichrist' the term 'man' supposes not only for those who are now, but also for those who will be. Hence it is extended to future ones. I say 'of a common term' because a discrete term is neither restricted nor extended.

One kind of ampliation is effected by a verb, as by the verb 'can', e.g. 'a man can be Antichrist'; another is effected by a name, e.g. 'it is possible that a man can be Antichrist'; another by a participle, e.g. 'a man is able (*potens*) to be Antichrist'; another by an adverb, e.g. 'a man is necessarily an animal'. For (in the last) 'man' is extended not only for the present but also for the future. And so there follows another division of ampliation: one kind of ampliation being in respect of supposita, e.g. 'a man can be Antichrist', another with respect to time, e.g. 'a man is necessarily an animal', as has been said.

Essentially the same doctrine but more thoroughly developed is found at the end of the 14th century in Albert of Saxony:

28.02 Ampliation is the taking of a term for one or more things beyond what is actually the case: for that or those things for which the proposition indicates (*denotat*) that it is used. Certain rules are established in this respect:

28.03 The first is this: every term having supposition in respect of a verb in a past tense is extended to stand for what was, e.g. when it is said: 'the white was black', 'the white' is taken in this proposition not only for what is white but for what was white.

28.04 Second rule: a term having supposition in respect of a verb in a future tense is extended to stand for what is or will be. . . .

28.05 Third rule: every term having supposition with respect to the verb 'can' is so extended as to stand for what is or can be. E.g. 'the white can be black' means that what is white or can be white, can be black. . . .

28.06 Fourth rule: A term having supposition in respect of the verb 'is contingent' is extended to stand for what is or can contingently be (*contingit esse*). And that is Aristotle's opinion in the first book of the *Prior* (*Analytics*). . . .

28.07 Fifth rule: A term subjected in a proposition in respect of a past participle, even though the copula of this proposition is a verb in the present, is extended to stand for what was. . . . E.g. in the proposition 'a certain man is dead' the subject stands for what is or has been.

28.08 Sixth rule: In a proposition in which the copula is in the present, but the predicate in the future, the subject is extended to stand for what is or will be. E.g. 'a man is one who will generate'; for this proposition indicates that one who is or will be a man is one who will generate.

28.09 Seventh rule: If the proposition has a copula in the present and a predicate that includes the verb 'can', as is the case with verbal names ending in '-ble' ('-*ibile*'), then the subject is extended to stand for what is or can be, e.g. when it is said: 'the man is generable'. For this is equivalent (*valet*) to: 'the man can be generated' in which 'man' is extended, according to the third rule, to stand for what is or can be. . . .

28.10 Eighth rule: all verbs which, although not in the present, have it in their nature to be able to extend to a future, past or possible thing as to a present one, extend the terms to every time, present, past and future. Such e.g. are these: 'I understand', 'I know', 'I am aware', 'I mean (*significo*)' etc.

20.11 Ninth rule: the subject of every proposition *de necessario* in the divided sense (cf. § 29, D.) is extended to stand for what is or can be. E.g. 'every *B* is necessarily *A*'; for this is equivalent to (*valet dicere*) 'Whatever is or can be *B*, is necessarily *A*'. . . .

28.12 Tenth rule: if no ampliating term is present in a proposition, its subject is not extended but this proposition indicates that (the subject stands) only for what is.

This text is a fine example of scholastic analysis of language. It introduces a notable enlargement of the doctrine of supposition, dividing the objects for which a term may stand into three temporal classes to which is added the class of possible objects. It can readily be seen that this doctrine makes an essential contribution to the problem of the so-called void class, since the expression 'void class' receives as many different denotata as there are kinds of ampliation. This can be compared with the modern methods of treating the problem (cf. § 46, A and B).

Albert's seventh, eighth and ninth rules also contain an analysis of modal propositions, but this subject will be considered in greater detail below (§ 33).

B. APPELLATION

Closely connected with ampliation is the so-called appellation, also relevant to the problem of the void class. The theory of it was already well developed in the 13th century, was further enlarged in the 14th when there were various theories different from that of the 13th.* We cite two 13th century texts, one from Peter of Spain and one from Shyreswood:

28.13 Appellation is the taking of a term for an existent thing. I say 'for an existent thing' since a term signifying a non-existent has no appellation, e.g. 'Caesar' or 'Anti-christ'

---

* For information on these points and much other instruction on the doctrines of supposition and appellation I am obliged to Prof. E. Moody.

etc. Appellation differs from supposition and signification in that appellation only concerns existents, but supposition and signification concern both existents and non-existents, e.g. 'Antichrist' signifies Antichrist and supposes for Antichrist but does not name (*appellat*) him, whereas 'man' signifies man and naturally supposes for existent as well as non-existent men but only names existent ones.

Of appellations one kind belongs to common terms such as 'man', another to singular terms such as 'Socrates'. A singular term signifies, supposes and names the same thing, because it signifies an existent, e.g. 'Peter'.

Further, of appellations belonging to common terms one kind belongs to a common term (standing) for the common thing itself, as when a term has simple supposition, e.g. when it is said: 'man is a species' or 'animal is a genus'; and then the common term signifies, supposes and names the same thing, as 'man' signifies man in general and supposes for man in general and names man in general. Another kind belongs to a common term (standing) for its inferiors, as when a common term has personal supposition, e.g. when it is said: 'a man runs'. Then 'man' does not signify, suppose and name the same thing; because it signifies man in general and supposes for particular men and names particular existent men.

28.14 Supposition belongs to (*inest*) a term in so far as it is under another. But appellation belongs to a term in so far as it is predicable of its (subordinate) things by means of the verb 'is'. . . . Some say therefore that the term put as subject supposes, and that put as predicate names. . . . It should also be understood that the subject-term names its thing, but not *qua* subject. The predicate-term on the other hand names it *qua* predicate.

The following from Buridan may serve as an example of 14th century theories:*

28.15 First it is to be understood that a term which can naturally suppose for something names all that it signifies or consignifies unless it be limited to what it stands for. . . . E.g. 'white' standing for men names whiteness, and 'great' greatness, and 'father' the past (act of) generation and someone

---

* These texts were communicated by Prof. E. Moody who also pointed out their great importance. He is to be thanked also for the main lines of the commentary.

else whom the father has generated, and 'the distant' names that from which it is distant and the space (*dimensionem*) between them by which it is made distant. . . .

28.16 A term names what it names as being somehow determinant (*per modum adiacentis aliquo modo*) or not determinant of that for which it stands or naturally can stand. . . .

Thirdly it is to be held that according to the different positive kinds of determination of the things named – the things for which the term stands – there are different kinds of predication, such as how, how many, when, where, how one is related to another, etc. It is from these different kinds of predication that the different predicaments are taken . . . (cf. **11.15**).

28.17 Appellative terms name differently in respect of an assertoric verb in the present and in respect of a verb in the past and in the future, and in respect of the verb 'can' or of 'possible'; since in respect of a verb in the present the appellative term – provided there is not ampliative term – whether it be put as subject or predicate, names its thing as something connected with it in the present, for which the term can naturally stand, and as connected with it in this or that manner, according to which it names.

This is a different doctrine from that of the 13th century, and seems to be of the highest importance. For according to it a term does not name what it stands for but something related to it by, it would seem, *any* relation. Buridan says this expressly for the term 'distant'. If A is distant from B 'distant' does not name A, but precisely B. That indicates a clear notion of relation-logic. Where we should write 'relation', Buridan has *adiacentia*. Especially important is **28.16** where Buridan goes so far as to say that absolute terms are definable by relations, an idea corresponding to the relative descriptions of **47.20**. Some interesting results would follow from the detailed working out of the basic notions of this text, e.g. a theory of plural quantification, but we have no knowledge of this being done in the Middle Ages.

C. ANALOGY

In the present state of research it is unfortunately impossible to present the scholastic theory of meaning with any hope of doing justice even only to its essentials. However, we shall treat of a further important point in this field, the theory of analogy. This is of direct relevance to formal logic, and fairly well explored. A single text from Thomas Aquinas will suffice:

28.18 Nothing can be predicated univocally of God and creatures; for in all univocal predication the sense (*ratio*) of the name is common to both things of which the name is univocally predicated ... and yet one cannot say that what is predicated of God and creatures is predicated purely equivocally. ... So one must say that the name of wisdom is predicated of God's wisdom and ours neither purely univocally nor purely equivocally, but according to analogy, by which is just meant: according to a proportion. But conformity (*convenientia*) according to a proportion can be twofold, and so a twofold community of analogy is to be taken account of. For there is a conformity between the things themselves which are proportioned to one another in having a determinate distance of some other relationship (*habitudinem*) to one another, e.g. (the number) 2 to unity, 2 being the double. But we also sometimes take account of conformity between two things which are not mutually proportioned, but rather there is a likeness between two proportions; e.g. 6 is conformed to 4 because as 6 is twice 3 so 4 is twice 2. The first conformity then is one of proportion, but the second of proportionality. So it is then that according to the first kind of conformity we find something predicated analogically of two things of which one has a relationship to the other, as being is predicated of substance and of accident owing to the relationship which substance and accident have (to one another), and health is predicated of urine and animals, since urine has some relationship* to the health of animals. But sometimes predication is made according to the second kind of conformity, e.g. the name of sight is predicated of corporeal sight and of intellect, because as sight is in the eye, so intellect is in the mind.

This is about the clearest text of the many in which Thomas Aquinas speaks of analogy (**28.19**). It has been only too often misunderstood, but deserves fairly thorough discussion from the historian of logic because of its historical as well as systematic significance. We therefore draw attention to the following points:

This text deals explicitly with a question of *semantics* – Thomas speaks of names – and it is noteworthy that he himself, like his best commentator Cajetan (**28.20**), almost always considers analogy as

---

* Reading *habitudinem* for *similitudinem*.

'of names'. Of course he does not mean mere utterances, but meaningful words, in accordance with the scholastic usage illustrated previously.

Now our text speaks of three classes of names: univocal, equivocal and analogous names. The last are intermediate between the two first. The class of analogous names falls into two sub-classes: those analogous according to a proportion, and those according to proportionality. Both these divisions originate with Aristotle (**10.29** and **10.31**), but the hasty indications of the *Nichomachean Ethics* are here developed into a systematic logical doctrine.

While the thomist doctrine of the first class of analogous names is here only of interest as showing an attempt to formalize the rules of their use, the theory of the second class, i.e. of names analogous according to proportionality, is nothing less than a first formulation of the notion of isomorphy (cf. **47.41**). That this is so can be seen as follows:

Let us note first that according to the text an analogous name of the second kind always refers to a relation or relata defined by one. Certainly something absolute is also implied by each of the subjects in such an analogy, but this is precisely different in each, and in that respect the name is equivocal. The community of reference consists only in regard to certain relations.

But it is not a matter of just one relation, rather of two *similar* ones. This is explicit in the text, only the example $(6:3 = 4:2)$ is misleading since we have there an identity of two relations. That Thomas is not thinking of such is shown by the illustrations, first in the domain of creatures (sight:eye — intellect:mind), then in God (divine being:God – creaturely being:creature). The ruling idea is then of a relation of similarity between two relations.

This relation between relations is such as to allow inference from what we know about one to something about the other, though at the same time we have the assertion: 'we cannot know what God is' (**28.21**). The apparent contradiction disappears when it is realized that we are dealing with isomorphy. For this does in fact allow one to transfer something from one relation to another, without affording any experience of the relata.

The use of a mathematical example is noteworthy, taken moreover from the only algebraic function then known. This is not only to be explained by the mathematical origin of the doctrine of analogy in Aristotle, but also perhaps by a brilliant intuition on the part of Aquinas who dimly guessed himself to be establishing a thesis about structure. In any case the text is of the utmost historical importance as being the first indication of a study of structure, which was to become a main characteristic of modern science.

§ 29. STRUCTURE AND SENSE OF PROPOSITIONS

A. DIVISION OF PROPOSITIONS

We give first a text of Albert of Saxony which summarizes the commonly received scholastic doctrine of the kinds of atomic (categorical) propositions:

29.01 Of proposition some are categorical, others hypothetical. But some of the categorical are said to be hypothetical in signification, such as the exclusive, exceptive and reduplicative propositions, and others besides.

Then of the categorical propositions that are not equivalent to the hypothetical in signification – such as 'man is an animal' and such-like – some are said to be assertoric (*de inesse*) or of simple inherence; others are said to be modal or of modified inherence. . . .

Again of categorical propositions of simple inherence some have ampliative subjects, as 'a man is dead', 'Antichrist will exist', the others do not have ampliative subjects, as 'man is an animal', 'stone is a substance' etc.

Again, of categorical propositions of simple inherence with ampliative subjects, some concern the present, others the past, others the future. . . .

Again, of categorical propositions about the present some are *de secundo adiacente*, others *de tertio adiacente*. An example of the first: 'man exists'; of the second: 'man is an animal'.

Again, of categorical propositions some have a non-compound extreme (term) (*de extremo incomplexo*), as 'man is an animal'; others have a compound extreme, as 'man or ass is man or ass'.

B. ANALYSIS OF PROPOSITIONS

Here we assemble a few aspects of the scholastic analysis of propositions. To begin with, this text of Thomas Aquinas, followed by one from Ockham, about the general structure:

29.02 In every true affirmative proposition the subject and predicate must signify somehow the same thing in reality but in different senses (*diversum secundum rationem*). And this is clear both in propositions with accidental predicate and in those with substantial. For it is evident that 'man' and 'white' are identical in suppositum and differing in sense, for the sense of 'man' is other than the sense of 'white'. And

180

likewise when I say: 'man is an animal', for that same thing which is man is truly an animal. For in one and the same suppositum there is both the sensible nature, after which it is called 'animal', and the rational nature, after which it is called 'man'. So that in this case too the predicate and subject are identical as to suppositum, but differing in sense. But this is also found in a way in propositions in which something (*idem*) is predicated of itself, inasmuch as the intellect treats as suppositum (*trahit ad partem suppositi*) what it posits as subject, but treats as form inhering in the suppositum what it posits as predicate. Hence the adage, that predicates are taken formally and subjects materially (cf. **27.08**). To the difference in sense there corresponds the plurality of predicate and subject; but the intellect signifies the real identity by the composition (of the two).

We have here actually *two* analyses of propositions. First an extensional one, which seems to have become classical in later Scholasticism. It can be reproduced thus: the proposition '*S* is *P*' is to be equated with the product of the following propositions: (1) there is at least one x such that both '*S*' and '*P*' stand (suppose) for x, (2) there is a property f such that '*S*' signifies f, (3) there is a property g such that '*P*' signifies g, (4) both f and g belong to x.

In the second analysis the subject is conceived as extensional, the predicate as intensional. The proposition '$A = A$' can be interpreted: (1) there is an x such that '*A*' stands for x, (2) there is a property f such that '*A*' signifies f, (3) f belongs to x. This analysis is applied in the text to a special kind of proposition, asserting an identity, but can evidently be applied generally.

Ockham gives another analysis:

29.03 It is to be said that it is not required for the truth of a singular proposition, which is not equivalent to many propositions, that subject and predicate should be really identical, nor that the predicated reality should be in the subject, nor that it should really inhere (*insit*) in the subject, nor that it should be really, extra-mentally, united to the subject. E.g. it is not required for the truth of this: 'that one is an angel', that the common term 'angel' should be in reality the same as what is posited as subject, nor that it should really inhere in it, nor anything of that kind, — but it is sufficient and necessary that subject and predicate should suppose for the same thing. And so in this: 'this is an angel', if subject and predicate suppose for the same thing, the proposition is true. And so it is not indicated (*denotatur*) that this has angelicity, or that angelicity is in it, or anything of this kind, but it is indicated that this is truly an angel, not that it is that predicate, but that it is that for which the predicate supposes.

An important text, but not readily intelligible to a modern reader. A possible, though not the only possible interpretation is this: it is sufficient and necessary for the truth of a proposition of this kind that the extension of subject and predicate should coincide. If that is so, he means to say that the predicate is not to be taken intensionally, but extensionally like the subject, as in Thomas's first analysis in **29.02**. Then Ockham gives a radically extensional interpretation of propositions.

The next text shows that what was said in **29.03** holds for other kinds of proposition as well:

29.04 For the truth of such (i.e. indefinite or particular propositions) it suffices that the subject and predicate stand for the same thing, if the proposition is affirmative.

C. ANALYSIS OF MODAL PROPOSITIONS: DICTUM AND MODUS

In the middle of the 13th century there arose a generally accepted doctrine about the structure of modal propositions. It is to be found in Albert the Great (**29.05**), Shyreswood (**29.06**), Peter of Spain (**29.07**), and in the *Summa Totius Logicae* (**29.08**). On account of its characteristic formalism we quote a youthful opusculum of Thomas Aquinas:

29.09 Since the modal proposition gets its name from '*modus*', to know what a modal proposition is we must know what a *modus* is. Now a *modus* is a determination of something effected by a nominal adjective determining a substantive, e.g. 'white man', or by an adverb determining a verb. But it is to be known that modes are threefold, some determining the subject of a proposition, as 'a white man runs', some determining the predicate, as 'Socrates is a white man' or 'Socrates runs quickly', some determining the composition of the predicate with the subject, as 'that Socrates is running is impossible', and it is from this alone that a proposition is said to be modal. Other propositions, which are not modal, are said to be assertoric (*de inesse*).

The modes which determine the composition are six: 'true', 'false', 'necessary', 'possible', 'impossible' and 'contingent'.

But 'true' and 'false' add nothing to the signification of assertoric propositions; for there is the same significance in 'Socrates runs' and it is true that Socrates runs' (on the one hand), and in 'Socrates is not running' and 'it is false that Socrates is running' (on the other). This does not happen with the other four modes, because there is not the same significance in 'Socrates runs' and 'that Socrates runs is impossible (or necessary)'. So we leave 'true' and 'false' out of consideration and attend to the other four.

Now because the predicate determines the subject and not conversely, for a proposition to be modal the four modes aforesaid must be predicated and the verb indicating composition must be put as subject. This is done if an infinitive is taken in place of the indicative verb in the proposition, and an accusative in place of the nominative. And it (the accusative and infinitive clause) is called 'dictum', e.g. of the proposition 'Socrates runs' the dictum is 'that Socrates runs' (*Socratem currere*). When then the dictum is posited as subject and a mode as predicate, the proposition is modal, e.g. 'that *Socrates* runs is possible'. But if it be converted it will be assertoric, e.g. 'the possible is that Socrates runs'.

Of modal propositions one kind concerns the dictum, another concerns things. A modal (proposition) concerning the dictum is one in which the whole dictum is subjected and the mode predicated, e.g. 'that Socrates runs is possible'. A modal (proposition) concerning things is one in which the mode interrupts the dictum, e.g. 'for Socrates running is possible' (*Socratem possibile est currere*). But it is to be known that all modals concerning the dictum are singular, the mode being posited as inherent in this or that as in some singular thing. But . . . modals concerning things are judged to be universal or singular or indefinite according to the subject of the dictum, as is the case with assertoric propositions. So that 'for all men, running is possible' is universal, and so with the rest. It should further be known that modal propositions are said to be affirmative or negative according to the affirmation or negation of the mode, not according to the affirmation or negation of the dictum. So that . . . this modal 'that Socrates runs is possible' is affirmative, while 'that Socrates runs is not possible' is negative.

There are two notable points in this text. First there is the very thorough formalism, the modal proposition being classified according to the place which the mode has in it. Then there is the explicit distinction of the two structures, one of which Aristotle made the basis of his modal logic (§ 15, B), the other of which Theophrastus adopted (§ 17, B). The modals *de re* correspond to the Aristotelian structure, in which the mode does not determine the 'composition' or, as we should say, the proposition as a whole, but 'the predicate'. Taking the proposition '*A* is possibly *B*' as *de re*, we could analyze it thus:

if x is A, then x is possibly B.

But the modals *de dicto* have the Theophrastan structure, according to which the fore-going proposition will be taken as *de dicto* and can be interpreted:

that A is B is possible.

D. COMPOSITE AND DIVIDED SENSES

Closely connected with that doctrine, classical in Scholasticism, is that of the composite and divided senses of propositions. It was developed out of the Aristotelian theory of the fallacies of division and composition (**11.22 f.**), and partly corresponds to the foregoing analysis of modal propositions (**29.09**), but extends to other kinds as well. It seems to have secured a quite central place in later scholastic logic. We cite first a text of Peter of Spain:

29.10 There are two kinds of composition. The first kind arises from the fact that some dictum can suppose for itself or a part of itself, e.g. 'that he who is sitting walks is possible'. For if the dictum 'that he who is sitting walks' is wholly subjected to the predicate 'possible', then the proposition is false and composite, for then opposed activities, sitting and walking, are included in the subject, and the sense is: 'he who is sitting is walking'. But if the dictum supposes for a part of the dictum, then the proposition is true and divided, and the sense is: 'he who is sitting has the power of walking'. To be distinguished in the same fashion is: 'that he who is not writing is writing is impossible'. For this dictum 'that he who is not writing is writing' is subjected to the predicate 'impossible',* but sometimes as a whole, sometimes in respect of a part of itself. And similarly: 'that a white thing is black is possible'. And it is to be known that expressions of this kind are commonly said to be *de re* or *de dicto*.

---

* Reading *impossibile* for *possibile*.

A twofold terminology can be seen here; the distinction *composita – divisa* corresponds to *de dicto – de re*. Peter also introduces the notion of supposition, while Thomas (**29.09**) proceeds wholly syntactically. Thomas has yet other expressions for the same idea:

29.11 Further (it is objected), if everything is known by God as seen in the present, it will be necessary that what God knows, is, as it is necessary that Socrates sits given that he is seen to be sitting. But this is not necessary absolutely, or as is said by some, by necessity of the consequent: rather conditionally, or by necessity of consequence. For this conditional is necessary: If he is seen to be sitting, he sits. Whence also, if the conditional is turned into a categorical, so that it is said: what is seen to be sitting, necessarily sits, evidently if this is understood as *de dicto* and composite, it is true; but understood as *de re* and divided, it is false. And so in these and all similar cases . . . people are deceived in respect of composition and division.

This gives us the two following series of expressions, corresponding member to member (the word *propositio* being understood with each): *de dicto, composita, necessaria necessitate consequentiae, necessaria sub conditione – de re, divisa, necessaria necessitate consequentis, necessaria absolute.*

Paul of Venice gives a peculiar variant of the doctrine of *de dicto* and *de re:*

29.12 Some say that always when the mode simply precedes or follows the expression with the infinitive, then the sense is definitely called 'composite' in every case, e.g. 'it is possible that Socrates runs', 'that Socrates runs (*Socratem currere*) is possible'. But when the mode occupies a place in the middle the sense is called 'divided', e.g. 'for Socrates it is possible to run'. Others on the other hand say that when the mode simply precedes, the sense is composite, as previously, but when it occupies a middle place or comes at the end, then the sense is divided, e.g. 'of *A* I know that it is true', 'that *A* is true is known by me'. And so with others similar.

But though these ways of speaking enjoy probability, yet they are not wholly true. . . . So I say otherwise, taking a position intermediate between them: when the mode simply precedes a categorical or hypothetical dictum, it effects the composite sense; and when it occurs between the verb and the first extreme, it is taken in the divided sense; but when it follows at the end, it can be taken in the composite or the divided sense.

This seemingly purely grammatical text is yet not without interest as showing how scholastic logic at the end of the 14th century was wholly bent on grasping the laws of everyday language. We find no essentially new range of problems in Paul beyond those of Thomas and Peter.

There is yet another interpretation of the composite and divided senses, first found in Peter, in a text which seems to adumbrate all the associated problems:

29.13 (The fallacy of) division is a false division of things that should be compounded. There are two kinds of division. The first arises from the fact that a conjunction can conjoin either terms or propositions, e.g. . . . 'five is even or odd'. Similarly: 'every animal is rational or irrational'. For if this conjunctive particle 'or' divides one proposition from another, it is false, and its sense is: 'every animal is rational or every animal is irrational'. If it disjoins one term from another, then it is true and its sense is: 'every animal is rational or irrational', in which the whole disjunctive complex is predicated. Similarly: 'every animal is healthy or sick', 'every number is even or odd'.

A more exact formulation of the same thought occurs in Burleigh:

29.14 'Every animal is rational or irrational.' The proof is inductive. The disproof runs: every animal is rational or irrational, but not every animal is rational, therefore every animal is irrational. The conclusion is false, the minor is not (false), therefore the major is. The consequence is evident from the locus of opposites (**16.18**).

Solution. The first (proposition) is multiple, according to composition and division. In the sense of composition it is true, in the sense of division it is false. Induction does not hold in the sense of division, because in the sense of division there is not a categorical proposition but a hypothetical of universal quantity; and thus the answer to the proof is clear.

To the disproof, I say the consequence does not hold in the sense of composition, nor is there room for an argument from the locus of opposites, for the locus of opposites is when one argues from a disjunctive and the negation of one part, to the other part; but in the sense of composition this is not a disjunctive but a categorical proposition.

The form of propositions of this kind in the composite sense could be expressed with variables thus:

(1) for every x: x is A or x is B.

In the divided sense the same proposition could be interpreted:

(2) for every x: x is A, or for every x: x is B.

If this interpretation is correct we have here an important theorem about the distribution of quantifiers. Yet Burleigh does not seem to have been thinking quite of (1), but rather of

(1') for every x: x is $(A$ or $B)$.

E. REFERENCE OF PROPOSITIONS

Finally we give a text in which the chief scholastic theories about the semantic correlate of propositions are listed. It is taken from Paul of Venice.

29.15 About the essence of the proposition . . . there are many opinions.

The first is that the significate of a true proposition is a circumstance (*modus*) of the thing and not the thing itself. . . .

29.16 The second opinion is that the significate of a true proposition is a composition of the mind (*mentis*) or of the intellect which compounds or divides. . . .

29.17 The third opinion, commonly received among the doctors of my (Augustinian) Order, in particular by Master Gregory of Rimini, is that the significate of a proposition is whatever in any way exists as a signifiable complex. And when it is asked whether such a signifiable is something or nothing, he answers that the name 'something' and its synonyms 'thing' and 'being' can be understood in three ways. (1) First in the widest sense, according to which everything signifiable, with or without complexity, truly or falsely, is called 'thing ' and 'something'. . . . (2) In a second way these (names) are taken for whatever is signifiable, with or without complexity, but truly, . . . (3) In a third way the aforesaid names are taken in such wise that they signify some existent essence or entity, and in this way, what does not exist is called 'nothing' . . . .. So this opinion says that the significate of a proposition is something, if one takes the afore-mentioned terms in the first or second way. . . .

29.18 The fourth opinion posits some theses. (1) The first is this: that no thing is the adequate or total significate of a mental proposition properly so called; since every such (proposition) signifies a variety of mutually distinct things, by reason of its parts to which it is equivalent in its signifying. And this is evident to everyone who examines the matter. Hence there is no total or adequate significate of such a proposition.

(2) The second thesis: whatever is signified by a mental proposition properly so called according to its total signification is also signified by any of its parts. . . .

(3) Third thesis: no dictum corresponding to a mental proposition properly so called, e.g. an expression in the infinitive mood taken as significant, supposes for any thing. For instance, if the dictum, i.e. the expression in the infinitive mood, 'that man is an animal', corresponding to the proposition 'man is an animal', is taken materially it stands for some thing, namely for the proposition to which it corresponds; but if it be taken significatively, i.e. personally, then according to the fourth opinion it stands for no thing. This is evident, since such an expression, so taken, signifies a number of things, viz. all those signified by the corresponding proposition, and so there would be no reason for it to suppose for one of its significates rather than another; hence (it supposes) either for each or for none. But nobody would say for each, since the expression 'that man is an animal' would signify an ass or suppose for an ass. Therefore for none. And what is said of that instance, holds for any other.

The four opinions there enumerated could be summed up thus in modern terminology; a proposition has for its semantical correlate (1) a real fact, (2) a psychical act (3) an objective content (the Stoic lekton), (4) nothing at all beyond what its parts already signify. In the 15th century there were very complicated and sharp disputes about this problem. But as it lies on the border-line of pure logic we shall omit consideration of them here (**29.19**).

II. PROPOSITIONAL LOGIC

§ 30. NOTION AND DIVISION OF CONSEQUENCES

A. HISTORICAL SURVEY

The theory of consequences is one of the most interesting scholastic doctrines. Essentially it is a development of Stoic propositional logic, though so far as is known it was constructed entirely anew, not in connection with the Stoic logoi (§ 21) but with certain passages of the *Hermeneia* and, above all, the *Topics*. All the same, fragments of the Stoic propositional logic did influence the Scholastics, mostly through the mediation of Boethius, though for a few we must suppose some other sources, as e.g. for the 'dog-syllogism' (**22.19**), which is found in Thomas Aquinas (**30.01**). But that these fragments were not the starting point is clear from the fact that, at least to begin with, they are not cited in the treatise on consequences, but in another on hypothetical syllogisms.

The name '*consequentia*' is Boethius's translation of Aristotle's ἀκολούθησις which occurs frequently in the *Hermeneia* (**30.02**) but not in any exact technical sense, rather for following quite in general. The word has the same sense in Abelard, though limited to logical relationships between terms (**30.03**),* and to some extent also in Kilwardby** (**30.04**) and Peter of Spain (**30.05**) E.g. in the latter we read of a *consequentia essentiae* (**30.06**).

In Ockham, on the other hand, and his successors the word has a sharply defined technical meaning, and signifies a relation of consequence between two propositions.

The following text from Kilwardby may serve as a good example of the earlier stage:

30.04 He (Aristotle) also says that something is a consequent (of something else) in part, and yet whatever follows from *A* follows from all that is contained under *A*, since what follows on the consequent follows on the antecedent, and so every consequent follows on the whole antecedent. . . .

It is to be answered to this, that (Aristotle) in this whole treatment (*Prior Analytics*) takes 'consequent' for the predicate and 'antecedent' for the subject. . . .

A further passage from Kilwardby is extremely instructive about this relationship:

---

* Vide Translator's Preface, B.
** Cited from transcriptions of two Oxford MSS (**30.04**) made by the translator.

30.07 Consequence is twofold, viz. essential or natural, as when a consequent is naturally understood in its antecedent, and accidental consequence. Of the latter kind is the consequence according to which we say that the necessary follows on anything. . . .

That shows that for Kilwardby a 'natural' and 'essential' consequence is only present when it is a matter of connection between terms. Thus for him the proposition 'every man runs, therefore there is a man who runs' would be natural, since 'each man' is 'naturally' included in 'every man'. In other words it is for him always based on term-logical relationships. He does also recognize purely propositional consequences such as the one he states: 'the necessary follows on anything', but these he considers only 'accidental' and of an inferior kind.

This opinion of Kilwardby's is of interest as showing that the Scholastics did *not* take the abstract propositional logic of the Stoics as their starting point, but the term-logic of Aristotle. Yet before very long they built on that basis a technically excellent pure logic of propositions that to the best of our knowledge was superior to that of the Megarians and Stoics.

Since the paper of Łukasiewicz (**30.08**) more works have been devoted to this propositional logic than to any other scholastic logical doctrine, and it is better known than most others (**30.09**). Yet we are still far from having a complete knowledge of it. We cannot here enumerate all the scholastic consequences that have been investigated in the 20th century, but must limit ourselves to texts defining the notion of *consequentia*, and then (§ 31) give a few examples.

B. DEFINITION OF CONSEQUENCE

Pseudo-Scotus gives the following definition of consequence:

30.10 A consequence is a hypothetical proposition composed of an antecedent and consequent by means of a conditional connective or one expressing a reason (*rationalis*) which signifies that if they, viz. the antecedent and consequent, are formed simultaneously, it is impossible that the antecedent be true and the consequent false.

Here a consequence is conceived as a proposition in almost word for word agreement with the Stoic definition (**19.15**) with only two considerable differences: (1) '*propositio*' means, not the lekton, but the thought, written and spoken proposition (cf. **26.03**); (2) the consequence corresponds to the compound and inferential sentences of the Stoics (**19.15**). Implication is defined in the Diodorean way

(**20.08**), though the time-variables might be thought to be missing; but comparison with the definition of consequence *ut nunc* (**30.12**, cf. **30.16**) shows that Diodorus's idea of 'for all times' is basic for the Scholastics too. They conducted a complicated discussion which shows that the range of problems considered was much wider than might be expected from what we have said here (cf. **30.17 f.**).

A noteworthy exception to the premise that a consequence is a proposition* is found in Burleigh :

30.11 It is also to be noted that the (contradictory) opposite of the antecedent does not follow from the opposite of the consequent in every valid consequence, but only in non-syllogistic consequences. For in syllogistic consequences the antecedent has no opposite, because a syllogistic antecedent is an unconnected plurality of propositions (*propositio plures inconiuncte*) and because such an antecedent has no opposite at all, it not being a proposition that is either simply or conjunctively one. But in a syllogistic consequence the opposite of one premiss follows from the opposite of the conclusion with the other premiss. And if from the opposite of the conclusion with one or other of the premisses there follows the opposite of the remaining premiss, then the original syllogism was valid. For that is how the Philosopher proves his syllogisms, viz. arguing from the opposite of the conclusion with one of the premisses, as can be seen in the first book of the *Prior Analytics*.

'*Propositio plures inconiuncte*' means here, as usually among the Scholastics (cf. **35.45**) not a compound proposition, not therefore a product of propositions, but a number of juxtaposed propositions. It follows that syllogisms, and so 'syllogistic consequences' are not propositions, and further that consequences were not always thought of as conditional propositions.

C. DIVISION OF CONSEQUENCES

Here again we begin with Pseudo-Scotus:

30.12 Consequences are divided thus: some are material, others are formal. A formal consequence is one which holds in all terms, given similar mutual arrangement (*dispositio*) and form of the terms. . . . A material consequence is one

---

* Prof. L. Minio-Paluello tells us in connection with Cod. Orleans 266, fol. 78 that this was already debated in the middle of the 12th century.

which does not hold in all terms given similar mutual arrangement and form so that the only variation is in the terms themselves. And such a consequence is twofold: one is simply true, the other true for the present (*ut nunc*). A simply true consequence is one reducible to a formal consequence by the addition of a necessary proposition. A correct material consequence true for the present is one which is reducible to a formal consequence by the addition of a true contingent proposition.

So there are three kinds of consequence: (1) formal, (2) simple material, (3) material *ut nunc*. The last two are reduced to the first, but by means of different kinds of proposition. For (2) there is required a necessary, and so always true, proposition, for (3) one must use a contingent proposition, one which is therefore true only at a certain time. An example of the reduction of (2) to (1) is: 'A man runs, therefore an animal runs' is reduced to a consequence of kind (1) by means of the proposition 'every man is an animal' when it is said: 'every man is an animal, a man runs, therefore an animal runs'. The newly introduced proposition is necessary, and so always true, hence the consequence reduced by its means to (1) is 'simply' valid, valid for all time.

Another definition is to be found in Ockham, along with a further division of formal consequence:

30.13 Of consequences, one kind is formal, another material. Formal consequence is twofold, since one holds by an extrinsic medium concerning the form of the proposition, such as these rules: 'from an exclusive to a universal (proposition) with the terms interchanged is a correct consequence', 'from a necessary major and an assertoric minor (premiss) there follows a necessary (conclusion)' etc. The other kind holds directly through an intrinsic medium and indirectly through an extrinsic one concerning the general conditions of the proposition, not its truth, falsity, necessity or impossibility. Of this kind is the following: 'Socrates does not run, therefore some man does not run'. The consequence is called 'material' since it holds precisely in virtue of the terms, not in virtue of some extrinsic medium concerning the general conditions of the proposition. Such are the following: 'If a man runs, God exists', 'man is an ass, therefore God does not exist' etc.

This text is most important, since Ockham here introduces a doctrine analogous to that of Whitehead and Russell in their distinction of formal and material implication (**44.11** ff.), analogous only, because the basic idea of implication is here Diodorean (**20.08**) instead of Philonian (**20.07**). Formal implications in this sense are further divided into two classes according as they hold in virtue of their component symbols or other propositions of the system.

These ideas are defined with some accuracy in a text of Albert of Saxony:

30.14 Of consequences, one kind is formal, another material. That is said to be a formal consequence to which every proposition which, if it were to be formed, would be a valid consequence, is similar in form, e.g. '*b* is *a*, therefore some *a* is *b*'. But a material consequence is one such that not every proposition similar in form to it is a valid consequence, or, as is commonly said, which does not hold in all terms when the form is kept the same; e.g. 'a man runs, therefore an animal runs'. But in these (other) terms the consequence is not valid: 'a man runs, therefore a log runs'.

We may compare **26.11** f. with this text, so far as concerns the notion of logical form, and indeed the former follows immediately on the latter.

Reverting to the distinction of simple and *ut nunc* consequences (**30.12**) with a similar reference to time-variables as in Diodorus Cronus (**20.08**, cf. **19.23**), Burleigh formulates this idea explicitly and accurately:

30.15 Of consequences, some are simple, some *ut nunc*. Simple are those which hold for every time, as: 'a man runs, therefore an animal runs'. Consequences *ut nunc* hold for a determinate time and not always, as: 'every man runs, therefore Socrates runs'; for that consequence does not hold always, but only so long as there is a man Socrates.

The first rule of consequence is this: in every valid simple consequence the antecedent cannot be true without the consequent. And so, if in any possible given case the antecedent could be true without the consequent, the consequence would not be valid. But in a consequence *ut nunc*, the antecedent *ut nunc*, i.e. for the (given) time for which the consequence holds, cannot be true without the consequent.

Buridan has a text on this subject, in which occurs the new idea of consequence for such and such a time *(ut tunc)*.

30.16 Of material consequences some are said to be consequences simply, since they are consequences without qualification, it being impossible for their antecedents to be true without their consequents. . . . And others are said to be consequences *ut nunc*, since they are not valid without qualification, it being possible for their antecedents to be true without their consequents. However, they are valid *ut nunc*, since things being exactly the same as they now are, it is impossible for the antecedent to be true without the consequent. And people often use these consequences in ordinary language (*utuntur saepe vulgares*), as when we say: 'the white Cardinal has been elected Pope' and conclude: 'therefore a Master in Theology has been elected Pope'; and as when I say: 'I see such and such a man' . . . you conclude 'therefore you certainly see a false man'. But this consequence is reduced to a formal one by the addition of a true, but not necessary, proposition, or of several true and not necessary ones, as in the examples given, since the white Cardinal is a Master in Theology and since such and such a man is a false man. In that way the following is a valid consequence: under the hypothesis that there are no men but Socrates, Plato and Robert, 'Socrates runs, Plato runs and Robert runs; therefore every man runs'. For this consequence is perfected by this true (proposition): 'every man is Socrates, Plato or Robert'.

And it is to be known that to this kind of consequences *ut nunc* belong permissive consequences, e.g. 'Plato says to Socrates: if you come to me I will give you a horse'. The proposition may be a genuine consequence, or it may be a false proposition and no consequence, since (1) if the antecedent is impossible, viz. because Socrates cannot come to Plato, then the consequence is simply speaking a genuine consequence, because from the impossible anything follows as will be said below. But if (2) the antecedent is false but not impossible, then the consequence is valid *ut nunc*, because from whatever is false anything follows, as will be said later, provided, however, that we restrict the name 'consequence *ut nunc*' to consequences *ut tunc*, whether concerning the past, future, or any other determinate time. But if the antecedent is true, so that Socrates will come to Plato, then perhaps we should say that it is still a genuine consequence because it can be made formal by the apposition* of true (propositions), when one knows whatever Plato wills to do in the future, that his wish will persist and that he will be able to carry it out; and when all circumstances are taken account

---

* Reading *appositas* for *oppositas*.

of according to which he wills it, and he suffers no hindrance, so that he will be able to and will do what and when he wills; if you then modify this proposition so that it is true according to the ninth book of the *Metaphysics*, i.e. 'Plato wills to give Socrates a horse when he comes to him; therefore Plato will give Socrates a horse'. If then these propositions about Plato's will and power are true, then Plato uttered a genuine consequence *ut nunc* to Socrates, but if they are not true he told Socrates a lie.

D. MEANING OF IMPLICATION

If the rooks and the crows cawed about the meaning of implication in the 2nd century B. c. (**20.06**), this occupation was surely intensified in the 15th century. For while the Megarian-Stoic school has bequeathed to us only four interpretations, Paul of Venice tells us of ten. Not all his definitions are comprehensible to us today, but perhaps this is due to textual corruptions. However, for the sake of completeness we give the whole list.

30.17 Some have said that for the truth of a conditional is required that the antecedent cannot be true without the consequent. . . .

Others have said that for the truth of a conditional it is not required that the antecedent cannot be true without the consequent in the divided sense, but it is required that it is not possible for the antecedent to be true without the consequent being true.

Thirdly people have said that for the truth of a conditional it is required that it is not possible that the antecedent of that consequence be true unless the consequent be true . . .

Fourthly people have said that for the truth of a conditional it is required that it is not possible that the antecedent be true while the consequent of that same antecedent is false without a fresh interpretation (*impositio*) . . . .

Fifthly people say that for the truth of a conditional it is required that if things are (*ita est*) as is signifiable by the antecedent, necessarily things are as is signifiable by the consequent. . . .

Sixthly people say that for the truth of a conditional it is required that it be not possible that things should be so and not so, referring to the significates of the antecedent and of the consequent* of that conditional. . . .

* Omitting *oppositi*.

195

Seventhly people say that for the truth of a conditional it is required that it is not possible for things to be so and not so, referring to the adequate significates of the antecedent and the consequent. . . .

Eighthly people say that for the truth of a conditional it is required that the consequent be understood in the antecedent. . . .

Ninthly people say that for the truth of a condition it is required that the adequate significate of the consequent be understood in the antecedent.

Tenthly people say that for the truth of a conditional it is required that the opposite of the consequent be incompatible with the antecedent. . . .

For the distinction between the first two of those definitions the following text of Buridan is instructive. *

30.18 Then there is the rule . . . , that the consequence is valid when it is impossible that things are as signified by the antecedent without their being as is signified by the consequent. And this rule can be understood in two ways.

In one way so that it would be a proposition concerning impossibility in the composite sense (the way in which it is usually intended) and the meaning then is that a consequence is valid when the following is impossible: 'If it is formed, things are as is signified by the antecedent, and are not as is signified by the consequent.' But this rule is invalid, since it justifies the fallacy: 'No proposition is negative, therefore some propositions are negative.'

In the other way, so that it would be a proposition concerning impossibility in the divided sense, so that the meaning is: a consequence is valid when whatever is stated in the antecedent cannot possibly be so without whatever is stated in the consequent being so. And it is clear that this rule would not prove the fallacy true; for whatever 'no proposition is negative' states, is possibly so, although things are not as the other (proposition of the fallacy) states; for if they were, affirmatives would persist but all negatives would be annihilated.

* This text was kindly communicated by Prof. E. Moody.

E. DISJUNCTION

The notion of implication is closely connected with that of disjunction. Hence two characteristic texts are in place to illustrate the problems connected with the latter. Peter of Spain writes:

30.19 For the truth of a disjunctive (proposition) it is required that one part be true, as 'man is an animal or crow is a stone', and it is allowed that both of its parts be true, but not so properly, as 'man is an animal or horses can whinny'. For its falsity it is required that both of its parts be false, as 'man is not an animal or horse is a stone'.

Peter's idea of disjunction is evidently rather hazy, for he wavers between the exclusive (**20.14**) and the non-exclusive (**20.18**) disjunction, describing the latter as 'less proper' though at the same time determining falsity in a way suitable to it alone. Which of the two is 'proper' must have been debated even in the 14th century, as can be seen from Burleigh's fine text:

30.20 Some say that for the truth of a disjunctive it is always required that one part be false, because if both parts were false it would not be a true disjunctive; for disjunction does not allow those things which it disjoins to be together, as Boethius says. But I do not like that. Indeed I say that if both parts of a disjunctive are true, the whole disjunctive is true. And I prove it thus. If both parts of a disjunctive are true, one part is true; and if one part is true, the disjunctive is true. Therefore (arguing) from the first to the last: if both parts of a disjunctive are true, the disjunctive is true.

Further, a disjunctive follows from each of its parts, but it is an infallible rule that if the antecedent is true, the consequent is true; therefore if each part is true the disjunctive is true.

I say therefore, that for the truth of a disjunctive it is not required that one part be false.

Burleigh therefore definitely sides with those who understand disjunction as non-exclusive. Also to be remarked in this text are the two propositional consequences formulated with exemplary exactness:

30.201 If A and B, then A.
30.202 If A, then A or B.

§ 31. PROPOSITIONAL CONSEQUENCES

The Scholastics made no explicit difference between consequences pertaining to propositional and to term-logic. Yet they usually, at least after Ockham, dealt with the former first. It is convenient in this connection to quote a text from Paul of Venice in which he collects the terminology used of so-called hypothetical propositions. After that we give three series of texts, one from Kilwardby (first half of the 13th century), one from Albert of Saxony (second half of the 13th century) and the third from Paul of Venice (first half of the 15th century). To those we add some texts from Buridan about consequences *ut nunc*. We cannot claim to survey even the essentials of scholastic propositional logic, for this is as yet too little explored. The texts cited serve only as examples of the problems considered and the methods applied.

A. HYPOTHETICAL PROPOSITIONS

31.01 Some posit five kinds of hypotheticals, some six, others seven, others ten, others fourteen etc. But leaving all those aside, I say that there are three and no more kinds of hypotheticals that do not coincide in significance, viz. the copulative, disjunctive, and conditional to which the rational is to be counted equivalent. For I do not see that the temporal, local and causal are hypothetical, still less those formed and constituted by other adverbial and connective particles. These are only hypothetical by similitude, e.g. 'I have written as you wanted', 'Michael answers as I tell him'. Similarly the comparative, e.g. 'Socrates is as good as Plato', 'Socrates is whiter than Plato'. Again, the relative, e.g. 'I see a man such as you see'. . . . Similarly the inhibitive, e.g. 'Socrates takes care than no-one confute him'. Again the elective, e.g. 'it is better to concede that your reply is bad than to concede something worse'. Similarly the subjunctive, e.g. 'I saw to it that you answered well'. Similarly the expletive, e.g. 'you may be moving but you are not running!' Thus by taking* the other particles in turn one can form a very great number of (pretended) hypotheticals.

B. KILWARDBY

We take a first series of consequences from Kilwardby's commentary on the *Prior Analytics* of Aristotle. Kilwardby does not

---

* Reading *discurrendo* for *distribuendo*.

always distinguish very clearly between propositional and term-relationships (cf. **30.04**), so that 'antecedent' and 'consequent' must sometimes be understood as referring to the subject and predicate of universal affirmative propositions.

31.02 What is understood in some thing or things, follows from it or from them by a necessary and natural consequence; and so of necessity if one of a pair of opposites is repugnant to the premisses (of a syllogism) the other follows from them.

31.03 If one of the opposites does not follow, the other can stand.

31.04 If one of the opposites stands, the other cannot.

31.05 What does not follow from the antecedent does not follow from the consequent.

31.06 What follows from the consequent follows from the antecedent.

31.07 What is compossible with one of two equivalents (*convertibilium*) is so with the other.

31.08 It is to be said that a negation can be negated, and so there is a negation of negation, but this second negation is really an affirmation, though accidentally (secundum quid) and vocally a negation. For a negation which supervenes on a negation destroys it, and in destroying it posits an affirmation.

31.09 If there necessarily follows from '*A* is white' '*B* is large', then from the denial (*destructio*) of the consequent: if *B* is not large, *A* is not white.

31.10 A disjunctive follows from each of its parts, and by a natural consequence; for it follows: if you sit, then you sit or you do not sit.

31.11 If the antecedent is contingent or possible, so is the consequent.

31.12 It is not necessary that what follows from the antecedent follows from the consequent.

C. ALBERT OF SAXONY

Secondly we give a series of texts from the *Perutilis Logica* of Albert of Saxony in which the doctrine of consequences can be seen in a highly developed state. Albert is here so closely dependent on Buridan that he often simply copies him. But there is much that he formulates more clearly, and the available text of Buridan is not so good as that of the *Perutilis Logica*. Buridan himself is not the original author of his doctrine of consequences; much of it comes from Ockham, and some even from Peter of Spain.

As in this whole section, the contemporary range of problems is only barely illustrated.

Albert's definitions of antecedent and consequent deserve to be quoted first:

31.13 That proposition is said to be antecedent to another which is so related to it that it is impossible that things be as is signifiable by it without their being as is in any way signifiable by the other, keeping fixed the use (*impositio*) of the terms.

Like all Scholastics of the 14th century and after, Albert makes a clear distinction between a *rule of consequence* and the *consequence* itself. A rule is a metalogical (more exactly a meta-metalogical) description of the form of a valid consequence. The consequence itself is a proposition having this form. That generally holds good; but some of Albert's rules are conceived as propositional forms like the Stoic inference-schemata (**21.22**) – cf. the fifth (**31.18**) – only with this difference, that the variables are here evidently metalogical, i.e. to be substituted with *names* of propositions, not with propositions themselves as is the case with the Stoic formulae.

31.14 The first (rule of simple consequence) is this: from an impossible proposition every other follows. Proof: from the nominal definitions of antecedent and consequent given in the first chapter. For if a proposition is impossible, it is impossible that things are as it indicates, and are not as any other indicates; therefore the impossible proposition is antecedent to every other proposition, and hence every proposition follows from an impossible one. This it is which is usually expressed: anything follows from the impossible. And so it follows: man is an ass, therefore a man runs; since the antecedent being impossible, if things are not as the consequent indicates, it is impossible that they should be as the antecedent indicates.

31.15 Second rule: A necessary proposition follows from any proposition. This is again proved by the nominal definitions of antecedent and consequent. For it is impossible that things should not be as a necessary proposition indicates, if they are as any other (proposition) indicates. Hence a necessary proposition is a consequent of any proposition. It follows therefore that this consequence is valid: 'a man runs, therefore God exists', or '(therefore) ass is an animal'.

The proofs of these two rules are very typical of the Scholastic approach to propositional logic and show how different it is both to that of the Megarian-Stoics and that of the moderns. The essential scholastic point is that a consequence does not unite two states of affairs but two propositions (in the scholastic sense, which includes the mental propositions, cf. **26.03**). Let '*P*' be the name of the proposition expressing the state of affairs *p*, and '*Q*' the name of the proposition expressing the state of affairs *q*, the proof of the first consequence can be presented thus:

As axiom is presupposed

31.151 If *p* cannot be the case then (*p* and *q*) cannot be the case.

Then the process is:

(1) *P* is impossible	(hypothesis)
(2) *p* cannot be the case	(by (1) and the definition of impossibility)
(3) (*p* and not *q*) cannot be the case	(by (2) and **31.151**)
(4) *Q* is the consequent of *P*	(by the definition and (3))
(5) *Q* follows from *P*	(by definition)

And this was to be proved, *Q* being any proposition.

Thus we can see that a metalogical thesis about a relationship (consequence) between propositions is proved through reduction to logical laws concerning relationships between states of affairs.

31.16 Third rule: (1) From any proposition there follows every other whose contradictory opposite is incompatible with it (the first). And (2) from no proposition does there follow another whose contradictory opposite is compatible with it, where (the expression) 'a proposition is compatible with another' is to be understood in the sense that the state of affairs (*sic esse*) which the one indicates is compatible with that which the other indicates. . . .

The first part of the rule is proved (thus): Let us suppose that the proposition *B* is incompatible with the proposition *A*. I say (then) that from *A* there follows the contradictory opposite of *B*, i.e. not-*B*. This is evident, for *A* and *B* are incompatible and therefore (either *A*) is impossible, so that every proposition follows from it, by the first rule; or *A* is possible, then necessarily if *A* is the case, either *B* or not-*B* is the case, since one part of a pair of contradictory opposites is always true. But it is impossible that if *A* is the case, *B* is the case, by hypothesis. Therefore it is necessary that if *A* is the case, not-*B* is the case. Therefore not-*B* follows from *A*.

The second part of the rule is proved (thus): if *A* and not-*B* are true together, then this holds: If *A* is the case, *B* is not the case. But since *B* and not-*B* are not true together, it is possible that if *A* is the case, *B* is not the case. Therefore *B* does not follow from *A*.

31.17 Fourth rule: for every valid consequence, from the contradictory opposite of the consequent there follows the contradictory opposite of the antecedent. This is evident, since on the supposition that *B* follows from *A*, I say that not-*A* follows from not-*B*. For either it is so, or it is possible that *A* and not-*B* are true together, by the previous rule. But it is necessary that if *A* is the case, *B* is the case. Therefore *B* and not-*B* will be true together, which is impossible, by the accepted (*communis*) principle 'it is impossible that two contradictories should be true together'. . . .

31.18 Fifth rule: if *B* follows from *A*, and *C* from *B*, then (1) *C* follows from *A*; and (2) *C* follows from everything from which *B* follows; and (3) what does not follow from *A*, does not follow from *B;* and (4) from everything from which *C* does not follow, *B* too does not follow. That is to say, in current terms, all the (following) consequences are valid: (1) Whatever follows from the consequent follows from the antecedent; (2) The consequent of this consequence follows from all that from which the antecedent follows; (3) What does not follow from the antecedent does not follow from the consequent; (4) The antecedent does not follow from that from which the consequent does not follow. This rule has four parts.

The first (part) is: If *B* follows from *A*, and *C* from *B*, then *C* follows from *A*. For on the supposition that *B* follows from *A*, if things are as *A* indicates, they are also as *B* indicates, by the nominal definition of antecedent and consequent. And on the supposition that *C* follows from *B*, if things are as *B* indicates, they are also as *C* indicates. Therefore, if things are as *A* indicates, they are also as *C* indicates. And accordingly *C* follows from *A*.

The second part is evident, since nothing from which *B* follows can be the case if *B* is not the case; and as *B* cannot be the case if *C* is not the case, it follows also: *C* follows from all from which *B* follows. And by 'being the case' is to be understood: being as *B* indicates . . . .

31.19 Sixth rule: (1) It is impossible that false follows from true. (2) It is also impossible that from possible follows impossible. (3) It is also impossible that a not necessary proposition follows from a necessary one. (The first part) is evident by the nominal definition of antecedent and consequent. For if things are as the antecedent indicates, they are also as the consequent indicates, and accordingly, when the antecedent is true, the consequent is true and not false. The second part is evident, for if things can be as the antecedent indicates, they can also be as the consequent indicates; and accordingly, when the antecedent is possible, the consequent also (is possible). The third part is evident, for if things necessarily are as the antecedent indicates, they must also (necessarily) be as the consequent indicates.

31.20 There follows from this rule: (1) if the consequent of a consequence is false, its antecedent is also false; (2) further, if the consequent of a consequence is impossible, its antecedent is also impossible; (3) further if the consequent of a consequence is not necessary, its antecedent also is not necessary.

And I purposely (*notanter*) say, 'if the consequent is not possible' and not 'if the consequent is not possibly true', since in this (consequence): 'every proposition is affirmative, therefore no proposition is negative', its antecedent is possible and its consequent too is possible, but although it is possible, it is impossible that it be true, as was said above. And yet true can follow from false, and possible can follow from impossible, and necessary can follow from not necessary, as is evident from Aristotle in the second (book) of the *Prior* (*Analytics*, ch. 2) (**16.32**)

31.21 Seventh rule: if *B* follows from *A* together with one or more additional necessary propositions, then *B* follows from *A* alone. Proof: *B* is either necessary or not necessary. If it is necessary, it follows from *A* alone, by the second rule, since the necessary follows from any (proposition). But if *B* is not necessary, then *A* is either possible or impossible. Suppose *A* is impossible then again *B* follows from *A* alone as also from A with an additional necessary proposition, by the first rule. Since from the impossible, anything follows. But suppose *A* is possible, then if *A* is the case it is impossible that *B* is not the case, or, if *A* is the case it is possible that *B* is not the case. On the first supposition, *B* follows from *A* alone, as also from *A* with an additional necessary proposition, by the nominal definition of antecedent and consequent. But supposing that if A is the case it is possible that B is not the case, then if A is the case, A and the additional necessary proposition must be true together. For it is impossible that* A should not be the case, since it is not possible that if A is the case, A is not the case. And accordingly, granted that A is the case, i.e. granted that things are as A indicates, it is necessary that they should be as A and the additional necessary proposition indicate. Therefore from A there follow A and the additional necessary proposition. And as B follows from A and the additional necessary proposition, one obtains the probandum by means of the first part of this rule, (viz.) that B follows from A alone, which was to be proved.

The rule could be formulated:

31.211 If C is necessary, then: if B follows from A and C, B follows from A alone,

and the proof is contained in the words: 'if A is the case, A and the additional necessary proposition must be the case' and the subsequent justification. For in fact, if C is necessary, then if we have A, we have A and C, and then if B follows from A and C, B follows from A. The passage previous to the words just quoted is therefore superfluous, but it has been retained as characteristic of the scholastic approach.

31.22 Eighth rule: every consequence of this kind is formal: 'Socrates exists, and Socrates does not exist, therefore a stick stands in the corner'. Proof: By formal consequence it follows: 'Socrates exists and Socrates does not exist, therefore Socrates exists', from a complete copulative proposition to one of its parts. Further it follows: 'Socrates exists and Socrates does not exist, therefore Socrates does not exist' by the same rule. And it further follows: 'Socrates exists, therefore either Socrates exists or a stick stands in the corner'. The consequence holds, since from every categorical proposition a disjunctive proposition is deducible (*infert*) of which it is a part. And then again: 'Socrates exists and Socrates does not exist; therefore (by the second part of this copulative proposition): Socrates does not exist; therefore a stick stands in the corner'. The consequence holds since the consequence is formal from a disjunctive with the denial (*destructio*) of one

* Omitting *necessariam.*

204

of its parts to the other. And so every proposition similar in form to this would be a valid consequence if it were formed. This rule is usually expressed in the following words: 'from every copulative consisting of contradictorily opposed parts, there follows any other (proposition by) formal consequence'.

This text is undoubtedly one of the peaks of scholastic propositional logic. Both the rule and its proof were part of the scholastic capital. It is to be found in Pseudo-Scotus in the form:

31.23 From every proposition evidently implying a contradiction, any other formally follows. So there follows for instance: 'Socrates runs and Socrates does not run, therefore you are at Rome.'

The proof in **31.22** relies on the following laws as axioms, which are expressly formulated:

31.221 If P and Q then P.
31.222 If P and Q then Q.
31.223 If P then, P or Q.
31.224 If P or Q, then, if not-P then Q.

The proof runs thus:

(1) P and not-P	(hypothesis)
(2) P	(by (1) and **31.221** with substitution of 'not-P' for 'Q')
(3) P or Q	(by (2) and **31.223** (cf. **31.10**))
(4) not-P	(by (1) and **31.222** with substitution of 'not-P' for 'Q')
(5) Q	(by (3), (4) and **31.224**)

And this was the probandum, Q being any proposition at all.

Of the laws used in this proof, **31.221–2** are to be found in Ockham (**31.24**) and were also familiar to Paul of Venice. **31.223** is the modern law of the factor, accepted by the Scholastics from the time of Kilwardby (**31.10**). **31.224** is the later modus tollendo ponens, analogous to the fifth indemonstrable of the Stoics (**22.08**), but using non-exclusive disjunction.

D. PAUL OF VENICE

Next we give some rules for copulative propositions, from Paul of Venice.

31.25 For the truth of an affirmative copulative (proposition) there is required and suffices the truth of both parts of the copulative. . . .

31.26 A corollary from this rule is the second: that for the falsity of an affirmative copulative the falsity of one of its parts is sufficient. . . .

31.27 The third rule is this: for the possibility of the copulative it is required and suffices that each of its principal parts is possible and each is compossible with each – or if there are more than two, with all. . . .

31.28 From this follows the fourth, viz.: for the impossibility of a copulative it is sufficient and requisite that one of its principal parts be impossible or that one be not compossible with the other, or the others. . . .

31.29 The fifth rule is this: for the necessity of an affirmative copulative, the necessity of every one of its parts. . . .

31.30 From this rule follows the sixth: that for the contingence of a copulative it is required and suffices that one of its categorical principal parts be contingent and compossible with the other, or with all others if there are more than two.

Similar rules for 'known', 'known as true', 'credible' follow.

For disjunctives, the same author gives the following rules, among others:

31.31 From what has been said (cf. **31.223**) there follow four corollaries. The first is: if there is an affirmative disjunctive . . . composed of two categoricals of which one is superordinate to the other by reason of a term or terms in it, the argument is valid to the superordinate part; it follows e.g.: you run or you are in motion, therefore you are in motion. . . .

31.32 The second corollary is this: if there is a disjunctive consisting of two categoricals of which one is possible, the other impossible, the argument to the possible part is valid. Hence it follows validly: 'there is no God, or you do not exist, therefore you do not exist'; 'you are an ass or you run, therefore you run'.

31.33 The third corollary is this: if there be formed a disjunctive of two categoricals that are equivalent (*convertibilibus*), the argument to each of them is valid, for it follows validly: 'there is no God or man is an ass, therefore man is an ass'. And from the same antecedent it follows that there is no God, since those categoricals, being impossible, are equivalent. It further follows: 'you are a man or you are risible, therefore you are risible', and it also follows that you are a man.

31.34 The fourth corollary is this: if a disjunctive be

formed of two categoricals of which one is necessary and the other contingent, the argument is valid to the necessary part. Hence it follows validly: 'you run or God exists, therefore God exists'. And it is not strange that all such consequences hold, for the consequent follows of itself immediately (*continue*) from each part of the disjunctive, hence it must follow too from the disjunctives themselves.

31.35 The eighth principal rule is this: from an affirmative disjunctive . . . to the negative copulative formed of the contradictories of the parts of the disjunctive is a valid argument. The proof is that the affirmative copulative formed of the contradictories of the parts of the disjunctive contradicts the disjunctive, therefore the contradictory of that copulative, formed by prefixing a negative, follows from the disjunctive. For example 'you run or you are in motion, therefore: not, you do not run and you are not in motion'; 'God exists or no man is an ass, therefore: not, there is no God and man is an ass'. Those consequences are evident, since the opposites of the consequents are incompatible with their antecedents, as has been said.

31.36 From that rule there follows as a corollary that from an affirmative copulative . . . to a negative disjunctive formed of the contradictories of the parts of the copulative is a valid argument. Hence it follows validly: 'you are a man and you are an animal, therefore: not, you are not a man or you are not an animal'. Similarly it follows: 'you are not a goat and you are not an ass, therefore: not*, you are a goat or you are an ass'. . . .

The last two texts contain two of the so-called 'de Morgan' laws. So far as is known, they first occur in Ockham (**31.37**) and Burleigh (**31.38**)**. The latter gives them in the form of equivalences.

31.39 If one argues from an affirmative conditional, characterized (*denominata*) by 'if', to a disjunctive consisting of the contradictory of the antecedent and the consequent*** of the conditional the consequence is formal. The proof is that this consequence is formal: 'if you are a man you are an animal; therefore, you are not a man or you are an animal'. And no one example is more cogent than another, therefore all are valid consequences.

---

  * Adding *non*.
 ** But Peter of Spain (*Tractatus Syncategorematum*) has the doctrine of **31.36**.
*** Reading *consequente* for *consequentis*.

E. RULES OF CONSEQUENCES UT NUNC

Buridan writes:

31.40 And it is to be noted that a proportionate conclusion is to be posited concerning consequences *ut nunc* (i.e. proportionate to that concerning simple consequences), viz. that from every false proposition there follows every other by a consequence *ut nunc*, because it is impossible that things being as they now are a proposition which is true should not be true. And so it is not impossible that it should be true, however anything else may not be true. And when the talk is of the past or future, then it can be called a consequence *ut nunc*, or however else you like to call it, e.g. it follows by a consequence *ut nunc* or *ut tunc* or even *nunc per tunc*: 'if Antichrist will not be generated, Aristotle never existed'. For though it be simply true that it is possible that Antichrist will not exist, yet it is impossible that he will not exist when things are going to be as they will be; for he will exist, and it is impossible that he will exist and that he will not exist.

We have here first of all the two classical 'paradoxical' laws of material implication:

31.401 If P is false then Q follows from P.
31.402 If P is true, then P follows from Q.

Buridan provides an example of (substitution in) the first of these laws, putting the proposition 'Antichrist will not be generated' for 'P', and 'Aristotle never existed' for 'Q'. The first proposition is, absolutely speaking, possible, so this cannot be a case of simple consequence (cf. the first rule, **31.14** *supra*), for that would require it to be absolutely impossible. But the consequence holds if taken *ut nunc*, since the proposition 'Antichrist will not be generated' will in fact be impossible in what will be the circumstances. Hence we have impossibility for that time (*ut tunc*) and so a consequence that holds for that time.

This shows that even consequence for a given time is defined by means of impossibility. The difference between it and simple consequence consists only in the kind of impossibility, absolute (for all times and circumstances) in the case of simple consequence, conditioned in that of consequence for a given time.

But impossibility *ut nunc* is defined as simple non-existence, and so the proposition 'Antichrist will not be generated' can be reckoned as impossible since Antichrist will in fact be generated. It follows that consequence *ut nunc* can be defined without the help of the modal functor, a proposition *ut nunc* being impossible simply when it is false.

Another law of consequence *ut nunc* comes from the same text of Buridan:

31.41 If a conclusion follows from a proposition together with one or more additional propositions, the same conclusion follows from that proposition alone by a consequence *ut nunc*.

This rule is analogous to the seventh rule given above for simple consequence (**31.21**), which shows that the whole system of simple consequences can be transformed into a system of consequences *ut nunc* by everywhere replacing 'necessary' by 'true' and 'impossible' by 'false' and similar simplifications.

Finally we remark that Buridan, so far as is now known, is the only scholastic logician to develop laws of consequence *ut nunc*, though he devoted much less space to them than to simple consequences. In Paul of Venice the subject of consequence *ut nunc* seems to have dropped out completely.

III. LOGIC OF TERMS

§ 32. ASSERTORIC SYLLOGISTIC

Contrary to a widespread opinion, the assertoric syllogistic was not only not the only, it was not even the chief subject of scholastic logic. The Scholastics, like most of the Commentators (**24.271** ff.), thought of syllogisms as rules (cf. **30.11**) rather than conditional propositions. The domain of syllogisms received a significant extension through the introduction of singular terms already in Ockham's time. But the new formulae thus derived will here be given separately under the heading 'Other Formulae' (§ 34) since they effect an essential alteration in the Aristotelian syllogistic. In the present section we shall confine ourselves to that part of the scholastic treatment which can still be deemed Aristotelian. Here, too, everything is treated purely metalogically (except in some early logicians such as Albert the Great), but that is quite in the Aristotelian tradition (**14.25** ff.).

The most important contributions are these: (1) the devising of numerous mnemonics for the syllogistic moods and their inter-relationships, culminating in the *pons asinorum*. (2) The systematic introduction and thorough investigation of the fourth figure. (3) The position and investigation of the problem of the null class, which has already received mention in connection with appellation (§ 28, B).

A. EARLY MNEMONICS

L. Minio-Paluello has recently made the big discovery of an early attempt to construct syllogistic mnemonics, in a MS of the early 13th century. This deprives of its last claims to credibility Prantl's legend of the Byzantine origin of such mnemonics.* The essentials are these:

32.06 It is to be remarked that there are certain notations (*notulae*) for signifying the moods. . . . The four letters *e, i, o, u* signify universal affirmatives, and the four letters *l, m, n, r* signify universal negatives, and the three** *a, s, t* signify

---

* Carl Prantl, relying on a single MS, ascribed to Michael Psellus (1018 to 1078/96) the Σύνοψις εἰς τὴν ᾿Αριστοτέλους λογικὴν ἐπιστήμην in which such mnemonics occur, and stated that the *Summulae* of Peter of Spain was a translation from that (**32.01**). In that opinion he was the victim of a great mistake, since M. Grabmann (**32.02**) following C. Thurot (**32.03**), V. Rose (**32.04**) and R. Stapper (**32.05**) has shown the Σύνοψις to be by George Scholarios (1400–1464) and a translation of the *Summulae*.
** Reading '3' for '4'.

particular affirmatives, and *b, c, d* signify particular negatives. So the moods of the first figure are shown in the following verse: *uio, non, est* (*?ost*), *lac, uia, mel, uas, erp, arc.* Thus the first mood of the first figure, signified by the notation *uio*, consists of a first universal affirmative and a subsequent universal affirmative, (and) concludes to a universal affirmative; e.g.: All man is animal and all risible is man, therefore all risible is animal. . . . The moods of the second figure are shown in the following verse: *ren, erm, rac*, obd.* . . . The moods of the third figure are shown in the following verse: *eua, nec, aut, esa, duc, nac.***

This is a very primitive technique, but at least it shows that the highly developed terminology of Peter of Spain*** had antecedents in Scholasticism itself.

We cite the relevant texts from the *Summulae Logicales*.

B. BARBARA-CELARENT

32.07 After giving a threefold division of propositions it is to be known that there is a threefold enquiry to be made about them, viz. What?, Of what kind?, How much? 'What?' enquires about the nature (*substantia*) of the proposition, so that to the question 'What?' is to be answered 'categorical' or 'hypothetical'; to 'Of what kind?' – 'affirmative' or 'negative'; to 'How much?' – 'universal', 'particular', 'indefinite', 'singular'. Whence the verse:

Quae ca vel hip, qualis ne vel aff, un quanta par in sin.
the questions being in Latin: quae?, qualis?, quanta?, and the answers: *categorica, hypothetica, affirmativa, universalis, particularis, infinita, singularis.*

So far as we know this is the first text in which the notions of quality and quantity occur. The full set of technical terms connected therewith, together with some others, appears in the next passage which resumes the doctrine of conversion.

32.08 The conversion of propositions having both terms in common but with the order reversed, is threefold; viz.

---

* MS has '*rachc*'.
** Personal thanks are due to Prof. L. Minio-Paluello for telling us of this MS and helping to restore the text.
*** This can not have originated with him. Prof L. Minio-Paluello informed me on 24. 6. 55 that he had found the word '*Festino*' in a MS dating at the latest from 1200.

simple, accidental, and by contraposition. Simple conversion is when the predicate is made from the subject and conversely, the quality and quantity remaining the same. And in this way are converted the universal negative and the particular affirmative. . . . The universal affirmative is similarly converted when the terms are equivalent (*convertibilibus*). . . .

Accidental conversion is when the predicate is made from the subject and conversely, the quality remaining the same, but the quantity being changed; and in this way the universal negative is converted into the particular negative, and the universal affirmative into the particular affirmative. . . .

The law of accidental conversion of the universal negative is not in Aristotle.

32.09 Conversion by contraposition is to make the predicate from the subject and conversely, quality and quantity remaining the same, but finite terms being changed to infinite ones. And in this way the universal affirmative is converted into itself and the particular negative into itself, e.g. 'all man is animal' – 'all non-animal is non-man'; 'some man is not stone' – 'some non-stone is not non-man'.*

Hence the verses:

A Affirms, *E* rEvokes**, both universal,
I affIrms, *O* revOkes**, both in particular.
Simply converts *fEcI*, accidentally *EvA*,
AstO by contra(position); and these are all the conversions.

The classical expressions *Barbara*, *Celarent*, etc. seem to have been fairly generally known about 1250. After describing the assertoric moods Peter of Spain introduced them thus:

32.10 Hence the verses:
Figure the first to every kind*** concludes,
The second only yields negations,
Particulars only from third figure moods.
Barbara, celarent, darii, ferion, baralipton,
Celantes, dabitis, fapesmo, frisesomorum.
Cesare. camestres, festino, baroco, darapti.
Felapto, disamis, datisi, bocardo, ferison.

---

* Reading *non homo.*
** *negat.*
*** viz. *problematis.*

32.11 In those four verses there are twenty-one expressions (*dictiones*) which so correspond to the twenty-one moods of the three figures that by the first expression is to be understood the first mood, and by the second the second, and so with the others. Hence the first two verses correspond to the moods of the first figure, but the third to the moods of the second save for its last expression. It is to be known therefore that by these four vowels, viz. *A*, *E*, *I*, *O* set in the aforesaid verses there are understood the four kinds of proposition. By the vowel *A* is understood the universal affirmative, by *E* the universal negative, by *I* the particular affirmative, by *O* the particular negative.

32.12 Further it is to be known that in each expression there are three syllables representing three propositions, and if there is anything extra it is superfluous, excepting *M* as will appear later. And by the first syllable is understood the major proposition, similarly by the second the second proposition, and by the third the conclusion; e.g. the first expression, viz. *Barbara*, has three syllables, in each of which *A* is set, and *A* set three times signifies that the first mood of the first figure consists of two universal affirmatives concluding to a universal affirmative; and thus it is to be understood about the other expressions according to the vowels there set.

32.13 Further it is to be known that the first four expressions of the first verse begin with these consonants, *B*, *C*, *D*, *F*, and all the subsequent expressions begin with the same, and by this is to be understood that all the subsequent moods beginning with *B* are reduced to the first mood of the first figure, with *C* to the second, with *D* to the third, with *F* to the fourth.

32.14 Further it is to be known that wherever *S* is put in these expressions, it signifies that the proposition understood by means of the vowel immediately preceding should be converted simply. And by *P* is signified that the proposition which is understood by means of the vowel immediately preceding is to be converted accidentally. And wherever *M* is put, it signifies that transposition of the premisses is to be effected. Transposition is to make the major minor and conversely. And where *C* is put, it signifies that the mood understood by means of that expression is to be reduced *per impossibile*.

Whence the verses:

SCHOLASTIC LOGIC

S enjoins simple conversion, *per accidens P*,
Transpose with *M, ad impossibile C.*
George Scholarios's Greek version of the four last verses of **32.10**
is not without interest (cf. **32.02 ff.**):

32.15 Γράμματα ἔγραψε γραφίδι τεχνικός,   (I)
      Γράμμασιν ἔταξε χάρισι πάρθενος ἱερόν·   (Ia)
      Ἔγραψε κάτεχε μέτριον ἄχολον.   (II)
      Ἅπασι σθεναρὸς ἰσάκις ἀσπίδι ὁμαλὸς φέριστος. (III)

Unlike the Latin ones, these verses are meaningful, and can be
rendered:
Letters there wrote with a style a scholar,
With letters there composed for the Graces a maiden a dedication.
She wrote: Cleave to the moderate, un-wrathful (man).
In all, that strength which like a shield is well-proportioned is
the best.

The names *Barbara, Celarent* etc. have survived the era of Scholasticism and are still in use today, unlike many other syllogistic
mnemonics. We give some examples of these others, and first some
which concern the technique of reducing moods of the second and
third figures (also of the 'indirect' moods of the first figure: **17.111 ff.**)
to moods of the first. For that purpose, Jodoc Trutfeder at the
beginning of the 16th century gave these expressions:

32.16

Baralipton	*Nes-*	*Celarent*
Celantes	*ci-*	*Darii*
Dabitis	*e-*	*Celarent*
Fapesmo	*ba-*	*Barbara*
Frisemom	*tis.*	*Darii*
Cesare	*O-*	*Ferio*
Camestres	*di-*	*Darii*
Festino	*e-*	*Celarent*
Baroco	*bam.*	*Barbara*
Darapti	*Le-*	*Celarent*
Felapton	*va-*	*Barbara*
Disamis	*re.*	*Celarent*
Datisi	*Ro-*	*Ferio*
Bocardo	*man-*	*Barbara*
Ferison	*nis.*	*Darii*

These expressions serve for the indirect process of Aristotle
(§ 14, D). Thus for instance from *Celarent*, by putting the contradictory opposite (*I*) of its conclusion (*E*) for the minor premiss (*A*)
there is concluded the contradictory of the latter (*O*), and one has

Festino. Applying this treatment to the major premiss one has *Disamis.* Evidently some further processes must be employed to get a few further moods. E.g. to get *Felapton* and *Darapti* from *Barbara* and *Celarent* respectively, one must first deduce *Barbari* and *Celaront* (**24.271** f.). So too in the case of *Dabitis* (**24.273**).

Further mnemonics that were used will be mentioned later (**32.24** and **32.38**).

C. BARBARI-CELARONT

Similar mnemonic expressions are found for the so-called 'sub-alternate' moods (**24.271–24.281**). A complete list with names appears in a text of Peter of Mantua that is in other respects very defective:

32.17 . . . the first (*formula*) . . . is usually signified by the expression *Barbara*. The second formula has premisses arranged in the way described which conclude to the particular affirmative or indefinite of the consequent of the first formula that we posited, and this we are wont to call *Barbari*. . . .

From the aforesaid (premisses) can also be concluded the particular negative of (i.e. corresponding to) the consequent of the aforesaid formula, which (new) formula we can call *Celaront*. . . .

The eighth formula, which is called *Baralipton*, follows from *Barbari*, by conversion of its conclusion. . . .

The ninth formula is called *Celantes* . . . from it follows the tenth, which is called *Celantos*; it concludes to a particular or indefinite conclusion. . . .

The second mood (of the second figure) can be gained from the aforesaid premisses (of the mood *Cesare*) by concluding to the particular that corresponds to (*Cesare*'s) conclusion, and is signified by the expression *Cesaro*. . . .

The next formula . . . is usually called *Camestres*. From it there follows another formula which we call *Camestro*.

So Peter of Mantua has five subalternate moods besides the nineteen moods of Peter of Spain, in fact the full twenty-four. But he has many others as well, commonly forming an 'indirect' mood corresponding to each of the others (applying the Aristotelian rules of § 13), e.g. a *Cesares* corresponding to *Cesare*. *Cesares* would look like this:

No man is stone;
All marble is stone;
Therefore no man is marble.

Contrast the following in *Camestres*:

All marble is stone;
No man is stone;
Therefore no man is marble.

The only difference between the two is in the order of the premisses, and to reckon them as distinct moods is an extreme of formalism. Peter of Mantua further forms such moods as *Barocos*, with the O-conclusion of *Baroco* converted (1) and other false formulas.*

D. THE FOURTH FIGURE

1. Among the Latins

We know of no scholastic logical text in Latin where the fourth figure in the modern sense can be found, though all logicians of the period develop the 'indirect moods of the first'. They are mostly aware of a fourth figure, but treat it as not distinct from the first, e.g. Albert the Great (**32.18**), Shyreswood (**32.19**), Ockham (**32.20**), Pseudo-Scotus (**32.21**), Albert of Saxony (**32.22**), Paul of Venice (**32.23**). We give an instance from Albert of Saxony.

32.22 (The syllogism is constituted) in a fourth way if the middle is predicated in the first premiss, subjected in the second. . . . But it is to be noted that the first figure differs from the fourth only by interchange of premisses which does nothing towards the deducibility or non-deducibility of the conclusion.

Some later logicians do recognize a 'fourth figure' but this again is not the modern one; only the first with interchanged premisses, as in the last text. This is very clear in Peter Tarteret and Peter of Mantua. We quote the first:

32.24 First (*dictum*): Taking 'figure' in a wide sense, the fourth figure is no different from the first but contained under it. Second: taking 'first figure' in a specific sense, a fourth figure is to be posited distinct from the first; and the fourth figure consists in this, that the middle is predicate in the major premiss, subject in the minor, e.g. 'all man is animal; all animal is substance; therefore all man is substance'.

* It should be understood in respect of this and the following sub-section that after Peter of Spain (generalizing the method of Boethius and Shyreswood for the second and third figures) it was usual to *define* the major and minor premisses as the first and second stated, and the extreme terms with reference to the premisses, not the conclusion. 48 moods in 4 figures can be (and sometimes were) correctly distinguished on this basis. 'Classical' failure to distinguish this from the method of Albalag (which goes back to Philoponus) resulted in many inconsistencies. (Ed.)

Third: there are four moods of the fourth figure, viz. *Bamana,
Camene, Dimari,* and *Fimeno.* They are reduced to the first
figure by mere exchange of premisses.

Peter of Mantua also has *Bamana* etc.

2. In Albalag

Yet a clearly formulated doctrine of the 'genuine' fourth figure is
to be found in a 13th century text of the Jewish philosopher Albalag.* This text, like the foregoing, seems to have been without
influence on the development of logic in the Middle Ages. It was
recently discovered by Dr. G. Vajda and has never been translated
into Latin. We quote it here at length for its originality, and because
it is instructive about the level of logic at that time.

32.25 In my opinion there must be four figures. For the
middle term can be subject in one of the two premisses and
predicate in the other in two ways: (1) the middle term is
subject in the minor, predicate in the major, (2) it is predicate
in the minor, subject in the major. The ancients only considered the second arrangement and called it the 'first figure'.
This admits of four moods which can yield a conclusion. But
the first arrangement, which I have found, admits of five
moods which can yield a conclusion. . . .

32.26 We say then that this new figure is subject to three
conditions: (1) one of its premisses must be affirmative, the
other universal; (2) if the minor premiss is affirmative, the
major will be universal; (3) if the major is particular, the
minor will be affirmative.

The conditions exclude eleven of the sixteen (theoretically
possible) moods; there remain therefore five which can yield
a conclusion.

32.27 (1) The minor particular affirmative, the major
universal negative:

Some white is animal.

No raven is white.

Some animal is not raven.

Then one can convert the minor particular affirmative and
the major universal negative and say:

Some animal is white,

No white is raven,

which yields the third mood of the first figure.

* This was kindly put at my disposal, together with a French translation, by
Dr. G. Vajda.

32.28 (2) The minor universal affirmative, the major universal negative:

All man is animal.

No man is raven.

Some animal is not raven.

Then one can get back to the third mood of the first figure by converting both premisses.

32.29 (3) The minor universal negative, the major universal affirmative:

No man is stone.

Every speaker is man.

No stone is speaker.

Exchanging the minor and major with one another, one comes back to the second mood of the first figure, of which the conclusion will be: 'No speaker is stone', and one only needs to convert this to obtain 'No stone is speaker'.

32.30 (4) Two affirmatives:

All composite is not eternal.

All body is composite.

Some not eternal is body.

Here one can interchange the minor and major premisses and reach the first figure, with conclusion: 'All body is not eternal' which can be converted to 'Some not eternal is body'.

32.31 (5) The minor universal affirmative, the major particular affirmative:

All man is speaker.

Some white is man.

Some speaker is white.

If one interchanges the minor and major premisses, one concludes in the first figure: 'some white is speaker' which will be converted as above. . . .

32.32 . . . the syllogism is formed with reference to a determinate proposition which is first established and laid down in the mind, and the truth of which one then tries to justify and manifest by means of the syllogism. Of the premisses, that containing the term which is predicate of this proposition is the major, that containing the subject is the minor.

Albalag here presents the modern definition of the syllogistic terms, not according to their extension, but formally, according to their places in the conclusion. The modern names of the moods he introduces are: *Fresison*, *Fesapo*, *Calemes*, *Bamalip* and *Dimaris* (cf. § 36, F).

There is missing only that corresponding to Peter of Mantua's *Celantos* (**32.17**), viz. *Calemop*. Albalag also formulates the general rules of the fourth figure, and uses the combinatorial method.

E. COMBINATORIAL METHOD

In Albert the Great we find a procedure taken over from the Arabs (**32.33**) by which all possible moods of the syllogism are first determined combinatorially, and the invalid ones then discarded. The relevant text runs:

32.34 It is to be known that with such an ordering of terms and arrangement of premisses (*propositionum*) sixteen conjugations result, yielded by the quantity and quality of the premisses. For if the middle is subject in the major and predicate in the minor, either (1) both premisses are universal, or (2) both are particular, or one (is) universal and the other particular and this in two ways: for either (3) the major is universal and the minor particular, or (4) conversely the major particular and the minor universal; these are the four gained by combinations of quantity. When each is multiplied by four in respect of affirmation and denial, there are sixteen conjugations in all, thus: if both (premisses) are universal either (1) both are affirmative, or (2) both negative, or (3) the major is affirmative and the minor negative, or conversely (4) the major is negative and the minor affirmative: and there are four conjugations. But if both are particular, there are again four conjugations . . . etc.

We may compare with that the text of Albalag (**32.25** ff.). Kilwardby uses similar methods.

F. INVENTIO MEDII, PONS ASINORUM

The Aristotelian doctrine of the *inventio medii* (**14.29**) was keenly studied by the Scholastics, and the schema of Philoponus (**24.35**) was not only taken over, but also further developed. It is to be found as early as Albert the Great, who probably found it in Averroes (**32.35**); Albert's version differs from that of Philoponus and Averroes only in the particular formulae employed. But as we find it in him, it became the foundation of the famous *pons asinorum*, so that it must be given in this form as well:

32.36

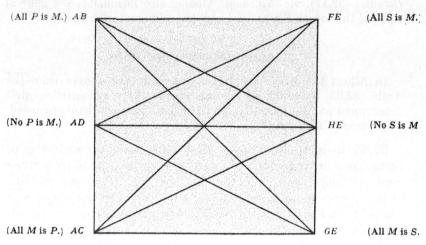

(All *P* is *M*.) *AB* · *FE* (All *S* is *M*.)

(No *P* is *M*.) *AD* · *HE* (No *S* is *M*.)

(All *M* is *P*.) *AC* · *GE* (All *M* is *S*.)

The further development of this figure is the *pons asinorum*, which must have been known to George of Brussels (**32.37**) since Thomas Bricot in a commentary on George's lectures gives the mnemonic words for it with the following explanation:

32.38 When the letters *A*, *E*, *I*, *O* are put in the third syllable they signify the quality and quantity of the conclusion to be drawn. . . . When the letters *A* and *E* are put in the first or second syllable, *A* signifies the predicate and *E* the subject. And each of the letters can be accompanied by three consonants; *A* with *B*, *C*, *D*, and then *B* signifies that the middle should follow on the predicate, *C* that it should be antecedent, *D* that it should be extraneous. Similarly *E* is accompanied by *F*, *G*, *H*, and then *F* signifies that the middle should follow on the subject, *G* that it should be antecedent, *H* that it should be extraneous. As is made clear in these verses:

E's the subject, *F* its sequent, *G* precedent, *F* outside;
A's the predicate, *B* its sequent, *C* precedent, *F* outside.
. . . To conclude to a universal affirmative, a middle is to be taken which is sequent to the subject and antecedent to the predicate; and this is shown by *Fecana*. . . . To conclude a particular affirmative in *Darapti*, *Disamis* and *Datisi*, a middle is to be taken which is antecedent to both extremes, as is made clear by *Cageti*. . . . To conclude to a universal negative in *Celarent* or *Cesare* a middle is to be taken which

Non pergunt aliqui per pons in ... ... caueti
Pontem ... leaue... ... ... cadent
Impedit hic ocul... ... sensus firm... ... dat & altos
In doctis saltus est sibi nulla talus

Horret equus talem ualidus ... ...tem
Du... n graditur cernens sit lic... ire potens
Non igitur rursum dico ueniant asinorum
Qui, sed eos retro nunc remanere uolo.

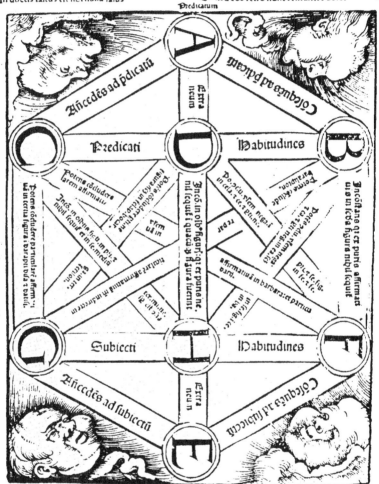

Asinus Mutat ab omni dum pons eo parte tremit
pgens Si nunc uadu labar cur cito regrediar

A... inus Heu... me qd facia ruo nec ... bet mihi qu...
cad... Aux...h...m, monitor qua dedit experior.

Pons Asinorum after Peter Tarteret (32.39)

is extraneous to the predicate and consequent on the subject, as is made clear by *Dafenes*. But if the inference is to be in *Camestres*, the middle must be extraneous to the subject and consequent on the predicate, as is made clear by *Hebare*. . . . For concluding to a particular negative in the third figure, the middle should be antecedent to the subject and extraneous to the predicate, as is made clear by *Gedaco*. . . . To conclude indirectly to a particular affirmative, the middle must be antecedent to the subject and consequent on the predicate, as is made clear by *Gebali*.

The mnemonic expressions given here employ the letters of Albert's figure, so that each expression corresponds to a line of the figure having the syllables of the mnemonic at its ends, a further syllable being added to show the quantity and quality of the corresponding conclusion. So this text of George's both illustrates the *pons asinorum* and helps to explain Albert's figure.

The *pons asinorum* itself we have found only in Peter Tarteret, with the following introduction:

32.39 That the art of finding the middle may be easy, clear and evident to all, the following figure is composed (*ponitur*) to explain it. Because of its apparent difficulty it is commonly called the 'asses' bridge' (*pons asinorum*) though it can become familiar and clear to all if what is said in this section (*passu*) is understood.

We give the schema itself in the preceding illustration.

G. THE PROBLEM OF THE NULL CLASS

The problem of the null class, i.e. of the laws of subalternation, accidental conversion (**14.12**, **32.08**) and the syllogistic moods dependent on them, has been much discussed in recent times (**46.01** ff.). It was already posed in the fourteenth century and solved by means of the doctrines of supposition and appellation. We give three series of texts, the first attributed to St. Vincent Ferrer, the second from Paul of Venice, the third from a neo-scholastic of the 17th century, a contemporary of Descartes, John of St. Thomas. Each gives a different solution.

1. St. Vincent Ferrer

32.40 Under every subject having natural supposition copulative descent can be made, with respect to the predicate, to all its supposita, whether such a subject supposes discretely*

---

* Reading *discrete* for *difinite*.

or particularly or universally. Therefore it follows validly: Man is risible, therefore this man is risible, and that man. . . .

32.41 But against this rule there are many objections. . . . (Sixth objection:). . . . In the propositions 'rain is water falling in drops', 'thunder is a noise in the clouds', the subjects have natural supposition. Yet it is not always permissible to descend in respect to the predicate to the supposita of the subject; for it does not follow: 'rain is water falling in drops, therefore this rain, and that rain, etc.'; since the antecedent is true even when there is no rain, as will be shortly said, and yet the consequent is not true nor even very intelligible, since when there is no rain (*nulla pluvia existente*) one cannot say 'this rain' or 'that rain', since a contradiction would be at once implied. In the same way must be judged the proposi- tion 'thunder is a noise etc.'

32.42 To the sixth objection it is to be said that that rule ... is understood (to hold) when such a subject has supposita actually (*in actu*) and not otherwise. For no descent can be made to the supposita* of anything except when it has them actually, since, as the objection rightly says, an evident con- tradiction would be implied. . . . Hence the consequence which concludes from a universal proposition to singular ones contained under it, e.g. 'every man runs, therefore Socrates runs and Plato runs', and 'every man is an animal, therefore Plato is an animal etc.', is called by some logicians 'conse- quence *ut nunc*'. And rightly so, since no such consequence is valid except for a determinate time, i.e. when Socrates and Plato and the other supposita actually exist.

32.43 Against the seventh objection it is to be briefly said that the subject of the proposition 'the rose is sweet- smelling' – or as one can also put it 'the rose smells sweet' – has personal supposition, and it follows validly 'therefore the rose exists (*est*)'. But if one says 'the rose is odoriferous' so that 'odoriferous' (*hoc quod dicitur odorifera*) expresses aptitude, then the subject has natural supposition and it does not follow: 'therefore the rose exists'. Hence being odoriferous is to the rose as living to mankind, and what has been said about the proposition 'man is living' must also be understood about this: 'the rose is odoriferous'.

---

* Reading *supposita* for *subjecta*.

The solution of the first text (**32.40–42**) consists then precisely in the exclusion of the null class (cf. § 46, B), 'null' being taken as 'actually null'. In other words: in the syllogistic every term must have appellation in the sense of Peter of Spain (**28.13f.**). In the second part (**32.43**) it is stipulated for subalternation that the subject must have personal (**27.17f.**) and not natural (**27.14**) supposition. This evidently presupposes that a term with personal supposition stands for really existent things. Thus we have the same solution as before.

2. *Paul of Venice*

32.44 The third rule is this: universal affirmative and particular or indefinite (affirmative, as also universal negative and particular or indefinite) negative (propositions) which have similarly and correctly supposing terms, are subalternate, and conversely, explicitly or implicitly, in the logical square (*figura*). Hence the following are subalternate: 'every man is an animal' and 'a certain man is an animal', and similarly: 'no man is an animal' and 'a certain man is not an animal'. I say 'correctly supposing terms', since the extremes must explicitly or implicitly stand for just the same thing, if it is a case of only one suppositum, for the same things, if it is a case of several. And so I say that (the following) are not subalternate: 'every man is an animal', 'a certain man is an animal', since under the supposition that there are no men, the universal would be true, but the particular false, contrary to the nature of subalterns. The reason why these are not subalternate is that the subjects do not stand for exactly the same thing. The subaltern of the former is therefore: 'man is an animal', and if one required a particular it must be this: 'a certain being which is a man is an animal'.

So Paul of Venice confines himself to stating the general rule that both propositions in a subalternation must have subjects with exactly the same supposition.

3. *John of St. Thomas*

John of St. Thomas deals with the problem of conversion.

32.45 Against the conversion of the universal affirmative, it is objected: the consequence 'every white man is a man, therefore a certain man is a white man' does not hold. For the antecedent is necessary, but the consequent can be false, in case no man in the world was white. . . .

The answer is that this (proposition) is not true in the sense in which the first proposition of which it is the converse is true. For when it is said: 'every white man is a man', with 'is' taken accidentally, for an existing man, this proposition in the argument given as an example is false, and its converse too. But when the 'is' abstracts from time and renders the proposition necessary, then 'white' will not be verified in the sense of existence, but according to possibility, i.e. independently of time, in the following sense: 'every possibly white man is a man', presupposing that no such exists. Accordingly the converse must be: 'therefore a certain man is a man who is possibly white', and thus this is true.

The following may serve as explanation: take the proposition (1) 'every Swiss king is a man'. By the rules of conversion (**14.11**, **32.08**) we may infer (2) 'a certain man is a Swiss king'. But (1) is true, (2) false. Therefore the rule of conversion employed is not valid. To this the Scholastics would answer that in (1) 'man' evidently stands for a possible man, not for a real one; it has therefore no appellation in the sense of **28.13**. And so if (1) is converted into (2), 'man' in (2) also supposes for possible men and in this sense (2) is true as well as (1).

A further interesting point is that singular terms always have appellation (**28.13**), so that the Scholastics attribute to proper names the same property with which the moderns endow descriptions (cf. § 46).

§ 33. MODAL SYLLOGISTIC

The history of scholastic modal syllogistic has been investigated from the modern point of view up to and inclusive of Pseudo-Scotus (**33.01**). We know that there was more than one system of modal logic in the Middle Ages and can to some extent follow the development.

A. ALBERT THE GREAT

The work of Albert the Great constitutes the starting point and, as his own text suggests (**33.02**), would seem to have drawn on Arabic sources. To begin with, he shows much the same doctrine as has been ascribed above (**29.09**); cf. also **23.10**, **29.12** to Thomas Aquinas and which is basic for the whole of Scholasticism (**33.03**), viz. the distinction of the composite (*composita, de dicto*) and the divided (*divisa, de re*) modal proposition, i. e. between that in which the modal functor governs the whole *dictum* and that in which it governs only a part. Later Albert gives a clear statement of the Aristotelian distinction of the two structures of the modal proposition in the divided sense:

33.04 That the predicate *A* possibly belongs to the subject *B* means one of these: (1) that *A* possibly belongs to that which is *B* and of which *B* is predicated in the sense of actual inherence, or (2) that *A* possibly belongs to that to which *B* possibly belongs.

There is added a third structure, unknown to Aristotle:

33.05 And if someone asks why the third meaning (*acceptio*) of the contingent is not given here, viz. that whatever is necessarily *B* is possibly *A*, since this is used in the mixing of the contingent and the necessary, it is to be answered that it is left sufficiently clear from what else has been determined about the mixing of the assertoric and the contingent.

The structure in question is this:
For all *x:* if *x* is necessarily *B*, *x* is possibly *A*.

It is significant that Albert the Great puts this doctrine at the beginning of the presentation of his theory of modal syllogisms in a special chapter entitled *De dici de omni et dici de nullo in propositionibus de contingenti* (**33.06**). What for Aristotle are marginal thoughts about the structure of modals by comparison with his main ideas (**15.13**), have here become fundamental.

We find then in Albert the Great a systematization of the Aristotelian teaching about the kinds of modal functors (**33.07**), and a thorough presentation of the syllogistic of the *Prior Analytics*.

B. PSEUDO-SCOTUS

Besides the four classical modal functors Pseudo-Scotus introduces others: 'of itself' (*per se*), 'true', 'false', 'doubtful' (*dubium*), 'known' (*scitum*), 'opined' (*opinatum*), 'apparent', 'known' (*notum*), 'willed' (*volitum*), 'preferred' (*dilectum*) (**33.08**), and so a number of 'subjective' functors. He formulates a long series of laws of modal propositional logic (modal consequences), among which are the following:

33.09 If the antecedent is necessary the consequent is necessary . . . and similarly with the other (positive) modes.

33.10 Modal (*de modo*) propositions in the composite sense with the (negative) modes 'impossible', 'false', 'doubtful' are not convertible like assertoric ones. Proof: for otherwise the (following) rules would be true: 'if the antecedent is impossible, the consequent is impossible', 'if the antecedent is doubtful, the consequent is doubtful'; but they are false. . . .

33.11 It follows: possibly no *B* is *A*, therefore possibly no *A* is *B*: since both (propositions) 'no *B* is *A*' and 'no *A* is *B*' follow from one another. So if one is contingent, the other is too: otherwise the contingent would follow from the necessary. . . .

33.12 If the premisses are necessary, the conclusion is necessary.

With the help of these and other laws known to us from the chapter on propositional consequences, Pseudo-Scotus proceeds to establish two systems of syllogistic, one with modal propositions in the composite, the other in the divided sense. As premisses he uses not only contingent but also (one-sidedly: (**15.071**) possible and impossible propositions. We cite only a few examples from his teaching on conversion:

33.13 Modal proposition in the composite sense are converted in just the same way as assertoric ones.

33.14 Affirmative possible (*de possibili*) propositions in the divided sense (in which the subject stands) for that which is, are not properly speaking converted. Proof: on the supposition that whatever is in fact running is an ass, the following is true: 'every man can run' in the sense that everything which is a man is able to run, but its converse is false: 'a certain runner can be a man'. . . . And I say 'properly speaking' on purpose, since (these propositions) can in a secondary sense be converted into assertorics. E.g. 'every man can run, therefore a certain thing that can run is a man'. . . .

33.15 The third thesis concerns affirmative possible propositions, in which the subject stands for that which can exist, for such affirmatives are converted in the same way as assertorics. . . .

33.16 As concerns necessary propositions, and first those which are to be understood in this (divided) sense with subject standing for what is, the first thesis is this, that affirmatives. . . are not converted; for supposing that God is creating, it does not follow: 'whatever is creating is necessarily God, therefore a certain God is creating necessarily'.

33.17 The second thesis is that negative necessary propositions with subject standing for what is, are not converted. . . .

33.18 Third thesis: that affirmative necessary propositions with subject standing for what can be are not properly speaking converted. . . .

33.19 Fourth thesis about necessary propositions with subject standing for what can be: universal negatives are simply converted, particular negatives not. Proof: since, as has been said earlier, the particular affirmative possible (proposition with subject standing) for what can be, converts simply, and it contradicts the universal negative necessary (proposition with subject standing) for what can be; so: if one of two contradictories is simply converted, so is the other, since when the consequent follows from the antecedent, the opposite of the antecedent follows from the opposite of the consequent.

C. OCKHAM

Pseudo-Scotus introduced 1. one-sidedly possible premisses into the syllogistic, 2. in the composite sense. Ockham has a further innovation: he treats also of syllogisms in which one premiss is taken in the composite, the other in the divided sense. At the same time the whole modal syllogistic is formally developed from its structural bases with remarkable acumen. We give only two examples:

33.20 As to the first figure it is to be known that when necessary premisses are taken in the composite sense, or when some are taken that are equivalent to those propositions in the composite sense, there is always a valid syllogism with a conclusion that is similar in respect of the composite or equivalent sense. . . . But when all the propositions are taken in the divided sense, or equivalent ones, a direct conclusion always follows, but not always an indirect. The first is evident because every such syllogism is regulated by *dici de omni* or (*dici*) *de nullo*. For by such a universal proposition it is denoted that of whatever the subject is said, of that the predicate is said. As by this: 'every man is necessarily an animal' is denoted that of whatever the subject 'man' is said, of that the predicate 'animal' is necessarily said. And the same holds good proportionately of the universal negative. Therefore adjoining a minor affirmative in which the subject (of the major) is predicated of something with the mode of necessity, the inference proceeds by *dici de omni* or *de nullo* (cf. **14.23**). Hence it follows validly: 'every man is necessarily an animal,

Socrates is necessarily a man, therefore Socrates is necessarily an animal'. But the indirect conclusion, viz. the converse of that conclusion with no other variation than the transposition of terms does not follow ... (There follows here the reason as in **33.16**). But if the major is taken in the composite sense, or an equivalent (proposition), and the minor in the divided sense, the conclusion follows in the composite sense and not in the divided. The first is evident, because it follows validly: 'This is necessary: every divine person is God, one creating is necessarily a divine person, therefore one creating is necessarily God'. But this does not follow: 'therefore this is necessary: one creating is God'.

But if the major is taken in the divided sense, or an equivalent (proposition), and the minor in the composite sense, the conclusion follows in the divided sense and in the composite sense. And the reason is that it is impossible that something (B) essentially (*per se*) or accidentally inferior (to A) should be necessarily predicated of something (C), so that the proposition ('C is B') would be necessary, without the proposition in which the superior (A) of that inferior (B) is predicated of the same (C) (viz. 'C is A') also being necessary.

So for every Aristotelian formula Ockham has the four: (1) with both premisses in the composite sense, like Theophrastus (cf. **17.15 f.**); (2) with both premisses in the divided sense, like Aristotle – as was concluded from the indications available (§ 15, B); (3) the major premiss composite, the minor divided; (4) the major premiss divided, the minor composite.

Another example is the following treatment of syllogisms with both premisses in the mode of simple (one–sided) possibility:

33.21 ... I here understand 'possible' in the sense of the possibility which is common to all propositions that are not impossible. And it is to be known that in every figure, if all the propositions be taken as possible in the compounded sense, or if equivalent ones to those be taken, the syllogism is invalid because inference would proceed by this rule: the premisses are possible, therefore the conclusion is possible, which rule is false. Hence it does not follow: 'that everything coloured is white is possible, that everything black is coloured is possible, therefore that everything black is white is possible'. .... And so the rule is false: the premisses are possible therefore the conclusion is possible. But this rule is true: if the premisses are possible and compossible, the conclusion is possible (cf. **31.27**) . . . But if the possible proposition be taken in the divided sense, or an equivalent one be taken, such as are propositions like 'every man can be white', 'a white thing can be black' etc. . . . there the subject can stand for things which are or for things which can be, i.e. for things of which it is verified by a verb in the present, or for things of which it is verified by a verb of possibility. . . . As if I say: 'every white thing can be a man', one sense is this: everything which is white can be a man, and this sense is true if there be nothing white but man. Another sense is this: everything which can be white can be a man, and this is false whether only man be white or something other than man. . . .

And it is to be known that if the subject of the major be taken for things which can be . . . however the subject of the minor be taken, the uniform syllogism is always valid and is regulated by *dici de omni* or *de nullo*, and the common principles of the assertoric syllogism hold. E.g. if one argues thus: 'every white thing can be a man – i.e. everything that can be white can be a man – every ass can be white, therefore every ass can be a man'. . . .

But if the subject of the major supposes for things which are, then such a uniform (syllogism) is not valid, for it does not follow: 'everything which is white can be a man, every ass can be white, therefore every ass can be a man'. For if there be nothing white but man, the premisses are true and the conclusion false. . . .

These examples may suffice to give an idea of the problems discussed.

We now give a summary of the different kinds of modal syllogism which Ockham considered. He distinguishes the following functors and kinds of functor: (1) 'necessary', (2) 'possible' (one-sidedly), (3) 'contingent' (two-sidedly, (4) 'impossible', (5) other modes (subjective). Further there are (6) the assertoric propositions. Ockham deals with syllogisms with premisses in the following combinations:

1–1	6–1			
2–2	6–2	1–2		
3–3	6–3	1–3	2–3	
4–4	6–4	1–4	2–4	
5–5	6–5	1–5	2–5	3–5

Altogether then he has eighteen classes. In each he discusses the four formulae mentioned above, and this in each of three figures – the analogates therefore of the nineteen classical moods. Theoretically this gives 1368 formulae, but many of them are invalid.

Here, however, as with Aristotle (§ 15, D), there are also many moods without analogues in the assertoric syllogistic, so that the total number of valid modal syllogisms for Ockham, in spite of the many invalid analogues, may reach about a thousand.

D. LOGIC OF PROPOSITIONS IN FUTURE AND PAST TENSES

The Scholastics did not look on propositions about the future and the past as modal, but they treated them quite analogously to modals. Two texts from Ockham illustrate this point:

33.22 Concerning the conversion of propositions about the past and the future, the first thing to be known is that every proposition about the past and the future, in which a common term is subject, is to be distinguished . . . in that the subject can suppose for what is or for what has been, if it is a proposition about the past . . . e.g. 'the white thing was Socrates' is to be distinguished, since 'white' can suppose for what is white or for what was white. But if the proposition is about the future, it is to be distinguished because the subject can suppose for what is or for what will be. . . . Secondly it is to be known that when the subject of such a proposition supposes for what is, then the proposition should be converted into a proposition about the present, the subject being taken with the verb 'was' and the pronoun 'which', and not into a proposition about the past. Hence this consequence is not valid: 'no white thing was a man, therefore no man was white', if the subject of the antecedent be taken for what is. For let it be supposed that many men both living and dead have been white, and that many other things are and have been white, and that no man is now white, then the antecedent is true and the consequent false. . . . And so it should not be converted as aforesaid but thus: 'no white thing was a man, therefore nothing which was a man was white'.

Then an example from syllogistic:

33.23 Now we must see how syllogisms are to be made from propositions about the past and the future. Here it is to be known that when the middle term is a common term, if the subject of the major supposes for things which are, the minor should be about the present and not the future or the past; for if the minor proposition was about the past and not the present such a syllogism would not be governed by *dici de omni* or *de nullo*, because in a universal major about the past with subject supposing for things which are, it is not denoted that the predicate is affirmed or denied by the verb in the past about whatever the subject is affirmed of by the verb in the past. But it is denoted that the predicate is affirmed or denied by the verb in the past about whatever the subject is affirmed of by a verb in the present. . . . But if the subject of the major supposes for things which have been, then one should not adjoin a minor about the present, because as is quite evident, the inference does not proceed by *dici de omni* or *de nullo;* but a minor about the past should be taken, and it makes no difference whether the subject of the minor supposes for things which are or things which have been. Hence this syllogism is invalid: 'every white thing was a man, an ass is white, therefore an ass was a man'. . . . What has been said about propositions concerning the past, is to be maintained proportionately for those about the future.

These principles are then applied to the syllogisms in the different figures.

§ 34. OTHER FORMULAE

In view of what we know about e.g. the composite and divided senses (**29.13**), and of our occasional discoveries of similar doctrines (**28.15** ff.), we must suppose that the Scholastics developed a number of logical theories not pertaining either to propositional logic or to syllogistic in the Aristotelian sense. But this field is hardly at all explored; e.g. we do not know whether they were acquainted with a more comprehensive logic of relations than that of Aristotle.

We cite a few texts belonging to such theories, viz. (1) a series of texts about non-Aristotelian 'syllogisms' with singular terms, (2) an analysis of the quantifiers 'ever' and 'some', (3) a 'logical square' of so-called 'exponible' propositions, i.e. of propositions equivalent to the product or sum of a number of categoricals. In that connection we finally give some theorems about the so-called *syllogismus obliquus*, which was not without importance for the later history of logic.

Here it must be stressed even more than usual, that these are only fragments concerning a wide range of problems that has not been investigated.

A. SYLLOGISMS WITH SINGULAR TERMS

A first widening of the Aristotelian syllogistic consists in the admission of singular terms and premisses.* Ockham already knows of the substitution that was to become classic:

34.01 Every man is an animal;
Socrates is a man;
Therefore, Socrates is an animal.

Here the minor premiss is singular. But Ockham also allows singular propositions as major premisses:

34.02 For it follows validly (*bene*): 'Socrates is white, every man is Socrates, therefore every man is white'. . . . And such a syllogism . . . is valid, like that which is regulated by *dici de omni* or *de nullo*, since just as the subject of a universal proposition actually stands for all its significates, so too the singular subject stands for all its significates, since it only has one.

The difference between a syllogism as instanced in **34.01** and the classical Aristotelian syllogism is only 'purely verbal' (**34.03**)!

This may well be termed a revolutionary innovation. Not only are singular terms admitted, contrary to the practice of Aristotle, but they are formally equated with universal ones. The ground advanced for this remarkable position is that singular terms are names of *classes*, just like universal terms, only in this case unit-classes. Therefore **34.02** is not propounding the syllogism as a substitution in the rule:

34.021 If 'for all x: if x is an S then x is a P' holds, and 'a is an S' holds, then it also holds: 'a is a P'.
– where 'S' and 'P' are to be thought of as class-names, 'a' as an individual name –, but as a substitution in:

34.022 If 'for all x: if x is an M then x is a P' holds, and 'for all x: if x is an S then x is an M' holds, then it holds: 'for all x: if x is an S then x is a P'

– where 'M', 'S' and 'P' are all class-names. In that case the *sole* difference between the Aristotelian and Ockhamist syllogisms is that the former is a proposition, the latter a rule. Admittedly the basis of the system is altered with the introduction of names for unit-classes.

Again, the syllogisms with singular terms that are usually attributed to Peter Ramus, are already to be found in Ockham.

34.02 contains one example; here is another:

* But **34.01** is Stoic. Vid. Sextus Empiricus, *Pyrr. Hyp.* B 164 ff.

34.04 Although it has been said above that one cannot argue from affirmatives in the second figure, yet two cases are to be excepted from that general rule. The first is, if the middle term is a discrete term, for then one can infer a conclusion from two affirmatives, e.g. it follows validly: 'every man is Socrates, Plato is Socrates, therefore Plato is a man'. And such a syllogism can be proved, because if the propositions are converted there will result an expository syllogism in the third figure.

The proof offered at the end of that text is evidently connected with the Aristotelian ecthesis (**13.13**), as is suggested by the scholastic term 'expository syllogism' and the following text from Ockham:

34.05 Besides the aforesaid syllogisms, there are also expository syllogisms, about which we must now speak. Where it is to be known that an expository syllogism is one which is constituted by two singular premisses arranged in the third figure, which, however, can yield both a singular, and a particular or indefinite conclusion, but not a universal one, just as two universals in the third figure cannot yield a universal. . . . To which it must be added that the minor must be affirmative, because if the minor is negative the syllogism is not valid. . . . If the minor is affirmative, whether the major is affirmative or negative, the syllogism is always valid.

Stephen de Monte summarizes this doctrine in systematic fashion:

34.06 But it is asked whether we can rightly syllogize by means of an expository syllogism in every figure; I say that we can. For affirmatives hold in virtue of this principle: when two different terms are united with some singular term taken singularly and univocally, in some affirmative copulative proposition from which the consequence holds to two universal affirmatives (*de omni*), such terms should be mutually united in the conclusion. . . . But negatives hold in virtue of this principle: whenever one of two terms is united with a singular term etc., truly and affirmatively, and the other negatively, such terms should be mutually united negatively, respect being had to the logical properties. . . .

Seven syllogisms arise in this way, two in each of the first and third figures, three in the second.

B. ANALYSIS OF 'EVERY' AND 'SOME'

34.07 We proceed to the signs which render (propositions) universal or particular. . . . Of such signs, one is the universal, the other is the particular. The universal sign is that by which it is signified that the universal term to which it is adjoined stands copulatively for its suppositum (*per modum copulationis*). . . . The particular sign is that by which it is signified that a universal term stands disjunctively for all its supposita. And I purposely say 'copulatively' when speaking of the universal sign, since if one says: 'every man runs 'it follows formally: 'therefore this man runs, and that man runs, etc.' But of the particular sign I have said that it signifies that a universal term to which it is adjoined stands disjunctively for all its supposita. That is evident since if one says: 'some man runs' it follows that Socrates or Plato runs, or Cicero runs, and so of each (*de singulis*). This would not be so if this term did not stand for all these (supposita); but it is true that this is disjunctive. Hence it is requisite and necessary for the truth of this: 'some man runs', that it be true of some (definite) man to say that he runs, i.e. that one of the singular (propositions) is true which is a part of the disjunctive (proposition): 'Socrates (runs) or Plato runs, and so of each', since it is sufficient for the truth of a disjunctive that one of its parts be true (cf. **31.10** and **31.223**).

This is the quite 'modern' analysis of quantified propositions (**44.03**) in the following equivalences:

34.071 (For all x: x is F) if and only if: (a is F) and (b is F) and (c is F) etc.

34.072 (There is an x such that x is F) if and only if: (a is F) or (b is F) or (c is F) etc.

Further remarkable is the express appeal to a propositional rule. In this text propositional logic is consciously made the basis of term-logic, and this is only one of many examples.

C. EXPONIBLE PROPOSITIONS

The so-called'exponible' propositions were scholastically discussed in considerable detail. They are those which are equivalent to a product or sum of a number of categoricals. There are three kinds, the exclusive, the exceptive, and the reduplicative. In view of the metalogical treatment we give the 'logical squares' of Tarteret for the first two kinds, with a substitution, also from him, and the mnemonic expressions:

34.08 *DIVES*   *ORAT*

'Only man is an animal' is thus expounded: CONTRARY   (1) man is an animal *and* (2) nothing which is not man is an animal.

'Only man is not an animal': (1) man is not an animal *and* (2) everything that is not man is an animal.

SUBALTERN   CONTRA-DICTORY   CONTRADICTORY   SUBALTERN

'Not only man is not an animal':   SUB-CONTRARY   (1) every man is an animal *or* (2) something which is not a man is not an animal

'Not only man is an animal': (1) man is not an animal *or* (2) something which is not man is an animal.

ANNO   *HELI*

34.09 *AMATE*   *PECCATA*

'Every man besides Socrates runs':

(1) every man who is not Socrates   CONTRARY runs *and* (2) Socrates is a man *and* (3) Socrates does not run.

'Every man besides Socrates does not run': (1) every man who is not Socrates does not run *and* (2) Socrates is a man and (3) Socrates runs.

235

'Not every man   SUB-   'Not every man
besides Socrates CONTRARY besides Socrates
does not run':   runs': (1) some
(1) some man who   man who is not
is not Socrates   Socrates does not
runs, *or* (2) Socra-   run *or* (2) Socrates
tes is not a man *or*   is not a man *or*
(3) Socrates does   Socrates runs.
not run.

IDOLES   *COMMODI*

The originality of the formal laws by substitution in which the consequences shown in these squares are gained, consists in their being a combination of the theory of consequences (especially the so-called 'de Morgan' laws, cf. **31.35**f.) with the Aristotelian doctrine of opposition (logical square: **12.09**f.). They are all valid, and one can only marvel at the acumen of those logicians who knew how to deduce them without the aid of a formalized theory. How complicated are the processes of thought underlying the given schemata can be shown by one of the simplest examples, in which *ANNO* follows from *DIVES*. *DIVES* must be interpreted thus:

(1) Some M is L, and: no not-M is L. From that there follows by the rule **31.222**:

(2) no not-M is L,

and from that in turn, by the law of subalternation (**24.29**, cf. **32.44**):

(3) some not-M is not L.

Applying the rule **31.10** (cf. **31.223**) one obtains:

(4) every M is L or some not-M is not L which was to be proved.

D. OBLIQUE SYLLOGISMS

The Aristotelian moods with 'indirect' premisses (**16.24**ff.) were also systematically elaborated and developed by the Scholastics. Ockham (**34.10**) already knew more than a dozen formulae of this kind. But so far as we know, no essentially new range of problems was opened up. We cite some substitutions in such moods from Ockham; their discovery has been quite groundlessly attributed to Jungius.

34.11 It also follows validly: 'every man is an animal, Socrates sees a man, therefore Socrates sees an animal'.

34.12 It follows validly: 'every man is an animal, an ass sees a man, therefore an ass sees an animal'.

34.13 It follows: 'no ass belongs to man, every ass is an animal, therefore some animal does not belong to man'.

§ 35. ANTINOMIES

A. DEVELOPMENT

Concerning also the search for solutions of antinomies in the Middle Ages insufficient knowledge is available for us to be able to survey the whole development here, though J. Salamucha devoted a serious paper to it (**35.01**). The connected problems seem to have been well known in the middle of the 13th century, but without their importance being realized. Albert the Great merely repeats the Aristotelian solution of the Liar (**35.02**), and again Giles of Rome (in the second half of the 13th century) only treats this antinomy briefly and quite in the Aristotelian way (**35.03**). Peter of Spain, whose *Summulae* treat of all the problems then considered important, considers the fallacy of what is 'simply and in a certain respect' (under which heading Aristotle deals with the Liar, cf. **23.18**) (**35.04**), but says nothing about antinomies.

However, two points are worth noting about Albert the Great; he is the first that we find using the expression 'insoluble' (*insolubile*) which later became a technical term in this matter, and then he has some formulations that are new, at least in detail. This can be seen in a passage from his *Elenchics*:

35.05 I call 'insoluble' those (propositions) which are so formed that whichever side of the contradictory is granted, the opposite follows. . . e.g. someone swears that he swears falsely; he swears either what is true, or not. If he swears that he swears falsely, and swears what is true, viz. that he swears falsely, nobody swears falsely in swearing what is true: therefore he does not swear falsely, but it was granted that he does swear falsely. But if he does not swear falsely and swears that he swears falsely, he does not swear what is true; therefore he swears falsely: because otherwise he would not swear what is true when he swears that he swears falsely.

By the time of Pseudo-Scotus the subject has become a burning one; he cites at least one solution that diverges from his own (**35.06**) and treats the question in two chapters of which the first bears the title 'Whether a universal term can stand for the whole proposition of which it is a part' (**35.07**). The answer is a decisive negative:

35.08 It is to be said that a part as part cannot stand for the whole proposition.

His solution, however, does not consist in an application of this principle, but is found in the distinction between the signified and the exercised act:

35.09 If it is said: 'I say what is false, therefore it is true that I say what is false', I answer that the consequence does not hold formally, as (also) it does not follow: 'man is an animal, therefore it is true to say that man is an animal', although the consequent is contained in the antecedent in the exercised act. Granted further that it follows, though not formally, I say that this other does not follow: 'I say that I say what is false, therefore in what I say I am simply truthful', or only in a certain respect and not simply. . . . Similarly it follows in some cases: 'What I say is true, therefore I am simply truthful', as (e.g.) here: 'It is true that I say that man is an animal, therefore I am simply truthful', viz. in those cases in which there is truth both in the act signified and the act exercised. But in our case (*in proposito*) there is falsity in the act signified and truth in the act exercised. It follows then: 'It is true that I exercise the act of speaking about what is false; therefore that about which I exercise it is false'.

A comparison of this text with **27.13** shows that we have here almost exactly the modern distinction between *use* and *mention*. But Pseudo–Scotus, employing the same terminology, teaches just the opposite to Burleigh.

These two examples are enough to show the state of affairs in the 13th century. When we come to Ockham the antinomies are no longer dealt with in sophistics, but in a special chapter *About Insolubles* (**35.10**). After that such a treatise becomes an essential part of scholastic logic. We pass over the further stages of development, which are mostly not known, and show how far the matter had got by the time of Paul of Venice at the end of the Middle Ages.

B. FORMULATION

1. The Liar

35.11 I compose the much-disputed insoluble by positing (1) that Socrates utters this proposition: 'Socrates says what is false', and this proposition is A, and (2) (that he) utters no other (proposition besides A), (where the proposition A) (3) signifies so exactly and adequately that it must not be varied in the present reply. That posited, I submit A and ask whether it is true or false. If it is said that it is true, contrariwise: it is consistent with the whole case that there is no other Socrates but this Socrates, and that posited, it follows that A is false. But if it is said that A is false, contrariwise: it is consistent with the whole case that there are two Socrateses of which the first says A, and the second that there is no God: if that is taken with the statement of the case, it follows that A is true.

35.12 I suppose therefore that Socrates, who is every Socrates, utters this and no other proposition: 'Socrates says what is false', which exactly and adequately signifies (what it says); let it be A. Which being supposed, it follows from what has been said that A is false; and Socrates says A, therefore Socrates says what is false. This consequence is valid, and the antecedent is true, therefore also the consequent; but the antecedent is A, therefore A is true.

Secondly it is argued: What is false is said by Socrates, therefore Socrates says what is false. The consequence holds from the passive to its active. But the antecedent is true, therefore also the consequent, and the antecedent is A, therefore A is true. Since, however, the antecedent is true, it is evident that its adequate significate is true. But it is a contradiction that it should be true.

Thirdly it is argued: the contradictory opposite of A is false, therefore A is true. The consequence holds and the antecedent is proved: for this: 'no Socrates says what is false' is false, and this is the contradictory opposite of A; therefore the contradictory opposite of A is false. The consequence and the minor premiss hold, and I prove the major: Since, A is false; but a certain Socrates says A; therefore a certain Socrates says what is false. Or thus: No Socrates says what is false; therefore no Socrates says the false A. The consequence holds from the negative distributed superordinate to its subordinate. The consequent is false, therefore also the antecedent.

2. *Other antinomies*

Besides this 'famous' insoluble there is a long series of similar antinomies that derive from it, of which we give some examples from Paul of Venice, omitting the always recurring words 'Socrates who is all Socrates' and 'which signify exactly as the terms suggest (*pretendunt*)':

35.13 Socrates . . . believes this: 'Socrates is deceived' . . . and no other (proposition).

35.14 Socrates believes this and no other: 'Plato is decciv-ed' . . . but Plato . . . believes this: 'Socrates is not deceived'.

35.15 Socrates . . . says this and nothing else: 'Socrates lies'.

35.16 'Socrates is sick'; 'Plato answers falsely (*male*)'; 'Socrates will have no penny'; ('Socrates will not cross the bridge');* where it is supposed that every sick man, and only one such, says what is false, and that every well man, and only one such, says what is true (and correspondingly for the three other cases). . . . On these suppositions I assert that Socrates . . . utters only the following: 'Socrates is sick' etc.

Those are the so-called 'singular insolubles'. There follow on them the 'quantified' ones:

35.17 I posit the case that this proposition 'it is false' is every proposition.

35.18 Let this be the case, that there are only two propositions, A and B, A false, and B this: 'A is all that is true'.

35.19 I posit that A, B and C are all the propositions, where A and B are true, and C is this: 'every proposition is unlike this' indicating A and B.

35.20 I posit that A and B are all the propositions, where A is this: 'the chimera exists' . . . and B this: 'every proposition is false'.

35.21 Let A, B and C be all the propositions . . . where A is this: 'God exists', B this: 'man is an ass', C** this: 'there are as many true as false propositions'.

35.22 The answer to be given would be similar on the supposition that there were only five propositions . . . of which two were true, two false, and the fifth was: 'there are more false than true (propositions)'.

* Inserted according to the words just following.
** The text has D.

Then some 'exponible' insolubles:

35.23 I posit that 'this is the only exclusive proposition' is the only exclusive (proposition). . . .

35.24 Let this be a fallacy about exceptives: 'no proposition besides A is false', supposing that this is A, and that it is every proposition.

35.25 I posit that A, B, and C are all the propositions . . . that A and B are true, and that C is this exclusive: 'every proposition besides the exclusive is true'.

35.26 The answer is similar . . . on the supposition that every man besides Socrates says: 'God exists', and that Socrates says only this: 'every man besides me says what is true'.

These are only a few examples from the rich store of late scholastic sophistic.

C. SOLUTIONS

1. The first twelve solutions

35.27 The first opinion states that the insoluble is to be solved by reference to the fallacy of the form of speech (**11.19**). . . . And if it is argued: 'Socrates utters this falsehood, therefore Socrates says what is false', one denies the consequence and says: 'This is the fallacy of the form of speech, because by reason of the (reference of the) speech the term 'false' supposes for 'Socrates etc.' in the antecedent, but for something else in the consequent. . . .

35.28 The second opinion solves the insolubles by the fallacy of false cause (**11.24**) . . . since the antecedent seems to be the cause of the consequent but is not. . . .

35.29 The third opinion says that when Socrates says 'Socrates says what is false', the word 'says', although in the present tense, ought to be understood for the time of the instant immediately preceding the time of utterance. Therefore it denies it (the proposition), saying that it is false. And then to the argument: 'this is false and Socrates says it, therefore Socrates says a false (proposition)', they say that the verb 'says' is verified for different times in the antecedent and consequent. . . .

35.30 The fourth opinion states that nobody can say that he says what is false or understand that he understands what is false, nor can there be any proposition on which an insoluble can be based. This opinion is repugnant to sense and thought.

For everybody knows that a man can open his mouth and form these utterances: 'I say what is false' or sit down and read similar ones. . . .

35.31 The fifth opinion states that when Socrates says that he himself says what is false, he says nothing. . . . This opinion is likewise false because in so saying, Socrates says letters, syllables, dictions and orations as I have elsewhere shown. Further Socrates is heard to speak, therefore he says something. Again they would have to say that if this, and no other, proposition was written: 'it is false', that nothing would be written, which is evidently impossible.

The fifth opinion counts the insoluble as deprived of sense.

35.32 The sixth opinion states that the insoluble is neither true nor false but something intermediate, indifferent to each. They are wrong too, because every proposition is true or false, and every insoluble is a proposition, therefore every insoluble is true or false. . . .

That is an effort to solve the antinomy in a three-valued logic.

35.33 The seventh opinion states that the insoluble is to be solved by reference to the fallacy of equivocation. For when it is said: 'Socrates says what is false' they distinguish about the 'saying' according to an equivocation: for it can signify saying that is exercised or that is thought (*conceptum*). And by 'saying that is exercised' is meant that which is in course of accomplishment; it expresses the judgment and is not completely a dictum. But by 'saying that is thought' is meant (what happens) when a man has said something or spoken in some way and immediately after he says that he says that, or speaks in that way. E.g. supposes that Socrates says 'God exists' and immediately after: 'Socrates says what is true'. This opinion says that when Socrates begins to say 'Socrates says what is false', if 'saying' be taken for exercised saying, it is true; but if for saying in thought, it is false. And if it is argued: 'nothing false is said by Socrates; and this is said by Socrates; therefore it is not false' – they say that the major is verified for saying in thought, and the minor for exercised saying, and so (the argument) does not conclude. But this solution is no use, for let it be supposed that the speech is made with exercised saying, and the usual deduction will go through. . . .

This solution corresponds with that of Pseudo-Scotus above (**35.09**).

35.34 The eighth opinion states that no insoluble is true or false because nothing such is a proposition. For although every or any insoluble be an indicative statement signifying according as its signification is or is not, yet this is not sufficient for it to be called a 'proposition'. Against this opinion it is argued that it follows from it that there are some two enunciations of which the adequate significate is one and the same, yet one is a proposition, the other not, as is clear when one supposes these: 'this is false' and 'this is false', indicating in both cases the second of them. . . .

This is again a quite 'modern' conception. Paul of Venice, and, it would seem, the majority of late Scholastics, did not like it.

35.35 The ninth opinion states that the insoluble is true or false, but not true and not false. . . .

Here the alternative '*A* is true or false' seems to be admitted, but '*A* is true' and '*A* is false' to be both rejected.

35.36 The tenth opinion solves the insoluble by reference to the fallacy of in a certain respect and simply (**11.24**), saying that an insoluble is a difficult paradox (*paralogismus*) arising from (a confusion between what is) in a certain respect and simply, due to the reflection of some act upon itself with a privative or negative qualification. So in solving, it says that this consequence is not valid: 'this false thing is said by Socrates, therefore a false thing is said by Socrates', supposing that Socrates says the consequent and not something else which is not part of it – because the argument proceeds from a certain respect to what is simply so; for the antecedent only signifies categorically, but the consequent hypothetically, since it signifies that it is true and that it is false. . . .

35.37 The eleventh opinion, favouring the opinion just expounded, states that every insoluble proposition signifies that it is true and that it is false, when understood as referring to its adequate significate. For, as is said, every categorical proposition signifies that that for which the subject and predicate suppose is or is not the same thing, and the being or not being the same thing is for the proposition, affirmative or negative, to be true; therefore every categorical proposition, whether affirmative or negative, signifies that itself is true, and every insoluble proposition falsifies itself; therefore every insoluble proposition signifies that it is true or that it is false. . . .

The last two opinions consider the insoluble to be equivalent to a copulative proposition. Why it should be so we shall see below (35.44).

35.38 The twelfth opinion, commonly held by all today, is that an insoluble proposition is a proposition which is supposed to be mentioned, and which, when it signifies precisely according to the circumstances supposed, yields the result that it is true and that it is false. E.g. if a case be posited about an insoluble, and it is not posited how that insoluble should signify, it is to be answered as though outside time: e.g. if it be supposed that Socrates says: 'Socrates says what is false' without further determination, the proposition advanced: 'Socrates says what is false' is to be doubted. But if it be supposed that the insoluble signifies as the terms suggest, the supposition is admitted and the insoluble is granted, and one says that it is false. And if it be said: 'this is false: "Socrates says what is false", therefore it signifies as it is not, but signifies that Socrates says what is false, therefore etc.' – the consequence is denied. But in the minor it should be added that it signifies precisely so, and if that is posited, every such supposition is denied. . . .

The 'time of obligation' here referred to is a technical term of scholastic discussion (*tractatus de obligationibus*: cf. § 26, D), on which very little research has so far been done. It means the time during which the disputant is bound to some (usually arbitrary) supposition.

2. *The thirteenth solution*

35.39 The thirteenth opinion states a number of conjuncts, some in the form of theses (*conclusionum*), others in the form of suppositions, others in the form of propositions or corollaries; but all these can be briefly stated in the form of theses and corollaries.

35.40 The first thesis is this: no created thing can distinctly represent itself formally, though it can do so objectively. This is clear, since no created thing can be the proper and distinct formal cognition of itself; for if something was to be so, anything would be so, since there would be no more reason in one case than in another. E.g. we say that the king's image signifies the king not formally but objectively, while the mental concept which we have of the king signifies the king not objectively but formally, because it is the formal cognition of the king. But if it be said that it represents itself distinctly, this will be objectively, by another concept *(notitia)* and not formally, by itself.

35.41 Second thesis: no mental proposition properly so-called can signify that itself is true or that itself is false. Proof: because otherwise it would follow that some proper and distinct cognition would be a formal cognition of itself, which is against the first thesis.

From this thesis it follows that the understanding cannot form a universal mental proposition properly so-called which signifies that every mental proposition is false, such as this mental (proposition): 'every mental proposition is false', understanding the subject to suppose for itself; nor can it form any mental proposition properly so-called which signifies that any other is false which in turn signifies that the one indicated by the first is false; nor any mental proposition properly so-called which signifies that its contradictory is true, as this one: 'this is true' indicating its contradictory. . . .

The last two texts contain a notably acute formulation of the veto on *circulus vitiosus* (**48.21**), and so of the most important modern idea about the solution of the antinomies.

35.42 The third thesis is this: a part of a mental proposition properly so-called cannot suppose for that same proposition of which it is a part, nor for the contradictory of that proposition; nor can a part of a proposition that signifies in an arbitrary way suppose for the corresponding mental proposition properly so-called. From which it follows that if this mental proposition is formed, and no other: 'every mental proposition is universal', it would be false.

35.43 Fourth thesis: there might be a vocal or written or mental proposition improperly so-called which had reflection on itself, because all such signify in an arbitrary way and not naturally, objectively but not formally. But a mental proposition properly so-called is a sign that represents naturally and formally, and it is not in our power that such a sign should signify whatever we want, as it is in the case of a vocal, written or mental sign improperly so-called.

From this thesis it follows that every insoluble proposition is a vocal, written or mental proposition improperly so-called; and a part of any such can suppose for the whole of which it is a part.

35.44 The fifth thesis is this: to every insoluble proposition there corresponds a true mental proposition properly so-called, and another one properly so-called, false. This is evident in the following: 'this is false' indicating itself, which corresponds to one such mental proposition, 'this is false', which is true. And the second part is proved. For this vocal proposition is false, therefore it signifies that a mental one is false, but not the one expressed, therefore another one which is true, viz. 'this is false', indicating the first mental one which indicates a vocal or written one.

35.45 From this thesis there follow some corollaries. First, that any insoluble proposition, and its contradictory too, is a manifold proposition (*propositio plures*) because there correspond to it a number of distinct (*inconiunctae*) mental propositions.

Second, there are some propositions, vocally quite similar and with terms supposing for the same things, one of which is a manifold proposition, but not the other. This is clear in the following: 'this is false' and 'this is false' where each 'this' indicates the second proposition.

Third corollary, every insoluble proposition is simultaneously true and false, and its contradictory likewise, because two mental propositions of which one is true and the other false contradict one another, though neither is simply true or simply false, but in a certain respect. . . .

3. The fourteenth solution

35.46 The fourteenth opinion, which is the basis of many of the preceding ones and so of those disputants who try rather to evade (the difficulties) than to answer, states that the insolubles are to be solved by means of the fallacy of the accident, according to which paradoxes (*paralogismi*) arise in two ways, by variation of the middle term or of one of the extremes. By variation of the middle, as when the middle supposes for something different in the major to what it supposes for in the minor, and conversely. And similarly when an extreme is varied. This opinion therefore says that when Socrates says 'Socrates says what is false', he says what is false. And then in reply to the argument: 'Socrates says this, and this is false, therefore Socrates says what is false' they deny the consequence, saying that here is a fallacy of the accident due to variation in an extreme; for the term 'false' supposes for something in the minor for which it does not suppose in the conclusion. Similarly if it is argued from the opposite saying of Socrates: 'nothing false is said by Socrates; this is false; therefore this is not said by Socrates', this is a fallacy of the accident due to variation of the middle; for the term 'false' supposes for something in the major for which it does not suppose in the minor.

To show that, they presuppose that in no proposition does a part suppose for the whole of which it is a part, nor is it convertible with the whole, nor antecedent to the whole. From which it is clear that the proposition 'Socrates says what is false, signifies that Socrates says what is false, not, however, the false thing that he says, but some false thing distinct from that; but because he only says that proposition, therefore it is false. . . .

This opinion has been met with already in Pseudo-Scotus (**35.06**) and is adopted by others too.

4. Preliminaries to the solution of Paul of Venice

After expounding fourteen opinions none of which are acceptable to him, Paul of Venice gives his own solution, and takes occasion to collect the current late-scholastic teachings relevant to the antinomies. We reproduce the essentials.

35.47 To explain the fifteenth opinion, which I know to be that of good (logicians) of old times, three chapters (*articuli*) are adduced. The first contains an explanation of terms, the second introductory suppositions, the third our purpose in the form of theses.

35.48 As to the first, this is the first division: every insoluble arises either from our activity or from a property of the expression (*vocis*). Our acts are twofold, some interior, others exterior. Interior are such as imagining, thinking etc.; exterior are bodily ones such as saying, speaking etc. Insolubles arising from our activity are: 'Socrates says what is false', 'Socrates understands what is false' etc. Properties of the expression are such as being subject, having appellation, being true or false, being able to be true, not being true of something other than itself, and so simply (*de se*) false, and not being false of itself or of something else. And so there arise from properties of the expression insolubles like these: 'it is false', 'nothing is true', 'the proposition is not verified of itself'. . . .

35.49 The second division is this: some propositions have reflection on themselves, some do not. A proposition having reflection on itself is one whose signification reflects on itself, e.g. 'it is every complex thing', or 'this is false', indicating itself. A proposition without reflection on itself is one whose significate is not referred to itself, e.g. 'God exists' and 'man is an ass'.

35.50 The third division is this: of propositions having reflection on themselves some have this reflection immediately, others have it mediately. . . .

35.51 The fourth division: of propositions having reflections on themselves, some have the property that their significations terminate solely at themselves, e.g. 'this is true', 'this is false', indicating themselves. But others have the property that their significations terminate both at themselves and at other things, e.g. 'every proposition is true', 'every proposition is false'. For they do not only signify that they alone are true or false, but that other propositions distinct from them are so too. . . .

35.52 It follows that no proposition has reflection on itself unless it contains a term that is appropriated to signify the proposition, such as are the terms 'true', 'false', 'universal', 'particular', 'affirmative', 'negative', 'to be granted', 'to be denied', 'to be doubted' and so on. But not every proposition containing such a term has to have reflection on itself, as is clear in these cases: 'it is false', when this is true, and again 'this is true' indicating 'God exists'; for such does not have reflection on itself, but its signification is directed solely to what is indicated etc. . . .

There again is the 'modern' notion of the vicious circle (**48.21**). Here are a few more preliminaries:

35.53 The first introductory supposition is this: that that proposition is true whose adequate significate is true, and if its being true contains no contradiction. . . .

35.54 Second supposition: that proposition is said to be false which falsifies itself or whose falsity arises not from the terms but from its false adequate significate. From which it follows that there is a false proposition with a true adequate significate, as is clear in the following: 'that is false', indicating itself. That it is false is evident, since it states that it is false, therefore it is false; and so its adequate significate is true, since it is true that it (the proposition) is false. It follows that every proposition which falsifies itself is false, and that not every proposition which verifies itself is true; since this: 'every proposition is true' verifies itself but is not true, as is evident.

35.55 The third supposition is this: two propositions are equivalent (*invicem convertuntur*) if their adequate significates are identical. For let A and B be two such propositions having the same adequate significate, and I argue thus: A and B have all extremes the same, vocally and in writing, and in thought, and similar copulas, and there is no indication belonging to one which does not belong to the other; then they are equivalent.

There follow some further preliminary suppositions taken from the generally received teaching about supposition and consequence. Finally this:

35.56 The last supposition is this: a part of a proposition can stand for the whole of which it is a part, as also for everything which belongs to it, without restriction, whether in thought or in writing or in speech.

Thereby is rejected the thirteenth opinion (**35.39** ff.), and with it the modern principle according to which an insoluble is not a proposition since it contains a part standing for the whole (**48.12** f.). This principle seems to be presupposed in various ways by the fourth (**35.30**), fifth (**35.31**), eighth (**35.34**), tenth (**35.36**), and eleventh (**35.37**) opinions.

The rejection of the thirteenth opinion means that the current modern distinction of language and meta-language was not adopted by Paul of Venice for his own solution. But it is explicitly accepted in the fifth thesis of the thirteenth opinion (**35.44**), more or less so in some of the other opinions.

5. *The solution of Paul of Venice*

Paul's own solution is very like that of the eleventh (**35.37**) and twelfth (**35.38**) opinions, and so we do not reproduce his long and difficult text. It consists essentially in a sharp distinction between the ordinary and 'exact and adequate' meaning of the insoluble proposition, where 'exact and adequate' connotes:

    (1) the semantic correlate, that to which it refers;

    (2) that the proposition itself is true.

This was said already in **35.57**, though without the use of 'exact and adequate', and with a universality that Paul does not approve. We repeat the main ideas, as they underlie his own solution. Some simplification will be effected, and formalization used. The first thing is to set out the antinomy, for which four extralogical axioms are employed:

(1) A signifies: A is false.

(2) If A signifies p, then A is true if and only if p.

(3) If A signifies p, then A is false if and only if not-p.

(4) A is false if and only if A is not true. (1) is the 'insoluble' proposition itself, (2)–(4) are various formulations of the Aristotelian definitions of truth and falsity (**10.35**). Substituting 'A is false' for 'p' in (2), we get by (1):

(5) A is true if and only if A is false, which with (4) gives:

(6) A is true if and only if A is not true, which in turn yields:

(7) A is not true,

and so by (4):

(8) A is false.

But if we put 'A is false' for 'p' in (3), we get:

(9) A is false if and only if A is not false, which immediately yields:

(10) A is not false,

in contradiction to (8). Here then is a genuine antinomy.

But the antinomy does not emerge if we operate with the 'exact and adequate' meaning instead of the simple one. (1) and (4) remain, but the other two axioms take on these forms:

(2') If A signifies p, then A is true if and only if [(1) A is true, and (2) p].

(3') If A signifies p, then A is false if and only if not [(1) A is true, and (2) p], since as has been said, a proposition has 'exact and adequate' signification when it signifies that it is itself true, and that what it states is as it is stated to be.

The first part of the deduction now goes through analogously to that given above, and we again reach:

(8') A is false.

But putting 'A is false' for 'p' in (3') gives:

(9') A is false if and only if not [(1) A is true, and (2) A is false]. to which we can apply the de Morgan laws (cf. **31.35**) to get:

(10') A is false if and only if either (1) A is not true, or (2) A is not false, i.e. in view of (4):

(11') A is false if and only if either (1) A is false or (2) A is not false.

As that alternation is logically true, being a substitution in the law of excluded middle (cf. **31.35**), the first part of the equivalence must also be true, giving us:

(12') A is false

which so far from being in contradiction to (8') is equiform with it. The antinomy is solved.

So far as we know, the medieval logicians only treated of semantical, not of logical antinomies. But the solutions contain all that is required for those as well.

SUMMARY

. In summary, we can make the following statements about medieval formal logic, in spite of our fragmentary knowledge:

1. Scholasticism created a quite *new variety* of formal logic. The essential difference between this and the one we found among the ancients, consists in its being an endeavour to abstract the laws and rules of a living (Latin) language, regard had to the whole realm of semantical and syntactical functions of signs.

2. This endeavour led to the codification of a far-reaching and thorough *semantics* and *syntax;* semiotic problems hold the forefront of interest, and nearly all problems are treated in relation to them.

3. Hence this logic is nearly entirely conducted in a *meta-language* (§ 26, B) with a clear distinction between rules and laws. Most of the theorems are thought of as rules and formulated descriptively.

4. The problem of *logical form* (§ 26, C) is posed and solved with great acumen.

5. Problems of *propositional logic* and technique are investigated as thoroughly and in as abstract a way as anywhere among the Megarian-Stoics.

6. *Assertoric term-logic* consists here essentially in a re-interpretation and acute development of syllogistic. But there are also other kinds of problem in evidence, such as that of plural quantification, of the null class, perhaps of relation-logic, etc.

7. *Modal logic*, both of propositions and terms, became one of the most important fields of investigation. Not only was the traditional system analysed with amazing thoroughness, but quite new problems were posed and solved, especially in the propositional domain.

8. Finally the problem of *semantical antinomies* was faced in really enormous treatises. Numerous antinomies of this kind were posited, and we have seen more than a dozen different solutions attempted. Between them they contain nearly every essential feature of what we know today on this subject.

So even in the present incomplete state of knowledge, we can state with safety that in scholastic formal logic we are confronted with a very original and very fine variety of logic.

PART IV

Transitional Period

§ 36. THE 'CLASSICAL' LOGIC

It is usual to put the close of the medieval period of history at the end of the 15th century. Of course that does not mean that typically scholastic ways of thought did not persist longer; indeed very important scholastic schools arose in the 16th and 17th centuries and accomplished deep and original investigations — it is enough to mention Cajetan and Vittoria. But there was no more research into formal logic; at most we find summaries of earlier results.

Instead there slowly grew up something quite new, the so-called 'classical' logic. Within this extensive movement which held the field in hundreds of books of logic for nearly four hundred years, one can distinguish three different tendencies: (1) humanism (inclusive of those later 17th century thinkers who were humanist in their approach to logic); it is purely negative, a mere rejection of Scholasticism; (2) 'classical' logic in the narrower sense; (3) more recent endeavours to broaden the bounds of (2). Typical examples of the three are L. Valla and Peter Ramus, the *Logique du Port Royal*, and W. Hamilton.

In what follows we shall first quote some passages to illustrate the general attitude of authors of books entitled 'Logic' in this period, then some that contain contributions to logical questions, whether scholastic or mathematico-logical, though these contributions are of small historical importance.

A. HUMANISM

Interest centres much more on rhetorical, psychological and epistemological problems than on logical ones. The humanists, and many 'classical' logicians after them, expressly reject all formalism. That they did not at the same time reject logic entirely is due to their superstitious reverence for all ancient thinkers, Aristotle included. But everything medieval was looked on as sheer barbarism, especially if connected with formal logic. Here is an instance. Valla writes:

36.01 I am often in doubt about many authors of the dialectical art, whether to accuse them of ignorance, vanity or malice, or all at once. For when I consider the numerous errors by which they have deceived themselves no less than others, I ascribe them to negligence or human weakness. But when on the other hand I see that everything they have transmitted to us in endless books has been given in quite a few rules, what other reason can I suppose than sheer pride? In amusing themselves by letting the branches of the vine

254

spread far and wide, they have changed the true vine into a wild one. And when – this is the worst – I see the sophisms, quibbles and misrepresentations which they use and teach, I can only kindle against them as against people who teach the art of piracy rather than navigation, or to express myself more mildly, knowledge of wrestling instead of war.

And again, about the third figure of the syllogism:

36.02 O trifling Polyphemus! O peripatetic family, that loves trifles! O vile people, whoever have you heard arguing like this? Indeed, who among you has ever presumed to argue so? Who permitted, endured, understood one who argued thus?

It is on these 'grounds' that the third figure is to be invalid! In another manner, but the content goes deeper, Descartes expresses himself:

36.03 We leave out of account all the prescription of the dialecticians by which they think to rule human reason, prescribing certain forms of discourse which conclude so necessarily that in relying on them the reason, although to some extent on holiday from the informative and attentive consideration (of the object), can yet draw some certain conclusion by means of the form.

Evidently such an attitude will not bring one to any logic. Peter Ramus holds a special position among the humanists. Though, at least in his first period, he was perhaps the most radical anti-Aristotelian, yet he succeeded in formulating on occasion some interesting thoughts, and published extensive treatises on formal logic. However, the following gives some idea of the general level of his logic:

36.04 Moreover, two further connected (i.e. conditional) moods were added by Theophrastus and Eudemus, in which the antecedent is negative and the consequent affirmative. The third connected mood, then, takes the contradictory of the antecedent and concludes to the contradictory (of the consequent), e.g.

If the Trojans have come to Italy without due permission, they will be punished;
but they came with permission,
therefore they will not be punished. . . .

36.05 The fourth connected mood takes the consequent and concludes to the antecedent: . . .

If nothing bad had happened, they would be here already;
but they are here,
therefore nothing bad has happened.

36.06 This mood is the rarest of all, but natural and useful, strict and correct, and it never produces a false conclusion from true premises. . . . *

Of course Theophrastus taught no such moods; both theorems are formally invalid and hold only by reason of the matter in particular cases. It is instructive to compare these thoughts with the treatment of similar problems in the Stoics (**22.04** f.) and Scholastics (§ 31).

B. CONTENT

In so bad a *milieu* logic could not last long, yet there were some thinkers among the humanists, Melanchthon for instance, who without being creative logicians, had a good knowledge of Aristotle. It was through them that in the 17th century the form of logic developed which we call the 'classical' in the narrower sense, partly among the so-called Protestant Scholastics, partly in Cartesian circles. Perhaps the most important representative work is the *Logique ou l'art de penser* of P. Nicole and A. Arnault. We describe the contents of this work, since they give the best survey of the problems considered in 'classical' logic.

The book has four parts, about ideas, judgments, arguments, and method. In the first part the Aristotelian categories (ch. 3) and predicables (ch. 7) are briefly considered, along with some points of semantics (*Des idées des choses et des idées des signes*, ch. 2), comprehension and extension (ch. 6). The other eleven chapters are devoted to epistemological reflections.

The second part roughly corresponds to the content of Aristotle's *Hermeneia*, and includes also considerations on definition and division (ch. 15–16).

In the third part the authors expound categorical syllogistic, apparently following Peter of Spain and so as a set of rules, but with use of singular premisses in the manner of Ockham (**34.01** f.). Four figures are recognized, with nineteen moods (the subaltern moods are missing). There follows a chapter on hypothetical syllogisms, and (ch. 12) a theory of *syllogismes conjonctifs* (the Stoic compounds) using formulas of term-logic, e.g.

---

* Admittedly these moods, as Professor A. Church has stated, do not appear in all editions. Perhaps Ramus saw his own mistake.

36.07 If there is a God, one must love him:
But there is a God;
Therefore one must love him.

Then there are some considerations about dialectical *loci*.

When we compare this with scholastic logic, the main things missing are the doctrines of supposition, consequences, antinomies, and modal logic. The main topics covered are those of the *Categories*, *Hermeneia*, and the first seven chapters of the first book of the *Prior Analytics*, but the treatment is often scholastic rather than Aristotelian, for which we instance the use of the mnemonics *Barbara*, *Celarent* etc. and the metalogical method of exposition.

The *Logica Hamburgensis* of J. Jungius (1635) is much better, and richer in content; but it did not succeed in becoming established. The *Logique ou l'art de penser*, also called the *Port Royal Logic*, became the standard text-book, a kind of *Summulae* of 'classical' logic. All other text-books mainly repeated its contents.

C. PSYCHOLOGISM

'Classical' logic is characterized not only by its poverty of content but also by its radical psychologism. Jungius provides a good example:

36.08 1. Logic is the art of distinguishing truth from falsity in the operations of our mind (*mentis*).

2. There are three operations of the mind: notion or concept, enunciation, and *dianoea* or discourse.

3. Notion is the first operation of our mind, in which we express something by an image; in other words a notion is a *simulacrum* by which we represent things in the mind. . . .

5. Enunciation is the second operation of the mind, so compounded of notions as to bring about truth or falsity. E.g. these are true enunciations: the sun shines, man is a biped, the oak is a tree. . . .

9. It is to be noted that a notion and the formation of a notion, an enunciation and the effecting of an enunciation, an argumentation and the construction of an argumentation are one and the same.

This is admittedly an extreme case. But when one thinks that the text is from Jungius, one of the best logicians of the 17th century, one cannot but marvel at the extent to which the understanding of logic has disappeared. Even Boole will maintain much this idea of logic.

Poor in content, devoid of all deep problems, permeated with a whole lot of non-logical philosophical ideas, psychologist in the worst sense, – that is now we have to sum up the 'classical' logic:

It may, however, be remarked that A. Menne (*Logik und Existenz*, 131, note 34) has propounded a distinction between an at least relatively pure 'classical' logic, and a 'traditional' philosophical and psychological logic, though these terms are commonly used synonymously. Of the former, J. N. Keynes (1906) may be taken as in every sense the best representative, but W. E. Johnson (1921) shows how relative is the distinction.

D. LEIBNIZ

Formed by this logic and its prejudices, modern philosophers such as Spinoza, the British empiricists, Wolff, Kant, Hegel etc. could have no interest for the historian of formal logic. When compared with the logicians of the 4th century B.C., the 13th and 20th centuries A.D. they were simply ignorant of what pertains to logic and for the most part only knew what they found in the Port Royal Logic.

But there is one exception, Leibniz (1646–1716). So far from being an ignoramus, he was one of the greatest logicians of all time, which is the more remarkable in that his historical knowledge was rather limited. His place in the history of logic is unique. On the one hand his achievement constitutes a peak in the treatment of a part of the Aristotelian syllogistic, where he introduced many new, or newly developed features, such as the completion of the combinatorial method, the exact working out of various methods of reduction, the method of substitution, the so-called 'Eulerian' diagrams, etc. On the other hand he is the founder of mathematical logic.

The reason why Leibniz is, nevertheless, named in *this* section, and *only* named, is that his great achievements in the realm of mathematical logic are little relevant to the history of problems, since they remained for long unpublished and were first discovered at the end of the 19th century when the problems he had dealt with had already been raised independently.

Only in one respect does he seem to have exercised a decisive influence, in forming the idea of mathematical logic. The pertinent passages will be quoted incidentally in the next section. Here we limit ourselves to quoting some of his contributions to syllogistic theory, and showing some of his diagrams.

E. COMPREHENSION AND EXTENSION

The idea underlying the distinction between comprehension and extension is a very old one: it is presupposed, for instance, in the *Isagoge* of Porphyry (**24.02** ff.); the scholastic doctrine of supposition has a counterpart of it in the theory of simple (**27.17** ff.) and personal (**27.24** ff.) supposition with an elaborate terminology. But the expressions *compréhension* and *étendue* are first found in the Port Royal Logic. Leibniz evidently has the idea, but without an established terminology.

We first cite an extract from his article *De formae logicae comprobatione per linearum ductus:*

36.09 Up to now we have assessed the quantities of terms in respect of (*ex*) the individuals. And when it was said: 'every man is an animal', it was meant (*consideratum est*) that all human individuals form a part of the individuals that fall under 'animal' (*esse partem individuorum animalis*). But in respect of (*secundum*) ideas, the assessment proceeds just conversely. For while men are a part of the animals, conversely the notion of animal is a part of the notion applying to man, since man is a rational animal.

So Leibniz had a fairly accurate idea of comprehension and extension, as well as of their inter-relationship. Now we come to the Port Royal Logic:

36.10 Now in these universal ideas (*idées*) there are two things (*choses*) which it is important to keep quite distinct: *comprehension and extension.*

I call the *comprehension* of an idea the attributes which it contains and which cannot be taken away from it without destroying it; thus the comprehension of the idea of triangle includes extension, figure, three lines, three angles, the equality of these three angles to two right-angles, etc.

I call the *extension* of an idea the subjects to which it applies, which are also called the inferiors of a universal term, that being called superior to them. Thus the idea of triangle in general extends to all different kinds of triangle.

F. THE FOURTH FIGURE AND SUBALTERN MOODS

Already in his youthful work *De arte combinatoria* Leibniz resumed the thought of Albalag (**32.25** ff.), without being acquainted with it, and proved that there is a fourth figure of assertoric syllogism (**36.11**). Later, he gave a complete and correct table of the twenty-four syllogistic moods, in which he deduced the moods of the second and third figures from those of the first, using the first reduction procedure of Aristotle (§ 14, D). We give a table which reproduces the deduction of the second and third figure moods, this time in the original language. '*Regressus*' means contraposition.

36.12

Barbara primae	ACD	ABC	ABD	*Barbara* primae	ACD	ABC	ABD
Regressus	ACD		OBD	Regr.		ABC	OBD
Ergo		OBC		Ergo	OCD		
Hinc *Baroco*				Hinc *Bocardo*			
secundae	ACD	OBD	OBC	tertiae	OBD	ABC	OCD

Celarent primae	ECD	ABC	EBD	*Celarent* primae	ECD	ABC	EBD
Regr.	ECD		IBD	Regr.		ABC	IBD
Ergo		OBC		Ergo	ICD		
Hinc *Festino*				Hinc *Disamis*			
secundae	ECD	IBD	OBC	tertiae	IBD	ABC	ICD

Darii primae	ACD	IBC	IBD	*Darii* primae	ACD	IBC	IBD
Regr.	ACD		EBD	Regr.		IBC	EBD
Ergo		EBC		Ergo	OCD		
Hinc *Camestres*				Hinc *Ferison*			
secundae	ACD	EBD	EBC	tertiae	EBD	IBC	OCD

Ferio primae	ECD	IBC	OBD	*Ferio* primae	ECD	IBC	OBD
Regr.	ECD		ABD	Regr.		IBC	ABD
Ergo		EBC		Ergo	ICD		
Hinc *Cesare*				Hinc *Datisi*			
secundae	ECD	ABD	EBC	tertiae	ABD	IBC	ICD

Barbari primae	ACD	ABC	IBD	*Barbari* primae	ACD	ABC	IBD
Regr.	ACD		EBD	Regr.		ABC	EBD
Ergo		OBC		Ergo	OCD		
Hinc *Camestres*				Hinc *Felapton*			
secundae	ACD	EBD	OBC	tertiae	EBD	ABC	OCD

Celaro primae	ECD	ABC	OBD	*Celaro* primae	ECD	ABC	OBD
Regr.	ECD		ABD	Regr.		ABC	ABD
Ergo		OBC		Ergo	ICD		
Hinc *Cesaro*				Hinc *Darapti*			
secundae	ECD	ABD	OBC	tertiae	ABD	ABC	ICD

(cf. **13.21, 13.22.**)

G. SYLLOGISTIC DIAGRAMS

The idea of representing class relations and syllogistic moods by geometrical figures was familiar to the ancient commentator (**24.34**); how far it was current among the Scholastics is not yet known. The use of circles is usually ascribed to L. Euler (1701–83) (cf. his *Lettres à une princesse d'Allemagne*, 1768), while that of straight lines is associated with the name of Lambert. But the former are to be found earlier in J. C. Sturm (1661) (**36.13**), and the latter in Alstedius (1614) (**36.14**). Schröder (**36.15**) notes that L. Vives was using angles and triangles in 1555.* Leibniz's use

---

* For the foregoing and some further details vid. A. Menne (**36.16**).

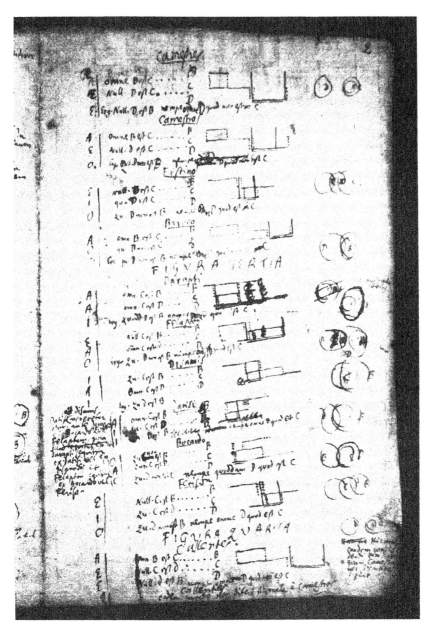

Syllogistic diagrams by Leibniz (**36.17**)

36.18

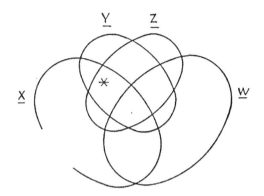

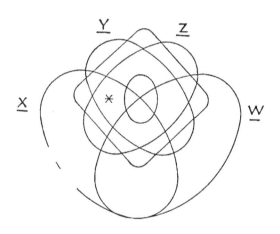

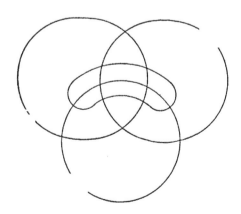

of circles and other diagrammatic methods remained unpublished till 1903. We reproduce a page of his MS (**36.17**) which contains both circular and rectilinear diagrams.

Such methods of presentation were much considered and further developed from the time of Euler onwards. J. Venn (1860) introduced ellipses for his investigations of the relations between more than three classes, and marked with a star every region representing a non-void class. Three of his diagrams are reproduced in (**36.18**) and a systematic development is considered by W. E. Hocking (**36.19**).

A different kind of diagram, mnemonic rather than expository of probative, due to Johnson, may be added here.

36.20 The attached diagram, taking the place of the mnemonic verses, indicates which moods are valid, and which are common to different figures. The squares are so arranged that the rules for the first, second and third figures also show the compartments into which each mood is to be placed, according as its major, minor or conclusion is universal or particular, affirmative or negative. The valid moods of the fourth figure occupy the central horizontal line.

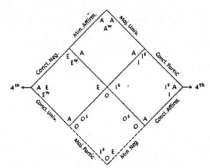

In the figure, the superscripts 'w' and 's' indicate the propositions that may be weakened or strengthened by subalternation.

H. QUANTIFICATION OF THE PREDICATE

While all points so far referred to fall within the general scheme of Aristotelian logic, Bentham's doctrine of the quantification of the predicate, usually ascribed to Hamilton, is directly opposed to Aristotle's teaching (**12.03**). At the same time, as can be seen from the texts, it is a development of the scholastic doctrine of exponibles. It has this historical importance, that it shows the kind of problem being considered by logicians at the time of Boole, and in some degree throws light on the origin of Boole's calculus.

We give two texts from G. Bentham (1827) first, then one from Hamilton (1860):

36.21 In the case where both terms of a proposition are collective entities, identity and diversity may have place:

1. Between *any* individual referred to by one term, and *any* individual referred to by the other. Ex.: The identity between equiangular and equilateral triangles.

2. Between *any* individual referred to by one term, and *any one of a part* only of the individuals referred to by the other. Ex.: The identity between men and animals.

3. Between *any one of a part* only of the individuals referred to by one, and *any one of a part* only of the individuals referred to by the other term. Ex.: The identity between quadrupeds and swimming animals.

36.22 Simple propositions, considered in regard to the above relations, may therefore be either affirmative or negative; and each term may be either universal or partial. These propositions are therefore reducible to the eight following forms, in which, in order to abstract every idea not connected with the substance of each species, I have expressed the two terms by the letters X and Y, their identity by the mathematical sign $=$, diversity by the sign $\parallel$, universality by the words *in toto*, and partiality by the words *ex parte*; or, for the sake of still further brevity, by prefixing the letters t and p, as signs of universality and partiality. These forms are,

$$
\begin{array}{llllllll}
1. & X \ in\ toto & = & Y \ ex\ parte & or & tX & = & pY \\
2. & X \ in\ toto & \parallel & Y \ ex\ parte & or & tX & \parallel & pY \\
3. & X \ in\ toto & = & Y \ in\ toto & or & tX & = & tY \\
4. & X \ in\ toto & \parallel & Y \ in\ toto & or & tX & \parallel & tY \\
5. & X \ ex\ parte & = & Y \ ex\ parte & or & pX & = & pY \\
6. & X \ ex\ parte & \parallel & Y \ ex\ parte & or & pX & \parallel & pY \\
7. & X \ ex\ parte & = & Y \ in\ toto & or & pX & = & tY \\
8. & X \ ex\ parte & \parallel & Y \ in\ toto & or & pX & \parallel & tY \\
\end{array}
$$

Hamilton writes:

36.23 The second cardinal error of the logicians is the not considering that the predicate has always a quantity in thought, as much as the subject; although this quantity be frequently not explicitly enounced, as unnecessary in the common employment of language; for the determining notion or predicate being always thought as at least adequate to, or coextensive with, the subject or determined notion, it is seldom necessary to express this, and language tends ever to elide what may safely be omitted. But this necessity recurs, the moment that, by conversion, the predicate becomes the subject of the proposition; and to omit its formal statement is to degrade Logic from the science of the necessities of thought, to an idle subsidiary of the ambiguities of speech. An unbiased consideration of the subject will, I am confident, convince you that this view is correct.

1°, That the predicate is as extensive as the subject is easily shown. Take the proposition, – 'All animal is man', or, 'All animals are men'. This we are conscious is absurd. . . . We feel it to be equally absurd as if we said, – 'All man is all animal', or ,'All men are all animals'. Here we are aware that the subject and predicate cannot be made coextensive. If we would get rid of the absurdity, we must bring the two notions into coextension, by restricting the wider. If we say – 'Man is animal', [*Homo est animal*], we think, though we do not overtly enounce it, '*All* man is animal'. And what do we mean here by *animal?* We do not think, *all*, but *some*, animal. And then we can make this indifferently either subject or predicate. We can think, – we can say, 'Some animal is man', that is, *some* or *all* man; and, *e converso*, 'Man (*some* or *all*) is animal', viz. *some* animal. . . .

2°, But, in fact, ordinary language quantifies the predicate so often as this determination becomes of the smallest import. This it does either directly, by adding *all*, *some*, or their equivalent predesignations to the predicate; or it accomplishes the same end indirectly, in an exceptive or limitative form.

Hamilton then proceeds to repeat, in dependence on the works of various 17th and 18th century logicians, the scholastic doctrine of the *exponibilia* (§ 34, C).

PART V

The mathematical variety of Logic

I. General Foundations

§ 37. INTRODUCTION TO MATHEMATICAL LOGIC

A. CHARACTERISTICS

The development of the mathematical variety of logic is not yet complete, and discussions still go on about its characteristic scope and even about its name. It was simultaneously called 'mathematical logic', 'symbolic logic' and 'logistic' by L. Couturat, Itelson and Lalande in 1901, and is sometimes simply called 'theoretical logic'. Even apart from the philosophical discussions as to whether or how far it is distinct from mathematics, there is no unanimity about the specific characteristics which distinguish it from other forms of logic.

However, there exists a class of writings which are generally recognized as pertaining to 'mathematical logic' ('logistic', 'symbolic logic' etc.). Analysis of their contents shows that they are predominantly distinguished from all other varieties of logic by two interdependent characteristics.

(1) First, a *calculus*, i.e. a formalistic method, is always in evidence, consisting essentially in the fact that the rules of operation refer to the *shape* and not the *sense* of the symbols, just as in mathematics. Of course formalism had already been employed at times in other varieties of logic, in Scholasticism especially, but it is now erected into a general principle of logical method.

(2) Connected with that is a deeper and more revolutionary innovation. All the other varieties of logic known to us make use of an *abstractive* method; the logical theorems are gained by abstraction from ordinary language. Mathematical logicians proceed in just the opposite way, *first constructing* purely formal systems, and later looking for an interpretation in every-day speech. This process is not indeed always quite purely applied; and it would not be impossible to find something corresponding to it elsewhere. But at least since Boole, the principle of such construction is consciously and openly laid down, and holds sway throughout the realm of mathematical logic.

Those are the essential features of mathematical logic. Two more should be added:

(3) The laws are formulated in an artificial language, and consist of symbols which resemble those of mathematics (in the narrower sense). The new feature here is that even the constants are expressed in artificial symbols; variables, as we have seen, have been in use since the time of Aristotle.

(4) Finally, until about 1930 mathematical logic formulated its

theorems in an object language, in this unlike the Scholastics, but in conformity with the ancients. That this is no essential feature is shown by more recent developments and the spread of metalogical formulation. But till 1930 the use of the object language is characteristic.

It may be further remarked that it can be said of mathematical logic, what was finally said about scholastic, that it is very rich and very formalistic. In wealth of formulae indeed, it seems to exceed all other forms of logic. It is also purely formal, being sharply distinguished from the decadent 'classical' logic by its avoidance of psychological, epistemological and metaphysical questions.

B. CHRONOLOGICAL SEQUENCE

G. W. Leibniz generally ranks as the original mathematical logician, but if he cannot count as the founder of mathematical logic it is because his logical works were for the most part published long after his death (the essentials by L. Couturat in 1901). However, he had some successors, the most important of whom were the brothers Bernoulli (1685), G. Plouquet (1763, 1766), J. H. Lambert (1765, 1782), G. J. von Holland (1764), G. F. Castillon (1803) and J. D. Gergonne (1816/17). * But no school arose.

One who did found a school, and who stands at the beginning of the continuous development of mathematical logic, is George Boole, whose first pioneer work, *The Mathematical Analysis of Logic*, appeared in 1847. In the same year Augustus de Morgan published his *Formal Logic*. Boole's ideas were taken further in different directions by R. L. Ellis (1863), W. S. Jevons (1864), R. Grassmann (1872), J. Venn (1880, 1881), Hugh McColl (1877/78), finally and chiefly by E. Schröder (1877, 1891–95).

Contemporaneous with the last-named are the works of a new group of mathematical logicians whose chief representatives are C. S. Peirce (1867, 1870), Gottlob Frege (1879), and G. Peano (1888). Of these three important thinkers only Peano founded a considerable school; Peirce and Frege went practically unnoticed. It was Bertrand Russell (1903) who discovered the thought of Frege and together with A. N. Whitehead combined it with his own discoveries in *Principia Mathematica* (1910–13), in which the symbolism of Peano was used.

D. Hilbert (1904) and L. E. J. Brouwer (1907, 1908) were active before the appearance of the *Principia*. J. Łukasiewicz published his first work in this field in 1910, St. Leśniewski in 1911. They were followed by A. Tarski (1921), R. Carnap (1927), A. Heyting (1929) and K. Gödel (1930).

---

* Figures in parentheses give the year of publication of the main work, then of the first subsequent important one.

These are only a few of the great number of mathematical logicians, which by now is beyond count.

C. FREGE

Among all these logicians, Gottlob Frege holds a unique place. His *Begriffsschrift* can only be compared with one other work in the whole history of logic, the *Prior Analytics* of Aristotle. The two cannot quite be put on a level, for Aristotle was the very founder of logic, while Frege could as a result only develop it. But there is a great likeness between these two gifted works. The *Begriffsschrift*, like the *Prior Analytics*, contains a long series of quite new insights, e.g. Frege formulates for the first time the sharp distinction between variables and constants, the concepts of logical function, of a many-place function, of the quantifier; he has a notably more accurate understanding of the Aristotelian theory of an axiomatic system, distinguishes clearly between laws and rules, and introduces an equally sharp distinction between language and meta-language, though without using these terms; he is the author of the theory of description; without having discovered, indeed, the notion of a value, he is the first to have elaborated it systematically. And that is far from being all.

At the same time, and just like Aristotle, he presents nearly all these new ideas and intuitions in an exemplarily clear and systematic way. Already in the *Begriffsschrift* we have a long series of mathematico-logical theorems derived from a few axioms 'without interruption' (*lückenlos*), as Frege says, for the first time in history. Various other mathematical logicians at the same time, or even earlier, expounded similar ideas and theories, but none of them had the gift of presenting all at once so many, often quite original, innovations in so perfect a form.

It is a remarkable fact that this logician of them all had to wait twenty years before he was at all noticed, and another twenty before his full strictness of procedure was resumed by Łukasiewicz. In this last respect, everything published between 1879 and 1921 fell below the standard of Frege, and it is seldom attained even today. The fate of Frege's work was in part determined by his symbolism. It is not true that it is particularly difficult to read, as the reader can assure himself from the examples given below; but it is certainly too original, and contrary to the age-old habits of mankind, to be acceptable.

All that we have said does not mean that Frege is the only great logician of the period now under consideration. We also have to recognize as important the basic intuitions of Boole, and many discoveries of Peirce and Peano, to name only these three. The very fact that Frege was a contemporary of Peirce and Peano forbids one to treat him as another Aristotle. But of all mathematical logicians he is undoubtedly the most important.

D. PERIODS

The history of mathematical logic can be divided into four periods.

1. *Prehistory:* from Leibniz to 1847. In this period the notion of mathematical logic arose, and many points of detail were formulated, especially by Leibniz. But there was no school at this time, and the continuous development had not yet begun. There were, rather, isolated efforts which went unnoticed.

2. The *Boolean* period, from Boole's *Analysis* to Schröder's *Vorlesungen* (vol. I, 1895). During this period there is a continuous development of the first form of mathematical logic. This form is principally distinguished from later ones in that its practitioners did not make the methods of mathematics their object of study, but contented themselves with simply applying them to logic.

3. The period of *Frege*, from his *Begriffsschrift* (1879) to the *Principia Mathematica* of Whitehead and Russell (1910–13). Frege, and contemporaneously Peirce and Peano, set a new goal, to find foundations for mathematics. A series of important logical ideas and methods were developed. The period reaches its peak with the *Principia* which both closes the preceding line of development and is the starting point of a new one, its fruitfulness being due in the first place to a thorough consideration and solution of the problem of the antinomies which had been a burning question since the end of the 19th century and had not previously found a solution in the new period.

4. The *most recent* period: since the *Principia*, and still in progress. This period can be sub-divided: the years from 1910 to 1930 are distinguished by the rise of metalogic, finitist in Hilbert, not so in Löwenheim and Skolem; after about 1930 metalogic is systematized in a formalistic way, and we have Tarski's methodology, Carnap's syntax, and the semantics of Gödel and Tarski in which logic and metalogic are combined. The 'natural' logics of Gentzen and Jaśkowski (1934) also belong here.

So we can say that the advance of metalogic is distinctive of the time since 1910, though new logical systems (in the object language) continue to appear: that of Lewis (1918), the many-valued systems of Post and Łukasiewicz (1920–21), the intuitionistic logic of Heyting (1930). Finally the very original systems of combinatorial logic by Schönfinkel (1924), Curry (1930), Kleene (1934), Rosser (1935) and Church (1936–41).

This fourth period will be touched on only very lightly, in some of its problems.

The following table gives an easy view of the temporal sequence of the logicians we have named. But it is to be noticed (1) that temporal succession does not always reflect actual influence; this will be discussed more in detail in the various chapters. (2) the subject developed so fast after 1870 that dates of births and deaths are little to the purpose; we have preferred to give those of publication of the chief logical works.

G. W. v. Leibniz

A. De Morgan 1847

G. Boole 1847
R. C. Ellis 1863
W. S. Jevons 1864

C. S. Peirce 1867–1870

R. Grassmann 1872
H. McColl 1877/78
E. Schröder 1877

G. Frege 1879
G. Peano 1888

D. Hilbert 1904
L. Brouwer 1907/8

B. Russell 1903
Principia 1910–1913

J. Łukasiewicz 1910
St. Leśniewski 1911
A. Tarski 1921
R. Carnap 1927
A. Heyting 1929
K. Gödel 1930

E. STATE OF RESEARCH

Mathematical logic is the best known form of logic, since many of its basic works, especially the *Principia*, so far from being past history are still in current use. Then again there have already been a number of historical studies of the period. Among these are the work of B. Jourdain (**37.01**), the historical sections of the works of C. I. Lewis (**37.02**) and J. Jorgensen (**37.03**). The treatise of H. Hermes and H. Scholz (**37.04**) is remarkably rich in historical information.

Since 1936 we have had as unique tools of research, a bibliography of mathematical logic from Leibniz to 1935, and the *Journal of Symbolic Logic* containing a current bibliography and excellent indexes. Both are as good as bibliograɪhy can be, under the editorship of A. Church who sees to them with exemplary punctuality and regularity. Among other contributions to the history of this period the numerous papers of R. Feys should be mentioned.

But still we do not know all about the period. L. Couturat's thorough and serious monograph on Leibniz needs completing on many points in the light of more recent systematic and historical research; there are also various other treatises on Leibniz's logic. Boole, too, has been fairly thoroughly investigated in recent years. But as yet there is no detailed treatment of Leibniz's successors, no monograph on Peirce, above all no thorough work on Frege's logic, without mentioning other less important logicians.

F. METHOD

For the reason stated in the introduction, we have tried to present the essential range of problems discussed in mathematical logic by means of texts containing little or no artificial symbols. This has proved feasible by and large, but not without exception; in particular, at least the basic methods have to be explained in terms of the contemporary symbolism, e.g. of Frege or the *Principia*. Then again, we have given the most important theorems in the various fields in symbolic formulation, in order to facilitate comparison with similar theorems developed in other periods.

The question of what time-limit to put is very difficult, and the various periods within the main one dovetail into each other in such a way as to make the drawing of sharp boundaries impossible. We have finally decided to close the exposition with the *Principia*, touching lightly on a few later developments which are either closely connected with matters discussed before 1910, or of special interest on their own account. That section (§ 49) is accordingly in the nature of an appendix.

The reader will only be able to appreciate the textual fragments that follow if, first, he is well acquainted with the fundamental concepts of *contemporary* mathematical logic (cf. § 5, B); second, he is able to abstract from the philosophy (ontology, epistemology, psychology etc.) of the various logicians. For never before have formal logicians been so divided by mutually opposed philosophies as here. We need only instance Frege's outspoken Platonism, and Boole's nominalism and even psychologism. But they have all developed essentially the same formal logic.

That is not to say that the individual philosophic views have been entirely without influence on the form of this or that system. But such influence has been much slighter than an unbiased observer might at first suppose. That the systems present such different appearances is due mainly to differences of immediate purpose (one may compare Boole with Frege, or Peano with Łukasiewicz), and to differences in the degree of exactness which are more marked here than in any other period.

271

§ 38. METHODS OF MATHEMATICAL LOGIC

Two essentially distinct methodological ideas seem to underlie mathematical logic. On the one hand it is a logic that uses a *calculus*. This was developed in connection with mathematics, which at first was considered as the ideal to which logic should approach. On the other hand mathematical logic is distinguished by the idea of *exact proof*. In this respect it is no hanger-on of mathematics, and this is not its model; it is rather the aim of logic to investigate the foundations and conduct of mathematics by means of more exact methods than have been customary among 'pure' mathematicians, and to offer to mathematics the ideal of strict proof.

In both respects the name 'mathematical logic' is justified, though for opposite reasons; first, because the new logic is a result of mathematics, then because it seeks to provide a basis for that science. But it would be a misunderstanding to conclude that mathematical logicians want to confine themselves to the consideration of quantities; their aim from the start has rather been to construct a quite general logic.

In what follows we illustrate both aspects with a series of texts which resume the development of mathematical logic.

A. LOGICAL CALCULUS

1. Lull

The idea of a mechanical process to facilitate inference is already present in the combinatorial arguments of the ancient Commentators, the Arabs and the Scholastics. We have given one example above (**32.34**), but of course it was only a matter of determining correct syllogistic moods. Raymond Lull (1235–1315) is the first to lay claim to a quite general mechanical procedure. It appears from the work of this remarkable man that he believed himself to have found a method which permits one to draw every kind of conclusion by means of a system of concentric, circular sheets or rings, of various sizes and mutually adjustable, with letters inscribed on their rims. Unfortunately Lull does not express the main ideas of this procedure at all clearly. However, it will be well to give at least a few passages from his *Ars Magna*, since his doctrine is not only one of the greatest curiosities in the history of logic, but also had some influence on Leibniz.

38.01 The understanding longs and strives for a universal science of all sciences, with universal principles in which the principle of the other, more special sciences would be implicit and contained as is the particular in the universal. . . .

38.02 This art is divided into thirteen parts, viz. the alphabet, the figures, definitions, rules, tables . . . (etc.).

The alphabet of this art is the following:

B signifies goodness, difference, whether, God, justice, avarice.

C signifies quantity, conformity, what, angel, prudence, throat.

We spare the reader the further enumeration of this alphabet. But we print a picture of the 'first figure' and here is part of the accompanying commentary:

38.03 There are four figures, as appears from this page. The first figure is signified by *A;* and it is circular, subdivided into nine compartments. In the first compartment is *B*, in the second *C*, etc. And it is said to be cruciform, in that the subject is turned into the predicate and conversely, as when one says: great goodness good greatness; eternal greatness, great eternity; God the good (*Deus bonus*), the good God (*bonus Deus*), and correspondingly for other (terms). By means of rotations of this kind the practitioner (*artista*) can see what is converted and what is not converted, such as 'God is good' and the like, which can be converted. But God and angel will not be converted, nor goodness and angel, nor its goodness and (its) greatness, and so on with the other terms.

This text is far from clear, and its consequences no clearer; it has, moreover, little relevance for genuine logic. But the mere idea of such a mechanical process was a fascinating one for many people in the 16th and 17th centuries.

2. Hobbes

Lull's ideas are to be found expressed in an extreme form three hundred years later, by Thomas Hobbes (1655). He made no attempt to carry them out, for like most modern philosophers Hobbes was no logician.

38.04 By *ratiocination* I mean *computation*. Now to compute, is either to collect the sum of many things that are added together, or to know what remains when one thing is taken out of another. *Ratiocination*, therefore, is the same with *addition* and *substraction* (*sic*); and if any man add *multiplication* and *division*, I will not be against it, seeing multiplication is nothing but addition of equals one to another, and division nothing but a substraction of equals one from another, as often as is possible. So that all ratiocination is comprehended in these two operations of the mind, addition and substraction.

This is, to be sure, rather the *jeu d'esprit* of a dilettante than a theory of mathematical logic; no inference can be interpreted in this way, and Hobbes never once tried to do it. The passage shows the mark of his extreme verbalism, inference being a mere accumulation of words. However, this text is historically important as having exercised some influence on Leibniz, and it is also characteristic of the mathematicism which largely dominated the new form of logic until Jevons. But perhaps no logician was so badly infected with it as Hobbes.

3. Leibniz

Leibniz had read Lull (**38.05**) and cites Hobbes too (**38.06**). But he has much more to offer than either of them. Like Lull, he is concerned with a universal basis for all sciences; like Lull again, his basic philosophy leads him to think of a purely combinatorial method. But this is now to take the form of a calculus, such as is employed in mathematics; logic is to be thought of as a generalized mathematics. Leibniz's most characteristic texts on this point are the following:

38.07 As I was keenly occupied with this study, I happened unexpectedly upon this remarkable idea, that an alphabet of human thought could be devised, and that everything could be discovered (*inveniri*) and distinguished (*dijudicari*) by the combination of the letters of this alphabet and by the analysis of the resulting words.

38.08 The true method should afford us a *filum Ariadnes*, i.e. a sensibly perceptible and concrete means to guide the mind, like the lines drawn in geometry and the forms of the operations which are prescribed to learners in arithmetic. Without this our mind could traverse no path without going astray.

38.09 To discover and prove truths, the analysis of ideas is necessary, . . . which corresponds to the analysis of (written) characters. . . . Hence we can make the analysis of ideas sensibly perceptible and conduct it as with a mechanical thread; since the analysis of the characters is something sensibly perceptible.

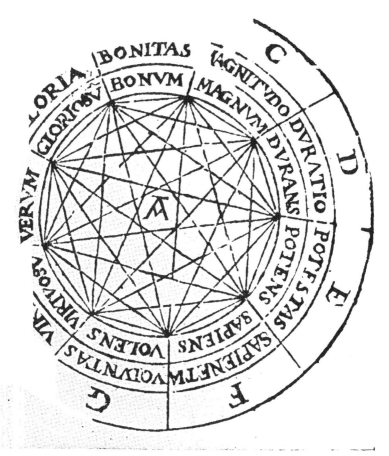

The "first figure" of Lull's "Ars Magna". Cf. 38.03

38.10 A *characteristic* of *reason*, by means of which truths would become available to reason by some method of calculation, as in arithmetic and algebra, so in every other domain, so long as it submits to the course of deduction.

38.11 Then, in case of a difference of opinion, no discussion between two philosophers will be any longer necessary, as (it is not) between two calculators. It will rather be enough for them to take pen in hand, set themselves to the abacus, and (if it so pleases, at the invitation of a friend) say to one another: *Calculemus!*

38.12 Ordinary languages, though mostly helpful for the inferences of thought, are yet subject to countless ambiguities and cannot do the task of a calculus, which is to expose mistakes in inference owing to the forms and structures of words, as solecisms and barbarisms. This remarkable advantage is afforded up to date only by the symbols (*notae*) of arithmeticians and algebraists, for whom inference consists only in the use of characters, and a mistake in thought and in the calculus is identical.

38.13 Hence it seems that algebra and the *mathesis universalis* ought not to be confused with one another. If indeed *mathesis* was to deal only with quantity, or with equals and unequals, or with mathematical ratio and proportion, there would be nothing to prevent algebra (which considers quantity in general) from being considered as their common part. But *mathesis* seems to underlie whatever the power of imagination underlies, insofar as that is accurately conceived, and so it pertains to it to treat not only of quantity but also of the arrangement (*dispositio*) of things. Thus *mathesis universalis*, if I am not mistaken, has two parts, the *ars combinatoria* concerned with the variety of things and their forms or qualities in general insofar as they are subject to exact inference, and the equal and the unequal; then *logistic* or *algebra*, which is about quantity in general.

There are here *two* different, though connected ideas: that of an 'alphabet of thought' and that of *mathesis universalis*. According to the first, one is to assign a symbol to every simple idea and solve all problems by combinations of these symbols. This is very consonant with Leibniz's philosophy, in particular with his doctrine of the strictly analytic character of all necessary propositions and of inference as a combining of elements. This philosophical view, questionable in itself, was yet fruitful for logic in that it led Leibniz to the notion of an artificial language (**38.12**) which, by contrast to ordinary languages, would be free from ambiguities. Therein Leibniz is the founder of *symbolic* logic as such, i.e. of the use of artificial symbols even for logical constants (and not only for variables as in all earlier forms of logic).

The other idea is that of *mathesis universalis* (**38.10**), i.e. of the application of calculation to all inferences, not only to those that are mathematical in the narrower sense. Leibniz does not advocate any mathematicism such as that of Hobbes: *mathesis universalis* is sharply distinguished from ordinary algebra (here strangely called 'logistic') and set in contrast to it (**38.13**). It is only the method that is to be applied to logic, and this is not any 'addition and subtraction' as with Hobbes, but simply formal operating with symbols. Of course the idea of a strictly formalistic logic, of constructing some meaningless system which is only interpreted later, such as we find in Boole, is not yet present. The calculus is to be a *filum Ariadnes* to assist the mind. The process envisaged is therefore basically the same as in the earlier logical tradition; formal laws are abstracted from meaningful sentences. But the principle of a formal process, i.e. of calculation, is here clearly expressed for the first time, so far as we know. In this, Leibniz is the founder of *mathematical* logic.

4. Lambert

Some further development of Leibniz's ideas is to be found in Lambert (1728–1777):

38.14 Let us see, then, how a more universal idea can be abstracted from the arithmetical and algebraic calculi. First, the idea of *quantity* must be got rid of, as being too special. You may put in its place *qualities, affections, things, truths, ideas* and whatever can be *discussed, combined, connected, separated and changed into ever new forms;* all and each of these substitutions can be made in accordance with the nature of things. For each of these operations and changes, with due differences allowed for, are applied to quantities.

Further, for the ideas of *equality, equation, ratio, relation, proportion, progression*, etc. which occur in arithmetic, more universal ones are to be substituted. So that in place of *equality* it will be convenient to introduce *identity*, in place of *equation identification*, if this word is taken in its active sense, in place of *proportion analogy*. And if the words *relation, progression* be retained, their meaning is to be extended, as ordinary usage suggests, so that they can be thought of as relations or progressions between the *things, qualities, affections*, *ideas* or *truths* to which the calculus is to be suited. And this is to be chiefly noted, that *those relations contribute no little to determining the form of the calculus, and that all those operations which the object of the calculus admits rest chiefly on them.*

5. *Gergonne*

Gergonne (1816/17) comes much closer to the idea of formalism:

38.15 It is constantly being said that reasoning must only be about objects of which one has a perfectly clear idea, yet often nothing is more false. One reasons, in practice, with words, just as one calculates with letters in algebra; and in the same way that an algebraic calculation can be carried out exactly without one having the slightest idea about the signification of the symbols on which one is operating, in the same way it is possible to follow a course of reasoning without any knowledge of the signification of the terms in which it is expressed, or without adverting to it if one knows it. . . . It is evident, for example, that one does not have to know the nature of the terms of a proposition in order to deduce its converse or subaltern when it admits of such. Doubtless one cannot dispense with a good knowledge of notions which are to be the immediate matter of judgment; but that is quite unnecessary for concluding to a judgment from a number of others already known to be correct.

This text is not altogether clear; Gergonne seems to equate the (Aristotelian) use of variables with formalism. But we can see the idea of formalism becoming clearer.

Gergonne also gave expression to an idea which is not without relevance to the symbolism of mathematical logic:

38.16 There is no known language in which a proposition exactly and exclusively expresses in which of our five relations both its component terms stand; such a language would have five kinds of proposition and its dialectic would be quite different from that of our languages.

He is referring there to five relationships between the extensions of two terms (or classes) which will be spoken of later (**40.12**).*

* We learned of this passage from a work of J. A. Faris.

6. Boole

We can find a clear idea of formalism, developed in an exemplary way, in the introduction to George Boole's epoch-making *The Mathematical Analysis of Logic* (1847), in this superior to much later works, e.g. the *Principia*.

38.17 They who are acquainted with the present state of the theory of Symbolical Algebra, are aware, that the validity of the processes of analysis does not depend upon the interpretation of the symbols which are employed, but solely upon the laws of their combination. Every system of interpretation which does not affect the truth of the relations supposed, is equally admissible, and it is thus that the same process may, under one scheme of interpretation, represent the solution of a question on the properties of numbers, under another, that of a geometrical problem, and under a third, that of a problem of dynamics or optics. This principle is indeed of fundamental importance; and it may with safety be affirmed, that the recent advances of pure analysis have been much assisted by the influence which it has exerted in directing the current of investigation.

But the full recognition of the consequences of this important doctrine has been, in some measure, retarded by accidental circumstances. It has happened in every known form of analysis, that the elements to be determined have been conceived as measurable by comparison with some fixed standard. The predominant idea has been that of magnitude, or more strictly, of numerical ratio. The expression of magnitude, or of operations upon magnitude, has been the express object for which the symbols of Analysis have been invented, and for which their laws have been investigated. Thus the abstractions of the modern Analysis, not less than the ostensive diagrams of the ancient Geometry, have encouraged the notion, that Mathematics are essentially, as well as actually, the Science of Magnitude.

The consideration of that view which has already been stated, as embodying the true principle of the Algebra of Symbols, would, however, lead us to infer that this conclusion is by no means necessary. If every existing interpretation is shewn to involve the idea of magnitude, it is only by induction that we can assert that no other interpretation is possible. And it may be doubted wither our experience is sufficient to render such an induction legitimate. The history of pure Analysis is, it may be said, too recent to permit us to set limits to the extent of its applications. Should we grant to the inference a high degree of probability, we might still, and with reason, maintain the sufficiency of the definition to which the principle already stated would lead us. We might justly assign it as the definitive character of a true Calculus, that it is a method resting upon the employment of Symbols, whose laws of combination are known and general, and whose results admit of a consistent interpretation. That to the existing forms of Analysis a quantitative interpretation is assigned, is the result of the circumstances by which those forms were determined, and is not to be construed into a universal condition of Analysis. It is upon the foundation of this general principle, that I purpose to establish the Calculus of Logic, and that I claim for it a place among the acknowledged forms of Mathematical Analysis, regardless that in its object and in its instruments it must at present stand alone.

From that Boole draws the explicit conclusion:

38.18 On the principle of a true classification, we ought no longer to associate Logic and Metaphysics, but Logic and Mathematics. . . . The mental discipline which is afforded by the study of Logic, *as an exact science*, is in species, the same as that afforded by the study of Analysis.

Leibniz and Lambert had already wanted to apply calculation to logic, and had used the idea of non-quantitative calculation. The epoch-making feature of Boole's text is the exemplarily clear account of the essence of calculation, viz. formalism, a process of which the 'validity does not depend upon the interpretation of the symbols which are employed, but solely upon the laws of their combination'. Boole is also aware of the possibility of interpreting the same formal system in different ways. This suggests that he did not think of logic as an abstraction from actual processes, as all previous logicians had done, but as a formal construction for which an interpretation is sought only subsequently. That is quite new, and in contrast with the whole tradition, Leibniz included.

7. Peirce

Finally we submit a text from Peirce's review of Schröder's logic (1896), which contains one of the best statements of the advantage to be looked for in a logical calculus.

38.19 It is a remarkable historical fact that there is a branch of science in which there has never been a prolonged dispute concerning the proper objects of that science. It is mathematics. Mistakes in mathematics occur not infrequently, and not being detected give rise to false doctrine, which may continue a long time. Thus, a mistake in the evaluation of a definite integral by Laplace, in his *Mécanique céleste*, led to an erroneous doctrine about the motion of the moon which remained undetected for nearly half a century. But after the question had once been raised, all dispute was brought to a close within a year. . . .

38.20 Hence, we homely thinkers believe that, considering the immense amount of disputation there has always been concerning the doctrines of logic, and especially concerning those which would otherwise be applicable to settle disputes concerning the accuracy of reasonings in metaphysics, the safest way is to appeal for our logical principles to the science of mathematics, where error can only long go unexploded on condition of its not being suspected. . . .

38.21 *Exact* logic will be that doctrine of the conditions of establishment of stable belief which rests upon perfectly undoubted observations and upon mathematical, that is, upon *diagrammatical*, or *iconic*, thought. We, who are sectaries of 'exact' logic, and of 'exact' philosophy, in general, maintain that those who follow such methods will, so far as they follow them, escape all error except such as will be speedily corrected after it is once suspected.

B. THEORY OF PROOF
1. Bolzano

A noteworthy precursor of modern proof-theory is Bernard Bolzano*.

38.22 If we now state that $M, N, O, \ldots$ are deducible from $A, B, C, \ldots$ and this in respect of the notions $i, j, \ldots$: we are basically saying, according to what has been said in § 155, the following: 'All ideal contents which in the place of $i, j, \ldots$ in the propositions $A, B, C, \ldots M, N, O, \ldots$ simultaneously verify the propositions $A, B, C, \ldots$ has the property of also simultaneously verifying the propositions $M, N, O. \ldots$' The

---

* Professor Hans Hermes drew our attention to this passage.
The rows of dots after the groups of letters are here part of the text.

most usual way of giving expression to such propositions is of course: 'If A, B, C, . . . are true: then also M, N, O, . . . are true.' But we often also say: 'M, N, O, . . . $follow$, or are $deducible$, or can be $inferred$ from A, B, C, . . . etc.' In respect of the notions i, j, . . . which we consider as the variables in these propositions, the same remark is applicable as in No. 1. But since according to § 155 No. 20 it is not at all the case with the relation of deducibility, as (it is) with the relations of mere compatibility, that a given content of propositions A, B, C, . . . on the one hand, and M, N, O, . . . on the other, can come into this relationship merely because we determine arbitrarily which notions therein are to count as variables: it is thus a rather startling statement when we say that certain propositions M, N, O, . . . can be brought into a relationship of deducibility with other propositions A, B, C, . . . by merely taking the notions pertaining to them as variable. But in such a judgment we only say that there are certain parts of the propositions A, B, C, . . . M, N, O, . . . which can be considered as variable, with the result that every ideal content which in the place of i, j, . . . makes all of A, B, C, . . . true, also makes all of M, N, O, . . . true. And thus we can easily see from § 137 how such a proposition must be expressed to bring out its logically constant parts. 'The notion of some parts of A, B, C, . . . M, N, O, . . . so constituted that every arbitrary ideal content which in their place verifies A, B, C, . . . always also verifies M, N, O, . . . has objectivity'. In ordinary speech propositions of this kind are expressed just like the preceding ones. It is only from other circumstances, e.g. from the context, that one can guess whether the speaker has in his mind *determinate* notions in respect to which the retation of deducibility is to be present, or whether he only inlends to intimate that there *are* such notions. Thus, e.g., it is easy enough to gather from the following proposition: 'if Caius is a man, and all men are mortal, then Caius, too, is mortal', that it is here intended to state the deducibility of the proposition: Caius is mortal, from the two propositions: Caius is a man, and, all men are mortal, in respect of the three notions; Caius, man and mortal. This next utterance on the other hand: 'If in all men there stirs an irresistible desire for permanence; if, too, the most virtuous must feel unhappy at the thought that he is one day to cease; then we are not wrong to expect of God's infinite goodness that he will not annihilate us in death' −

this would be subject to the reproach of extreme obscurity, since its sense is not that the said propositions stand in a relationship of deducibility when some of their notions (which still have to be ascertained) have been taken as variable. By such an utterance it is only intended to state that notions are present such as to warrant inference from the truth of the antecedent to the truth of the consequent; but it does not as yet tell one which these notions properly are.

2. Frege

While that text of Bolzano's contains important ideas about the concept of deduction or deducibility, the modern development of this second aspect of mathematical logic begins with Frege. We take the essential texts from the *Grundgesetzen der Arithmetik* (1893); but it can easily be shown that most of what is said in them was already known to this great logician by 1879.

38.23 In my *Grundlagen der Arithmetik* I have tried to make it plausible that arithmetic is a branch of logic and does not need to take its grounds of proof either from experience or intuition. This will now be confirmed in the present book, by the fact that the simplest laws of numbers can be deduced by logical means alone. But at the same time this shows that considerably higher demands must be made on the process of proof than is usual in arithmetic. A region of some ways of inference and deduction must be previously delimited, and no step may be made which is not in accordance with one of these. In the passage, therefore, to a new judgment, one must not be satisfied with the fact that it is evidently correct, as mathematicians nearly always have been up to now, but one must analyze it into its simple logical steps, which are often by no means a few. No presupposition may remain unremarked; every axiom which is needed must be discovered. It is just the tacit presuppositions, that are made without clear consciousness, which obscure understanding of the epistemological character of a law.

38.24 The ideal of a strict scientific method in mathematics, such as I have here tried to realize, and which could well be called after Euclid, I might describe thus. It cannot indeed be required that everything should be proved, since that is impossible; but one can see to it that all propositions which are used without being proved, are expressly stated as such, so that it is clearly known on what the whole structure rests. The effort, then, must be to reduce the number of these primitive laws as far as possible, by proving everything which can be proved. Further, and here I go beyond Euclid, I require that all methods of inference and deduction which are to be applied, shall be previously presented. Otherwise it is impossible to ensure with certainty that the first requirement is fulfilled. I think that I have now attained this ideal in essentials. Stricter requirements could only be made in a few points. In order to secure greater mobility, and not to fall into excessive prolixity, I have allowed myself to make tacit use of the commutability of antecedents, and of the identification of like antecedents, and have not reduced the ways of inference and deduction to the smallest number. Those who know my small book *Begriffsschrift* will be able to gather from it how the strictest requirements could be forthcoming here as well, but also that this would bring with it a notable increase in size.

Frege is correct here in claiming Euclid as his predecessor, insofar as Euclid was the first to carry out the idea of an axiomatic system in *mathematics*. But it would have been much better to refer to Aristotle (**14.02**, **14.05**), for what Frege offers is an important sharpening of the Aristotelian concept of an axiomatic system. His first requirement is that all presuppositions should be formulated expressly and without gaps. Then he makes an explicit distinction between the laws and the methods of inference and deduction, i.e. the rules of inference. This is not altogether new (cf. **22.12–22.15**, **30.11**. § 31, C), but is stated with greater clarity than ever before. Finally, Frege can be contrasted with Leibniz, Boole and other earlier writers in his laying down of a quite new requirement: 'considerably higher demands must be made on the notion of proof than is usual in arithmetic'. With that, mathematical logic enters on its second phase.

38.23 and **38.24**, along with the citations from Boole, are texts of far-reaching influence on the concept of mathematical logic. In this connection two further quotations, dating from 1896, may be added.

38.25 Words such as 'therefore', 'consequently', 'since' suggest indeed that inference has been made, but say nothing of the principle in accordance with which it has been made, and could also be used without misuse of words where there is no logically justified inference. In an inquiry which I here have in view, the question is not only whether one is convinced of the truth of the conclusion, with which one is usually satisfied in mathematics; but one must also bring to consciousness the reason for this conviction and the primitive laws on which it rests. Fixed lines on which the deductions must move are necessary for this, and such are not provided in ordinary language.

38.26 Inference is conducted in my symbolic system (*Begriffsschrift*) according to a kind of calculation. I do not mean this in the narrow sense, as though an algorithm was in control, the same as or similar to that of ordinary addition and multiplication, but in the sense that the whole is algorithmic, with a complex of rules which so regulate the passage from one proposition or from two such to another, that nothing takes place but what is in accordance with these rules. My aim, therefore, is directed to continuous strictness of proof and utmost logical accuracy, along with perspicuity and brevity.

Frege's program of thorough proof was later carried out in mathematics by Hilbert with a view to pure formality. The texts can be referred to in O. Becker (**38.27**). It was Łukasiewicz who applied it to logical systems with complete strictness. We shall give an example in the chapter on propositional logic (**43.45**).

C. METALOGIC

The idea of a metalogic was an inevitable result of the combination of Boole's formalism and Frege's theory of proof. For once formulae had been distinguished from rules, and the former treated with strict formalism, 'after the fashion of an algorithm' as Frege says, then the rules had to be interpreted as meaningful and having content. At once the rules are seen as belonging to a different level to the formulae. The notion of this second level appears first in connection with mathematics as that of metamathematics in Hilbert. We cite his lecture *Die logischen Grundlagen der Mathematik* (1923):

38.28 The basic idea of my theory of proof is this:
Everything that goes to make up mathematics in the accepted sense is strictly formalized, so that mathematics proper, or mathematics in the narrower sense, becomes a stock of formulae. . . .
Beyond mathematics proper, formalized in this way, there is, so to speak, a new mathematics, a metamathematics, which is needed to establish the other securely. In it, by contrast to the purely formal ways of inference in mathematics proper,

inference which has regard to the subject matter is applied, though merely to establish the freedom from contradiction of the axioms. In this metamathematics we operate with the proofs of mathematics proper, these last themselves forming the object of the inference that regards the matter. In this way the development of the total science of mathematics is achieved by a continual exchange which is of two kinds: the gaining of new provable formulae from the axioms by means of formal inference, and on the other hand the addition of new axioms along with the proof of freedom from contradiction by means of inference having regard to the matter.

The axioms and provable propositions, i.e. formulae, which arise in this process of exchange, are representations of the thoughts which constitute the usual processes of mathematics as understood up to now, but they are not themselves truths in an absolute sense. It is the insights which are afforded by my theory of proof in regard to provability and freedom from contradiction which are rather to be viewed as the absolute truths.

This important text goes beyond the bounds of this chapter in that it touches not only on proof-theory but also on the concept of logic and its relations to mathematics, since Hilbert here limits meaningful inference to the proof of freedom from contradiction, in accordance with his special philosophy of mathematics. The important point for our purpose is chiefly the sharp distinction between the formalized, and so in Boole's sense meaningless, calculus on the one hand, and the meaningful rules of inference on the other. This idea, too, was first expressed by Frege, when he required enumeration of all 'ways of inference and deduction' as distinct from axioms (cf. **38.24**). But Frege did not think of the axioms and theorems as meaningless, however formally he considered them. Here on the contrary it is a case of inscriptions considered purely materially.

A new stage in the understanding of formalization has thus been reached. The doctrine in Hilbert is, of course, limited to mathematics – he speaks of metamathematics. But soon this idea was to be extended to logic, and this came about in the Warsaw School. The expression 'metalogic' first occurs in a paper by Łukasiewicz and Tarski of 1930 (**38.29**).

Parallel to the work of the Warsaw School is that which R. Carnap was carrying on in Vienna at the same time.

We cite now a text of Tarski's, the founder of systematic metalogic. He forms the starting-point for the most recent developments which will not be pursued here.

Tarski wrote in 1930:

38.30 Our object in this communication is to define the meaning, and to establish the elementary properties, of some important concepts belonging to the *methodology of the deductive sciences*, which, following Hilbert, it is customary to call *metamathematics*.

Formalized deductive disciplines form the field of research of metamathematics roughly in the same sense in which spatial entities form the field of research in geometry. These disciplines are regarded, from the standpoint of metamathematics, as sets of *sentences*. Those sentences which (following a suggestion of S. Leśniewski) are also called *meaningful sentences*, are themselves regarded as certain inscriptions of a well-defined form. The set of all sentences is here denoted by the symbol '*S*'. From the sentences of any set X certain other sentences can be obtained by means of certain operations called *rules of inference*. These sentences are called the *consequences of the set* X. The set of all consequences is denoted by the symbol '*Cn* (X)'.

An exact definition of the two concepts, of sentence and of consequence, can be given only in those branches of metamathematics in which the field of investigation is a concrete formalized discipline. On account of the generality of the present considerations, however, these concepts will here be regarded as primitive and will be characterized by means of a series of axioms.

§ 39. THE CONCEPT OF LOGIC

As has been seen above (§ 38) Boole (**38.17**), Peirce (**38.19**) and with them the other mathematical logicians of the 19th century considered logic to be a branch of mathematics, this last being described not with reference to its object but its method, the application of a calculus. However, at the end of the 19th century there arose considerable disagreement about the relationship of logic to mathematics, a disagreement which at the same time concerned the answer to the question whether logic can be developed purely formally as a system of symbols, or whether it necessarily involves an interpretation of the symbols. So there were two problems, but both concerned with the concept of logic. Three main positions took shape: the logistic, the formalistic (not in the sense in which 'formalism' is used in the last and in subsequent sections) and the intuitionistic. We shall illustrate their main features with some texts.

A. THE LOGISTIC POSITION

On the logistic position there is no essential distinction between logic and mathematics, inasmuch as mathematics can be developed out of logic; more exactly, inasmuch as all mathematical terms can be defined by logical ones, and all mathematical theorems can be deduced from true logical axioms. Frege is the originator of this line of thought, which attained its fullest development in the *Principia Mathematica* of Whitehead and Russell, written precisely to provide a thorough proof of the logistic thesis.

1. Frege: semantics

Frege's theory of logic is closely connected with his semantics (a word which we always use here in the sense of Morris (**5.01**), not in Tarski's technical sense). On this point we shall here recall briefly only that logic for Frege was not a game with symbols but a science of objective thoughts (*Gedanken*), i.e. of ideal propositions (and so of *lecta* in the sense of **19.04** ff.). The premisses must be true, formalism is only a means. To begin with, we give a text about the first point:

39.01 By the word 'sentence' (*Satz*) I mean a sign which is normally composite, regardless of whether the parts are spoken words or written signs. This sign must naturally have a sense (*Sinn*). I shall here only consider sentences in which we assert or state something. We can translate a sentence into another language. In the other language the sentence is different from the original one, since it consists of different components (words) differently compounded; but if the translation is correct, it expresses the same sense. And the sense is properly just that which matters to us. The sentence has a value for us through the sense which we apprehend in it, and which we recognize as the same in the translation too. This sense I call 'thought' (*Gedanke*). What we prove is not the sentence but the thought. And it makes no difference what language we use for that purpose. In mathematics people speak indeed of a proof of a *Lehrsatz* when they understand by the word *Satz* what I call 'thought' – or perhaps they do not sufficiently distinguish between the verbal or symbolic expression and the thought expressed. But for clarity it is better to make this distinction. The thought is not perceptible to the senses, but we give it an audible or visible representative in the sentence. Hence I say 'theorem' rather than 'sentence', 'axiom' rather than 'primitive sentence', and by theorems and axioms I understand true thoughts. This further implies that thoughts are not something subjective, the product of our mental activity; for the thought, such as we have in the theorem of Pythagoras, is the same for everyone, and its truth is quite independent of whether it is or is not thought by this or that man. Thinking is to be viewed not as the production of thought but as its understanding.

Here, in another terminology, we have exactly the Stoic doctrine that logic deals with lecta, and the third scholastic view (28.17) according to which propositions stand for ideal structures.

On the question of the truth of premisses, Frege says:

39.02 Nothing at all can be deduced from false premisses. A mere thought which is not accepted as true, cannot be a premiss. Only when I have accepted a thought as true can it be a premiss for me; mere hypotheses cannot be used as premisses. Of course, I can ask what consequences follow from the supposition that A is true without having accepted the truth of A; but the result then involves the condition: *if A is true.* But that is only to say that A is not a premiss, since a true premiss does not occur in the judgment inferred.

Frege thus holds a kind of absolutest doctrine closely approximating to the Aristotelian theory of ἀπόδειξις (14.02) but apparently still more radical.

We append now a characteristic text about the use of quotation-marks, in which Frege's high degree of exactness finds expression – a degree that has been too seldom attained since.

39.03 People may perhaps wonder about the frequent use of quotation-marks; I use them to distinguish the cases where I am speaking of the symbol itself, from those where I am speaking of what it stands for. This may seem very pedantic, but I consider it necessary. It is extraordinary how an inexact manner of speaking and writing, which was originally perhaps used only for convenience, can in the end lead thought astray after one has ceased to notice it. Thus it has come about that numerals are taken for numbers, names for what they name, what is merely auxiliary for the proper object of arithmetic. Such experiences teach us how necessary it is to demand exactness in ways of talking and writing.

2. Frege: Logic and Mathematics

39.04 Under the name 'formal theory' I shall here consider two modes of conception, of which I subscribe to the first and endeavour to refute the second. The first says that all arithmetical propositions can, and hence should, be deduced from definitions alone by purely logical means. . . . Out of all the reasons which support this view I shall here adduce only one, which is based on the comprehensive applicability of arithmetical doctrines. One can in fact number pretty well everything that can be an object of thought: the ideal as well as the real, concepts and things, the temporal and the spatial, events and bodies, methods as well as propositions; numbers themselves can be in turn numbered. Nothing is actually required beyond a certain definiteness of delimitation, a certain logical completeness. From this there may be gathered no less than that the primitive propositions on which arithmetic is based, are not to be drawn from a narrow domain to the special character of which they give expression, as the axioms of geometry express the special character of the spatial domain; rather must those primitive propositions extend to everything thinkable, and a proposition of this most universal kind is rightly to be ascribed to logic.

From this logical or formal character of arithmetic I draw some conclusions.

First: no sharp boundary between logic and arithmetic is to be drawn; considered from a scientific point of view both constitute a single science. If the most universal primitive propositions and perhaps their immediate consequences are attributed to logic, and the further development to arithmetic, it is like wanting to detach a special science of axioms from geometry. Yet the partitioning of the whole domain of knowledge among the sciences is determined not only by theoretical but also by practical considerations, so that I do not wish to say anything against a certain practical separation. But it must not become a breach as is now the case to the detriment of both. If this formal theory is correct, logic cannot be so fruitless as it may appear to a superficial consideration – of which logicians are not guiltless. And there is no need for that attitude of reserve on the part of many mathematicians towards any philosophic justification of whatever is real, at least insofar as it extends to logic. This science is capable of no less exactness than mathematics itself. On the other hand logicians may be reminded that they cannot learn to know their own science thoroughly if they do not trouble themselves about arithmetic.

39.05 My second conclusion is that there is no special arithmetical kind of inference such that it cannot be reduced to the common inference of logic.

39.06 My third conclusion concerns definitions, as my second concerned kinds of inference. In every definition something has to presupposed as known, by means of which one explains what is to be understood by a name or symbol. An angle cannot be well defined without presupposing knowledge of a straight line. Now that on which a definition is based may itself be defined; but in the last resort one must always come to something indefinable, which has to be recognized as simple and incapable of further resolution. And the properties which belong to these foundation stones of science, contain its whole content in embryo. In geometry these properties are expressed in the axioms, to the extent that these are independent of one another. Now it is clear that the boundaries of a science are determined by the nature of its foundation stones. If, as in geometry, we are originally concerned with spatial structures, the science, too, will be limited to what is spatial. Since then arithmetic is to be independent of all particular properties of things, that must hold for its foundations: they must be of a purely logical kind. The conclusion follows that everything arithmetical is to be reduced by definitions to what is logical.

3. Russell

Frege's postulates were first taken up by Giuseppe Peano – though without direct dependence on Frege – then by Bertrand Russell. The latter extended the logistic thesis to geometry and mathematical disciplines in general.

39.07 The general doctrine that all mathematics is deduction by logical principles from logical principles was strongly advocated by Leibniz. . . . But owing partly to a faulty logic, partly to belief in the logical necessity of Euclidean Geometry, he was led into hopeless errors. . . . The actual propositions of Euclid, for example, do not follow from the principles of logic alone; . . . . But since the growth of non-Euclidean Geometry, it has appeared that pure mathematics has no concern with the question whether the axioms and propositions of Euclid hold of actual space or not: this is a question for applied mathematics, to be decided, so far as any decision is possible, by experiment and observation. What pure mathematics asserts is merely that the Euclidean propositions follow from the Euclidean axioms – *i.e.* it asserts an implication: any space which has such and such properties has also such and such other properties. Thus, as dealt with in pure mathematics, the Euclidean and non-Euclidean Geometries are equally true: in each nothing is affirmed except implications. . . .

39.08 Thus pure mathematics must contain no indefinables except logical constants, and consequently no premisses, or indemonstrable propositions, but such as are concerned exclusively with logical constants and with variables. It is precisely this that distinguishes pure from applied mathematics.

How and to what extent this program was carried out, cannot here be pursued. Reference may be made to Becker (**39.09**). In conclusion we should like only to illustrate Frege's definition of number by means of purely logical concepts, especially with a view to comparing it with a similar discovery in the Indian logic of the 17th century (**54.17**).

4. Frege: number

39.10 To illuminate matters it will be good to consider number in connection with a judgment where its primitive manner of application occurs. If when I see the same outward appearances I can say with the same truth: 'this is a group of trees' and 'these are five trees' or 'here are four companies' and 'here are 500 men', no difference is made to the individual or to the whole, the aggregate, but to my naming. But this is only the sign of the substitution of one concept by another. This suggests an answer to the first question of the previous paragraph, that number involves a statement about a concept. This is perhaps most evident for the number 0. When I say: 'Venus has 0 moons', there is no moon or aggregate of moons there about which anything can be said; but to the *concept* 'moon of Venus' there is attributed a property, viz. that of comprising nothing under it. When I say: 'the emperor's carriage is drawn by four horses', I apply the number four to the concept 'horse which draws the emperor's carriage'. . . .

39.11 Among the properties which are predicated of a concept I do not, of course, understand the notes which make up the concept. These are properties of the things which fall under the concept, not of the concept. Thus 'right-angled' is not a property of the concept 'right-angled triangle'; but the proposition that there is no right-angled, rectilineal, equilateral triangle, states a property of the concept 'right-angled, rectilineal, equilateral triangle', attributing to it the number 0.

39.12 In this respect existence is like number. The affirmation of existence is nothing else than the denial of the number 0. Since existence is a property of the concept, the ontological proof of the existence of God fails of its purpose....

It would also be false to deny that existence and unicity can ever be notes of concepts. They are only not notes of *that* concept to which the manner of speech might lead one to ascribe them. E.g. when all concepts belonging only to one object are collected under one concept, uniqueness is a note of this concept. The concept 'moon of the earth', for instance, would fall under it, but not the so-called heavenly body. Thus a concept can be allowed to fall under a higher one, under a concept, so to speak, of second order. But this relationship is not to be confused with that of subordination.

Frege's definition of number was later interpreted by Russell extensionally, when he took numbers as classes of classes (**39.13**).

B. FORMALISM

The formalists, too, see no essential difference between logical and mathematical formulae, but they understand both formalistically and think of the single system composed of them as a system of symbols. Evidence and truth of the axioms have no part to play: but freedom from contradiction is everything. The founder of formalism is David Hilbert, the essentials of whose thought on logic is contained in the text given earlier (**38.28**). Here we add only a brief passage from a letter to Frege in 1899 or 1900:

39.14 You write: 'From the truth of the axioms it follows that they do not contradict one another'. I was very interested to read this particular sentence of yours, because for my part, ever since I have been thinking, writing and lecturing about such matters, I have been accustomed to say just the reverse: if the arbitrarily posited axioms are not in mutual (*sic*) contradiction with the totality of their consequences, then they are true – the things defined by the axioms exist. That for me is the criterion of truth and existence.

For the rest, it is not easy to find texts to illustrate Hilbert's thought before 1930; for that and the later development Becker may again be consulted (**39.15**).

It should be noted that formalism has been very important for the concept of logic, quite apart from its value as a theory. Logic having been previously viewed as a calculus, it is henceforth ever more and more transposed onto the level of metalogic. After Hilbert, it is not the formulae themselves but the rules of operation by which they are formed and derived that are more and more made the object of logical investigation.

C. INTUITIONISM

By contrast to the logisticians and formalists, the intuitionists make a sharp distinction between logic and mathematics. Mathematics is not, for them, a set of formulae, but primarily a mental activity the results of which are subsequently communicable by means of language. In language, as used by mathematicians, certain regularities are observed, and this leads to the development of a logic. Thus logic is not presupposed by, but abstracted from mathematics. Once that has been done, it can then be formalized, but this is a matter of secondary importance. *

Intuitionism has a fairly long history in mathematics: L. Kronecker and H. Poincaré are precursors; H. Weyl is reckoned a 'semi-intuitionist'. But L. E. J. Brouwer ranks as the founder of the school, and intuitionistic logic was first properly formulated (and formalized) by A. Heyting in 1930.

From the standpoint of formal logic it is to be noted that the intuitionists, as they themselves say, admit the principle of *tertium exclusum* only under certain limitations. In this respect their doctrine belongs to those 'heterodox' logics of which we shall speak in § 49.

We give one text from Heyting and one from Brouwer:

39.16 Intuitionistic mathematics is an activity of thought, and every language – even the formalistic – is for it only a means of communication. It is impossible in principle to establish a system of formulae that would have the same value as intuitionistic mathematics, since it is impossible to

---

* Special thanks are due to Prof. E. W. Beth for much information in this connection, as generally for his help with the composition of this fifth part.

reduce the possibilities of thought to a finite number of rules that thought can previously lay down. The endeavour to reproduce the most important parts of mathematics in a language of formulae is justified exclusively by the great conciseness and definiteness of this last as compared with customary languages, properties which fit it to facilitate penetration of the intuitionistic concepts and their application in research.

For constructing mathematics the statement of universally valid logical laws is not necessary. These laws are found as it were anew in every individual case to be valid for the mathematical system under consideration. But linguistic communication moulded according to the needs of everyday life proceeds according to the form of logical laws which it presupposes as given. A language which imitated the process of intuitionistic mathematics step by step would so diverge in all its parts from the usual pattern that it would have to surrender again all the useful properties mentioned above. These considerations have led me to begin the formalization of intuitionistic mathematics once again with a propositional calculus.

The formulae of the formalistic systems come into being by the application of a finite number of rules of operation to a finite number of axioms. Besides 'constant' symbols they also contain variables. The relationship between this system and mathematics is this, that on a determinate interpretation of the constants and under certain restrictions on substitution for variables every formula expresses a correct mathematical proposition. (E.g. in the propositional calculus the variables must be replaced only by senseful mathematical sentences.) If the system is so constructed as to fulfil the last-mentioned requirement, its freedom from contradiction is thereby guaranteed, in the sense that it cannot contain any formula which would express a contradictory proposition on that interpretation.

The formalistic system can also be considered mathematically for its own sake, without reference to any interpretation. Freedom from contradiction then takes on a new meaning inasmuch as contradiction is defined as a definite formula; for us this method of treatment is less to the fore than the other. But here questions come in about the independence and completeness of the axiom-system.

39.17 The differences about the rightness of the new formalistic foundations and the new intuitionistic construction of mathematics will be removed, and the choice between the two methods of operation reduced to a matter of taste, as soon as the following intuitions (*Einsichten*) have been generally grasped. They primarily concern formalism, but were first formulated in intuitionist literature. This grasp is only a matter of time, since they are results purely of reflection, containing nothing disputable, and necessarily acknowledged by everyone who has once understood them. Of the four intuitions this understanding and acknowledgement has so far been attained for two in the formalistic literature. Once the same state of affairs has been reached for the other two, an end will have been put to disputes about foundations in mathematics.

FIRST INTUITION. *The distinction between the formalistic endeavours to construct the 'mathematical stock of formulae' (formalistic idea of mathematics) and an intuitive (meaningful) theory of the laws of this construction, as also the understanding that for the last theory the intuitionistic mathematics of the set of natural numbers is indispensable.*

SECOND INTUITION. *The rejection of the thoughtless application of the logical theorem of tertium exclusum, as also the awareness first, that investigation of the credentials and domain of validity of the said theorem constitutes an essential object of mathematical foundational research; second, that this domain of validity in intuitive (meaningful) mathematics comprises only finite systems.*

THIRD INTUITION. *The identification of the theorem of tertium exclusum with the principle of the solubility of every mathematical problem.*

FOURTH INTUITION. *The awareness that the (meaningful) justification of formalistic mathematics through proof of its freedom from contradiction involves a vicious circle, since this justification depends on the (meaningful) correctness of the proposition that the correctness of a proposition follows from the freedom from contradiction of this proposition, i.e. from the (meaningful) correctness of the theorem of tertium exclusum.*

II. THE FIRST PERIOD

§ 40. THE BOOLEAN CALCULUS

The system of mathematical logic inaugurated by Boole in 1847 holds a special place in history in that it admits of two interpretations, in class-logic and propositional logic. In this section we shall consider the abstract calculus itself and its classical interpretation, reserving the propositional interpretation to the following section.

The growth of Boole's calculus can be summarized as follows: De Morgan is its precursor (though his chief work was published contemporaneously with Boole's in 1847); Boole set out the main lines of the system in that year; but his exposition lacks the concept of the logical sum which first appears in Peirce (1867), Schröder (1877), and Jevons (1890), as also the concept of inclusion, originally introduced by Gergonne (1816) and clearly formulated by Peirce in 1870. Schröder's system (1890) ranks as the completion of this growth, though perhaps Peano's (1899) may here be counted as the real close.

A. DE MORGAN

Boole's calculus emerged in a way from the 'classical' endeavours to broaden the Aristotelian syllogistic (**36.15** f.). This can be most clearly seen from the syllogistic of Augustus de Morgan.

40.01 I shall now proceed to an enlarged view of the proposition, and to the structure of a notation proper to represent its different cases.

As usual, let the universal affirmative be denoted by A, the particular affirmative by I, the universal negative by E, and the particular negative by O. This is the extent of the common symbolic expression of propositions: I propose to make the following additions for this work. Let one particular choice of order, as to subject and predicate, be supposed established as a standard of reference. As to the letters X, Y,. Z, let the order always be that of the alphabet, XY, YZ, XZ Let x, y, z, be the contrary names of X, Y, Z; and let the same order be adopted in the standard of reference. Let the four forms when choice is made of an X, Y, Z, be denoted by $A_,$, $E_,$, $I_,$, $O_,$; but when the choice is made from the contraries, let them be denoted by A', E', I', O'. Thus with reference to Y and Z, "Every Y is Z" is the $A_,$ of that pair and order: while "Every y is z" is the A'. I should recommend $A_,$ and A'

to be called the *sub-A* and the *super* - A of the pair and order in question: the helps which this will give the memory will presently be very apparent. And the same of $I_{\prime}$ and I', etc.

Let the following abbreviations be employed; – $X)\,Y$ means "Every X is Y". $X.\,Y$ means "No X is Y". $X{:}Y$ means "Some Xs are not Ys". XY means "Some Xs are Ys".

Later, De Morgan developed a different symbolism. We give its description and a comparative table, from a paper of 1856:

40.02 Let the subject and predicate, when specified, be written before and after the symbols of quantity. Let the enclosing parenthesis, as in $X)$ or $(X$, denote that the name-symbol X, which would be enclosed if the oval were completed, enters universally. Let an excluding parenthesis, as in $)X$ or $X($, signify that the name-symbol enters particularly. Let an even number of dots, or none at all, inserted between the parentheses, denote affirmation or agreement; let an odd number, usually one, denote negation or non-agreement.

40.03   *Universals*

Former memoir.	Notation of my Work on Logic.	Both.	Notation now proposed.	Proposition expressed in common language.
A	A_1	$X\,)\,Y$	$X\,))\,Y$	Every X is Y
a	A^1	$x\,)\,y$ or $Y\,)\,X$	$x\,))\,y$ or $X\,((\,Y$	Every Y is X
E	E_1	$X\,)\,y$ or $X\,.\,Y$	$X\,))\,y$ or $X\,).(\,Y$	No X is Y
e	E^1	$x\,)\,Y$ or $x\,.\,y$	$x\,))\,Y$ or $X\,(.)\,Y$	Everything is X or Y o rboth

Particulars

I	I_1	XY	$X\,()\,Y$	Some Xs are Ys
i	I^1	xy	$x\,()\,y$ or $X\,)(\,Y$	Some things are neither Xs nor Ys
O	O_1	Xy or $X:Y$	$X\,()\,y$ or $X\,(.(\,Y$	Some Xs are not Ys
o	O^1	xY or $Y:X$	$x\,()\,Y$ or $X\,).)\,Y$	Some Ys are not Xs

B. BOOLE

Boole, who was the first to outline clearly the program of mathematical logic, was also the first to achieve a partial execution. In this respect there is a great likeness between his relationship to Leibniz and that of Aristotle to Plato. For with Boole as with Aristotle we find not only ideas but a system.

This system of Boole's can be described thus: it is in the first place closely allied to arithmetic, in that it uses only arithmetical symbols and has only one law that diverges from those of arithmetic, viz. $x^n = x$. All its procedures are taken over from simple algebra; Boole has no conscious awareness of purely logical methods (even of those which are intuitively used in algebra), e.g. of the rules of detachment and substitution. As a matter of fact, even the basic law mentioned makes very little difference to the algebraic character of his system – which is algebra limited to the numbers 0 and 1.

Boole's mathematicism goes so far – and this is the second main characteristic of his doctrine – that he introduces symbols and procedures which admit of no logical interpretation, or only a complicated and scarcely interesting one. Thus we meet with subtraction and division and numbers greater than 1.

From the logical point of view it is to be noted that disjunction (symbolized by '$x + y$') is taken as exclusive, and that inclusion is expressed by means of equality. Both lead to difficulties and unnecessary complications; both are the result of the tendency to mathematicize.

A third and special characteristic is that the system possesses two interpretations, in classical and propositional logic.

Altogether, in spite of its defects, Boolean algebra is a very successful piece of logic. Boole resembles Aristotle both in point of originality and fruitfulness; indeed it is hard to name another logician, besides Frege, who has possessed these qualities to the same degree, after the founder.

1. Symbolism and basic concepts

40.04 Proposition I. All the operations of the Language, as an instrument of reasoning, may be conducted by a system of signs composed of the following elements, viz.:

1st. Literal symbols as x, y, etc., representing things as subjects of our conceptions.

2nd. Signs of operation, as $+$, $-$, $\times$, standing for those operations of the mind by which the conceptions of things are combined or resolved so as to form new conceptions involving the same elements.

3rd. The sign of identity, $=$.

And these symbols of Logic are in their use subject to definite laws, partly agreeing with and partly differing from the laws of the corresponding symbols in the science of Algebra.

40.05 Let us employ the symbol 1 or unity, to represent the Universe, and let us understand it as comprehending every conceivable class of objects whether actually existing or not, it being premised that the same individual may be found in more than one class, inasmuch as it may possess more than one quality in common with other individuals. Let us employ the letters X, Y, Z, to represent the individual members of classes, X applying to every member of one class, as members of that particular class, and Y to every member of another class as members of such class, and so on, according to the received language of treatises on Logic.

Further let us conceive a class of symbols x, y, z, possessed of the following character.

The symbol x operating upon any subject comprehending individuals or classes, shall be supposed to select from that subject all the Xs which it contains. In like manner the symbol y, operating upon any subject, shall be supposed to select from it all individuals of the class Y which are comprised in it, and so on.

When no subject is expressed, we shall suppose 1 (the Universe) to be the subject understood, so that we shall have

40.051 $x = x$ (1),

the meaning of either term being the selection from the Universe of all the Xs which it contains, and the result of the operation being in common language, the class X, i.e. the class of which each member is an X.

From these premises it will follow, that the product xy will represent, in succession, the selection of the class Y, and the selection from the class Y of such individuals of the class X as are contained in it, the result being the class whose members are both Xs and Ys. . . .

From the nature of the operation which the symbols x, y, z, are conceived to represent, we shall designate them as elective symbols. An expression in which they are involved will be called an elective function, and an equation of which the members are elective functions, will be termed an elective equation. . . .

1st. The result of an act of election is independent of the grouping or classification of the subject.

Thus it is indifferent whether from a group of objects considered as a whole, we select the class X, or whether we divide the group into two parts, select the Xs from them separately, and then connect the results in one aggregate conception.

We may express this law mathematically by the equation

$(\mathbf{40.052})\ x\,(u + v) = xu + xv,$

$u + v$ representing the undivided subject, and u and v the component parts of it.

2nd. It is indifferent in what order two successive acts of election are performed.

Whether from the class of animals we select sheep, and from the sheep those which are horned, or whether from the class of animals we select the horned, and from these such as are sheep, the result is unaffected. In either case we arrive at the class of *horned sheep*.

The symbolical expression of this law is

$(\mathbf{40.053})\ xy = yx.$

3rd. The result of a given act of election performed twice, or any number of times in succession, is the result of the same act performed once. . . . Thus we have

$(\mathbf{40.054})\ xx = x,$

or $\quad x^2 = x:$

and supposing the same operation to be n times performed, we have

$(\mathbf{40.055})\ x^n = x,$

which is the mathematical expression of the law above stated.

The laws we have established under . . . symbolical forms . . . are sufficient for the base of a Calculus. From the first of these it appears that elective symbols are *distributive*, from the second that they are *commutative*; properties which they possess in common with symbols of *quantity*, and in virtue of which, all the processes of common algebra are applicable to the present system. The one and sufficient axiom involved in this application is that equivalent operations performed upon equivalent subjects produce equivalent results.

The third law . . . we shall denominate the index law. It is peculiar to elective symbols.

2. Applications

We now give two examples of the application of these principles in Boole's work. The first concerns the law of contradiction.

40.06 That axiom of metaphysicians which is termed the principle of contradiction, and which affirms that it is impossible for any being to possess a quality, and at the same time not to possess it, is a consequence of the fundamental law of thought, whose expression is $x^2 = x$.

Let us write this equation in the form

(**40.061**) $x - x^2 = 0$

whence we have

(**40.062**) $x(1 - x) = 0$;   (1)

both these transformations being justified by the axiomatic laws of contradiction and transposition. . . . Let us for simplicity of conception, give to the symbol x the particular interpretation of *men*, then $1 - x$ will represent the class of 'not-men'. . . . Now the formal product of the expressions of two classes represents that class of individuals which is common to them both. . . . Hence $x(1 - x)$ will represent the class whose members are at once 'men', and 'not-men', and the equation (1) thus expresses the principle, *that a class whose members are at the same time men and not men does not exist.* In other words, that *it is impossible for the same individual to be at the same time a man and not a man.* Now let the meaning of the symbol x be extended from the representing of 'men', to that of any class of beings characterized by the possession of any quality whatever; and the equation (1) will then express that it is impossible for a being to possess a quality and not to possess that quality at the same time. But this is identically that 'principle of contradiction' which Aristotle has described as the fundamental axiom of all philosophy. . . .

The above interpretation has been introduced not on account of its immediate value in the present system, but as an illustration of a significant fact in the philosophy of the intellectual powers, viz., that what has been commonly regarded as the fundamental axiom of metaphysics is but the consequence of a law of thought, mathematical in its form.

The second example is taken from the application of Boole's methods in the domain of syllogistic.

40.07 The equation by which we express any Proposition concerning the classes X and Y, is an equation between the symbols x and y, and the equation by which we express any proposition concerning the classes Y and Z, is an equation between the symbols y and z. If from two such equations we eliminate y, the result, if it do not vanish, will be an equation between x and z, and will be interpretable into a Proposition concerning the classes X and Z. And it will then constitute the third member, or Conclusion, of a Syllogism, of which the two given Propositions are the premises.

The result of the elimination of y from the equations

$$ay + b = 0,$$

$$(14)$$

$$a' y - b' = 0,$$

is the equation $ab' - a' b = 0$ (15).

40.08 Ex(ample). AA, Fig. 1, and by mutation of premises (change of order), AA, Fig. 4.

All Ys are Xs, $y (1 - x) = 0$, or $(1 - x) y = 0$,

All Zs are Ys, $z (1 - y) = 0$, or $zy - z = 0$.

Eliminating y by (15) we have

$$z (1 - x) = 0,$$

All Zs are Xs.

In both these texts Boolean methods are being applied to traditional problems, involving logical relationships between *two* objects (classes, propositions). But the interesting thing about this calculus for our history is that it is applicable to more than two objects, so that it oversteps the limits of the 'classical' logic. An instance is given later (**41.03**).

C. THE LOGICAL SUM

The original Boolean calculus had two main defects from the logical point of view, both occasioned by its extreme mathematicism; disjunction was treated as exclusive, and there was no symbol to hand for inclusion, though that is fundamental in logic. The first defect was remedied by Jevons, who was strongly opposed to this mathematicism and introduced non-exclusive disjunction.

49.09 There are no such operations as addition and subtraction in pure logic. . .

40.10 Now addition, subtraction, multiplication, and division, are alike true as modes of reasoning in numbers, where we have the logical condition of a unit as a constant restriction. But addition and subtraction do not exist, and do not give true results in pure logic, free from the conditions of number.

For instance take the logical proposition –
$$A + B + C = A + D + E$$
meaning *what is either A or B or C is either A or D or E*, and *vice versa*. There being no exterior restriction of meaning whatever, except that some terms must always have the same meaning, we do not know which of A, D, E, is B, nor which is C; . . . . The proposition alone gives us no such information.

Much clearer is Charles S. Peirce, also an opponent of Boole's mathematicism (1867). He uses an appropriate though still primitive symbolism.

40.11 Let the sign of equality with a comma beneath it express numerical identity. . . . Let $a +\!\!, b$ denote all the individuals contained under a and b together. The operation here performed will differ from arithmetical addition in two respects: first, that it has reference to identity, not to equality, and second, that what is common to a and b is not taken into account twice over, as it would be in arithmetic. The first of these differences, however, amounts to nothing, inasmuch as the sign of identity would indicate the distinction in which it is founded; and therefore we may say that
(1) If No a is b $a +\!\!, b =\!\!, a + b$.
It is plain that
(2) $a +\!\!, a =\!\!, a$
and also, that the process denoted by $+\!\!,$ and which I shall call the process of *logical addition*, is both commutative and associative. That is to say
(3) $a +\!\!, b =\!\!, b +\!\!, a$
and
(4) $(a +\!\!, b) +\!\!, c =\!\!, a +\!\!, (b +\!\!, c)$.

This is the *third* time that non-exclusive disjunction is discovered, cf. Galen (**20.18**) and Burleigh (**30.20**).

A symbolism quite different from that of mathematics is first met with in Peano (**41.20**).

D. INCLUSION

The introduction of the concept of inclusion and a symbol for it has a fairly long history. The modern symbol appears thirty years before Boole's *Analysis* and quite independently of his calculus in J. D. Gergonne's *Essai de dialectique rationelle*, 1816/17. (The parentheses enclosing the italic capitals in this text are Gergonne's.)

40.12 We have chosen the signs to characterize these relations in the way which seems best for linking the sign to the thing signified, and this is an endeavour which we think of some importance, however puerile it may appear at first. The letter (H), initial letter of the word *Hors* (outside) designates the system of two ideas completely outside one another, as are the two vertical strokes of this letter. These two strokes can next be considered as crossed to form the letter (X) intended to recall the system of two ideas which, as it were, somehow intersect. Finally the two strokes can be identified so as to form the letter (I) which we use to represent the system of two ideas which exactly coincide with one another; this letter is, moreover, the initial letter of the word *Identity*, the denomination suitable to the kind of relation in question. It may also be noted that the three letters (H, X, I) are symmetrical, like the relations they are intended to recall, so that they are not liable to change their appearance by being reversed. But this is not the case with the letter (C) which on being reversed changes into $(\Im)$; hence we have reserved this letter to recall a relation in which the two ideas play different parts, a relation which is not at all reciprocal. This letter is, moreover, the initial letter common to both of the words *Containing* and *Contained*, which well express the relative situation of the two ideas.

But it was Charles S. Peirce who in 1870 systematically elaborated the concept of inclusion.

40.13 *Inclusion in* or *being as small as* is a *transitive* relation. The consequence holds that

$$\text{If} \quad x \prec y,$$
$$\text{and } y \prec z,$$
$$\text{then } x \prec z.$$

(Footnote) I use the sign $\prec$ in place of $\leq$. My reasons for not liking the latter sign are that it cannot be written rapidly enough, and that it seems to represent the relation it expresses as being compounded of two others which in reality are complications of this. It is universally admitted that a higher conception is logically more simple than a lower one under it. Whence it follows from the relations of extension and comprehension, that in any state of information a broader concept is more simple than a narrower one included under it. Now all equality is inclusion in, but the converse is not true; hence inclusion in is a wider concept than equality, and therefore logically a simpler one. On the same principle, inclusion is also simpler than being less than. The sign $\leqq$ seems to involve a definition by enumeration; and such a definition offends against the laws of definition.

Schröder introduces and explains the symbol of inclusion from the start:

40.14 Examples of categorical judgements of the simplest kind are propositions accepted as true in chemistry:
'Gold is metal' – 'Common salt is sodium chloride'. –
Even to these we can very easily link the basic contrasts needed in our science.
Both statements have the same copula. . . . Yet the *factual* relation between the subject and predicate of the statement is essentially different in the first and in the second case, insofar as conversely *metal is not always gold*, while, *sodium chloride is also common salt*. This difference is not expressed in a way apparent to the eye in the original statements.
If it is now desired to exhibit the factual relation between subject and predicate by a relative symbol *more exactly than those statements do*, a symbol must be chosen for the first example different from that for the second. One might write:
$$gold \subset metal \qquad common\ salt = sodium\ chloride$$
40.15 The other symbol $\subset$ can be read . . . *'subordinated'*. It is called the *symbol of subordination* and a statement such as
$$a \subset b,$$
a *'subordination'*. The symbol is shaped similarly to, and to some extent in imitation of, the 'inequality symbol' of arithmetic, viz. the symbol $<$ for *'less* [than]'. As is well known, this can be read backwards as 'greater', $>$, and it is easily impressed on the memory together with its meaning if one bears in mind that the symbol broadens from the smaller to the larger value, or points from the larger value towards the smaller. Analogously, our symbol of subordination, when read backwards in the reversed position, $\supset$, i.e. reading again from left to right, will mean *'superordinated'*. The original subordination may also be written backwards as a *superordination'*:
$$b \supset a,$$
and this expression means just the same as the original one.

40.16 The copula 'is' is sometimes used to express one, sometimes the other of the relations which we have shown by means of the symbols $\subset$ and $=$. For its exhibition a symbol composed of both the two last, $\in$, is chiefly recommended, as being immediately, and so to say of itself, intelligible, and readily memorizable. In fullest detail, this symbol is to be read as 'subordinated or equal'. . . .

A statement of the form

$a \in b$

is called a *subsumption*, the symbol $\in$ the *symbol of subsumption*.

E. PEANO

The term of this whole development is to be found in the symbolism which Giuseppe Peano published in 1889. This comprises essentially more than the Boolean calculus and at the same time brings the latter to its final form. Its essentials will be given below (**41.20**).

III. PROPOSITIONAL LOGIC

§ 41. PROPOSITIONAL LOGIC: BASIC CONCEPTS AND SYMBOLISM

We speak first of the development of proposition-determining functors and other fundamental parts of propositional logic. This was first formulated, in the modern period of logic, by Boole – actually as the second possible interpretation of his calculus (1847). A more exact exposition appears in McColl (1877). Frege's *Begriffsschrift* (1879) marks a new beginning, in this as in so many other regions of formal logic. In connection with Frege's doctrine of implication we give also two important texts from Peirce.

Later, Peano (1889) introduced a symbolism which is notably easier to read than Frege's; Russell's displays only inessential variations from it. But the symbolism which Łukasiewicz later constructed, in dependence on Frege, is basically different from Peano's.

A. BOOLE

We read in the *Analysis:*

41.01 Of the conditional syllogism there are two, and only two formulae.

1st The constructive,

If *A* is *B*, then *C* is *D*,

But *A* is *B*, therefore *C* is *D*.

2nd The destructive,

If *A* is *B*, then *C* is *D*,

But *C* is not *D*, therefore *A* is not *B*.

. . . If we examine either of the forms of conditional syllogism above given, we shall see that the validity of the argument does not depend upon any considerations which have reference to the terms *A*, *B*, *C*, *D*, considered as the representatives of individuals or of classes. We may, in fact, represent the Propositions *A* is *B*, *C* is *D*, by the arbitrary symbols *X* and *Y* respectively, and express our syllogisms in such forms as the following:

If *X* is true, then *Y* is true,

But *X* is true, therefore *Y* is true.

Thus, what we have to consider is not objects and classes of objects, but the truths of Propositions, namely, of those elementary Propositions which are embodied in the terms of our hypothetical premises.

41.02 If we confine ourselves to the contemplation of a given proposition X, and hold in abeyance every other consideration, then two cases only are conceivable, viz. first that the given Proposition is true, and secondly that it is false. As these cases together make up the Universe of the Proposition, and as the former is determined by the elective symbol x, the latter is determined by the symbol $1 - x$.

But if other considerations are admitted, each of these cases will be resolvable into others, individually less extensive, the number of which will depend upon the number of foreign considerations admitted. Thus if we associate the Propositions X and Y, the total number of conceivable cases will be found as exhibited in the following scheme.

	Cases	*Elective expressions*
1st	X true, Y true	xy
2nd	X true, Y false	$x(1-y)$
3rd	X false, Y true	$(1-x)y$
4th	X false, Y false.	$(1-x)(1-y)$.

41.03 And it is to be noted that however few or many those circumstances may be, the sum of the elective expressions representing every conceivable case will be unity. Thus let us consider the three Propositions. X, It rains, Y, It hails, S, It freezes. The possible cases are the following:

	Cases	*Elective expressions*
1st	It rains, hails, and freezes,	xyz
2nd	It rains and hails, but does not freeze	$xy(1-z)$
3rd	It rains and freezes, but does not hail	$xz(1-y)$
4th	It freezes and hails, but does not rain	$yz(1-x)$
5th	It rains, but neither hails nor freezes	$x(1-y)(1-z)$
6th	It hails, but neither rains nor freezes	$y(1-x)(1-z)$
7th	It freezes, but neither hails nor rains	$z(1-x)(1-y)$
8th	It neither rains, hails, nor freezes	$(1-x)(1-y)(1-z)$
		$1 = $ sum

PROPOSITIONAL LOGIC

41.04 . . . To express that a given Proposition X is true.

The symbol $1 - x$ selects those cases in which the Proposition X is false. But if the Proposition is true, there are no such cases in its hypothetical Universe, therefore
$$1 - x = 0,$$
or $\qquad\qquad x = 1.$

To express that a given Proposition X is false.

The elective symbol x selects all those cases in which the Proposition is true, and therefore if the Proposition is false,
$$x = 0.$$

These principles are then applied just like those of the logic of classes, to syllogistic practice.

The similarity of the table of four cases in **41.02** with Philo's matrix of truth-values (**20.07**) is to be noticed. As has already been said, the Boolean calculus had no symbol for implication, nor yet one for negation; both are introduced by means of more complex formulae. In place of the logical sum, Boole had the notion of exclusive disjunction. Hence it is that propositional logic is made to appear as a discipline co-ordinate with, if not subordinate to, the logic of classes, by contrast to the clear insight possessed by the Stoics and Scholastics into its nature as basic.

B. McCOLL

Passing over the development that occurred between 1847 and 1877, mainly due to Jevons and Peirce, we now give instead a text from Hugh McColl (1877) in which propositional logic is emancipated from the calculus of classes, and endowed with all the symbols just mentioned. In a way this text marks the highest level of mathematical logic before Frege.

41.05 *Definition 1.* – Let any symbols, say A, B, C, etc., denote statements [or propositions] registered for convenience of reference in a table. Then the equation $A = 1$ asserts that the statement A is *true*; the equation $A = 0$ asserts that the statement A is false; and the equation $A = B$ asserts that A and B are equivalent statements.

41.06 *Definition 2.* – The symbol $A \times B \times C$ or ABC denotes a compound statement, of which the statements A, B, C may be called the *factors*. The equation $ABC = 1$ asserts that *all the three statements are true*; the equation $ABC = 0$ asserts that all the three statements are *not* true, *i.e.* that at least *one* of the three is false. Similarly a compound statement of any number of factors may be defined.

309

41.07 *Definition 3.* – The symbol $A + B + C$ denotes an *indeterminate* statement, of which the statements A, B, C may be called the terms. The equation $A + B + C = 0$ asserts that all the three statements are *false*; the equation $A + B + C = 1$ asserts that all the three statements are *not* false, *i.e.*, that at least *one* of the three is true. Similarly an indeterminate statement of any number of terms may be defined.

41.08 *Definition 4.* – The symbol A' is the *denial* of the statement A. The two statements A and A' are so related that they satisfy the two equations $A + A' = 1$ and $AA' = 0$; that is to say, one of the two statements (either A or A') must be true and the other false. The same symbol (*i.e.* a dash) will convert any complex statement into its denial. For example, $(AB)'$ is the denial of the compound statement $AB. \ldots$

41.09 *Definition 5.* – When only *one* of the terms of an indeterminate statement $A + B + C + \ldots$ can be true, or when no two terms can be true at the same time, the terms are said to be *mutually inconsistent* or *mutually exclusive*.

41.10 *Definition 12.* – The symbol $A:B$ [which may be called an *implication*] asserts that the statement A implies B; or that whenever A is true B is also true.

Note. – It is evident that the implication $A:B$ and the equation $A = AB$ are equivalent statements.

C. FREGE

1. Content and judgment

A new period of propositional logic begins with Gottlob Frege. His first work, the *Begriffsschrift* of 1879, already contains in brief an unusually clear and thorough presentation of a long series of intuitions unknown to his immediate predecessors, while those already familiar are better formulated. To start with we choose a text relevant rather to semantics than logic, in which this great thinker introduces of his propositional logic with the 'judgment-stroke':

41.11 A judgment is always to be expressed by means of the sign

$$\vdash$$

This stands to the left of the sign or complex of signs in which the content of the judgment is given. If we *omit* the little vertical stroke at the left end of the horizontal stroke, then the judgment is to be transformed into *a mere complex of ideas;* the author is not expressing his recognition or non-recognition of the truth of this. Thus, let

⊢— A

mean the judgment: 'unlike magnetic poles attract one another'. In that case

—— A

will not express this judgment; it will be intended just to produce in the reader the idea of the mutual attraction of unlike magnetic poles – so that, e.g., he may make inferences from this thought and test its correctness on the basis of these. In this case we *qualify* the expression with the words *'the circumstance that'* or *'the proposition that'*.

Not every content can be turned into a judgment by prefixing ⊢— to a symbol for the content; e.g., the idea 'house' cannot. Hence we distinguish contents that *are*, and contents that *are not, possible contents of judgment*.

As a constituent of the sign ⊢— *the horizontal stroke combines the symbols following it into a whole; assertion, which is expressed by the vertical stroke at the left end of the horizontal one, relates to the whole thus formed.* The horizontal stroke I wish to call the *content-stroke*, and the vertical the *judgment-stroke*. The content-stroke is also to serve the purpose of relating any sign whatsoever to the whole formed by the symbols following the stroke. *The content of what follows the content-stroke must always be a possible content of judgment.*

2. Implication

Frege then introduces the Philonian concept of implication, though, unlike Peirce (**41.14**) he knows nothing in this connection of Philo or the Scholastics. It is remarkable that he proceeds almost exactly like Philo.

41.12 If A and B stand for possible contents of judgment, we have the four following possibilities:

      (i) A affirmed, B affirmed;
      (ii) A affirmed, B denied;
      (iii) A denied, B affirmed;
      (iv) A denied, B denied.

stands for the judgment that *the third possibility is not*

realized, but one of the other three is. Accordingly, the denial of

$$\begin{array}{l} \rule[0.5ex]{1.5em}{0.4pt}\!\!\!\top\!\!-\! A \\ \quad\;\; \rule[-0.5ex]{0.4pt}{1.5ex}\!\!\!\llcorner\!-\! B \end{array}$$

is an assertion that the third possibility is realized, i.e. that
A is denied and *B* affirmed.

From among the cases where

$$\begin{array}{l} \rule[0.5ex]{1.5em}{0.4pt}\!\!\!\top\!\!-\! A \\ \quad\;\; \llcorner\!-\! B \end{array}$$

is affirmed, the following may be specially emphasized:

(1) *A* is to be affirmed. – In this case the content of *B* is
quite indifferent. Thus, let ⊢— *A* mean: 3 × 7 = 31; let *B*
stand for the circumstance of the sun's shining. Here only
the first two cases out of the four mentioned above are
possible. A causal connection need not exist between the two
contents.

(2) *B* is to be denied. – In this case the content of *A* is
indifferent. E.g., let *B* stand for the circumstance of perpetual
motion's being possible, and *A* for the circumstance of the
world's being infinite. Here only the second and fourth of the
four cases are possible. A causal connection between *A* and *B*
need not exist.

(3) One may form the judgment

$$\begin{array}{l} \vdash\!\!\top\!-\! A \\ \quad\;\;\; \llcorner\!-\! B \end{array}$$

without knowing whether *A* and *B* are to be affirmed or denied.
E.g., let *B* stand for the circumstance of the Moon's being in
quadrature with the Sun, and *A* the circumstance of her
appearing semi-circular. In this case we may render

$$\begin{array}{l} \vdash\!\!\top\!\dashv\! A \\ \quad\;\;\; \llcorner\!-\! B \end{array}$$

by means of the conjunction 'if'; 'if the Moon is in quadrature
with the Sun, then she appears semi-circular'. The causal
connection implicit in the word 'if' is, however, not expressed
by our symbolism; although a judgment of this sort can be
made only on the ground of such a connection. For this connection is something general, and as yet we have no expression
for generality.

The text needs some explanations. First, Frege uses '*A*' for the
consequent and '*B*' for the antecedent – contrary to ordinary usage,
but like Aristotle; so the antecedent stands in the *lower* place. So

the schema excludes only the case where the antecedent (*B*) is true and the consequent (*A*) is false; in all the other three cases the proposition is true. Thus we have just the same state of affairs as in Philo (**20.07**): the schema is a symbol of Philonian implication. It signifies 'if *B*, then *A*' in the Philonian sense of 'if'.

Important is the stress laid on the fact that implication has *nothing* to do with the causal connection between the facts signified by the antecedent and consequent. .

D. PEIRCE

Philonian implication alone continued to be used in mathematical logic up to 1918 – unlike usage in the Stoic and Scholastic periods. One of the best justifications of this concept which seems so odd to the man in the street, is to be found in a fairly late text of Peirce's, dated 1902.

41.13 To make the matter clear, it will be well to begin by defining the meaning of a hypothetical proposition, in general. What the usages of language may be does not concern us; language has its meaning modified in technical logical formulac as in other special kinds of discourse. The question is what is the sense which is most usefully attached to the hypothetical proposition in logic? Now, the peculiarity of the hypothetical proposition is that it goes out beyond the actual state of things and declares what *would* happen were things other than they are or may be. The utility of this is that it puts us in possession of a rule, say that 'if *A* is true, *B* is true', such that should we hereafter learn something of which we are now ignorant, namely that *A* is true, then by virtue of this rule, we shall find that we know something else, namely, that *B* is true. There can be no doubt that the Possible, in its primary meaning, is that which may be true for aught we know, that whose falsity we do not know. The purpose is subserved, then, if throughout the whole range of possibility, in every state of things in which *A* is true, *B* is true too. The hypothetical proposition may therefore be falsified by a single state of things, but only by one in which *A* is true while *B* is false. States of things in which *A* is false, as well as those in which *B* is true, cannot falsify it. If, then, *B* is a proposition true in every case throughout the whole range of possibility, the hypothetical proposition, taken in its logical sense, ought to be regarded as true, whatever may be the usage of ordinary speech. If, on the other hand, *A* is in no case true, throughout the range of possibility, it is a matter of indifference whether the hypothetical be understood to be true or not, since it is useless. But it will be more simple to class it among true propositions, because the cases in which the antecedent is false do not, in any other case, falsify a hypothetical. This, at any rate, is the meaning which I shall attach to the hypothetical proposition in general, in this paper.

Also of interest is the following remark of the same logician (1896):

41.14 Although the Philonian views lead to such inconveniences as that it is true, as a consequence *de inesse*, that if the Devil were elected president of the United States, it would prove highly conducive to the spiritual welfare of the people (because he will not be elected), yet both Professor Schröder and I prefer to build the algebra of relatives upon this conception of the conditional proposition. The inconvenience, after all, ceases to seem important, when we reflect that, no matter what the conditional proposition be understood to mean, it can always be expressed by a complexus of Philonian conditionals and denials of conditionals.

E. APPLICATIONS OF HIS SYMBOLISM BY FREGE

Some examples of the applications of Frege's implication-schema will make his main ideas clearer.

41.15 The vertical stroke joining the two horizontal ones is to be called the *conditional-stroke.* . . . Hence it is easy to see that

$$
\begin{array}{l}
\vdash \ \begin{array}{c} \rule[0.5ex]{1.5em}{0.4pt} \end{array} \!\!\!\! \begin{array}{l} A \\ B \end{array} \\
 \rule[0.5ex]{1.5em}{0.4pt}\ \varGamma
\end{array}
$$

denies the case in which A is denied, B and $\varGamma$ are affirmed. This must be thought of as compounded of

$$
\rule[0.5ex]{2em}{0.4pt} \ \begin{array}{l} A \text{ and } \varGamma \\ B \end{array}
$$

just as

314

$$\overline{}\!\!\!\!\underset{\displaystyle\smash{\rule{0pt}{1.2ex}}}{\rule{0pt}{0pt}}\left\lceil\begin{array}{l}A\\B\end{array}\right.$$

is from A and B. Thus we first have the denial of the case in which

$$\overline{}\left\lceil\begin{array}{l}A\\B\end{array}\right.$$

is denied, Γ is affirmed. But the denial of

$$\overline{}\left\lceil\begin{array}{l}A\\B\end{array}\right.$$

signifies that A is denied and B is affirmed. Thus we obtain what is given above.

41.16 From the explanation given in § 5 (**41.12**) it is obvious that from the two judgments

$$\vdash\left\lceil\begin{array}{l}A\\B\end{array}\right. \text{ and } \vdash B$$

there follows the new judgment $\vdash$ A. Of the four cases enumerated above, the third is excluded by

$$\vdash\left\lceil\begin{array}{l}A\\B\end{array}\right.$$

and the second and fourth by:

$$\vdash B,$$

so that only the first remains.

41.17 Let now X for example signify the judgment

$$\vdash\left\lceil\begin{array}{l}A\\B\end{array}\right.$$

— or one which $\vdash\left\lceil\begin{array}{l}A\\B\end{array}\right.$ contains as a particular case. Then I write the inference thus:

$$(X)\!: \quad \dfrac{\vdash B}{\vdash A.}$$

Here it is left to the reader to put together the judgment

$$\vdash\left\lceil\begin{array}{l}A\\B\end{array}\right.$$

from $\vdash$ B and $\vdash$ A, and see that it tallies with the cited judgment X.

F. NEGATION AND SUM IN FREGE

Frege uses the same schemata, together with the 'negation-stroke', to express the logical sum.

41.18 If a small vertical stroke is attached to the lower side of the content-stroke, this shall express the circumstance of the content's not being the case. Thus, e.g., the meaning of

$$\vdash_{\!\top} A:$$

is: 'A is not the case'. I call this small vertical stroke the *negation-stroke*.

41.19 We now deal with some cases where the symbols of conditionality and negation are combined.

$$\vdash_{\!\!\top}\!\!\!\begin{array}{c} A \\ B \end{array}$$

means: 'the case in which B is to be affirmed and the negation of A is to be denied does not occur'; in other words, 'the possibility of affirming both A and B does not exist', or 'A and B are mutually exclusive'. Thus only the three following cases remain:

> A affirmed, B denied;
> A denied, B affirmed;
> A denied, B denied.

From what has already been said, it is easy to determine the meaning possessed by each of the three parts of the horizontal stroke preceding A.

$$\vdash_{\!\!\top}\!\!\!\begin{array}{c} A \\ B \end{array}$$

means: 'the case in which A is denied and negation of B is affirmed does not exist'; or, 'A and B cannot both be denied'. There remain only the following possibilities:

> A affirmed, B affirmed;
> A affirmed, B denied;
> A denied, B affirmed.

A and B between them exhaust all possibilities. Now the words 'or', 'either – or', are used in two ways. In its first meaning,

$$\text{'}A \text{ or } B\text{'}$$

means just the same as

$$\vdash_{\!\!\top}\!\!\!\begin{array}{c} A \\ B, \end{array}$$

i. e. that nothing besides A and B is thinkable. E.g., if a gaseous mass is heated, then either its volume or its pressure increases. Secondly, the expression

$$\text{`}A \text{ or } B\text{'}$$

may combine the meaning of

$$\vdash\!\!\top\!\!\begin{array}{c} A \\ \underline{\quad} B \end{array} \quad \text{and that of} \quad \vdash\!\!\top\!\!\begin{array}{c} A \\ \underline{\top} B \end{array}$$

so that (i) there is no third possibility besides A and B, (ii) A and B are mutually exclusive. In that case only the following two possibilities remain out of the four:

A affirmed, B denied;

A denied, B affirmed.

Of these two uses of the expression 'A or B' the more important is the first, which does not exclude the coexistence of A and B; and we shall use the word 'or' with this meaning. Perhaps it is suitable to distinguish between 'or' and 'either – or', regarding only the latter as having the subsidiary meaning of mutual exclusion.

G. PEANO'S SYMBOLISM FOR PROPOSITIONAL LOGIC

Frege's symbolism has the unusual feature of being two-dimensional. In that it diverges from the historical practice of mankind which has almost always expressed its thoughts in one-dimensional writing. It must be admitted that this revolutionary novelty has much to be said for it – it notably widens the expressive possibilities of writing. But this was too revolutionary; Frege's symbolism did not prove generally intelligible, and the subsequent development took place in another direction. Schröder made no reference to it in 1892, Russell admitted in 1903 that he had learned much from Frege when he had met his system, but not having known it he followed Peano. Modern mathematical logic, though its authors have less depth of thought than Frege, has adopted Peano's symbolism. For this reason we quote a text from Peano's *Arithmetices Principia* (1889) in which he lays down this intuitively clear and meaningful symbolism for propositional logic.

41.20 *I. Concerning punctuation*

By the letters a, b, ... x, y, ... x', y' ... we indicate any undetermined beings. Determined beings we indicate by the signs or letters P, K, N. . . .

For the most part we shall write signs on one and the same line. To make clear the order in which they are to be conjoined we use *parentheses* as in algebra, or *dots* . : ∴ :: etc.

That a formula divided by dots may be understood, first the signs which are separated by no dots are to be collected, afterwards those separated by one dot, then those by two dots, etc.

E.g. let $a, b, c, \ldots$ be any signs. Then $ab \cdot cd$ signifies $(ab)(cd)$; and $ab \,.\, cd : ef \,.\, gh \therefore k$ signifies $(((ab)\,(cd))\,((ef)\,(gh)))\,k$.

Signs of punctuation may be omitted if there are formulae with different punctuation but the same sense; or if only one formula, and that the one we wish to write, has the sense.

To avoid danger of ambiguity we never make use of . : as signs of arithmetical operations.

The only form of parentheses is (). If dots and parentheses occur in the same formula, signs contained in parentheses are to be collected first.

II. Concerning propositions

By the sign P is signified a *proposition*.

The sign $\cap$ is read *and*. If a, b are propositions; then $a \cap b$ is the simultaneous affirmation of the propositions a, b. For the sake of brevity we shall commonly write ab in place of $a \cap b$.

The sign $-$ is read *not*. Let a be a P; then $-a$ is the negation of the proposition a.

The sign $\cup$ is read *or* (*vel*). Let a, b be propositions; then $a \cup b$ is the same as $- :-a.-b$.

[By the sign V is signified *verum* or *identity*; but we never use this sign.]

The sign Λ signifies *falsum* or *absurdum*.

[The sign C signifies *is a consequence*; thus bCa is read b *is a consequence of the proposition* a. But we never use this sign.]

The sign $\supset$ signifies *is deduced* (*deducitur*): thus $a \supset b$ signifies the same as bCa.

H. LATER DEVELOPMENT OF SYMBOLISM FOR PROPOSITIONAL LOGIC

Peano's successors introduced only minor alterations to his symbolism. First Russell (1903), who writes 'v' instead of '$\cup$', and '$\sim$' instead of '$-$', then Hilbert and Ackermann (1928) who write a stroke over a letter for negation, and '∞' for the equivalence-sign '≡' of Frege and Russell. M. H. Sheffer (1928) introduced '|' as a sign for 'not both'.

The Polish school, on the other hand, developed two symbolic languages essentially different from Peano's; those of St. Leśniewski and J. Łukasiewicz. We shall not go into the first, which is peculiar and little used, but the symbolism of Łukasiewicz deserves brief exposition, both for its originality and its exactness. The essential feature is that all predicates (called by Łukasiewicz 'functors') stand *in front of* their arguments; thus all brackets and dots are dispensed with, without any ambiguity arising.

The various sets of symbols may be compared thus:

McColl	A'	$+$	$\times$	$:$	$=$	
Peano	$-p$	$\cup$	$\cap$	$\supset$	$=$	
Russell	$\sim p$	v	.	$\supset$	$\equiv$	
Hilbert	$\overline{A}$		&	$\rightarrow$	∞	
Łukasiewicz	Np	A	K	C	E	D (i.e. NK)

Thus Łukasiewicz writes 'Cpq' for '$p \supset q$', and 'Apq' for '$p \lor q$'. An example of a more complex formula is '$CCpqCNqNp$' instead of '$p \supset q . \supset . \sim q \supset \sim p$'.

§ 42. FUNCTION, VARIABLE, TRUTH-VALUE

While nearly everything mentioned so far is within the scope of Stoic and Scholastic logic – though the new logicians knew hardly anything of the achievements of their predecessors, – the concepts of function, variable, and truth-value, without effecting anything radically new, yet produce so marked a development of the old concept of logical form as to deserve distinct and thorough treatment.

After an introductory quotation from De Morgan (1858) concerning logical form in general, we give Frege's fundamental text on the concept of function (1893), the explanation and development of Frege's thought from Russell and the *Principia* (1903 and 1910), and finally the extension of the concept of function to many-place functions by Peirce (1892) and Frege (1893). For the doctrine of the variable in mathematical logic we have a quotation from Frege's *Begriffsschrift* (1879) and Russell's elaboration of the ideas therein (1903 and 1910). As to truth-values, two texts from Frege (1893) and one from Peirce (1885) are to hand.

In conclusion we exhibit some examples of modern truth-matrices (truth-tables, tables of truth-values), by which propositional functors are defined, taking these from Peirce (1902) and Wittgenstein (1921); the decision procedure based on them is illustrated from Kotarbiński (1929).

A. LOGICAL FORM

An important text of De Morgan's make a fitting start. It dates from 1858, and shows a very clear idea of logical form. It may be compared with Buridan's definition of logical form (**26.12**): the thought is the same, but more developed, in that abstraction is made from the sense of the logical constants.

42.01 In the following chain of propositions, there is exclusion of matter, form being preserved, at every step: —

		Hypothesis
(Positively true)	Every man is animal	
	Every man is Y	Y has existence
	Every X is Y	X has existence
	Every X —— Y	—— is a *transitive* relation
	α of X —— Y	α a fraction $<$ or $= 1$
(Probability β)	β of X —— Y	β a fraction $<$ or $= 1$

The last is *nearly* the purely formal judgment, with not a single material point about it, except the transitiveness of the copula. But 'is' is more intense than the symbol ——, which means only transitive copula: for 'is' has transitiveness, and more. Strike out the word *transitive*, and the last line shews the pure form of the judgment.

The foregoing table is to be understood in the sense that the conditions formulated in one row, hold for all subsequent rows; thus, e.g., the relation shown by the stroke ('——') in the two last rows must be transitive, since this is laid down in the preceding row.

Neither De Morgan nor any other logician can remain at so high a level of abstraction as is here achieved. Basically, this is a rediscovery of the scholastic concept of form, made through a broadening of the mathematical concept of function, for which we refer to Peirce (**42.02**) and Frege.

B. CONCEPT OF FUNCTION: FREGE

We now give Frege's fundamental text (1893):

42.03 If we are asked to state what the word 'function' as used in mathematics originally stood for, we easily fall into saying that a function of x is an expression formed, by means of the notations for sum, product, power, difference, and so on, out of 'x' and definite numbers. This attempt at a definition is not successful because a function is here said to be an *expression*, a combination of signs, and not what the combination designates. Accordingly another attempt would be made: we could try 'reference of an expression' instead of 'expression'. There now appears the letter 'x' which indicates a number, not as the sign '2' does, but indefinitely. For different numerals which we put in the place of 'x', we get, in general, a different reference. Suppose, e.g., that in the expression '$(2 + 3 \cdot x^2)\, x$', instead of 'x' we put the number-signs '0', '1', '2', '3', one after the other; we then get correspondingly as the reference of the expression the numbers 0, 5, 28, 87. Not one of the numbers so referred to can claim to be our function. The essence of the function comes out rather in the correspondence established between the numbers whose signs we put for 'x' and the numbers which then appear as the reference of our expression – a correspondence which is represented intuitively by the course of the curve whose equation is, in rectangular co-ordinates, '$y = (2 + 3.\, x^2)\, x$'. In general, then, the essence of the function lies in the part of the expression which is there over and above the 'x'. The expression of a *function needs completion, is 'unsaturated'*. The letter 'x' only serves to keep places open for a numerical sign to be put in and complete the expression; and thus it enables us to recognize the special kind of need for a completion that constitutes the peculiar nature of the function symbolized above. In what follows, the Greek letter 'ξ' will be used instead of the letter 'x'. This 'keeping open' is to be understood in this way: All places in which 'ξ' stands must always be filled by the same sign and never by different ones. I call these places *argument-places*, and that whose sign or name takes these places in a given case I call the *argument of the function* for this case. The function is completed by the argument: I call what it becomes on completion the *value* of the function for the argument. We thus get a name of the value of a function for an argument when we fill the argument-places in the name of the function with the name of the argument. Thus, e.g., '$(2 + 3.\, 1^2)\, 1$' is name of the number 5, composed of the function-name '$(2 + 3.\, \xi^2)\, \xi$' and '1'. The argument is not to be reckoned in with the function, but serves to complete the function, which is 'unsaturated' by itself. When in the sequel an expression like 'the function $\Phi\, (\xi)$' is used, it is always to be observed that the only service rendered by 'ξ' in the symbol for the function is that it makes the argument-places recognizable; it does not imply that the essence of the function becomes changed when any other sign is substituted for 'ξ'.

The following remarks will assist understanding of this pioneer passage. In mathematical usage the word 'function' has two references, usually not very clearly distinguished. On the one hand it stands for an *expression* (formula) in which a variable occurs, on the other for the 'correspondence between numbers' for which such an expression stands, and so for some kind of lecton or in general, for that for which the expression stands, (which in any case is not a written symbol). Frege makes a sharp distinction between these two references, and allows only the *second* to the word 'function' – conformably with his general position that logic (and mathematics) has as its object not symbols but what they stand for. It is important to understand this, because Russell and nearly all logicians after him will speak of expressions and formulae as 'functions', unlike Frege.

However, this opposition is irrelevant to the basic logical problems considered here. Frege, too, makes use of analysis of expressions to convey his thought, and what he states in the text just quoted, holds good for *every* interpretation of the word 'function'. He introduces, namely, three fundamental concepts: 1. of the argument and argument-place, 2. of a value, 3. of an 'unsaturated' function, i.e. one containing a variable.

C. PROPOSITIONAL FUNCTION: RUSSELL

Russell who knew the work of Frege well, followed his ideas but with some divergences. He seems to start from the Aristotelian concept of proposition rather than from the mathematical concept of function, and as already said, apparently interprets the word 'function' as the name of an expression or written formula. In the *Principles* (1903) he writes:

42.04 It has always been customary to divide propositions into subject and predicate; but this division has the defect of omitting the verb. It is true that a graceful concession is sometimes made by loose talk about the copula, but the verb deserves far more respect than is thus paid to it. We may say, broadly, that every proposition may be divided, some in only one way, some in several ways, into a term (the subject) and something which is said about the subject, which something I shall call the *assertion*. Thus 'Socrates is a man' may be divided into *Socrates* and *is a man*. The verb, which is the distinguishing mark of propositions, remains with the assertion; but the assertion itself, being robbed of its subject, is neither true nor false. . . .

If this text is compared with **12.04** and similar passages in Aristotle, it can be seen that Russell here opts for the original Aristotelian analysis of propositions against that of the later 'classical' logic. In this connection he seems to have been the first to formulate expressly the idea that when the subject is replaced by a variable, the resulting formula – the propositional function – is no longer a proposition. The same problem is still more explicitly treated in the *Principia:*

42.05 By a 'propositional function' we mean something which contains a variable x, and expresses a proposition as soon as a value is assigned to x. That is to say, it differs from a proposition solely by the fact that it is ambiguous: it contains a variable of which the value is unassigned. . . .

42.06 The question as to the nature of a function is by no means an easy one. It would seem, however, that the essential characteristic of a function is *ambiguity*. Take, for example, the law of identity in the form 'A is A', which is the form in which it is usually enunciated. It is plain that, regarded psychologically, we have here a single judgment. But what are we to say of the object of judgment? We are not judging that Socrates is Socrates, nor that Plato is Plato, nor any other of the definite judgments that are instances of the law of identity. Yet each of these judgments is, in a sense, within the scope of our judgment. We are in fact judging an ambiguous instance of the propositional function 'A is A'. We appear to have a single thought which does not have a definite object, but has as its object an undetermined one of the values of the function 'A is A'. It is this kind of ambiguity that constitutes the essence of a function. When we speak of 'φx', where x is not specified, we mean one value of the function, but not a definite one. We may express this by saying that 'φx' *ambiguously denotes* φa, φb, φc, etc., where φa, φb, φc, etc. are the various values of 'φx'.

D. MANY-PLACE FUNCTIONS

Perhaps even more important than the broadening of the concept of function to include non-mathematical domains, is the extension to many-place functions achieved by Frege and Peirce. The resulting extension of the Aristotelian subject-predicate schema is something quite new in formal logic. Our first text is Peirce's (1892):

42.07 If upon a diagram we mark two or more points to be identified at some future time with objects in nature, so as to give the diagram at that future time its meaning; or if in any written statement we put dashes in place of two or more demonstratives or pro-demonstratives, the professedly incomplete representation resulting may be termed a *relative rhema*. It differs from a relative *term* only in retaining the 'copula', or signal of assertion. If only one demonstrative or pro-demonstrative is erased, the result is a *non-relative rhema*. For example, '--- buys --- from --- for the price of ---', is a relative rhema; it differs in a merely secondary way from

'--- is bought by --- from --- for ---',

from '--- sells --- to --- for ---',

and from '--- is paid by --- to --- for ---'.

On the other hand, '--- is mortal' is a non-relative rhema.

42.08 A rhema is somewhat closely analogous to a chemical atom or radicle with unsaturated bonds. A non-relative rhema is like a univalent radicle; it has but one unsaturated bond. A relative rhema is like a multivalent radicle. The blanks of a rhema can only be filled by terms, or, what is the same thing, by 'something which' (or the like) followed by a rhema; or, two can be filled together by means of 'itself' or the like. So, in chemistry, unsaturated bonds can only be saturated by joining two of them, which will usually, though not necessarily, belong to different radicles. If two univalent radicles are united, the result is a saturated compound. So, two non-relative rhemas being joined give a complete proposition. Thus, to join '--- is mortal' and --- 'is a man', we have 'X is mortal and X is a man', or some man is mortal. So likewise, a saturated compound may result from joining two bonds of a bivalent radicle; and, in the same way, the two blanks of a dual rhema may be joined to make a complete proposition. Thus, '--- loves ---', 'X loves X', or something loves itself.

Frege, a year later, writes in the same sense:

42.09 So far we have only spoken of functions of one argument; but we can easily make the transition to *functions with two arguments*. These *need a double completion* in that after a completion by one argument has been effected, a function with one argument is obtained. Only after another completion do we reach an object, which is then called the *value* of the function for the two arguments. Just as we made use of the letter 'ξ' for functions with one argument, so we now use the letters 'ξ' and 'ζ' to express the twofold unsaturatedness of functions with two arguments, as in '$(ξ + ζ)^2 + ζ$'. In substituting, e.g., '1' for 'ζ' we saturate the function to the extent that in $(ξ + 1)^2 + 1$ we are left with a function with only one argument. This way of using the letters 'ξ' and 'ζ' must always be kept in view when an expression such as 'the function Ψ (ξ, ζ)' occurs (cf. **42.03**). . . . I call the places in . which 'ξ' appears, *ξ-argument-places*, and those in which 'ζ' appears, *ζ-argument-places*. I say that the ξ-argument-places are mutually *cognate* and similarly the ζ-argument-places, while I call a ξ-argument-place *not cognate* to a ζ-argument-place.

The functions with two arguments $ξ = ζ$ and $ξ > ζ$ always have a truth-value as value [at least when the signs '$=$' and '$>$' are appropriately explained]. For our purposes we shall call such functions relations. E.g., 1 stands to 1 in the first relation, and generally every object to itself, while 2 stands to 1 in the second relation. We say that the object Γ *stands to* the object Δ in the relation Ψ (ξ, ζ) if Ψ (Γ, Δ) is the True. Similarly we say that the object Δ *falls under* the concept Φ (ξ), if Φ (Δ) is the True. It is naturally presupposed here, that the function Φ (ξ) always has a truth-value. (*Footnote of Frege's*: A difficulty occurs which can easily obscure the true state of affairs and so cast doubt on the correctness of my conception. When we compare the expression 'the truth-value of this, that Δ falls under the concept Φ (ξ)' with 'Φ (Δ)', we see that to 'Φ ( )' there properly corresponds 'the truth-value of this, that ( ) falls under the concept Φ (ξ)' and not 'the concept Φ (ξ)'. Thus the last words do not properly signify a concept [in our sense], though the form of speech makes it seem as if they do. As to the difficulty in which language thus finds itself, cf. my paper *On Concept and Object*.)

E. THE VARIABLE

1. Frege

Variables, introduced by Aristotle, were subsequently regularly used both in logic and mathematics. A reflective concept of variable is already to be found in Alexander of Aphrodisias (**24.08**). In mathematical logic the concept of variable is first explicitly introduced by Frege.

42.10 The symbols used in the general theory of magnitude fall into two kinds. The first consists of the letters; each letter represents either an indeterminate number or an indeterminate function. This indeterminateness makes it possible to express by means of letters the general validity of propositions; e.g.: $(a + b) c = ac + bc$. The other kind contains such symbols as $+, -, \vee, 0, 1, 2$; each of these has its own proper meaning.

I adopt this fundamental idea of distinguishing two kinds of symbols (which unfortunately is not strictly carried out in the theory of magnitude – *footnote of Frege's*: Consider the symbols 1, log, sin, Lim. –) *in order to make it generally applicable in the wider domain of pure thought.* Accordingly, I divide all the symbols I use into *those that can be taken to mean various things* and *those that have a fully determinate sense.* The first kind are *letters*, and their main task is to be the expression of *generality*. For all their indeterminateness, it must be laid down that a letter *retains* in a given context the meaning once given to it.

2. Russell

42.12 The idea of a variable, as it occurs in the present work, is more general than that which is explicitly used in ordinary mathematics. In ordinary mathematics, a variable generally stands for an undetermined number or quantity. In mathematical logic, any symbol whose meaning is not determinate is called a *variable*, and the various determinations of which its meaning is susceptible are called the *values* of the variable. The values may be any set of entities, propositions, functions, classes or relations, according to circumstances. If a statement is made about 'Mr A and Mr B', 'Mr A' and 'Mr B' are variables whose values are confined to men. A variable may either have a conventionally-assigned range of values, or may (in the absence of any indication of the range of values) have as the range of its values all determinations which render the statement in which it occurs significant. Thus when a text-book of logic asserts that 'A is A', without any indication as to what A may be, what is meant is that *any* statement of the form 'A is A' is true. We may call a variable *restricted* when its values are confined to some only of those of which it is capable; otherwise we shall call it *unrestricted*. Thus when an unrestricted variable occurs, it represents any object such that the statement concerned can be made significantly (*i.e.* either truly or falsely) concerning that object. For the purposes of logic, the unrestricted variable is more convenient than the restricted variable, and we shall always employ it. We shall find that the unrestricted variable is still subject to limitations imposed by the manner of its occurrence, *i.e.* things which can be said significantly concerning a proposition cannot be said significantly concerning a class or a relation, and so on. But the limitations to which the unrestricted variable is subject do not need to be explicitly indicated, since they are the limits of significance of the statement in which the variable occurs, and are therefore intrinsically determined by this statement. This will be more fully explained later.

To sum up, the three salient facts connected with the use of the variables are: (1) that a variable is ambiguous in its denotation and accordingly undefined; (2) that a variable preserves a recognizable identity in various occurrences throughout the same context, so that many variables can occur together in the same context each with its separate identity; and (3) that either the range of possible determinations of two variables may be the same, so that a possible determination of one variable is also a possible determination of the other, or the ranges of two variables may be different, so that, if a possible determination of one variable is given to the other, the resulting complete phrase is meaningless instead of becoming a complete unambiguous proposition (true or false) as would be the case if all variables in it had been given any *suitable* determinations.

F. TRUTH-VALUES

Truth-values, which are of great importance in formal logic, form a special kind of value. The idea is already present in the Megarian school (**20.07**), but its expression and first description comes from Frege. His doctrine is linked to his own semantics, according to which every proposition is a name for truth or falsity, and in this he has not been generally followed, but the concept of truth-value has been accepted by all.

We give first a text of Frege's:

42.13 But that indicates at the same time that the domain of values for functions cannot remain limited to numbers; for if

I take as arguments of the function $\xi^2 = 4$ the numbers $0, 1, 2, 3$, in succession, I do not get numbers. '$0^2 = 4$', '$1^2 = 4$', '$2^2 = 4$', '$3^2 = 4$', are expressions now of true, now of false thoughts. I express this by saying that the value of the function $\xi^2 = 4$ is the *truth-value* either of what is true or of what is false. From this it can be seen that I do not intend to assert anything by merely writing down an equation, but that I only designate a truth-value; just as I do not intend to assert anything by simply writing down '2^2' but only *designate* a number. I say: 'The *names* '$2^2 = 4$' and '$3 > 2$' *stand for* the same truth-value' which I call for short *the True*. In the same manner '$3^2 = 4$' and '$1 > 2$' *stand for* the same truth-value, which I call for short *the False*, just as the name '2^2' *stands for* the number 4. Accordingly I say that the number 4 is the *reference* of '4' and of '2^2', and that the True is the reference of '$3 > 2$'. But I distinguish the *sense* of a name from its *reference*. The names '2^2' and ' $2 + 2$' have not the same *sense*, nor have '$2^2 = 4$' and '$2 + 2 = 4$'. The sense of the name for a truth-value I call a *thought*. I say further that a name *expresses* is its sense, and what it *stands for* is its reference. I *designate* by a name that which it stands for.

The function $\xi^2 = 4$ can thus have only two values, the True for the arguments $+ 2$ and $- 2$ and the False for all other arguments.

Also the domain of what is admitted as argument must be extended – indeed, to objects quite generally. *Objects* stand opposed to functions. I therefore count as an object everything that is not a function: thus, examples of objects are numbers, truth-values, and the *ranges* to be introduced further on. The names of objects – or *proper names* – are not therefore accompanied by argument-places, but are 'saturated', like the objects themselves.

42.14 I use the words, 'the function $\Phi(\xi)$ has the same *range* as the function $\Psi(\xi)$', to stand for the same thing as the words, 'the functions $\Phi(\xi)$ and $\Psi(\xi)$ have the same value for the same arguments'. This is the case with the functions $\xi^2 = 4$ and $3.\xi^2 = 12$, at least if numbers are taken as arguments. But we can further imagine the signs of evolution and multiplication defined in such a manner that the function $(\xi^2 = 4) = (3.\xi^2 = 12)$ has the True as its value for any argument whatever. Here an expression of logic may also be used: 'The concept *square root of 4* has the same extension as the concept *something whose square when trebled makes 12'*. With those functions whose value is always a truth-value we can therefore say 'extension of the concept' instead of 'range of the function', and it seems suitable to say that a *concept* is a function whose value is always a truth-value.

Independently of Frege, Peirce developed similar thoughts in 1885. His treatment of truth-values is more formalistic and not tied to any particular semantic theory. However, this formalism enabled him to formulate one which seems to qualify him to be regarded as a precursor of many-valued logics.

42.15 According to ordinary logic, a proposition is either true or false, and no further distinction is recognized. This is the descriptive conception, as the geometers say; the metric conception would be that every proposition is more or less false, and that the question is one of amount. At present we adopt the former view.

42.16 Let propositions be represented by quantities. Let **v** and **f** be two constant values, and let the value of the quantity representing a proposition be **v** if the proposition is true and be **f** if the proposition is false. Thus, x being a proposition, the fact that x is either true or false is written

$$(x - \mathbf{f})\,(\mathbf{v} - x) = 0.$$

So

$$(x - \mathbf{f})\,(\mathbf{v} - y) = 0$$

will mean that either x is false or y is true. . . .

42.17 We are, thus, already in possession of a logical notation, capable of working syllogism. Thus, take the premisses, 'if x is true, y is true', and 'if y is true, z is true'. These are written

$$(x - \mathbf{f})\,(\mathbf{v} - y) = 0$$
$$(y - \mathbf{f})\,(\mathbf{v} - z) = 0.$$

Multiply the first by $(\mathbf{v} - z)$ and the second by $(x - \mathbf{f})$ and add. We get

$$(x - \mathbf{f})\,(\mathbf{v} - \mathbf{f})\,(\mathbf{v} - z) = 0,$$

or dividing by $\mathbf{v} - \mathbf{f}$, which cannot be 0,

$$(x - \mathbf{f})\,(\mathbf{v} - z) = 0;$$

and this states the syllogistic conclusion, 'if x is true, z is true'.

42.18 But this notation shows a blemish in that it expresses propositions in two distinct ways, in the form of quantities, and in the form of equations; and the quantities are of two kinds, namely those which must be either equal to f or to v, and those which are equated to *zero*. To remedy this, let us discard the use of equations, and perform no operations which can give rise to any values other than f and v.

42.19 Of operations upon a simple variable, we shall need but one. For there are but two things that can be said about a single proposition, by itself; that it is true and that it is false,

$$x = v \text{ and } x = f.$$

The first equation is expressed by x itself, the second by any function, φ, of x, fulfilling the conditions

$$\varphi v = f \quad \varphi f = v.$$

This simplest solution of these equations is

$$\varphi x = f + v - x.$$

G. TRUTH-MATRICES
1. Peirce

The standpoint revealed in the last text comes near to defining propositional functors by means of truth-values. Tabular definitions of this kind have already been met with in the Stoic-Megarian school (**20.07** ff.), later on in Boole, though without explicit reference to truth-values, and finally in Frege's *Begriffsschrift* (**41.12**). Peirce has the notion quite explicitly, and in connection, moreover, with ancient logic, in 1880:

42.20 There is a small theorem about multitude that it will be convenient to have stated, and the reader will do well to fix it in his memory correctly. . . . If each of a set of m objects be connected with some one of a set of n objects, the possible modes of connection of the sets will number n^m. Now an assertion concerning the value of a quantity either admits as possible or else excludes each of the values v and f. Thus, v and f form the set m objects each connected with one only of n objects, *admission* and *exclusion*. Hence there are, n^m, or 2^2, or 4, different possible assertions concerning the value of any quantity, x. Namely, one assertion will simply be a form of assertion without meaning, since it admits either value. It is represented by the letter, x. Another assertion will violate the hypothesis of dichotomies by excluding both values. It may be represented by $\bar{x}$. Of the remaining two, one will admit v and exclude f, namely $\underset{\sim}{x}$; the other will admit f and exclude v, namely $\bar{x}$.

Now, let us consider assertions concerning the values of two quantities, x and
y. Here there are two quantities, each
of which has one only of two values; so
that there are 2^2, or 4, possible states of
things, as shown in this diagram.

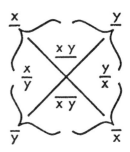

Above the line, slanting upwards to
the right, are placed the cases in which
x is v; below it, those in which x is f.
Above the line but slanting downward
to the right, are placed the cases in which y is v; below it,
those in which y is f. Now in each possible assertion each of
these states of things is either admitted or excluded; but not
both. Thus m will be 2^2, while n will be 2; and there will
be n^m, or 2^2, or 16, possible assertions. . . .

Of three quantities, there are 2^3, or 8, possible sets of
values, and consequently 2^8, or 256, different forms of propositions. Of these, there are only 38 which can fairly be said to
be expressible by the signs [used in a logic of two quantities].
It is true that a majority of the others might be expressed
by two or more propositions. But we have not, as yet, expressly
adopted any sign for the operation of compounding propositions. Besides, a good many propositions concerning three
quantities cannot be expressed even so. Such, for example,
is the statement which admits the following sets of values:

x	y	z
v	v	v
v	f	f
f	v	f
f	f	v

Moreover, if we were to introduce signs for expressing
[each of] these, of which we should need 8, even allowing the
composition of assertions, still 16 more would be needed to
express all propositions concerning 4 quantities, 32 for 5,
and so on, *ad infinitum.*

2. *Wittgenstein*

The same doctrine was systematically elaborated about 1920 by
J. Łukasiewicz, E. L. Post and L. Wittgenstein. We give the relevant
text from the last:

42.21. With regard to the existence of n atomic facts there are $K_n = \sum\limits_{\nu=0}^{n} \binom{n}{\nu}$ possibilities.

It is possible for all combinations of atomic facts to exist, and the others not to exist.

42.22 To these combinations correspond the same number of possibilities of the truth – and falsehood – of n elementary propositions.

42.23 The truth-possibilities of the elementary propositions mean the possibilities of the existence and non-existence of the atomic facts.

42.24 The truth-possibilities can be presented by schemata of the following kind ('T' means 'true, 'F' 'false'. The rows of T's and F's under the row of the elementary propositions mean their truth-possibilities in an easily intelligible symbolism).

p	q	r
T	T	T
F	T	T
T	F	T
T	T	F
F	F	T
F	T	F
T	F	F
F	F	F

p	q
T	T
F	T
T	F
F	F

p
T
F

42.25 . . . The truth-possibilities of the elementary propositions are the conditions of the truth and falsehood of the propositions.

42.26 It seems probable even at first sight that the introduction of the elementary propositions is fundamental for the comprehension of the other kinds of propositions. Indeed the comprehension of the general propositions depends *palpably* on that of the elementary propositions.

42.27 With regard to the agreement and disagreement of a proposition with the truth-possibilites of n elementary propositions there are $\sum\limits_{\varkappa=0}^{K_n} \binom{K_n}{\varkappa} = L_n$ possibilities.

42.28 . . . Thus *e.g.*

p	q	
T	T	T
F	T	T
T	F	
F	F	T

is a propositional sign.

42.29 . . . Among the possible groups of truth-conditions there are two extreme cases.

In the one case the proposition is true for all the truth-possibilities of the elementary propositions. We say that the truth-conditions are *tautological*.

In the second case the proposition is false for all the truth-possibilities. The truth-conditions are *self-contradictory*.

In the first case we call the proposition a tautology, in the second case a contradiction.

42.30 The proposition shows what it says, the tautology and the contradiction that they say nothing.

The tautology has no truth-conditions, for it is unconditionally true; and the contradiction is on no condition true.

Tautology and contradiction are without sense.

(Like the point from which two arrows go out in opposite directions.)

(I know, *e.g.* nothing about the weather, when I know that it rains or does not rain.)

42.31 Tautology and contradiction are, however, not nonsensical; they are part of the symbolism, in the same way that '*O*' is part of the symbolism of Arithmetic.

The name 'tautology' and the last quotation show the peculiar (extremely nominalist) tendency underlying Wittgenstein's semantic views. It is diametrically opposed to Frege's tendency and from his point of view misleading.

H. DECISION PROCEDURE OF LUKASIEWICZ

The tables of values constructed in the texts just cited provide a decision procedure for propositional functions, i.e. a procedure which enables one to decide whether a function is a logical law (whether it becomes a true proposition for every correct substitution). The basic idea of such a procedure is present in Schröder (**42.32**). It was developed by E.L. Post (**42.33**) and was known to J. Łukasiewicz at the same time (**42.34**). It is set out in full in the manuals of Hilbert and Ackermann (**42.35**), 1928, and T. Kotarbinski, 1929. We quote Kotarbinski's text, because of its clarity. The author writes 'p'' for 'not p', and uses '$+$', '$<$', '$=$', as signs of addition, implication and equivalence respectively.

42.36 We shall now give a very simple method of verification for the propositional calculus, which enables one to verify the correctness of every formula in this domain [viz. the zero-one method of verification]. We stipulate for this purpose that it is permitted to write, say, zero for a false proposition, and one for a true. With the help of this symbolism we now investigate whether a given formula becomes a true proposition for all substitutions of propositions for propositional variables – always under the condition that the same (proposition) is substituted for the same (variable), or whether on the other hand it becomes a false proposition for some substitutions. In the first case it is a valid formula, in the second an invalid one. . . .

We recollect in this connection: (1) that the negation of a true proposition is always a false proposition, and conversely; (2) that the logical product is true only when both factors are true; (3) that the logical sum is always true when at least one of its parts is true, and false only in the case that both its parts are false; (4) that implication is false only when its antecedent is true and its consequent false; (5) that equivalence is true only when both sides are true or both false; but when one side is true, the other false, then the whole equivalence is false. If, for example, we put zero for p and one for q in a formula, then this formula can be further simplified by writing a zero in place of the product of p and q wherever this occurs throughout the formula – and analogously in the case of the other functions. . . .

If, after the application of all possible substitutions of zero and one for propositional variables in a given formula, and after carrying out the . . . simplifications described, the formula always reduces to a one, then it is true. But if it is zero for even a single choice of substitutions, it is invalid.

To have an example, we verify the formula of transposition . . .

$$(p < q) = (q' < p')$$

1. We suppose that true propositions have been substituted both for p and for q. Our formula then takes on the form

$$(1 < 1) = (1' < 1').$$

Simplifying it by Rule (1), we get:
$$(1 < 1) = (0 < 0)$$
. . . further . . . we get
$$1 = 1$$
which . . . we can replace by
$$1.$$

The process is then repeated with the other three possible substitutions.

§ 43. PROPOSITIONAL LOGIC AS A SYSTEM

In the last two paragraphs we have spoken of the basic concepts and one of the main methods of modern propositional logic. Now we come on to show the second, axiomatic, method at work, in some sample sections reproduced from different propositional systems.

These sections will be taken from the systems of McColl (1877), Frege (1879 and 1893), Whitehead and Russell (1910) – here we insert a text from Peirce, connected with the Sheffer stroke – and finally Łukasiewicz (1920). In this last system, two-valued propositional logic seems to have reached the term of its development.

A. McCOLL

The ensuing texts, which are a continuation of the definitions in **41.05** ff., contain rules for an algebraic system of propositional logic, constructed in the spirit of Boole. It may be compared with the non-algebraic system of Łukasiewicz (**43.45**). It may be remarked that while this algebraic style has been for the most part superseded, there have also been quite recent algebraic systems (Tarski).

43.01 *Rule 1.* – The rule of ordinary algebraical multiplication applies to the multiplication of indeterminate statements, thus:
$$A(B + C) = AB + AC; (A + B) (C + D) = AC + AD + BC + BD;$$
and so on for any number of factors, and whatever be the number of terms in the respective factors.

43.02 *Rule 2.* – Let A be any statement whatever, and let B be any statement which is implied in A [and which must therefore be true when A is true, and false when A is false]; or else let B be any statement which is admitted to be true independently of A; then [in either case] we have the equation $A = AB$. As particular cases of this we have $A = AA =$

335

$AAA = $ etc., as repetition neither strengthens nor weakens the logical value of a statement. Also,
$A = A(B+B') = A(B+B')(C+C') = $ etc., for
$B+B' = 1 = C+C' = $ etc. [see Def. 4] (**41.08**).

    43.03 *Rule 3.* $- (AB)' = AB' + A'B + A'B'$
$$= AB' + A'(B+B') = AB' + A'$$
$$= A'B + B'(A+A') = A'B + B',$$
for $A+A' = 1$ and $B+B' = 1$. Similarly we may obtain various equivalents (with mutually inconsistent terms) for $(ABC)'$, $(ABCD)'$, etc.

    43.04 *Rule 4.* $- (A+B)' = A'B'$; $(A+B+C)' = A'B'C'$; and so on.

    43.05 *Rule 5.* $- A+B = \{(A+B)'\}' = (A'B')'$
$$= AB' + (A'+A)B = AB' + B$$
$$= A'B + A(B'+B = A'B + A.$$
Similarly we get equivalents (with mutually inconsistent terms) for $A+B+C, A+B+C+D$, etc.

    43.06 *Rule 11.* $-$ If $A:B$, then $B':A'$. Thus the implications $A:B$ and $B':A'$ are equivalent, each following as a necessary consequence of the other. This is the logical principle of 'contraposition'.

    43.07 *Rule 12.* $-$ If $A:B$, then $AC:BC$, whatever the statement C may be.

    43.08 *Rule 13.* $-$ If $A:\alpha$, $B:\beta$, $C:\gamma$, then $ABC:\alpha\beta\gamma$, and so on for any number of implications.

    43.09 Rule *14.* $-$ If $AB=0$, then $A:B'$ and $B:A'$.

    43.10 *Definition 13.* $-$ The symbol $A \div B$ asserts that A does *not* imply B; it is thus equivalent to the less convenient symbol $(A:B)'$.

    43.11 *Rule 15.* $-$ If A implies B and B implies C, then A implies C.

    43.12 *Rule 16.* $-$ If A does not imply B, then B' does not imply A'; in other words, the non-implications $A \div B$ and $B' \div A'$ are equivalent.

    43.13 *Rule 17.* $-$ If A implies B but does not imply C, then B does not imply C in other words, from the two premises $A:B$ and $A \div C$, we get the conclusion $B \div C$.

    43.14 The following formulae are all either self-evident or easily verified, and some of them will be found useful in abbreviating the operations of the calculus: $-$

    (1) $1' = 0, 0' = 1$;
    (2) $1 = 1 + a = 1 + a + b = 1 + a + b + c$, etc.;

(3) $(ab + a'b')' = a'b + ab'$,
$(a'b + ab')' = ab + a'b'$;
(4) $a : a + b : a + b + c$, etc.;
(5) $(\alpha + A)(\alpha + B)(\alpha + C) \ldots = \alpha + ABC \ldots$;
(6) $(a : b) : a' + b$;
(7) $(a = b) = (a : b)(b : a)$;
(8) $(a = b) : ab + a'b'$;
(9) $(A : a)(B : b)(C : c) \ldots : (ABC \ldots : abc \ldots)$;
(10) $(A : a)(B : b)(C : c) \ldots : (A + B + C \ldots : a + b + c + \ldots)$;
(11) $(A : x)(B : x)(C : x) \ldots = (A + B + C + \ldots : x)$;
(12) $(x : A)(x : B)(x : C) \ldots = (x : ABC \ldots)$;
(13) $(A : x) + (B : x) + (C : x) + \ldots : (ABC \ldots : x)$;
(14) $(x : A) + (x : B) + (x : C) + \ldots : (x : A + B + C + \ldots)$.

B. FREGE'S RULES OF INFERENCE

One of Frege's most important intuitions concerned the distinction between theorems and rules of inference. This is already to be found in the *Begriffsschrift* (**43.15**), where he uses only a single rule; in the *Grundgesetze* he adopts several for reasons of practical convenience, of which we give four:

43.16 *If the lower member of a proposition differs from a second proposition only in lacking the judgment-stroke, one can conclude to another proposition which results from the first by suppression of that lower member.*

'Lower member', i.e. antecedent. The sense is therefore: Given '⊢— if B, then A' and further '⊢— B', then we may suppress B in the conditional proposition to obtain '⊢— A'. This is the *modus ponendo ponens* (**22.04**).

43.17 A lower member may be exchanged with its upper member, if at the same time the truth-value of each is *changed*.

Thus, given 'if B, then A', one may write 'if not A, then not B'; this is the rule of simple contraposition (**31.17**, cf. **43.22** [28]).

43.18 *If the same combination of symbols occurs as upper member in one proposition and lower member in another, one can conclude to a proposition in which the upper member of the second appears as upper member, and all lower members of the two, save the one mentioned, as lower members. But lower members which occur in both, need only be written once.*

337

Given 'if C, then B' and 'if B, then A', one may write 'if C, then A'. This is the rule corresponding to the law of syllogism (cf. **31.18**).

43.19 *If two propositions correspond in their upper members, while a lower member of one differs from a lower member of the other only in respect of a preceding negation-stroke, then we can conclude to a proposition in which the corresponding upper member appears as upper member, and all lower members of the two, with the exception of the two mentioned, as lower members. Lower members which occur in both are only to be written down once.*

Frege's concrete example (**43.20**) is this: Given 'if e, then if not d, then: if b, then a' and 'if e, then if d, then: if b, then a', one may write: 'if e, then: if b, then a'.

Łukasiewicz, deriving from Frege, formulates the difference between thesis and rule, and states the most important rule, as follows:

43.21 A *logical thesis* is a proposition in which besides logical constants there occur only propositional or name-variables and which is true for all values of the variables that occur in it. A *rule of inference* is a direction which empowers the maker of inference to derive new theses on the basis of already admitted theses. Thus e.g. the laws of identity given above are logical theses, while the following 'rule of detachment' is a rule of inference:

Whose admits as true the implication 'if α, then β' and the antecedent 'α' of this implication, has the right to admit as true also the consequent 'β' of this implication.

Thus for Łukasiewicz, 'logical thesis' covers both axioms and derived propositions.

C. PROPOSITIONAL LAWS FROM THE BEGRIFFSSCHRIFT

Space prevents us from giving Frege's propositional schemata (corresponding to Łukasiewicz's theses) in the original symbolism; Instead, we translate some of them into Peano-Russellian.

43.22 01. $a \supset . b \supset a$

02. $c \supset . b \supset a : \supset : c \supset b . \supset . c \supset a$

03. $b \supset a . \supset : . c \supset . b \supset a : \supset : c \supset b . \supset . c \supset a$

04. $b \supset a . \supset : c \supset . b \supset a : . \supset : . b \supset a : \supset : c \supset b . \supset . c \supset a$

05. $b \supset a : \supset : c \supset b . \supset . c \supset a$

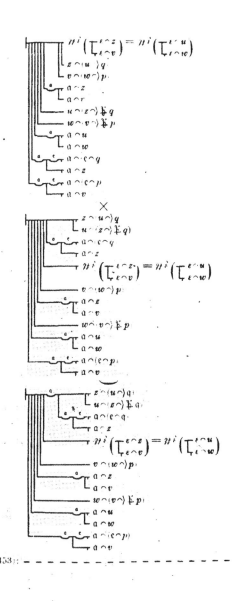

An example of Frege's Symbolism taken from "Begriffsschrift", p. 56.

06. $c \supset . b \supset a :. \supset :. c : \supset : d \supset b . \supset . d \supset a$
07. $b \supset a :. \supset :. d \supset . c \supset b : \supset : d . \supset . c \supset a$
08. $d \supset . b \supset a : \supset : b . \supset . d \supset a$
09. $c \supset b : \supset : b \supset a . \supset . c \supset a$
10. $e \supset . d \supset b : \supset a :. \supset . d \supset . e \supset b : \supset a$
11. $c \supset b . \supset . a : \supset . b \supset a$
12. $d \supset : c . \supset . b \supset a :. \supset :. d : \supset : b . \supset . c \supset a$
13. $d \supset : c . \supset . b \supset a :. \supset :. b : \supset : d . \supset . c \supset a$
14. $e \supset :. d : \supset : c . \supset . b \supset a :: \supset :: e :. \supset :. b : \supset :$
    $d . \supset . c \supset a$
15. $e \supset :. d : \supset : c . \supset . b \supset a :: \supset :: b :. \supset :. e \supset : d .$
    $\supset . c \supset a$
16. $e \supset :. d \supset : c \supset . b \supset a :: \supset :: e \supset :. d : \supset : b \supset . c \supset a$
17. $d \supset : c . \supset . b \supset a :. \supset :. c \supset : b . \supset . d \supset a$
18. $c \supset . b \supset a : \supset :. d \supset c : \supset : b \supset . d \supset a$
19. $d \supset . c \supset b : \supset :. b \supset a : \supset : d \supset . c \supset a$
20. $e \supset : d \supset . c \supset b :: \supset :: b \supset a :. \supset :. e \supset : d . \supset . c \supset a$
21. $d \supset b . \supset a : \supset :. d \supset c . \supset : c \supset b . \supset a$
22. $f \supset :: e \supset :. d : \supset : c . \supset . b \supset a :: . \supset :: . f \supset :: e \supset :. d$
    $\supset : b \supset . c \supset a$
23. $d \supset : c . \supset . b \supset a :. \supset :: e \supset d . \supset :. c \supset : b . \supset . e \supset a$
24. $c \supset a . \supset : c \supset . b \supset a$
25. $d \supset . c \supset a : \supset :. d \supset : c \supset . b \supset a$
26. $b \supset . a \supset a$
27. $a \supset a$
28. $b \supset a . \supset . \sim a \supset \sim b$
29. $c \supset . b \supset a : \supset : c \supset . \sim a \supset \sim b$
30. $b \supset . c \supset a : \supset . c \supset . \sim a \supset \sim b$
31. $\sim \sim a \supset a$
32. $\sim b \supset a . \supset . \sim a \supset \sim \sim b : \supset : \sim b \supset a . \supset . \sim a$
    $\supset b$
33. $\sim b \supset a . \supset . \sim a \supset b$
34. $c \supset . \sim b \supset a : \supset : c \supset . \sim a \supset b$
35. $c \supset . \sim b \supset a : \supset : \sim a \supset . c \supset b$
36. $a \supset . \sim a \supset b$
37. $\sim c \supset b . \supset a : \supset . c \supset a$
38. $\sim a . \supset . a \supset b$
39. $\sim a \supset a . \supset . \sim a \supset b$
40. $\sim b \supset : \sim a \supset a . \supset a$
41. $a \supset \sim \sim a$
42. $\sim \sim (a \supset a)$
43. $\sim a \supset a . \supset . a$

44. $\sim a \supset c . \supset : c \supset a . \supset a$
45. $\sim c \supset a . \supset . \sim a \supset c : \supset : . \sim c \supset a : \supset : c \supset a . \supset a$
46. $\sim c \supset a . \supset : c \supset a . \supset . a$
47. $\sim c \supset b . \supset : . b \supset a . \supset : c \supset a . \supset a$
48. $d \supset . \sim c \supset b : \supset : . b \supset a . \supset : c \supset a . \supset . d \supset a$
49. $\sim c \supset b . \supset : . c \supset a . \supset : b \supset a . \supset a$
50. $c \supset a . \supset : . b \supset a . \supset : \sim c \supset b . \supset a$
51. $d \supset . c \supset a : \supset : : b \supset a . \supset : . d \supset : \sim c \supset b . \supset a$
52. $c \equiv d . \supset . f(c) \supset f(d)$
53. $f(c) \supset : c \equiv d . \supset f(d)$
54. $c \equiv c$
55. $c \equiv d . \supset . d \equiv c$
56. $d \equiv c . \supset . f(d) \supset f(c)$
57. $c \equiv d . \supset . f(d) \supset f(c)$

D. WHITEHEAD AND RUSSELL

Passing over Peano, we come now to the *Principia Mathematica* of Whitehead and Russell (Vol. 1, 1910).

1. Primitive symbols and definition

Besides variables, Frege's sign of assertion '⊢' and Peano's dots and brackets, the *Principia* uses only two undefined primitive symbols: '$\sim$' and 'v'. 'p' is read as 'not p', '$p \vee q$' as 'p or q' the alternation being non-exclusive (**43.23**).

Implication is defined:

43.24 *1.01. $p \supset q . = . \sim p \vee q$ Df.

2. Axioms (Primitive Propositions)

43.25 *1.1. Anything implied by a true elementary proposition is true. Pp. (Footnote: The letters "Pp" stand for "primitive proposition", as with Peano.)

The above principle ... is not the same as "if p is true, then if p implies q, q is true". This is a true proposition, but it holds equally when p is not true and when p does not imply q. It does not, like the principle we are concerned with, enable us to assert q simply, without any hypothesis. We cannot express the principle symbolically, partly because any symbolism in which p is variable only gives the *hypothesis* that p is true, not the *fact* that it is true.

43.26 *1.2. ⊢ : $p \vee p . \supset p$ Pp.

This proposition states: "If either p is true or p is true, then

340

p is true". It is called the "principle of tautology", and will be quoted by the abbreviated title of "Taut". It is convenient for purposes of reference, to give names to a few of the more important propositions; in general, propositions will be referred to by their numbers.

43.27 *1.3. $\vdash : q . \supset . p \vee q$ Pp.

This principle states: "If q is true, then 'p or q' is true". Thus *e.g.* if q is "to-day is Wednesday" and p is "to-day is Tuesday", the principle states: "If to-day is Wednesday, then to-day is either Tuesday or Wednesday". It is called the "principle of addition". . . .

43.28 *1.4. $\vdash : p \vee q . \supset . q \vee p$ Pp.

This principle states that "p or q" implies "q or p". It states the permutative law for logical addition of propositions, and will be called the "principle of permutation". . . .

43.29 *1.5. $\vdash : p \vee (q \vee r) . \supset . q \vee (p \vee r)$ Pp.

This principle states: "If either p is true, or 'q or r' is true, then either q is true, or 'p or r' is true". It is a form of the associative law for logical addition, and will be called the 'associative principle'. . . .

43.30 *1.6. $\vdash :: . q \supset r . \supset : p \vee q . \supset . p \vee r$ Pp.

This principle states: "If q implies r, then 'p or q' implies 'p or r'". In other words, in an implication, an alternative may be added to both premiss and conclusion without impairing the truth of the implication. The principle will be called the "principle of summation", and will be referred to as "Sum".

3. Statement of proofs

Two examples will explain the method of proof used in the *Principia*:

43.31 *2.02. $\vdash : q . \supset . p \supset q$

Dem.

$$\left[\text{Add} \frac{\sim p}{p} \right] \vdash : q . \supset . \sim p \vee q \qquad (1)$$

$$(1) . (*1.01) \vdash : q . \supset . p \supset q$$

This is to be read: take 'Add', i.e. **43.27**:

$$q . \supset . p \vee q$$

and in it substitute '$\sim p$' for 'p'; we obtain

$$q . \supset . \sim p \vee q$$

As according to **43.24** '$\sim p \vee q$' and '$p \supset q$' have the same meaning, the latter can replace the former in (1), which gives the proposition to be proved; it corresponds to the Scholastic *verum sequitur ad quodlibet*.

That proof is a very simple one; a slightly more complicated example is:

43.32 *2.3. $\vdash : p \vee (q \vee r) . \supset . p \vee (r \vee q)$

Dem.

$$\left[\text{Perm} \ \frac{q, \, r}{p, \, q} \right] \vdash : q \vee r . \supset . r \vee q :$$

$$\left[\text{Sum} \ \frac{q \vee r, \, r \vee q}{q, \quad r} \right] \supset \vdash : p \vee (q \vee r) . \supset . p \vee (r \vee q)$$

4. Laws

43.33 The most important propositions proved in the present number are the following: . . .

*2.03. $\vdash : p \supset \sim q . \supset . q \supset \sim p$

*2.15. $\vdash : \sim p \supset q . \supset . \sim q \supset p$

*2.16. $\vdash : p \supset q . \supset . \sim q \supset \sim p$

*2.17. $\vdash : \sim q \supset \sim p . \supset . p \supset q$

These four analogous propositions consitute the "principle of transposition" . . .

*2.04. $\vdash :. p . \supset . q \supset r : \supset : q . \supset . p \supset r$

*2.05. $\vdash :. q \supset r . \supset : p \supset q . \supset . p \supset r$

*2.06. $\vdash :. p \supset q . \supset : q \supset r . \supset . p \supset r$

These two propositions are the source of the syllogism in Barbara (as will be shown later) and are therefore called "the principle of the syllogism" . . .

*2.08. $\vdash . p \supset p$

I.e. any proposition implies itself. This is called the "principle of identity" . . .

*2.21. $\vdash : \sim p . \supset . p \supset q$

I.e. a false proposition implies any proposition.

Next the *Principia* gives a series of laws concerning the logical product (**43.34**). At their head stand the two definitions:

43.35 *3.01. $p . q . = . \sim (\sim p \vee \sim q)$ Df

where "$p . q$" is the og a product of p and q.

*3.02. $p \supset q \supset r . =\!\text{l.} \ p \supset q . q \supset r$ Df

This definition serves merely to abbreviate proofs.

43.36 The principal propositions of the present number are the following:

*3.2. $\vdash :. p . \supset : q . \supset . p . q$

I. e. "p implies that q implies $p . q$", *i.e.* if each of two propositions is true, so is their logical product.

*3.26. $\vdash : p . q . \supset . p$

*3.27. $\vdash : p . q . \supset . q$

I.e. if the logical product of two propositions is true, then each of the two propositions severally is true.

*3.3. $\vdash :. p . q . \supset . r : \supset : p . \supset . q \supset r$

I.e. if p and q jointly imply r, then p implies that q implies r. This principle (following Peano) will be called "exportation", because q is "exported" from the hypothesis . . .

*3.31. $\vdash :. p . \supset . q \supset r : \supset : p . q . \supset . r$ . . .

*3.35. $\vdash : p . p \supset q . \supset . q$

I.e. "if p is true, and q follows from it, then q is true". This will be called the "principle of assertion". . . .

*3.43. $\vdash :. p \supset q . p \supset r . \supset : p . \supset . q . r$

I.e. if a proposition implies each of two propositions, then it implies their logical product. This is called by Peano the "principle of composition". . . .

*3.45. $\vdash :. p \supset q . \supset : p . r . \supset . q . r$

I.e. both sides of an implication may be multiplied by a common factor. This is called by Peano the "principle of the factor" . . .

*3.47. $\vdash :. p \supset r . q \supset s . \supset : p . q . \supset . r . s$

43.37 This proposition (*3.47), or rather its analogue for classes, was proved by Leibniz, and evidently pleased him, since he calls it "praeclarum theorema".

43.38 *3.24. $\vdash . \sim (p . \sim p)$

The above is the law of contradiction.

Next equivalence is introduced (**43.39**):

43.40 When each of two propositions implies the other, we say that the two are *equivalent*, which we write "$p \equiv q$". We put *4.01. $p \equiv q . = . p \supset q . q \supset p$ Df

. . . two propositions are equivalent when they have the same truth-value.

43.41 The principal propositions of this number are the following:

*4.1 $\vdash : p \supset q . \equiv . \sim q \supset \sim p$

*4.11. $\vdash : p \equiv q . \equiv . \sim p \equiv \sim q$ . . .

*4.2. $\vdash . p \equiv p$

*4.21. $\vdash : p \equiv q . \equiv . q \equiv p$

*4.22. $\vdash : p \equiv q \,.\, q \equiv r \,.\, \supset \,.\, p \equiv r$

These propositions assert that equivalence is *reflexive, symmetrical* and *transitive*.

*4.24. $\vdash : p \,.\, \equiv \,.\, p \,.\, p$

*4.25. $\vdash : p \,.\, \equiv \,.\, p \vee p \quad \ldots$

*4.3. $\vdash \,.\, p \,.\, q \,.\, \equiv \,.\, q \,.\, p \quad \ldots$

*4.31. $\vdash : p \vee q \,.\, \equiv \,.\, q \vee p \quad \ldots$

*4.32. $\vdash : (p \,.\, q) \,.\, r \,.\, \equiv \,.\, p \,.\, (q \,.\, r)$

*4.33. $\vdash : (p \vee q) \vee r \,.\, \equiv \,.\, p \vee (q \vee r) \quad \ldots$

*4.4. $\vdash :.\, p \,.\, q \vee r \,.\, \equiv : p \,.\, q \,.\, \vee \,.\, p \,.\, r$

*4.41. $\vdash :.\, p \,.\, \vee \,.\, q \,.\, r : \equiv \,.\, p \vee q \,.\, p \vee r$

The second of these forms (*4.41) has no analogue in ordinary algebra.

*4.71. $\vdash :.\, p \supset q \,.\, \equiv : p \,.\, \equiv \,.\, p \,.\, q$

I.e. p implies q when, and only when, p is equivalent to $p \,.\, q$. This proposition is used constantly; it enables us to replace any implication by an equivalence.

*4.73. $\vdash :.\, q \,.\, \supset : p \,.\, \equiv \,.\, p \,.\, q$

I.e. a true factor may be dropped from or added to a proposition without altering the truth-value of the proposition.

43.42 *5.1. $\vdash : p \,.\, q \,.\, \supset \,.\, p \equiv q$

I.e. two propositions are equivalent if they are both true. . . .

*5.32. $\vdash :.\, p \,.\, \supset \,.\, q \equiv r : \equiv : p \,.\, q \,.\, \equiv \,.\, p \,.\, r \quad \ldots$

*5.6. $\vdash :.\, p \,.\, \sim q \,.\, \supset \,.\, r : \equiv : p \,.\, \supset \,.\, q \vee r$

E. SHEFFER'S FUNCTOR

In 1921 H. M. Sheffer showed that all propositional functors could be defined in terms of a single one, namely the 'stroke' ('|'). '$p \mid q$' means the same as 'not p or not q'. This was adopted in the second edition of the *Principia* (**43.43**). But there is another functor which will serve the same purpose and this was found by Peirce in 1880. Here is his text:

43.44 For example, $x \curlywedge y$ signifies that x is f and y is f. Then $(x \curlywedge y) \curlywedge z$, or $\overline{x \curlywedge y} \curlywedge z$, will signify that z is f, but that the statement that x and y are both f is itself f, that is, is *false*. Hence, the value of $x \curlywedge x$ is the same as that of $\bar{x}$; and the value of $x \curlywedge x \curlywedge x$ is f, because it is necessarily false; while the value of $\overline{x \curlywedge y} \curlywedge \overline{x \curlywedge y}$ is only f in case $x \curlywedge y$ is v; and $(x \curlywedge x \curlywedge x) \curlywedge (\,\overline{x \curlywedge x \curlywedge x}\,)$ is necessarily true, so that its value is v.

With these two signs, the vinculum (with its equivalents,

parentheses, brackets, braces, etc.) and the sign ⅄, which I will call the *ampheck* (from ἀμφηκής , cutting both ways), all assertions as to the values of quantities can be expressed.

Thus,

x is $\overline{x \mathbin{⅄} x} \mathbin{⅄} \overline{x \mathbin{⅄} x}$

$\bar{x}$ is $x \mathbin{⅄} x$

$x : \vee : \bar{x}$ is $(x \mathbin{⅄} x \mathbin{⅄} x) \mathbin{⅄} (x \mathbin{⅄} x \mathbin{⅄} x)$

$x \cdot \bar{x}$ is $x \mathbin{⅄} x \mathbin{⅄} x$

$-(x\bar{x}y\bar{y})$ is $\overline{\overline{x \mathbin{⅄} y} \mathbin{⅄} (x \mathbin{⅄} y \mathbin{⅄} x \mathbin{⅄} y)} \mathbin{⅄} \big\{ (\overline{x \mathbin{⅄} y \mathbin{⅄} x \mathbin{⅄} y}) \mathbin{⅄} \overline{x \mathbin{⅄} y} \big\}$

$x\bar{x}y\bar{y}$ is $x \mathbin{⅄} y \mathbin{⅄} (x \mathbin{⅄} y \mathbin{⅄} x \mathbin{⅄} y)$

$x \equiv y$ is $\overline{(x \mathbin{⅄} y \mathbin{⅄} y)} \mathbin{⅄} \overline{(x \mathbin{⅄} x \mathbin{⅄} y)}$

$-(x \equiv y)$ is $x \mathbin{⅄} y \mathbin{⅄} \overline{(x \mathbin{⅄} x \mathbin{⅄} y \mathbin{⅄} y)}$

$x \vee y$ is $\overline{x \mathbin{⅄} y \mathbin{⅄} x \mathbin{⅄} y}$

$\bar{x} \vee \bar{y}$ is $\overline{(x \mathbin{⅄} x \mathbin{⅄} y \mathbin{⅄} y)} \mathbin{⅄} (x \mathbin{⅄} x \mathbin{⅄} y \mathbin{⅄} y)$ [or $x \mathbin{⅃} y$]

$\bar{x} \vee y$ is $\overline{(x \mathbin{⅄} y \mathbin{⅄} y)} \mathbin{⅄} (y \mathbin{⅄} x \mathbin{⅄} y)$

or $[(y \mathbin{⅄} x \mathbin{⅄} x) \mathbin{⅄} (y \mathbin{⅄} x \mathbin{⅄} x)]$

$x \cdot y$ is $\overline{x \mathbin{⅄} x \mathbin{⅄} y \mathbin{⅄} y}$

$\bar{x} \cdot y$ is $\overline{x \mathbin{⅄} x \mathbin{⅄} y}$ or $x \mathbin{⅄} y \mathbin{⅄} y$

F. ŁUKASIEWICZ'S STATEMENT OF PROOFS

Finally we give an example of the statement of propositional proofs in the very exact form developed by Łukasiewicz in 1920. The text quoted here dates from 1934, and is chosen for its brevity and clarity.

43.45 The logical systems based on axioms are strictly *formalized*, i.e. the correctness of derivations can be checked without reference to or even knowledge of the meaning of the symbols used in them, provided only one knows the rules of inference.

In illustration two examples of formalized proofs are given.

a) Proof of the law of identity 'Cpp' from the propositional axioms:

1 $CCpqCCqrCpr$

2 $CCNppp$

3 $CpCNpq$

  1 q/Csq × 4   [substitution of 'Csq' for 'q']

4 $CCpCsqCCCsqrCpr$

  4 s/Np × 5   [substitution of 'Np' for 's']

5 $CCpCNpqCCCNpqrCpr$

$5 \times C3 - 6$ [detachment of *6* on the basis of *5* and *3*]
6 CCCNpqrCpr
$6 \, q/p, r/p \times 7$ [substitution of '*p*' for '*q*' and '*r*']
7 CCCNpppCpp
$7 \times C\, 2 - 8$ [detachment of *8* on the basis of *7* and *2*]
8 Cpp
. . .

IV. LOGIC OF TERMS

§ 44. PREDICATE LOGIC

The matter so far discussed corresponds to the Megarian-Stoic doctrine and the Scholastic theory of *consequentiae*, with the exception of the first interpretation of the Boolean calculus which is comparable to the Aristotelian (assertoric) syllogistic as being also a logic of terms. But in the second period of mathematical logic, i.e. mainly since Frege, two other forms of term-logic were developed. These are linked together in contrast to Boole's calculus (in its classical interpretation) essentially in the following respects:

1. The Boolean calculus is purely extensional: it treats of classes, i.e. extensions of concepts. The calculus has no means at its disposal of dealing with meanings, much less of distinguishing them from classes. Now, on the other hand, in the new logic of terms, meaning and extension are treated in sharp distinction, so that we have *two* different doctrines: the logic of predicates, treating of meaning, and the logic of classes, treating of extensions.

2. Within the logic of classes, the Boolean calculus has no place for individuals; in this respect it resembles the Aristotelian logic, or more exactly, its authors confused the relation of an individual to a class with that of one class to another, like Ockham and the 'classical' logicians (confused, therefore, the Aristotelian relations of species and genus). These are now kept clearly distinct.

3. The Boolean calculus expresses the Aristotelian quantifiers 'all' and 'some' as operations on classes; it can therefore say, for instance, that all A is B, or that A and B intersect. But it does this by means of relations between classes and the universe, without using the concept of the individual. Now, on the other hand, we meet one of the most interesting contributions made by mathematical logic, viz. quantifiers 'all' and 'some' applied to individuals. In contrast to the Aristotelian tradition, these quantifiers are conceived as separate from the quantified function and its copula, and are so symbolized.

We shall speak first of the development of the doctrine of quantifiers, which begins, so far as we know, with Frege (1879). But the doctrine in the form given it by Frege, which is superior to all subsequent ones, remained at first quite unknown, until eventually Russell helped to establish it. Hence it must have been developed independently of Frege by Mitchell (1883), Peirce (1885) (cf. **44.02**) and Peano (1889). In the second place we give two texts about the concepts of free and bound variables, first explicitly introduced by Peano (1897), as it seems. Formal implication, which is closely connected with that, also derives from Peano (1889), but was thoroughly expounded by Peirce (1896). After that we make a selection of laws of predicate-logic from the *Principia*, and finally illustrate the theory of identity as found in Frege (1879) and Peirce (1885).

A. QUANTIFIERS

For the reasons stated we begin with Mitchell.

1. Mitchell

Mitchell writes:

44.01 Let F be any logical polynomial involving class terms and their negatives, that is, any sum of products (aggregants) of such terms. Then the following are respectively the forms of the universal and the particular propositions: –

All U is F, here denoted by F_1
Some U is F, here denoted by Fu.

These two forms are so related that

$$\overline{\overline{F}}_1 + Fu = \infty$$
$$\overline{F}_1 Fu = 0 \ \ ;$$

that is, F_1 and Fu are negatives of each other; that is $\overline{(F_1)} = Fu$. The two propositions F_1 and Fu satisfy the one equation

$$F_1\overline{F}_1 = 0,$$

and are 'contraries' of each other. Whence, by taking the negative of both sides, we get $Fu + Fu = \infty$; that is Fu and $\overline{F}u$ are 'sub-contraries' of each other. The line over the F in the above does not indicate the negative of the proposition, only the negative of the predicate, F. The negative of the proposition F_1 is not $\overline{F}_1$, but $(\overline{F}_1)$, which, according to the above $=$ Fu.

One might at first think that 'F_1' simply signifies 'all 1 are F', but this is not so; the subscript is not a subject, but precisely an index or quantifier which says that what 'F' represents holds universally, and correspondingly for 'Fu'. This is the first step in the separation of the quantifier from the function, though this is still not too clear. In the continuation of that text, Mitchell introduces the symbols ‚Π' and ‘Σ', but *not* as quantifiers.

2. Peirce

The doctrine is very clear in Peirce:

44.02 We now come to the distinction of *some* and *all*, a distinction which is precisely on a par with that between truth and falsehood; that is, it is descriptive.

All attempts to introduce this distinction into the Boolean algebra were more or less complete failures until Mr. Mitchell showed how it was to be effected. His method really consists in making the whole expression of the proposition consist of two parts, a pure Boolean expression referring to an individual and a Quantifying part saying what individual this is. Thus, if k means 'he is a king', and h, 'he is happy',

the Boolean $\qquad (\overline{k} + h)$

means that the individual spoken of is either not a king or is happy. Now, applying the quantification, we may write

$$\text{Any } (\overline{k} + h)$$

to mean that this is true of any individual in the (limited) universe, or

$$\text{Some } (\overline{k} + h)$$

to mean that an individual exists who is either not a king or is happy.

44.03 In order to render the notation as iconical as possible we may use Σ for *some*, suggesting a sum, and Π for *all*, suggesting a product. Thus $\Sigma_i x_i$ means that x is true of some one of the individuals denoted by i or

$$\Sigma_i x_i = x_i + x_j + x_k + \text{etc.}$$

In the same way, $\Pi^2 x^2$ means that x is true of all these individuals, or

$$\Pi_i x_i = x_i x_j x_k, \text{ etc.}$$

If x is a simple relation, $\Pi_i \Pi_j x_{ij}$ means that every i is in this relation to every j, $\Sigma_i \Pi_j x_{ij}$ means that some one i is in this relation to every j, $\Pi_j \Sigma_i x_{ij}$ that to every j some i or other is in this relation, $\Sigma_i \Sigma_j x_{ij}$ that some i is in this relation to some j. It is to be remarked that $\Sigma_i x_i$ and $\Pi_i x_i$ are only *similar* to a sum and a product; they are not strictly of that nature, because the individuals of the universe may be innumerable.

We have already met the basic idea of this text, having seen it explicitly formulated by Albert of Saxony (**34.07**), so that this is a re-discovery. Quite new, on the other hand, is the clear separation of the quantifier from the formula quantified.

3. Peano

Peirce's notation was adopted by Schröder (**44.04**) and today is still used in Łukasiewicz's symbolism. But Peano's is more widely established, since its essentials were taken over in the *Principia*. The Italian logician introduces it in these words:

44.05 If the propositions *a*, *b*, contain undetermined beings, such as *x*, *y*, ..., i.e. if there are relationships between the beings themselves, then $a \supset_{x,y,} ... b$ signifies: whatever *x*, *y*, ..., may be, *b* is deduced from the proposition *a*. To avoid risk of ambiguity, we write only $\supset$ instead of $\supset_{x,y,} ....$

4. Frege

Now we come to Frege's *Begriffsschrift:*

44.06 In the expression for a judgment, the complex symbol to the right of ⊢— may always be regarded as a function of one of the symbols that occur in it. *Let us replace the argument with a Gothic letter, and insert a concavity in the content-stroke, and make this same Gothic letter stand over the concavity*: e.g.:

$$\vdash\!\!\!\frown^{\mathfrak{a}}\!\!\!\smile\!\!- \quad \Phi\,(\mathfrak{a})$$

This signifies the judgment that the function is a fact whatever we take its argument to be. A letter used as a functional symbol, like Φ in $\Phi\,(A)$, may itself be regarded as the argument of a function; accordingly, it may be replaced by a Gothic letter, used in the sense I have just specified. The only restrictions imposed on the meaning of a Gothic letter are the obvious ones: (i) that the complex of symbols following a content-stroke must still remain a possible content of judgment (**41.11**); (ii) that if the Gothic letter occurs as a functional symbol, account must be taken of this circumstance. *All further conditions imposed upon the allowable substitutions for a Gothic letter must be made part of the judgment.* From such a judgment, therefore, we can always deduce any number we like of *judgments with less general content*, by substituting something different each time for the Gothic letter; when this is done, the concavity in the content-stroke vanishes again. The horizontal stroke that occurs to the left of the concavity in

$$\vdash\!\!\!\frown^{\mathfrak{a}}\!\!\!\smile\!\!- \quad \Phi\,(\mathfrak{a})$$

is the content-stroke for (the proposition) that $\Phi\,(\mathfrak{a})$ holds good whatever is substituted for $\mathfrak{a}$; the stroke occurring to the right of the concavity is the content-stroke of $\Phi\,(\mathfrak{a})$ – we must here imagine something definite substituted for $\mathfrak{a}$.

By what was said before about the meaning of the judgment-stroke, it is easy to see what an expression like

$$—\!\!\frown\!\!\overset{\mathfrak{a}}{\smile}\!\!\frown\!\!— X\ (\mathfrak{a})$$

means. This expression may occur as part of a judgment, as in

$$\vdash\!\!\frown\!\!\overset{\mathfrak{a}}{\smile}\!\!\frown\!\!— X\ (\mathfrak{a}),\qquad \vdash\overline{\underset{\underset{\displaystyle\smile\overset{\mathfrak{a}}{}\!\!— X\ (\mathfrak{a})}{\rule{0pt}{0pt}}}{\hspace{3em}A}}$$

It is obvious that from these judgments we cannot infer less general judgments by substituting something definite for $\mathfrak{a}$, as we can from

$$\vdash\!\!\frown\!\!\overset{\mathfrak{a}}{\smile}\!\!\frown\!\!— X\ (\mathfrak{a})$$

$\vdash\!\!\frown\!\!\overset{\mathfrak{a}}{\smile}\!\!\frown\!\!— X\ (\mathfrak{a})$ serves to deny that $X\ (\mathfrak{a})$ is always a fact whatever we substitute for $\mathfrak{a}$. But this does not in any way deny the possibility of giving $\mathfrak{a}$ some meaning Δ such that $X\ (\Delta)$ is a fact. $\vdash\overline{\underset{\underset{\displaystyle\smile\overset{\mathfrak{a}}{}— X\ (\mathfrak{a})}{\rule{0pt}{0pt}}}{\hspace{3em}A}}$

means that the case in which $—\!\!\frown\!\!\overset{\mathfrak{a}}{\smile}\!\!\frown\!\!— X\ (\mathfrak{a})$ is affirmed and A denied does not occur. But this does not in any way deny the occurrence of the case in which $X\ (\Delta)$ is affirmed and A denied; for, as we have just seen, $X\ (\Delta)$ may be affirmed and, nevertheless, $—\!\!\frown\!\!\overset{\mathfrak{a}}{\smile}\!\!\frown\!\!— X(\mathfrak{a})$ denied. Thus here likewise we cannot make an arbitrary substitution for $\mathfrak{a}$ without prejudice to the truth of the judgment. This explains why we need the concavity with the Gothic letter written on it; *it delimits the scope of the generality signified by the letter. A Gothic letter retains a fixed meaning only within its scope;* the same Gothic letter may occur within various scopes in the same judgment, and the meaning we may ascribe to it in one scope does not extend to any other scope. The scope of one Gothic letter may include that of another, as is shown in

$$\vdash\!\!\frown\!\!\overset{\mathfrak{a}}{\smile}\overline{\underset{\underset{\displaystyle\smile\overset{\mathfrak{e}}{}— B(\mathfrak{a},\ \mathfrak{e})}{\rule{0pt}{0pt}}}{\hspace{3em}A(\mathfrak{a})}}$$

In this case *different* letters must be chosen; we could not replace $\mathfrak{e}$ by $\mathfrak{a}$. It is naturally legitimate to replace a Gothic letter everywhere in its scope by some other definite letter, provided that there are still different letters standing where different letters stood before. This has no effect on the context. *Other substitutions are permissible only if the concavity directly follows the judgment-stroke,* so that the scope of the Gothic letter is constituted by the content of the whole judgment. Since this is a specially important case, I shall introduce the following abbreviation: *an italic letter is always*

351

to have as its scope the content of the whole judgment, and this scope is not marked out by a concavity in the content-stroke. If an italic letter occurs in an expression not preceded by a judgment-stroke, the expression is senseless. *An italic letter may always be replaced by a Gothic letter that does not yet occur in the judgment*; in this case the concavity must be inserted immediately after the judgment-stroke. E.g. for

$$\vdash X\,(a)$$

we may put

$$\vdash\!\!\!\underset{\mathfrak{a}}{\smile}\!\!\!\vdash X\,(\mathfrak{a})$$

since a occurs only in the argument-position within $X\,(a)$.

Likewise it is obvious that from

$$\vdash \begin{array}{l} \Phi\,(a) \\ A \end{array}$$

we may deduce

$$\vdash\!\!\!\underset{\mathfrak{a}}{\smile}\!\!\!\vdash \begin{array}{l} \Phi\,(\mathfrak{a}) \\ A \end{array}$$

if A is an expression in which a does not occur, and a occupies only argument-positions in Φ (a). If $\underset{\mathfrak{a}}{\smile}\ \Phi\,(a)$ is denied, we must be able to specify a meaning for a such that $\Phi\,(a)$ is denied. Thus if $\quad \Phi\,(a)$ were denied and A affirmed, we should have to be able to specify a meaning for a such that A was affirmed and $\Phi\,(a)$ denied. But since we have

$$\vdash \begin{array}{l} \Phi\,(a) \\ A \end{array}$$

we cannot do so; for this formula means that whatever a may be the case in which $\Phi\,(a)$ would be denied and A affirmed does not occur. Hence we likewise cannot both deny $\underset{\mathfrak{a}}{\smile}$ $\Phi\,(\mathfrak{a})$ and affirm A: i.e.

$$\vdash\!\!\!\underset{\mathfrak{a}}{\smile}\!\!\!\vdash \begin{array}{l} \Phi\,(\mathfrak{a}) \\ A. \end{array}$$

44.07 We may now consider certain combinations of symbols.

$$\vdash\!\!\!\underset{\mathfrak{a}}{\smile}\!\!\!\vdash X\,(\mathfrak{a})$$

means that we can find something, say Δ, such that $X\,(\Delta)$ is denied. We may thus render it as: 'there are some things that have not the property X'.

The sense of

$$\vdash\!\!\!\underset{\mathfrak{a}}{\smile}\!\!\!\top X\,(\mathfrak{a})$$

is different. This means: 'Whatever $\mathfrak{a}$ may be, $X\,(\mathfrak{a})$ must always be denied', or 'there is not something with the property X', or (calling something that has the property X, a X) 'there is no X'.

⌐╰┰ Λ (a) is denied by
├┰╰┰ Λ (a)

This may therefore be rendered as 'there are Λ 's'.

This an extremely important text. Frege quite clearly teaches the separation of quantifier and quantified function, introduces the concept of 'bound variable' (though without so naming it), defines the existential quantifier, and investigates what happens when there is more than one quantifier.

B. APPARENT VARIABLES

1. Peano

The expressions 'real' and 'apparent variable' derive from Peano (1897):

44.08 In these explanations we say that a letter in a formula is *real* or *apparent*, as the case may be, according as the value of the formula depends or does not depend on the name of this letter. Thus in $\int_0^1 x^m dx$ the letter x is apparent and the letter m real. All letters occuring in a theorem are apparent, since its truth is independent of the names of the letters.

The expressions 'free' and 'bound variable' are used today in just the same sence.

2. Whitehead and Russell

It is strange that the problem of quantification is only superficially touched on in Russell's *Principles of Mathematics* (1903). But it is thoroughly treated in *Principia Mathematica* (1910), from the introduction to which comes the following passage:

44.09 Corresponding to any propositional function φx, there is a range, or collection, of values, consisting of all the propositions (true or false) which can be obtained by giving every possible determination to x in φx. A value of x for which φx is true will be said to "satisfy" φx. Now in respect to the truth or falsehood of propositions of this range three important cases must be noted and symbolized. These cases are given by three propositions of which one at least must be true. Either (1) all propositions of the range are true, or (2) some propositions of the range are true, or (3) no proposition of the range is true. The statement (1) is symbolized by "$(x) . \varphi x$", and (2) is symbolized by $(\exists x) . \varphi x. \ldots$ The symbol "$(x) . \varphi x$" may be read "φx always", or "φx is always true", or "φx is true for all possible values of x". The symbol "$(\exists x) \cdot \varphi x$" may be read "there exists an x for which φx is true", or "there exists an x satisfying φx", and thus conforms to the natural form of the expression of thought.

44.10 *Apparent variables.* The symbol "$(x) \cdot \varphi x$" denotes one definite proposition, and there is no distinction in meaning between "$(x) \cdot \varphi x$" and "$(y) \cdot \varphi y$" when they occur in the same context. Thus the "x" in "$(x) \cdot \varphi x$" is not an ambiguous constituent of any expression in which "$(x) \cdot \varphi x$" occurs; ... The symbol "$(x) \cdot \varphi x$" has some analogy to the symbol

$$\text{"}\int_b^a \varphi(x) \, dx\text{"}$$

... The x which occurs in "$(x) \cdot \varphi x$" or ($\exists x$) $\cdot \varphi x$" is called (following Peano) an 'apparent variable' ... A proposition in which x occurs as an apparent variable is not a function of x. Thus *e.g.* "$(x) \cdot x = x$" will mean "everything is equal to itself". This is an absolute constant, not a function of a variable x.

C. FORMAL IMPLICATION

The theory of what Russell calls 'formal implication' is closely connected with that of quantification. It is already suggested by Peano (**44.05**) in the formula $a \supset_x b$, but Peirce is the first to explain it clearly:

44.11 Now let us express the categorical proposition, 'Every man is wise'. Here, we let mi mean that the individual object i is a man, and wi mean that the individual object i is wise. Then, we assert that, 'taking any individual object of the universe, i, no matter what, either that object, i, is not a man or that object, i, is wise'; that is, whatever is a man is wise. That is, 'whatever i can indicate, either mi is not true or wi is true! The conditional and categorical propositions are expressed in precisely the same form; and there is absolutely no difference, to my *mind*, between them. The *form* of relationship is the same.

Russell writes:

44.12 For the technical study of Symbolic Logic, it is convenient to take as a single indefinable the notion of a formal implication, *i.e.* of such propositions as "x is a man implies x is a mortal, for all values of x" – propositions whose general type is: "$\varphi(x)$ implies $\psi(x)$ for all values of x", where $\varphi(x)$, $\psi(x)$, for all values of x, are propositions. The analysis of this notion of formal implication belongs to the principles of the subject, but is not required for its formal development.

The suggestion for study which Russell makes here, has not been taken up so far as we know.

44.13 It is to be observed that "x is a man implies x is a mortal" is not a relation of two propositional functions, but is itself a single propositional function having the elegant property of being always true. For "x is a man" is, as it stands, not a proposition at all, and does not imply anything; ...

D. LAWS OF ONE-PLACE PREDICATES

After what has been said, we can here confine ourselves to some remarks and examples from the *Principia*:

44.14 We have proved in *3.33 that

$$p \supset q \,.\, q \supset r \,.\, \supset \,.\, p \supset r \,.$$

Put $p =$ Socrates is a Greek,
         $q =$ Socrates is a man,
         $r =$ Socrates is a mortal.

Then we have "if 'Socrates is a Greek' implies 'Socrates is a man', and 'Socrates is a man' implies 'Socrates is a mortal', it follows that 'Socrates is a Greek' implies 'Socrates is a mortal'". But this does not of itself prove that if all Greeks are men, and all men are mortals, then all Greeks are mortals.

Putting
$$\varphi x \,.\, = \,.\, x \text{ is a Greek,}$$
$$\psi x \,.\, = \,.\, x \text{ is a man,}$$
$$\chi x \,.\, = \,.\, x \text{ is a mortal,}$$
we have to prove
$$(x) \,.\, \varphi x \supset \psi x : (x) \,.\, \psi x \supset \chi x : \supset : (x) \,.\, \varphi x \supset \chi x. \ldots$$
We shall assume in this number, . . . that the propositions of *1–*5 (cf. **43.26–42**) can be applied to such propositions as $(x) \,.\, \varphi x$ and $(\exists x) \,.\, \varphi x$. . . . We need not take $(\exists x) \,.\, \varphi x$ as a primitive idea, but may put

*10.01. $(\exists x) \,.\, \varphi x \,.\, = \,.\, {\sim} (x) \,.\, {\sim}\varphi x$ Df

44.15 *10.1. $\vdash : (x) \,.\, \varphi x \,.\, \supset \,.\, \varphi y$

I.e. what is true in all cases is true in any one case.

*10.11. If φy is true whatever possible argument y may be, then $(x) . \varphi\, x$ is true. . . .

*10.23. $\vdash :. (x) . \varphi\, x \supset p . \equiv : (\exists x) . \varphi x . \supset . p$

I.e. if φx always implies p, then if φx is ever true, p is true.

*10.24. $\vdash : \varphi y . \supset . (\exists x) . \varphi x$

I.e. if φy is true, then there is an x for which φx is true. This is the sole method of proving existence-theorems.

*10.27. $\vdash :. (z) . \varphi z \supset \psi z . \supset : (z) . \varphi z . \supset . (z) . \varphi z$

I.e. if φz always implies ψz, then "φz always" implies "ψz always".

44.16 *10.26. $\vdash :. (z) . \varphi z \supset \psi z : \varphi x : \supset . \psi x$

This is one form of the syllogism in Barbara. *E.g.* put $\varphi z . = . z$ is a man, $\psi z . = . z$ is mortal, $x = $ Socrates. Then the proposition becomes: "If all men are mortal, and Socrates is a man, then Socrates is mortal".

Another form of the syllogism in Barbara is given in *10.3 (cf. **44.17**). The two forms, formerly wrongly identified, were first distinguished by Peano and Frege. . . .

*10.271. $\vdash :. (z) . \varphi z \equiv \psi z . \supset : (z) . \varphi z . \equiv . (z) . \psi z$

*10.28. $\vdash :. (x) . \varphi x \supset \psi x . \supset : (\exists x) . \varphi x . \supset . (\exists x) . \psi x$

*10.281. $\vdash :. (x) . \varphi x \equiv \psi x . \supset : (\exists x) . \varphi x . \equiv . (\exists x) . \psi x$

44.17 *10.3. $\vdash :. (x) . \varphi x \supset \psi x : (x) . \psi x \supset \chi x : \supset . (x) . \varphi x \supset \chi\ x$

44.18 *10.35. $\vdash :. (\exists x) . p . \varphi x . \equiv : p : (\exists x) . \varphi x$

44.19 *10.42. $\vdash :. (\exists x) . \varphi x . v . (\exists x) . \psi x : . (\exists x) . \varphi x \ v \ \psi x$

*10.5. $\vdash :. (\exists x) . \varphi x . \psi x . \psi x . \supset : (\exists x) . \varphi x : (\exists x) . \psi x$

44.20 The converse of the above proposition is false . . . while *10.42 states an equivalence. . . .

44.21 *10.51. $\vdash :. \sim\{ (\exists x) . \varphi x . \psi x \} . \equiv : \varphi x . \supset_x . \sim \psi x$

The distinction between the two forms of syllogism in *Barbara* consists, when expressed in Aristotelian terms, in the fact that in **44.17** the minor premiss is a universal proposition, in **44.16** a singular one. The false identification of the two, of which Russell speaks, is not Aristotelian, but first found in Ockham (**34.01**).

E. LAWS OF MANY-PLACE PREDICATES

The concept of a many-place function (**42.07** ff.) led Frege to plural quantification. This is not to be confused with quantification of the predicate (**36.15** ff.), since what is here quantified is not the predicate, but two parts of the subject of predication.

We cite the most important laws which inter-relate such propositions from the *Principia*.

44.22 *11.1. ⊦ : $(x, y) \cdot \varphi (x, y) \cdot \equiv \cdot (y, x) \cdot \varphi (x, y)$
44.23 *11.23. ⊦ : $(\exists x, y) \cdot \varphi (x, y) \cdot \equiv \cdot (\exists y, x) \cdot \varphi (x, y)$
44.24 *11.26. ⊦ :. $(\exists x) : (y) \cdot \varphi (x, y) : \supset : (y) : (\exists x) \cdot \varphi (x, y)$
... Note that the converse of this proposition is false. $\exists.g.$ let
$\varphi (x, y)$ be the propositional function 'if y is a proper fraction,
then x is a proper fraction greater than y'. Then for all values
of y we have $(\exists x) \cdot \varphi (x, y)$, so that $(y) : (\exists x) \cdot \varphi(x, y)$ is
satisfied. In fact '$(y) : (\exists x) \cdot \varphi(x, y)$' expresses the proposition:
'If y is a proper fraction, then there is always a proper fraction
greater than y'. But '$(\exists x) : (y) \cdot \varphi(x, y)$' expresses the proposition: 'There is a proper fraction which is greater than any
proper fraction', which is false.

44.24 is a re-discovery of a theorem from the doctrine of compounded and divided sense (**29.10** ff.)

F. IDENTITY

One logical two-place predicate which has special importance is
identity. In the Boolean period it was introduced without definition. In later mathematical logic it was defined — conformably with
an idea of Aristotle's (**16.13**) — by means of one-place predicates
and implication or equivalence. Leibniz formulated this thought in
his *principe des indiscernables*, on ontological grounds and, as it
seems, without the help of a mathematical-logical symbolism. The
first definition in mathematical logic is to be found in Frege.

44.25 Equality of content differs from conditionality and
negation by relating to names, not to contents. Elsewhere,
names are mere proxies for their content, and thus any phrase
they occur in just expresses a relation between their various
contents; but names at once appear *in propria persona* so
soon as they are joined together by the symbol for equality of
content; for this signifies the circumstance of two names'
having the same content. Thus, along with the introduction
of a symbol for equality of content, all symbols are necessarily
given a double meaning – the same symbols stand now for
their own content, now for themselves. At first sight this
makes it appear as though it were here a matter of something
pertaining only to *expression*, not to *thought;* as though we
had no need of two symbols for the same content, and therefore no need of a symbol for equality of content either.
In order to show the unreality of this appearance, I choose the
following example from geometry. Let a fixed point A lie

on the circumference of a circle, and let a straight line rotate around this. When this straight line forms a diameter, let us call the opposite end to A the point B corresponding to this position. Then let us go on to call the point of intersection of the straight line and the circumference, the point B corresponding to the position of the straight line at any given time; this point is given by the rule that to continuous changes in the position of the straight line there must always correspond continuous changes in the position of B. Thus the name B has an indeterminate meaning until the corresponding position of the straight line is given. We may now ask: What point corresponds to the position of the straight line in which it is perpendicular to the diameter? The answer will be: The point A. The name B thus has in this case the same content as the name A; and yet we could not antecedently use just one name, for only the answer to the question justified our doing so. The same point is determined in a double way:

(1) It is directly given in experience;

(2) It is given as the point B corresponding to the straight line's being perpendicular to the diameter.

To each of these two ways of determining it there answers a separate name. The need of a symbol for equality of content thus rests on the following fact: The same content can be fully determined in different ways; and *that*, in a particular case, *the same* content actually is given by *two ways of determining it*, is the content of a *judgment*. Before this judgment is made, we must supply, corresponding to the two ways of determination, two different names for the thing thus determined. The judgment needs to be expressed by means of a symbol for equality of content, joining the two names together. It is clear from this that different names for the same content are not always just a trivial matter of formulation; if they go along with different ways of determining the content, they are relevant to the essential nature of the case. In these circumstances the judgment as to equality of content is, in *K*ant's sense, synthetic. A more superficial reason for introducing a symbol for equality of content is that sometimes it is convenient to introduce an abbreviation in place of a lengthy expression; we then have to express equality of content between the abbreviation and the original formula.

$$\vdash (A \equiv B)$$

is to mean: *the symbol A and the symbol B have the same*

conceptual content, so that A can always be replaced by B and conversely.

This analysis is remarkably like that of Thomas Aquinas (**29.02**). Only, as is evident, Frege conceives identity as a relation between two *names*, and so defines it in a meta-language. Later mathematical logicians have not followed him in this, but have thought of identity as a relation between objects. This modern definition (which also corresponds to Aristotle's thought) is to be found first in Peirce:

44.26 We may adopt a special token of second intention, say 1, to express identity, and may write 1_{ij}. But this relation of identity has peculiar properties. The first is that if i and j are identical, whatever is true of i is true of j. This may be written

$$\Pi_i \, \Pi_j \, \{ 1_{ij} + \bar{x}_i + x_j \} \ldots$$

The other property is that if everything which is true of i is true of j, then i and j are identical. This is most naturally written as follows: Let the token, q, signify the relation of a quality, character, fact, or predicate to its subject. Then the property we desire to express is

$$\Pi_i \, \Pi_j \, \Sigma_k \, (1_{ij} + \bar{q}_{ki} \, q_{kj}) \cdot$$

And identity is defined thus

$$1_{ij} = \Pi_k \, (q_{ki} \, q_{kj} + \bar{q}_{ki} \, \bar{q}_{kj}).$$

That is, to say that things are identical is to say that every predicate is true of both or false of both. It may seem circuitous to introduce the idea of a quality to express identity; but that impression will be modified by reflecting that $q_{ki} \, q_{kj}$[*] merely means that i and j are both within the class or collection k. If we please we can dispense with the token q, by using the index of a token and by referring to this in the Quantifier just as subjacent indices are referred to. That is to say, we may write

$$1_{ij} = \Pi_x \, (x_i \, x_j + \bar{x}_i \, \bar{x}_j).$$

§ 45. THE LOGIC OF CLASSES

The so-called 'pure' logic of classes, i.e. the theory of relations between classes, was developed as the first interpretation of the Boolean calculus. But as already stated, this had no means of expressing the relation of an individual to a class to which it belonged.

---

[*] Reading $q_{ki} \, q_{kj}$ instead of $q_{ki} \, q_{jk}$

Further, the concept of class was taken as primitive, not defined. Here the later growth of mathematical logic brought two important novelties: first, the introduction of the concept of the relation between an individual and a class as distinct from that of class inclusion; second, the reduction of classes to properties (predicates), through definition.

A. INDIVIDUAL AND CLASS. CONCEPT OF ELEMENT

The first of these novelties is to be found, like so many others, originating in Frege's *Begriffsschrift* (1879). Just ten years later it appears also in Peano, who did not then know the *Begriffsschrift*. Here again Frege's work, though earlier and better than Peano's, remained without influence till Russell (1903). For this reason we begin with Peano:

45.01 *Concerning classes*
By the symbol K is signified a *class*, or aggregation of beings.

The symbol ε signifies *is (est)*. Thus $a \varepsilon b$ is read *a is a b; a ε K* signifies *a is a class; a ε P* signifies *a is a proposition.*

In place of $-(a \varepsilon b)$ we shall write $a -\varepsilon b;$ the symbol $-\varepsilon$ signifies *is not;* i.e.:
$$a -\varepsilon b . = : -a \varepsilon b.$$
The symbol $a, b, c \varepsilon m$ signifies: $a, b,$ and c are m; i.e.:
$$a, b, c \varepsilon m . = : a \varepsilon m . b \varepsilon m . c \varepsilon m.$$
Let a be a class; then $-a$ signifies the class constituted by the individuals which are not a.
$$a \varepsilon K . \supset : x \varepsilon -a . = . x -\varepsilon a.$$

B. MEANING AND EXTENSION

Only then could the problem of priority as between meaning and extension be posed with full accuracy. Frege was a convinced intensionalist, i.e. he emphatically maintained the priority of meaning – of concept, in his terminology – over extension, i.e. over class. His clearest formulation of this was in a communication to Jourdain in 1910 – later, then, than Russell's statement of the problem of antinomies:

45.02 In my fashion of regarding concepts as functions, we can treat the principal parts of logic without speaking of classes, as I have done in my *Begriffsschrift*, and the difficulty does not come into consideration. Only with difficulty did I resolve to introduce classes (or extents of concepts), because the matter did not appear to me quite

360

secure – and rightly so, as it turned out. The laws of numbers are to be developed in a purely logical manner. But the numbers are objects, and in Logic we have only two objects, in the first place: the two truth values. Our first aim, then, was to obtain objects out of concepts, namely, extents of concepts or classes. By this I was constrained to overcome my resistance and to admit the passage from concepts to their extents. And, after I had made this resolution, I made a more extended use of classes than was necessary, because by that many simplifications could be reached. I confess that, by acting thus, I fell into error of letting go too easily my initial doubts, in reliance on the fact that extents of concepts have for a long time been spoken of in Logic. The difficulties which are bound up with the use of classes vanish if we only deal with objects, concepts, and relations, and this is possible in the fundamental part of Logic. The class, namely, is something derived, whereas in the concept – as I understand the word – we have something primitive. Accordingly, also the laws of classes are less primitive than those of concepts, and it is not suitable to found Logic on the laws of classes. The primitive laws of Logic should contain nothing derived. We can, perhaps, regard Arithmetic as a further developed Logic. But, in that, we say that in comparison with the fundamental Logic, it is something derived. On this account I cannot think that the use of arithmetical signs ('+', '−', ':') is suitable in Logic. The sign of equality is an exception; in Arithmetic it denotes, at bottom, identity, and this relation is not peculiar to Arithmetic. It must be doubtful *a priori* that it is suitable to constrain Logic in forms which originally belong to another science.

We saw that Peano introduced the concept of the relation between individual and class, i.e. the concept of element (ε). On the most obvious interpretation he conceived the matter extensionally.

In 1903 Russell formulated the problem thus:

45.03 *Class* may be defined either extensionally or intensionally. That is to say, we may define the kind of object which is a class, or the kind of concept which denotes a class: this is the precise meaning of the opposition of extension and intension in this connection. But although the general notion can be defined in this two-fold manner, particular classes, except when they happen to be finite, can only be defined intensionally, *i.e.* as the objects denoted by such and such concepts. I believe this distinction to be purely psychological: logically, the extensional definition appears to be equally applicable to infinite classes, but practically, if we were to attempt it, Death would cut short our laudable endeavour before it had attained its goal.

Points to be noted here, and often neglected, are: (1) no modern logician is extensionalist in the sense of adopting exclusively a logic of classes, without a logic of predicates. (2) For class-logic itself there are two bases possible, an extensional and an intensional. (3) Russell – but not all logicians mentioned, Frege for instance – is of the opinion that these bases are to be theoretically equated. (4) But he admits that in practice the foundation of class-logic, and so of the extensional aspect of term-logic, must be intensional.

From the concept of extensionality touched on here, we must distinguish another, mentioned in the *Principia* in connection with propositional functions. For the *Principia* uses an intensional method of defining classes, in the sense that it uses the concept of propositional function in which there occurs a name of a property – and so a predicate. But a propositional function itself can be conceived either intensionally or extensionally. The most important text on this subject in the *Principia* is this:

45.04 When two functions are formally equivalent, we shall say that they have the same *extension*. ... Propositions in which a function φ occurs may depend, for their truth-value, upon the particular function φ, or they may depend only upon the extension of φ. In the former case, we will call the proposition concerned an *intensional* function of φ; in the latter case, an *extensional* function of φ. Thus, for example, $(x) . \varphi x$ or $(\exists x) . \varphi x$ is an extensional function of φ, because, if φ is formally equivalent to ψ, i.e. if $\varphi x . \equiv x . \psi x$, we have $(x) . \varphi x . \equiv . (x) . \psi x$ and $(\exists x) . \varphi x . \equiv . (\exists x) . \psi x$. But on the other hand 'I believe $(x) . \varphi x$' is an intensional function, because, even if $\varphi x . \equiv x . \psi x$, it by no means follows that I believe $(x) . \psi x$ provided I believe $(x) . \varphi x$.

C. THE PLURAL ARTICLE

Frege was the first to state a purely intensional definition (in the first sense) of classes. He could do this because he had at his disposal a symbol which transformed a function into its range of values: so that '*F* belongs to all *x*' becomes 'the *x*-s to which *F* belongs'. Frege's text is as follows:

45.05 Our symbolism must also be able to show the transformation of the universality of an equation into an equation between ranges of values. Thus, for instance, for

$$\text{`}\underbrace{}_{a}\quad a^2 - a = a.(a-1)\text{'}$$

I write '$\grave{\epsilon}\,(\epsilon^2 - \epsilon) = \grave{\alpha}\,(\alpha . (\alpha - 1))$'
where by '$\grave{\epsilon}\,(\epsilon^2 - \epsilon)$' I understand the range of values of the function $\xi^2 - \xi$, by '$\grave{\alpha}\,(\alpha . (\alpha - 1))$' that of $\xi . (\xi - 1)$. Similarly $\grave{\epsilon}\,(\epsilon^2 = 4)$ is the range of values of the function $\xi^2 = 4$, or, as we can also say, the comprehension of the concept *square root of four.*

After Frege, and evidently independently of him, Peano developed a similar idea. His theory is not entirely intensional, in that he uses the concept of element (ϵ) in his definition of classes.

45.06 Let a be a K(i.e.class). Let us write the symbol $x\epsilon$ before the symbol a; by the convention P2 (cf. **45.01**) we obtain the proposition

$$x \,\epsilon\, a$$

which contains the variable letter x. Now we make the convention that in writing the symbol $\overline{x\,\epsilon}$ before this proposition, the formula

$$\overline{x\,\epsilon}\,(x\,\epsilon\,a)$$

again represents the class a.
This convention is usefully applied which the proposition containing the variable letter x is not yet reduced to the form $x\,\epsilon\,a$. Let p be a proposition containing the variable letter x; the formula $\overline{x\,\epsilon}\,p$ indicates the class of 'x-es which satisfy the condition p'.
The symbol $\overline{x\,\epsilon}$ can be ready by the phrase 'the x-es which'.
Example: $1 \,\epsilon\, \overline{x\,\epsilon}\,(x^2 - 3x + 2 = 0)$
'unity is a root of the equation in parentheses'.
Let us note that in the formula $\overline{x\,\epsilon}\,p$ the letter x is apparent; the value of the formula does not change if we substitute for the letter x another letter y, in the symbol $\overline{x\,\epsilon}$ and in the proposition p.

D. DEFINITION OF CLASSES BY FUNCTIONS

In the text just quoted Peano comes near to an intensional definition of classes, when he speaks of a condition p. This idea receives explicit formulation in the *Principia*, where Russell and Whitehead write '$\hat{x}$' for 'the x-s which . . .'. Their basic definition is this:

45.07 *20.03. Cls = $\hat{\alpha}\{(\exists\,\varphi)\,.\,\alpha = \hat{z}\,(\varphi\,!\,z)\}$ Df

This is the definition of the class of classes, and so (on an intensional interpretation) of the concept of class as such. The class of classes, symbolized by 'Cls', is identical with *those* α *-s* ($\hat{\alpha}$) for which there is a property φ such that α is identical with the z-s of which φ is true. (The point of exclamation means that the last function has the name of an individual as argument and is elementary.)

The sense of this rather complicated and abstract definition becomes clear in this law which is deduced with its aid:

45.08 *20.3. $\vdash\,:\,x\,\varepsilon\,\hat{z}\,(\psi z)\,.\,\equiv\,.\,\psi x$

i.e. 'x is an element of the class of the z-s such that ψz, if and only if ψx'.

E. PRODUCT AND INCLUSION OF CLASSES

Peano succeeded in defining relations between classes by means of the definite article and quantifiers, propositional functions being presupposed. We cite two examples of such definitions from the *Formulaire* (1897) and a discussion of the difference between being an element and being included in a class.

45.09 Let a and b be classes; by $a \frown b$ we indicate the class $\overline{x}\,\varepsilon\,(x\,\varepsilon\,a\,.\,x\,\varepsilon\,b)$.

45.10 Thus the logical product of Ks (classes) has been defined by the logical product of P (proposition)s, the latter being taken as a primitive idea.

45.11 *Implication and Inclusion.*

Let a and b be Ks. In place of the proposition

$x\,\varepsilon\,a\,.\,\supset x\,.\,x\,\varepsilon\,b$

'whatever x may be, if it is an a, it is also a b', we shall write the formula, which no longer contains the apparent letter x,

$a \supset b$

which can be read: 'all a is b', or 'the class a is contained in the class b'.

45.12 The symbols ε and $\supset$, which we have introduced, and the symbol $=$, well known to the reader ... have different significations, though they sometimes correspond to the same words in language. E.g.:

'7 *is the* sum of 3 and 4' can be rendered as '7 = 3 + 4' ...

'7 *is a* prime number' can be rendered as '7 ε Np' ...

'All multiples of 6 are multiples of 3' can be rendered by '$N \times 6 \supset N \times 3$'.
These symbols also obey different laws.

§ 46. EXISTENCE

Within mathematical logic, at least since Schröder, there have been two sets of problems concerning existence. The first is in connection with the question of the so-called null class, already raised in the Middle Ages; for with the admission of such a class certain difficulties arise in the Aristotelian syllogistic. The second is concerned with propositions in which existence is ascribed to an individual, and has led to the important logical doctrine of description as found in Frege and Russell.

A. THE NULL CLASS

We treat here of the essentials on both these points.

The concept of the null class, containing no elements, was tacitly introduced in Boole's *Analysis*, in that Boole simply took over zero from algebra as the symbol of such a class. This occurs as follows, in his interpretation of the proposition 'all Xs are Ys'.

46.01 As all the Xs which exist are found in the class Y, it is obvious that to select out of the Universe all Ys, and from these to select all Xs, is the same as to select at once from the Universe all Xs.

Hence $\qquad xy = x,$

or $\qquad x(1 - y) = 0, \qquad (4).$

There is then a dissymmetry in Boole, since he introduces the universal class (1) explicitly (**40.05**), but, so to say, tacitly smuggles in the null class (0). This dissymmetry is removed in Schröder, both concepts being introduced side by side in parallel fashion.

46.02 *Two special domains* are now to be introduced into the algebra of logic, for the names of which . .. the numerals 0 and 1 recommend themselves. These too we shall explain by means of the relation-symbol of inclusion, for the

| Definition (2×) of the 'iden- | Definition (2+) of the 'iden- |
| tically null' | tically one' |

follows from our positing as *universally valid*, i.e. as to be admitted for *every* domain a of our manifold, the subsumption

$\qquad 0 \in a \qquad\qquad\qquad\qquad a \in 1$

365

That means to say:

0 is what we call a domain which stands in the relation of inclusion to every domain *a, which is contained in every domain of the manifold.*	1 is what we call a domain to which every domain *a* stands in the relation of inclusion, *in which every domain of the manifold is contained.*

46.03 Purely on didactical grounds . . . meanwhile, the interpretation which the symbols 0 and 1 will have, may be already briefly given here in advance: 0 will represent to us an *empty* domain. . . . .

Schröder then draws from his definition, the consequence that 'nothing' is 'subject of every predicate' (**46.04**).

B. NULL CLASS AND ASSERTORIC SYLLOGISTIC

The concept of the null class leads once more to the positing of the scholastic problem of the validity of certain theorems in the assertoric syllogistic. On this point we have, exceptionally a thorough historical investigation in Albert Menne's excellent work (**46.05**). The discussion of this problem took, in brief, this course:

Leibniz met with certain difficulties in his assertoric syllogistic: he was unable to deduce the four moods whose names contain '*p*', which was the cause of his constantly building new systems without finding any of them satisfactory. Boole deduced all the moods apart from those four and the five subalternate ones, expressing the Aristotelian propositions in the fashion aforesaid (**40.08**). But he said nothing about the non-deducibility of the nine others. Venn and Schröder, however, went into the problem. Schröder says:

46.06 *From the stand-point of our theory* we must now describe a number of these (syllogistic) moods as *incorrect,* viz. all those inferences by *means of which a particular judgment is drawn from purely universal premisses.* On closer inspection we shall see that these are *enthymemes* which tacitly omit an essential premiss – but as soon as this is explicitly formulated and added to complete the other premisses, then they evidently depend on three premisses and so cease to be simple' syllogisms, and even 'syllogisms' at all.

The missing premiss is formulated thus:

46.07 The inference only holds good when to the stated premisses the further assumption $a \neq 0$ is added as another premiss, i.e. the supposition that there *are* individuals of the class of the subject.

Hence two Aristotelian rules are rejected:

46.08 Hence it is to be noted: that *an inference by sub-alternation is not permissible in exact logic.*

46.09 It is ... further to be noted: *Of the conversions in traditional logic only the conversio pura is permissible in exact logic* (i.e. not the *conversio per accidens*: cf. **32.08**).

The moods in question here are: *Darapti, Felapton, Bamalip, Fesapo* and the five subalternate moods: *Barbari, Celaronl, Cesaro, Camestrop, Calemop.*

It may be asked whether the interpretation given by Boole and Schröder to the Aristotelian propositions is the only possible one? Further development has shown that it is not. If 'all . . . are . . .' and 'some . . . are . . .' are taken as undefined symbols, a correct system can be constructed in which all the Aristotelian moods are valid. The following axioms, due to Łukasiewicz, are sufficient – apart from metalogical suppositions – to yield such a system. We translate them into ordinary language.

1. All *A-s* are *A*
2. Some *A-s* are *A*
3. *Barbara*
4. *Datisi*

By introducing a term-negation, one can even limit oneself to 1, 2 and 4, as I. Thomas has shown (**46.10**). The Aristotelian system has also been developed as an exact, demonstrably consistent (46.11) system, in which the traditional syllogisms are to hand as *simple* syllogisms – contrary to the statement of Schröder cited above. It is true that the system involves some further presuppositions, but this is so of every system of term-logic, not excluding Schröder's.

C. DESCRIPTION

1. The definite article: Frege

Along with the problem of the null class, there has been posed in mathematical logic also that of the question: 'what is it that properly exists?' Frege was the first to give an answer to this, to the effect that existence is a property of the concept, not of the object (**39.11–12**). On the other hand, Frege introduced the concept of description (corresponding to the singular definite article), in dependence on his ideas about definitons of classes (**45.02**). His most important text on this subject is ithe following:

46.13 If we allowed ourselves to assert as universally valid the equation of '$\grave{\epsilon} (\Delta = \epsilon)$' with '$\Delta$', we should have in the form '$\grave{\varepsilon}\,\Phi\,(\varepsilon)$' a substitute for the definite article in language. For if it were supposed that $\Phi\,(\xi)$ was a concept under which that object Δ – and only this – fell, $\overline{}\!\underset{a}{\smile}\!\overline{}\,\Phi\,(a) = (\Delta = a)$ would be the True, and so $\grave{\varepsilon}\,\Phi\,(\varepsilon) = \grave{\varepsilon}\,(\Delta = \varepsilon)$ would also be the True, and consequently on our equation of '$\grave{\varepsilon}\,(\Delta = \varepsilon)$' with '$\Delta$', $\grave{\varepsilon}\,\Phi\,(\varepsilon)$ would be the same as Δ; i.e. in the case that $\Phi\,(\xi)$ is a concept under which one and only one object falls, '$\grave{\varepsilon}\,\Phi\cdot(\varepsilon)$, denotes this object. But this is of course not possible, since that equation, in its universality, must be admitted to fail. However, we can get some assistance by introducing the function

$$\diagdown\xi$$

with the stipulation that two cases are to be distinguished:

1) if there corresponds to the argument an object Δ, in such a way that $\grave{\varepsilon}\,(\Delta = \varepsilon)$ is the argument, the value of the function $\diagdown\,\xi$ is Δ itself;

2) if there corresponds to the argument no object Δ, in such a way that $\grave{\varepsilon}\,(\Delta = \varepsilon)$ is the argument, the argument itself is the value of the function $\diagdown\,\xi$.

Accordingly $\diagdown\,\varepsilon\,(\Delta = \varepsilon) = \Delta$ is the True, and '$\diagdown\,\grave{\varepsilon}\,\Phi\,(\varepsilon)$' stands for the object falling under the concept $\Phi\,(\xi)$, when $\Phi\,(\xi)$ is a concept under which one and only one object falls; in all other cases '$\diagdown\,\grave{\varepsilon}\,\Phi\,(\varepsilon)$' stands for the same thing as '$\grave{\varepsilon}\,\Phi\,(\varepsilon)$'. Thus, e.g., $2 = \diagdown\,\grave{\varepsilon}\,(\varepsilon + 3 = 5)$ is the true, since 2 is the only object falling under the concept

what added to 3 yields 5

– presupposing a proper definition of the sign of addition – ...

Here we have a substitute for the definite article in speech, which serves to form proper names from conceptual phrases. E.g. from the word

'positive square root of 2'

which stand for a concept, we form the proper name

'the positive square root of 2'.

There is a logical danger here. For if we want to form the proper name 'the square root of 2' from the words 'square root of 2', we make a logical mistake, since this proper name would be ambiguous and even lacking in reference without further stipulations. If there were no irrational numbers, which has indeed been maintained, the proper name 'the positive square root of 2' would be lacking in reference, at least according to the immediate sense of the words, without further stipulations. And if we purposely assigned a reference to this proper name, this would have no connection with its formation, and it could not be inferred that there is a positive square root of 2, though we should be only too ready to infer this. This danger concerning the definite article is here quite removed, since '\ è Φ (ε)' always has a reference, whether the function Φ (ξ) is not a concept, or is a concept under which more than one or no object falls, or whether again it is a concept under which one and only one concept falls.

2. Logical existence

Frege's theory was adopted by Russell in the 20th century, and further developed. This came about in peculiar circumstances. Russell himself, in 1901, introduced the distinction between real and logical existence:

46.14 Numbers, the Homeric gods, relations, chimeras and four-dimensional spaces all have being, for if they were not entities of a kind, we could make no propositions about them. Thus being is a general attribute of everything, and to mention anything is to show that it is.

Existence, on the contrary, is the prerogative of some only amongst beings. To exist is to have a specific relation to existence – a relation ... which existence itself does not have.

The distinction is not very profound – compared with the Thomistic theory of *ens rationis* (**26.04** ff.) it seems incomplete: it confuses such different kinds of beings as relations, mathematical structures and fictitious heroes. But the text is interesting because two years later A. Meinong formulated very similar ideas which became the starting-point of Russell's theory of description. We cite a text from Meinong's famous *Über Annahmen*.

46.15 If anyone forms the judgment e.g. 'a *perpetuum mobile* does not exist', it is clear that the object of which existence (*Dasein*) is here denied, must have properties, and even characteristic properties, for without such the belief in non-existence can have neither sense nor justification; but the possession of properties is as much as to say a manner of being ('*sosein*' – Meinong's quotes). This manner of being, however, does not presuppose any existence, which is rather, and rightly, just what is denied. The same could be shown analogously about knowledge of components. By keeping in general, as has often been found helpful, to knowledge of, or the effort to know, how the object under consideration was conceived in two stages, the grasping of the object and the judging about it, it at once becomes evident that one may say: objects are grasped, so to speak, in their manner of being; what is then judged, and eventually assented to, is the being, or a further manner of being, of what is grasped in that manner of being. This manner of being, and through it that which is in this manner, is comprehensible without limitation to existence, as the fact of negative judgments shows; but to that extent our comprehension finds something given about the objects, without respect to how the question of existence or non-existence is decided. In this sense 'there are' also objects which do not exist, and I have expressed this in a phrase which, while somewhat barbarous, as I fear, is hard to better, as 'externality (*Aussersein*) of the pure object'.

A year later Meinong had extended this doctrine also to 'impossible' objects·

46.16 There is, then, no-doubt that what is to be an object of knowledge does not in any way have to exist. . . . The fact is of sufficient importance for it to be formulated as the principle of the independence of manner of being from existence, and the domain in which this principle is valid can best be seen by reference to the circumstance that there are subject to this principle not only objects which in fact do not exist, but also such as cannot exist because they are impossible. Not only is the oft-quoted golden mountain golden, but the round square too is as surely round as it is square. . . . To know that there are no round squares, I have to pass judgment on the round square. . . . Those who like paradoxical expressions, can therefore say: there are objects of which it is true that there are no objects of that kind.

Nobody will deny that Meinong's doctrine is certainly paradoxical. But it is also simply false: it is not necessary to pass judgment on a round square in order to know that there are no round squares. That a philosopher of Meinong's quality could commit so grave – and so perilous – an error, is due to his not conducting an exact logical analysis of the matters at issue, i.e. more precisely, that he was not acquainted with Frege's doctrine of description. This was first brought into notice by Russell.

3. Description in Russell

It should be obvious that Russell's earlier theory (46.14) coincides with that of Meinong; though Russell goes further than Meinong in ascribing to Homeric gods etc. not merely a special manner of being but simply being. However, it seems that Meinong's clear formulation induced Russell to reject this doctrine and therewith his own earlier theory. He took over instead the theory of Frege and proceeded to develop it. In his paper *On Denoting* (1905) he wrote:

46.17 The evidence for the above theory is derived from the difficulties which seem unavoidable if we regard denoting phrases as standing for genuine constituents of the propositions in whose verbal expressions they occur. Of the possible theories which admit such constituents the simplest is that of Meinong. This theory regards any grammatically correct denoting phrase as standing for an *object*. Thus 'the present King of France', 'the round square', etc. are supposed to be genuine objects. It is admitted that such objects do not *subsist*, but, nevertheless, they are supposed to be objects. This is in itself a difficult view; but the chief objection is that such objects, admittedly, are apt to infringe the law of contradiction. It is contended, for example, that the existent present King of France exists, and also does not exist; that the round square is round, and also not round, etc. But this is intolerable; and if any theory can be found to avoid this result, it is surely to be preferred.

The above breach of the law of contradiction is avoided by Frege's theory. . . .

The theory of description is now introduced as follows, where Russell begins with an analysis of description:

46.18 By a 'denoting phrase' I mean a phrase such as any one of the following; a man, some man, any man, every man, all men, the present King of England, the present King of France, the centre of mass of the solar system at the first instant of the twentieth century, the revolution of the earth round the sun, the revolution of the sun round the earth. Thus a phrase is denoting solely in virtue of its *form*. We may distinguish three cases: (1) A phrase may be denoting, and yet not denote anything; e.g., 'the present King of France'. (2) A phrase may denote one definite object; e.e. 'the present King of England' denotes a certain man. (3) A phrase may denote ambiguously; e.g. 'a man' denotes not many men, but an ambiguous man. The interpretation of such phrases is a matter of considerable difficulty. . . .

46.19 My theory, briefly, is as follows. I take the notion of the *variable* as fundamental; I use '$C(x)$' to mean a proposition (Footnote: More exactly a propositional function.) . . . where x, the variable, is essentially and wholly undetermined. Then we can consider the two notions '$C(x)$ is always true' and '$C(x)$ is sometimes true'. Then *everything* and *nothing* and *something* (which are the most primitive of denoting phrases) are to be interpreted as follows:

C(everything) means '$C(x)$ is always true';
C(nothing) means '"$C(x)$ is false" is always true';
C(something) means 'It is false that "$C(x)$ is false" is always true'.

Here the notion '$C(x)$ is always true' is taken as ultimate and indefinable, and the others are defined by means of it. *Everything*, *nothing*, and *something* are not assumed to have any meaning in isolation, but a meaning is assigned to *every* proposition in which they occur. . . .

Next Russell interprets the proposition, 'I met a man' as '"I met x, and x is human" is not always false', and sets out the theory of formal implication already described (**44.11** ff.). There follows the theory of definite description:

46.20 It remains to interpret phrases containing *the*. These are by far the most interesting and difficult of denoting phrases . . . *the*, when it is strictly used, involves uniqueness. . . . Thus when we say 'x was *the* father of Charles II' we not only assert that x had a certain relation to Charles II, but also that nothing else has this relation. The relation in question, without the assumption of uniqueness, and without any denoting phrases, is expressed by 'x begot Charles II'. To get an equivalent of 'x was the father of Charles II' we must add, 'If y is other than x, y did not beget Charles II', or, what is equivalent, 'If y begot Charles II, y is identical with x'. Hence 'x is the father of Charles II' becomes: 'x begot Charles II; and "if y begot Charles II, y is identical with x" is always true of y'.

46.21 The whole realm of non-entities, such as 'the round square', 'the even prime other than 2', 'Apollo', 'Hamlet', etc., can now be satisfactorily dealt with. All these are denoting phrases which do not denote anything. . . . So . . . 'the round square is round' means 'there is one and only one entity x which is round and square, and that entity is round', which is a false proposition, not, as Meinong maintains, a true one. 'The most perfect Being has all perfections; existence is a perfection; therefore the most perfect Being exists' becomes:

'There is one and only one entity x which is most perfect; that one has all perfections; existence is a perfection; therefore that one exists'. As a proof, this fails for want of a proof of the premiss 'there is one and only one entity x which is most perfect'.

4. Symbolism

a. Peano

It only remained to introduce a suitable symbolism. This had already been created by Peano in connection with that used to define classes, and so with the plural article (cf. **45.06**):

46.22 Let p be a P (i.e. proposition) containing a letter x; the formula $x \ni p$ represents the class of x-s which satisfy the condition p.

The sign $\ni$ can be read as the word 'which'. . . .

Let us call the class $x \ni p$, a; the proposition $x \, \varepsilon \, a$ coincides with p; then every P containing a letter x, that is to say every condition in x, is reducible to the form $x \, \varepsilon \, a$, where a is a determinate Cls (i.e. class).

We also have $x \ni (x \, \varepsilon \, a) = a, \, x \, \varepsilon \, (x \ni p) = p$; the two signs, $x \, \varepsilon$ and $x \ni$ represent inverse operations.

46.23 Let a be a class: a signifies: 'there are a-s, a-s exist'.

46.24 $\iota \, x = y \ni (y = x) \quad \{ = (\text{equal to } x) \} \qquad$ Df
$y \, \varepsilon \, \iota \, x \, . = . \, y \, \varepsilon \, (\iota \, x) : a \supset \iota \, x \, . = a \supset (\iota \, x) :$
$a = \iota \, x \, . = . \, a = (\iota \, x) \qquad$ Df

. . . This sign ι is the first letter of the word ἴσος. So $\iota \, x$ designates the class formed by the object x, and $\iota \, x \cup \iota \, y$ the class composed of the objects x and y.

46.25 $a \, \varepsilon \, \text{Cls}. \, \exists \, a : x, y \, \varepsilon \, a \, . \supset x,y, \, . \, x = y : = y : \supset : z = \imath \, a \, .$
$\qquad = . \, a = \iota \, z \, \ldots$
$a \, \varepsilon \, \text{Cls} . \, a = \iota \, x \, . \supset . \, x = \imath \, x \, \ldots$

Let a be a class containing a sole individual x. That is the case when there are a-s and two individuals of the class a are necessarily equal. In that case $\imath \, a \ldots$ which can be read 'the a' indicates the individual x which forms the class a.

MATHEMATICAL VARIETY OF LOGIC

b. Principia

The most important definitions in this connection in the *Principia* are these:

46.26 *24.01. $V = \hat{x}\,(x = x)$ Df .

       *24.02. $\Lambda = - V$ Df

'V' corresponds to Boole's '1', 'Λ' to his '0'.

46.27 *24.03. $\exists\,!\,\alpha\,. = .\,(\exists x)\,.\,x\,\varepsilon\,\alpha$ Df

46.28 *14.01. $[(\imath x)\,(\varphi x)\,.\,\psi\,(\imath x)(\varphi x)\,. = :(\exists b) : \varphi x\,.\equiv_x$
$.\,x = b : \psi\,b$ Df

Here '$(\imath x)\,(\varphi x)$' is an 'incomplete symbol' and is to be read 'the x such that φx'; '$\psi\,(\imath x)\,(\varphi x)$' ascribes the property ψ to the x so described. The whole *14.01 is to mean: there is at least one b such that ψb (at the end), and for all x: φx if and only if $x = b$.

46.29 *14.02. $E\,!\,(\imath x)\,(\varphi x)\,. = :(\exists b) : \varphi x\,.\equiv_x.\,x = b$
    Df

To say that *the x*, such that φx, exists, means to say that there is just one x such that φx, i.e. one and only one such.

V. OTHER DOCTRINES

§ 47. LOGIC OF RELATIONS

The formal logic of relations is one of the chief new creations of mathematical logic. Anticipations of it are, indeed, to be found in antiquity (Aristotle, **16.20**ff.: Galen, **24.36**) and among the Scholastics (cf. **35.12**), but there is no developed theory before Lambert in the 18th century. Here we show the development from 1847, beginning with the basic doctrines in De Morgan (1847), and going on to Peirce (1883), and Russell (1903 and 1910). We close with some texts on the ancestral relation and isomorphy.

A. LAYING THE FOUNDATIONS

1. De Morgan

The real founder of the modern logic of relations is De Morgan' of whom Peirce, himself a great logician, said that he 'was one of the best logicians that ever lived and unquestionably the father of the logic of relatives' (**47.01**).

One pioneer text of De Morgan's has already been quoted (**42.01**); the following series comes from a paper of 1860:

47.02 I now proceed to consider the formal laws of relation, so far as is necessary for the treatment of the syllogism. Let the names X, Y, Z, be singular: not only will this be sufficient when *class* is considered as a unit, but it will be easy to extend conclusions to quantified propositions.

47.03 Let $X. .LY$ signify that X is some one of the objects of thought which stand to Y in the relation L, or is one of the Ls of Y. *Let* $X. LY$ signify that X is not any one of the Ls of Y. Here X and Y are *subject* and *predicate*: these names having reference to the mode of entrance in the relation, not to order of mention. Thus Y is the predicate in $LY . X$, as well as in $X . LY$.

This is certainly a remarkable extension of the concept of subject and predicate. De Morgan's successors did not adopt it.

47.04 When the predicate is itself the subject of a relation, there may be a composition: thus if $X . . L(MY)$, if X be one of the Ls of one of the Ms of Y, we may think of X as an 'L of M' of Y, expressed by $X . . (LM)Y$, or simply by $X . . LMY$.

De Morgan has thus introduced the concept of the relative product.

47.05 We cannot proceed further without attention to forms in which *universal* quantity is an inherent part of the compound relation, as belonging to the notion of the relation itself, intelligible in the compound, unintelligible in the separated component.

47.06 We have thus three symbols of compound relation; LM, an L of an M; LM', an L of every M; L, M, an L of none but Ms. No other compounds will be needed in syllogism, until the premises themselves contain compound relations.

47.07 The converse relation of L, L^{-1}, is defined as usual: if $X \mathrel{..} LY$, $Y \mathrel{..} L^{-1}$: if X be one of the Ls of Y, Y is one of the L^{-1}s of X. And L^{-1} may be read 'L-*verse* of X'. Those who dislike the mathematical symbol in L^{-1} might write L^{-1}. This language would be very convenient in mathematics: $\varphi^{-1}x$ might be the 'φ-verse of x' read as 'φ-verse x'.

Relations are assumed to exist between any two terms whatsoever. If X be not any L of Y, X is to Y in some not-L relation: let this *contrary* relation be signified by l; thus $X . LY$ gives and is given by $X \mathrel{..} lY$. Contrary relations may be compounded, though contrary terms cannot: Xx, both X and not-X, is impossible; but Llx, the L of a *not*-L of X, is conceivable. Thus a man may be the partisan of a non-partisan of X.

47.08 Contraries of converses are converses: thus not-L and not-L^{-1} are converses. For $X \mathrel{..} LY$ and $Y \mathrel{..} L^{-1}X$ are identical; whence $X \mathrel{..}$ not-LY and $Y \mathrel{..} (\text{not-}L^{-1})X$, their simple denials, are identical; whence not-L and not-L^{-1} are converses.

Converses of contraries are contraries: thus L^{-1} and (not-$L)^{-1}$ are contraries. For since $X \mathrel{..} LY$ and $X \mathrel{..}$ not-LY are simple denials of each other, so are their converses $Y \mathrel{..} L^{-1}X$ and $Y \mathrel{..} (\text{not-}L)^{-1}X$; whence L^{-1} and (not-$L)^{-1}$ are contraries.

The contrary of a converse is the converse of the contrary: not-L^{-1} is (not-$L)^{-1}$. For $X \mathrel{..} LY$ is identical with Y. not-$L^{-1}X$ and with $X . (\text{not-}L) Y$, which is also identical with Y. (not-$L)^{-1}X$. Hence the term not-L-verse is unambiguous in meaning though ambiguous in form.

If a first relation be contained in a second, then the converse of the first is contained in the converse of the second: but the contrary of the *second* in the contrary of the *first*.

The conversion of a compound relation converts both components, and inverts their order.

47.09 A relation is *transitive* when a relative of a relative is a relative of the same kind; as symbolized in $LL))L$, whence $LLL))LL))L$; and so on.

A transitive relation has a transitive *converse*, but not necessarily a transitive *contrary*; for $L^{-1}L^{-1}$ is the converse of LL, so that $LL))L$ gives $L^{-1}L^{-1})) L^{-1}$.

2. Peirce

47.10 A dual relative term, such as 'lover', 'benefactor', 'servant', is a common name signifying a pair of objects. Of the two members of the pair, a determinate one is generally the first, and the other the second; so that if the order is reversed, the pair is not considered as remaining the same.

Let A, B, C, D, etc., be all the individual objects in the universe; then all the individual pairs may be arrayed in a block, thus:

$A:A$	$A:B$	$A:C$	$A:D$	etc.
$B:A$	$B:B$	$B:C$	$B:D$	etc.
$C:A$	$C:B$	$C:C$	$C:D$	etc.
$D:A$	$D:B$	$D:C$	$D:D$	etc.
etc.	etc.	etc.	etc. etc.	

A general relative may be conceived as a logical aggregate of a number of such individual relatives. Let l denote 'lover'; then we may write

$$l = \Sigma_i \, \Sigma_j \, (l)_{ij} \, (I:J)$$

where $(l)_{ij}$ is a numerical coefficient, whose value is 1 in case I is a lover of J, and 0 in the opposite case, and where the sums are to be taken for all individuals in the universe.

Peirce therefore takes relations extensionally, as classes of pairs.

47.11 Every negative term has a negative (like any other term) which may be represented by drawing a straight line over the sign for the relative itself. The negative of a relative includes every pair that the latter excludes, and vice versa. Every relative has also a *converse*, produced by reversing the order of the members of the pair. Thus, the converse of "lover" is "loved". The converse may be represented by drawing a curved line over the sign for the relative, thus: $\breve{l}$. It is defined by the equation

$$(\bar{l})_{ij} = (l)_{ji}.$$

The following formulae are obvious, but important:

$$\bar{l} = l \qquad\qquad \check{l} = l$$

$$\bar{\check{l}} = \check{\bar{l}}$$

$$(l \prec b) = (\bar{b} \prec \bar{l}) \qquad (\check{l} \prec b) = (\check{l} \prec \check{b}).$$

Relative terms can be aggregated and compounded like others. Using + for the sign of logical aggregation, and the comma for the sign of logical composition (Boole's multiplication, here to be called non-relative or internal multiplication), we have the definitions

$$(l+b)_{ij} = (l)_{ij} + (b)_{ij}$$

$$(l,b)_{ij} = (l)_{ij} \times (b)_{ij}.$$

The first of these equations, however, is to be understood in a peculiar way: namely, the + in the second member is not strictly addition, but an operation by which

$$0 + 0 = 0 \qquad 0 + 1 = 1 + 0 = 1 + 1 = 1.$$

That is to say that Peirce, unlike Boole, uses non-exclusive disjunction (**40.11**).

47.12 The main formulae of aggregation and composition are

$$\begin{cases} \text{If } l \prec s \text{ and } b \prec s, \text{ then } l + b \prec s. \\ \text{If } s \prec l \text{ and } s \prec b, \text{ then } s \prec l, b. \end{cases}$$

$$\begin{cases} \text{If } l + b \prec s, \text{ then } l \prec s \text{ and } b \prec s. \\ \text{If } s \prec l, b, \text{ then } s \prec l \text{ and } s \prec b. \end{cases}$$

$$\begin{cases} (l + b), s \prec l, s + b, s. \\ (l + s), (b + s) \prec l, b + s. \end{cases}$$

The subsidiary formulae need not be given, being the same as in non-relative logic.

47.13 We come now to the combination of relatives. Of these, we denote two by special symbols; namely, we write

lb for lover of a benefactor,

and

$l \dagger b$ for lover of everything but benefactors.

The former is called a particular combination because it implies the *existence* of something *loved by* its relate and *a benefactor of* its correlate. The second combination is said to be *universal*, because it implies the *non-existence* of anything except what is either loved by its relate or a benefactor of its correlate.

In the first case, (lb), we have, as can be seen from the formula given below (**47.14**), a situation like this: x (relate) loves y, and y is a benefactor of z (correlate); so the relation holds between x and z, provided always that there is (at least) one y which is loved by x and is a benefactor of z.

47.14 The combination lb is called a relative product, $l \dagger b$ a relative sum. The l and b are said to be undistributed in both, because if $l \prec s$, then $lb \prec sb$ and $l \dagger b \prec s \dagger b$; and if $b \prec s$, then $lb \prec ls$ and $l \dagger b \prec l \dagger s$.

The two combinations are defined by the equations

$$(lb)_{ij} = \Sigma_x \, (l)_{ix} \, (b)_{xj}$$
$$(l \dagger b)_{ij} = \Pi_x \, \{(l)_{ix} + (b)_{xj}\}$$

The sign of addition in the last formula has the same signification as in the equation defining non-relative multiplication.

Relative addition and multiplication are subject to the associative law. That is,

$$l \dagger (b \dagger s) = (l \dagger b) \dagger s,$$
$$l \, (bs) = (lb) \, s.$$

Two formulae so constantly used that hardly anything can be done without them are

$$l \, (b \dagger s) \prec lb \dagger s,$$
$$(l \dagger b) \, s \prec l \dagger bs.$$

The former asserts that whatever is lover of an object that is benefactor of everything but a servant, stands to everything but servants in the relation of lover of a benefactor. The latter asserts that whatever stands to any servant in the relation of lover of everything but its benefactors, is a lover of everything but benefactors of servants. The following formulae are obvious and trivial:

$$ls + bs \prec (l + b) \, s$$
$$l, b \dagger s \prec (l \dagger s), (b \dagger s).$$

Unobvious and important, however, are these:

$$(l + b) \, s \prec ls + bs$$
$$(l \dagger s), (b \dagger s) \prec l, b \dagger s.$$

There are a number of curious development formulae. . . .

We pass over Frege, Peano and Schröder – a text of Frege's will be given later (**47.30**ff.) – and go on at once to Russell.

3. Russell

Russell strangely seems at first to have adopted an intensional view of relations.

47.15 Peirce and Schröder have realized the great importance of the subject (i.e. of the logic of relations), but unfortunately their methods, being based, not on Peano, but on the older Symbolic Logic derived (with modifications) from Boole, are so cumbrous and difficult that most of the applications which ought to be made are practically not feasible. In addition to the defects of the old Symbolic Logic, their method suffers technically (whether philosophically or not I do not at present discuss) from the fact that they regard a relation essentially as a class of couples, thus requiring elaborate formulae of summation for dealing with single relations. This view is derived, I think, probably unconsciously, from a philosophical error: it has always been customary to suppose relational propositions less ultimate than class-propositional (or subject-predicate propositions, with which class-propositions are habitually confounded), and this has led to a desire to treat relations as a kind of classes. However this may be, it was certainly from the opposite philosophical belief, which I derived from my friend Mr. G. E. Moore, that I was led to a different formal treatment of relations. This treatment, whether more philosophically correct or not, is certainly far more convenient and far more powerful as an engine of discovery in actual mathematics.

Certainly experience has shown clearly that the extensional view is more convenient. We read in the Principia:

4. Principia

47.16 A *relation*, as we shall use the word, will be understood in extension: it may be regarded as the class of couples (x, y) for which some given function $\psi(x, y)$ is true.

47.17 The following is the definition of the class of relations:
*21.03. Rel $= \hat{R}\{(\exists \varphi) . R = \hat{x}\hat{y} \; \varphi \mathbin{!} (x, y)\}$ Df
Similar remarks apply to it as to the definition of 'Cls' (*20.03) (cf. **45.07**). . . . The notation 'xRy' will mean 'x has the relation R to y'. This notation is practically convenient, and will, after the preliminaries, wholly replace the cumbrous notation $x\{\hat{x}\hat{y} \; \varphi(x, y)\} y$.

The most important basic notions of relation-logic in the *Principia* are these:

47.18 (23.01. $R \subset S . = : xRy . \supset_{x,y} . xSy$ Df

*23.02 $R \frown S = \hat{x}\hat{y}\,(xRy\,.\,xSy)$ Df

*23.03 $R \smile S = \hat{x}\hat{y}\,(xRy\,.\,\vee\,.\,xSy)$ Df

*23·04 $\doteq R = \hat{x}\hat{y}\{\,\sim(xRy)\,\}$ Df

47.19 The universal relation, denoted by $\dot{V}$, is the relation which holds between any two terms whatever of the appropriate types, whatever these may be in the given context. The null relation, Λ, is the relation which does not hold between any pair of terms whatever, its type being fixed by the types of the terms concerning which the denial that it holds is significant. A relation R is said to *exist* when there is at least one pair of terms between which it holds; 'R exists' is written '$\exists\,!\,R$'. . . .

*25.01. $\dot{V} = \hat{x}\hat{y}\,(x = x\,.\,y = y)$ Df

*25.02. $\Lambda = \doteq\dot{V}$ Df

*25.03. $\exists\,!\,R\,.\,=\,.\,(\exists\,x,y)\,.\,xRy$ Df

47.20 The general definition of a descriptive function is:

*30.01. $R^{\prime}y = (\imath\,x)\,(xRy)$ Df

That is, '$R^{\prime}y$' is to mean 'the term x which has the relation R to y'. If there are several terms or none having the relation R to y, all propositions about $R^{\prime}y$, i.e. all propositions of the form '$\varphi(R^{\prime}y)$', will be false. The apostrophe in '$R^{\prime}y$' may be read 'of'. Thus if R is the relation of father to son, '$R^{\prime}y$' means 'the son of y'; in this case, all propositions of the form '$\varphi(R^{\prime}y)$' will be false unless y has one son and no more (cf. **46.20**).

47.21 If R is a relation, the relation which y has to x when xRy is called the *converse* of R. Thus *greater* is the converse of *less, before* of *after, husband* of *wife.* The converse of identity is identity, and the converse of diversity is diversity. The converse of R is written $\breve{R}$ (read 'R-converse'). When $R = \breve{R}$, R is called a symmetrical relation, otherwise it is called *not-symmetrical.* When R is incompatible with $\breve{R}$, R is called *asymmetrical.* Thus 'cousin' is symmetrical, 'brother' is not-symmetrical (because when x is the brother of y, y may be either the brother or the sister of x), and 'husband' is asymmetrical.

47.22 Given any relation R, the class of terms which have the relation R to a given term y are called the referents of y, and the class of terms to which a given term x has the relation R are called the *relata* of x. We shall denote by $\overrightarrow{R}$ the relation of the class of referents of y to y, and by $\overleftarrow{R}$ the relation of the class of relata of x to x. . . . $\vec{R}$ and $\overset{\leftarrow}{R}$ are chiefly useful for the same of the descriptive functions to which they give rise; thus $\vec{R}{}^{\text{‘}}y = \hat{x}\,(xRy)$ and $\overset{\leftarrow}{R}{}^{\text{‘}}x = \hat{y}\,(xRy)$. Thus *e.g.* if R is the relation of parent to son, $\vec{R}{}^{\text{‘}}y$ the parents of y, $\overset{\leftarrow}{R}{}^{\text{‘}}x$ the sons of x. If R is the relation of less to greater among numbers of any kind, $\vec{R}{}^{\text{‘}}y =$ numbers less than y, and $\overset{\leftarrow}{R}{}^{\text{‘}}x =$ numbers greater than x. When $\vec{R}{}^{\text{‘}}y$ exists, $R{}^{\text{‘}}y$ is the class whose only member is $R{}^{\text{‘}}y$. But when there are many terms having the relation R to y, $\vec{R}{}^{\text{‘}}y$, which is the class of those terms, supplies a notation which cannot be supplied by $R{}^{\text{‘}}y$. And similarly if there are many terms to which x has the relation R, $\overset{\leftarrow}{R}{}^{\text{‘}}x$ supplies the notation for these terms. Thus for example let R be the relation 'sin', *i.e.* the relation which x has to y when $x = \sin y$. Then 'sin$'x$' represents all values of y such that $x = \sin y$, *i.e.* all values of $\sin^{-1} x$ or arcsin x. Unlike the usual symbol, it is not ambiguous, since instead of representing some one of these values, it represents the class of them.

The definitions of $\vec{R}$, $\overset{\leftarrow}{R}$, . . . are as follows:

*32.01. $\vec{R} = \hat{\alpha}y\,\{\,\alpha = \hat{x}\,(xRy)\,\}$ Df

*32.02. $\overset{\leftarrow}{R} = \hat{\beta}\,\hat{x}\{\,\beta = \hat{y}\,(xRy)\,\}$ Df

47.23 If R is any relation, the *domain* of R, which we denote by D$'R$, is the class of terms which have the relation R to something or other; the *converse domain*, $\mathbb{Q}'R$, is the class of terms to which something or other has the relation R; and the *field*, $C'R$, is the sum of the domain and the converse domain. (Note that the field is only significant when R is a homogeneous relation.)

The above notations D$'R$, $\mathbb{Q}'R$, $C'R$ are derivative from the notations $D, \mathbb{Q}, C$ for the relations, to a relation, of its domain, converse domain, and field respectively. We are to have

$$\mathrm{D}'R = \hat{x}\{\,(\exists\,y)\,.\,xRy\,\}$$
$$\mathbb{Q}'R = \hat{y}\{\,(\exists\,x)\,.\,xRy\,\}$$
$$C'R = \hat{x}\{\,(\exists\,y):xRy\,.\,\mathrm{v}\,.\,yRx\,\};$$

hence we define D, $\mathbb{Q}$, C as follows:

*33·01. $\mathrm{D} = \hat{\alpha}\hat{R}\,[\alpha = \hat{x}\{\,(\exists\,y)\,.\,xRy\,\}]$ Df

*33.02. $\mathbb{Q} = \hat{\beta}\hat{R}\,[\beta = \hat{y}\{\,(\exists\,x)\,.\,xRy\,\}]$ Df

*33.03. $C = \hat{\gamma}\hat{R}\,[\gamma = \hat{x}\{\,(\exists\,y):xRy\,.\,\mathrm{v}\,.\,yRx\,\}]$ Df

The letter C is chosen as the initial of the word "campus".

47.24 The relative product of two relations R and S is the relation which holds between x and z when there is an intermediate term y such that x has the relation R to y and y has the relation S to z. Thus *e.g.* the relative product of *brother* and *father* is *paternal uncle*; the relative product of *father* and *father* is paternal grandfather; and so on. The relative product of R and S is denoted by "$R \mid S$"; the definition is:

*34.01. $R \mid S = \hat{x}\hat{z}\{ (\exists y) . xRy . ySz \}$ Df ...

The relative product of R and R is called the square of R; we put

*34.02. $R^2 = R \mid R$ Df
*34.03. $R^3 = R^2 \mid R$ Df

47.25 We have to consider the relation derived from a given relation R by limiting either its domain or its converse domain to members of some assigned class. A relation R with its domain limited to members of α is written "$\alpha \uparrow R$"; with its converse domain limited to members of β, it is written "$R \upharpoonright \beta$"; with both limitations, it is written "$\alpha \uparrow R \upharpoonright \beta$". Thus *e.g.* "brother" and "sister" express the same relation (that of a common parentage), with the domain limited in the first case to males, in the second to females. "The relation of white employers to coloured employees" is a relation limited both as to its domain and as to its converse domain. We put

*35.01. $\alpha \uparrow R = \hat{x}\hat{y} (x \, \varepsilon \, \alpha . xRy)$ Df

with similar definitions for $R \upharpoonright \alpha$ and $\alpha \uparrow R \upharpoonright \beta$.

46.26 $P \Gamma \alpha$ is defined as follows:

*36.01. $P \Gamma \alpha = \alpha \uparrow P \upharpoonright \alpha$ Df

We thus have

*36.13. $\vdash : x (P \Gamma \alpha) y . \equiv . x, y \, \varepsilon \, \alpha . xPy$

47.27 We introduce what may be regarded as the plural of $R'y$. "$R'y$" was defined to mean "the term which has the relation R to y". We now introduce the notation "$R``\beta$" to mean 'the terms which have the relation $R$ to members of $\beta$". Thus if $\beta$ is the class of great men, and $R$ is the relation of wife to husband, $R``\beta$ will mean "wives of great men". If β is the class of fractions of the form $1-1/2^n$ for integral values of n, and R is the relation "less than", $R``\beta$ will be the class of fractions each of which is less than some member of this class of fractions, *i.e.* $R``\beta$ will be the class of proper fractions. Generally, $R``\beta$ is the class of those referents which have relata that are members of β.

We require also a notation for the relation of $R``\beta$ to β.

This relation we will call R_ε. Thus R_ϑ is the relation which holds between two classes α and β when α consists of all terms which have the relation R to some member of β.

A specially important case arises when $R'y$ always exists if $y \, \varepsilon \, \beta$. In this case, $R``\beta$ is the class of all terms of the form $R'y$ when $y \, \varepsilon \, \beta$. We will denote the hypothesis that $R'y$ always exists if $y \, \varepsilon \, \beta$ by the notation $E!! \, R``\beta$, meaning "the R's of β's exist".

The definitions are as follows :

*37.01. $R``\beta = \hat{x}\{ (\exists y) . y \, \varepsilon \, \beta . xRy \}$ Df

*37.02. $R\varepsilon = \hat{\alpha}\hat{\beta}\,(\alpha = R``\beta)$ Df

47.28 A *one-many* relation is a relation R such that, if y is any member of $\Box'R$, there is one, and only one, term x which has the relation R to y, *i.e.* $\overrightarrow{R}'y \, \varepsilon \, 1$. Thus the relation of father to son is one-many, because every son has one father and no more. The relation of husband to wife is one-many except in countries which practise polyandry. (It is one-many in monogamous as well as in polygamous countries, because, according to the definition, nothing is fixed as to the number of relata for a given referent, and there *may* be only one relatum for each given referent without the relation ceasing to be one-many according to the definition.) The relation in algebra of x^2 to x is one-many, but that of x to x^2 is not, because there are two different values of x that give the same value of x^2.

47.29 A relation R is called *many-one* when, if x is any member of $D'R$, there is one, and only one, term y to which x has the relation R, $i..e$ $\overleftarrow{R}'x \, \varepsilon \, 1$. Thus many-one relations are the converses of one-many relations. When a relation R is many-one, $\overleftarrow{R}'x$ exists whenever $x \, \varepsilon \, D'R$.

A relation is called *one-one* when it is both one-many and many-one, or, what comes to the same, when both it and its converse are one-many.

B. SERIES

One of the most important parts of the logic of relations is the doctrine of series of relations, which plays a notable part in mathematics and other sciences (e.g. Biology). It is based on the theory of the relative product (**47.13**f.), and makes use of the difficult concept of the ancestral relation, which Frege was the first to define exactly. We give first some texts from the *Begriffsschrift*, then the elaboration of the concept in the *Principia*.

1. Frege

47.31 If from the proposition that ƀ has a property F, it can be universally, whatever ƀ may be, concluded that every result of the application of a process f to ƀ has the property F, then I say: 'the property F is hereditary in the f-series'.

47.32 If the property F is hereditary in the f-series: if x has the property F and y is the result of applying the process f to x: then y has the property F.

47.33 If from the two propositions, that every result of applying the process f to x has the property F, and that the property F is hereditary in the f-series, whatever F may be, it can be concluded that y has the property F, then I say: 'y succeeds x in the f-series'.

47.34 If x has the property F which is hereditary in the f-series, and if y succeeds x in the f-series, then y has the property F.

47.35 If y succeeds x in the f-series, and if z succeeds y in the f-series, then z succeeds x in the f-series.

47.36 If from the circumstance that ҽ is a result of applying the process f to ƀ, whatever ƀ may be, it can be concluded that every result of applying f to ƀ is the same as ҽ, then I say: 'the process f is unequivocal'.

47.37 If x is a result of applying the unequivocal process f to y, then every result of applying the process f to y belongs to the f-series that begins with x.

2. Principia

47.38 Mathematical induction is, in fact, the application to the number-series of a conception which is applicable to all relations, and is often very important. The conception in question is that which we shall call the *ancestral relation* with respect to a given relation. If R is the given relation, we denote the corresponding ancestral relation by "R_*"; the name is chosen because, if R is the relation of parent and child, R_* will be the relation of ancestor and descendant − where, for convenience of language, we include x among his own ancestors if x is a parent or a child of anything.

It would commonly be said that a has to z the relation of ancestor to descendant if there are a certain number of intermediate people b, c, d, . . . such that in the series a, b, c, d, . . . z each term has to the next the relation of parent and child. But this is not an adequate definition, because the dots in

$$"a, b, c, d, \ldots z"$$

represent an unanalysed idea.

47.39 Let us call μ a *hereditary class with respect to R* if $\breve{R}"\mu \subset \mu$, *i.e.* if successors of μ's (with respect to R) are μ's. Thus, for example, if μ is the class of persons named Smith, μ is hereditary with respect to the relation of father to son. If μ is the Peerage, μ is hereditary with respect to the relation of father to surviving eldest son. If μ is numbers greater than 100, μ is hereditary with respect to the relation of ν to ν + 1; and so on. If now a is an ancestor of z, and μ is a hereditary class to which a belongs, then z also belongs to this class. Conversely, if z belongs to every hereditary class to which a belongs, then (in the sense in which a is one of his own ancestors if a is anybody's parent or child) a must be an ancestor of z. For to have a for one's ancestor is a hereditary property which belongs to a, and therefore, by hypothesis, to z. Hence a is an ancestor of z when, and only when, a belongs to the field of the relation in question and z belongs to every hereditary class to which a belongs. This property may be used to define the ancestral relation; *i.e.* since we have

$$aR_* z . \equiv : a \varepsilon C'R : \breve{R}"\mu \subset \mu . a \varepsilon \mu . \supset \mu . z \varepsilon \mu$$

$$R_* = \hat{a}\hat{z}\{a \varepsilon C'R : \breve{R}"\mu \subset \mu . a \varepsilon \mu . \supset \mu . z \varepsilon \mu\} \qquad \text{Df}$$

We then have

$$\vdash : a \varepsilon C'R . \supset . \overleftarrow{R}_* 'a = \hat{z}\{\breve{R}"\mu \subset \mu . a \varepsilon \mu . \supset \mu . z \varepsilon \mu\}.$$

Here $\overleftarrow{R}_* 'a$ may be called 'the descendants of a'. It is the class of terms of which a is an ancestor.

C. ISOMORPHY

Finally, with the help of relational concepts, another doctrine can be developed which is important for many sciences, viz. that of isomorphy or ordinal similarity. Essentially this is a matter of the identity of two formal structures, i.e. of two networks of relations, similar only in their purely formal properties, but in those identical. We have already met an anticipation of this theory in the Middle Ages (**28.18** ff.). It is first presented in detail in the *Principia*. There too, the concept of isomorphy is applied to the theory of types, fundamental for the system, as a result of which we get the theory of so-called systematic ambiguity (**48.23**).

47.40 Two series generated by the relations P and Q

respectively are said to be ordinally similar when their terms can be correlated as they stand, without change of order.

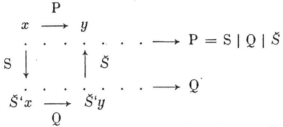

In the accompanying figure, the relation S correlates the members of $C'P$ and $C'Q$ in such a way that if xPy, then $(\check{S}'x) Q (\check{S}'y)$, and if zQw, then $(S'z) P (S'w)$. It is evident that the journey from x to y (where xPy) may, in such a case, be taken by going first to $\check{S}'x$, thence to $\check{S}'y$, and thence back to y, so that $xPy . \equiv . x (S \mid Q \mid \check{S}) y$, i.e. $P = S \mid Q \mid \check{S}$. Hence to say that P and Q are ordinally similar is equivalent to saying that there is a one-one relation S which has $C'Q$ for its converse domain and gives $P = S \mid Q \mid \check{S}$. In this case we call S a *correlator* of Q and P.

We denote the relation of ordinal similarity by "smor", which is short for "similar ordinally". Thus

$$P \text{ smor } Q . \equiv . (\exists S) . S \, \varepsilon \, 1 \longrightarrow 1 . C'Q = \mathrm{\alpha}'S . P = S \mid Q \mid \check{S}$$

§ 48. ANTINOMIES AND THEORIES OF TYPES

A. HISTORICAL SURVEY

Former endeavours to solve the problem of semantic antinomies (§§ 23 and 35) seem to have fallen into complete oblivion in the time of the 'classical' decadence. Nor did the mathematical logicians know anything about them until Rüstow (**48.01**), with the sole exception of Peirce, who had read Paul of Venice and given a subtle commentary on him in this respect (**48.02**); but even Peirce seems to have attended only to *one* of the numerous solutions quoted above (§ 35).

At the end of the 19th century the problem re-emerged, and in a new form. Besides the 'Liar' a whole series of antinomies are found which are not semantic but logical, i.e. which arise without the use of any metalinguistic expressions. And they are genuine antinomies, i.e. contradictions deducible from intuitively evident axioms by means of no less correct rules (which differentiates them from simple contradictions). In spite of the fact that the antinomies are clearly seen to be of this character, they are often called by the gentler name of 'paradoxes'.

The history of the problem of antinomies in our time is, briefly, as follows. Between 1895 and 1897 C. Burali-Forti (**48.03**) and G. Cantor (**48.04**) independently stated the first *logical* antinomy (of the set of all ordinal numbers). But logicians considered this antinomy to be a matter of mathematics in the narrow sense, and gave it little attention: people were already accustomed to the fact that what were ordinarily considered to be unassailable parts of mathematics had been in difficulties right from the time of Zeno of Elea. In 1902 B. Russell constructed his celebrated antinomy of the class of all classes, which was first published by Frege (**48.05**) who also proposed an improvement on it (**48.06**). Subsequently many fresh antinomies, some logical, some semantic, have appeared. Up to now more than a dozen genuinely different ones are known.

Naturally, logicians began to seek solutions, as they had done in antiquity and in the Middle Ages. To begin with, two attempts were made: Russell's ramified theory of types (1908) and Zermelo's theory (**48.07**). The latter was markedly mathematical in character, and cannot be expounded here. In 1910 the *Principia* was constructed according to the ramified theory. In 1921 L. Chwistek simplified this by his construction of the simple theory of types, which received further development and confirmation at the hands of P. Ramsey in 1926. Both assisted towards clarification by applying the theory of types to expressions, whereas Russell had not determined its semantic character. This line of development was terminated by St. Leśniewski's theory of semantic levels (**48.08**). Parallel with this work on the theory of types, new experiments were constantly being made to simplify it, or find an alternative. The plan of this work does not allow us to go further into the more recent developments. We confine ourselves, accordingly, to the antinomies themselves, and the two forms of the theory of types. We shall further add illustrations of two doctrines closely connected with the ramified theory of types, viz. that of the axiom of reducibility and that of systematic ambiguity.

B. THE ANTINOMIES

We now give some texts in which antinomies are formulated; others can be found in Becker (**48.04**). Our present texts always speak of contradictions, not antinomies, as the two had not then been distinguished; but antinomies are always intended.

We read in the *Principia*:

48.09 We shall begin by an enumeration of some of the more important and illustrative of these contradictions, and shall then show how they all embody vicious-circle fallacies, and are therefore all avoided by the theory of types. It will be noticed that these paradoxes do not relate exclusively to the ideas of number and quantity. Accordingly no solution can be adequate which seeks to explain them merely as the result of some illegitimate use of these ideas. The solution must be sought in some such scrutiny of fundamental logical ideas as has been attempted in the foregoing pages.

48.10 (1) The oldest contradiction of the kind in question is the *Epimenides*. . . . The simplest form of this contradiction is afforded by the man who says "I am lying"; if he is lying, he is speaking the truth, and vice versa (cf. **23.10** ff.).

48.11 (2) Let w be the class of all those classes which are not members of themselves. Then, whatever class x may be, "x is a w" is equivalent to "x is not an x". Hence, giving to x the value w, "w is a w" is equivalent to "w is not a w".

This is Russell's own famous antinomy of the class of all classes. It differs from those mentioned so far in that it contains no semantic expressions such as 'I say', 'I lie', '. . . is true' etc., no statements about statements. Antinomies of this new kind are called 'logical' to distinguish them from the semantic ones.

48.12 (3) Let T be the relation which subsists between two relations R and S whenever R does not have the relation R to S. Then, whatever relations R and S may be, "R has the relation T to S" is equivalent to "R does not have the relation R to S". Hence giving the value T to both R and S, 'T has the relation T to T" is equivalent to "T does not have the relation T to T".

48.13 (5) The number of syllables in the English names of finite integers tends to increase as the integers grow larger, and must gradually increase indefinitely, since only a finite number of names can be made with a given finite number of syllables. Hence the names of some integers must consist of at least nineteen syllables, and among these there must be a least. Hence "the least integer not nameable in fewer than nineteen syllables" must denote a definite integer; in fact, it denotes 111,777. But "the least integer not nameable in fewer than nineteen syllables" is itself a name consisting of eighteen syllables; hence the least integer not nameable in fewer than nineteen syllables can be named in eighteen syllables, which is a contradiction.

This is another semantic antinomy. In the same context Russell gives three others, those of Burali-Forti, Richard, and the least indefinable ordinal number. We give the second in Richard's own words:

48.14 I am going to define a certain set (*ensemble*) of numbers which I shall call the set E, by means of the following considerations:

Let us write all the arrangements of the twenty-six letters of the French alphabet (taken) two by two, arranging these arrangements in alphabetic order; then all the arrangements three by three, ranged in alphabetic order; then those four by four, etc. These arrangements may contain the same letter repeated several times; they are arrangements with repetition.

Whatever whole number p may be, every arrangement of the twenty-six letters p by p will be found in this table, and as everything that can be written with a finite number of words is an arrangement of letters, everything that can be written will be found in the table of which we have just shown the manner of construction.

As numbers are defined by means of words, and the latter by means of letters, some of these arrangements will be definitions of numbers. Let us cancel from our arrangements all those which are not definitions of numbers.

Let u_1 be the first number defined by an arrangement, u_2 the second, u_3 the third, etc.

There have thus been arranged in a determinate order *all the numbers defined by means of a finite number of words.*

Therefore: all the numbers that can be defined by means of a finite number of words form a denumerable set.

This now is where the contradiction lies. We can form a number which does not belong to this set.

'Let p be the n-th decimal of the n-th number of the set E; let us form a number having zero for its integral part, $p + 1$ for its n-th decimal if p is equal neither to eight nor to nine, and otherwise unity.'

This number N does not belong to the set E. If it was the n-th number of the set E, its n-th figure would be the n-th decimal figure of that number, which it is not.

I call G the group of letters in inverted commas.

The number N is defined by the words of the group G, *i.e.* by a finite number of words; it ought therefore to belong to the set E. But we have seen that it does not belong.

That is the contradiction.

Richard then tries to show that the contradiction is only apparent.

C. ANTICIPATIONS OF THE THEORY OF TYPES

Peano's distinction between ε and ⊃ (**45.12**) can be regarded as already a beginning of the later theory of types. An idea of Schröder's which plays the same part in his system as that distinction in Peano's, is a much closer approach. *

48.16 In the last example, the subsumption $0 \notin 1$, it can further easily be shown that it is not in fact permissible to understand by 1 a class so extensive, as it were so completely open, as the 'universum of discussability' depicted above.

As has been shown, 0 is to be contained in *every* class which can be selected from the manifold, 1, so that $0 \notin a$ holds, 0 is to be subject to *every* predicate.

If now we were to understand by a, *the class of those classes which are equal to* 1, [and this would certainly be permissible, if we could include in 1 everything conceivable], * then this class comprises essentially only *one* object, viz. the symbol 1 itself or the totality of the manifold which constitutes its reference – *but beyond that also 'nothing', in view of* 0. But if 1 and 0 constitute the class of those objects which can be equated with 1, not only: $1 = 1$, but *also*: $0 = 1$, must be admitted. Since a predicate which belongs to a class [here the predicate: being identically equal to 1] must also belong to every individual of this class, ...

In such a manifold, in which $0 = 1$ holds, all possibility of distinguishing two classes or even individuals, is antecedently excluded; everything would here be all the same ('*wurst*').

48.17 These considerations show, *that Boole's universal interpretation of* 1 *was*, in fact, *too extreme*.

In the actual calculus of domains, the subsumption $0 \notin a$ can, as we have seen, be held as valid without limitation, e.g. for the domain a for a manifold of points, 1.

But now the question must be answered, how far the laws of the calculus can be carried over also to the manifold formed of *all possible* classes, of *any objects of thought whatever*.

---

*This text of Schröder's was brought to our notice by a paper of Prof. A. Church (**48.15**). The author kindly made available this work which is obtainable only with difficulty.
** The square brackets are Schröder's.

It has been shown that it is not permissible to leave this manifold, 1, completely undetermined, wholly unlimited or open, since some possible formulations of the predicate-class a . . . prove not to be permissible. How then are we to secure that the rules of the calculus, when applied to it, . . . can no longer lead to contradiction?

I shall try to give the answer to this difficult question.

First of all, we are concerned with a manifold of any kind of 'things' – objects of thought in general – as 'elements' or '*individuals*'. These may be (in whole or in part) given from the start, or may be (in the other part or in whole) somehow determined only conceptually. But they cannot remain completely undetermined, as has already been shown.

In order that the symbols 0 and 1 etc. may be applicable according to the rules of the calculus in this manifold, certain stipulations must be made concerning how the elements of this manifold are given or determined conceptually.

As a first stipulation we have already specified in § 7, in postulate $((1+))$*, that: the elements of the manifold must be all of them consistent, 'compatible' with one another. *Only in this case do we symbolize* the manifold by 1.

48.18 If the elements of the manifold are consistent, they can be *arbitrarily* collected together into systems, 'domains' of its elements, and distinguished within it. In other words, any *classes* of individuals can be selected from the manifold even for the purpose of distributive application. . . .

By that process of arbitrary selection of classes of individuals of the manifold originally envisaged, there [in general] arises, is produced, a *new*, much more extensive manifold, viz. that of the domains or classes of the previous one. . . .

The new manifold could be called the 'second power' of the former – but better its '*first* . . . *derived* manifold'.

From that in turn a new, still more extensive manifold can be derived, which is to be called the derivate of the first derivate, or the *second derivate*. And so on.

As can be seen from the foregoing considerations, the meaning of the identical 1 in the first manifold cannot extend to that on the second, still less to that in still higher derived manifolds.

And in order that the subsumption (2+) can be held as

---

*The parentheses are Schröder's.

valid even in the original manifold, it is necessary [and sufficient] from the start *that among the elements given as 'individuals' there should be no classes comprising as elements individuals of the same manifold.*

It is remarkable that Frege did not perceive the significance of this doctrine. In his review of Schröder's *Vorlesungen* (**48 · 19**), he even strongly opposed it. We give Frege's text, since it is so formulated as almost to lead one to suppose that he is attacking the simple theory of types.

48.20 Herr Schröder derives from this the conclusion that the original manifold 1 must be so made up that, among the elements given as individuals within it, there are found no classes that, for their part, contain within themselves as individuals any elements of the same manifold. This expedient, as it were, belatedly gets the ship off the sandbank; but if she had been properly steered, she could have kept off it altogether. It now becomes clear why at the very outset, in shrewd prevision of the imminent danger, a certain manifold was introduced as the theatre of operation, although there was no reason for this in the pure domain-calculus. The subsequent restriction of this field for our logical activities is by no means elegant. Whereas elsewhere logic may claim to have laws of unrestricted validity, we are here required to begin by delimiting a manifold with careful tests, and it is only then that we can move around inside it.

D. THE RAMIFIED THEORY OF TYPES

We come now to Russell's ramified theory of types in its first formulation (1908).

48.21 A *type* is defined as the range of significance of a propositional function, *i.e.* as the collection of arguments for which the said function has values. Whenever an apparent variable occurs in a proposition, the range of values of the apparent variable is a type, the type being fixed by the function of which "all values" are concerned. The division of objects is necessitated by the reflexive fallacies which otherwise arise. These fallacies, as we saw, are to be avoided by what may be called the "vicious circle principle"; *i.e.* "no totality can contain members defined in terms of itself". This principle in our technical language becomes: "whatever contains an apparent variable must not be a possible value of that variable". Thus whatever contains an apparent variable must be of a different type from the possible values of that variable; we will say that it is of a *higher* type. Thus the apparent variables contained in an expression are what determines its type. This is the guiding principle in what follows.

Propositions which contain apparent variables are generated from such as do not contain these apparent variables by processes of which one is always the process of generalization, *i.e.* the substitution of a variable for one of the terms of the proposition, and the assertion of the resulting function for all possible values of the variable. Hence a proposition is called a *generalized* proposition when it contains an apparent variable. A proposition containing no apparent variable we will call an *elementary* proposition. It is plain that a proposition containing an apparent variable presupposes others from which it can be obtained by generalization; hence all generalized propositions presuppose elementary propositions. In an elementary proposition we can distinguish one or more *terms* from one or more *concepts;* the *terms* are whatever can be regarded as the *subject* of the proposition, while the concepts are the predicates or relations asserted of these terms. The terms of elementary propositions we will call *individuals;* they form the first and lowest type. . . .

By applying the process of generalization to individuals occuring in elementary propositions, we obtain new propositions. The legitimacy of this process requires only that no individuals should be propositions. That this is so, is to be secured by the meaning we give to the word *individual.* We may define an individual as something destitute of complexity; it is then obviously not a proposition, since propositions are essentially complex. Hence in applying the process of generalization to individuals, we run no risk of incurring reflexive fallacies.

Elementary propositions together with such as contain only individuals as apparent variables we will call *first-order propositions*. These form the second logical type.

We have thus a new totality, that of *first-order propositions*. We can thus form new propositions in which first-order propositions occur as apparent variables. These we will call *second-order propositions;* these form the third logical type.

Thus *e.g.* if Epimenides asserts "all first-order propositions affirmed by me are false", he asserts a second-order proposition; he may assert this truly, without asserting truly any first-order proposition, and thus no contradiction arises.

The above process can be continued indefinitely. The *n* + 1th logical type will consist of all propositions of order *n*, which will be such as contain propositions of order *n* − 1 but of no higher order, as apparent variables. The types obtained are mutually exclusive, and thus no reflexive fallacies are possible so long as we remember that an apparent variable must always be confined within one type.

In practice, a hierarchy of functions is more convenient than one of propositions. Functions of various orders may be obtained from propositions of various orders by the method of *substitution*. If p is a proposition, and a a constituent of p, let '$p/a;x$' denote the proposition which results from substituting x for a wherever a occurs in p. Then p/a, which we will call a *matrix*, may take the place of a function; its value for the argument x is $p/a;x$, and its value for the argument a is p. . . . The order of a matrix will be defined as being the order of the proposition in which the substitution is effected.

In the same connection we adduce a further text, from the *Principia*, which has two points of interest. First, the idea expounded is very close to one expounded by Paul of Venice (**35.41—43**; **35.49** ff.); second, the text contains the essentials of the *simple* theory of types.

48.22 An analysis of the paradoxes to be avoided shows that they result from a certain kind of vicious circle. The vicious circles in question arise from supposing that a collection of objects may contain members which can only be defined by means of the collection as a whole. Thus, for example, the collection of *propositions* will be supposed to contain a proposition stating that "all propositions are either true or false". It would seem, however, that such a statement could not be legitimate unless "all propositions" referred to some already definite collection, which it cannot do if new propositions are created by statements about "all propositions". We shall, therefore, have to say that statements about "all propositions" are meaningless. More generally, given any set of objects such that, if we suppose the set to have a total, it will contain members which presuppose this total, then such a set cannot have a total. By saying that a set has "no total", we mean, primarily, that no significant statement can be made about "all its members".

E. SYSTEMATIC AMBIGUITY

The application of the theory of types to expressions containing the word 'true' and suchlike issues at once in the thesis that words of this kind are ambiguous. This is formulated in the *Principia* as follows:

48.23 Since "$(x).\varphi x$" involves the function $\varphi \hat{x}$, it must according to our principle, be impossible as an argument to φ. That is to say, the symbol '$\varphi \{ (x) . \varphi x \}$' must be meaningless. This principle would seem, at first sight, to have certain exceptions. Take, for example, the function "$\hat{p}$ is false", and consider the proposition "$(p).p$ is false". This should be a proposition asserting all propositions of the form "p is false". Such a proposition, we should be inclined to say, must be false, because "p is false" is not always true. Hence we should be led to the proposition
  "$\{ (p) . p$ is false $\}$ is false",
i.e. we should be led to a proposition in which "$(p) . p$ is false" is the argument to the function '$\hat{p}$ is false' which we had declared to be impossible. Now it will be seen that "$(p) . p$ is false", in the above, purports to be a proposition about all propositions, and that, by the general form of the vicious-circle principle, there must be no propositions about *all* propositions. Nevertheless, it seems plain that, given any function, there is a proposition (true or false) asserting all its values. Hence we are led to the conclusion that "p is false" and "q is false" must not always be the values, with the arguments p and q, for a single function "$\hat{p}$ is false". This, however is only possible if the word "false" really has many different meanings, appropriate to propositions of different kinds.

That the words "true" and "false" have many different meanings, according to the kind of proposition to which they are applied, is not difficult to see. Let us take any function $\varphi \hat{x}$, and let a be one of its values. Let us call the sort of truth which is applicable to φa "*first* truth". (This is not to assume that this would be first truth in another context; it is merely to indicate that it is the first sort of truth in our context.) Consider now the proposition $(x) . \varphi x$. If this has truth of the sort appropriate to it, that will mean that every value φx has "first truth". Thus if we call the sort of truth that is appropriate to $(x) . \varphi x$ "*second* truth", we may define "$\{(x) . \varphi x\}$ has second truth" as meaning "every value for $\varphi \hat{x}$ has first truth", *i.e.* "$(x) . (\varphi x$ has first truth)".

48.24 It will be seen that, according to the above hierarchy no statement can be made significantly about "all a-functions" where a is some given object. Thus such a notion as "all properties of a", meaning "all functions which are true with the argument a", will be illegitimate. We shall have to distinguish the order of function concerned. We can speak of "all predicative properties of a", "all second-order properties of a", and so on. (If a is not an individual, but an object of order n, "second-order properties of a" will mean "functions of order $n + 2$ satisfied by a".) But we cannot speak of "*all* properties of a". In some cases, we can see that some statement will hold of "all nth-order properties of a", whatever value n may have. In such cases, no practical harm results from regarding the statement as being about "all properties of a", provided we remember that it is really a number of statements, and not a single statement which could be regarded as assigning another property to a, over and above all properties. Such cases will always involve some systematic ambiguity, such as that involved in the meaning of the word 'truth', as explained above (cf. **48.23**). Owing to this systematic ambiguity, it will be possible, sometimes, to combine into a single verbal statement what are really a number of different statements, corresponding to different orders in the hierarchy. This is illustrated in the case of the liar, where the statement "all A's statements are false" should be broken up into different statements referring to his statement of various orders, and attributing to each the appropriate kind of falsehood.

It should be clear that the authors of the *Principia* do not go far enough in suggesting that these different statements are combined only into a single *verbal* statement; for all the statements in question evidently share the same formal *structure*. We have in fact a case of isomorphy (**47.41**). It is remarkable that the name used for this kind of isomorphy, 'systematic ambiguity', is an exact translation of the common Scholastic expression *aequivocatio a consilio*, synonymous with 'analogy' (**28.18** ff.); for isomorphy is precisely analogy.

F. THE AXIOM OF REDUCIBILITY

Closely connected with the ramified theory of types and systematic ambiguity is the axiom of reducibility used in the *Principia*. The expression 'predicative function' used in this context is defined thus:

48.25 We will define a function of one variable as *predicative* when it is of the next order above that of its argument, *i.e.* of the lowest order compatible with its having that argument. If a function has several arguments, and the highest order of function occurring among the arguments is the nth, we call the function predicative if it is of the $n + 1$th order, i.e. again, if it is of the lowest order compatible with its having the arguments it has. A function of several arguments is predicative if there is one of its arguments such that, when the other arguments have values assigned to them, we obtain a predicative function of the one undetermined argument.

48.24 follows soon after, and the passage continues:

48.26 The axiom of reducibility is introduced in order to legitimate a great mass of reasoning, in which, prima facie, we are concerned with such notions as 'all properties of a' or 'all a-functions', and in which, nevertheless, it seems scarcely possible to suspect any substantial error. In order to state the axiom, we must first define what is meant by 'formal equivalence'. Two functions $\varphi\hat{x}$, $\psi\hat{x}$ are said to be 'formally equivalent' when, with every possible argument x, φx is equivalent to ψx, i.e. φx and ψx are either both true or both false. Thus two functions are formally equivalent when they are satisfied by the same set of arguments. The axiom of reducibility is the assumption that, given any function $\varphi\hat{x}$, there is a formally equivalent *predicative* function, i.e. there is a predicative function which is true when φx is true and false when φx is false. In symbols, the axiom is:

$$\vdash : (\exists\, \psi) : \varphi\, x \, . \equiv_x . \, \psi!\, x \, .$$

For two variables, we require a similar axiom, namely: Given any function $\varphi\,(\hat{x}, \hat{y})$, there is a formally equivalent predicative function, *i.e.*

$$\vdash : (\exists\, \psi) : \varphi\,(x, y) \, . \equiv_{x, y} . \, \psi\,!\,(x, y).$$

This text has two points of interest. First, it contains quantified predicates (functors), like Peirce's definition of identity (**44.26**); this must eventually lead to the construction of the so-called higher predicate calculus, though this is not to be found till some time after the *Principia*. In the *Principia*, with few exceptions, only arguments, not functors, are quantified. Secondly, it is clear that the axiom of reducibility is a further case of isomorphy, so that one usually speaks, with systematic ambiguity, of *the* reducibility axiom. The authors of the *Principia* themselves admit (14.27) that it is not at all evident, and as an axiom it is not proved. Its justification lies wholly in its convenience, which is no great logical recommendation. Hence logicians have concerned themselves to dispense with it.

G. SIMPLE THEORY OF TYPES

1. Chwistek

L. Chwistek was the first (1921) to propose discarding this axiom and the complications of the ramified theory of types:

48.28 Thus a theory of logical types seems to be an absolutely necessary basis of every modern formal logic which is going to retain the fundamental operations of the algebra of logic. . . .

But when we ask whether Russell's theory of types fully serves its purpose, we must say this. According to this theory every object has a determinate logical type and every domain of validity of an argument consists of objects which belong to the same logical type.

But the converse does not hold, since an object of given type can belong to the domain of validity of arguments of functions with different types. Two functions which have different types and the same domain of validity of their arguments we shall call, with Russell, functions of different ranks (i.e. orders; cf. **48.21**).

Russell now posits that there is a lowest rank of functions, those characterized by containing no apparent variables, i.e. which can be envisaged without use of the concepts 'for all x' and 'for some x'. . . .

And for Russell's theory of types a certain axiom (the so-called axiom of reducibility) is essential. . . .

I should now like to show that the adoption of this axiom straightway leads to the reconstruction of Richard's antinomy.

There follows the reconstruction of this antinomy within a system containing the axiom of reducibility, and Chwistek goes on:

48.29 Thus the axiom of reducibility appears as a contradictory supposition, and hence we cannot agree without reserve to Russell's theory of types.

If we were to share the hesitations of many logicians about the theoretical worth of Richard's method, it would be clear that there is no real basis for distinguishing between ranks of propositional functions. In any case Russell's theory of types needs a critical overhaul. . . .

48.30 Finally I may be allowed to say something about the results of my endeavours over many years to reconstruct the system of Russell and Whitehead without the axiom of reducibility.

If we deny any theoretical value to Richard's antinomy, formal logic, obtains an essential simplification, since, though we still have to do with types, we no longer have orders of functions, so that we can briefly speak of 'all properties' of a thing. In this way we can at once obtain a system, different from that of Russell and Whitehead, having the same theoretical value.

But the freedom from contradiction of this systems remains very doubtful, and apart from this, the following most important question remains to be answered:

Is a system of formal logic possible, which would be based on the general theory of types, without the axiom of reducibility, and which would not have to adopt any new axioms?

I am in a position to give an affirmative answer to this question, having succeeded in constructing such a system, and in particular in establishing the theory of cardinal and inductive numbers without any additional hypothesis beyond what is already present in the system of Russell and Whitehead.

2. Ramsey

Ramsey reached the same conclusion in 1925. He lays particular emphasis on the distinction between logical and semantic antinomies:

48.31 It is not sufficiently remarked, and the fact is entirely neglected in *Principia Mathematica*, that these contradictions fall into two fundamentally distinct groups, which we will call A and B. The best known ones are divided as follows: –

A.　(1) The class of all classes which are not members of themselves.

　　(2) The relation between two relations when one does not have itself to the other.

　　(3) Burali Forti's contradiction of the greatest ordinal.

B.　(4) 'I am lying'.

(5) The least integer not nameable in fewer than nineteen syllables.

(6) The least indefinable ordinal.

(7) Richard's Contradiction.

(8) Weyl's Contradiction about 'heterologisch' *.

Footnote of Ramsey's: *For the first seven of these see *Principia Mathematica*, 1 (1910), 63. For the eighth see Weyl, *Das Kontinuum*, 2.

The principle according to which I have divided them is of fundamental importance. Group A consists of contradictions, which, were no provision made against them, would occur in a logical or mathematical system itself. They involve only logical or mathematical terms such as class and number, and show that there must be something wrong with our logic or mathematics. But the contradictions of Group B are not purely logical, and cannot be stated in logical terms alone, for they all contain some reference to thought, language, or symbolism, which are not formal but empirical terms. So they may be due not to faulty logic or mathematics, but to faulty ideas concerning thought and language. If so, they would not be relevant to mathematics or to logic, if by 'logic' we mean a symbolic system, though, of course, they would be relevant to logic in the sense of the analysis of thought.

48.32 A theory of types must enable us to avoid the contradictions; Whitehead and Russell's theory consisted of two distinct parts, united only by being both deduced from the rather vague 'Vicious-Circle Principle'. The first part distinguished propositional functions according to their arguments, i.e. classes according to their members; the second part created the need for the Axiom of Reducibility by requiring further distinctions between orders of functions with the same type of arguments.

We can easily divide the contradictions according to which part of the theory is required for their solution, and when we have done this we find that these two sets of contradictions are distinguished in another way also. The ones solved by the first part of the theory are all purely logical; they involve no ideas but those of class, relation and number, could be stated in logical symbolism, and occur in the actual development of mathematics when it is pursued in the right direction.

* more exactly, Grelling's.

Such are the contradiction of the greatest ordinal, and that of the class of classes which are not members of themselves. With regard to these Mr. Russell's solution seems inevitable.

On the other hand, the second set of contradictions are none of them purely logical or mathematical, but all involve some psychological term, such as meaning, defining, naming or asserting. They occur not in mathematics, but in thinking about mathematics; so that it is possible that they arise not from faulty logic or mathematics, but from ambiguity in the psychological or epistemological notions of meaning and asserting. Indeed, it seems that this must be the case, because examination soon convinces one that the psychological term is in every case essential to the contradiction, which could not be constructed without introducing the relation of words to their meaning or some equivalent.

It can be seen how sharply Ramsey distinguishes between object- and metalanguage. But it is to be noted that he does not use these expressions, and can only conceive the domain of relations between signs and significates psychologically or epistemologically. In the course of later developments, this domain became separated (by Leśniewski, and above all by Tarski) and denoted as that of semantics.

The simple theory of types proposed in the last text is not at all such a simple matter as an uninitiated reader might at first suppose. The axiom of reducibility is replaced by so-called pseudo-definitions, or alternatively, by axioms about the existence of classes, and the freedom from contradiction of these axioms is not an easy question; so that the theory under consideration does not lack its problems. *

We cannot here pursue this question, nor the later development of the whole matter.

§ 49. SOME RECENT DOCTRINES

As an appendix, we shall speak briefly in this paragraph of a few of the problems and doctrines that have arisen since the *Principia*. It will only be a matter of some examples of the enormous development characteristic of the fourth period of mathematical logic (vide § 37), which does not properly fall within our scope.

We must forgo speaking of doctrines which constitute a break with tradition, such as those concerning the 'natural logics'

*Thanks are due to Prof. E. W. Beth for important information on this point.

as also of the numerous and often pioneer insights into semantic questions. None of this yet belongs to history, and has, moreover, only slight connection with what has so far been expounded.

Up to 1918 all mathematical logicians – unlike the Megarians, Stoics and Scholastics – used only one notion of implication, the Philonian (**20.07**) or material (**41.13 f.**). Hence the mathematical logic of that time was exclusively assertoric, a logic without modalities, or in other words, a two-valued logic. It supposed only two values, truth and falsity. The only exception, to our knowledge, is the system of McColl (**49.01**). In 1918 C. I. Lewis introduced a new notion of implication and with it a modal logic, since when a whole series of non-Philonian implications have been propounded and elaborated, i.e. many-valued logics have been developed. We mention here two such systems, Lewis's system of 'strict implication' (1918) and Łukasiewicz's three-valued logic (which he discovered in 1917).

Gödel's famous theorem, his account of which we give in conclusion, belongs to another domain of problems.

A. STRICT IMPLICATION: LEWIS

Lewis formulated the idea of 'strict implication' as early as 1913 (**49.02**). The following texts date from 1918:

49.03 The fundamental ideas of the system are similar to those of MacColl's *Symbolic Logic and its Applications*. They are as follows:

1. *Propositions*: p, q, r, etc.
2. *Negation*: $- p$, meaning 'p is false'.
3. *Impossibility*: $\sim p$, meaning 'p is impossible', or 'It is impossible that p be true'.
4. *The logical product*: $p \times q$ or pq, meaning 'p and q both', or 'p is true and q is true'.
5. *Equivalence*: $p = q$, the defining relation.

Systems previously developed, except MacColl's, have only two truth-values, 'true' and 'false'. The addition of the idea of impossibility gives us five truth-values, all of which are familiar logical ideas:

(1) p, 'p is true'.
(2) $- p$, 'p is false'.
(3) $\sim p$, 'p is impossible'.
(4) $- \sim p$, 'It is false that p is impossible' i.e., 'p is possible'.
(5) $\sim - p$, 'It is impossible that p be false' i.e., 'p is necessarily true'.

403

49.04 The dyadic relations of propositions can be defined in terms of these truth-values and the logical product, *pq*.

1.01 *Consistency.* $p \circ q = - \sim (pq)$.   Def.

$\sim (pq)$, 'It is impossible that *p* and *q* both be true' would be '*p* and *q* are *in*consistent'. Hence $- \sim (pq)$, 'It is *possible* that *p* and *q* both be true', represents '*p* and *q* are consistent'.

1.02 *Strict Implication.* $p \dashv q = \sim (p - q)$.   Def.

1.03 *Material Implication.* $p \subset q = - (p - q)$.   Def.

1.04 *Strict Logical Sum.* $p \wedge q = \sim (-p - q)$. Def.

1.05 *Material Logical Sum.* $p + q = - (-p - q)$.   Def.

1.06 *Strict Equivalence.* $(p = q) = (p \dashv q)(q \dashv p)$.   Def.

. . . .

1.07 *Material Equivalence.* $(p \equiv q) = (p \supset q)(q \supset p)$.   Def.

Lewis thought that his 'strict' implication resembled the ordinary 'if – then' more closely than does material implication. But this seems not to be the case. While avoiding the classical 'paradoxes of implication' (**31.411–412. 43.22** [01] and [36]), it brings its own paradoxes (cf. **31.14**f.), as the following theorems of Lewis's system show:

49.05 ... an ... analogy holds between material implication, $p \supset q$, and strict implication, $p \dashv q$.

3.41 $(p \subset q) \dashv (-q \subset -p)$

If *p* materially implies *q*, then '*q* is false' materially implies '*p* is false'.

3.42 $-p \dashv (p \supset q)$

If *p* is false, then *p* materially implies any proposition *q*.

3.43 $(p \subset -p) \dashv -p$

If *p* materially implies its own negation, then *p* is false.

3.44 $[p \subset (q \subset r)] \dashv [q \subset (p \subset r)]$

. . . .

2.62 $(p \dashv q) \dashv (-q \dashv -p)$

If *p* strictly implies *q*, then '*q* is false' strictly implies '*p* is false'.

3.52 $\sim p \dashv (p \dashv q)$

If *p* is impossible (not self-consistent, absurd), then *p* strictly implies any proposition, *q*.

3.53 $(p \dashv -p) \dashv \sim p$

If *p* strictly implies its own negation, then *p* is impossible (not self-consistent, absurd).

3.54 $[p \dashv (q \subset r)] \dashv [q \dashv (p \subset r)]$

We may add certain further theorems which are consequences of the above.

3.45 $p \dashv (q \subset p)$

If *p* is true, then every

3.55 $\sim -p \dashv (q \dashv p)$

If *p* is necessarily true,

| proposition, *q*, materially implies *p*. | then *p* is strictly implied by any proposition, *q*. |

More such laws follow in the original.

B. MANY-VALUED LOGICS: LUKASIEWICZ

Many-valued logics were an important discovery. J. Łukasiewicz discovered a system of this kind in 1917 and lectured on it to the Philosophical Society in Lwów in 1920 (**49.06**). In the same year E. L. Post independently published another such system (**49.07**). We cite a passage on the subject from a lecture by Łukasiewicz in 1929, for its comparatively ready comprehensibility.

49.08 One could, however, adopt a position which is incompatible with the principle of two-valued logic. According to this position logical propositions can have values other than truth and falsity. A proposition of which we do not know whether it is true or false, may have no determinate value of truth or falsity but may have a third, undetermined value. One may think, for instance, that the proposition 'I shall be in Warsaw in a year's time' is neither true nor false, but has the third, undetermined value, which we can symbolize by '½'. But we can go still further and ascribe infinitely many values to propositions, values which lie between falsity and truth. In this case we should have an analogy with the calculus of probability, in which we ascribe infinitely many degrees of probability to different events. In this way we should obtain a whole heap of many-valued logics; three-valued, four-valued, etc. and finally an infinitely-valued logic. Symbols other than '1' and '0', such as are used in proofs of independence, would thus correspond with propositions having different degrees of truth, in logics with a corresponding number of values. Actually, it is the method of proving the independence of propositions in the theory of deduction which has occasioned our researches into many-valued logics.

In three-valued logic tables for implication and negation must be set up, analogous to those which we have in two-valued logic. Those given here seem to me very intuitive.

C	0	½	1	*N*
0	1	1	1	1
½	½	1	1	½
1	0	½	1	0

Thus every meaningful expression would be true in threevalued logic if for all substitutions of the symbols '0', '½', '1' for variable expressions, they yielded always '1' when the reduction had been completed according to the accompanying table. It is easy to verify that in a three-valued logic thus understood, our axioms 1 ('*CCpqCCqrCpr*') and 3 ('*CpCNpq*') are true. But axiom 2 ('*CCNppp*') is not true. For the substitution p/½ gives us

$$CCN\ \tfrac{1}{2}\ \tfrac{1}{2}\ \tfrac{1}{2} = CC\ \tfrac{1}{2}\ \tfrac{1}{2}\ \tfrac{1}{2} = C\ 1\ \tfrac{1}{2} = \tfrac{1}{2}.$$

It follows from the table given, that every sentence of three-valued logic is also a sentence of two-valued logic (but evidently not conversely). Three-valued logic can be exhibited as an axiomatic system, in the same way as that in which we have thought of the (two-valued) theory of deduction. Then we should not need to appeal to the given table proving sentences.

In infinitely-valued logic we suppose that propositions can take infinitely many values; we co-ordinate them with the rational numbers satisfying the condition $0 \leqslant x \leqslant 1$. For such a logic it is evidently impossible to set up a table, since this would have to have infinitely many rows and columns. We determine the properties of implication and negation for infinitely-valued logic in the following way, premising that p and q are rational numbers in the interval $0 - 1$:

if $p \leqslant q$, then $Cpq = 1$; if $p > q$, then
$Cpq = 1 - p + q;\ Np = 1 - p.$

From these equations there follow the properties of implication and negation which they were given in three-valued logic. From the said equations one can see that when the arguments of implication and negation do not go beyond the interval of the rational numbers $(0, 1)^{*}$, then the values of implication and negation, too, do not go beyond this interval.

In the many-valued logic we adopt the following definitions:

$Apq = CCpqq, Kpq = NANpNq, Epq = KCpqCqp.$

We have already spoken of the definitions given for alternation and equivalence. The definition of conjunction is based on the De Morgan laws.

Infinitely-valued logic is a proper part of two-valued logic; mostly, those sentences of two valued logic are not true in it, on which certain kinds of apagogic inferences are based.

The relationship of many-valued logics to the two-valued

---

*Lukasiewicz has the parentheses.

reminds one of the relationship of non-Euclidean geometries to the geometry of Euclid. Like the non-Euclidean geometries, so too the many-valued logics are internally consistent, but different from the two-valued logic. Without deciding the question of the truth of one of these logics, we remark that the two-valued logic has this superiority: it is much simpler than the many-valued logics. In any case, the many-valued logics have proved useful, in leading to the method of finding independence.

Wajsberg axiomatized three-valued logic in 1931 (**49.09**). The question of the interpretation of these systems is still not clarified. While many logicians – e.g. Bernays (**49.10**) – think that they admit of no ready interpretation and so can hardly count as 'logics', H. Reichenbach has shown that the theory of Quantum Mechanics can be axiomatized on the basis of Łukasiewicz's three-valued logic, which cannot be done on the basis of two-valued logic (**49.11**).

C. GÖDEL'S THEOREM

As a final text from the history of problems treated in mathematical logic we choose K. Gödel's celebrated paper of 1931. It belongs to methodology rather than logic, but its great importance for the latter justifies its finding a place here.

49.12 As is well known, the development of mathematics in the direction of greater exactness has led to the formalization of many of its domains in such a way that proof can be carried through in accordance with a few mechanical rules. The most extensive formal systems so far constructed are the system of *Principia Mathematica* [PM][1] on the one hand, and the axiom-system for set-theory due to Zermelo and Fraenkel [further developed by J. v. Neumann] on the other. Both these systems are so comprehensive that all contemporary methods of proof used in mathematics have been formalized in them, i.e. have been reduced to a few axioms and rules of inference. Hence the conjecture suggests itself that these axioms and rules of inference are sufficient to decide *all* mathematical questions which can be completely formally expressed in the said systems. In what follows, it will be shown that this is not the case, but that in both the systems mentioned there are even relatively simple problems from the theory of the familiar integers[4] which cannot be decided on the basis of the axioms. This circumstance is not due at all to the special nature of these systems, but holds for a very large class of formal systems, to which there belong in particular all those formed from these two by the addition of a finite number of axioms[5], it being presumed that no false theorems of the kind specified in foot-note[4] become provable through the added axioms.

We first sketch, before going into details, the main ideas of the proof, naturally without laying claim to exactness. The formulae of a formal system [we here confine ourselves to the system of PM] are finite material sequences of basic symbols [variables, logical constants, and parentheses or punctuation-marks], and it is easy to specify exactly *which* sequences of basic symbols are meaningful formulae and which are not.[6] Analogously, from the formal point of view proofs are only finite sequences of formulae [with definite statable properties]. For metamathematical purposes it is naturally indifferent what objects are taken as basic symbols, and we opt for using natural numbers[7] as such. Accordingly, a formula becomes a finite sequence of natural numbers[8] and a proof becomes a finite sequence of finite sequences of natural numbers. Metamathematical concepts [theorems] thus become concepts [theorems] about natural numbers or sequences of such,[9] and consequently expressible [at least in part] in the symbols of the system PM itself. In particular, it can be shown that the concepts 'formula', 'proof', 'provable formula', are definable in the system PM, i.e. it is possible to produce a formula $F(v)$, for instance, in PM, having a free variable v [of the type of a sequence of numbers],[10] such that $F(v)$ states when meaningfully interpreted: v is a provable formula. Now we state an undecidable sentence of the system PM, i.e. a sentence A such that neither A nor *not-A* is provable, in the following way:

A formula of PM with just one free variable, and that of the type of the natural numbers [class of classes] we will call a *class-symbol*. We think of class-symbols as somehow ordered in a sequence[11], denote the n-th by $R(n)$, and note that the concept 'class-symbol', as also the ordering relation R, can be defined in PM. Let α be an arbitrary class-symbol; by $[\alpha; n]$ we denote the formula which arises from the class-symbol α when the free variable is replaced by the symbol for the natural number n. The ternary relation $x = [y; z]$ can also be shown to be definable in PM. Now we define a class K of natural numbers, as follows:

$$n \ \varepsilon \ K \ \equiv \ \overline{Bew} \ [R \ (n); \ n]^{11\mathrm{a}} \qquad\qquad [1]$$

[where *Bew* x signifies: x is a provable formula]. Since the concepts occurring in the definiens are all definable in PM, so is the concept K, formed from them, i.e. there is a class-symbol S^{12} such that the formula $[S; \ n]$ states when meaningfully interpreted, that the natural number n belongs to K. As a class-symbol, S is identical with a determinate $R(q)$, i.e.

$$S \ = \ R(q)$$

holds for a determinate natural number q. We now show that the sentence $[R(q); \ q]^{13}$ is undecidable in PM. For on the supposition that the sentence $[R(q); \ q]$ was provable, it would also be true, i.e. according to what has been said q would belong to K, and so by [1] $\overline{Bew} \ [R(q); \ q]$ would hold, in contradiction to the supposition. But if on the contrary the negation of $[R(q); \ q]$ was provable, then $\overline{n \ \varepsilon \ K}$ would hold, i.e. $Bew \ [R(q); \ q]$. Thus $[R(q); \ q]$ as well as its negation would be provable, which is again impossible.

The analogy of this argument with the antinomy of Richard (**48.14**) leaps to the eye; it is also closely comparable with the 'Liar'[14] (**23.10** ff., **35.11** ff., **48.10**), since the undecidable sentence $[R(q); \ q]$ states that q belongs to K, i.e., by [1], that $[R(q); \ q]$ is not provable. We thus have a sentence that states its own unprovability.[15] The method of proof just expounded can be applied to every formal system which, firstly, when meaningfully interpreted, disposes of sufficient means of expression to define the concepts occurring in the foregoing considerations [in particular the concept 'provable formula'], and in which, secondly, every provable formula is also meaningfully true. The exact carrying out of the foregoing proof that follows will have the task, among others, of replacing the second of those requirements by a purely formal and much weaker one.

From the observation that $[R(q); \ q]$ states its own unprovability, it at once follows that $[R(q); \ q]$ is true, since $[R(q); \ q]$ *is indeed* unprovable [since undecidable]. The sentence that is undecidable in the system PM has thus been decided by metamathematical considerations. The exact analysis of this remarkable circumstance leads to surprising results concerning proofs that formal systems are free from contradiction. These will be considered more closely in Section 4 Theorem (XI).

[1]Cf. the summary of the results of this work in *Anzeiger der Akad. d. Wiss. in Wien* [math.-naturw. Kl.] 1930 Nr. 19. . . .

[4]I.e. more exactly, there are *un*decidable sentences in which besides the logical constants − [not], v [or], (x) [for all], = [identical with], there occur no other concepts than + [addition], . [multiplication], both applying to natural numbers, the prefix (x) also being applicable only to natural numbers.

[5] Only such axioms being reckoned distinct in PM as are not differentiated merely by alteration of types.

[6] Here and in what follows we always understand by 'formula of PM' a formula written without abbreviations [i.e. without application of definitions]. Definitions serve only to procure shorter expressions and are therefore dispensable with in principle.

[7] I.e. we model the basic symbols on the natural numbers in an unambiguous way. . . .

[8] I.e. a co-ordination of a segment of the number series with natural numbers. [Numbers cannot be put in a spatial order.]

[9] In other words: the procedure described yields an isomorphic model of the system PM in the domain of arithmetic, and all metamathematical considerations can be equally well treated in this isomorphic model. This is done in the sketched proof that follows, i.e. by 'formula', 'sentence', 'variable' etc. *we are always to understand the corresponding objects in the isomorphic model.*

[10] It would be quite easy [only rather lengthy] actually to write out this formula.

[11] E.g. according to increasing sums of terms, and for equal sums, lexicographically.

[11a] The stroke across the top denotes negation.

[12] Again there is not the least difficulty in actually writing out the formula S.

[13] Note that '$[R(q); q)]$' or '$[S; q]$', which means the same thing, is merely a *metamathematical description* of the undecidable sentence. But as soon as the formula S has been ascertained, it is of course possible to determine also the number q, and so effectively to write out the undecidable sentence itself.

[14] Every epistemological antinomy can be subjected to an undecidability-proof of this kind.

410

[15] Contrary to intuition, such a sentence involves nothing essentially circular, since it first states the unprovability of a quite definite formula [viz. the q-th in the lexicographical ordering on a definite substitution], and only then [as it were casually] does it appear that this formula is precisely the one in which it has itself been expressed.

D. COMBINATORY LOGIC

In a lecture at Göttingen in 1920 (edited by H. Behmann in 1924 (**49.13**)) M. Schönfinkel laid the foundations of a new development which in certain respects has no parallel in other varieties of logic. We have seen successful efforts made to reduce the number of undefined propositional functors (§ 43 E) and to define the existential quantifier in terms of the universal (cf. **44.14**); the new endeavour is to dispense with the use of variables, part of the primitive capital of formal logic (cf. § 9 B, a, (aa)). Schönfinkel states his program as follows:

44.14 It is agreeable to the axiomatic method . . . that one should not only do one's best to restrict the number and content of the *axioms*, but also to reduce as far as possible the number of the basic undefined concepts. . . . The progress so far made along this road prompts the effort towards a further step . . . to try to eliminate even the remaining basic concepts of proposition, propositional function and variable by suitable reduction. To investigate and follow up such a possibility more closely would be valuable not only from the point of view of methodological endeavour to obtain the greatest possible unity of thought, but also from a certain philosophical or, if preferred, aesthetic point of view. For the variable in a logical proposition serves only as a mark distinctive of certain argument-places and operators as mutually relevant, and hence is to be characterized as a subsidiary concept, properly speaking unsuited to the purely constant, 'eternal' nature of a logical proposition.

It seems to me very remarkable that even this goal we have set can be attained, in the sense, moreover, that the reduction is achieved by means of three basic concepts.

Schönfinkel then introduces five 'functions' of general applicability, by the following definitional equations:
the identity function I: $Ix = x$;
the constant function C: $Cxy = x$;
the permuting function T: $T\,\Phi xy = \Phi yx$;
the compounding function Z: $Z\Phi\chi x = \Phi(\chi x)$;

the amalgamating function $S: S\Phi\chi x = (\Phi x)\,(\chi x)$,
and shows that S and C can be used to define the others:

$$I = SCC,$$
$$Z = S(CS)C,$$
$$T = S(ZZS)(CC).$$

The more properly logical *incompatibility function* U is then explained by means of the Sheffer-stroke and the universal quantifier:

$$Ufg = fx \mid {}^x gx$$

44.15 We now have the remarkable fact that every logical formula can be expressed not only by means of the several functions I, C, T, Z, S, U, but actually by means of C, S and U.

As an example, he reduces the proposition:

$$\text{(f) (Eg) (x) } \overline{fx \,\&\, gx}$$

(symbolism of Hilbert, cf. § 41 *H*) to the form:

$$U[S(ZUU)U]\,[S(ZUU)\,U].$$

Further researches in this direction have been made by H. B. Curry (1930), J. B. Rosser (1935), A. Church (1941), R. Feys (1946) and P. Rosenbloom (1950).

SUMMARY

In summary, we can make the following points about the results achieved in the period of mathematical logic of which we have treated (up to the *Principia*):

1. Mathematical logic again presents us with a *highly original* variety of logic; for in contrast to all the other known forms of this science, it proceeds *constructively*, i.e. by investigating logical laws in an artificial language that it has devised. Such artificial languages exhibit very simple syntactical and semantic relations, as compared with natural languages, with the result that formal logic has undergone a change very like that effected by Galileo in the domain of physics. Instead of the immediate, but complex facts, the simpler underlying connections can now be investigated.

2. In comparison with that fundamental novelty, the constant. and after Boole deliberate, increase in *formalism* is less revolutionary, since formalism was highly developed also among the Stoics and Scholastics. But we know of no such thorough-going application of this method as in mathematical logic.

3. With the help of the new principle of constructivity and of formalism, many *old intuitions were recaptured and considerably developed* in the course of this period, intuitions which had been lost to view in the barbaric 'classical' period. We may instance the concept of logical form, the distinction between language and

metalanguage, between propositional and term-logic, the problem of semantic antinomies, and some aspects of other semantic problems.

4. Further, we here find a long series of *quite new discoveries*. First and foremost, the problem of '*complete proof*' was posed and fully solved. The analysis of propositions was carried out by new means, though still in an Aristotelian sense, namely by applying the concepts of *functor* and *argument*, and by *quantifiers*. This led to problems of *many-place functors* and *plural quantification* which had not been known before. The distinction between the *logic of predicates* and that of *classes* was not indeed quite new, having been treated in the Scholastic doctrine of supposition, but it now comes to be very sharply made. The *logic of relations* seems to be quite a new creation, notwithstanding some hints in Aristotle, Galen and the Scholastics, as also the theory of description and the *logical antinomies*. These are only a few examples.

5. After all that, it must seem rather surprising that, up to and including the *Principia*, there is here *less* logical strictness (particularly as concerns the distinction of language and metalanguage) than in the best texts of Megarian-Stoic and scholastic logic. Frege is the only exception. Even Lewis's explanations (cf. **49.05**) lack precision. But this weakness was overcome after the *Principia*, so that logic attained once more a very high level of exactness.

6. Finally, the large number of logical formulae stated and investigated is characteristic of mathematical logic. Often this is due to a purely mechanical development and brings no interesting information, but often enough a much greater positive contribution is made than by the other forms of logic, especially in the logic of terms.

Thus there can be no doubt that in this period formal logic once more attained one of its peaks of development.

413

PART VI

The indian variety of Logic

§ 50. INTRODUCTION TO INDIAN LOGIC

A. HISTORICAL SURVEY

A sketch of the history of formal logic in India will be more intelligible to the reader if it is prefaced with some account of the basic evolution of Indian thought, which is but little known in the West.

With some simplification we can put the beginning of systematic thought in India in the last centuries B.C. Various religious, psychological and metaphysical conceptions are indeed known before that, but they first take on systematic form in the classical texts that survive from that time, texts called 'Sūtra' by the Brahmins – the word means both a statement of doctrine and a work consisting of such. Of these texts six are Brahmanic in character, the *Sāṃkhya-kārīka*, the *Yoga-, Pūrva-mīmāṃsā-, Vedānta-, Nyāya-* and *Vaiśeṣika-sūtra*. The last seems to have been first edited in about the first century A.D., the *Nyāya-sūtra* first about 200; their contents, however, are ascribed at least in part to an earlier period. Every one of these Sūtras has occasioned a swarm of commentaries, commentaries on commentaries, commentaries of the third order etc., and nearly the whole philosophical literature of India consists of commentaries. The teachings of these schools can be characterized thus:

Sāṃkhya: dualistic ontology and cosmogony.
Yoga: systematization of mythical and ascetical practice.
Pūrva-mīmāṃsā: monistic metaphysics.
Nyāya: epistemology, logic, and methodology.
Vaiśeṣika: realistic ontology and systematics.
These bodies of teaching often supplement one another, e.g. those of the *Vaiśeṣika* and *Nyāya*.

Besides the Brahmans there arose, among others, two further religious communions: the Buddhists and the Jins (for this spelling rather than 'Jains' see **50.01**). Both took shape in the 6th century B.C. and in the centuries round the beginning of our era developed highly speculative systems of thought which first found expression in some fundamental texts. Buddhism is of over-riding importance to us. It is divisible into two great tendencies: the Hīnāyāna (the little vehicle) and the Mahāyāna (the great vehicle). Within these two main streams again various schools arose. The chief schools of the Hīnāyāna are the pluralistic-realistic Sarvāstivāda and the phenomenalistic Santrāntika schools. In the Mahāyāna the first development was the negativistic relativism of the Mādhyamikas. The movement culminated in the idealism of the Vijñānavāda school. From among the followers of this last there should be mentioned at least the two brilliant brothers, the saintly Asaṅga, and Vasubandhu who was perhaps one of the most productive thinkers the history of philosophy has to show.

Indian philosophy quickly developed permanent controversies, but also fruitful exchange of thought between the different schools. From the 8th century on, Buddhism lost ground and within Brahmanism the Vedānta gained the upper hand, mainly owing to a series of prominent thinkers of whom the most important is Śaṅkara, 8–9th century. The final result, manifest even in the 10th century, is a unification: the Vedānta absorbed some doctrines of the other schools and also much Buddhist thought, and the controversies - such as that between the radical (advaita) pantheism of Śaṅkara and the moderate opinions of Rāmānuja (11th century) took place entirely within the Vedantic school.

Essentially, we can speak of three main periods of Indian logic which roughly coincide with the three millennia of its history:

antiquity: approximately to the beginning of our era, the time of as yet unsystematic thought.

classical period: the first millennium A.D., marked on the one hand by controversies between schools, on the other by the construction of developed systems.

modern period: the second millennium A.D., with predominance of the Vedanta.

B. EVOLUTION OF FORMAL LOGIC

Formal logic (nyāya-śāstra) developed in India, as in Greece, from the methodology of discussion. Such a methodology was already systematically constructed in the 2nd century B.C. The first ideas which can be said to be formal-logical occur indeed as early as the Vaiśeṣika-sūtra (1st century A.D.), but the history of Indian formal logic properly begins with the Nyāya-sūtra (edited in the 2nd century A.D.). This 'logical' sūtra (so characterized by its very name) was the foundation of all Indian logical thought.

After the final redaction of the Nyāya-sūtra the next five to six centuries display controversies between the Buddhist, Brahmanist and also Jinist logicians. In all three camps logic was keenly cultivated. Among the most important thinkers are in the Naiyāyikaś*, Vatsyāyana (5–6th cent.) (50.02),** Uddyotakara (7th cent.) (50.03) and Vācaspati Miśra (10th cent.)***; in the Vaiśeṣikas primarily

---

* I.e. among the followers of the Nyāya. The most important of other such names are 'Mīmāṃsaka' for a follower of the Mīmāṃsa, 'Vedantin' for a follower of the Vedānta, but simply 'Vaiśeṣika' for a follower of the Vaiśeṣika.

** According to Shcherbatskoy, Vatsyāyana might possibly be a contemporary of Dignāga's, but D. Ingalls puts him in the 4th century (communication by letter).

*** This thinker has been generally ascribed to the 9th century, but I follow P. Hacker who puts him in the 10th (50.04). Prof. D. Ingalls was kind enough to draw my attention to Hacker's work.

Praśastapāda (5–6th cent.) (**50.05**), in the Mīmāmsakas Kumārila (7th cent.) (**50.06**). Perhaps still more important than those is the Buddhist Vasubandhu (4–5th cent.) (**50.07**) and his brilliant pupil Dignāga (5–6th cent.) (**50.08**). quite the greatest Indian logician, who founded an idealistic but unorthodox Vijñānavada-school. To this school there belong among others the commentator on Dignāga, Dharmakīrti (7th cent.) (**50.09**), and *his* commentator Dharmottara (8–9th cent.) (**50.10**). In the same centuries occurred the crystallization of formal logic which is plainly present in the 7th; a genuine and correct, though still in many ways elementary formal logic has developed from the methodology of public discussion.

To the third period of Indian philosophy there corresponds a new epoch of logic, that of the Navya-Nyāya, the new Nyāya. Given shape by the *Tattva-cintāmani*, the great work of Gaṅgeśa (14th cent.) (**50.11**), this logic was developed with the utmost subtlety in a spirit remarkably like that of late western Scholasticism, though the basic ideas and methods are quite different.

Of the innumerable logicians of this period the best known are Jayadeva (15th cent.) (**50.12**), Ragunātha (16th cent.) (**50.13**), Mathurānātha (**50.14**), Jagadīśa (17th cent.) (**50.15**), and the author of a compendium not unlike the *Summulae Logicales*, Annambhaṭṭa (17th cent.) (**50.16**).

Today the study of Indian logic has been re-introduced in India along with the resumption of speculative Vedantic thought (Sri Aurobindo). But it is not yet possible to form a judgment about this development.

We set out the most important names and dates in a table:

Pre-logical methodology of discussion

THE OLD SCHOOL

Nyāya-sūtra (final redaction in 2nd century A.C.)

NAIYĀYIKAS	BUDDHISTS	OTHERS
	Vasubandhu (4–5 c.)	
Vatsyāyana (5–6 c.)		
	Dignāga (5–6 c.)	Praśastapāda (5–6 c.)
Uddyotakara (7 c.)		Kumārila (7 c.)
	Dharmakīrti (7 c.)	
	Dharmottara (8–9 c.)	
	Śāntaraksita (8 c.)	
Vācaspari Miśra (10 c.)		(Prābhākara)
Udayana (end 10 c.)		Śrīdhara (ca. 991)

418

THE NEW SCHOOL

Gaṅgeśa	14 c
Jayadeva	1425–1500
Ragunātha	ca. 1475 – ca. 1550
Mathurānātha	ca. 1600 – ca. 1675
Jagadīśa	ca. 1600
Annambhaṭṭa	after 1600.

C. STATE OF RESEARCH

The present (1955) state of research in the field of Indian logic has a certain resemblance to that in the field of western Scholastic logic. Most of the logical texts are still unpublished, and many, especially the Buddhist ones, are only available in Tibetan or Chinese translations; many too are no longer extant. But the publication of these texts would at first bring little result – unlike the Scholastic case, since an extensive philological formation would be required before they could be read in the originals, while people so equipped have commonly not studied systematic logic. We are even worse off for translations than for editions; only very few texts (**50.17**) have been completely translated. Of others we have only fragments in western languages, in many cases nothing at all.

On the other hand we already have a number of scientific compendia and a comprehensive history of the literature of Indian logic by S. C. Vidyābhūṣaṇa (1921). But this is similar to Prantl's work in that an understanding of logical doctrine is not to be looked for (though it is very important in other respects), and then again many remarks on the literary history need revision.

Monographs fall into two groups. One derives from the work of indologs, whose logical formation stems from the so-called 'classical' logic. The most important works are those of A. B. Keith (1921), H. N. Randle (1930) and Th. Shcherbatskoy (1932). Useful as they are, they yet contain (especially the monumental work of Shcherbatskoy on Buddhist logic) so many misunderstandings of systematic questions, that their results need to be thoroughly revised. The second group is composed of a few writings by indologs formed in mathematical logic, e.g. the works of St. Schayer (1932-3), the commentary of A. Kunst (1939) – both belonging to the school of Łukasiewicz – and the monograph of D. Ingalls (1951) which is perhaps the most important in the field.

This is all very sad. Even on points of purely literary history there is great uncertainty. In Indological studies one is accustomed indeed to find the dating of a thinker fluctuating between two centuries, but this prejudices the possibility of solving various problems and important questions, e.g. the as yet obscure relation between Dignāga and Praśastapāda, while even so prominent a logician as Vācaspati Miśra can be ascribed to the 9th or 10th century indifferently. The content too of Indian logic is in great part unexplored. Ingalls' work revealed to the historian of logic a new intellectual world, that of the Navya-Nyāya, of which, at least in the west, very little was known. The mass of logical problems touched on there is so great that a generation of well-qualified investigators is needed to clear it up thoroughly. The same can be said of the classical period.

To summarize, although much is still obscure, or even unknown, we have a certain insight into the development of Indian logic at the beginning of the classical period, and are even perhaps already in a state to understand in some degree the *rise* of definitely formal logic. Further we have some knowledge of what may be called the final form of this logic in the Navya-Nyāya. But that is all. We cannot as yet speak of a history of logical problems in India.

D. METHOD

In spite of this unsatisfactory state of research it seems indispensable to give a brief exposition of some Indian problems, primarily those concerning the rise of formal logic. For, defective as is our knowledge of other aspects, this one can actually be followed better in India than in Greece. The evolution that we here describe in a way parallel to the other case, took in fact very much longer in India, so that the growth of a logical problematic can be seen in much more detail than in the west.

It seems useful to complete our exposition with some details of later logic, presenting only fragments which have been in essentials taken over from Ingalls. Those doctrines are stressed which either illustrate the specific character of Indian logic or may be of interest from the standpoint of systematic logic. Of the many details not touched on, we may mention the highly developed sophistic.

That our brief survey, entirely dependent on translations, is after all very unsatisfactory, should be evident *a priori*. Thanks to the help of competent indologs who are also logicians we yet hope that we have given the essentials. For the rest, it seemed better in the context of this book to give an incomplete exposition of Indian logic than to omit it entirely, for it, and it alone, serves the historian in the most important task of making a comparison.

Minor alterations made to the translations we have used, are not noted. Additions made by the original translators and by ourselves are alike put in parentheses.

§ 51. THE PRECURSORS

A. MILINDA-PAÑHA

In order to give some impression of the spirit in which the discussions were conducted which gave rise to Indian logic, we begin with a passage from the Buddhist work *Milinda-pañha*. It relates a conversation between the Greek king Menander, who ruled over the Punjab and part of what later became the United Provinces about 150 B.C., and the sage Nāgasena. The work itself dates from much later. Nāgasena's words reveal a world of discussion not unlike that which we meet in Plato.

51.01 The king said: 'Excellent Nāgasena, would you like to hold further discussion with me?'

'If you are willing to discuss like a wise man, O king, yes, indeed; but if you want to discuss like a king, then no.'

'How do the wise discuss, excellent Nāgasena?'

'In the discussions of the wise, O king, there is found unrolling and rolling up, convincing and conceding; agreements and disagreements are reached. And in all that, the wise suffer no disturbance. Thus it is, O king, that the wise discuss.'

B. KATHĀVATTHU

We can see how such a discussion was conducted, and the strictly defined rules that guided it, from another Buddhist work, the *Kathāvatthu*, perhaps contemporaneous with the last text. Here is a discussion between two disputants about the knowability of the human soul.

51.02 *Anuloma* ('The way forward')

Theravādin: Is the soul known in the sense of real and ultimate fact?

Puggalavādin: Yes.

Theravādin: Is the soul known *in the same* way as a real and ultimate fact is known?

Puggalavādin: Nay, that cannot truly be said.

Theravādin: Acknowledge your refutation:

(1) If the soul be known in the sense of a real and ultimate fact, then indeed, good sir, you should also say, the soul is known in the same way as [any other] real and ultimate fact [is known].

(2) That which you say here is wrong, namely, (*a*) that we

ought to say, 'the soul is known in the sense of a real and ultimate fact', but (*b*) we ought not to say, the soul is known in the same way as [any other] real and ultimate fact [is known].

(3) If the latter statement (*b*) cannot be admitted, then indeed the former statement (*a*) should not be admitted.

(4) In affirming the former statement (*a*), while

(5) denying the latter (*b*), you are wrong.

51.03 *Paṭikamma* ('The way back')

Puggalavādin: Is the soul not known in the sense of a real and ultimate fact?

Theravādin: No, it is not known.

Puggalavādin: Is it unknown in the same way as any real and ultimate fact is [*known*]?

Theravādin: Nay, that cannot truly be said.

Puggalavādin: Acknowledge the rejoinder:

(1) If the soul be not known in the sense of a real and ultimate fact, then indeed, good sir, you should also say: not known in the same way as any real and ultimate fact is known.

(2) That which you say here is wrong, namely, that (*a*) we ought to say 'the soul is not known in the sense of a real and ultimate fact', and (*b*) we ought not to say: 'not known in the same way as any real and ultimate fact is known'.

If the latter statement (*b*) cannot be admitted, then indeed the former statement (*a*) should not be admitted either.

In affirming (*b*), while denying (*a*), you are wrong.

Anuloma and *Paṭikamma* are only two of the five phases of the 'first refutation' (*paṭhama niggaha*). On this first, there follow the second, third, fourth and fifth, differing only in small details such as 'everywhere', 'always' and 'in everything'; then come four more in which 'known' and 'unknown' replace one another.

It can hardly be denied that this procedure, which evidently follows a fixed rule of discussion, seems to us rather too long and complicated. But it is hard to understand how Randle (**51.04**) could conclude from it that the author of the *Kathāvatthu* had no respect for logic. For our text shows clearly that the disputants not only apply definite and accepted rules of formal logic, but almost formulate them expressly.

St. Schayer also saw this (**51.05**). But in speaking of 'anticipations of propositional logic' in the *Kathāvatthu*, he seems to go to far. One could indeed think of the various statements as substitutions in the following propositional formulae:

422

51.021   (1) If p, then q;
therefore (2) not: p and not q;
therefore (3) if not q, then not p.
51.031   (1) If not p, then not q;
therefore (2) not: not p and not not q;
therefore (3) if not not q, then not not p.

But that would be to credit the Indian thinkers with a power of abstraction which they possessed no more than the pre-Aristotelians. The rules applied by our author are rather to be interpreted like those we found among the early Greeks (cf. § 7, D), rules, then, which rather correspond to the following formulae of the logic of terms:

51.022   (1) If A is B, then A is C;
therefore (2) not: (A is B) and not (A is C);
therefore (3) if not (A is C), then not (A is B).
51.032   (1) If A is not B, then A is not C;
therefore (2) not: (A is not B) and not (A is not C);
therefore (3) If not (A is not C), then not (A is not B).

Here we note that **51.03** results from **51.02** on substitution of 'A is not B' for 'A is B' and of 'A is not C' for 'A is C', which might suggest that some propositional rules were already in conscious use. But abstract formulation of such rules is nowhere to be found in this context, and the substitutions show that the thought revolved round the fixed subject A.

It should further be noticed that the passage from (1) to (2) involves a term-logical analogue of a well-known definition of implication (cf. **31.13**; **49.04** [1.03]), and that (2) and (3) together constitute a kind of law of contraposition (**31.20**, **43.22** [28]) or rather a *modus tollendo tollens* in a term-logical version (cf. **16.16**).

The important point historically, is that the beginning of Indian logic corresponds so closely to that of Greek logic.

C. THE TEN-MEMBERED FORMULA

It may be that the *Kathāvatthu* exhibits a level to which the methodology of discussion did not often attain at that time; certainly we find many later texts which are further removed from formal logic. An extract from the *Daśavaikālika-niryukti* of the younger Bhadrabāhu, a Jin, may serve as an example. He lived before 500 A.D., perhaps about 375 (**51.06**). The importance of this text is that it shows one a process from which the later five-membered syllogism may have developed.

51.07 (1) The proposition (*pratijña*): 'to refrain from taking life is the greatest of virtues.'

(2) The limitation of the proposition (*pratijña-vibhakti*): 'to refrain from taking life is the greatest of virtues, according to the jinist Tīrthaṅkaras.'

(3) The reason (*hetu*): 'to refrain from taking life is the greatest of virtues, because those who so refrain are loved by the gods, and to do them honour is an act of merit for men.'

(4) The limitation of the reason (*hetu-vibhakti*): 'none but those who refrain from taking life are allowed to remain in the highest place of virtue.'

(5) The counter-proposition (*vipakṣa*): 'but those who despise the jinist Tīrthaṅkaras and take life are said to be loved by the gods, and men regard doing them honour as an act of merit. Again, those who take life in sacrifices are said to be residing in the highest place of virtue. Men, for instance, salute their fathers-in-law as an act of virtue, even though the latter despise the jinist Tīrthaṅkaras and habitually take life. Moreover, those who perform animal sacrifices are said to be beloved of the gods.'

(6) The opposition to the counter-proposition (*vipakṣa-pratiṣedha*): 'those who take life as forbidden by the jinist Tīrthaṅkaras do not deserve honour, and they are certainly not loved by the gods. It is as likely that fire will be cold as that they will be loved by the gods, or to do them honour will be regarded by men as an act of merit. Buddha, Kapila and others, though really not fit to be worshipped, were honoured for their miraculous sayings, but the jinist Tīrthaṅkaras are honoured because they speak absolute truth'.

(7) An instance or example (*dṛṣṭanta*): 'the *Arhats* and *Sādhus* do not even cook food, lest in so doing they should take life. They depend on householders for their meals.'

(8) Questioning the validity of the instance or example (*āśaṅkā*): 'the food which the householders cook is as much for the *Arhats* and *Sādhus* as for themselves. If, therefore, any insects are destroyed in the fire, the *Arhats* and *Sādhus* must share in the householders' sin. Thus the instance cited is not convincing.'

(9) The meeting of the question (*āśaṅkāpratiṣedha*): 'the *Arhats* and *Sādhus* go to the householders for their food without giving notice, and not at fixed hours. How, therefore, can it be said that the householders cooked food for the *Arhats* and *Sādhus*? Thus the sin, if any, is not shared by the *Arhats* and *Sādhus*.'

(10) Conclusion (*nigamana*): 'to refrain from taking life is therefore the best of virtues, for those who so refrain are loved by the gods, and to do them honour is an act of merit for men.'

§ 52. VAIŚEṢIKA- AND NYĀYA-SŪTRA

So far we have spoken of the precursors of Indian logic; now we shall consider the first step in its development, which takes place mainly in the two sister sūtras, the *Vaiśeṣika-* and *Nyāya-sūtra*. The *Vaiśeṣika-sūtra* is older, and in most respects more important for logic; but the *Nyāya-sūtra* underlies the whole later development of Indian logic, constituting, indeed, its *Organon*.

First we give the doctrine of categories from the *Vaiśeṣika-sūtra*, then some short passages from the same source about inference, and finally go on to the *Nyāya-sūtra* and its five-membered syllogism.

A. VAIŚEṢIKA-SŪTRA

1. Doctrine of categories

52.01 The supreme good (results) from the knowledge, produced by a particular piety, of the essence of the predicables, substance, attribute, action, genus, species, and combination, by means of their resemblances and differences.

Earth, water, fire, air, ether, time, space, self, and mind (are) the only substances.

Attributes are colour, taste, smell, and touch, numbers, measures, separateness, conjunction and disjunction, priority and posteriority, understandings, pleasure and pain, desire and aversion, and volitions.

Throwing upwards, throwing downwards, contraction, expansion and motion are actions.

The resemblance of substance, attribute, and action lies in this that they are existent and non-eternal, have substance as their combinative cause, are effect as well as cause, and are both genus and species.

The resemblance of substance and attribute is the characteristic of being the originators of their congeners.

52.02 Substance-ness, attribute-ness, and action-ness are both genera and species.

(The statement of genera and species has been made) with the exception of the final species.

Existence is that to which are due the belief and usage, names '(It is) existent', in respect of substance, attribute and action.

Existence is a different object from substance, attribute and action.

And as it exists in attributes and actions, therefore it is neither attribute nor action.

(Existence is different from substance, attribute and action) also by reason of the absence of genus-species in it.

2. Inference

Besides the doctrine of categories, the *Vaiśeṣika-sūtra* contains the first Indian account of inference known to us.

52.03 'It is the effect or cause of, conjunct with, contradictory to, or combined in, this' – such is (cognition) produced by the mark of inference.

'It is its' (– this cognition is sufficient to cause an illation to be made); whereas (the introduction of) the relation of effect and cause arises from a (particular) member (of the argument).

Hereby verbal (cognition is) explained.

Reason, description, mark, proof, instrument – these are not antonyms.

(Comparison, presumption, sub-sumption, privation, and tradition are all included in inference by marks), because they depend, for their origin, upon the cognition, namely, 'It is its'.

B. NYĀYA-SŪTRA

1. Text

As has been said, the *Nyāya-sūtra*, the 'logical' sūtra, constitutes the fundamental text for the whole of Indian logic. We cite some passages in the translation of Vidyābhusana (**52.04**), for their pioneer character:

52.05 1. Supreme felicity is attained by the knowledge about the true nature of sixteen categories, viz. means of right knowledge, object of right knowledge, doubt, purpose, familiar instance, established tenet, members, confutation, ascertainment, discussion, wrangling, cavil, fallacy, quibble, futility, and occasion for rebuke.

2. Pain, birth, activity, faults and misapprehension – on

the successive annihilation of these in the reverse order, there follows release.

3. Perception, inference, comparison and word (verbal testimony) – these are the means of right knowledge.

4. Perception is that knowledge which arises from the contact of a sense with its object and which is determinate, unnameable and non-erratic.

5. Inference is knowledge which is preceded by perception, and is of three kinds, viz., a priori, a posteriori and 'commonly seen'.

6. Comparison is the knowledge of a thing through its similarity to another thing previously well known.

7. Word (verbal testimony) is the instructive assertion of a reliable person.

8. It is of two kinds, viz., that which refers to matter which is seen and that which refers to matter which is not seen.

52.06 25. A familiar instance is the thing about which an ordinary man and an expert entertain the same opinion.

26. An established tenet is a dogma resting on the authority of a certain school, hypothesis, or implication.

27. The tenet is of four kinds owing to the distinction between a dogma of all the schools, a dogma peculiar to some school, a hypothetical dogma, and an implied dogma.

32. The members (of a syllogism) are proposition, reason, example, application, and conclusion.

33. A proposition is the declaration of what is to be established.

34. The reason is the means for establishing what is to be established, through the homogeneous or affirmative character of the example.

35. Likewise through heterogeneous or negative character.

36. A homogeneous (or affirmative) example is a familiar instance which is known to possess the property to be established and which implies that this property is invariably contained in the reason given.

37. A heterogeneous (or negative) example is a familiar instance which is known to be devoid of the property to be established and which implies that the absence of this property is invariably rejected in the reason given.

38. Application is a winding up, with reference to the example, of what is to be established as being so or not so.

39. Conclusion is the re-stating of the proposition after the reason has been mentioned.

The part of this text that we find most interesting is that containing sūtras 32–39, which give what is, so far as we know, the first description of the five-membered syllogism. The classic and constantly repeated example – as standard as the western 'all men are mortal, Socrates is a man, etc.' – is the following:
 Proposition: There is fire on the mountain;
 Reason: Because there is smoke on the mountain;
 Example: As in a kitchen – not as in a lake;
 Application: It is so;
 Conclusion: Therefore it is so.
Before attempting to comment on this formula, we should like to listen to the first commentator on the *Nyāya-sūtra*.

2. Vātsyāyana's commentary

We cite, in the version of Jhā (**52.08**), Vātsyāyana's remarks on some of the 'members':

52.09 The 'statement of the proposition' is that assertion which speaks of the subject which is intended to be qualified by the property which has to be made known or proved.
52.10 That which 'demonstrates' – i.e. makes known or proves – the probandum – i.e. the property to be proved (as belonging to the subject), – through a property common to the example, is the 'statement of the probans'. That is to say, when one notices a certain property in the subject (with regard to which the conclusion is to be demonstrated) and notices the same property also in the example, and then puts forward that property as demonstrating (or proving) the probandum, – this putting forward of the said property constitutes the 'statement of the probans'. As an example (in connection with the conclusion 'sound is not eternal') we have the statement 'because sound has the character of being a product'; as a matter of fact everything that is a product, is not eternal.

On this text the translator, Jhā, remarks: 'The term *sādhya* is used in the present text rather promiscuously. It stands for the probandum, the predicate of the conclusion, and also for the subject, the thing in regard to which that character is to be demonstrated.'

52.11 The 'statement of the probans' is that also which demonstrates the probandum through dissimilarity to the example (i.e. through a property that belongs to the example and not to the probandum). 'How?' For example, 'sound is non-eternal, because it has the character of being produced, – that which has *not* the character of being produced is always eternal'.

52.12 For instance in the reasoning 'sound is non-eternal, because it has the character of being produced', what the probans 'being produced' means is that being produced, it ceases to be, – i.e. loses itself. – i.e. is destroyed. Here we find that being produced is meant to be the means of proving (i.e. the probans) and being non-eternal is what is proved (the probandum); and the notion that there is the relation of means and end between the two properties can arise only when the two are found to co-exist in any one thing; and it arises only by reason of 'similarity' (of a number of things in every one of which the two properties are found to coexist). So that when one has perceived the said relation in the familiar instance, he naturally infers the same in the sound also; the form of the inference being: 'Sound also is non-eternal, because it has the character of being produced, just like such things as the dish, the cup and the like. And this is called 'statement of the example' (*udāharaṇa*), because it is what is the means of establishing, between the two properties, of the relation of means and end.

53.13 When the example cited is the homogeneous one, which is similar to the subject, e.g. when the dish is cited as the example to show that it is a product and is non-eternal, we have the 're-affirmation' or 'application' stated in the form 'sound is so', i.e. 'sound is a product; where the character of being a product is applied to the subject *sound*.

When the example cited is the heterogeneous one, which is dissimilar to the subject, e.g. when the soul is cited as an example of the substance which, not being a product, is eternal, – the 're-affirmation' of 'application' is stated in the form 'sound is not so', where the character of being a product is reasserted of the subject *sound* through the denial of the application of the character of not being produced. Thus there are two kinds of re-affirmation, based upon the two kinds of example.

3. Interpretation

Combining these explanations, we get the following scheme:

(1) We want to prove a property – not being eternal – of a subject – sound. This purpose is expressed in the 'proposition'.

(2) To effect it, we use the 'reason', which consists in another property – being produced – that we have noticed in sound.

(3) We next exemplify the matter in, say, a dish, which is produced and is not eternal, showing that these two properties co-exist in the dish and other things of that kind. This is the 'example'. It can also be formulated negatively, as when we adduce something in which absence of the probandum accompanies absence of the reason; in the classic example this is a lake.

(4) Having done that, we assert that the same connection between being produced and not being eternal occurs in the subject – sound. This is the 'application'.

(5) And so we conclude that in sound too, not being eternal must occur.

The reader accustomed to western logic may find this process strange, but the Indian formula loses its strangeness, and even seems quite natural, when it is remembered that it is not the result of reflexion about the Platonic διαίρεσις, but merely the fixing of a method of discussion. The following sequence is quite natural in discussion:

A.: I state that *S* has the character *P* (1)

B.: Why?

A.: Because *S* has the character *M* (2).

B.: So what?

A.: Well, both *M* and *P* characterize *X*, and neither of them *Y* (3). So it is in our case (4). Therefore *S* has the character *P* (5).

That is just the form of our 'syllogism'. But what logical formula underlies it? That question formed the subject of a centuries-long discussion in India, of which we have only partial knowledge and understanding. Some details are given in the next chapter. One point already emerges from the *Nyāya-sūtra* and Vātsyāyana, that we should not look for any universal premisses, not, therefore, for a syllogism of the western kind. Vātsyāyana does once say 'all' (**52.10**); but this should be regarded as accidental, for there is nothing of the kind in the *Nyāya-vārttika* uf Uddyotakara. Later history also shows how difficult the Indian logicians found it to grasp the universal. The original formula of the sūtras is simply an argument by analogy from some individuals to others, rhetorical rather than logical in character. Neither the sūtras nor Vātsyāyana have achieved a properly formal logic.

It has been objected to this interpretation of the formula that besides the 'syllogism' the sūtras give another means of knowledge, the 'comparison' (cf. **52.05**, 3 to 7). But this is again an argument by analogy, so that we should have to accept two such arguments in the sūtras. However, the objection is not sound, since the 'comparison (*upamāna*) was expounded in the Nyāya tradition, not as an argument from analogy in the ordinary sense, but as one of a quite special (metalinguistic) kind, an argument about a name. This can best be seen in the *Tarka-Saṃgraha*, a late text, but true to the *Nyāya* tradition:

52.14 Comparison (*upamāna*) is the efficient cause of knowledge of similarity. This (in its turn) is knowledge of the relation between a name and the thing it names. . . . Example: Whoso does not know the gayal, hears from some forester that it is like the domestic ox; going into the forest and remembering this saying, he sees an object like a domestic ox. At once there arises in him knowledge by similarity: 'That is what is called a "gayal".'

So, following the plain text of the sūtra and Vātsyāyana, we may take the pretended 'syllogism' not as a syllogism but as a formula for inference by analogy, of a rhetorical kind. We shall now see how this became a genuine law, or rule, of formal logic.

§53. THE RISE OF FORMAL LOGIC

A. MAIN STAGES OF DEVELOPMENT

What Plato is to Aristotle in formal logic, the Nyāya-sūtra is to, say, Dharmakīrti, save that the Nyāya-sūtra lacks that idea of universal law which in Plato opened the way to the rise of western logic. It was this idea which brought about the speedy emergence of logical form in the west. But in India, logic took shape very slowly, in the course of centuries and under the auspices of methodology. However, it is just this step-by-step, 'natural' development of Indian logic which gives it its great historical interest.

Though only partially acqainted with this development, we can determine some of its phases. Their order of succession is not altogether clear, but we can be certain of their occurrence and sometimes of their temporal relationship. Thus we obtain the following scheme:

First step: The establishment of a formal rule of syllogism (the *trairūpya*) based on examples. According to G. Tucci (**53.01**) Vasubandhu will have known this.

Second step: Dignāga developed the *trairūpya* into a formal syllogistic – the 'wheel of reasons' (*hetu-cakra*). Uddyotakara carried this further still.

Third step: The components of the syllogism were reduced to three, the probandum no longer being resumed in the conclusion,

431

and the application being dropped. A distinction is also made between a syllogism for oneself and a syllogism for another (*sva-artham* and *para-artham*); the first comprises three stages, the second the classic five. Dharmottara says (**53.02**) that Dignāga was the first to make this distinction, with which opinion Shcherbatskoy agrees (**53.03**).

Fourth step: The word '*eva*' ('*only*') was added to the *trairūpya;* this radically changed the exemplification from a mere exhibition of examples to a universal premiss. This addition is not to be found in the 5th century, but seems to have been generally accepted in the 7th, being found, for example, in Dharmakīrti (**53.04**).

Fifth step: The concept of universal law emerged. There were two technical terms in this connection: the 'not occurring elsewhere' of the Jins (*anyathānupapannatva*), and 'pervasion' (*vyāpti*). Both were used in the 7th century. There were of course earlier premonitions; e.g. the word '*vyāpaka*' and its cognates often occurs in Vātsyāyana, but in a physical sense. The same author once has '*vyāpakatvam*' in a logical sense (**53.05**), but this may be a later addition since the word is missing in several manuscripts*. Contrary to the opinion of Shcherbatskoy (**53.06**), we can be sure that Vasubandhu knew as little of 'universal connection' as Dignāga, but in the 8th century Sāntarakṣiṭa and Kamalaśīla rejected it as a basis for syllogism.

The emergence of the concept of universal law marks Indian thought as having attained to the level of formal logic. Examples continue to be used, but only as a concession to the needs of communication; once clearly elaborated, the syllogistic formula has no need of examples. Often, in fact, the word 'example' merely marks the statement of universal connection (cf. **53.26**).

B. TERMINOLOGY

Before exemplifying in texts the development that has been sketched, we briefly elucidate the more important technical terms in the accompanying table.** They are not easily translated into western languages, as the concepts they refer to cannot be paired off with those of the Greeks, and they are, moreover, nearly all ambiguous.

---

* Prof. D. Ingalls has remarked on this.
** Prof. C. Regamey has helped greatly in drawing up this table. For examination of the technical terms, cf. Randle (**53.07**).

TECHNICAL TERMS

Sanskrit	Classic example	Meaning	Transla-tions	Symbol
pakṣa	mountain	object of discussion	subject	S
linga *lakṣaṇa*	smoke	sign, mark characteristic	mark, midd-le term	M
hetu	1) smoke 2) because of smoke	1) reason 2) justifi-cation	1) reason 2) justifi-cation	M
dṛṣṭānta	cowherd lake	example	example	
sapakṣa	cowherd	example like the *pakṣa*	*sapakṣa*	XP
vipakṣa	lake	example unlike the *pakṣa*	*vipakṣa*	X-not-P
sādhya	1) fire 2) mountain	predicate to be proved, often also 2) = *pakṣa*	probandum	1) P 2) S
dharma	fieriness smokiness	quality, form	quality	
dharmin	the mountain is *dharmin* in respect of fieriness and smokiness	subject of the quality,	bearer of the quality	
pakṣadharma	the moun-tain's being fiery	possession of the *dharma* by the *pakṣa*		S-as-M
anumeya		1) *pakṣa* 2) *sādhya* (1) 3) *pakṣa-dharma*	*probandum*	1) S 2) P 3) S as having

C. THE THREE-MEMBERED SYLLOGISM

Our first text is a methodological one from Dignāga, directed against the Nyāya, and with a remarkably modern sound:

53.08 There are only two means of cognition (*pramānas*), I mean inference and direct perception, for those such as communication, analogy (*upamāna*) etc. are contained in these two. There are only two means of cognition by means of which we can grasp a thing in itself (*svalakṣana*) and its universality (*sāmānylakṣana*); there is no other object of cognition than these two (and no other) that can be grasped by one of these means of cognition.

The great Indian logician goes on to state that the syllogism – every syllogism – needs only three components:

53.09 We maintain that just as an undoubtedly valid syllogism is attained by someone for himself, (so too) an undoubtedly valid syllogism is produced in another's reason. It shows the connection (of the probandum) with the *pakṣadharma* (i.e. the subject as qualified by the middle term), and the exclusion of everything separated from the probandum.

The reason (*hetu*) is formulated to show that the *pakṣadharma* is present in the probandum; the example is formulated to show that it is inseparably linked with it; the proposition is formulated to show the probandum.

Hence no other component is required for the formulation of a syllogism, beyond those stated. In saying this I contradict the opinion of those logicians who count the desire for knowledge (*jijñāsā*), the application and the conclusion as components of the syllogism.

Here it could be objected that if this is so, the giving of the example is not a special component, since it only makes clear the sense of the reason. (I answer that) though this is true in essentials, yet the statement of the reason is only to say that this has the nature of what it is to be *pakṣadharma* – it cannot show that it is present in cases of presence (of the probandum), absent in cases of absence (of the probandum). Consequently it is necessary to adduce distinctly the positive (*sapakṣa*) and negative (*vipakṣa*) examples.

So Dignāna's three-membered syllogism consists of justification, examples and proposition, i.e. of the second, third and first stages of the classic five-stage syllogism, application (4) and conclusion (5) being dropped. After this reduction the classic example becomes:
Proposition: There is fire on the mountain,
Reason: Because there is smoke on the mountain;
Example: as in the kitchen, where there is fire, not as in the lake, where there is no fire.

But something more important underlies this formula, namely the thought of an inseparable connection of *M* with *P*. The thought is only expressed in passing, but it is there. Yet this connection can only be intuited in examples, and Dignāga's logic is not ready to dispense with them, as the last quotation shows. This point can be still more clearly seen in the doctrines of the *lrairūpya* and the 'wheel of reasons'.

D. THE THREE-MEMBERED RULE: *TRAIRŪPYA*

In Praśastapāda this rule, the name of which means 'the three characteristics (of the reason)', has the following form:

53.10 What is conjoined with the probandum, and has been found in what possesses the probandum, and is always absent in its absence, is the mark (*liṅga*) which brings about inference.

Dignāga writes:

53.11 It is evident that this is the only valid rule of inference: if (1) the presence of this definite mark (*liṅga*) in the subject (*pakṣa*) has been stated, and if we remember that (2) the same mark is certainly in everything similar to the subject (*sapakṣa*), but (3) absolutely absent in everything unlike it (*vipakṣa*), then the result of the inference is certainly valid.

It cannot be denied that this text has its obscurities, and both Indians of old and modern Europeans have exercised great subtlety in trying to elucidate it. But Dignāga's practice, in relation to his 'wheel of reasons' shows that he is considering the following three-membered formula:
  (1) *M* occurs in *s* (smoke on the mountain);
  (2) *M* occurs in *XP* (smoke in the kitchen, which fire has);
  (3) *M* does not occur in *X*-not-*P* (no smoke in the lake, which no fire has);
  therefore *P* occurs in *S*.

E. WHEEL OF REASONS: *HETU-CAKRA*

Dignāga elaborated the *lrairūpya* in a table called the 'wheel of reasons' (*helu-cakra*), the first Indian attempt at a formal logic. Here is a metalogical formulation of the 'wheel':

53.12 A middle term or quality of the subject of inference (*pakṣa-dharma*) first takes three forms, according as it does or does not reside in the two possible ways in the *sapakṣa*. And in each of these three possible cases the middle term does or does not reside in the two ways in the *vipakṣa*. . . . Among these a middle term which is present in (either of) the two ways in the *sapakṣa*, and is absent in the *vipakṣa*, is a valid reason. What differs from this is either contradictory or inconclusive.

The two possible ways of the middle term being in the *sapakṣa* are: (1) that M is in all, (2) that M is in some; there is also the third possibility, not here mentioned, that (3) M is in no *sapakṣa*. That is why Dignāga speaks of 'three possible cases'. Similarly there are three cases in regard to the *vipakṣa*, that M can be in all, some or none. Thus there are nine possible cases in all. Symbolizing the three cases by 'A', 'I' and 'E', we get the following table, where the first letter relates to the *sapakṣa*, the second to the *vipakṣa*:

1. AA	2. AE	3. AI
4. EA	5. EE	6. EI
7. IA	8. IE	9. II

Of these moods only two, viz. 2 and 8, are valid. Dignāga worked all this out in terms of substitutions: but we only have his text in a translation by Vidyābhūṣana from the Tibetan, and as it does not seem reliable (**53.13**), we do not quote it. Instead, here is a short summary by Vācaspati Miśra in his *Nyāya-varttika-tātparya-ṭīkā:* ·

53.14 The nine middle terms used to prove eternality and the other probanda are: knowable, product, non-eternal; product, audible, effect of volition; non-eternal, effect of volition, intangible.

Uddyotakara completed this table in the following way: first he considers cases in which there is no *sapakṣa*, or it may be, *vipakṣa*, which gives seven further moods. using 'Λ' for these cases, we get:

10. $A\Lambda$	11. $I\Lambda$	12. $E\Lambda$
11. ΛA	14. ΛI	15. ΛE
	16. $\Lambda\Lambda$	

of which 10, 11 and 15 are valid, so that we now have five valid moods in all (**53.15**).

Uddyotakara then goes on to consider the ocurrence or non-occurrence of the middle term in the subject, and other circumstances besides, so that in sum his valid and invalid moods are not less than 176. Those in which the *hetu* is compound (and which Prof. D. Ingalls has pointed out to the author) deserve special attention. And example is: 'A word is not eternal, because it can be named and is an object of knowledge'.

Primitive and pre-logical as all this may seem, it should not be overlooked that the *hetu-cakra* contains some historically interesting details. A first point to note is that the Indians do not admit four kinds of proposition like Aristotle (cf. **12.06**) and the Scholastics, but only three, since they interpret 'Some S is P' not as 'at least some' but as 'at least some and not all' .Thus the 'I' in the foregoing table corresponds to the logical product of I and O in the Scholastic sense. This would give a logical triangle in place of the western logical square.

Also to be noted in the *hetu-cakra* is the evident tendency to extensionalism. That *sapakṣa* and *vipakṣa* are conceived as classes (and apparently by Uddyotakara and Dharmakīrti the subject, *pakṣa*, too) gives the effect of quantification; so that Indian logic was well on the way to extensional thought.

It should finally be emphasized that poor as this logic is, it is none the less formal: these thinkers tried to construct their syllogistic, like Aristotle, out of abstract relationships between classes as such, not out of concrete substitutions.

F. 'EVA'

Dharmakīrty extended the *trairūpya* by means of '*eva*' which can be applied to either subject or predicate. The formula runs:

In subject *eva*
In *sapakṣa eva*
In *vipakṣa eva* not

which means:

In subject *wholly*
In similar *only*
In dissimilar *never* (**53.16**).

G. UNIVERSAL CONNECTION

The syllogistic of Dignāga is still very much tied to examples; even he still bears the stamp of the methodological tradition. Liberation from this tradition seems to have been first achieved outside the Buddhist schools, and in the shape of a doctrine of universal connection between reason (*hetu*) and probandum (*sādhya*), or subject (*pakṣa*) and reason. Two varieties of this doctrine are known, one intensional, propounded by a Jin, Pātrasvāmin (probably 7th century); and one extensional, first clearly in evidence with Kumārila, a Mīmāṃsaka (7th century). The next five passages are the pertinent ones from Pātrasvāmin and the commentary of Kamalaśīla (Buddhist).

53.17 (Text) Can one not already assert the validity of an argumentation in respect of otherwise-non-occurrence (*anyathānupapannatva*)? Thus even reasons having the three marks (*trirūpahetus*) in a syllogism which satisfies these conditions, are powerless, if otherwise-non-occurrence is lacking.

53.18 (Commentary) Explanation of the expression 'otherwise-non-occurrence': The expression 'otherwise-non-occurrence' consists of two parts and means that (otherwise: *anyathā*, i.e.) apart from the probandum (*sādhya*) there is no occurrence (*anūpapannatva*) (of the reason): that the reason only occurs in the probandum.

53.19 (Text) As reason is postulated one to which belongs otherwise-non-occurrence. This is a (sufficient) reason whether it is charcterized by *one* mark, or by *four*, or *not by four*.

The single mark here, is otherwise-non-occurrence, the three others are those postulated by the *trairūpya*.

53.20 (Text) Just as people say of a father that he has *one* son, even though he has three sons, because this son is the only good one, so too this matter is to be understood.

The good son is, of course, otherwise-non-occurrence. Hence:

53.21 (Text) The relation of necessary concomitance is nowhere present in reasons having the three marks (*trirūpahetus*). . . . Only those arguments have validity, in which is present otherwise-non-occurrence. The two examples (*dṛṣṭantas*) may or may not be the case, for they are not the efficient cause (of the conclusion). Where otherwise-non-occurrence is wanting, what use are the three (marks of the *trairūpya*)? When otherwise-non-occurrence is there, (again) what use are the three?

This radical doctrine did not succeed in establishing itself. A similar but more extensional theory, that of *vyāpti*, later became generally accepted. It is not easy to translate '*vyāpti*'; 'pervasion' seems to correspond best with the original sense of the word. A.Kunst uses 'implication', but it must be remembered that there is no question of a relation between two propositions, but either between two classes, or a class and its element (as in Kumārila), or, as for most of the Naiyāyikas, between two properties (essences) in accordance with the intensionalist standpoint of the school. The following text of Kumārila, the first in which we find a definition of *vyāpti*, gives clear expression to the first of these ways of understanding the matter:

53.22 The pervaded (*vyāpya*) is what has equal or less extension in space and time; its pervader (*vyapaka*) is what has equal or more extension. This means that when the pervaded thing is apprehended, its pervader is apprehended:

for not otherwise would the relation of pervaded and pervader hold between the two.

H. FINAL FORM OF THE DOCTRINE

1. Text

Passing over the whole vast discussion about *vyāpti* which went on in the Navya-Nyāya from the time of Gaṅgeśa (14th century), we give just one further text, from the *Tarkasaṃgraha* of Annambhaṭṭa (17th century). This small book corresponds closely to the *Summulae Logicales*, only coming at the end instead of the beginning of the development; it contains the essential and generally accepted doctrines of the 'new' Nyāya school.

53.23 Consideration (*parāmarśa*) is the knowledge of the fact that the subject (*pakṣa*) possesses a certain property (*dharma*), (knowledge which is) qualified by *vyapti*. Example: This mountain has smoke which does not occur without fire – that is the consideration; the knowledge which arises from it (viz.) 'The mountain has fire' is the conclusion.

Vyāpti is a law of concomitance (of this type): Everywhere where there is smoke, there is fire.

The quality of being a certain property of the subject (*pakṣa-dharmatā*) is the fact for the 'contained' (i.e. the reason – smoke) of being on the mountain.

53.24 There are two kinds of inference (*anumāna*): that for oneself, and that for another. (Inference) for oneself is that which is the cause of the conclusion (drawn) for oneself. Example: As a result of repeated observations in the kitchen etc. one has gained the (knowledge of the) law of concomitance: 'Everywhere where there is smoke, there is fire'. (Then) one goes on the mountain and, conceiving a doubt as to whether there is fire on this mountain, when one perceives smoke on it, one remembers the law of concomitance: 'Everywhere where there is smoke, there is fire'. From that there arises the knowledge: 'There is smoke on this mountain, which is inseparably associated with fire'. That is what is called the 'consideration of the mark (or middle term). From that there arises the knowledge: 'There is fire on this mountain' as conclusion. Such is an inference made for oneself.

53.25 But when, having deduced fire from smoke, one uses a five-membered expression to tell someone else, that is inference for another. Example: The mountain is fiery, because smoky. All that is smoky is fiery, like the hearth. So

439

here; therefore it is so. By means of this exposition of the mark, the other also recognizes (that there is) fire.

53.26 The five members are proposition, reason, example, application, conclusion. 'The mountain is fiery' – that is the proposition. 'Because smoky' – that is the reason. 'All that is smoky is fiery' – that is the example. 'So here' – that is the application. 'Therefore it is so' – that is the conclusion.

2. Interpretation

If we disregard the psychology, which here plays a considerable part, these points come to light:

(1) The Indian syllogism is not a thesis, but a rule, like the Stoic and Scholastic syllogisms.

(2) Structurally it is Ockhamist rather than Aristotelian, since the 'reason' always corresponds to a singular proposition.

(3) Yet the formulation rather suggests a formula of modern mathematical logic, than an Ockhamist syllogism, viz.:

> For all x: if x is A, then x is B;
> but a is A;
> therefore a is B.

(4) The Indian formula also contains an express justification of the major premiss. In this respect there seems to be a difference between the classic Nyāya logicians and the *Tarkasaṃgraha*. The latter, and later, text fairly evidently envisages an inductive proof, while the earlier thinkers intuit the connection of two essences in an individual.

(5) It should be evident that we are still in a logic of terms.

Modest as these results may seem to a western logician, the text cited undoubtedly attains to the level of genuine formal logic, though it is very far for from being formalistic.

§ 54. SOME OTHER LOGICAL DOCTRINES

In spite of his indifference to logic, even Shcherbatskoy was able to show that later Indian logic contained many interesting doctrines of formal logic. Thanks to the notable study of selected texts from the Navya-Naiyāyikas by D. Ingalls, we are now acquainted with some of them. But Ingalls' book is the first of its kind, and does not yet permit us to survey the whole range of Indian problems. Hence we limit ourselves to brief mention of the most important ones that he considers.

First of all we want to explain the extraordinary appearance of the later Indian logical texts. The first thing that strikes a western reader is the completely negative form of nearly every sentence. In

440

the simplest case, the Navya-Naiyāyikas, instead of writing 'the mountain is smoky' put something like 'not-mountain-ness qualifies the locus of not-being-smoky'. This form seems to have originated in the Buddhist doctrine of *apoha* (exclusion), the consequences of which were taken over by the Navya-Nyāya.

A. APOHA

We read in Dignāga:

54.01 Therefore the meaning of a word consists in a repudiation of the discrepant meaning.

About which a Buddhist commentator, Jinendrabuddhi, says:

54.02 Is the view of a double meaning, really a different view? The mistake found in this view (i.e. the mistake that it contradicts the text of Dignāga), will it not also extend to this (other view)? No, it will not. For the repudiation of the contrary is the exclusive meaning (of every word). And there is no contradiction (with the statement of Dignāga), because the 'own' meaning of the word is just repudiation of the contrary (and nothing else).

A word, then, signifies not what something is, but what it is not. However, this doctrine was not always maintained in its radical sense. E.g. Kamalaśīla differentiates three kinds of negation. One of them is defined:

54.03 Simple negation means, e.g., that a cow is not a non-cow.

And although Kamaśīla expressly says:

54.04 We have never admitted that the meaning of a word is pure negation.

Still, that 'not not-being-cow' is the pattern of all subsequent logical language.

B. DEFINITIONS OF *VYĀPTI*

As a first sample of the problems considered in the Navya-Nyāya, we give a text from the *Tattva-cintāmaṇi*, containing five of the definitions of *vyāpti* which Gangeśa rejects. It must be emphasized that this text is one of the simpler ones, and much more readily comprehensible than the commentaries which have attempted to 'elucidate' it.

54.05 What is pervasion (*vyāpti*)? It is not simply non-deviation (of the subject from the probandum, *sādhya*), for it is not this (viz. non-deviation defined as):

(1) non-occurrence (of the subject) to the locus of absence of the *sādhya;* nor

(2) non-occurrence to the locus of that absence of the *sādhya* (which absence occurs) in what is different from a locus of the *sādhya;* nor

(3) the possession of a different locus from that of a mutual absence whose counter-positive is a locus of the *sādhya;* nor

(4) (the subject's) being the counter-positive of an absence which is in all loci of the absence of the *sādhya;* nor

(5) non-occurrence in that which is something other than the locus of the *sādhya;*

since if the *sādhya* is wholly positive, *vyāpti* is none of the kinds of non-deviation defined above.

For us to have any understanding of this text – a relatively easy one, be it remembered – the means afforded by mathematical logic are indispensable, and we shall use, in essentials, the symbolism of the *Principia* in its logic of relations (**46.17** ff.). Taking *vyāpti* as inclusion between predicates (cf. commentary on **53.21**), we read '*gCs*' as 'the relation of *vyāpti* holds between *g* and *s*'. The names of the various relations employed in the definitions we abbreviate as follows: occurrence in, absence from, difference from, being in, '*V*', '*A*', '*D*', '*I*', being counter-positive of, being locus of '*G*', '*L*.' Then, neglecting quantifiers, the definitions can be given thus:

1. $g\,C\,s \equiv g\,(\div V \mid L \mid A)\,s$
2. $g\,C\,s \equiv g\,(\div V \mid L \mid A)\,s$ i.e. $\equiv g\,(-V \mid L \mid V \mid L \mid D)\,s$
3. $g\,C\,s \equiv g\,(L \mid D \mid G \mid L)\,s$
4. $g\,C\,s \equiv g\,(G \mid A \mid I \mid L \mid A)\,s$
5. $g\,C\,s \equiv g\,(\div V \mid D \mid L\,)\,s$

Prefixing universal quantifiers to these equivalences, we get the abbreviated formulae:

1. $C = \div V \mid L \mid A$
2. $C = \div V \mid L \mid V \mid L \mid D$
3. $C = L \mid D \mid G \mid L$
4. $C = G \mid A \mid I \mid L \mid A$
5. $C = \div V \mid D \mid L$

The degree of abstraction is evidently very high. The formulae can be further simplified if one takes I, L and V as simple inherence, D and G as non-identity, A as the negation of inherence; then the first definition, for example, could be read:

1. $gCs \equiv . (x) \sim (gx . \sim sx),$

which by a well known equivalence (cf. **31.13**) yields:

$$\equiv . (x). gx \supset sx$$

a. formal implication (cf. **44.11–13**). Such a simplification, however, would be a violation of the text, since the Navya-nyāya logicians distinguished all these relations sharply, but the reduction we have made does show that they were concerned with essentially the same problem as the Megarians (**20.05**ff.), Scholastics (**30.10**ff.) and now again the moderns (**49.03**ff.), the problem of defining 'if – then'.

While we shall not go further into the widely different positions adopted about this matter, it may be remarked that Gangeśa formulates in this text only a few of the definitions of *vyāpti* that were current in India; according to the *Nyāya-kośa* 13 correct and 21 incorrect ones had been given (**54.06**).

C. SOME BASIC CONCEPTS

We now confine ourselves to the enumeration of some basic concepts of the Navya-nyāya, and in dependence on Ingalls. We choose the following points:

The Navya-nyāya regularly operates with a twofold abstraction: first, from a concrete object, say a man, *devadatta*, devadatta-ness was abstracted; from this in turn a further abstraction was made, yielding what it is to be devadatta-ness, or devadatta-ness-ness. The same abstractions were regularly applied to relations. With the help of such concepts the Indian logicians were able to express very complicated matters in a purely intentional way, without any use of quantifiers.

The Navya-nyāya has a whole series of concepts corresponding to the western subject and predicate, or argument and functor. One such pair, which seems to be basic, is locus (*adhikaraṇa*) and superstratum (*ādheya*); but the superstratum can have a threefold relationship to the locus, being in it by inherence, contact or particular determination (**54.07**).

Another pair is that of the determinandum and the determinans (*viśeṣya* and *viśeṣaṇa*). The determinandum seems to be a concrete object, the determinans a property, whether a specific (*jāti*) or 'imposed' property (*upādhi*) – we may compare the Aristotelian concepts of species and accident (**11.09**f.), (**54.08**).

A third pair is that of the limitor and the limited (*avacchedaka* and *avacchinna*). Among various meanings, this is fundamental: if a concrete A is determined by a property B, then the abstract of B is limited by the abstract of A. E.g., take 'the mountain has fire'; then the mountain is determined both by mountainness and fieriness; it is then said that it is determined by fieriness limited by mountainness (**54.09**).

As to identity, the Navya logicians seem not to have had a technical term for our *numerical* identity in Aristotle's sense (**11.11**, cf. **44.26**). Instead, they always used specific identity (**11.11**) for

443

which they had at least three synonyms: (1) *A* has the same nature as *B* (*A B-svarūpa*); this was called 'essential identity' (*tat-svarūpatā*); (2) *A* has self-identity with *B* (*AB-tādātmya*); (3) *A* is precisely *B* (*A B eva*) (**54.10**).

In the matter of negation, Gaṅgeśa already has a whole series of concepts. Two classes of such concepts can be distinguished among the later logicians:

(1) mutual absence (*anyonyābhāva*), consisting in the denial of identity, e.g. 'fire is the locus of absence of water'; this negation was also expressed by 'is different from' (*bhinna*).

(2) Relative absence (*saṃsargābhāva*), denial of a relation other than identity, e.g. 'the lake has absence of fire' where contact is the relation denied. There are various sub-classes of relational absence, of which permanent absence (*atyantābhāva*) is the most important (**54.11**).

This line of thought is further complicated in that our logicians regularly speak of an opposite, (*abhāvīya-pratiyogi*) which they apparently conceive of as an object, and a concrete one, so that they are able to form an abstract from it, and limit this, and so on. If now the opposed-ness of absence is limited by a specific property, the resulting absence is called specific absence (*sāmānyābhāva*), but if by an individual property, an individual absence (viśeṣābhāva). The following gives an example of specific absence:

54.12 A lake is a locus of constant absence of fire, the opposedness to which is limited by fieriness and contact.

This means that the relation of contact does not exist between lakes and fieriness.

By speaking not of fire but of fieriness in such formulae, the Nāvya-Nyāya can express what western logic tries to express by a quantified formula, in our case, by saying : 'There is *no* fire in a lake'. The Nāvya-Nyāya logic is thoroughly intensional, in a way often sought after in the west, but never achieved.

In connection with different kinds of negation, there was a vast discussion about what corresponds to the western law of double negation (**20.04**; **43.22** [31]; cf. also **54.03**). A sample of this discussion follows.

D. THE LAW OF DOUBLE NEGATION

In the light of the fore-going, the next text, even if not thoroughly comprehensible, at least enables one to guess at its meaning. We read in Mathurānātha:

54.13 (The above objection should not be made,) for this reason: Absence of a constant absence is essentially identical with the counter-positive (of the constant absence). Therefore, difference from pot is essentially identical with an absence the counter-positiveness to which is limited by counter-absence of difference from pot. Therefore even pot-ness, although it is the limitor of counter-positiveness to difference from pot, in so far as it is essentially identical with constant absence of difference from pot, is still the counter-positive itself of difference from pot and subsists by inherence.

54.14 The following theory should not be held: Although in other cases absence of constant absence is essentially identical with the counter-positive (to the constant absence), still an absence limited by constant absence of difference from pot etc. is not essentially identical with difference from pot etc., but is only essentially identical with constant absence of pot-ness. . . .

The logician expresses his opinion about that as follows:

54.15 Such a theory cannot be upheld, for wherever one perceives a pot, there one does not perceive constant. absence of a pot, and there one may say there is absence of constant absence of a pot. Accordingly absence of constant absence of pot is essentially identical with pot.

The last sentence expressly formulates the law of double negation. Mathurānātha goes on:

54.16 In just the same way, wherever one perceives difference from pot, there one does not perceive constant absence of difference from pot, and there one may say there is absence of constant absence of difference from pot. Accordingly, an absence the counter-positiveness to which is limited by constant absence of difference from pot is simply different from pot.

That is to say, not from pot-ness. Here we even have something like a law of triple negation. But it should be noticed that not all these negations are of the same kind.

E. RELATION LOGIC, DEFINITION OF NUMBER

The foregoing gives only a sample of the range of problems considered by the Nāvya-Nyāya. They include also various questions about the logical sum and product, obscured in their syntax by the difficulty of being sure in Sanskrit whether expressions are to be taken as sentences or terms. We shall not explore them further. The logic of relations is also elaborated, or rather a doctrine about kinds of relation and relational abstracts. Of special interest is the relation called '*paryāpti*' (*paryāpti-sambandha*), about which Mathurānātha writes:

54.17 But still, if one admits the theory that two-ness is related by *paryāpti* to two and not to each, the definition will be so wide as to apply in false inference where the reason occurs by *paryāpti*, e.g., 'It is a pot because it is both a pot and a cloth'. Here the reason, pot-and-cloth-ness, does not occur in the locus of not-potness by *paryāpti*, which is the limiting relation of being-reason, for common sense tells us that just 'pot' (i.e. locus of potness) is not 'both pot and cloth', so locus of not-potness' is not 'both pot and cloth'.

The essential point here for us, is not the discussion about the rightness of the inference in question, but the description of *paryāpti*, which is a relation between the number 2 and a class with two elements, not between the latter and its individuals. This resembles Frege's definition of number.

SUMMARY

In spite of our insufficient knowledge of Indian logic, we can say in summary:

1. In India too a *formal logic* developed, and so far is known, without the influence of Greek logic. That it really was a formal logic is shown by the fact that the formulae constructed by the Indian thinkers concern the fundamental question of logic, the question of 'what follows from what' (**54.18**). These formulae, moreover, were thought of as universally valid.

2. But it is quite a *different variety of logic* to that we are accustomed to in the west. There are two great differences; Indian logic has *no variables*, and its tendency is *notably intensional*, whereas western logic is predominantly extensional.

3. This intensional tendency led to an extremely interesting range of problems, not yet wholly comprehensible to us, and to a logical analysis of quite a different kind to that developed in the west. This is most evident in the formulation of very complicated matters *without quantifiers*, also in the strange doctrine of *repeated abstraction*, and so on.

4. Indian logic seems to be almost entirely *lacking in propositional logic;* its logic of classes and predicates roughly corresponds to syllogistic, while remaining more rudimentary than the latter. On the other hand it has a very interesting and subtle doctrine of *formal implication*, a remarkably abstract and complex *theory of*

negation, and some theorems in the domain of *relational logic* such as did not develop in the west till Frege and Russell.

5. In the present state of research it is difficult to attempt comparison with the western varieties of logic. The general impression is that while important problems of formal logic were unknown to the Indians e.g. antinomies, truth-tables, yet in some matters they attained the heights of logical subtlety and abstract treatment, to such a degree that the west could learn a great deal from them, granted more thorough research and more adequate interpretation.

6. But the most interesting thing about this variety of logic is that in quite different circumstances and without being influenced by the west, it developed in many respects the *same problems* and reached the *same solutions*. Examples are the syllogism of the *Tarka-Saṃgraha* and Mathurānātha's definition of number.

Once more then, it can be said that we meet here an original and interesting variety of genuine formal logic.

REFERENCES

BIBLIOGRAPHY

INDICES

I. REFERENCES

All titles are so abbreviated that they can easily be found in the Bibliography, with the following exceptions:

'AM'	for 'Sextus Empiricus, Adversus Mathematicos'
'Analysis'	for 'G. Boole, The Mathematical Analysis of Logic'
'BL'	for 'S(h)c(h)erbatskoy, Buddhist Logic I'
'BS'	for 'G. Frege, Begriffsschrift'
'CP'	for 'C. S. Peirce, Collected Papers'
'Dial.'	for 'Petrus Abaelardus, Dialectica' ed. De Rijk
'DL'	for 'Diogenes Laertius, De clarorum philosophorum vitis'
'EIL'	for 'H. N. Randle, Indian logic in the early schools'
'GP'	for 'Leibniz, Die philosophischen Schriften. Ed. C. I. Gerhardt'
'HIL'	for 'S. C. Vidyābhūṣana, History of Indian Logic'
'LM'	for 'Paulus Venetus, Logica Magna'
'MG'	for 'Migne, Patrologiae cursus completus, Patres Ecclesiae Graecae'
'ML'	for 'Migne, Patrologiae cursus completus Patres Ecclesiae Latinae'
'MNN'	for 'D. H. H. Ingalls, Materials for the study of Navya-Nyāya Logic'
'NS (Jhā)'	for 'The Nyāya-Sūtras of Gautama, with Vātsyāyana's Bhāṣya and Uddyotakara's Vārtika. Trans. . . . by M. G. Jhā'
'NSV'	for 'The Nyāya-Sūtras of Gotama, Trans. S. C. Vidyābhusana' (Allahabad, 1913)
'PM'	for 'A. N. Whitehead and B. Russell, Principia Mathematica'
'PL'	for 'Albert of Saxony, Logica Albertucii Perutilis Logica'
'Prantl'	for 'C. Prantl, Geschichte der Logik im Abendlande'
'Pyrrh. Hyp.'	for 'Sextus Empiricus, Πυρρωνείων ὑποτυπώσεων libri 3'
'SL'	for 'William of Ockham, Summa Logicae'
'Sum'	for 'Petrus Hispanus, Summulae Logicales, ed. Bocheński'
'TS'	for 'Annambhaṭṭa, Le compendium des topiques (Tarka-Sam-graha). Texte, trad., comm. par A. Foucher'

Roman and Arabic figures following an abbreviated title, refer to the volume and page respectively. Exceptions, and the significance of further figures, will be evident if the work is consulted.

1.01 Introduction to Math. Logic note 252 .– **02** Prantl II note 235. – **03** Meta-logicon I, 5; cf. Prantl II note 234. – **04** Dialectica I, 165, 16 f. – **05** Dial. IV, 485, 37 ff.; 486, 8-19. – **06** Dial. III, 310, 13 ff. – **07** Dial. III, 287, 13 ff. – **08** Dial. II, 239, 8 and 13. – **09** Dial. III, 340, 21 f. – **10** Dial. III, 395, 6 ff. – **11** Dial. V, 544, 15 ff. – **12** Logica nostrorum petitioni sociorum (Geyer) 506, 26-28. – **13** Dial. I, 118, 4 ff. – **14** Dial. IV, 494, 1 ff. – **15** Dial. IV, 472, 34-36. – **16** Dial. IV, 481, 35 ff. – **17** ib. 482, 20 ff.

2.01 Schola in liberales artes, col. 1–30. – **02** Op. omnia I. – **03** ib. col. 130. – **04** A brief account (Works II), 693. – **05** Kritik d. r. V. (B), 7 f. – **06** Prantl. – **07** Prantl I 408. – **08** ib. 402. – **09** ib. 474 f. – **10** ib. 477. – **11** ib. 488. – **12** Prantl II 8. – **13** ib. – **14** Prantl III 2. – **15** ib. 89. – **16** ib. 107. – **17** ib. 108. – **18** Prantl IV 1 ff. – **19** ib. 2. – **20** System 16–94. – **21** A short history. – **22** Die Stoa. – **23** So Prantl, Janet-Séailles, Adamson, and also Pohlenz. – **24** Die arist. Theorie. – **25** Gredt, Elementa I 64 (n. 68). – **26** Scholz, Geschichte. – **27** Łukasiewicz, Zur Geschichte.

3.01 Cf. Bibliography 6.5.

5.01 Morris, Foundation; Morris, Signs. – **02** PM I 144 (*10.26). – **30** Cf. Menne, Logik und Existenz.

REFERENCES

6.01 DL VIII 57; AM VII 6. – **02** Met. M 4, 1078b 17–32, esp. 27–29.

7.01 Soph. El. 34, 183b17–23 and 34–36. – **02** Simplic., In Phys. 140, 29–33. – **03** ib. 141, 2–8. Cf. Diels, Vors. I 255f.; Zeller I/I 592f. – **04** Simplic., In Phys. 562, 4f. – **05** Theait. 171 A–B. – **06** Diels, Vors. II 279–283. – **07** Rose, 2nd ed., n. 50; 3rd. ed., n. 51 (Alex. Aph.). Also: Walzer, n. 2. – **08** Rose, ib. (Elias). Also: Walzer, ib. – **09** Rose, ib. (Anonym. Scholiast). Also: Walzer, ib. Cf. Rose ib. (Lactantius).

8.01 Tim. 47 B–C. – **02** Gorg. 507 A. – **03** Euthyphr. 12 A. – **04** Prot. 350 C–E. – **05** Soph. 218 D - 221 C. – **06** An. Pr. A 31, 46a31–b25.

9.01 Aristoteles, Werk und Geist. – **02** An. Pr. A 1, 24a1ff. – **03** Top. A 1, 100a25ff. – **04** An. Pr. A 1, 24a28ff. – **05** vid. Bibliography 2.73. – **06** Aristoteles, Grundlegung. – **07** Die Entwicklung. – **08** Pr. and Post. Analytics 6–23. – **09** Die arist. Theorie. – **10** Arist. Syllogistic; cf. Bocheński, Anc. Form. Log.

10.01 An. Post. A 22, 84a7f. – **02** ib. A 32, 88a18 and 30. – **03** An. Pr. B 16, 65a36f.; A 30, 46a9f.; B 23, 68b9ff.; Top. A 1, 100a22 and 29f.; cf. Bonitz, 183. – **04** Top. A 14, 105b20–34. – **05** ib. A 1, 100a18ff. and 25–b25. Cf. An. Pr. A 1, 24b18–22. – **06** An. Pr. A 4, 25b26–31. – **07** ib. A 1. 24a16f. and 24b16ff. (omission in b17f. with Ross.) – **08** An. Post. A 10, 76b24f. – **09** Herm. 2, 16a19f. – **10** ib. 3, 16b6ff. – **11** ib. 4, 16b26–29. – **12** ib. 5, 17a8f. – **13** ib. 2, 16a19f. and 27ff.; 4, 17a1f. – **14** ib. 5, 17a17ff. – **15** ib. 3, 16b19ff. – **16** ib. 2, 16a19ff. – **17** ib. 22ff.; 4, 16b32f. – **18** ib. 7, 17a38ff. – **19** ib. 2, 16a30ff. – **20** ib. 32f. – **21** ib. 3, 16b6ff. – **22** ib. 11ff. – **23** ib. 16ff. – **24–25** ib. 4, 16b26ff. – **26** ib. 6, 17a8f. – **27** ib. 5, 17a37f. – **28** ib. 1, 16a2f. – **29** Cat. 1, 1a1ff., but confirmed by several genuine passages (cf. Bonitz, 734B): e.g. Soph. El. 19, 177a9ff. – **30** Soph. El. 4. 165b30ff. – **31** Eth. Nic. A 6, 1096b25–29. – **32** Met. E, 1027b25ff. – **33** Herm. 1, 16a9–14. – **34** ib. 4, 17a2–7. – **35** ib. 9, 18a40–b3.

11.01 Top. A 2, 101a26–b3. – **02** ib. A 4, 101b13–16. – **03** ib. 38–36. – **04** ib. A 12, 105a10ff. – **05** ib. B 2, 109a34–38. – **06** ib. A 4, 101b17–23. – **07** ib. A 5, 101b37–102a2. – **08** ib. 102a18–22. – **09** ib. 31f. – **10** 102b4–8. – **11** ib. A 7, 103a7–14. – **12** Cat. 4, 1b25–2a4. The other enumerations of the categories are in: Phys. A 7, 190a31; Eth. Nic. A 4, 1096a23; An. Post. A 22, 83a21; Phys. E 1, 225b5; Met. Δ 7, 1017a25. Cf. Bocheński, Anc. Form. Log., Cat. 34, note 11 and Prantl I 207, note 356. – **13** Top. A 9, 103b20–37. – **14** Cat. 4, 1b25f.; cf. 5, 2a11ff. – **15** An. Pr. A 37, 49a6ff. – **16** Met. B 3, 998b22–27. – **17** An. Pr. B 16–21, 64b27–67b26. – **18** Soph. El. 1, 165a2–13. – **19** ib. 4, 165b23–27. – **20** ib. 30–34. – **21** ib. 166a6–14. – **22** ib. 23–31. – **23** ib. 33ff. – **24** ib. 166b21–27. – **25** ib. 166b32f. – **26** ib. 167a7ff. – **27** ib. 21–27. – **28** ib. 36–40. **29** ib. 167b1–30; cf. **16.15**.

12.01 Top. A 2, 109b18ff.; B 8, 113b15ff. – **02** Cat. 10, 11b17–23. – **03** Herm. 7, 17a37–b16. – **04** An. Pr. A 1, 24a16–20. – **05** ib. A 27, 43a25–43. Cf. Lukasiewicz, Arist. Syllogistic, 5ff. – **06** Sugihara, Particular and indefinite propositions. – **07** E.g. An. Pr. A 4, 26a29f.; A 7, 29a27ff. – **08** In An. Pr. 30, 29ff. – **09** An. Pr. B 15, 63b23–30; cf. B 8, 59b8–11. – **10** Herm. 7, 17b26f. – **11** ib. 38–18a6. – **12** Top. B 1, 109a3–6; Γ 6, 119a34ff. – **13** An. Pr. A 5, 27b21. – **14** Herm. 10, 20a19–22. – **15** ib. 13, 22a21–22b22. – **16** ib. 10, 20a23–26. – **17** An. Pr. A 46, 51b36–52a14. – **18** ib. B 22, 68a20. – **19** Met. Γ 3, 1005b19f. – **20** An. Pr. A 46, 51b36–40. – **21** Met. Γ 6, 1011b16. – **22** ib. 20f. – **23** Top. B 7, 113a25f. – **24** Herm. 7, 17b20–23. – **25** Met. Γ 3, 1005b23f. – **26** ib. 32ff. – **27** Aristotle on the law of contradiction. Cf. Lukasiewicz, O zasadzie; Salamucha, Pojęcie dedukcji. – **28** An. Post. A 11, 77a10–18. – **29** An. Pr. B 15, 63b41–64a4. – **30** Herm. 9, 18a28–31. – **31** Met. Γ 8, 1012b10–13. – **32** Herm. 9, 18a39–b1 and 19a39–b4.

13.01 An. Pr. A 4, 25b32–35. – **02** ib. 37ff. – **03** ib. 40–26a2. – **04** ib. 26a2–9; cf. Lukasiewicz, Arist. Syllogistic, 67ff. – **05** An. Pr. A 4, 26a17–25. – **06** ib.

25–29. – **07** ib. A 5, 26b34 ff. – **08** ib. 27a5–9. – **09** ib. 9–15. – **10** ib. 32–36. – **11** ib. 36–b1. – **12** ib. A 6, 28a10 ff. – **13** ib. 18–26. – **14** ib. 26–30. – **15** ib. 28b7–11. – **16** ib. 11–14. – **17** ib. 17–21. – **18** ib. 33 ff. – **19** ib. A 27, 43a25–43. – **20** ib. A 23, 41a13–18. – **21** ib. A 7, 29a19–26. – **22** ib. B 1, 53a3–14. – **23** ib. 15–30.

14.01 An. Pr. A 4 25b26–31. – **02** An. Post. A 2, 71b9–24. – **03** ib. A 7, 75a39–b2. – **04** ib. A 14, 79a17–32. – **05** ib. A 3, 72b18–73a4. – **06** An. Pr. A 7, 29b1–11. – **07** ib. 11–15. – **08** ib. A 4, 25b24 f.; A 5, 27a1 f.; A 6, 28a15 f. – **09** ib. A 1, 24b22–26. – **10–12** ib. A 2, 25a15–22. – **13** ib. 22–26. – **17** ib. A 25, 41b36–42a5. – **18** Arist. Syllogistic 34 f. – **19** An. Pr. B 9, 60a35–b2. – **21** ib. B 10, 61a5–15. – **22** ib. B 8–10. – **23** ib. A 1, 24b26–30. – **24** ib. A 41; 49b14–20. – **25** ib. A 24, 41b6 f. – **26** ib. A 25, 41b36 ff. – **27** ib. 42a32 f. – **28** ib. A 24, 41b26–31. – **29** ib. A 26 f., 43a16–24.

15.01 An. Pr. A 2, 25a1 f. – **02** ib. A 9, 30a39 f. – **03** ib. A 14, 33a26 f. – **04** ib. A 10, 30b37–40. Cf. ib. A 13, 32b8 ff.; Phys. B 9, 199b34 ff.; De som. et vig. 455b26; De part. an. A 1, 639b24 ff. and 642a9 ff. – **05** Herm. 9, 19a23 ff. – **06** An. Pr. A 15, 34b7–18. – **07** Herm. 9, 19a23 ff. – **08** An. Pr. A 13, 32a18 ff. – **09** Met. Θ 3, 1047a24 ff. – **10** Becker, Die arist. Theorie, 76 ff., 83 ff. – **11** An. Pr. A 3, 25a36–b18. – **12** An. Pr. A 13, 32b4–22. – **13** ib. 25–29. – **14** Herm. 13, 22a ff. – **15** An. Pr. A 16, 37a20–26. – **16** ib. A 13, 32a29–35. – **17** ib. A 3, 25a26–36. – **18** ib. 40–b2. – **19** ib. 25b16 f. – **20** ib. 17 f. – **21** ib. 25a40–b2. – **22** ib. A 9, 30a15–23. – **23** ib. A 14, 33a5–17. – **24** Cf. Becker, Die arist. Theorie, 50 ff. and Ross on An. Pr. A 15, 34a25 ff. – **25** An. Pr. A 15, 34a1–b27.

16.01 An. Pr. A 32, 47a22–35. – **02** ib. A 44, 50a16–28. – **03** ib. 29–38. – **04** ib. A 29, 45b15–20. – **05** ib. A 44, 50a39–b4. – **06** In An. Pr. 389,32–390,1. – **07** Top. B 8, 113b17 f. – **08** ib. Δ 4, 124b7 f. – **09** ib. B 8, 113b19 ff. – **10** ib. B 1, 109a3–6; cf. Γ 6, 119a34 ff. – **11** ib. B 8, 113b34 ff. – **12** ib. Γ 6, 119a39–b5. – **13** ib. H 1, 152a31–37. – **14** Soph. El. 24, 179a37 ff. – **15** ib. 5, 167b1 ff. – **16** An. Pr. B 4, 57b1 ff. – **17** Soph. El. 28, 181a28 ff. – **18** Top. B 6, 112a24–30. – **19** An. Pr. A 46, 52a39–b13. – **20** Top. B 8, 114a18 f. – **21** ib. Γ 6, 119b3 f. – **22** ib. B 10, 114b40–115a2. – **23** PM I 291 (on ʽ37.62). – **24** An. Pr. A 36, 48a40–b9. – **25** ib. 48b10–14. – **26** ib. 14–19. – **27** ib. 20–27. – **28** Top. B 10, 114b38–115a14. – **29** An. Pr. B 2, 53b12 f. – **30** ib. 23 f. – **31** ib. A 15, 34a5 ff. – **32** ib. B 2, 53b7–10. – **33** ib. B 4, 57a36 f.

17.01 Cf. Bocheński, La log. de Théophraste, 27 ff. – **02** ib. 128 ff. – **03** Ammonius, De int. comm., 65,31–66,9 (on 17a6). – **04** ib. 90, 18 f. (on 17a38). – **05** Brandis, Scholia, 145 A, 30–34 (on 24a15). – **06** Arist., org. graec., ed. Waitz, I 40 (on 17b16). – **07** Alex. Aph., In An. Pr. I, XII, 3–10. – **08** Alex. Aph., In An. Pr. 379, 9 ff. (on 49b30). – **09** ib. 31, 4–10 (on 25a4). – **10** ib. 69, 36 ff. – **11** ib. 109, 29–110,2 (on 29a19). – **12** ib. 41, 21 ff. (on 25b19). – **13** ib. 220, 9–16 (on 25b19). Cf. Brandis, Scholia, 150 A, 7 and Ammonius, In An. Pr. I (Schol.) 45, 42–46,1. – **14** Alex. Aph., In An. Pr. 158, 24 f. and 159, 8–13 (on 32a9). – **15** ib. 124, 8–13 (on 30a15). Cf. ib. 173,32–174,19 (on 33b25) and 119, 7 ff.; Philop., In An. Pr. 205, 13 and 123, 15 ff. and 129, 16 ff.; Ammonius, In An. Pr. I (Schol.) 38, 38 ff. and 40, 2 ff. and 40, 37 ff. – **16** Alex. Aph., In An. Pr. 132, 23–27. – **17** ib. 124, 21–25. – **18** Simplic., In de caelo 552,31–553,4. – **19** Galen, Inst., 8, 6 ff. and 32, 11 ff. – **20** Alex. Aph., In An. Pr. 389,32–390,3 (on 50a39). – **21** Philop., In An. Pr. 242, 18–21 (on 40b17). – **22** Alex. Aph., In An. Pr. 326, 20–327, 18; cf. Philop. In An. Pr. 302, 9–23.

18.01 DL II 106. – **02** ib. 108. – **03** ib. 109. – **04** ib. 111 f. – **05** ib. 113. – **06** ib. 114. – **07** DL VII 1. – **08** ib. 2. – **09** ib. 16. – **10** ib. 25. – **11** ib. 168. – **12** ib. 179. – **13** ib. 180.

19.01 DL VII 39. – **02** ib. 40. – **03** ib. 41 f. – **04** AM VIII 11. – **05** DL VII 63. – **06** AM VII 38. – **07** DL VII 43 f. – **08–09** ib. 57. – **10** ib. 58. – **11** Stoic Logic 16. – **12** DL VII 65 f. – **13** ib. 68. – **14** AM VIII 96 f. – **15** DL VII 71 ff. – **16** Diog.

REFERENCES

Laert., Leben und Meinungen, trans. O. Apelt. – **17** Seneca, Ad Luc. epist. 58, 12. – **18** ib. 15. – **19** Simplic., In Cat. 66,32–67,2. – **20** Vid. Trendelenburg, Gesch. d. Kategorienlehre, 221 ff. – **21** AM VIII 11. – **22** Cf. AM VII 243 f. – **23** Alex. Aph., In An. Pr. 183,42–184,6. – **24** Epict. Diss. II 19, 1. – **25** Comm. Peri Herm. (ed. Meiser) I 234,22–235,11.

20.01–**02** Apul., Peri Herm. 267 (Opera III 177, 26 f.). – **03** Galen, Inst. III 9,11–16 and IV 11, 5–14. – **04** DL VII 69 f. – **05** AM VIII 112. – **06** AM I (rec. Bekker) 309. – **07** AM VIII 113 f. – **08** ib. 115 ff. – **09** Pyrr. Hyp. B 111. – **10** DL VII 73. – **11** Hurst, Implication, 491; Zeller III/I 105, note 5. – **12** Cf. Mates, Stoic Logic, 48. – **13** Pyrr. Hyp. B 112. – **14** AM VIII 282. – **15** Aul. Gell., Noct. Att. XVI 8. – **16** Pyrr. Hyp. B 191. – **17** Galen, Inst. IV 9,17–10,2. – **18** ib. V 11,24–12,8. – **19** Aul. Gell., Noct. Att. XVI 8. – **20** Galen, Inst. XIV 34, 14–17. – **21** ib. III 9, 8 ff. – **22** Galen and the logic, 46 ff. – **23** Cf. v. d. Driessche, Le "De syllogismo".

21.01 Pyrr. Hyp. B 135 f. – **02** ib. B 137. – **03** Heintz, Studien, 62 f. and 195. Cf. Mates, Stoic Logic, 110, note 26, and Pyrr. Hyp. B 113. – **04** DL VII 76. – **05** Alex. Aph., In An. Pr. 262, 28–32. – **06** DL VII 77. Cf. Pyrr. Hyp. B 137 and 145; AM VIII 415. – **07** Pyrr. Hyp. B 138. – **08** Stoic Logic 111. – **09** Pyrr. Hyp. B 140. – **10** DL VII 78. – **11** Alex. Aph., In An. Pr. 373, 29–35. – **12** ib. 22, 17 ff.; cf. 345, 29 f. – **13** ib. 345, 27 ff. – **14** ib. 21,30–22, 1. – **15** ib. 20,10 ff. Cf. Apul., Peri Herm. 272 (Opera III 184, 26–30). – **16** Alex. Aph., In An. Pr. 18,15 ff.; cf. his In Top. 10,6 ff. On the difference between the two kinds mentioned in **21.15** and **21.16** cf. Prantl I 446, note 122; 447, note 125; 476, note 185. – **17** AM VIII 443. Cf. Pyrr. Hyp. B 186. – **18** Apul., Peri Herm. 272 (Opera III 184, 19–23). Cf. Alex. Aph., In Top. 8, 16–19. – **19** Alex. Aph., In An. Pr. 18, 4 ff. – **20** DL VII 79. – **21** AM VIII 223–228. – **22** ib. 227. – **23** Galen, Inst. VI 15, 8–16,7. Cicero, Top. 56. Mart. Capella, Opera IV, 420. Boethius, Comm. Peri Herm. (ed. Meiser) I 351. – **24** DL VII 77. – **25** AM VIII 306.

22.01 Mates, Stoic Logic, 63 f. – **02** DL VII 79. Cf. Pyrr. Hyp. B 156. – **03** ib. 156 f. – **04**–**05** ib. 157. – **06**–**07** ib. 158. – **08** ib. For **22.04**–**22.08** cf. also DL VII 80 f. Further texts are collected in Mates, Stoic Logic, 68. – **09** Cicero, Top., 57; Mart. Capella, Opera IV, 419 f. – **10** Cf. Mates, Stoic Logic, 78; note 77. – **11** Galen, De plac. (Opera, ed. Kühn, V, 1823) II/III, 224. – **12** Apul., Peri Herm. 277 f. (Opera III 191, 5–10). – **13** Alex. Aph., In An. Pr. 278, 11–14. – **14** ib. 274, 21–24. – **15** AM VIII 231. – **16** AM VIII 229–233. – **17** AM VIII 234 ff. – **18** Cicero, Top., 57. – **19** Pyrr. Hyp. A 69. – **20** Mates, Stoic Logic, 80, note 82. – **21** Origenes, Contra Celsum VII 15 (MG 11, 1441A–1444A). – **22** AM VIII 281. With another substitution: Pyrr. Hyp. B. 186.

23.01 Cf. Prantl I 50–58. – **02** Tit. 1, 12. – **03** Diels, Vors. I 32. – **04** Euthyd. 283 E–286 E. Cf. Rüstow, Lügner 30 ff. – **05** Soph. El. 25,180b2–7. – **06** DL V 49. – **07** Cf. the inventory in Rüstow, Lügner, 61–65, after DL VII 196 ff. – **08** Athenaeus Nauc., Deipnos. IX, 401 E. – **09** Lügner, 40 f. – **10** Cicero, Acad. Rel. cum Lucullo 95. – **11** Aul. Gell., Noct. Att. XVIII 2, 10. – **12** Cicero, Acad. Rel. cum Lucullo 96. – **13** Hieronymus, Opera I/I, Ep. Part. I, ep. LXIX (ad Oceanum 2) 681. – **14** Ps.-Acronius, Scholia II 1, 46. – **15** Anonymus (Sophonias), In Soph. El. 58, 31 f.; cf. 119, 25–120, 1. – **16** Augustinus, Contra Acad. III 13, 29. – **17** Alex. Aph. (Michael Eph.), In Soph. El. 171, 18 f. (on 180b2–16). – **18** Soph. El. 25, 180b2–7. – **19** Rüstow, Lügner, 50. – **20** Stoicorum Veterum Fragmenta II 298 a (106 f.). The text is adopted as edited by Rüstow, Lügner, 73,22–74,25.

24.01 Stakelum, Galen and the logic. – **02** Isagoge 1, 2 f. – **03** ib. 4, 21–27. – **04** ib. 15, 15 f. – **05** ib. 2, 15 f. – **06** ib. 3, 5–14. – **07** Alex. Aph., In An. Pr. 34, 17–20 (on 25a14). – **08** ib. 53,28–54,2 (on 25b37). – **09** De syll. hyp. I 837 D–838 A. – **10** ib. 835 A–C. – **11** Cf. v. d. Driessche, Le "De syllogismo", 298 and Bocheński, La log. de Théophraste, 87 ff. – **12** De syll. hyp. 846 A, 848 A, 852

REFERENCES

A, B, 854 C, D, 872 B, C, 873 A, B, 874 A. Cf. also v. d. Driessche, Le "De syllogismo'", 294–299. – 13 De syll. hyp. 875 A, B. – 14 Cf. v. d. Driessche, Le "De syllogismo", 294–299. – 15 De syll. hyp. 845 B. – 16 ib. 864 D. – 17 ib. 856 B. – 18 ib. 858 B. – 19 ib. 859 D. – 20 ib. 861 B. – 21 ib. 864 B. – 22 ib. 864 D. – 23 ib. 874 D. – 24 Le "De syllogismo", 296. – 25 De syll. hyp. 875 A. – 26 The full list in v. d. Driessche, Le "De syllogismo", 306 f. – 27 Apul., Peri Herm. 280 (Opera III 193, 16–20). – 28 Galen, Inst. XI 26, 5 ff. reading πρῶτον for τρίτον in 26, 6. – 29 Apul., Peri Herm. 269 (Opera III 180, 18). – 30 Published in: Kalbfleisch, Über Galens Einleitung, 707. – 31 Galen, Inst. XII 26, 13–17. – 32 Arist. Syllogistic, 38–42. – 33 Ammonius, In An. Pr. I, IX, 23–30. – 34 ib. IX, 41 – X, 11. There follow further examples and similar schemes. – 35 Philop., In An. Pr. 274. – 36 Galen, Inst. XVI 38, 12–20. – 37 ib. 39, 15 ff.

25.01 Zur Geschichte. – 02 Logika zdań; Die Aussagenlogik. – 03 SL I (ed. Boehner), XII. – 04 Cf. Sext. Emp., Opera ed. Mutschmann I, X. The translation is to be found in: Paris, Bibl. Nat., Cod. lat. 14700, fol. 83–132. – 05 Bibliogr. 3.53.

26.01 Sum 1.02–1.05. – 02 Sum 6.01. – 03 SL I 1, 11–19. – 04 In Met. Arist. 4, 4; 574. – 05 Sum. theol. I 28, 1, ad 2. – 06 De potentia 7, 9, c. – 07 SL I 12, 6–67. – 08 PL I 9, 4va. – 09 Shyreswood, Syncategoremata, 48. – 10 SL I 4, 3–22. – 11 PL IV 1, 24rb. – 12 Tract. cons., cap. 7. – 13 Medieval logic, 78–91.

27.01 Intr. 74,11–75,4. – 02 De potentia 9, 4, c. – 03 Sum. theol. I 39, 5, ad 5. – 04 SL I 63, 2 f. Cf. Moody, Truth, 21 ff. – 05 Intr. 75, 9–14. – 06 ib. 76, 11–24. – 07 In lib. Peri Herm. I, 5, 6. – 08 Sum. theol. III 16, 7, ad 4. – 09 SL I 64, 1 f. – 10 Comm. in text. Petri Hispani (on Sum 6.07). – 11 De supp. dial. 69 f. – 12 ib. 70. – 13 De puritate 21, 22–32 (219, 1–9). – 14 Sum 6.04. – 15 LM I 2, 16ra. – 16 Vid. reference for **27.10.** – 17 Sum 6.05. – 18 ib. 6.06. – 19 ib. 6.07. – 20 Sum. theol. III 16, 7, c. – 21 SL I 65, 6–14. – 22 E.g. PL II 1, 11ra. – 23 LM I 2, 18ra. – 24 SL I 65, 1 ff. – 25 Sum 6.08. – 26 ib. 6.09. – 27 ib. 6.10. – 28 ib. 6.11. – 29 ib. 9.1. – 30 Moody, Truth, 23.

28.01 Sum 9.2 and 9.3. – 02–12 PL II 10, 15ra–16rb. – 13 Sum 10.01–10.03. – 14 Shyreswood, Intr., 82, 6–17. – 15–17 Sophismata, cap. 4 (cf. p. 204, note). – 18 De veritate 2, 11, c. – 19 The most important are, in chronological order: Script. sup. Sent. I, prol. 1, 2, ad 2; ib. d. 19, 5, 2; ib. d. 35, 1, 4; De veritate 2, 11, ad 6; Sum. Contra Gent. I 34; De potentia 7, 7; In Met. Arist. 4, 1 and 5, 8; In X lib. Eth. Arist. I 7; Sum. theol. I, 13, 5. The best historical treatment of the question is in M. T. L. Penido, Le rôle, 12–53, which also contains a bibliography (pp. 12). This is supplemented by: Wyser, Thomas v. Aquin, 56 and Wyser, Der Thomismus, 79 f. – 20 De nominum analogia, lines 1469–1534. – 21 Sum. theol. I 3, proem.

29.01 PL III 1, 17ra. – 02 Sum. theol. I 13, 12, c. – 03 SL II 2, 25vb. – 04 SL II 3, 26rb. – 05 Lib. II Peri Herm. B II 1; 440 A, 2. – 06 Intr. 40, 10 ff. – 07 Sum 1.28. – 08 Summa totius logicae I 7, 11–13; 82 ff. – 09 De prop. mod. 5–16. – 10 Sum 7.26. – 11 Sum. Contra Gent. I 67. – 12 LM I 21, 76va. – 13 Sum 7.29. – 14 De puritate 92,29–93,10 (246, 32 ff.). – 15–18 LM II 11, 162ra–163rb. – 19 Cf. Elie, Le complexe.

30.01 Sum. theol. I/II 13, 2, ad 3. – 02 E.g. Herm. 14a30, 33, 35; 14b12, 15, 28; 15a6, 8; 22a14. The verb ἀκολουθέω is still more frequent: ib. 14a31; 15a27; 20a20; 21b35; 22a33; 22b3, 12, 15, 18, 22, 25 ff., 30; 23a20, 33. – 03 Abelard, Topica (Ouvrages, ed. Cousin) 529, 538, 541 and often. (Cf. Petrus Abaelardus, Dialectica, ed. L. M. De Rijk, index, p. 614.). – 04 In An. Pr., MS Merton College Oxford 289 and 280 (referred to as A and B respectively) A 65b, B 72a. References in parentheses are to Thomas, Maxims in Kilwardby. – 05 Sum 1.31, 3.33, 3.34, 7.58, 7.61. – 06 Sum 3.34. – 07 In An. Pr., A 81a, B 87b (137, 31). – 08 Zur Geschichte, esp. 121 ff. – 09 Salamucha, Logika zdań; Bocheński, De

REFERENCES

consequentiis; Boehner, Does Ockham know; Moody, Truth, 64–100. – **10** In An. Pr. I 10, 7; 104 Bf. – **11** De puritate 9, 16–29 (207, 31 ff.). – **12** In An. Pr. I 10, 8 ff.; 105 A–B. – **13** SL III 3, 1. Text according to Salamucha, Logika zdań, 215. – **14** PL IV 1, 24ra–b. – **15** De puritate 1, 17–30 (199, 20 ff.). – **16** Tract. cons, a, IIIv. – **17** LM II 9, 134va–135ra. A different enumeration in PL III 5, 19va. – **18** Sophismata, cap. 8, Sophisma 2. – **19** Sum 1.23. – **20** De puritate 91, 3–19 (245, 8 ff.).

31.01 LM II 6, 124va. – **02** In An. Pr., A 42c, B 48a. – **03** ib. A 42c, B 48b (142, 52). – **04** ib. A 43b, B 49a, (143, 55). – **05** ib. (142, 48). – **06** ib. A 43c, B 49b, (142, 49). – **07** ib. A 73d, B 80c, (145 end). – **08** ib. A 77b, B 83d–84a (144, 63). – **09** ib. A 80d, B 87b, (137, 27). – **10** ib. A 81a, B 87b, (137, 30). – **11** ib. A 37d, B 43b, (146 end). – **12** ib. A 45c, B 51c, (139, 40). – **13** PL IV 1, 24ra. – **14** PL IV 2, 24rb. – **15** PL IV 2, 24rb–va. – **16–18** PL IV 2, 24va. – **19** PL IV 2, 24va–b. – **20–21** PL IV 2, 24vb. – **22** PL IV 2, 24vb–25ra. – **23** In An. Pr. II, 3, 3; 184 A–B. – **24** SL II 32, 35ra. – **25–30** LM II 9, 129vb–130ra. – **31–32** LM II 9, 133vb. – **33** LM II 9, 133vb–134ra. – **34–36** LM II 9, 134ra. – **37** SL II 32,35ra–b and 33, 35rb. Critical text in: Salamucha, Logika zdań, 230 notes 44 and 47. – **38** De puritate 10,25–11, 2 (209, 4 ff.). – **39** LM II 9, 136vb. – **40** Tract. cons. I 8, 1 (after Moody, Truth, 98 f.). – **41** ib. (after Moody, Truth, 99).

32.01 Prantl I 658 and II 266. – **02** Hands. Forschungen und Funde. – **03** vid. Bibliogr. 3.91, all three items. – **04** Pseudo-Psellus und Petrus Hispanus. – **05** Die Summulae Logicales; Papst Johannes XXI. – **06** Cod. lat. Mon.4652,111r–112v. – **07** Sum 1.11. – **08** Sum 1.18 f. – **09** Sum 1.20 f. – **10** Sum 4.17. – **11** Sum 4.18. – **12** Sum 4.19 – **13** Sum 4.20. – **14** Sum 4.21. – **15** After Prantl II 282 f. (from Cod. graec. Mon. 548, which the author has seen). – **16** Summulae tot. log. (after Prantl IV 242, note 391). – **17** Logica magistri P. M., fol. 1 of tractatus syllogismorum, ra–vb. – **18** Lib. I Pr. An. II 2, 488 A and V 1, 609 A ff. – **19** Intr. 51, 22–26. – **20** SL II 1, 2; 36ra. – **21** In An. Pr. I 34; 168 Bff. – **22** PL IV 7, 29ra. – **23** LM II 13, 172ra. – **24** Exp. mag. P. T. sup. text. log. Arist. 55vb–56ra. – **25–32** Paris, Bibl. Nat., Cod. héb. 956, 109/110. – **33** Cf. Algazel, Logica et philosophia, cap. 4 (Prantl II 375, note 268) and Averroes, Priorum resolutionum (Prantl II 389, note 320) and **32.26** supra. – **34** Lib. I Pr. An. II 2, 488 A–B. – **35** Cf. Prantl II 393. – **36** Lib. I Pr. An. VI 3, 635 A–B. – **37** Thomas Bricot, Cursus optimarum quaestionum. Cf. Prantl IV 200, note 125. – **38** Thomas Bricot, Cursus optimarum quaestionum. 127vb. Text in Prantl IV 201, note 129. – **39** Mag. P. T. comm. in Isag. Porph. et lib. log. Arist., 59v. Text in Prantl IV 206, note 165. – **40** De supp. dial. 20. – **41** ib. 21 f. – **42** ib. 33. – **43** ib. 41 f. – **44** LM II 6, 113vb–114ra. – **45** Ars logica, quaest. disp. 7, 3; 195 A–B.

33.01 Bocheński, Z historii; cf. his Notes historiques. – **02** Lib. I Pr. An. I 1, 460 A. – **03** Lib.II Peri Herm. B II 1, 440 A. – **04** Lib. I Pr. An. IV 2, 540 B. Cf. Bocheński, Z historii, 62. – **05** Lib. I Pr. An. IV 2, 542 B. Cf. Bocheński, Z historii, 62. – **06** Lib. I Pr. An. IV 2, 540 Bff. – **07** Vid. Bocheński, Z historii, 67. – **08** In An. Pr. I 25, 5 ff.; 143 A–B. – **09** ib. 5; 143 A. – **10** ib. 6; 143 A. – **11.** ib. 30, 7; 159 A. – **12** ib. 27, 2; 148 B. – **13** ib. 25, 4; 142 B. – **14** ib. 26, 13; 146 B. – **15** ib. 15; 146 B. – **16** ib. 17; 147 A. – **17** ib. 18; 147 A. – **18** ib. 19; 147 B. – **19** ib. 20; 147 B. – **20** SL III 1, 20; 41rb. – **21** SL III 1, 23; 42ra. – **22** SL II 22, 32vb. – **23** SL III 1, 17; 40va–b.

34.01 SL III 1, 3; 36rb. – **02** SL III 1, 8; 38va. – **03** SL III 1, 20; 41rb. – **04** SL III 1, 13; 39vb. – **05** SL III 1, 16; 40rb–va. – **06** Ars insolubilis (not paged). – **07** PL III 2, 17vb. – **08** Comm. in text. Petri Hispani, de exponibilibus, 58va–b. – **09** ib. 68rb. – **10** SL III 1, 9; 38va–b and 12; 39va–b and 15; 40rb.

35.01 Pojawienie się. – **02** Soph. El. II 2, 3, 3; 694 B and 1, 3, 1; 559 A and 2, 3, 3; 696 A–697 A. – **03** Exp. sup. lib. El. Arist. Text in Salamucha, Pojawienie się, 37, note 64. – **04** Sum 7.46 ff. – **05** Soph. El. II 2, 3, 3; 696 B. – **06** In lib. El. LIII 2, 76 A–B. – **07** ib. LII ,73 A. – **08** ib. LII 4, 75 A. – **09** ib. LIII 3, 76 B. –

456

REFERENCES

10 SL III 3, 45; 71va–b. – **11** LM II 15, 196va. (All texts to **35.57** from LM II 15.) – **12** 196vb. – **13–14** 197rb. – **15** 197va. – **16** 197vb. – **17–19** 198rb. – **20** 198va. – **21** 198va–b. – **22–25** 198vb. – **26** 199ra. – **27** 192rb. – **28** 192rb–va. – **29–34** 192va. – **35–37** 192vb. – **38** 192vb–193ra. – **39–43** 194rb. – **44** 193rb–va. – **45** 193va. – **46** 194ra. – **47– 51** 194va. – **52–54** 194vb. – **55** 194vb–195ra. – **56** 195ra. – **57** 196vaff.

36.01 Dial. disp. (In: Opera) 693f. – **02** ib. 738f. – **03** Regulae (Oeuvres X) 405f. – **04** Dial. lib. duo, 215. – **05** ib. 216. – **06** ib. 217. – **07** Arnault and Nicole, La logique (Paris 1752), 241. – **08** Log. Hamb., 1. – **09** De form. log. 300. – **10** Arnault and Nicole, La logique (Paris 1752); 31. – **11** De arte comb. 52. – **12** De form. syll. 413f. – **13** Universalia Euclidea, 86ff. (Vid. Addit. to Bibliog.). – **14** Cf. Erdmann, Logik (1892), 247. – **15** Schröder, Vorlesungen I, 155; Vives, De censura veri, 607. – **16** Logik und Existenz, 46f. – **17** Bibl. Hannov. Phil. VII B IV 2r; cf. Couturat, Fragm. 295ff. – **18** On the diagrammatic, 7f. – **19** Two extensions (vid. Addit. to Bibliog.). – **20** Logic II, 97f. (Vid. Addit. to Bibliog.). – **21** Outline 130f. – **22** ib. 133f. – **23** Lectures II, 258f.

37.01 The development. – **02** A survey. – **03** A treatise. – **04** Math. Logik.

38.01 Ars magna et ultima, 218. – **02** ib. 219. – **03** ib. 220. – **04** El. philos. sect. I de corp. 1, 1, 2; (Opera I) 3. – **05** Brief an d. Herzog Johann Friedrich, 58 (cf. Couturat, La logique, 83, note 1) and Brief an Remond, 619f. cf. Couturat, La logique, 39, note 2). – **06** De arte comb. 64. – **07** Abhdlg. ohne Überschr., die characteristica universalis betr., 185. – **08** Brief an Galloys, 181 (cf. also GP VII, 22). – **09** From the Analysis linguarum (text after Couturat, La logique, 91, note 4). – **10** an C. Rödeken, 32. – **11** Abhdlg. ohne Überschr., Vorarb. z. allg. Charakteristik (I), 200. – **12** Abhdlg. ohne Überschr., Vorarb. z. allg. Charakteristik (II), 205. – **13** De ortu, progr. et nat. alg., 205. – **14** De univ. calc. 442f. – **15** Essai de dial. rat., 211, note. – **16** ib. 199. – **17** Analysis 3f. – **18** Analysis 13. – **19** The regener. logic (CP III) 268. – **20** ib. 269. – **21** ib. 271. – **22** Wissenschaftslehre II 198ff. – **23** Grundgesetze I 1. – **24** ib. I, p. vi. – **25** Über die Begr.-schr. d. Herrn Peano 362f. – **26** ib. 364f. – **27** Grundlagen d. M. 370ff. – **28** Log. Grundlagen 152f. – **29** Untersuchungen 30. – **30** Über einige fundamentale Begriffe 22f.

39.01 Über Log. u. Math. 5. – **02** Frege to Jourdain 1910; in: Jourdain, The development, 240. – **03** Grundgesetze I 4. – **04** Über formale Theorien 94f. – **05** ib. 95. – **06** ib. 96. – **07** Principles 5. – **08** ib. 8. – **09** Grundlagen d. M. 317f. – **10** Grundlagen d. A. 59. – **11** ib. 64. – **12** ib. 65. – **13** Vid. Becker, Grundlagen d. M. 322. – **14** Unbekannte Briefe Freges uber die Grundlagen 17. – **15** Grundlagen d. M. 351ff. – **16** Heyting, Die formalen Regeln d. int. Logik, 3f. – **17** Brouwer, Intuit. Betrachtungen, 48f.

40.01 Formal logic 60. – **02** On the symbols 86f. – **03** ib. 91. – **04** An investigation 27. – **05** Analysis 15ff. – **06** An investigation 49ff. – **07** Analysis 31f. – **08** Analysis 34. – **09** Pure logic 70. – **10** ib. 71. – **11** On an improvement (CP III) 3f. – **12** Essai de dial. rat. 194f. – **13** Descr. of a notation (CP III) 28. – **14** Vorlesungen I 127. – **15** ib. 129. – **16** ib. 132f.

41.01 Analysis 48f. – **02** Analysis 49f. – **03** Analysis 50. – **04** Analysis 51. – **05–08** The calculus (Vol IX) 9. – **09** ib. 10. – **10** ib. 177. – **11** BS 1f. – **12** BS 5ff. – **13** On the algebra of logic. A contribution (CP III) 218f. – **14** The regenerated logic (CP III) 280. – **15** BS 6. – **16** BS 7. – **17** BS 8. – **18** BS 10. – **19** BS 10f. – **20** Arithm. Princ. VIIf.

42.01 On the syll. no. III 178. – **02** The simp. math. (CP IV) 208f. – **03** Grundgesetze I 5f. – **04** Principles 39. – **05** PM I 38. – **06** PM I 39. – **07** The critic of arg. (CP III) 262. – **08** ib. 262f. – **09** Grundgesetze I 8. – **10** BS 1. – **11** Principles 89–94. – **12** PM I 4f. – **13** Grundgesetze I 6f. – **14** ib. 7f. – **15–16** On the algebra of logic. A contribution (CP III) 214. – **17–19** ib. 215. – **20** The simp. math. (CP IV) 212f. – **21** Tractatus 4.27. – **22** ib. 4.28. – **23** ib. 4.3. – **24** ib. 4.31. – **25** ib.

REFERENCES

4.41. – **26** ib. 4.411. – **27** ib. 4.42. – **28** ib. 4.442. – **29** ib. 4.46. – **30** ib. 4.461. – **31** ib. 4.4611. – **32** Vorlesungen I, § 9 and II, 1, § 32. – **33** Introduction 163–185. – **34** Cf. Hermes-Scholz, Math. Logik, p. 16, note 16 (Bibliogr. 1.22). – **35** Grundzüge. – **36** Elementy 192 ff.

43.01–**05** The calculus (Vol. IX) 10. – **06** ib. 177. – **07–09** ib. 178. – **10–13** ib. 180. – **14** ib. (Vol. X) 16. – **15** Vid. **38.24** supra, and BS 25 f. – **16** Grundgesetze I 26 B. – **17** ib. 27 B. – **18** ib. 29 B. – **19** ib. 30 B–31 A. – **20** ib. 30. B. – **21** Bedeutung d. log. Analyse 77. – **22** BS 26–51. – **23** PM I 93. – **24–25** ib. 94. – **26–29** ib. 96. – **30** ib. 97. – **31** ib. 100. – **32** ib. 104. – **33** ib. 99. – **34** ib. *3ʲ 109 ff. – **35** ib. 109. – **36** ib. 110 f. – **37** ib. 113. Cf. Leibniz, Ad specimen calculi, 223. – **38** PM I 111. – **39** ib. 115 ff. – **40** ib. 115. – **41** ib. 116. – **42** ib. 123. – **43** ib. xvi. Cf. Sheffer, A set of five, and the literature listed in PM I xlv f. – **44** The simp. math. (CP IV) 215 f. – **45** Bedeutung d. log. Analyse 80 f.

44.01 On a new algebra 74 f. – **02** On the algebra of logic. A contribution (CP III) 227. – **03** ib. 228. – **04** Vorlesungen I, § 15. – **05** Arithm. Princ. IX. – **06** BS 19–22. – **07** BS 22 f. – **08** Formulaire 2, 1; 23. – **09** PM I 15. – **10** PM I 16. – **11** The regener. logic (CP III) 281. – **12** Principles 11. – **13** ib. 38. – **14** PM I 138. – **15** ib. 139. – **16** ib. 144. – **17** ib. 145. – **18** ib. 146. – **19** ib. 148. – **20** ib. 140. – **21** ib. 149. – **22** ib. 153. – **23–24** ib. 154. – **25** BS 13 ff. – **26** On the algebra of logic. A contribution (CP III) 233 f.

45.01 Arithm. Princ. X. – **02** In: Jourdain, The development, 251. – **03** Principles 69. – **04** PM I 187. – **05** Grundgesetze I 14 f. – **06** Formulaire 2, 1; 30. – **07** PM I 190. – **08** PM I 193. – **09** Formulaire 2. 1; 31. – **10** ib. 32. – **11** ib. 28. – **12** ib. 29.

46.01 Analysis 21. – **02** Vorlesungen I 188. – **03** ib. 189. – **04** ib. 238. – **05** Logik und Existenz (Bibliogr. 1.23). – **06** Vorlesungen II, 1; 220. – **07–08** ib. 244. – **09** ib. 247. – **10** CS (n). – **11** Slupecki, Zhadań (Additions to Bibliogr.); cf. Lukasiewicz, Aristotle's Syllogistic and I. Thomas, A new decision procedure. – **12** Menne, Logik und Existenz, §§ 6 ff., and 125, 31.33. – **13** Grundgesetze I 18 ff. – **14** Existence and being (Principles)449. – **15** Über Annahmen 79. – **16** Über Gegenstandstheorie 7 ff. – **17** On denoting 482 f. – **18** ib. 479. – **19** ib. 480. – **20** ib. 481 f. – **21** ib. 491. – **22** Formulaire 2, 3; 7. – **23** ib. 20. – **24** ib. 22. – **25** ib. 23. – **26–27** PM I 216. – **28** ib. 173. – **29** ib. 174.

47.01 On the algebra of logic. A contribution (CP III) 237. – **02–05** On the syll. no. IV 341. – **06–07** ib. 342. – **08** ib. 342 f. – **09** ib. 346. – **10** A theory of prob. inf. (CP III) 195. – **11** ib. 195 f. – **12** ib. 196. – **13** ib. 196 f. – **14** ib. 197 f. – **15** Principles 24. – **16** PM I 200. – **17** ib. 201. – **18** ib. 213. – **19** ib. 228. – **20** ib. 232. – **21** ib. 238. – **22** ib. 242. – **23** ib. 247. – **24** ib. 256. – **25** ib. 265. – **26** ib. 277. – **27** ib. 279. – **28** ib. 418. – **29–30** ib. 419. – **31** BS 58. – **32** BS 59. – **33** BS 61 f. – **34** BS 64. – **35** BS 71. – **36** BS 77. – **37** BS 80. – **38** PM I 543. – **39** ib. 544. – **40** PM II 295.

48.01 Der Lügner. – **02** Grounds of validity (CP V) 210 ff. – **03** Una questione. – **04** Cf. Becker, Grundlagen d. M., 308 and Fraenkel & Bar-Hillel, Le problème, 225 f. – **05** Grundgesetze II 253. – **06** Cf. Sobociński, l'analyse (1949), 220–228. – **07** Beweis; Untersuchungen. – **08** Cf. Ajdukiewicz, Syntaktische Konnexität, – **09–12** PM I 60. – **13** ib. 61. – **14** Lettre 295 f. – **15** Schröder's anticipation. – **16** Vorlesungen I 245. – **17** ib. 246 f. – **18** ib. 247 f. – **19** Kritische Beleuchtung. – **20** ib. 439 f. – **21** Math. logic as based 236 f. – **22** PM I 37. – **23** PM I 41 f. – **24** PM I 55. – **25** PM I 53. – **26** PM I 56. – **27** PM I 59. – **28** Über die Antinomien 238 f. – **29–30** ib. 241. – **31** The foundations 20 f. – **32** ib. 76 f.

49.01 Symbolic logic. – **02** Interesting theorems. – **03** A survey 292. – **04** ib. 293. – **05** ib. 303. – **06** Vid. Sobociński, In memoriam Jan Lukasiewicz, 21 (Bibliogr. Additions); Lukasiewicz, 0 logice. – **07** Introduction. – **08** Elementy 116 ff. – **09** Aksjomatyzacja. – **10** In: Gonseth Entretiens 1941, 104 f. – **11** Phil.

REFERENCES

found. of quant. mech. – **12** Über formal unentscheidbare 173 ff. – **13** Schönflnkel, Über die Bausteine, 304 f. – **14** ib.

50.01 Regamey, Die Religionen, 211, note 190. – **02** BL 49; cf. EIL 18 ff. – **03** EIL 32 ff.; cf. BL 49. – **04** Hacker, Jayantabhaṭṭa. – **05** EIL 26 f. and BL 50. – **06** EIL 37 f. – **07** Regamey, Buddhist. Philos., 41 .(Here, and for other Buddhists, I follow Regamey). Cf. BL 32 and EIL 24. – **08** Regamey, Buddhist. Philos., 66; EIL 27; BL 31 f. – **09** Regamey, Buddhist. Philos., 67; EIL 34; BL 31 f. – **10** Regamey, Buddhist. Philos., 68. – **11** Cf. Bhattacaryya, Baṅgalir Sarasvat (I owe this text to Prof. D. Ingalls). – **12** MNN 6 ff. – **13** MNN 9 ff. – **14–15** MNN 20 ff. – **16** TS. – **17** Vid. Bibliogr. 6.2.

51.01 Die Fragen des Milindo 49. – **02–03** HIL 235 ff., cf. Points of controversy 8 ff. – **04** EIL 14. – **05** Studien II 90 ff. – **06** HIL 165. – **07** HIL 166 ff.

52.01 Die Lehrsprüche 310–320. – **02** ib. 334 ff. – **03** ib. 430 ff. – **04** NSV. – **05** NSV 1–4. – **06** NSV 8–13. – **07** Cf. EIL 174, note 3. – **08** NS (Jhā). – **09** NS (Jhā) I 320. – **10** ib. 343. – **11** ib. 354. – **12** ib. 385 f. – **13** ib. 396. – **14** TS 149.

53.01 Pre-Diṅnāga X, note 3. – **02** Nyāyabinduṭīkā 42. Cited in: BL 290; Keith, Indian logic, 106; EIL 160. – **03** BL 291. – **04** BL 244. – **05** NS (Jhā) I 497. – **06** BL 236. – **07** EIL 180–189. – **08** Nyāyamukha 50. – **09** ib. 44 f. – **10** Bhāṣya; EIL 181. – **11** Nyāyamukha 44. – **12** Fragments from Diṅnāga J 29 f. – **13** HIL 298. – **14** Fragments from Diṅnāga J 32. – **15** EIL 233 ff. – **16** BL 244 f. – **17** Kunst, Probleme 11. – **18–19** ib. 12. – **20** ib. 13. – **21** ib. 14. – **22** Śloka varttika, annumāna 5; EIL 231. – **23** TS (anumāna 1 f.) 120-126. Cf. Annambhaṭṭas Tarkasaṃgraha, trans. Hultzsch, 29–32. – **24** TS 126 f. – **25** TS 128. – **26** TS 129.

54.01 Pramāṇa-samuccaya V 11; BL 461. – **02** BL 463. – **03–04** BL 474. – **05** MNN 86. – **06** ib. 29. – **07** ib. 43. – **08** ib. 40. – **09** ib. 49. – **10** ib. 67 ff. – **11** ib. 54 ff. – **12** cf. MNN 56. – **13** MNN 102. – **14–16** ib. 103. – **17** MNN 122.

II. BIBLIOGRAPHY

CONTENTS

460

6. THE INDIAN VARIETY OF LOGIC

Introductory remarks

This is the first attempt at a comprehensive bibliography for the history of logic. We have concentrated on listing as completely as possible writings cited in the present work, the chief works of the most important logicians, and the more recent literature relevant to the history of formal logic. The bibliography also mentions, though not so completely, works of the following kinds: older general accounts of the history of formal logic, the more important older works on points of detail, those dealing with the literary history of logical works, and finally general bibliographical works and books of reference for the history of philosophy, mathematics etc. containing matter of importance for the history of logic.

Special thanks are due for their help in this matter to Professors O. Gigon (Berne), P. Wyser (Fribourg) and C. Regamey (Lausanne/Fribourg).

Within each sub-section the titles are listed alphabetically by authors; each author's works are given chronologically so far as possible, otherwise alphabetically by titles. Collected editions, often also principal works, appear in the first places.

No work is mentioned more than once, and then in the most general section to which it is relevant.

Long titles are not always given in full, and resulting abbreviations are *not* indicated. Sub-titles are nearly always omitted. 'Ebda.' after a title indicates that the work so labelled appeared in the same place as that immediately preceding, or in the immediately preceding work itself.

If a work appeared in a collection, the name under which the latter must be looked for is only given when different from that of the author of the work.

It has been decided on grounds of economy to reproduce the bibliography photographically from the German edition. For this edition some additions have been made at the end.

Abbreviations

'A.'	for	'Edition'.
'AHDLM'	for	'Archives d'histoire doctrinales et littéraires du moyen-age'
'BESP'	for	'Bibliographische Einführungen in das Studium der Philosophie' (cid. *1.111.*: Bocheński).
'Couturat, Log.'	for	'Couturat, La logique de Leibniz d'après des documents inédits'
'Cout.Op.'	for	'Opuscules et fragments inédits de Leibniz. Ed. L. Couturat'
'Franc. Stud.'	for	'Franciscan Studies'
'Franz. Stud.'	for	'Franziskanische Studien'
'𝔤'		indicates the edition used for the German edition of this book.
'GM'	for	'Leibniz, Mathematische Schriften. Hrsg. C. I. Gerhardt'
'JRAS(GB)'	for	'Journal of the Royal Asiatic Society of Great Britain and Ireland'
'JSL'	for	'The Journal of Symbolic Logic'
'RE'	for	'Paulys Realenzyklopädie' (vid. *2.12*. The Roman figure indicates the row, the first Arabic numeral the half-volume, the second the column.)
'S', 's', 'S.', 'S.a.', 's.', 's.a.'	for	'Vid.', 'Et vid.', 'vid.', 'et vid.'
'WZKM'	for	'Wiener Zeitschrift für die Kunde des Morgenlandes'

1. GENERAL

1.1. History of logic and mathematics
1.11. Bibliography
1.111. Philosophical bibliography

Bibliographie de la philosophie. Hrsg. Inst. Int. de Philosophie (früher: de collaboration philos.). Paris 1937 ff.

Bocheński, I. M. (Hrsg.): Bibliograph. Einführungen in das Studium der Philosophie. Bern 1948 ff. (= BESP).

de Brie, G. A.: Bibliographia Philosophica 1934—1945. I: Bibliographia Historiae Philosophiae. Bruxellis 1950. II: Bibliographia Philosophiae. Antverpiae 1954.

Répertoire bibliographique de la Rev. Philos. de Louvain (bis 1944: Revue Néoscolastique de Philos.). Louvain 1946 ff.

Ueberweg, F.: Grundriß der Geschichte der Philosophie. 5 Bde. Letzte A.: (mit Bibliogr. bis ca. 1926). Neudr. Basel 1951—1953.

1.112. Mathematical bibliography

Becker, O., und J. E. Hofmann: Geschichte der Mathematik. Bonn 1950.

1.12. General accounts, works of reference
1.121. For philosophy

Ueberweg (1.111.)

1.122. For mathematics

Becker, O.: Grundlagen der Mathematik. Freiburg i. Br. und München 1954. S. a. 1.112.

Bell, E. T.: The development of mathematics. New York, London 1940. 2., überarb. A. 1945.

Bense, M.: Konturen einer Geistesgeschichte der Mathematik. 2. A. Hamburg 1948.

Beth, E. W.: De wijsbegeerte der wiskunde van Parmenides tot Bolzano (Die Philosophie der Mathematik von Parmenides bis Bolzano). Antwerpen, Nijmegen 1944.

Boll, M.: Les étapes des mathématiques. Paris 1941. 5. A. 1948.

Cantor, M.: Vorlesungen über die Geschichte der Mathematik. 3. A. 4 Bde. Leipzig 1907 ff.

1.123. On philology

Steinthal, H.: Geschichte der Sprachwissenschaft. 2. A. Berlin 1890.

1.2. General history of logic
1.21. Bibliography

Beth, E. W.: Symbol. Logik und Grundlegung der exakten Wissenschaften. BESP 3. Bern 1948.

Church, A.: A Bibliography of symbolic logic, in: JSL 1, 1936, 121—218.

— Additions and corrections to a bibliography of symbolic logic. Ebda. 3, 1938, 178—212.

Weitere Ergänzungen und Korrekturen am Schluß der Buchbesprechungen in zahlreichen späteren Heften von JSL.

— Journal of Symbolic Logic, The. 1936 ff.

S. a. Rabus und Ziehen (1.24.).

BIBLIOGRAPHY

1.22. Recent works on all or several periods

Beth, E. W.: Summulae logicales. Groningen 1942.
— Verleden en toekomst der wetenschappelijke wijsbegeerte (Vergangenheit
   u. Zukunft d. wissenschaftl. Philos.), in: De gids 107, 1943, 1—13.
— Geschiedenis der logica (Geschichte der Logik). Den Haag 1944. 2. A. 1948.
— Les fondements logiques des mathématiques. Paris, Louvain 1950. 2. A. 1955.
Bocheński, I. M.: Notiones historiae logicae formalis, in: Angelicum 13, 1936, 109
   bis 123.
— L'état et les besoins de l'histoire de la logique formelle, in: Actes du Xe Con-
   grès Intern. de Philos., Amsterdam 1949, 1062—1064. Poln. in: Przegl.
   Filoz. 44, 1948, 389—394.
— Spitzfindigkeit, in: Festgabe an die Schweizer Katholiken. Freiburg (Schweiz)
   1954, 334—352.
Czeżowski, T.: Logika. Warszawa 1949.
De Cesare, E. A.: Evolución de la lógica, in: Rev. de cienc. econ. 1941, 1—8.
Enriques, F.: Évolution de la logique. Paris 1926.
Ferrater Mora, J.: Esquema para una historia de la lógica, in: Asomante (San
   Juan, Puerto Rico) 4, 1948, 5—16.
Feys, R.: De ontwikkeling van het logisch denken (Die Entwicklung des log.
   Denkens). Antwerpen, Nijmegen 1949.
Glanville, J. J.: The confrontation of logics, in: The New Scholasticism 28, 1954,
   187—198. (Besprechungen.)
Granell, M.: Lógica. Madrid 1949.
Greniewski, H.: Elementy logiki formalnej. Warszawa 1955.
Hermes, H., und H. Scholz: Mathematische Logik. In: Enzyklopädie der Ma-
   thematischen Wissenschaften, Bd. 1, 1. Teil, A. Leipzig 12. A. 1952.
Jørgensen, J.: A treatise of formal logic. 3 Bde. Copenhagen, London 1931.
— Indledning til logikken og metodelaeren (Einf. in die Logik und Methodolo-
   gie). Kopenhagen 1942.
Kaczorowski, S.: Logika tradycyjna (Die tradit. Logik). Lwów 1938.
Perez Ballestar, J.: Un curso de historia de la lógica, in: Teoría (Madrid) 2, 1954,
   171—176.
Reymond, A.: Les principes de la logique et la critique contemporaine. Paris
   1932.
Scholz, H.: Geschichte der Logik. Berlin 1931.
— Was ist Philosophie? Berlin 1940.

1.23. Recent works on special points

Beth, E. W.: Historical studies in traditional philos., in: Synthese 5, 1946/47,
   248—260.
— Les relations de la dialectique à la logique, in: Dialectica 2, 1948, 109—119.
Bocheński, I. M.: Z historii logiki zdań modalnych. Lwów 1938. Franz.:
— Notes historiques sur les propositions modales, in: Rev. des Sciences Philos.
   et Théol. 26, 1937, 673—692.
— De consequentiis scholasticorum earumque origine, in: Angelicum 15, 1938,
   92—109.
Clark, J. T.: Conventional logic and modern logic. Woodstock (Md.) 1952.
Costello, H. T.: Old problems with new faces in recent logic, in: Stud. in the
   hist. of ideas. New York 1918, 249—267.
Dürr, K.: Alte und neue Logik, in: Jb. der Schweiz. Philos. Ges. 2, 1942, 104—122.
— Die Entwicklung der Dialektik von Platon bis Hegel, in: Dialectica 1, 1947,
   45—62.
Enriques, F.: Per la storia della logica. Bologna 1922. Deutsch: Zur Geschichte
   der Logik. Üb. L. Bieberach. Leipzig, Berlin 1927. Engl.: The historic
   development of logic. Üb. J. Rosenthal. New York 1929.

BIBLIOGRAPHY

Heimsoeth, H.: Zur Geschichte der Kategorienlehre, in: Nicolai Hartmann, Der Denker und sein Werk. Hrsg. H. Heimsoeth und R. Heiss. Göttingen 1952.
Korcik, A.: Przyczynek do historii rachunku zdań. (A contribution to the history of propositional calculus.), in: Studia Logica (Warszawa) 1, 1953, 247—253.
Łukasiewicz, J. : Zur Geschichte der Aussagenlogik, in: Erkenntnis, 5, 1935/36, 111—131. Poln.: Z historii logiki zdań, in: Przegl. filoz. 37, 1934, 417—437.
Menne, A.: Logik und Existenz. Meisenheim (Glan) 1954.
Rüstow, A.: Der Lügner. Leipzig 1910.

1.24. Older general accounts

Adamson, R.: A short history of logic. London, Edinburgh 1911.
Bachmann, C. Fr.: System der Logik. Leipzig 1828 (569—644).
Blakey, R.: Historical sketch of logic. London, Edinburgh 1851.
— Essay on Logic. London 2. A. 1848. (Bibliogr. Anhang.)
Barthélemy-Saint-Hilaire, J.: De la logique d'Aristote. Paris 1838 (II, 93—355).
Calker, Fr.: Denklehre oder Logik und Dialektik nebst einem Abriß der Geschichte und Literatur derselben. Bonn 1822 (13—198).
Eberstein, W. L. G. v.: Versuch einer Geschichte der Logik und Metaphysik bey den Deutschen von Leibniz bis auf gegenwärtige Zeit. Halle 2. A. I 1794, II 1799.
Fabricius, J. A.: Specimen elencticum historiae logicae etc. Hamburg 1699. (Auch in: Opusc. hist.-crit.-liter. Sylloge. Hamburg 1738, 161—184.)
Franck, A.: Esquisse d'une histoire de la logique, précédée d'une analyse étendue de l'organum d'Aristote. Paris 1838.
Frobesius, J. N.: Bibliographia logica, in: Wolfii logica in compendium redacta. Helmstedt 1746.
Gassendi, P.: De logicae origine et varietate, in: Opera. Lugduni 1658, I, 35—66.
Harms, Fr.: Die Philosophie in ihrer Geschichte. II: Geschichte der Logik (Hrsg. Lasson). Berlin 1881.
Hoffmann, F.: Grundriß der reinen allgemeinen Logik. Würzburg 2. A. 1855.
— Grundzüge einer Geschichte des Begriffs der Logik in Deutschland von Kant bis Baader (Vorrede u. Einleitung zu Baaders Werken). Leipzig 1851.
Janet, P., und G. Séailles: Histoire de la Philosophie. Paris 10. A. 1918.
Keckermann, B.: Opera omnia I. Genevae 1614.
— Praecognitorum Logicorum Tractatus III. Hannover 1598, 2. A. 1604 (76—203).
Metz, A.: Institutiones logicae. Bamb. und Wirceburg 1796 (230—248).
Prantl. C.: Geschichte der Logik im Abendlande. 4 Bde. Leipzig 1855—1870. Manuldruck: Leipzig 1927 (g).
Ragnisco: Storia critica delle categorie. 2 Bde. Napoli 1870.
Rabus, L.: Logik und System der Wissenschaften. Erlangen, Leipzig 1895.
Ramus, P.: Schola in liberales artes, grammaticam, rhetoricam, dialecticam, physicam, metaphysicam. Basilea 1569.
Reiffenberg, de: Principes de logique, suivis de l'histoire et de la bibliographie de cette science. Bruxelles 1833 (289—408).
Reimann, J. Fr.: Critisierender Geschichts-Calender von der Logica. Frankfurt am Main 1699.
Rösser, C.: Institutiones logicae. Wirceburg 1775 (183 ff.).
Syrbius, J. J.: Institutiones philosophiae rationalis eclecticae. Jena 1717, 2. A. 1726 (Einleitung).
Trendelenburg, A.: Geschichte der Kategorienlehre. Berlin 1846.
— Logische Untersuchungen. Leipzig 1870.
Ueberweg, Fr.: System der Logik und Geschichte der logischen Lehren. Bonn. 1. A. 1857, 4. A. 1874 (15—66). 5. A. 1882 (15—94).
Venn, J.: Symbolic Logic. London 1881 (Einl. u. 405—444).
Walchius, J. G.: Historia logicae, in: Parerga academica. Lipsiae 1721 (453—848).
Ziehen, Th.: Lehrbuch der Logik auf positivistischer Grundlage mit Berücksichtigung der Geschichte der Logik. Bonn 1920.

2. THE GREEK VARIETY OF LOGIC

2.1. History of ancient philosophy
2.11. Bibliography

Année Philologique: Bibliographie critique et analytique de l'antiquité gréco-latine.Publiée parJules Marouzeau. (Bibliographie derJahre 1924ff.) Paris 1928 ff.
Gigon, O.: Antike Philosophie. BESP 5. Bern 1948.

2.12. General accounts, works of reference

Enriques, F., und G. de Santillana: Histoire de la pensée scientifique. Paris 1936—1937.
Gomperz, Th.: Die griechischen Denker. 3 Bde. Leipzig 1907.
Heath, T. L.: A history of Greek mathematics. 2 Bde. Oxford 1921.
— A manual of Greek mathematics. Oxford 1931.
Oxford Classical Dictionary, The. Ed. M. Cary u. a.. Oxford 1949.
Paulys Realenzyklopädie der klassischen Altertumswissenschaft. Neue Bearbeitung von G. Wissowa, W. Kroll, K. Mittelhaus, K. Ziegler. Stuttgart 1894 — 1938 (= RE).
Praechter, K.: Die Philosophie des Altertums. Basel 13. A. 1953 (unv. Nachdr. d. 12. A. 1926). (Bd. 1 v. Ueberweg: *1.111.*)
Reidemeister, K.: Das exakte Denken der Griechen. Hamburg 1949.
Zeller, E.: Die Philosophie der Griechen in ihrer geschichtlichen Entwicklung. Leipzig. I/I 1923 (7. A.); I/II 1920 (6. A.); II/I 1922 (5. A.); II/II 1922 (4. A.); III/I 1909 (4. A.); III/II 1923 (5. A.).

2.2. Editions of texts, translations

Alexander Aphrodisiensis: In Aristotelis Analyticorum Priorum Librum I Commentarium. Ed. M. Wallies. Berolini 1883.
— In Aristotelis Topicorum Libros octo commentaria. Ed. M. Wallies. Berolini 1891.
— In Aristotelis Metaphysica Commentaria. Ed. M. Hayduck. Berolini 1891.
— (Michael Ephesius): In Sophisticos Elenchos. Ed. M. Wallies. Berolini 1898.
Ammonius: In Aristotelis Analyticorum Priorum librum I commentarium. Ed. M. Wallies. Berolini 1899.
— In Aristotelis de Interpretatione commentarius. Ed. A. Busse. Berolini 1897.
Anonymus (Sophonias): In Sophisticos Elenchos paraphrasis. Ed. M. Hayduck. Berolini 1884.
Apuleius Madaurensis: Opera quae supersunt. III: De philosophia libri. Ed. P. Thomas. Lipsiae 1938.
Aristoteles graece. Rec. I. Bekker, in: Aristotelis opera, ed. Acad. reg. bor. I-II. Berolini 1831.
— Organum graece. Ed. Theodorus Waitz. 2 Bde. Lipsiae 1844—1846.
— Categoriae et Liber de Interpretatione. Rec. L. Minio-Paluello. Oxonii 1949.
— Prior and Posterior Analytics. A revised text with introduction and commentary by W. D. Ross. Oxford 1949.
— Topica cum libro de sophisticis elenchis. E schedis Ioannis Strache ed. M. Wallies. Lipsiae 1923.
— Physics. A revised text with introduction and commentary by W. D. Ross. Oxford 1936.
— De anima libri III. Ed. G. Biehe. 3. A. Lipsiae 1926, cur. O. Apelt.
— On the soul. Parva naturalia. On breath. Ed. W. S. Hett. London 1935.
— De somno et vigilia. Graece et latine ed. H. J. Drossaart Lalofs. Leiden 1943.
— Parts of animals, in: A. L. Peck, Movements of animals and progression of animals. Ed. E. S. Forster. London 1937.
— Traité sur les parties des animaux (Griech. und franz.). Ed. J. M. Le Blond. Paris 1945.

BIBLIOGRAPHY

— Metaphysics. A revised text with introduction and commentary by W. D. Ross. 2 Bde. Oxford 1924. Neudruck 1948.
— Ethica Nicomachea. Rec. Franciscus Susemihl. Lipsiae 1887.
— quae ferebantur librorum fragmenta, in: Aristotelis opera, ed. Acad. reg. bor. V (ed. V. Rose). Lipsiae 1886.
— Dialogorum Fragmenta. Ed. R. Walzer. Firenze 1934.
— Philosophische Werke. Üb. E. Rolfes. Organon. Leipzig 1918—1925. N. A. 1948.
— The Works of Aristotle. Transl. into English under the editorship of Sir W. D. Ross. 12 Bde. Oxford 1908—1952 (Einzelne Bände in Neuauflagen).
— Waitz, Th.: s. Organum graece.
S. a. *2.75.*: Trendelenburg, Elementa.
Arnim, I. ab: s. Stoicorum Vet. Fragm.
Athenaeus Naucratica: Dipnosophistarum Libri XV. Rec. G. Kaibel. 3 Bde. Lipsiae 1887—1890 (II: Libri VI—X).
Augustinus, S. Aurelius: Opera, Sect. I, Pars III: Contra Academicos libri tres. Rec. P. Knöll. Vindobonae, Lipsiae 1922.
Aulus Gellius: Noctium Atticorum libri XX. Ed. M. Hertz et C. Hosius. 2 Bde. Lipsiae 1903 (g).
— Les Nuits Attiques. Üb. M. Mignon. III: Livres XIV—XX (lat. und franz.). Paris 1934.
Bekker, I.: Anecdota Graeca. Ed. R. Schneider et G. Uhlig. Lipsiae 1878—1910.
Bocheński, I. M.: Elementa Logicae Graecae. Romae 1937.
Boethius, A. M. T. S.: Commentarii in librum Aristotelis περὶ ἑρμενείας. Ed. G. Meiser. Lipsiae. Pars Prior 1877. Pars Posterior 1880.
— In librum Aristotelis de Interpretatione Commentaria, in: Opera omnia. Acc. J.-P. Migne. ML 64. Petit-Montrouge, Paris 1860.
— De syllogismo categorico libri duo. Ebda.
— De syllogismo hypothetico libri duo. Ebda.
Brandis, C. A.: Scholia in Aristotelem, in: Aristotelis opera, ed. Acad. reg. bor. IV. Berolini 1836.
Capella: s. Martianus.
Cassiodorus: De artibus ac disciplinis liberalium litterarum, in: Magni Aurelii Cassiodori opera omnia. Tom. Post. ML 70. Parisiis 1847, Sp. 1149—1220.
Cicero, M. T.: Scripta quae manserunt omnia. Fasc. 42: Academicorum reliquiae cum Lucullo. Rec. O. Plasberg. Lipsiae 1922.
— Topica, in: Opera Rhetorica. Ed. G. Friedrich. Lipsiae 1893.
— Divisions de l'art oratoire. Topiques. Ed. H. Bornecque. Paris 1924.
— Scripta quae manserunt. Rec. C. F. W. Mueller. IV, I: Academica. De finibus bonorum et malorum. Tusculanes disputationes. Lipsiae 1889.
— Tusculanes I. Ed. G. Fohlen. Paris 1931.
— De natura Deorum. Academica. Ed. H. Rackham. London 1933.
— Traité du destin (De fato). Ed. A. Yon. Paris 1944.
David: In Porphyrii Isagogen commentarium. Ed. A. Busse. Berolini 1904.
Diels, H.: s. Die Fragmente der Vorsokratiker u. Doxographi Graeci.
Diogenes Laertius: De clarorum philosophorum vitis, dogmatibus et apophtegmatibus. Ed. C. G. Cobet. Parisiis 1888.
— Lifes of eminent philosophers, with an English translation by R. D. Hicks. 2 Bde. London, Cambridge (Mass.) 1950—1951.
— Leben und Meinungen berühmter Philosophen. Üb. u. erl. v. Otto Apelt. 2 Bde. Leipzig 1921.
Doxographi Graeci: Ed. H. Diels. Berolini 1929.
Epictetus: Dissertationes ab Ariano digestae. Rec. H. Schenkl. Lipsiae 1916.
Eustratius: In Analytica Posteriora Commentarium. Ed. M. Hayduck. Berolini 1907.
Festa, N.: I frammenti degli Stoici antichi. Bari 1935.
Fragmente der Vorsokratiker, Die. Griech. u. deutsch v. H. Diels. 6. A. hrsg. v. W. Kranz. 3 Bde. Berlin 1951—1952.

BIBLIOGRAPHY

Galenus: Institutio logica. Ed. C. Kalbfleisch. Lipsiae 1896.
— Opera omnia, in: Medicorum Graecorum opera. Ed. C. C. Kühn. Lipsiae
1821—1830.
Glossaria Latina. Ed. W. M. Lindsay e. a.. IV. London 1930.
Hieronymus, S. Eusebius: Opera, Sect. I, Pars I: Epistularum Pars I (Ep.
I—LXX). Rec. Isidorus Hilberg. Vindobonae, Lipsiae 1910.
Lucianus: ed. N. Nilen. I. Lipsiae 1906.
Martianus Capella: Opera. Ed. A. Dick. Leipzig 1925.
Mates, B.: Stoic logic. Berkeley (Diss.), Los Angeles 1953 (SS. 95—131:
Übers. stoischer Fragm.).
Origenes: Werke. Bd. 2: Buch V—VIII gegen Celsus. Hrsg. Dr. P. Koetschau.
Leipzig 1899.
— Opera omnia I. Acc. et rec. J.-P. Migne. MG 11. Petit-Montrouge, Paris 1857.
Paulus, Hl.: Πρὸς Τίτον, in: Novum Testamentum Graece et Latine. Ed. H. J.
Vogels. II. Düsseldorf 1922.
Philipson, Robert: Il frammento logico Fiorentino, in: Riv. di fllol. e di erud.
class. 7, 1929, 495—507.
Philodemus: On methods of inference. Ed. Ph. and E. A. De Lacy, Lancaster
(Pa.) 1941.
Philo Alexandrinus: Opera quae supersunt II. Rec. P. Wendland. Berolini 1897.
Philoponus, Ioannes: In Aristotelis Analytica Priora commentaria. Ed. M.
Wallies. Berolini 1905.
— In Aristotelis Analytica Posteriora Commentaria cum Anonymo in librum II.
Ed. M. Wallies. Berolini 1919.
Platon: Opera. Rec. I. Burnet. Oxonii 1899—1906.
— Œuvres complètes. (Mehrere Mitarbeiter.) 13 Bde. Paris 1920 ff.
— Sämtliche Werke (in deutscher Übersetzung). 3 Bde. I Berlin, II u. III
Heidelberg, o. J. (g. Unsere Platonzitate sind mit wenigen Änderungen
dieser Ausgabe entnommen.)
Plotin: Ennéades. Ed. E. Bréhier. Paris 1924—1938.
— Opera I. Ed. P. Henry und H.-P. Schwyzer. Paris, Bruxelles 1951.
Plutarch: Moralia. Ed. G. N. Bernadakis. Leipzig 1908.
Porphyrius: Isagoge et in Aristotelis Categorias Commentarium. Ed. A. Busse.
Berolini 1887.
Pseudoacronius: Scholia in Horatium Vetustiora. Rec. O. Keller. II: Scholia in
Sermones, Epistulas Artemque Poeticam. Lipsiae 1904.
Seneca, Lucius Annaeus: Ad Lucilium Epistularum Moralium quae supersunt.
Ed. Otto Hense. Lipsiae 1898.
Sextus Empiricus: ex rec. I. Bekkeri. Berlin 1842 (g f. 20.06).
— Opera. Rec. H. Mutschmann, I: Πυρρωνείον ὑποτυπώσεων libros 3 continens.
Lipsiae 1912. II: Adversus Dogmaticos libros quinque (Adversus Mathe-
maticos libros VII—XI) continens. Lipsiae 1914 (g).
Simplicius: In Aristotelis Categorias commentarium. Ed. C. Kalbfleisch. Berolini
1907.
— In Aristotelis De caelo commentaria. Ed. H. L. Heiberg. Berolini 1894.
— In Aristotelis Physicorum liber. Ed. H. Diels. Berolini, lib. I—IV 1892, lib.
V—VIII 1895.
Stephanus: In librum Aristotelis de interpretatione Commentarium. Ed. M.
Hayduck. Berolini 1885.
Stoicorum Veterum Fragmenta. Ed. I. ab Arnim. Lipsiae 1923.
Straton von Lampsakos. Ed. Fr. Wehrli. Basel 1950.
Themistius: Quae fertur in Analytica Priora paraphrasis. Ed. M. Wallies.
Berolini 1884.
— In Analyticorum Posteriorum paraphrasis. Ed. M. Wallies. Berolini 1900.
Theophrastus Eresius: Opera quae supersunt omnia. III: fragmenta continens.
Ed. Fr. Wimmer. Lipsiae 1872.
— (Logische Fragmente) in: Bocheński, La logique de Théophraste (*2.3.*).

469

BIBLIOGRAPHY

2.3. Recent works on formal logic

Becker, A.: Bestreitet Aristoteles die Gültigkeit des „Tertium non datur" für Zukunftsaussagen ?, in: Actes du Congr. Int. de Philos. Scient. VI. Paris 1936, 69—74.
— Die aristotelische Theorie der Möglichkeitsschlüsse. (Diss. Münster i. W.) Berlin 1933.
Beth, E. W.: Historical studies in traditional philosophy, in: Synthese 5, 1946/1947, 248—260.
— Deux études de philosophie grècque, in: Mélanges philos., Amsterdam 1948.
— The prehistory of research into foundations, in: British Journ. of Philos. of Science 3, 1952.
— Le paradoxe du „sorite" d'Eubulide de Mégare, in: La vie et la pensée, Paris 1954.
Bocheński, I. M.: La logique de Théophraste. Fribourg 1947.
— Non-analytical laws and rules in Aristotle, in: Methodos 3, 1951, 70—80. S. a. 1.23.
— Ancient Formal Logic. Amsterdam 1951.
Bornstein, B.: Jeszcze o początkach logiki matematycznej u Platona (Weiteres über Grundlagen der mathematischen Logik bei Platon), in: Przegl. klas. 5, 1939, 90—100.
— Początki logiki geometrycznej w filozofii Platona (Grundlagen der geometrischen Logik in der Philosophie Platons), in: Przegl. klas. 4, 1938, 529—545.
Chisholm, R. M.: Sextus Empiricus and modern empiricism, in: Philos. of science 8, 1941, 371—384.
Czeżowski, T.: Arystotelesa teorja zdań modalnych (Aristoteles' Theorie der modalen Aussagen), in: Przegl. filoz. 39, 1936, 232—241.
de Lacy, Ph.: Stoic categories as methodological principles, in: Trans. Amer. Philos. Ass. 76, 1945, 246—263.
Dopp, J.: Un exposé moderne de la syllogistique d'Aristote (Bespr. v.: Łukasiewicz, Aristotle's syllogistic), in: Rev. philos. de Louvain 50, 1952, 284—305.
Dürr, K.: Aussagenlogik im Mittelalter, in: Erkenntnis 7, 1938, 160—168.
— Moderne Darstellung der platonischen Logik, in: Mus. Helvet. 2, 1945, 166—194.
— Bemerkungen zur aristotelischen Theorie der modalen Formen, in: Archiv f. Philos. 1, 1947, 81—93.
— The propositional logic of Boethius. Amsterdam 1951. S. a. 1.23.: Die Entwicklung.
Ferrater Mora, J.: Dos obras maestras de historia de la logica, in: Notas y Est. de Filos. (S. Miguel de Tucuman) 4, 1953, 145—158.
Guggenheimer, H.: Über ein bemerkenswertes logisches System aus der Antike, in: Methodos 3, 1951, 150—164.
Heitzman, M. W.: The philosophical foundations of the Aristotelian logic and the origin of the syllogism, in: Proc. Amer. Cath. Philos. Ass., 1954, 131—142.
Henle, P.: A note on the validity of Aristotelian logic, in: Philos. of Science 2, 1935, 111—113.
— On the fourth figure of the syllogism, in: Philos. of Science 16, 1949, 94—104.
Hurst, M.: Implication in the 4th Century B. C., in: Mind, 44, 1935, 484—495.
Husic, I.: Aristotle on the law of contradiction and the basis of syllogism, in: Mind 15, 1906, 95—102 (Über An. Post. A 11, 77a10—22).
Jordan, Z.: Platon odkrywcą metody aksjomatycznej (Platon, der Entdecker der axiomatischen Methode), in: Przegl. filoz. 40, 1937, 57—67.
Kempski, J. v.: C. S. Peirce und die ἀπαγωγή des Aristoteles, in: Kontrolliertes Denken (Festschr. Britzelmayr), München 1951, 56—64.
Kłósak, K.: Teoria indeterminizmu ontologicznego a trójwartościowa logika zdań prof. Jana Łukasiewicza (Die Theorie des ontologischen Indeterminismus und die dreiwertige Aussagenlogik von Prof. Jan Lukasiewicz), in: Ateneum Kapł. (Włoclawek) 49, 1948, 209—230.

BIBLIOGRAPHY

Klósak, K.: Konieczność wyjścia poza logika dwuwartościową (Die Notwendig-keit des Hinausgehens über die zweiwertige Logik). Ebda. 50, 1949, 105—116.
Korcik, A.: Teorja konwersji zdań asertorycznych u Arystotelesa w świetle teorji dedukcji (Die Lehre von der Umkehrung der assertorischen Aussagen bei Aristoteles im Lichte der Deduktionslehre). Wilno 1937.
— Teoria sylogizmu zdań asertorycznych u Arystotelesa na tle logiki tradycyj-nej. (Die Lehre von den Syllogismen aus assertorischen Aussagen bei Aristo-teles auf dem Hintergrund der traditionellen Logik). Lublin 1948.
— Zdania egzystencjalne u Arystotelesa (Existenzaussagen bei Aristoteles), in: Polonia Sacra (Kraków) 6, 1954, 46—50.
Koyré, A.: Epiménide le menteur. Paris 1947.
Krokiewicz, A.: O logice stoików (Über die stoische Logik), in: Kwartalnik Filoz. 17, 1948, 173—197.
Larguier des Bancels, J.: La logique d'Aristote et le principe du tiers exclu, in: Rev. de théol. et de philos. 14, 1926, 120—124.
Leśniak, K.: Filodemosa traktat o indukcji (Der Traktat des Philodemos über die Induktion), in: Studia Logica (Warszawa) 2, 1955, 77—111 (Engl. Zu-sammenfassung 147—150).
Lukasiewicz, J.: O zasadzie sprzeczności Arystotelesa. Kraków 1910. Zusammen-fassung:
— Über den Satz des Widerspruchs bei Aristoteles, in: Bull. Int. de l'Acad. des Sciences de Cracovie, Cl. d'hist. et de philos., 1910. Krakau 1910.
— O logice stoików (Über die stoische Logik), in: Przegl. Filoz. 30, 1927, 278 f.
— O sylogistyce Arystotelesa (Über die aristotelische Syllogistik), in: Spra-wozd. Polskiej Akad. Umiej. 44, 6. Kraków 1939.
— Aristotle's syllogistic from the standpoint of modern formal logic. Oxford 1951.
— A system of modal logic, in: Journ. of Comp. Syst. (St. Paul, Minn.) 1, 1953, 111—149 (bes. 117—119).
— On a controversial problem of Aristotle's modal syllogistic, in: Dom. Stud. 7, 1954, 114—128.
S. a. 1.22.
Mates, B.: Diodorean implication, in: Philos. Rev. 1949, 234—242.
— Stoic logic and the text of Sextus Empiricus, in: Amer. Journ. of Philol. 70, 1949, 290—298.
— Stoic logic. Berkeley (Diss.), Los Angeles 1953.
Menne, A.: S. 1.23.
Northrop, F. S. C.: An internal inconsistency in Aristotelian logic, in: The Monist 38, 1928, 193—210.
— A reply, emphasizing the existential import of propositions. Ebda. 39, 1929, 157—159.
Platzeck, E. W.: La evolución de la lógica griega. Barcelona, Madrid 1954.
— Von der Analogie zum Syllogismus. Paderborn 1954.
Popkin, R. H.: An examination of two inconsistencies in Aristotelian logic, in: The philos. review 56, 1947, 670—681.
Prior, A. N.: Łukasiewicz's symbolic logic. (Besp. v. Lukasiewicz, Aristotle's syllogistic from the standpoint ...), in: The Australas. Journ. of Philos. 30, 1952, 33—46.
— The logic of negative terms in Boethius, in: Franc. Stud. 13, 1953, 1—6.
— Three-valued logic and future contingents, in: The Philos. Quart. (St. An-drews) 3, 1953, 317—326.
— Diodorean modalities. Ebda. 5, 1955, 205—213.
Reidemeister, K.: Mathematik und Logik bei Plato. Leipzig 1942.
Robinson, R.: Plato's consciousness of fallacy, in: Mind 51, 1942, 97—114.
— Plato's earlier dialectic. Ithaca (N. Y.) 1941.
Salamucha, J.: Pojęcie dedukcji u Arystotelesa i św. Tomasza z Akwinu (Der Be-griff der Deduktion bei Aristoteles und beim hl. Thomas von Aquin). Wars-zawa 1930.

471

BIBLIOGRAPHY

Sanchez-Mazas, M.: Las recientes investigaciones de historia de la lógica antigua: La escuela de Łukasiewicz, in: Seminario de Lógica Matemática, Inst. „Luis Vives", Madrid 1953/1954, 177—180.

Scholz, H.: Die Axiomatik der Alten, in: Blätter f. deutsche Philos. 4, 1930/1931, 259—278.

— Logik, Grammatik, Metaphysik, in: Arch. f. Rechts- u. Sozialphilos. 36, 1944, 393—433, und in: Arch. f. Philos. 1, 1947, 39—80.

S. a. *1.22.*: Geschichte, Was ist Philosophie?

Stakelum, J. W.: Galen and the logic of propositions. (Diss. Angelicum) Romae 1940.

— Why „Galenian Figure'"? in: The New Scholasticism 16, 1942, 289—296.

Sugihara, T.: The axiomatization of the Aristotelian modal logic, in: Memoirs of the Lib. Art College, Fukui University, 2, 1953, 53—60.

— Particular and indefinite propositions in Aristotelian logic. Ebda. 3, 1954, 77—86.

Thomas, I.: Boethius' locus a repugnantibus, in: Methodos 3, 1951.

Vailati, G.: La teoria Aristotelica della definizione, in: Riv. di filos. e scienze aff. (Padova) 5, 1903. Auch in: Scritti di G. Vailati (1863—1909), (Leipzig, Florenz) 1911, 487—499.

— A proposito d'un passo del Teeteto e di una dimostrazione di Euclide, in: Riv. di filos. e scienze aff. (Padova) 6, 1904. Auch in: Scritti, 516—527.

van den Driessche, R.: Le „De syllogismo hypothetico" de Boèce, in: Methodos 1, 1949, 293—307.

(Virieux)-Reymond, Ant.: Points de contact entre la logique stoïcienne et la logique russellienne, in: Actes du Congr. Int. de Philos. Scientif. VIII. Paris 1936, 20—23.

Virieux-Reymond, Ant.: Le „Sunemménon" stoïcien et la notion de la loi scientifique, in: Studia Philosophica (Basel) 9, 1949.

— La logique stoïcienne, in: Actes du Xième Congr. Int. de Philos. Amsterdam 1949, 718 f.

— La logique et l'épistémologie des stoïciens. Lausanne 1949.

Wedberg, A.: The Aristotelian theory of classes, in: Ajatus (Helsinki) 15, 1948/49, 299—314.

2.4. Works covering the whole period, or several thinkers and schools

S. Bocheński: Z historii, Notes (*1.23.*); Ancient Form. Logic (*2.3.*). Heitzman (*2.3.*); Łukasiewicz (*1.23.*); Platzeck (*2.3.*); Rüstow (*1.23.*); Vailati: A proposito (*2.3.*).

Altenburg, G. M.: Die Methode der Hypothesis bei Plato, Aristoteles und Proklus. Marburg 1905.

Cherniss, H.: Aristotle's criticism of Plato and the Academy I. Baltimore 1944.

Fritz, K. von: Philosophie und sprachlicher Ausdruck bei Demokrit, Plato und Aristoteles. New York 1938.

Hambruch, E.: Logische Regeln der platonischen Schule in der aristotelischen Topik. Berlin 1904.

Hoffmann, E.: Die Sprache und die archaische Logik. Tübingen 1925.

Kapp, E.: Greek foundations of traditional logic. New York 1942.

Lohmann, J.: Das Verhältnis des abendländischen Menschen zur Sprache, in: Lexis 3, 1952, 5—49.

— Vom ursprünglichen Sinn der aristotelischen Syllogistik (Der Wesenswandel der Wahrheit im griechischen Denken), in: Lexis 2, 1949, 205—236.

Stenzel, J.: Logik, in: RE I 25. Stuttgart 1926, 991—1011.

— Zahl und Gestalt bei Platon und Aristoteles. Leipzig 1924.

Vacca, G.: Sul concetto di probabilità presso i Greci, in: Giorn. dell'Ist. Ital. degli Attuari 7, 1936.

2.5. The beginnings

Ş. Krokiewicz (*2.3.*)

Beth, E. W.: Gorgias van Leontini als wijsgeer, in: Alg. Nederl. Tijdschr. v. Wijsbeg. en Psych. 35, 1941/1942.
Burnet, J.: Early greek philosophy. London 4. A. 1948.
Calogero, G.: I primordi della logica antica, in: Annali d. R. Scuola Norm. Sup. di Pisa (Lettere ... II, IV, II). Bologna 1935, 121—138.
— Studi sull' eleatismo. Roma 1932.
Deman, Th.: Le témoignage d'Aristote sur Socrate. Paris 1942.
Dupréel, E.: Les sophistes. Neuchâtel 1948.
Festugière, A. J.: Socrate. Paris 1934. Deutsch: Sokrates. Speyer 1950.
Fränkel, H.: Wege und Formen frühgriechischen Denkens. München 1955.
Gigon, O.: Der Ursprung der griechischen Philosophie. Basel 1945.
— Gorgias über das Nichtsein, in: Hermes 1936, 186 ff.
Hoffmann, E.: Die Sprache .... (*2.4.*).
Magalhaes-Vilhena, V. de: Le problème de Socrate. Paris 1952. (Mit großer Bibliogr.)
Nestle, W.: Vom Mythos zum Logos. Die Selbstentfaltung des griechischen Denkens von Homer bis auf die Sophistik und Sokrates. Stuttgart 1940.
— Die Schrift des Gorgias „Über die Natur oder über das Nichtseiende", in: Hermes 1922, 551 ff.
Ranulf, S.: Der eleatische Satz vom Widerspruch. Kopenhagen 1924.
Snell, B.: Die Ausdrücke für den Begriff des Wissens in der vorplatonischen Philosophie. Berlin 1924.
— Die Entdeckung des Geistes. Hamburg 1946.
Stenzel, J.: Sokrates, in: RE II 5. Stuttgart 1927, 811—890.
Wilson, J. Cook: On the possibility of a conception of the Enthymema earlier than that found in the Rhet. and the Pr. Anal., in: Trans. Oxford Philol. Soc. 1883/84, 5 f.
Untersteiner, M.: I sofisti (ohne Ort) 1949.

2.6. Plato
2.61. Bibliography

Gigon, O.: Platon. BESP 12. Bern 1950.

2.62. General accounts, works of reference

Astius, Fr.: Lexicon Platonicum. 2 Bde. Lipsiae 1835—1836.
Friedländer, P.: Platon. Bd. 1. 2., erw. und verb. A. Berlin 1954.
Hoffmann, E.: Platon. Zürich 1950.
Wilamowitz-Moellendorff, U. v.: Platon. 2 Bde. Berlin 3. A. 1929.

2.63. Plato's logic

S. Beth: Les relations (*1.23.*); Bornstein (*2.3.*); Jordan (*2.3.*); Dürr: Die Entwicklung (*1.23.*), Moderne Darstellung (*2.3.*); Reidemeister (*2.3.*); Robinson (*2.3.*); Vailati: A proposito (*2.3.*).

Goldschmidt, V.: Les dialogues de Platon. Structure et méthode dialectique. Paris 1947.
— Le paradigme dans la dialectique platonicienne. Paris 1947.
Grenet, P.: Les origines de l'analogie philosophique dans les dialogues de Platon. Paris 1948.
Schaerer, R.: La dialectique platonicienne dans ses rapports avec le syllogisme et la méthode cartésienne, in: Rev. de Théol. et de Philos. 1948, 24—50.

Stenzel, J.: Studien zur Entwicklung der platonischen Dialektik von Sokrates zu Aristoteles. Leipzig, Berlin 2. A. 1931.
Taliaferro, R. Catesby: Plato and liberal arts: a plea for mathematical logic, in: The New Scholasticism 11, 1937, 297—319.

2.7. Aristotle
2.71. Bibliography

Aristoteles, in: Gesamtkatalog der Preußischen Bibliotheken. Berlin 1934 (Sonderdruck).
Gohlke, P.: Überblick über die Literatur zu Aristoteles, in: Jahrb. f. d. Fortschr. d. klass. Altertumswiss. 54, 1928 (Bd. 216), 65—110; 55, 1929 (Bd. 220), 265—328.
Philippe, M.-D.: Aristoteles. BESP 8. Bern 1948.
Schwab, M.: Bibliographie d'Aristote. Paris 1896.
S. a. Heitzman (2.3.) u. Owens (2.72.).

2.72. General accounts, works of reference

Bonitz, H.: Index Aristotelicus (Aristotelis opera, ed. Ac. reg. bor. V.). Berolini 1870.
Boutroux, E.: Études d'histoire de la philosophie. Aristote. Paris 1897.
Gohlke, P.: Aristoteles und sein Werk. Paderborn 2. A. 1952.
Grote, G.: Aristotle. London 3. A. 1883.
Hamelin, O.: Le système d'Aristote. Paris 1920.
Kappes, M.: Aristoteles-Lexikon. Paderborn 1894.
Mansion, A.: Introduction à la Physique aristotélicienne. Louvain, Paris 2. A. 1945.
Mansion, S.: Le jugement d'existence chez Aristote. Paris 1946.
Owens, J.: The doctrine of being in the Aristotelian Metaphysics. Toronto 1951.
Robin, L.: Aristote. Paris 1944.
Ross, W. D.: Aristotle. London 2. A. 1930.
Wilamowitz-Moellendorff, U. v.: Aristoteles und Athen. 2 Bde. Berlin 1893.
Wilpert, P.: Die Lage der Aristoteles-Forschung, in: Ztschr. f. Philos. Forsch. 1, 1946, 247—260.
Wilson, J. C.: Aristotelian studies. London 1879.
Zürcher, J.: Aristoteles. Werk und Geist. Paderborn 1952. (Bespr.: Deutsche Lit.-Ztg. 76, 1955, 263—269.)

2.73. Works on authenticity and development

Bernays, J.: Die Dialoge des Aristoteles in ihrem Verhältnisse zu seinen übrigen Werken. Berlin 1863.
Bignone, E.: L'Aristotele perduto e la formazione di Epicuro. 2 Bde. Firenze 1936.
Bonitz, H.: Aristotelische Studien. 5 Bde. Wien 1862—1867.
— Über die Categorien Aristotelis, in: Sitz.-B. der Wiener Akad. 10, 1853, 591—645.
Brandis, Chr.: Über die Reihenfolge der Bücher des aristotelischen Organons, in: Abh. der Berl. Akad. 1833.
Case, Th.: On the development of Aristotle, in: Mind 34, 1925, 80—86.
de Rijk, L.-M.: The authenticity of Aristotle's Categories, in: Mnemosyne, Sect. IV, 4, 1951, 129—159.
Dupréel, E.: Aristote et le traité des catégories, in: Arch. f. Gesch. d. Philos. 22, 1909, 230 ff.
Düring, I.: Notes on the history of the transmission of Aristotle's writings, in: Göteborgs Högskolas Årsskrift, 56, 1950, 37—70, u. sep. Göteborg 1950.
Fritz, K. v.: Der Ursprung der aristotelischen Kategorienlehre, in: Arch. f. Gesch. d. Philos. 40, 1931, 449—496.

Gercke, A.: Ursprung der aristotelischen Kategorien, in: Arch. f. Gesch. d. Philos. 4, 1891, 421—441.
Gohlke, P.: Die Entstehung der aristotelischen Lehrschriften. Berlin 1933.
— Die Entstehung der aristotelischen Logik. Berlin 1936.
Husic, I.: The authenticity of Aristotle's Categories, in: Journ. of Philos. 36, 1939, 427—431.
Jäger, W.: Aristoteles. Grundlegung einer Geschichte seiner Entwicklung. Berlin 1923. — Engl., üb. v. R. Robinson, Oxford 1934. — Ital., üb. v. G. Calogero, Firenze 1935.
Louis, P.: Sur la chronologie des oeuvres d'Aristote, in: Bull. de l'Ass. G. Budé 5, 1948, 91—95.
Maier, H.: Die Echthheit der aristotelischen Hermeneutik, in: Arch. f. Gesch. d. Philos. 13, 1900, 23—72.
Mansion, A.: La génèse de l'œuvre d'Aristote d'après les travaux récents, in: Rev. Néosc. de Philos. 29, 1927, 307—341 u. 423—466.
Moraux, P.: Einige Bemerkungen über den Aufbau von Aristoteles' Schrift De caelo, in: Mus. Helv. 6, 1949, 157—165.
— Les listes anciennes des ouvrages d'Aristote. Louvain 1951.
Rose, V.: De Aristotelis librorum ordine et auctoritate commentatio. Berolini 1854.
Ross, W. D.: The discovery of the syllogism, in: Philos. Rev. 48, 1939, 251—272.
Shute, R.: On the history of the process by which the Aristotelian writings arrived at their present form. Oxford 1888.
Solmsen, F.: Die Entwicklung der aristotelischen Logik und Rhetorik. Berlin 1936.
— Boethius and the history of the Organon, in: Amer. Journ. of Philol. 31, 1944, 69—74.
Stocks, J. L.: The composition of Aristotle's logical works, in: Class. Quart. 1933, 115—124.
Textor, A.: De Hermeneiae Aristotelis capitibus I—XI. Berolini 1870.
Waitz, Th.: De Hermeneiae Aristotelis capitibus I—X. Magdeburgi 1844.
Wallies, M.: Zur Textgeschichte der Ersten Analytik, in: Rhein. Mus. f. Philol., N. F. 72, 1917/18, 626—632.

2.74. Commentaries on the logical works

S. Alexander Aph. (2.2.); Simplicius (2.2.); Averroes (3.2.); Thomas v. Aquin (3.2.); Ross, in: Aristoteles, Pr. and Post. Analytics (2.2.).

Pacius, J.: In Porphyrii Isagogen et Aristotelis Organon commentarius. 1605.
Zabarella, J.: In duos Aristotelis Libros Posteriores Analyticos Commentarii. Venetiis. Tertia ed. 1587.
— Opera logica. Venetiis 1578. Coloniae 1603 u. 1697.

2.75. Aristotle's logic

S. Becker; Bocheński: Non-analytical; Czeżowski; Husic; Kłosak; Korcik; Larguier de Bancels; Lukasiewicz: O zasadzie, Üb. den Satz, O sylogistyce, Ar. syllogistic, On a controv. probl.; Prior: Three-valued; Salamucha; Sugihara; Vailati: La teoria; Wedberg (alle: 2.3.).

Apostle, H. G.: Aristotle's philosophy of mathematics. Chicago 1952.
Apelt, O.: Die Kategorienlehre des Aristoteles, in: Beitr. z. Gesch. d. griech. Philos. Leipzig 1891, 101—216.
Arpe, C.: Das τί ἦν εἶναι bei Aristoteles. Berlin 1938.
Barth, T.: Das Problem der Vieldeutigkeit bei Aristoteles, in: Sophia 10, 1942, 11—30.
Barthélemy Saint-Hilaire, J.: De la logique d'Aristote. Paris 1838.
Calogero, G.: I fondamenti della logica Aristotelica. Firenze 1927.

Consbruck, M.: Ἐπαγωγή und Theorie der Induktion bei Aristoteles, in: Arch. f. Gesch. d. Philos. 5, 1892, 301—321.
de Rijk, L. M.: The place of the categories of being in Aristotle's philosophy. Utrecht 1952. (Auch üb. d. Wahrheitsbegriff.)
della Seta, U.: La dottrina del sillogismo in Aristotele. Roma 1911.
Dominczak, S.: Les jugements modaux chez Aristote et les scolastiques. Louvain 1923.
Dulac, H.: The Peri Hermeneias: its place in logic and its order, in: Laval Théol. et Philos. 5, 1949, 161—169.
Einarson, B.: On certain mathematical terms in Aristotle's logic, in: Amer. Journ. of Philol. 1936, 35—54 u. 151—172.
Gohlke, P.: Die Entstehung der aristotelischen Prinzipienlehre. Tübingen 1954.
Heath, T.: Mathematics in Aristotle. Oxford 1949.
Heiberg, J. L.: Mathematisches zu Aristoteles, in: Abh. z. Gesch. d. math. Wiss. 1904, 1—49.
Heidel, W. A.: The necessary and the contingent in the Aristotelian system. Chicago 1896.
Husic, I.: On the Categories of Aristotle, in: Philos. Rev. 13, 1904, 514—528.
Le Blond, J.-M.: Eylogos et l'argument de convenance chez Aristote. Paris 1938.
— Logique et méthode chez Aristote. Paris 1939.
— La définition chez Aristote, in: Gregorianum 20, 1939, 351—380.
Lee, H. D. P.: Geometrical method and Aristotle's account of the first principles, in: Class. Quart. 29, 1935, 113—129.
Maier, H.: Die Syllogistik des Aristoteles. 3 Bde. Tübingen 1896—1900. Neudr.: Leipzig 1936.
Miller, J.-W.: The structure of Aristotle's logic. London 1938.
Moser, S.: Zur Lehre der Definition bei Aristoteles I. Innsbruck 1935.
Muskens, G. L.: De vocis ΑΝΑΛΟΓΙΑΣ significatione ac usu apud Aristotelem. Groningen 1943.
Pastore, A.: Sul compito della filosofia secondo la logica del pontenziamento con vestigi d'intuizione logica in Aristotele, in: Arch. di filos. 10, 1940, 463 bis 480.
Picard, J.: Syllogismes catégoriques et hypothétiques, in: Rev. de métaph. et de mor. 1936, 231—267 u. 403—430.
Prantl, C.: Über die Entwicklung der aristotelischen Logik aus der platonischen Philosophie, in: Abh. Bayer. Akad. 7, 1, 1853, 129—211.
Pró, D. F.: La concepción de la lógica en Aristóteles, Santo Tomás y Hegel, in: Philosophia (Mendoza) 2, 1945, 229—263; 3, 1946, 71—78 u. 275—290.
Rassow, H.: Aristotelis de notionis definitione doctrina. Berolini 1843.
Ross, W. D.: Some thoughts on Aristotle's logic, in: Proc. of the Arist. Soc. 40, 1939/40, I—XVIII.
Scheu, M.: The categories of being in Aristotle and St. Thomas. Washington 1944.
Shorey, N.: Συλλογισμοὶ ἐξ ὑποθέσεως in Aristotle, in: Amer. Journ. of Philol. 10, 1889, 430—462.
Simon, Y. R.: Aristotelian demonstration, in: The modern Schoolman 25, 1948, 183—190.
Solmsen, Fr.: The discovery of the syllogism, in: Philos. Rev. 50, 1941.
Thiel, N. M.: Die Bedeutung des Wortes HYPOTHESIS bei Aristoteles. Fulda 1919.
Trendelenburg, F. A.: Das τὸ ἐνὶ εἶναι, τὸ ἀγαθῷ εἶναι, etc. und das τὸ τί ἦν εἶναι bei Aristoteles, in: Rhein. Mus. 2, 1828, 457—483.
— De Aristotelis categoriis prolusio academica. Berolini 1833.
— Elementa logices Aristoteleae. Berolini 1845. N. A. 1852.
Usowicz, A. C. M.: De Aristotelis circa definitionem doctrina commentatorum sententiis illustrata, in: Collectanea Theologica (Leopoli) 19, 1938, 273—317.
Zahlfleisch, I.: Über die Aristotelischen Begriffe ὑπάρχειν, ἐνδέχεσθαι, ἐξ ἀνάγκης ὑπάρχειν, in: Progr. d. Gymn. Ried, 1878.

2.76. Theophrastus

S. Becker (*2.3.*); Bocheński: La logique (*2.3.*), Z historii, Notes (*1.23.*); Lukasiewicz: On a controv. probl. (*2.3.*).

Barbotin, E.: La théorie aristotélicienne de l'intellect d'après Théophraste. Louvain, Paris 1954.

Usener, H.: Analecta Theophrastea, in: Kleine Schriften. Leipzig, Berlin 1912.

2.8. The Megarian Stoic school. Period of the commentators
2.81. Bibliography

S. Mates, Stoic logic (*2.3.*).

Perler, O.: Patristische Philosophie. BESP 18. Bern 1950.

2.82. General accounts of Stoic philosophy

Barth, P.: Die Stoa. Stuttgart 6. A. 1946.
Bevan, E.: Stoics and Sceptics. Oxford 1913.
Bréhier, E.: Chrysippe. Paris 1910.
Goldschmidt, V.: Le système stoicien et l'idée de temps. Paris 1953.
Pohlenz, M.: Die Stoa. 2 Bde. Göttingen 1948.
Rieth, O.: Grundbegriffe der stoischen Ethik. Berlin 1934.
Stock, St. G.: Stoicism. London 1908.
S. a. Zeller III (*2.12.*).

2.83. Stoic logic

S. Bocheński: De consequentiis; Lukasiewicz: Zur Geschichte; Rüstow (alle *1.23.*). — Beth: Le paradoxe; Chisholm; de Lacy; Dürr: Aussagenlogik, The propositional; Hurst; Koyré; Leśniak; Lukasiewicz: O logice; Mates; Prior: The logic; van den Driessche; Virieux-Reymond (alle *2.3.*).

Bréhier, E.: La théorie des incorporels dans l'ancien stoïcisme. Paris 1928.
Brochard, V.: Sur la logique des Stoïciens, in: Arch. f. Gesch. d. Philos. 5, 1892, 449—468.
Heintz, W.: Studien zu Sextus Empiricus, ed. R. Harder. Halle 1932.
Kalbfleisch, K.: Über Galens Einleitung in die Logik, in: Jahrb. f. class. Philol. 23, Suppl.-Bd., Leipzig 1897.
Kochalsky, A.: De Sexti Empirici adversus logicos libris quaestiones criticae. (Diss.) Marburg 1911.
Minio-Paluello, L.: Gli Elenchi Sofistici: redazioni contaminate . . ., frammenti dell'ignoto commento d'Alessandro d'Afrodisia tradotti in Iatino, in: Riv. di fílos. neosc. 46, 1954, 223—231.
— The genuine text of Boethius' translation of Aristotle's Categories, in: Med. and Renaiss. Stud. 1, 1943, 151—177.
Moraux, P.: Alexandre d'Aphrodise, exégète de la noétique d'Aristote. Liège, Paris 1942.
Schmekel, A.: Die positive Philosophie in ihrer geschichtlichen Entwicklung. Berlin 1938.
Théry, G.: Alexandre d'Aphrodise. Kain 1926.
Volait, G.: Die Stellung des Alexander von Aphrodisias zur aristotelischen Schlußlehre. Halle 1907.
Zeller, E.: Über den κυριεύων des Megarikers Diodorus, in: Sitz.-B. der Preuß. Akad. 1882, 151—159.

2.9. Other ancient systems

S. Guggenheimer u. Leśniak (*2.3.*).

3. THE SCHOLASTIC VARIETY OF LOGIC

3.1. Scholastic philosophy
3.11. Bibliography

Bourke, V. J.: Thomistic bibliography. St. Louis 1945.
Bulletin Thomiste. Hrsg. Société thomiste. Le Saulchoir, Étiolles-Paris 1924 ff.
Gesamtkatalog der Wiegendrucke. Hrsg. v. d. Komm. f. d. Gesamtkat. d. Wiegendrucke. Leipzig 1925 ff.
Giacon, C.: Il pensiero cristiano con particolaro riguardo alla scolastica. Milano 1943.
Hurter, H.: Nomenclator literarius theologiae catholicae. 3. A. 5 Bde. (Bd. V in 2 T.). Innsbruck 1903—1913.
Kristeller, P. O.: Latin manuscript books before 1600. New York 1948. Auch in: Traditio 6, 1948, 227—317.
Lang, A., u. a. (Hrsg.): Aus der Geisteswelt des Mittelalters. Münster 1935. (Bibliogr. der Werke von M. Grabmann bis 1934.)
Mandonnet, P., und J. Destrez: Bibliographie thomiste. Le Saulchoir, Kain 1921.
Michelitsch, A.: Kommentatoren zur Summa Theologiae des hl. Thomas von Aquin. Graz, Wien 1924.
Quétif, J., und J. Echard: Scriptores Ordinis Praedicatorum. Paris, I u. II 1719—1721, III (ed. Coulon und Papillon) 1910—1934.
Russell, J. C.: Dictionary of writers of thirteenth century in England. London 1936.
Schäfer, O.: Johannes Duns Scotus. BESP 22. Bern 1953.
— Bibliographia de vita et operibus Johannis Duns Scoti (19. u. 20. Jahrh.). Romae 1955.
Stroick, C.: Les derniers ouvrages de Mgr. Grabmann, in: Rev. de l'Univ. d'Ottawa, Sect. spéc. 22, 1952, 36*—66*.
van Steenberghen, F.: Philosophie des Mittelalters. BESP 17. Bern 1950.
Thomistische Literaturschau, in: Divus Thomas (Freiburg, Schweiz) 4 ff., 1926 bis 1953, u. in: Freiburger Zeitschrift für Philos. u. Theologie, 1 ff., 1954 ff.
Wyser, P.: Thomas von Aquin. BESP 13/14. Bern 1950.
— Der Thomismus. BESP 15/16. Bern 1951.
S. a. Geyer, Grabmann u. de Wulf (*3.12.*).

3.12. General accounts, works of reference

Axters, S.: Scholastiek Lexikon. Latijn-Nederlandsch. Antwerpen 1937.
Chartularium Universitatis Parisiensis . . ., cont. H. Denifle aux. A. Chatelain. 4 Bde. Parisiis 1889—1897.
du Cange, C. D.: Glossarium mediae et infimae latinitatis. Frankfurt 1681. Basel 1762. Neudr. in 10 Bden. Paris 1937—1938.
Geyer, B.: Die patristische und scholastische Philosophie. Basel 12. A. 1951 (Unv. Nachdr. d. 11. A. v. 1927). (Bd. II v. Ueberweg: *1.111.*)
Gilson, E.: La Philosophie au Moyen Age. Paris 2. verm. A. 1947.
Glorieux, P.: Répertoire des maîtres en théologie de Paris au XIIIe siècle. 2 Bde. Paris 1933.
Grabmann, M.: Storia della teologia cattolica della fine dell'epoca patristica ai tempi nostri. Übers v. G. di Fabio. Milano 2. verb. A. 1939.
Klibanski, R.: The continuity of the platonic tradition. London 1939.
Krumbacher, K.: Geschichte der byzantinischen Literatur. München 1891.
Landgraf, A. M.: Einführung in die Geschichte der theologischen Literatur der Frühscholastik. Regensburg 1948.
Little, A. G.: The Grey Friars at Oxford. London 1892.
Signoriello, N.: Lexicon peripateticum philosophico-theologicum. Roma 5. umg. A. 1931.

de Wulf, M.: Histoire de la philosophie médiévale. 3 Bde. Louvain 6. A. 1934
   1936, 1947.
S. a. Prantl (*1.24.*) III—IV.

3.2. Editions of texts (including MSS cited)

Abälard: S. Peter Abälard.
Adam Balsamiensis Parvipontani: Ars disserendi. Ed. L. Minio-Paluello. Roma
   1955.
Aegidius Columna: s. Egidius Romanus.
Albalag: Paris, Bibl. Nat., Cod. héb. 109—110.
Albert der Große: Opera. Ed. Jammy. Lugd. 1651.
— Opera omnia. Ed. L. Vivès. 38 Bde. Paris 1890—1899. Bde. I und II: Lo-
   gica. 1890.
— Alberti Magni ad logicam pertinentia. Venetiis 1532.
— Alberti Magni ,,De antecedentibus ad logicam", in: Teoresi 9 (2—3), 177—242.
   (Teildr. Diss. Freiburg/Schw. 1951.)
— Liber II Perihermenias, in: Opera omnia. Ed. A. Borgnet. Parisiis 1890 ff,
   Bd. I.
— Liber I Priorum Analyticorum. Ebda.
— Soph. El. Ebda. Bd. II.
Albert von Sachsen: Logica Albertucii Perutilis Logica. Venetiae 1522.
— Expositio aurea et admodum utilis super artem veterem edita per venerabi-
   lem inceptorem fratrem Guilielmum de Occham cum quaestionibus Alberti
   parvi de Saxonia. Bononiae 1496.
— Quaestiones subtilissimae Albert de saxonia super libros posteriorum. Vene-
   tiis 1497.
— Sophismata Alberti de Saxonia nuper emendata. Paris 1495.
— Tractatus obligationum. Lugduni 1498.
   S. a.: Wilhelm v. Ockham, Expositio aurea . . .
Alexander Sermoneta: Excellentissimi artium et medicinae doctoris magistri
   Alexandri Sermonete cum dubiis reverendi magistri Pauli pergulesis: necnon
   eximii Gaetani de Thiemis quibusdam declaratinis (sic!) in consequentias
   Strodi commentariolu (sic!) feliciter incipit. Venetiae 1488.
— Consequentiae Strodi cum commento Alexandri Sermonete, Declarationes
   Gaetani in easdam consequentias, Dubia magistri Pauli pergulensis, Obliga-
   tiones eiusdem strodi, Consequentiae Ricardi de Ferabrich, Expositio
   Gaetani super easdem. Venetiis 1507.
Algazel: Logica et Philosophia Algazelis Arabi. Venet. 1506, 1536 u. o. J.
Alkuin (Flaccus Albinus): Opera didascalia. De dialectica. In: B. Flacci Albini
   seu Alcuini Opera omnia II (ML 101). Petit-Montrouge 1851, Sp. 949—976.
Anonymus: Argumenta communia ad inferendum sophistice unamquamque
   propositionem esse veram vel falsam. Basileae 1511.
— Explanatio in nonnulla Petri Burdegalensis, quem Hispanum dicunt, volu-
   mina, cum interrogationum ex iis elicibilium et Sophismatum Alberthi
   Saxonis expeditione. O. O. u. J.
— Mainzer Summula: Modernorum summulae logicales . . . a magistris collegii
   Moguntini regentibus de modernorum doctrina sunt studiosissime inno-
   vatae . . . Spirae 1489.
— Promptuarium argumentorum dialogice ordinatorum . . . Coloniae 1496.
— Pulcerrimus tractatus de modo opponendi et respondendi . . . O. O. u. J.
   (Köln?).
— Thesaurus sophismatum circa tractatus parvorum logicalium, iuxta dispu-
   tativum processum magistrorum regentiae bursae Montis in praeclarissima
   universitate Coloniensi singulis secundis, quartis et sextis feriis quam diutis-
   sime observatum, ad perfectum neophicorum inibi studentium lucubratissime
   collectus. Coloniae 1495, 1501.
Antonius Andreas: Scripta seu expositiones Antonii Andreae super artem veterem et super Boetium de divisionibus. Venetiis 1492, 1508 u. 1517.

479

BIBLIOGRAPHY

Antonius Coronel, aus Segovia: Super librum Praedicamentorum Aristotelis secundum utriusque viae, realium scilicet et nominalium, principia commentaria. (Paris) 1513.
— Prima pars Rosarii magistri Anthonii Coronel... Secunda pars rosarii Logices magistri Anthonii Coronel... (Paris) 1512.
— In posteriora Aristotelis Commentaria. (Paris) um 1510.
— Tractatus exponibilium et fallaciarum. (Paris) 1511.
— Acutissimi artium interpretis magistri Iohannis maioris in Petri Hyspani summulas commentaria. Lugduni 1505.
Antonius de Fantis: Tabula generalis rerum scibilium sive mare magnum Scoticarum speculationum ex universis sententiarum voluminibus. Venetiis 1617.
— Habes in hoc volumine candidissime lector difficilem totius disciplinae rationalis provinciam ... habes philosophorum difficultates ... quas ... eximius doctor Antonius de Fantis elucubravit ... Venetiis 1504.
— Quinque illustrium auctorum formalitatum libelli. Venetiis 1588.
Antonius Silvester: Dialecticis sititoribus quaestionum pars prima super summularum Buridani tractatum primum. Paris (1511 ?).
Apollinaris Offredus (Cremonensis): Absolutissima commentaria una cum quaestionibus in primum Aristotelis Posteriorum Analyticorum librum. Ed. Ant. Honoratus. Cremona 1581.
— Suppositiones, in: Logica Magistri Petri Mantuani. Venetiis 1492 (unpaginiert).
Aristotelis: Analytica Posteriora, translatio anonyma. Ed. L. Minio-Paluello (Aristoteles Latinus IV/2). Bruge, Paris 1953.
— Analytica Posteriora Gerardo Cremonensi interprete. Ed. L. Minio-Paluello (Aristoteles Latinus IV/3). Bruge, Paris 1954.
Armand von Beauvoir: De declaratione difficilium terminorum, tam theologicalium quam philosophiae ac logicae. Coloniae 1502.
Arnold von Luyde (de Tungris): Epitomata, quae vulgo reparationes dicuntur, lectionum et exercitiorum logicae veteris ac novae Aristotelis secundum divi Alberti ... Coloniae 1507 (auch 1496 u. 1500).
— Reparationes lectionum et exercitiorum tractatuum parvorum logicalium Petri Hyspani ... Reparationes ... per artium liberalium magistrum ac sacrae theologiae licentiatum Arnoldum Tungerio ... collectae. Coloniae 1500.
Averroes: Opera. 11 Bde. Venetiis 1550—1552. (Die wichtigsten logischen Schriften in Bd. 1; auch in: Aristotelis Opera latine, Venet. 1552).
Avicenna: Avicennae peripat. philosophi ac medicorum facile primi opera in lucem redacta. Venetiis 1495, 1508.
— La logique du fils de Sina, communément appelé Avicenne, etc. Transl. Vattier. Paris 1658.
Bartholomäus Arnoldi (de Usingen) Compendium Novum totius logicae ... O. O. u. J.
— Summa compendiaria totius logicae in famatissimo studio Erphurdiensi per magistrum Bartholomeum Arnoldi de Usingen collecta. ... (Basel) 1507.
— Exercitium veteris artis in studio Erffordiensi collectum per Magistrum Bartholomeum arnoldi de Usingen instauratum atque emendatum.... Erfordiae 1514.
— Exercitium novae logicae ... per Ioannem Canappum. (Erfurt) 1516.
Bartholomaeus Manzolus: Dubia super logicam Pauli Veneti iuxta viam realium philosophorum praesertim S. Thomae extricata et resoluta ... (Venedig) 1523.
Baudry, L. (Hrsg.): La querelle des futurs contingents. Louvain 1465—1475. Textes inédits. 1950.
Benedictus Victorius Faventinus (Bononiensis): Opusculum ... in Tisberum de sensu composito ac diviso cum ... collectaneis in suppositiones Pauli Veneti. Bononiae 1504.
— Examinatio Quaestionis De Instanti Gualterii Burlei ... Digressiones De Unitate Scientiae, De Essentialibus Sillogismi, Et in quo genere fiat motus. Bologna 1505.
S. a. d. dritte unt. Wilh. Hentisberus genannte Werk.

480

BIBLIOGRAPHY

Bernardinus Petri: De sensu composito et diviso . . . Neapoli 1514.

Boetius von Dacien: S. Grabmann, Die Sophismatenliteratur (*3.41.*).

Buridan: S. Johannes Buridanus.

Burleigh: S. Walter Burleigh.

Cajetanus de Thienis: S. Alexander Sermoneta, Excellentissimi . . .

— Erläuterungen zu den Sophismata des Hentisberus, in: Tractatus gulielmi Hentisberi de sensu composito et diviso . . . Venetiis 1494.

Cajetanus de Vio: S. Thomas de Vio Caietanus.

Caspar Lax: Termini magistri Gasparis Lax Secundo revisl et emendati per ipsum . . . O. O. u. J. (1512?).

— Obligationes . . . Parisius 1512.

— Insolubilia . . . Parisius 1512.

Cod. lat. Mon. 4652. (g **32.06**).

Collegii Conimbricensis: Commentaria in universam Dialecticam Aristotelis. Coloniae 1611.

Cousin, V. (Hrsg.): Fragments de philosophie du moyen-âge. Paris 1840. 2. A. 1850.

David Cranston: Tractatus Insolubilium et Obligationum . . . de novo recognitus per magistrum Guillermum mandreston et magistrum Anthonium silvestri . . . cum obligationibus Strodi . . . O. O. u. J. (Paris ?).

Dominicus Soto: Commentarii in Aristotelis dialecticam. Salamancae 1544.

Duns Scotus: S. Johannes Duns Scotus.

Egidius Romanus (de Colonna): Expositio in artem veterem, videlicet in universalibus, praedicamentis, postpraedicamentis, sex principiis et Periermenias. Venet. 1507, 1582; Bergomi 1591.

— Expositio super libros Priorum. Venet. 1516.

— Expositio super libros Posteriorum Aristotelis. Venet. 1500.

— Expositio super libros Elenchorum Aristotelis. Venet. 1500. (g)

— In libros Perihermeneias expositio. Venetiis 1507.

— In libros priorum analeticorum Aristotelis Expositio et interpretatio. Venetiis 1499, 1504, 1516, 1522.

— Expositio supra libros elenchorum Aristotelis. Venetiis 1496, 1499, 1530.

— In libros Posteriorum Aristotelis profundissima commentaria. Venetiis 1496, 1499, 1530.

Erasmus Wonsidel (aus Wunsiedel): Exercitium totius veteris artis . . . 2 Teile. Liptzk 1511.

Faventinus Blanchellus Menghus: Zwei Kommentare zu den Summulae des Paulus Venetus u. d. Titeln „Expositio" und „Quaestiones", in: Pauli Veneti summulae cum commentariis Menghi Faventini . . . ac quaestionibus eiusdem . . . per Franciscum de Macerata revisa. Venetiis 1498.

Ferdinand von Enzinas: Primus tractatus Summularum. Parisiis 1528.

— Oppositionum liber primus. Parisiis 1528.

Franciscus Mayron: Quodlibettales quaestiones fertilissimae. Venetiis 1507, 1520.

— Contenta in volumine per . . . dom. Hieronymum de Nuciarellis Romanum correcta et emendata, lector, invenies: Passus super universalia et praedicamenta . . . Francisci Maironis (auch sep. Bononiae 1479) . . . De primo principio complexo eiusdem . . . De univocatione entis. Venetiis 1517.

Franciscus Taegius: Lectura in libellum Thomae Aquinatis de fallaciis. Pavia 1511.

Franciscus Toletus: Commentaria in universam Aristotelis logicam. Parisiis 1586.

Gaetanus de Thienis: S. Radulph Strodus.

Georg Benegnus: Artis dialecticae praecepta vetera ac nova . . . Romae 1520.

Georg von Brüssel: Expositio . . . in logicam Aristotelis, una cum Magistri Thome bricoti textu de novo inserto . . . Lugduni 1504. Wörtlich stimmt damit überein:

— Cursus optimarum quaestionum super totam logicam . . . O. O. u. J.

— Expositio Georgii super summulis magistri Petri Hispani . . . Lugduni 1489.

— Interpretatio . . . in summulas magistri Petri Hispani una cum magistri Thomae Bricot quaestionibus . . . Parisiorum 1497.

481

BIBLIOGRAPHY

— Interpretatio ... in summulas magistri Petri Hispani una cum magistri Thomae Bricot quaestionibus ... Lugduni 1515.

S. a. Thomas Bricot.

Georgios Scholarios: Cod. graec. Mon. 548.

Gerhard Harderwyk: Commentaria in quattuor libros novae logicae secundum processum bursae Laurentianae Coloniensis ... per honorabilem ... Gerardum herdarwiccensem actu regentem et per Udalricum zell proprie lyskirchen ... characterizati. (Köln) 1494.

— Copulata Petri Hyspani secundum processum bursae Laurentii ... Commentum ... per magistrum Gerardum de Harderwyck ... (Köln) 1488, 1492, 1504.

Gilbertus Porretanus: Liber de sex principiis Gilberto Porretae adscriptus ... Ed. A. Heyse OFM., rec. D. Van Den Eynde OFM. Münster i. W. 2. A. 1953.

— Kommentar zu Pseudo-Boethius, De Trinitate, in: Boethii Opera, Basileae 1570, 1128—1273.

Gregor Breytkopf (Bredekopf, Laticephalus): Excerpta Libr. Posteriorum Aris. cum commentariolo. (Leipzig) 1506.

— Compendium, sive Parvulus Antiquorum totam paene complectens logicen ... O. O. 1509 u. 1513.

— Parvorum logicalium opusculum de suppositione scilicet Ampliatione, Restrictione, et Appellatione, Insuper de Expositione et Consequentiis. Liptzigk 1507.

— Tractatus de inventione medii. Tractatulus propositionum modalium respiciens difficultates. Hexastichon ... ad lectorem etc. ... O. O. u. J. (Leipzig).

Gregor Reisch: Margarita philosophica. 1496 u. öfter bis 1583.

Gregor von Rimini (Ariminensis): Lectura super Primo et Secundo Sententiarum. Ed. Paulus Genazano. Venetiis 1532.

Heinrich von Gent: Quaestiones logicales, in: Magistri Henrici Gendovensis ... tripartitio. Ed. A. Ventura. Bononiae 1701.

Heinrich von Gorkum: Circa initium compendii magistri Henrici de Gorichem ..., quo ... ea, quae in libro Posteriorum Aristotelis quodam velamine proponuntur, in lucem aurorae ... apertissime secernuntur ... Coloniae 1506.

Heinrich Greve: Parva logicalia ... O. O. u. J.

Herveus Natalis (Brito): Tractatus de secundis intentionibus. Parisiis 1489, Venetiis 1513.

— Liber de intentionibus incipit. O. O. u. J.

Hieronymus von Hangest: Problemata logicalia ... (Paris) 1516.

Hieronymus de Marcho: Compendium praeclarum quod parva logica seu summulae dicitur ... (Köln) 1507.

Hieronymus Pardus: Medulla dyalectices ... (Paris) 1505.

Hieronymus Savonarola: Compendium logicae. Lipsiae 1516. Auch in: Compendium totius philosophiae, Venetiis 1534 u. 1542, II, 63 ff.

Hugo von St. Viktor: Eruditionis didascaliae libri Septem. In: Opera omnia II (ML 176), Petit-Montrouge 1854, 739—838.

Jacobus Almain: Tractatus quinque consequentiarum. (Laut Prantl IV, 4 ff. verloren.)

Jacob Faber Stapulensis: In libros logices Paraphrasis. ... (Paris) 1525.

— Introductiones in Suppositiones, Praedicabilia, Divisiones, Praedicamenta, Librum de enuntiatione, Libros Priorum, Posteriorum, Locos, Fallacias, Obligationes, Insolubilia. Gedr. in d. unter Jodocus Clichtoveus angeg. Werk.

Jacobus Riccius: Incipiunt quaedam obiectiones et annotata super logica Pauli Veneti. 1488.

Jodocus Clichtoveus: Introductiones artificiales in Logicam Iacobi Fabri Stapulensis ... Iodoci item Clichtovei in Terminorum cognitionem Introductio, cum altera de Artium divisione, eiusdem in utraque Annotatiunculis. Lugduni 1540; (Paris) 1505, 1536. (Die Introductio einzeln als: Fundamentum logicae [mit Kommentar des Joh. Cäsarius]. Paris 1560.)

Jodoc Trutfeder Isenacensis: Summulae totius logicae ... Erphurdiae 1501.
— Epitome seu breviarium dialecticae... Erphordiae 1512. (Um An. post., Top.
   und Soph. El. verkürzte A. der Summulae.)
Johann Altenstaig: Dialectica ... (Hagenau) 1514.
Johannes Antonius Scotus Neapolitanus: De demonstratione potissima quae-
   stio unica, in: Egidius Romanus, In libros pr. anal. Arist. Expositio, Vene-
   tiis 1516, 83 v ff.
Joannes a Sancto Thoma: Ars Logica. Nova ed. a B. Reiser. Taurini 1930.
— Cursus philosophicus tomi 3. Romae 1636—1637. Tom. I, Logica, auch:
   Parisiis 1883.
Johannes Buridanus: Perutile compendium totius logicae ... cum praeclaris-
   sima solertissimi viri Joannis Dorp expositione, Parisiis 1487, Venetiis 1489,
   1499.
— Commentum Johannis Dorp super textu summularum Johannis Buridani
   nuperrime castigatum a Johanne Maioris cum aliquibus additionibus eius-
   dem. (Paris) 1504. (Dasselbe wie vorher, nur vermehrt um eine Quaestio des
   Joh. Majoris).
— Consequentiae. (Paris) 1495.
— Perutile compendium totius logicae ... (Venedig) 1499. (Auch u. d. T.: Summa
   de dialectica.)
— Sophismata Buridani. (Paris), o. J. (ca. 1496).
— Textus summularum magistri Joh. Bur. cur. Joh. Dorp. Parisiis 1487.
— Tractatus consequentiarum magistri i. b.... Parisius o. J. (unpaginiert). (g)
Joannes de Cornubia = Verf. des In An. Priora (?) und In An. Post. des Pseudo-
   (Duns) Scot. S. Johannes Duns Scotus (Pseudo).
Johannes Damascenus: St. John Damascene, Dialectica. Version of Robert
   Grosseteste. Ed. O. A. Colligan. St. Bonaventure (N. Y.), Louvain, Pader-
   born 1953.
Johannes Dolz: Termini cum principiis necnon pluribus aliis ipsius dialectices
   difficultatibus ... Parisius o. J. (um 1510?).
— Disceptationes super primum tractatum summularum ... (Paris) 1512.
— Sillogismi magistri Ioh. Dolz ... (Paris) 1511.
Johannes Dorp: Ioh. Dorp recognitus et auctus. Summulae Buridani. Cum
   expositione ... Iohannis Dorp. recognitae a ... Iohanne Maiore. ... Lug-
   duni 1510. S. a. Joh. Buridanus.
Johannes Dullaert: Quaestiones ... in librum praedicamentorum Aristotelis.
   (Paris 1523).
— Quaestiones super duos libros Perihermenias Aristotelis ... (Paris) 1515.
Johannes Duns Scotus: Opera omnia. 12 Bde. Lugduni 1639 (= Ed. Wadding).
— Opera omnia. 26 Bde. (Vivès) Parisiis 1891—1895.
— Super universalia Porphyrii quaestiones acutissimae; in: Op. omnia (Vivès)
   I, 51—435.
— In librum Praedicamentorum questiones, in: Op. omnia (Vivès) I, 437—538.
— In I et II Perihermeneias questiones, in: Op. omnia (Vivès) I, 539—579.
— In duos libros Perihermeneias. Operis secundi quod appellant questiones
   octo. In: Op. omnia (Vivès) I, 581—601.
Johannes Duns Scotus (Pseudo): In librum I et II Priorum Analyticorum Ari-
   stotelis Quaestiones, in: Op. omnia (Vivès) II, 81—197.
— (Joh. de Cornubia): In librum I et II Posteriorum Analyticorum Aristotelis
   quaestiones. In: Op. omnia (Vivès) II, 199—347.
— In libros Elenchorum Aristotelis quaestiones. In: Op. omnia (Vivès) II,
   1—50.
Johann Eck (Johann Mayr): Aristotelis Stagyritae Dialectica; cum quinque
   vocibus Porphyrii Phoenicis; Argyropilo traductore ... facili explanatione
   declarata ... (Augsburg) I: 1516, II: 1517.
— In summulas Petri Hispani ... explanatio. (Augsburg) 1516.
— Logices exercitamenta Appellata parva logicalia. Argentinae 1507.
— Elementarius Dialecticae ... Augustae Vindelicorum 1517, 1518.

BIBLIOGRAPHY

Johannes Faber de Werdea: Exercitata parvorum logicalium secundum viam modernorum. (Reutlingen) 1487.

Johannes Gebwiler: Magistralis Totius Parvuli artis Logices compilatio ... Basileae 1511.

Johannes Gerson: Opera. 5 Bde. (Antwerpen) 1706. Darin: De conceptibus. De modis significandi. De concordantia metaphysicae cum logica.

Johann von Glogau: Exercicium Novae Logicae Seu Librorum Priorum Et Elenchorum ... (Krakau) 1511.

— Liber posteriorum analeticorum. (Krakau) 1499.

— (?): Commentarium secundum Modernam doctrinam in Tractatus logices Petri Hispani Primum et Quartum. Item Commentarium in Tractatus parvorum logicalium Marsilii ... Itemque De Descensu, De positione propositionum in esse, De Statu, De Alienatione. (Hagenau) 1503.

Johannes Gratiadei von Ascoli: Commentaria ... in totam artem veterem Aristotilem. Venet. 1493.

Johann Heynlin (Johannes a Lapide): Libri artis logicae Porphyrii et Aristotelis cum explanatione ... Basileae o. J.

— Tractatus ... de propositionibus exponibilibus, cum tractatu de arte solvendi importunas sophistarum argumentationes. Basileae, o. J.

Johannes Magistri: Quaestiones veteris artis perutiles ... Zweiter Teil: Quaestiones admodum utiles ... explanative nove logice arestotelis. Heidelberg 1488.

— Dicta circa summulas magistri pe. his ... O. O. u. J. (Mainz 1490?).

Johannes Majoris Scotus: In Petri Hyspani summulas commentaria. Lugduni 1505.

— Libri quos in artibus ... emisit. Lugduni 1516.

— Introductorium perutile in Aristotelicam Dialecticen, duos Terminorum Tractatus, ac Quinque Libros Summularum complectens. (Paris) 1508, 1527.

— Quaestiones Logicales. (Paris) 1528.
S. a. Johannes Dorp.

Johannes de Monte: Summulae ... super Petrum Hispanum. Venetiis 1500.

Johannes Parreut: Textus veteris artis ... Item exercitata circa hoc secundum doctrinam Modernorum ... Viennensis 1507. Auch: (Ingolstadt) 1492, (Nürnberg) 1494, (Hagenau) 1501.

Johannes Raulin: S. Nicolaus Amans.

Johannes von Salisbury (Saresberiensis): Opera. Ed. Giles, Oxoniae 1848.

— The Metalogicon of John of Salisbury. Transl. with an Introd. by D. D. McGarry. Berkeley 1955.

Johannes Versor: Quaestiones super artem veterem. (3 Inkunabeln o. O. u. J., u. öfters bis: Köln) 1503.

— Super omnes libros novae logicae. O. O. u. J. u. (Köln) 1486, 1497, 1503.

— Kommentare zu Petrus Hispanus (zahlr. Inkunabeln, u. später bis: Venedig) 1572.

Isidorus Hispalensis: Etymologiarum libri XX. In: Opera omnia, Tom. III u. IV (ML 82), Petit-Montrouge 1850, 73—728.

Kajetan: S. Thomas de Vio Caietanus.

Kilwardby: S. Robert Kilwardby.

Konrad von Buchen (Wimpina): Congestio Textus Nova Proprietatum logicalium cum commentatione non vulgari ... O. O. u. J.

Konrad von Halberstadt: De logica. (Vgl. Prantl III, 201, 24 ff.)

Konrad Pschlacher: Parvorum logicalium liber. Viennae 1516.

Lambertus de Monte: Copulata pulcherrima ... in veterem artem Aresto ... Coloniae 1488, 1490.

— Copulata pulcerrima in novam logicam Arestotelis. Coloniae 1493 (auch: O. J., 1488, 1505, 1511).

— Erläuterungen zu Petrus Hispanus. Häufig mit dem Text des Petrus gedruckt. Ohne diesen Text: Coloniae 1487.

484

BIBLIOGRAPHY

Laurentianus Florentinus: In librum Aristotelis de elocutione. In: Egidius Romanus, In libros pr. anal. Arist. Expositio ... Venetiis 1516.

Magnus Hundt: Compendium totius logices, quod a nonnullis Parvulus Antiquorum appellatur. Liptzk ... 1511.

Marsilius de Inghen: Quaestiones perutiles ... super libris priorum analecticorum Aristotelis. In: Egidius Romanus, In libros pr. anal. Arist. Expositio ... Venetiis 1516.

— Erläuterung der ersten Analytiken. Ebda.

— Textus dialectices de suppositionibus, ampliationibus, appellationibus, restrictionibus, alienationibus, et duabus consequentiarum partibus abbreviatus ... In: Copulata Petri Hyspani secundum processum bursae Laurentii ... Commentum ... per magistrum Gerardum de Harderwyck ... (Köln) 1488. Und in:

— Commentaria in summulas Petri Hispani albertocentonus continentia ... secundum processum bursae laurentianae Colon ... 1492. Viennae 1512, 1516.

Martin Molenfelt: Tractatus obligatorium. In: Petrus Tartaretus, Expos. sup. summulis, Parisiis 1494, Friburgi 1494.

Martin Pollich(ius): Cursus Logici commentariorum nostra collectanea. Liptzk 1512.

Mauritius Hibernicus (de Portu hibernico): Lectura acuratissima Mauritii Hibernici ... super ysagogis Porphyrii, Modorum quoque significandi seu grammaticae speculativae ... Venetiis 1512.

Michael von Breslau: Introductorium dyalecticae, quod Congestum Logicum appellatur ... Argentiae 1515.

Michael von Paris (Parisiensis): Quaestiones ... in Tractatum parvorum logicalium Petri Hispani. Cracoviae 1512.

Michael Psellus: Σύνοψις τῶν πέντε φωνῶν καὶ τῶν δέκα κατηγοριῶν. Venet. 1532.

— Synopsis organi Aristotelis Michaele Psello auctore. Ed. El. Ehinger. 1597. (Text des cod. graec. Mon. 548).

— Synopsis organi Aristotelici. Ed. El. Ehinger. Wittenberg 1597. (Griech. Text mit lat. Übers.).

Nicolaus Amans: Dubia, in: Iohannis Raulin cum plerisque dubiis Nicolai amantis passim annexis in logicam aristotelis Commentarium ... Paris, o. J.

Nicolaus de Orbellis (oder Dorbellus): Logicae brevis expositio = Logica = Summula philosophiae rationalis (= Kom. zu den Summulae). (Parma) 1482, Venet. 1489, 1500, 1516, (Basel) 1498, 1503.

Nicolaus Tinctor: Dicta tinctoris super Summulas Petri hyspani. (Reutlingen oder Tübingen) 1486.

Ockham: S. Wilhelm v. Ockham.

Olivier von Siena: Tractatus rationalis scientiae. (Siena) 1491.

Pamphilus de Monte: Logica ... Bononiae 1522.

Paulus Pergulensis: Compendium perclarum ad introductionem iuvenum in facultate logicae. O. O. u. J.

— Logica magistri Pauli Pergulensis. Venetiis 1498.

— Dubia (zu den) Consequentiae Strodi. Gedr. in d. unt. Alexander Sermoneta genannten Werken.

Paulus Soncinas (Barbus): Expositio magistri ... super artem veterem. Venetiis 1499, in: Universalia seu Isagogen Porphyrii et Aristotelis praedicamenta expositio. Ed. Iac. Rossetti. Venet. 1587.

Paulus Venetus (Paolo Nicoletti): Summulae seu logicae institutiones. Mediolani 1474. Venetiis 1488.

— Quadratura. Venetiis 1493.

— Expositio in libros posteriorum Aristotelis. Venetiis 1486.

— Sophismata. Venetiis 1493.

— Logica Magna (Pars 1 und 2). Venetiis 1499.

— Logica ...: Summa totius dialecticae ... (Venedig) 1544.

BIBLIOGRAPHY

Peter Abälard: Philosophische Schriften. Hrsg. und unters. v. Dr. B. Geyer. Münster i. W. 1933. (Darin: Introductiones.)
— Dialectica. First complete ed. with intr. by L. M. de Rijk. Assen (Niederl.) 1955.
— Opera in unum collecta V. Cousin adjuv. C. Jourdain. 2 Bde. Paris 1849 bis 1859.
— Ouvrages inédits d'Abélard. Ed. V. Cousin. Paris 1836. (Darin: Dialectica, Topica.)
Peter von Ailly: Destructiones modorum significandi. Conceptus et insolubilia secundum viam nominalium . . . O. O. u. J.
— Tractatus exponibilium magistri Petri de Aillyaco. Parisiis 1494.
Petrus Bruxellensis: Acutissimae quaestiones et quidem perutiles in singulos Aristotelis logicales libros . . . (Paris) 1514.
— Summularum artis dialecticae utilis admodum interpretatio . . . (Paris) 1508.
Petrus Hispanus: Summulae Logicales. Ed. I. M. Bocheński. (Turin) 1947 (g). (Prantl III, 33,11—73,20 nennt 48 alte A.)
— The Summulae logicales of Peter of Spain. Ed. J. P. Mullally. Notre-Dame (Ind.) 1945. (Teil-Abdr. aus Wiegendr. m. engl. Übers.)
Petrus Mantuanus: Logica Magistri Petri Mantuani (unpaginiert). O. O. u. J.; Paviae 1483; Venetiis 1492.
Petrus Nigri: Clipeus Thomistarum. (Venedig) 1504 u. öfters.
Petrus Tartaretus: Commentarium . . . in Textum Petri Hispani. O. O. u. J. (Auch: Parisiis 1494, Friburgi 1494, o. O. 1500, Venetiis 1504, 1514, 1621.)
— Expositio . . . super textus logices Aristotelis . . . Venetiis 1503.
— . . . commentarii in Isagogas Porphyrii et libros logicorum Aristotelis accuratissime recogniti. (Basel) 1514 (Staatsbibl. München). (Auch: Paris 1494, Lugduni 1500, 1509, Venetiis 1504, 1514, 1591, 1621.)
— . . . commentarii in isagogas Porphyrii et libros logicorum Aristotelis . . . Basileae 1517.
— In universam philosophiam opera. Venetiis 1614.
Philipp Mucagata: Opera . . . In logicam. Venetiis 1494.
Pseudo-Scot: S. Johannes Duns Scotus (Pseudo).
Radulph Strodus: Consequentiae Strodi, cum commento Alexandri Sermoneta. (Venedig) 1493.
— Consequentiae Strodi cum commento Alexandri Sermonetae, Declarationes Gaetani in easdem consequentias, Dubia magistri Pauli Pergulensis, Obligationes eiusdem Strodi, Consequentiae Ricardi de Ferabrich, Expositio Gaetani super easdem. Venetiis 1507.
S. a. Alexander Sermoneta.
Raimundus Lullus: Opera omnia. Ed. I. Salzinger. Moguntiae 1721—1742.
— Opera ea, quae ad adinventam ab ipso artem universalem scientiarum artiumque omnium . . . pertinent etc. Argentorati 1617. (Auch: 1609, 1651.)
— L'Ars compendiosa de R. Lulle. Avec une étude sur la Bibliographie et le fond Ambrosien de Lulle par C. Ottaviano. Paris 1930.
Richard von Capsalis: Dicta sexdecim . . . de futuris contingentibus, in: Expositio aurea . . . super Artem veterem . . . per . . . Guilielmum de Occham cum quaestionibus Albert parvi de Saxonia. Bononiae 1496.
Richard Feribrigus (od. Ferabrich): Consequentiae. Gedr. im zweiten unt. Alexander Sermoneta gen. Werk.
Robert Caubraith: Quadrupertitum in Oppositiones, Conversiones, Hypotheticas et Modales. Parisiis 1516.
Robert Grosseteste (Capito oder Lincolniensis): Commentaria . . . in libros posteriorum Aristotelis . . . Scriptum Gualterii Burlei super eosdem libros posteriorum. Venetiis 1497.
Robert Holkot: In quatuor libros Sententiarum quaestiones argutissimae . . . Lugduni 1497 u. öfters.
Robert Kilwardby: In Analytica Priora. Hss. Merton College Oxford 289 u. 280.

BIBLIOGRAPHY

Auszüge in: I. Thomas, Maxims in Kilwardby, u. Kilwardby on conversion (*3.3.*).

Robert von Lincoln: S. Walter Burleigh, 4. gen. Werk.

Samuel Casinensis: Opus, quod liber ysagogicus inscribitur ... Mediolani 1494.

Savonarola: S. Hieronymus Savonarola.

Sextus Empiricus: Πυρρωνείον ὑποτυπώσεων. Lat. Übers. in: Paris, Bibl. Nat., Cod. lat. 14700, 83—132.

Shyreswood: S. Wilhelm v. Shyreswood.

Silvester Maurus: Aristotelis opera omnia quae exstant brevi paraphrasi et ... expositione illustrata. 4. Bde. I: Logica, Rhetorica, Poetica. Ed. Fr. Ehrle. Parisiis 1855—1856.

Silvester Mazolinus de Prieria: Compendium dialecticae ... Venetiis 1496.

— Apologia ... in dialecticam suam cum explanatione clarissima totius materiae intentionalis. Bononiae 1499.

Simon de Lendenaria: Recollectae supra sophismatibus Hentisberi. Gedr. in d. unter Wilhelm Hentisberus zuerst gen. Werk.

Stephanus de Monte: Ars insolubilis (unpaginiert). O. O. 1490. (Auch: Paviae 1490.)

Summa Totius Logicae Aristotelis: S. Thomas v. Aquin (Pseudo).

Thomas von Aquin: Scriptum super Sententiis Magistri Petri Lombardi. Ed. P. Mandonnet et M. F. Moos. 4 Bde. Paris 1929 ff.

— Summa Theologiae cum Commentariis Caietani. In: Opera omnia iussu Leonis XIII edita, IV—XII, Romae 1888—1906.

— Summa Theologiae. Ed. P. Caramello. Cum textu et rec. Leonina. 4 Bde. Roma 1948.

— Summa Theologiae. 5 Bde. Ottawa 1941—1945.

— Summa contra Gentiles cum Commentariis Ferrariensis, in: Opera omnia iussu Leonis XIII edita, XIII—XV, Romae 1920—1930.

— Summa contra Gentiles (Editio Leonina manualis). Romae 1934.

— In libros Perihermenias Aristotelis expositio (c. 1—10, 19—31). In: Opera omnia iussu Leonis XIII edita I, Romae 1882.

— In Metaphysicam Aristotelis Commentaria. Hrsg. M.-R. Cathala. Taurini 3. A. 1935.

— In decem libros Ethicorum Aristotelis ad Nicomachum Expositio. Ed. R. M. Spiazzi. Taurini 2. A. 1949.

— Quaestiones disputatae de potentia, in: Quaestiones disputatae II, ed. R. Spiazzi. Taurini 8. A. 1949.

— Quaestiones disputatae de veritate, in: Quaestiones disputatae I, ed. R. Spiazzi. Taurini 8. A. 1949.

— De fallaciis, in: Opuscula omnia IV, ed. P. Mandonnet. Paris 1927.

— De demonstratione, in: Opuscula omnia V, ed. P. Mandonnet. Paris 1927.

— De quattuor oppositis. Ebda.

— De natura generis. Ebda.

— De natura accidentis. Ebda.

— De propositionibus modalibus, ed. I. M. Bocheński, in: I. Bocheński, S. Thomae Aq. de modalibus opusc. et doct. (*3.3.*).

Thomas von Aquin (Pseudo): Summa totius logicae Aristotelis, in: Opuscula omnia V, ed. P. Mandonnet. Paris 1927.

— De natura syllogismorum. Ebda.

— De inventione medii. Ebda.

Thomas Bricot: Cursus optimarum questionum super philosophiam Aristotelis ... secundum viam modernorum: ac secundum cursum magistri Georgii (Bruxellensis). O. O. u. J.

— Incipiunt quaestiones super totam logicam cum interpretatione textus secundum cursum magistri Georgii (Bruxellensis). O. O. u. J.

— Textus totius logices ... abbreviatus. (Basel) 1492.

S. a. Georg von Brüssel.

Thomas Claxton: Quaestiones de distinctione inter esse et essentiam reali. —

BIBLIOGRAPHY

Quaestiones de analogia entis. Ed. M. Grabmann, in: Acta Pont. Acad. Romanae S. Thomae ... 8, 1943, 92—153.

Thomas von Erfurt: Tractatus de modis significandi sive Grammatica speculativa, in: Joh. D. Scot, Op. omnia (Vivès) I, 1—50.

Thomas Murner: Logica memorativa Chartiludium logicae, sive totius dialecticae memoria ... Argentinae 1509.

Thomas de Vio Caietanus: Commentaria in Porphyrii Isagogen ad Praedicamenta Aristotelis. Ed. I. M. Marega. Romae 1934.

— Commentaria in Praedicamenta Aristotelis. Ed. M.-H. Laurent. Romae 1939.

— De nominum analogia. De conceptu entis. Ed. P. Zammit. Roma 1934.

Vincenz von Beauvais: Speculum doctrinale, 4. Buch. Argentorati 1473, (Nürnberg) 1486.

Vinzenz Ferrer: De suppositionibus dialecticis, in: Œuvres de Saint Vincent Ferrier I, éd. Le Père Fages. Paris 1909.

Walter Burleigh: De puritate artis logicae tractatus longior. With a rev. ed. of the Tractatus brevior. Ed. Ph. Boehner. St. Bonaventure (N. Y.), Louvain, Paderborn 1955.

— De puritate artis logicae. Ed. Boehner. St. Bonaventure (N. Y.), Louvain 1951. (g)

— Super artem veterem Porphyrii et Aristotelis expositio ... Venetiis 1485.

— Commentaria Roberti Linconiensis in libros posteriorum Aristotelis cum textu seriatim inserto. Scriptum Gualterii Burlei super eosdem ... Venetiis 1497.

— Summa totius logicae. Venetiis 1508.

S. a. Robert Grosseteste.

Wilhelm Hentisberus (Tysberus): Tractatus ... de sensu composito et diviso. Regulae ... cum sophismatibus ... etc. Venetiis 1494.

— Probationes conclusionum. (Pavia) 1483.

— De sensu composito et diviso (mit Kommentar des Benedictus Victorius). Bononiae 1504.

Wilhelm Manderston: Compendiosa Dialectices Epitome ... quaestio de futuro contingenti. Parrhisiis 1528.

Wilhelm von Ockham: Expositio super primum librum Perihermeneias, Kap. I, ed. Ph. Boehner, in: Traditio 4, 1946, 320—335. Kap. II, ed. ders., in: The tractatus de praedestinatione..., 1945, 104—113.

— Logica Magistri Ocham ... cur. Joh. Dorp. Parisiis 1488.

— ... summa totius logice ... Venetiis 1522. (g)

— Summa totius logicae ... Parisiis 1488; Bononiae 1498; Venetiis 1508, 1591; Oxoniae 1675 u. öfters.

— Summa Logicae. Pars Prima. Ed. Ph. Boehner. St. Bonaventure (N. Y.), Louvain 1951. (g)

— Summa Logicae. Pars Secunda et Tertiae Prima. St. Bonaventure (N. Y.), Louvain, Paderborn 1954.

— Summa totius logicae, Pars III, Kap. 30, ed. Ph. Boehner, in: The tractatus de praedestinatione..., 1945.

— Expositio aurea et admodum utilis super artem veterem edita ... cum quaestionibus Alberti parvi de Saxonia. Bononiae 1496.

— The tractatus de praedestinatione et de praescientia dei et de futuris contingentibus of William of Ockham. Ed. ... Ph. Boehner. St. Bonaventure (N. Y.) 1945.

— The tractatus de successivis attributed to William Ockham. Ed. Ph. Boehner. St. Bonaventure (N. Y.), Louvain 1944.

— Expositionis in libros artis logicae prooemium. Expositio in libros Porphyrii de praedicabilibus. Ed. E. A. Moody. (Im Druck).

— Quodlibeta, z. T. ins Engl. übers. in: R. McKeon, Selections from Mediaeval Philosophers, II (Scribners), 1930, 351—359 und 360—421.

— Quodlibeta septem. Parisiis 1487; Argentinae 1491.

— Dialogus inter magistrum et discipulum. Lugduni 1495.

488

Wilhelm von Shyreswood: Die Introductiones in logicam des W. v. S. Literar-
hist. Einl. u. Textausg. v. M. Grabmann. München 1937.
— (William Sherwood): Syncategoremata, ed. J. R. O'Donnell, in: Mediev.
Stud. 3, 1941, 46—93.

3.3. Recent works on formal logic

S. Bocheński *1.22.*, *1.23.*; Lukasiewicz *1.23.*
Bendiek, J.: Scholastische und mathematische Logik, in: Franz. Stud. 31, 1949,
13—48.
— Die Lehre von den Konsequenzen bei Pseudo-Scotus. Ebda. 34, 1952, 205
bis 234.
Bocheński, I. M.: Logistique et logique classique, in: Bull. Thom. 4, 1934/36,
240—248.
— Duae „consequentiae' Stephani de Monte, in: Angelicum 12, 1935, 397—399.
— De consequentiis Scholasticorum earumque origine. Ebda. 15, 1938, 1—18.
— Sancti Thomae Aquinatis de modalibus opusculum et doctrina. Ebda. 17,
1940, 180—218.
— On analogy, in: The Thomist 11, 1948, 424—447.
— Wstęp do teorii analogii, in: Roczn. Filos. (Lublin) 1, 1948, 64—82 (franz.
Zusammenfassung: 319 f.).
— Communications sur la logique mediévale, (zusammengef.) in: JSL 20,
1955, 90 f.
Boehner, Ph.: Der Aristotelismus im Mittelalter, in: Franz. Stud. 22, 1935,
338—347.
— Ein Gedicht auf die Logik Ockhams. Franciscus Landinus: in laudem logi-
cae Ockham. Ebda. 26, 1939, 78—85.
— Zur Echtheit der „Summa Logicae" Ockhams. Ebda. 190—193.
— Ockham's Tractatus de praedestinatione et de praescientia Dei et de futuris
contingentibus and its main problems, in: Proc. Amer. Cath. Philos. Ass. 16,
1941, 177—192.
— The text tradition of Ockham's „Ordinatio", in: The New Scholasticism
16, 1942, 203—241.
— The „notitia intuitiva" of non-existents according to William Ockham, in:
Traditio 1, 1943.
— The medieval crisis of logic and the author of the Centiloqium attributed
to Ockham, in: Franc. Stud. 25, 1944, 151—170.
— El sistema de lógica escolástica. Estudio historico y critico, in: Rev. de la
Univ. Nac. de Córdoba (Arg.) 31, 1944, 1599—1620.
— The tractatus de praedestinatione et de praescientia dei et de futuris con-
tingentibus of William Ockham. Ed. with a study on the mediaeval pro-
blem of three-valued logic by Ph. B. St. Bonaventure (N. Y.), Louvain 1945.
— Ockham's theory of truth, in: Franc. Stud. 5, 1945, 138—161.
— Scotus' teaching according to Ockham. Ebda. 6, 1946, 100—107 u. 362—375.
— Ockham's theory of signification. Ebda. 143—170.
— Ockham's theory of supposition and the notion of truth. Ebda. 261—292.
— Bemerkungen zur Geschichte der De Morganschen Gesetze in der Scholastik,
in: Arch. f. Philos. 4, 1951, 113—146.
— Does Ockham know of material implications?, in: Franc. Stud. 11, 1951,
203—230.
— Medieval Logic. An outline of its development from 1250 — c. 1400. Man-
chester 1952.
— In memoriam Philotheus Boehner OFM. 1901—1955, in: Franc. Stud. 15,
101—105.
— Ein Beitrag zur mittelalterlichen Suppositionstheorie. Amsterdam (Ange-
kündigt.)
— The Life, Writings, and Teachings of William Ockham. Edinburgh. (Im
Druck).

BIBLIOGRAPHY

Britzelmayr, W.: Über die älteste formale Logik in deutscher Sprache, in: Ztschr. f. Philos. Forsch. 1, 1947, 46 ff.

Dürr, K.: Aussagenlogik im Mittelalter, in: Erkenntnis (Den Haag) 7, 1938, 160—168.

Ferrater Mora, J.: De Boecio a Alberto de Sajonia: Un fragmento de historia de la logica, in: Imago mundi 1, 1954, 3—22.

Henry, D. P.: Numerically definite reasoning in the Cur Deus homo, in: Dom. Stud. 6, 1953, 48—55.

Michalski, K.: Le problème de la volonté à Oxford et à Paris au XIVe siècle, in: Stud. philos. (Leopoli) 2, 1937, 233—365.

Moody, E. A.: The logic of William of Ockham. New York, London 1935.

— Ockham, Buridan and Nicholas of Autrecourt, in: Franc. Stud. 7, 1947, 113—146.

— Ockham and Aegidius of Rome. Ebda. 9, 1949, 417—442.

— Truth and consequence in mediaeval logic. Amsterdam 1953.

— Comment (betr.: Bergmann, Some remarks on the ontology of Ockham), in: Philos. Rev. 63, 1954, 572—576.

Morduhai-Boltovskoi, D.: Insolubiles in scholastica et paradoxos de infinito de nostro tempore, in: Wiad. Matem. 47, 1939, 111—117.

Platzeck, E. W.: Die Lullsche Kombinatorik, in: Franz. Stud. 34, 1952, 36 ff.

Prior, A. N.: Modality de dicto and modality de re, in : Theoria (Lund) 18, 1952, 174—180.

— The parva logicalia in modern dress, in: Dom. Stud. 5, 1952, 78—87.

— On some consequentiae in Walter Burleigh, in: The New Scholasticism 27, 1953.

Salamucha, J.: Logika zdań u Wilhelma Ockhama, in: Przegl. filoz. 38, 1935, 208—239.

— Die Aussagenlogik bei Wilhelm von Ockham, üb. v. J. Bendiek, in: Franz. Stud. 32, 1950, 97—134.

— Pojawienie się zagadnień antynomialnych na gruncie logiki średniowiecznej (Erscheinung der Antinomien-Probleme in der mittelalterlichen Logik), in: Przegl. Filoz. 40, 1937 u. Sonderdruck.

— Zestawienie scholastycznych narzędzi logicznych z narzędziami logistycznymi (Vergleich logischer Techniken der Scholastik mit logistischen Techniken), in: Myśl katolicka ... (5.33.), 35—49. (Franz. Zus.fssg. 167 ff.).

Saw, R. L.: William of Ockham on terms, propositions and meaning, in: Proc. Arist. Soc. 42, 1941/42, 45—64.

Scholz, H.: Die mathematische Logik und die Metaphysik, in: Philos. Jb. d. Görres-Ges. 51, 1938, 257—291.

Swieżawski, St.: Les intentions premières et les intentions secondes chez Jean Duns Scot, in: AHDLM 9, 1934, 205—260.

Thomas, I.: Material implication in John of St. Thomas, in: Dom. Stud. 3, 1950, 180.

— Farrago logica. Ebda. 4, 1951, 69—79 (69—71: Historical Notes).

— Saint Vincent Ferrer's De suppositionibus. Ebda. 5, 1952, 88—102.

— Kilwardby on conversion. Ebda. 6, 1953, 56—76.

— Maxims in Kilwardby. Ebda. 7, 1954, 129—146.

3.4. Works on literary history and development. Older works covering the whole or large parts of medieval logic
3.41. Literary history and development

Callus, D. A.: Introduction of Aristotelian learning to Oxford, in: Proc. British Acad. 29.

Ferreira, J.: As Sumulas Logicais de Pedro Hispano e os sus comentadores. Sonderdr. aus: Colectanea de Estudos 3, 1952 (3), Braga 1952.

Grabmann, M.: Die Geschichte der scholastischen Methode. 2 Bde. Freiburg i. Br. 1909—1911.
— Die Entwicklung der mittelalterlichen Sprachlogik (Tractatus de modis significandi), in: Philos. Jb. d. Görres-Ges. 35, 1922, 121—135 u. 199—214; und in: Mittelalt. Geistesleben I, 104—141.
— Forschungsziele und Forschungswege auf dem Gebiete der mittelalterlichen Scholastik und Mystik, in: Mittelalt. Geistesleben I, 1—64.
— Mittelalterliches Geistesleben. München I 1926, II 1936.
— Bearbeitungen und Auslegungen der aristotelischen Logik aus der Zeit von Peter Abaelard bis Petrus Hispanus, in: ·Abh. d. Preuß. Akad. 1937, phil.-hist. Kl., 5.
— Kommentare zur aristotelischen Logik aus dem 12. und 13. Jh., in: Sitz.-Ber. d. Preuß. Akad., phil.-hist. Kl., 18, 1938.
— Ungedruckte lateinische Kommentare zur aristotelischen Topik aus dem 13. Jh., in: Arch. f. Kultur-Gesch. 28, 1938 (2).
— Methoden und Hilfsmittel des Aristotelesstudiums im Mittelalter, in: Sitz-. Ber. d. Bayer. Akad., phil.-hist. Abt., 1939, 5.
— Die Sophismatenliteratur des 12. u. 13. Jh. mit Textausgabe eines Sophisma des Boetius von Dacien. Münster 1940.
— Thomas von Erfurt und die Sprachlogik des mittelalterlichen Aristotelismus, in: Sitz.-Ber. d. Bayer. Akad., phil.-hist. Abt., 1943, 2.
Hunt, R. W.: The introductions to the „Artes" in the twelfth century, in: Studia mediaev. in hon. R. J. Martin, Brugis 1948, 85—112.
Isaac, J.: Le PERI HERMENEIAS en occident de Boèce à Saint Thomas. Paris 1953.
Michalski, K.: Les sources du criticisme et du scepticisme dans la philosophie du XIVe siècle. Cracovie 1924.
— Le criticisme et le scepticisme dans la philosophie du XIVe siècle, in: Bull. int. de l'Ac. Polon. d. sciences et d. lettres, Cl. d'Hist. et d. Phil., An. 1925, Cracovie 1926, 41—122.
— Les courants philosophiques à Oxford et à Paris pendant le XIVe siècle. Ebda., Cracovie 1922, 63—68.
S. a. *3.53.*, *3.91.* u. *3.92.*

3.42. Aristoteles latinus

Grabmann, M.: Aristoteles im zwölften Jahrhundert, in: Mediaev. Stud. 12, 1950, 123—162.
— Guglielmo di Moerbeke O. P. il traduttore delle opere di Aristotele. Roma 1946.
— I divieti ecclesiastici di Aristotele sotto Innocenzo III e Gregorio IX. Roma 1941.
Jourdain, A. L. M. M.: Recherches critiques sur l'art et l'origine des traductions latines d'Aristote. Paris 1819 u. 1843.
Lacombe, G.: Aristoteles latinus. Codices descripsit G. L. . . . (mit) A. Birkenmayer, M. Dulong, A. Franceschini. Pars prior: Roma 1939. Pars posterior, supplementibus indicisque instr. L. Minio-Paluello: Cambridge 1955 (S. 769—1388).
Minio-Paluello, L.: Gli Elenchi Sofistici (*2.83.*).
— The genuine text . . . (*2.83.*).
— Note sull' Aristotele latino medievale, in: Riv. di Filos. Neoscol. 42, 1950, 222—237; 43, 1951, 97—124; 44, 1952, 389—412; 46, 1954, 211—231.
— Iacobus Veneticus Grecus, canonist and translator of Aristotle, in: Traditio 8, 1952, 265—304.
— La tradizione semitico-latina del testo dei Secondi Analitici (Note sull' Aristotele latino medievale IV), in: Riv. di Filos. Neoscol. 43, 1951, 97—124.
— L'ignota versione moerbekana dei Secondi Analitici usata da S. Tomaso (Note sull'Aristotele latino medievale V). Ebda. 44, 1952, 389—397.

— Aristoteles Latinus: Codices II. Cambridge 1955. (S. soeben: Lacombe.)
— The text of Aristotle's Topics and Elenchi: the Latin tradition, in: The Class. Quart. 49, 1955, 108—118.
— The text of the Categoriae: the Latin tradition. Ebda. 39, 1945, 63—74.
van Steenberghen, F.: Aristote en Occident. Les origines de l'aristotélisme parisien. Louvain 1946.

3.43. General treatments of logic

Eibl, H.: Über einige Axiome scholastischen Denkens, in: Arch. f. Gesch. d. Philos. 29, 1924, 8—20.
Elie, H.: Le complexe significabile. Paris 1936.
Hellin, J. M.: El principio de identidad comparada según Suárez, in: Pensiamento 6, 1950, 435—463; 7, 1951, 169—202.
Klibansky, R.: The Rock of Parmenides. Medieval views on the origin of dialectic. In: Mediev. and Renaiss. Stud. 1941/43, 178—186.
Preti, G.: Studi sulla logica nel medioevo. II: Natura (oggetto, scopi, metodo) della logica. In: Riv. crit. di storia d. filos. 8, 1953, 680—697.
Rotta, P.: La filosofia del linguaggio nella patristica e nella scolastica. Torino 1909.
— La filosofia del linguaggio nel medioevo, in: Riv. d. Filos. Neosc. 32, 1940, 453—458.
Rucker, P.: Mathematik und Philosophie . . . Verwendung der mathematischen Methode in der Philosophie. Patristik und Scholastik. In: Phil. Jb. d. Görres-Ges. 53, 1940, 17—29 u. 234—245.
Xiberta, B. M.: Enquesta historica sobre el principio d'identidad comparada, in: Estud. Franc. 45, 1933, 291—336.

3.5. Arabian and Jewish philosophy and logic
3.51. Bibliography

de Menasce, P. J.: Arabische Philosophie. BESP 6. Bern 1948.
Sauvaget, J.: Introduction à l'histoire de l'Orient musulman; éléments de bibliographie. Paris 1943.
Vajda, G.: Jüdische Philosophie. BESP 19. Bern 1950.

3.52. Works of reference

Brockelmann, C.: Geschichte der arabischen Literatur. Weimar, I 1898, II 1902; Supplementband I—III Leiden 1937—1942.
Encyclopedia, The Universal Jewish: Hrsg. Isaac Landmann. 10 Bde. New York 1939 ff.
Enzyklopädie des Islams: Hrsg. Houtsma, Wensinck, Heffening, Gibb und Lévy-Provençal. 4 Bde. und 1 Erg.bd. Leiden und Leipzig 1913—1938. (Register-band noch unveröffentlicht. Vgl. BESP 6, 6 f.).

3.53. Arabian and Jewish logic

Dieterici, Fr.: Die Logik und Psychologie der Araber im 10. Jahrhundert, Leipzig 1868.
Djorr, K.: Les versions syro-arabes des Catégories d'Aristote (Diss. Paris 1946). Beirut?
Madkour, I.: L'organon d'Aristote dans le monde arabe. Paris 1934.
Pollak, I.: Die Hermeneutik des Aristoteles in der arabischen Übersetzung des Ishaq Ibn Honain. Leipzig 1913.
Sauter, K.: Die peripatetische Philosophie bei den Syrern und Arabern, in: Archiv f. Gesch. d. Philos. 17, 1904, 516—534.

3.6. Thomas Aquinas
3.61. Bibliography

S.: Bourke, Bull. Thomiste, Mandonnet u. Wyser (*3.11.*).

3.62. General accounts, works of reference

Chenu, M.-D.: Introduction a l'étude de saint Thomas d'Aquin, Montreal, Paris 1950.

Gilson, E.: Le thomisme. Paris, 6. verb. A. 1948

Grabmann, M.: Einführung in die Summa Theologiae des hl. Thomas von Aquin. Freiburg i. Br., 2. verm. A. 1928.

— Die Werke des hl. Thomas von Aquin. Münster i. W., 3. st. erw. A. 1949.

Manser, G. M.: Das Wesen des Thomismus. Freiburg i. Ü., 3. erw. A. v. P. Wyser, 1949.

Petrus a Bergamo: Tabula aurea. Bononiae 1477. Basileae 1478 u. öfters.

Schütz, L.: Thomas-Lexikon. Paderborn 1895. Nachdr. New York 1949.

3.63. His logic

S.: Bocheński, De consequentiis, Z historii, Notes (*1.23.*); S. Thomae Aqu. de modalibus (*3.3.*). Salamucha, Pojęcie (*2.3.*)

Grabmann, M.: Der Wissenschaftsbegriff des hl. Thomas v. Aquin, in: Jahresber. d. Görres-Ges. 1932/33, Köln 1934, 7*—44*.

— De fontibus historicis logicam S. Thomae de Aquino illustrantibus, in: Acta Pont. Acad. Romanae S. Thomae Aqu. 1936/37. Sonderdr. (Rom) 1938.

Mansion, A.: Date de quelques commentaires de saint Thomas sur Aristote (De interpretatione, De anima, Metaphysica), in: Studia mediaev. in hon. R. J. Martin, Brugis 1948, 271—287.

Lachance, J.: Saint Thomas dans l'histoire de la logique, in: Et. d'hist. littér. et doctr. du XIIIᵉ siècle 1, 1932, 61—104.

Manthey, Fr.: Die Sprachphilosophie des hl. Thomas von Aquin. Paderborn 1937.

Richard, T.: Philosophie du raisonnement dans la science d'après Saint Thomas. Paris (1919).

Simonin, H. D.: La notion d',,Intentio" dans l'œuvre de Saint Thomas d'Aquin, in: Rev. d. sc. philos. et theol. 19, 1930, 445—463.

Scheu, M.: The categories of being in Aristotle and St. Thomas (Diss.). Washington 1944.

Vacant, A.: La parole et le langage selon St. Thomas et selon Duns Scot, in: Ann. de Philos. Chrét. 119, vol. 21, 1889/90, 479—495 u. 529—547.

Warnach, V.: Erkennen und Sprechen bei Thomas von Aquin, in: Divus Thomas (Freiburg i. Ü.) 15, 1937, 189—218 u. 263—290; 16, 1938, 161—196.

— Das äußere Sprechen und seine Funktion nach der Lehre des heiligen Thomas v. Aq. Ebda. 16, 1938, 393—419.

3.64. Doctrine of analogy

S.: Bocheński, On analogy (*3.3.*).

Anderson, J. F.: The band of being. An essay on analogy and existence. St. Louis 1954.

Blanche, F. A.: L'analogie, in: Rev. de philos. 23, 1923, 248—270.

— La notion d'analogie dans la philosophie de St. Thomas d'Aq., in: Rev. d. sc. philos. et théol. 10, 1921, 169—193.

— Sur le sens de quelques locutions concernant l'analogie dans la langue de St. Thomas d'Aquin. Ebda. 52—59.

Gazzana, A.: L'analogia in S. Tommaso e nel Gaetano, in: Gregorianum 24, 1943, 367—383.

Goergen, A.: Die Lehre von der Analogie nach Kardinal Cajetan und ihr Verhältnis zu Thomas von Aquin. (Diss.) Speyer 1938.

Habbel, J.: Die Analogie zwischen Gott und Welt nach Thomas von Aquin. Regensburg 1928.

Landry, B.: L'analogie de proportion chez St. Thomas d'Aquin, in: Rev. néoscol. de philos. 24, 1922, 257—280.

— L'analogie de proportionnalité chez St. Thomas d'Aquin. Ebda. 454—464.

Palacios, L. E.: La analogía de la lógica y la prudencia en Juan de Santo Tomás, in: La Cienc. tom. 69, 1945, 221—235.

Pénido, M. T. L.: Le rôle de l'analogie en théologie dogmatique. Paris 1931.

Phelan, G. B.: St. Thomas and analogy. Milwaukee 1941.

Ramirez, J.: De analogia secundum doctrinam aristotelico-thomisticam, in: La Cienc. tom. 24, 1921, 20—40 u. 195—214 u. 337—357; 25, 1922, 17—38.

3.7. Duns Scotus and Pseudo-Scotus
3.71. Bibliography

S.: Schäfer (3.11.).

Bettoni, E.: Vent'anni di studi scotistici (1920—1940). Saggio bibliografico. Milano 1943.

Minges, P.: Die skotistische Literatur des 20. Jahrhunderts, in: Franz. Stud. 4, 1917, 49—67 u. 177—198.

3.72. General accounts, works of reference

Fernández Garzía, M.: Lexicon scholasticum ... in quo termini ... philosophiam ac theologiam spectantes a b. Ioanne Duns Scoto declarantur. Ad Claras Aquas 1910.

Gilson, E.: Jean Duns Scot. Introduction à ses positions fondamentales. Paris 1952.

Harris, C. R. S.: Duns Scotus. Oxford 1927.

Longpré, E.: La philosophie du bienheureux Duns Scot. Paris 1924.

3.73. Logic and theory of analogy

S.: Bendiek, Die Lehre; Swieżawski, Les intentions (beide 3.3.); Bocheński: Z historii; Notes; De consequentiis (1.23.).

Barth, T.: De fundamento univocationis apud Ioannem Duns Scotum, in: Antonianum 14, 1939, 181—206 u. 277—298 u. 373—392.

— Zum Problem der Eindeutigkeit, in: Philos. Jb. d. Görres-Ges. 85, 1942, 300—321.

Belmond, S.: Analogie et univocité d'après J. Duns Scot, in: Études Franc. 2(?) 1951, 173—186.

Heidegger, M.: Die Kategorien- und Bedeutungslehre des Duns Scotus. Tübingen 1916.

Minges, P.: Beitrag zur Lehre des Duns Scotus über die Univokation des Seinsbegriffes, in: Philos. Jb. d. Görres-Ges. 20, 1907, 306—323.

Schmaus, M.: Die Quaestio des Petrus Sutton OFM. über die Univokation des Seins, in: Coll. Franc. 3, 1933, 5—25.

Shircel, C. L.: The univocity of the concept of being in the philosophy of John Duns Scot. Washington (Diss. Cath. Univ.) 1942.

Werner, K.: Die Sprachlogik des Johannes Duns Scotus, in: Sitz-Ber. d. Wiener Akad. 85, 1877, 545—597.

3.8. William of Ockham
3.81. Bibliography

Federhofer, F.: Ein Beitrag zur Bibliographie und Biographie des W. von Ockham, in: Phil. Jb. d. Görres-Ges. 38, 1925, 26—48.

Heynck, V.: Ockham-Literatur 1919—1949, in: Franz. Stud. 32, 1950, 164—183.

3.82. General accounts and important details

Abbagnano, N.: Guglielmo di Ockham. Lanciano 1931.
Baudry, L.: Guillaume d'Ockham. I. Paris 1950.
— A propos de la théorie occamiste de la relation, in: AHDLM 9, 1934.
— Les rapports de Guillaume d'Occam et de Walter Burleigh. Ebda.
— Sur trois manuscrits occamiste. Ebda. 9—10, 1935/36, 129—162.
Doncoeur, P.: Le nominalisme de Guillaume d'Occam. La théorie de la rela-
tion, in: Rev. néoscol. de philos. 23, 1921, 5—25.
Giacon, C.: Guglielmo di Occam. 2 Bde. Milano 1941.
Hofer, J.: Biographische Studien über Wilhelm von Ockham, in: Archivum
Franciscanum Historicum 6, 1913, 211—233 u. 439—465 u. 654—669.
Lindsay, J.: The logic and metaphysics of Occam, in: The Monist 30, Oct. 1920,
521—547.

3.83. His logic

S.: Boehner, Moody, Salamucha, Saw (*3.3.*).

de Lagarde, G.: Un exemple de logique ockhamiste, in: Rev. du Moyen-âge
latin 1, 1945, 237—258.
Menges, M. C.: The concept of univocity regarding the predication of God and
creature according to William Ockham. St. Bonaventure (N. Y.), Louvain,
Paderborn 1952.
Moody, E. A.: The logic of William of Ockham. New York, London 1935.
Webering, D.: Theory of demonstration according to William Ockham. St. Bo-
naventure (N. Y.), Louvain, Paderborn 1953.
Weinberg, J.: Ockham's conceptualism, in: Philos. Rev. (New York) 50, 1941,
523—528.

3.9. Other logicians
3.91. Peter of Spain

Grabmann, M.: Handschriftliche Forschungen und Funde zu den philosophi-
schen Schriften des Petrus Hispanus, in: Sitz.-Ber. d. Bayer. Akad., phil.-
hist. Abt., 1936, 9.
Prantl, C.: M. Psellus und Petrus Hispanus. Leipzig 1867.
Rose, V.: Pseudo-Psellus und Petrus Hispanus, in: Hermes 2, 1867, 146 f. u. 465 ff.
Simonin, H. D.: Les Summulae Logicales de Petrus Hispanus, in: AHDLM 5,
1930, 267—278.
Stapper, R.: Die Summulae Logicales des Petrus Hispanus und ihr Verhältnis
zu Michael Psellus, in: Festschr. z. elfhundertj. Jubil. d. dt. Campo Santo in
Rom, Freiburg i. Br. 1897, 130—138.
— Papst Johannes XXI. Münster i. W. 1898.
Thurot, Ch.: Bespr. v. Prantl, Geschichte d. Logik im Abendlande, in: Rev.
crit. d'hist. et de litt. 1867, 1. Sem., Nr. 13, 194—203.
— Bespr. v. Prantl, Michael Psellus und Petrus Hispanus. Ebda. 2. Sem., Nr. 27,
4—11.
— De la logique de Pierre d'Espagne, in: Rev. archéol. 10, 1864, 267—281.

3.92. Various

Baeumker, Cl.: Die „Impossibilia" des Sigers von Brabant, in: Beitr. z. Gesch.
d. Philos. d. Mittelalters II. Münster i. W. 1898.
Bibliographia Albertina, in: S. Rituum Congregatione (sic), Extensionis · · ·
addito doctoris titulo . . . B. Alberti Magni . . . Romae 1931.
Doyle, J.: John of St. Thomas and mathematical logic, in: The New Scholasticism 27, 1953, 3—38.
Grabmann, M.: De Thoma Erfordiensi auctore Grammaticae quae Ioanni Duns

Scoto adscribitur speculativae, in: **Archivum Franciscanum Historicum 15,** 1922, 273—277.
— Die italienische Thomistenschule des XIII. und beginnenden XIV. Jahrhunderts, in: Grabmann, Mittelalterl. Geistesleben I, München 1926, 332 bis 391.
— Bate, Heinrich (Verf. d. In An. Post. v. Ps.-Scot), in: Lexik. f. Theol. u. Kirche II, Freiburg i. Br. 1931, 35.
— Die Stellung des Kardinals Cajetan in der Geschichte des Thomismus und der Thomistenschule, in: Grabmann, Mittelalterl. Geistesleben II, München 1936, 602—613. S. a.: Gazzana u. Goergen (*3.64.*).
— Ein tractatus de universalibus und andere logische Inedita aus dem 12. Jahrh. im Cod. lat. 2486 der Nationalbibliothek in Wien, in: Mediaev. Stud. 9, 1947, 56—70.
— Einzelgestalten aus der mittelalterlichen Dominikaner- und Thomistenschule, in: Grabmann, Mittelalterl. Geistesleben II, München 1936, 512—613.
— Forschungen zur Geschichte der ältesten deutschen Thomistenschule des Dominikanerordens. Ebda. I, München 1926, 392—431.
— Mitteilungen über Werke des Adam von Bocfeld aus Ms. lat. quart. 906 der Preußischen Staatsbibliothek in Berlin, in: Divus Thomas (Freiburg/Schw.) 1939, 1.
Minio-Paluello, L.: The „ars disserendi" of Adam of Balsham „Parvipontanus" (Adam von Petit-Pont), in: Mediaev. and Renaiss. Stud. 3, 1954, 116—169.
Reis, L.: The predicables and Predicaments in the Totius Summa logicae Aristotelis. New York 1936.
Weinberg, J.: Nicolaus of Autrecourt. Princeton 1948.
S. a.: Palacios (*3.64.*).

4. THE PERIOD OF TRANSITION

4.1. General
4.11. Bibliography

S.: Frischeisen-Köhler/Moog, Windelband (*4.12.*); Rabus, Ziehen (*1.24.*).

Lemcke, J.: Versuch einer Jungius-Bibliographie, in: Beiträge zur Jungius-Forschung (Festschr. d. Hamburgischen Universität), hrsg. A. Meyer, Hamburg 1929, 88—93.

4.12. General accounts

Fischer, K.: Geschichte der neueren Philosophie. Mannheim, Heidelberg 1854 ff. Letzte v. F. selbst bes. A.: Jubiläumsausg. 1897 ff.
Frischeisen-Köhler, M. u. W. Moog: Die Philosophie der Neuzeit bis zum Ende des XVIII. Jhs. Basel 13. A. 1953 (Unv. Nachdr. d. 12. A. v. 1924). (Bd. III v. Ueberweg: *1.111.*)
Österreich, T. K.: Die deutsche Philosophie des XIX. Jhs. und d. Gegenwart. Basel 13. A. 1951 (Unv. Nachdr. d. 12. A. v. 1924). (Bd. IV v. Ueberweg: *1.111.*)
— (Hrsg.) Die Philosophie des Auslandes vom Beginn des 19. Jhs. bis auf die Gegenwart. Basel 13. A. 1953 (Unv. Nachdr. d. 12. A. v. 1928). (Bd. V v. Ueberweg: *1.111.*)
Windelband, W.: Lehrbuch der Geschichte der Philosophie. Hrsg. H. Heimsoeth. 14. erg. A. Tübingen 1948.

BIBLIOGRAPHY

4.2. Editions of texts

Aemstelredamus, A.: S. Agricola, De inventione 1570.

Agricola, R.: De inventione dialectica. 1480. (Und mehrere Ausgaben im 16. Jahrh.)

— Epitome commentariorum dialecticae inventionis Rodolphi Agricolae per Bartolomeum Latomum. Coloniae 1532. (Ausz. aus d. vorangeh. Werk.)

— Libellus de formando studio ... cuius auctores sunt ... Rod. Agricola, Erasm. Roterodamus, Phil. Melanchthon. U. a. Coloniae 1532.

— De inventione dialectica libri omnes ... scholiis illustrati Ioannis Phrissemii, Alardi Aemstelredami, Reinardi Hadamarii, quorum scholia ... congressit Ioannes Noviomagus. Coloniae 1570.

Aldrich, H.: Artis logicae compendium. 1691, und häufig später.

Alstedius, J. H.: Compendium I: systematis logici; II: gymnasii logici. Herbornae 1611.

— Logicae systema harmonicum ... Herbornae Nassov. 1614.

— Compendium logicae harmonicae ... Herbornae Nassov. 1615.

— Claris artis Lullianae et verae logices duos in libellos tributa. Argentorati 1633.

Arnauld, A. und P. Nicole: La logique ou l'art de penser. Paris 1662, Amsterdam 1675.

(—) La logique ou l'art de penser. Nouv. éd., rev. et corr. Paris (1752). (g)

Bartholinus, C.: Logicae peripateticae praecepta ita perspicue atque breviter scholiis exemplisque illustrata etc. Ed. sexta. Francofurti 1621. (1. A. wohl 1611).

Baynes, T. S.: An essay on the new analytic of logical forms. Edinburgh 1850.

Beneke, F. E.: Syllogismorum analyticorum origines et ordo naturalis. Berolini 1839.

Bentham, G.: Outline of a new system of logic. London 1827.

Bentham, J.: Essay on logic, in: The works of J. B., ed. John Bowring, Bd. VIII, Edinburgh 1843, 213—294.

Bergius, C.: Artificium Aristotelico-Lullio-Rameum, in quo per artem intelligendi, logicam etc. Bregae 1615.

Beurhusius, F.: S. Ramus, Dialecticae libri duo ... Francoforti 1591.

— Defensio Petri Rami dialecticae etc. 1588.

— Paedagogia logica (in drei Teilen). 2. Teil: Colon. 1588. 3. Teil: 1596.

Carpentarius (Charpentier) J.: Universae artis disserendi descriptio ex Aristotelis logico organo collecta etc. Paris 1. A. 1560, 2. A. 1564.

— Animadversiones in libros III institutionum dialecticarum Petri Rami. Paris 1554.

— Ad expositionem disputationis de methodo, contra Thessalum Ossatum ... responsio. Paris 1564.

— Compendium in communem artem disserendi. Paris 1565.

Clauberg, J.: Logica vetus et nova. Duisburg 1556, Amstelodami 1654.

— Opera omnia Philosophica. Amstelodami 1691.

— Logica contracta. Tiguri 1700.

Clericus (Leclerc) J.: Logica s. Ars ratiocinandi. Amst. 1698.

Condillac, E. Bonnot de: Logique. Paris 1780.

Cramer, D.: Disputatio de principiis logicae Aristoteleae partibus ... Witebergae 1593.

— Viginti duae disputationes logicae. Vitemb. 1593. (Gegen Ramus.)

Crusius, C. A.: De summis rationis principiis. Lips. 1752.

Descartes, R.: Regulae ad directionem ingenii, in: Œuvres de Descartes, ed. Ch. Adam et P. Tannery, X, Paris 1908.

Dieterich (Dietericus) C.: Epitome praeceptorum dialecticae etc. Lipsiae 1636.

— Institutiones logicae et rhetoricae. Giessae 1609.

Drobisch, M. W.: Neue Darstellung der Logik nach ihren einfachsten Verhältnissen. 4. A. Leipzig 1875.

497

BIBLIOGRAPHY

Erasmus von Rotterdam: S. Agricola, Libellus.
Erdmann, B.: Logik. 1. Band: Logische Elementarlehre. Halle 1892. 2., völlig umg. A. 1907.
Euler, L.: Lettres à une princesse d'Allemagne sur quelques sujets de physique et de philosophie, 1768—1772. Deutsche Übersetzung: Leipzig 1773—1780. S. a. Lambert, Briefwechsel zw. L. E. und J. H. Lambert (5.2.).
Fonseca, Petrus: Institutionum dialecticarum libri 8. Coloniae 1623.
Freigius, J. Th.: Ciceronianus Joan. Thomae Freigii in quo: ex Ciceronis monumentis Ratio instituendi locos communes demonstrata ... Basileae 1575.
— Trium artium logicarum, grammaticae, dialecticae et rhetoricae breves succinctiae ... Basileae 1568.
— Questiones Logicae et Ethicae. Basileae 1574.
— Logicae Rameae triumphus. Basileae 1583.
— Rhetorica, poetica, logica, ad usum rudiorum in epitomen redactae ... Noribergae 1585.
Goclenius, R.: Problematum logicorum ... pars I—IV. Marpurgi 1590—1595. Dasselbe, aber pars I—V: 1594—1596.
— Questiones et disputationes logicae. Marpurgi 1594.
— ... partitionum dialecticarum ex Platone, Aristotele, Cicerone, Philippo ... et aliis ... libri duo. Francofurti 1595, 2. A. 1598.
— Praxis logica ex privatis eius lectionibus. Francofurti 1595. (Auch in d. 2. A. von „partitionum" enthalten.)
— Explicatio quorundam locorum obscuriorum, quae occurrunt in doctrina de ratione solvendi fallaces conclusiunculas. Marpurgi 1597.
— Ratio solvendi vitiosas argumentationes: pars critices: ad institutiones dialecticas pertinens. Marpurgi 1597; 1611.
— ... isagoge in Organum Aristotelis ... Francofurti 1598.
— Commentariolus de ratione definiendi. In usum academiae Marpurgensis. Francofurti 1600.
— De tropo definiendi. Marpurg. 1602.
— Institutionum logicarum libri tres. Marpurgi I: 1608, II und III: 1605.
— ... controversiae logicae et philosophiae, ad praxin logicam directae ... Marpurgi 1609.
Gredt, J.: Elementa philosophiae aristotelico-thomisticae I. Ed. quinta Friburgi Brisgoviae 1929.
Hadamarius, R.: S. Agricola, De inventione 1570.
Hamilton, W.: Lectures on logic by Sir W. H., I und II in einem Band; Edinburgh, London 1860 (Voll. III und IV der Lectures on Metaphysics and Logic by Sir W. H., ed. H. L. Mansel and John Veitch). Auch als: Lectures on logic. 2 Bde. Edinburgh 1866.
Hermann, C.: Philosophische Grammatik. Leipzig 1858.
Höfler, A.: Logik. 2. A. Wien und Leipzig 1922.
Horneius, C.: Institutiones logicae. 2. A. Francof. 1653.
Husserl, E.: Logische Untersuchungen. 2 Bde. Halle 1900—1901. 2., umgearb. A. in 3 Bänden: Halle 1913—1921.
Itterus, M. A.: Synopsis philosophiae rationalis seu Nucleus praeceptorum logicorum etc. 2. A. Francof. 1660.
Jungius, J.: Logica Hamburgensis. Hamburgi 1635, 1638, 1681 (g).
Kant, I.: Die falsche Spitzfindigkeit der vier syllogistischen Figuren erwiesen. Königsberg 1762.
— Kritik der reinen Vernunft, 2. A. 1787. In: Kants gesammelte Schriften, hrsg. v. d. Kgl. Preuß. Akad. d. Wiss., Bd. 3 (= Erste Abteilung: Werke, Dritter Band). Berlin 1904.
Keckermann, B.: Gymnasium Logicum. Libri tres. Hannoviae 1608.
— Opera omnia. Genevae 1614.
— Resolutio systematis logici maioris in tabellas pleniores, quam quae antehac fuerunt. Hanoviae 1621.

498

Keckermann, B.: Systema logicae. ... Hanoviae 1620. (Auch frühere Ausgaben.)
— Systema logicae minus. Hanoviae 1618.
Keynes, J. N.: Studies and exercices in formal logic including a generalization of logical processes in their application to complex inferences. 4. ed. re-written and enlarged. London 1906. Neudr. London 1928.
Kircher, A.: Ars magna sciendi s. combinatoria. Amstelod. 1669.
— Polygraphia nova et universalis ex combinatoria arte detecta. (Rom) 1663.
Langius, J. C.: Inventum novum quadrati logici universalis in trianguli quoque formam commode redacti. Giss. 1714.
Latomus, Bartolomeus: S. Agricola, Epitome.
Lipps, T.: Grundzüge der Logik. Hamburg 1893. Unv. Neudr. Leipzig, Hamburg 1912.
Mansel, H. L.: The limits of a demonstrative science considered in a letter to the Rev. W. Whewell. Oxford 1853.
Martinus, J.: Institutionum logicarum libri VIII. Wittebergae 1610.
— Logicae peripateticae per dichotomias in gratiam Ramistarum resolutae libri II. 4. A. Wittebergae 1614; 5. A. 1616.
— Praelectiones extemporaneae in systema logicum B. Keckermanni. 1617.
Melanchthon, Ph.: Erotemata dialectices. Wittenberg 1541. Neudr. in: Corpus Reformatorum, Halle und Braunschweig 1834 ff., Bd. XIII.
  S. a. Agricola, Libellus; Ramus, Dialecticae libri duo ... Francoforti 1591.
Mill, J. St.: A system of logic rationative and inductive. 2 Bde. London 1843, 9. A. 1875, Volksausg. 1884. Deutsch v. J. Schiel: Braunschweig 1849 und öfters.
— Gesammelte Werke. Deutsch hrsg. v. Th. Gomperz, Leipzig 1869 ff.
Niphus, A.: Aristotelis Περὶ ἑρμηνείας liber. Parisiis 1540.
Noviomagus, Joh.: S. Agricola, De inventione 1570.
Pesch, T.: Institutiones logicales secundum principia S. Thomae Aquinatis ad usum scholasticum accomodavit T. P. 2 Teile, 3 Bde. (Freiburg i. Br.) 1888 bis 1890.
Pfänder, A.: Logik. 2. A. Halle 1929.
Phrissemius, Joh.: S. Agricola, De inventione 1570.
Piscator, J.: Animadversiones in dialecticam P. Rami exemplis Sacr. literarum passim illustratae. 2. A. Francofurt 1582.
Poiret, P.: Tractatus de vera methodo inveniendi verum. Amstelodami 1692.
Ramus, P.: Dialecticae libri duo: et his e regione comparati Philippi Melan. thonis (sic!) dialecticae libri quatuor; cum explicationum et collationum notis ... auctore Frederico Beurhusio. Editio secunda. Francoforti 1591.
— Petri Rami ... dialecticae libri duo ... Parisiis 1556. (g)
— Aristoteleae animadversiones. Paris 1543.
— Schola in liberales artes, grammaticam, rhetoricam, dialecticam, physicam, metaphysicam. Basilea 1569.
— Dialecticae partitiones. (Paris) 1543. Als Institutionum dialecticarum libri III 1553 und als Dialecticae libri II 1556 wieder erschienen.
— Institutionum dialecticarum libri III. Parisiis 1549.
— Dialectique. 1555.
— Prooemium reformandae Parisiensis Academiae, in: Opera, Basileae 1569, 1061 ff.
— Defensio pro Aristotele adv. Jac. Schecium. Laus. 1571.
Reid, Th.: A brief account of Aristotle's logic, with remarks, in: The works of Th. R. ... Preface, notes ... by Sir W. Hamilton ... Vol. II. 8. A. Edinburgh 1880, 681—714.
Saurius, M. J.: Syntagmatis logici VI. Stetini 1656.
Scharfius, J.: Manuale logicum. 8. A. Witteberg 1657. Auch als: Medulla manualis logici Scharfiani. 3. A. Jena 1656.
Schegk, J.: De demonstratione libri XV, novum opus, Galeni librorum eiusdem argumenti jacturam resarciens. Basil. 1564.
Scheibler, Ch.: ... opus logicum. Marpurgi Cattorum 1634.

BIBLIOGRAPHY

— Opus logicam quatuor partibus universum hujus artis systema comprehendens. Ed. novissima. Genevae 1651.
Sigwart, Chr. von: Logik. Freiburg i. Br. I 1873, II 1878. 2. A. 1889.
Sigwart, H. C. W.: Handbuch zu Vorlesungen über die Logik. Tübingen 1818.
— Handbuch der theoretischen Philosophie. Tübingen 1820.
Snell(ius), R.: Commentarius doctissimus in dialecticam Petri Rami. Sigenae Nassov. 1597.
Sturmius, J.: Partitionum dialecticorum libri 3. Argentorati 1591.
Talaeus, A.: Opera ... (Darin: In Topica Ciceronis ad Trebatium. In Paradoxa ad M. Brutum.) Ed. J. Th. Freigius. Basileae 1576.
— Rhetorica e Petri Rami praelectionibus observata. Francofurti 1579, 1582; Bernae 1616; und andere Ausg.
— ... rhetoricae libri duo, Petri Rami praelectionibus illustrati. Basileae 1569.
Thompson, W.: Outlines on the necessary laws of thought. London 1842. 8. A. 1882.
Timplerus, C.: Logicae systema methodicum libris V comprehensum etc. Hanoviae 1612.
Tschirnhaus, E. W. Graf v.: Medicina mentis s. artis inveniendi praecepta generalia. Amsterdam 1687, Leipzig 1695.
Ueberweg, F.: System der Logik und Geschichte der logischen Lehren. 5. A. Bonn 1882.
Valla, L.: Dialecticae disputationes contra Aristotelicos, in: Opera. Basileae 1540.
Vedel(ius), N.: Rationale theologicum seu de necessitate et vero usu principiorum rationis ac philosophiae in controversiis theologicis libri tres. Genevae 1628.
Vives, L.: De disciplinis libri XX. (Antwerpen) 1531. Coloniae 1536.
— Gesamtausgabe, Valent. Edet. 1785.
Wallis, J.: Institutio logicae. Oxon. 1687, und häufig später.
Watts, I.: Logic or the rihgt use of reason in the enquiry after truth etc. London 1724. (Deutsch: Leipzig 1765.)
— Supplement to his treatise of logic. London 1741.
Weigel, E.: Analysis Aristotelica ex Euclide restituta etc. Jenae 1658.
— Universi corporis pansophici caput summum etc. Jenae 1673.
Weise, Chr.: Doctrina logica. Zittau 1681. Lips., Francof. 1690.
— Nucleus logicae. Zittau 1691. Lips. 1706. Gießen 1712.
— Curieuse Fragen über die Logica. Leipzig 1700.
Wendelinus, M. F.: Logicae Institutiones. Servestae 1648.
Whately, R.: Elements of logic, London 1826. 4. A. 1831, 9. A. 1848.
Wilkins, J.: The mathematical and philosophical works of J. W. London 1708.
— An essay towards a real character and a philosophical language; an alphabetical dictionary. London 1668.
Wolff, Chr.: Vernünftige Gedanken von den Kräften des menschlichen Verstandes und ihrem richtigen Gebrauch in der Erkenntnis der Wahrheit. Halle 1712, 1754.
Wundt, W.: Logik. Stuttgart 1911—20.

4.3. Literature

Anschutz, R. P.: The logic of J. St. Mill, in: Mind 58, 1949, 277—305.
Beth, E. W.: Kants Einteilung der Urteile in analytische und synthetische, in: Alg. Nederl. Tijdschr. v. Wijsb. en Psych. 46, 1953/54.
— Nieuwentyt's significance for the philosophy of science, in: Synthese, 1955.
Broad, C. D.: Dr. J. N. Keynes, in: Nature 164, 1949, 1031 f.
Dürr, K.: Die Entwicklung der Dialektik (1.23.).
— Les diagrammes logiques de Leonhard Euler et de John Venn, in: Actes Xme Congr. Int. de Philos., Amsterdam 1949, 720 f.
— Die Syllogistik des Johannes Hospinianus, in: Synthese (Bussum, Niederlande) 9, 5, 472—484.

Faust, A.: Die Dialektik Rudolf Agricolas, in: Arch. f. Oesch. d. Philos. 34, 1922, 117—135.
Göldel, R. W.: Die Lehre von der Identität in der deutschen Logik-Wissenschaft seit Lotze ... Mit einer Bibliographie zur ... Identitäts-Lehre ... seit der Mitte des 19. Jahrh. Leipzig 1935.
Kückelhahn, L.: Johannes Sturm. Leipzig 1872.
Meyer-Abich, A.: Joachim Jungius — ein Philosoph vor Leibniz, in: Beiträge zur Leibniz-Forschung I, Reutlingen 1947, 138—152.
Noel, G.: Logique de Condillac. Paris 1902.
Pró, D. F.: La concepción de la lógica en Aristoteles, Santo Tomás y Hegel, in: Philosophia (Mendoza) 2, 1945, 229—263; 3, 1946, 71—78 u. 275—290.
Schmidt, C.: La vie et les travaux de Jean Sturm. Strasbourg 1855.
Stammler, G.: Deutsche Logikarbeit seit Hegels Tod als Kampf von Mensch, Ding und Wahrheit. I: Berlin 1936.
Ushenko, A.: The logics of Hegel and Russell, in: Philos. and. phenomenol. research 10, 1949, 107—114.
Wojtowicz, T.: Die Logik von Johann Jakob Breitinger 1701—1776. (Diss. Zürich) Paris 1947.

5. THE MATHEMATICAL VARIETY OF LOGIC

5.1. General
5.11. Bibliography

Anonymer Verfasser: Notice biographique (Eine Biographie Feys' und Bibliographie seiner Schriften), in: Synthese 7, 1948/49, 447—452.
Beth, E. W.: Logica en grondslagenonderzoek 1940—1945 (Logik und Grundlagenforschung 1940—1945), in: Alg. Nederl. Tijdschr. v. Wijsb. en Psych. 38, 1946, 103—108.
— Symbolische Logik und Grundlegung der exakten Wissenschaften. BESP 3. Bern 1948.
Church, A.: A bibliography of symbolic logic, in: JSL 1, 1936, 121—218.
— A bibliography of symbolic logic — Part II, in: JSL 3, 1938, 178—212. Sep.: Providence (R. I.) 1939.
— Brief bibliography of formal logic, in: Proc. of the Amer. Acad. of Arts and Sciences 80, 1952, 155—172.
Denonn, L. E.: Bibliography of the writings of Bertrand Russell to 1944. In: The philos. of B. Russell. Ed. by P. A. Schilpp. Evanston, Chicago 1944, 743—790.
Dürr, K.: Der logische Positivismus. BESP 11. Bern 1948.
Feigl, H.: Selected bibliography of logical empiricism, in: Rev. int. de philos. (Brüssel) 4, 1950, 95—102.
Fraenkel, A.: Einleitung in die Mengenlehre. Berlin, 2. A. 1923, 3. A. 1928.
Henle, P., H. M. Kallen, S. K. Langer (hrsg.): Henry M. Sheffer. A bibliography, in: Structure, method and meaning. Essays in honor of Henry M. Sheffer. New York 1951, XV f.

* Es ist in der mathematischen Logik nicht leicht, historische Forschung von systematischer zu unterscheiden. Zudem besteht schon eine musterhafte Bibliographie für die mathematische Logik (von A. Church). So beschränkt sich dieser 5. Abschnitt auf die Titel derjenigen Schriften, (1) die in diesem Werk zitiert sind, (2) die als die wichtigsten angesehen werden, (3) die einen ausgesprochen historischen Charakter haben.

Für Schriften, die nicht in Kongreßsprachen verfaßt sind, ist zu beachten, daß ab 1936 fast alles Angegebene im JSL besprochen ist.

BIBLIOGRAPHY

Leggett, H. W.: Bertrand Russell (s. unten: *5.7.*).
Lewis, C. I.: A survey of symbolic logic (s. unten: *5.2.*).
Lowe, V. und R. C. Baldwin: Bibliography of the writings of Alfred North Whitehead to November, 1941 (with selected reviews). In: The philos. of A. N. Whitehead. Ed. by P. A. Schilpp. Evanston, Chigago 1941, 703—725.
Mac Lane, S.: Symbolic logic, in: The Amer. math. monthly 46, 1939, 289—296.
Martin, N. M.: Postscript. In: J. Jørgensen, The development of logical empiricism, Chicago 1951, 91—99.
Schröder, E.: Vorlesungen über die Algebra der Logik (exakte Logik), I und II/2. (*5.2.*)
Venn, J.: Symbolic logic. London 1881. 2. A. 1894.
Zeitschrift für mathematische Logik und Grundlagen der Mathematik. Hrsg. G. Asser und K. Schröter. Berlin.

5.12. History of philosophy and mathematics

Schmidt, A.: Mathematische Grundlagenforschung (Enzykl. d. math. Wiss. Bd. I, T. I, 2). Leipzig 1950. (Darin Bibliographie.)

5.2. Texts

Ajdukiewicz, K.: Die syntaktische Konnexität, in: Studia philos. (Leopoli) 1, 1935, 1—27.
Behmann, H.: Beiträge zur Algebra der Logik, in: Math. Annalen 86, 1922, 163—229.
Bocheński, I. M.: On the categorical syllogism, in: Dom. Stud. 1, 1948, 35—57.
Bolzano, B.: Wissenschaftslehre. 4. Bde. Neudr., 2. verb. A. hrsg. W. Schultz, Leipzig I—II 1929, III 1930, IV 1931.
Boole, G.: Collected logical works. Ed. P. E. B. Jourdain. 2 Bde. Chicago, New York 1916. 2. A. 1940. 3. A. New York 1951.
— The mathematical analysis of logic, being an essay toward a calculus of deductive reasoning. London, Cambridge 1847. Neudr. in: G. Boole's Coll. log. works; u.: Oxford 1948, 1951 (g).
— The calculus of logic, in: The Cambridge and Dublin math. Journal 3, 1848, 183—198. Neudr. in: G. Boole's Coll. log. works I.
— An investigation of the laws of thought, on which are founded the mathematical theories of logic and probabilities. London 1854. Neudr. ebda.
— Studies in logic and probability. Ed. R. Rhees. London 1952.
Brouwer, L. E. J.: Over de grondslagen van de wiskunde (Über die Grundlagen der Mathematik). (Diss.) Amsterdam, Leipzig 1907.
— De onbetrouwbaarheid der logische principes (Die Unzuverlässigkeit der logischen Prinzipien), in: Tijdschr. v. wijsbeg. 2, 1908, 152—158. Neudr. in: Brouwer, Wiskunde-waarheid-werkelijkheid, Groningen 1919.
— Intuitionisme en formalisme. Groningen 1912. Neudr. ebda. Engl.: Intuitionism and formalism, übers. v. A. Dresden, in: Bull. Amer. Math. Soc. 20, 1913—1914, 81—96.
— Begründung der Mengenlehre unabhängig vom logischen Satz vom ausgeschlossenen Dritten, in: Verh. Kon. Akad. Amsterdam (Sect. 1) 12, 5, 1918 u. 12, 7, 1919.
— Intuitionistische Betrachtungen über den Formalismus, in: Sitz.-Ber. Preuß. Akad., Phys.-math. Kl., 1928, 48—52. Auch in: Kon. Akad. Amsterdam, Proc., 31, 1928, 374—379.
Burali-Forti, C.: Una questione sui numeri transfiniti, in: Rend. Circolo Matem. Palermo 11, 1897, 154—164.
Carnap, R.: Logische Syntax der Sprache. Wien 1934. Engl.: The logical syntax of language. New York 1937.
— Introduction to semantics. Cambridge (Mass.) 1942 (od. 46).

502

BIBLIOGRAPHY

Carnap, R.: Meaning and necessity. A study in semantics and modal logic. Chigago 1947.

Castillon, G. F.: Mémoire sur un nouvel algorithme logique, in: Mém. Acad. R. Sc. et Belles-Lettres (Berlin) 53, 1805, Cl. de philos. spéc., 3—24.

Chwistek, L.: Zasada sprzeczności w świetle nowszych badań Bertranda Russella (Das Widerspruchsprinzip im Lichte der neuesten Forschungen Bertrand Russells), in: Rozpr. Akad. Um. (Kraków), Wydz. hist.-filoz. 2, Ser. 30, 1912, 270—334.

— Antynomje logiki formalnej, in: Przegl. filoz. 24, 1921, 164—171.

— Über die Antinomien der Prinzipien der Mathematik, in: Math. Zeitschr. 14, 1922, 236—243.

— Zasady czystej teorji typów (Prinzipien der reinen Typentheorie), in: Przegl. filoz. 25, 1922, 359—391.

— The theory of constructive types, in: Roczn. Pol. Tow. Matem. 2, 1924, 9—48; 3, 1925, 92—141.

— Über die Hypothesen der Mengenlehre. in: Math. Zeitschr. 25, 1926, 439 bis 473.

— The limits of science. Üb. H. C. Brodie u. A. P. Coleman. Einl. u. Anh. v. H. C. Brodie. London 1947, New York 1948.

Couturat, L.: Besp. v. Schröder, Vorlesungen über die Algebra der Logik, Bde. I und II/1, in: Bull. d. sc. mathém., 2. S., 24, 1900, 49—68.

Curry, H. B.: Grundlagen der kombinatorischen Logik, in: Amer. journ. of math. 52, 1930, 509—536 u. 789—834.

Delboeuf, J. R. L.: Logique algorithmique, in: Rev. philos. de la Fr. et de l'Etr., 1876, 225—252 u. 335—355 u. 545—595. Neudr. Liège, Bruxelles 1877.

De Morgan, A.: Formal logic or the calculus of inference, necessary and probable. London 1847. Neudr. (hrsg. A. E. Taylor) Chicago, London 1926.

— On the symbols of logic, the theory of syllogism, and in particular of the copula, and the application of the theory of probabilities to some questions of evidence, in: Trans. Cambr. Philos. Soc. 9, 1856, 79—127.

— On the syllogism, no. III, and on logic in general. Ebda. 10, 1864, 173—230.

— On the syllogism, no. IV, and on the logic of relations. Ebda. 331—358.

Ellis, R. L.: The mathematical and other writings of Robert Leslie E. Ed. W. Walton. Cambridge 1863.

— Notes on Boole's Laws of Thought. Ebda. 391—393.

Frege, G.: Rechnungsmethoden, die sich auf eine Erweiterung des Größenbegriffes gründen. (Habil.-Schr.) Jena 1874.

— Über eine Weise, die Gestalt eines Dreiecks als complexe Größe aufzufassen, in: Jenaische Zeitschr. f. Naturwiss. 12, 1878, Suppl.-Heft, S. XVII.

— Begriffsschrift, eine der arithmetischen nachgebildete Formelsprache des reinen Denkens. Halle 1879.

— Über Anwendungen der Begriffsschrift, in: Sitz.-Ber. Jenaisch. Ges. f. Medizin u. Naturwiss. für das Jahr 1879, 29—33.

— Über die wissenschaftliche Berechtigung einer Begriffsschrift, in: Zeitschr. f. Philos. u. philos. Krit. 81, 1882, 48—56.

— Über den Zweck der Begriffsschrift, in: Jenaische Zeitschr. f. Naturwiss. 16, 1883, Suppl.-Heft, 1—10.

— Die Grundlagen der Arithmetik. Eine logisch-mathematische Untersuchung über den Begriff der Zahl. Breslau 1884. Unv. Neudr. Breslau 1934 (g). Deutsch-engl. Ausg.: The Foundations of Arithmetic. Transl. J. L. Austin. Oxford 1950. Einzelne Stellen übers. v. Jourdain in: The Monist 25, 1915, 481—494; 26, 1916, 182—199; 27, 1917, 114—127. Vgl.: Frege, Aritmetica e logica.

— Über formale Theorien der Arithmetik, in: Jenaische Zeitschr. f. Naturwiss. 19, 1886, Suppl.-Heft, 94—104.

— Über das Trägheitsgesetz, in: Zeitschr. f. Philos. u. philos. Krit. 98, 1891, 145—161.

503

BIBLIOGRAPHY

— Function und Begriff. Jena 1891.
— Über Sinn und Bedeutung, in: Zeitschr. f. Philos. u. philos. Krit. 100, 1892, 25—50. Engl. (üb. M. Black) in: Philos. Rev. 57, 1948, 207—230.
— Über Begriff und Gegenstand, in: Vierteljahrschr. f. wiss. Philos. 16, 1892, 192—205. Engl.: On concept and object, üb. P. Geach, in: Mind 60, 1951, 169—180.
— Le nombre entier, in: Rev. de métaph. et de mor. 3, 1895, 73—78.
— Kritische Beleuchtung einiger Punkte in E. Schröders Vorlesungen über die Algebra der Logik, in: Arch. f. syst. Philos. 1, 1895, 433—456.
— Über die Begriffsschrift des Herrn Peano und meine eigene, in: Ber. d. math.-phys. Cl. d. Kgl. Sächs. Ges. d. Wiss. 48, 1897, 361—378.
— Lettera del sig. G. Frege all'Editore (datiert v. Jena, 29. Sept. 1896), in: Rev. de mathém. (Riv. di matem.) 6, 1896—1899, 53—59.
— Über die Zahlen des Herrn H. Schubert. Jena 1899.
— Grundgesetze der Arithmetik. Begriffsschriftlich abgeleitet. 2 Bde. Jena 1893—1903. §§ 86—137 engl. in: Frege against the formalists, in: Philos. Rev. 59, 1950, 70—93 u. 202—220 u. 332—345.
— Über die Grundlagen der Geometrie I, in: Jahrbücher d. Dt. Mathem.-Ver. 12, 1903, 319—324; II: 368—375; III/1: 15, 1906, 293—309; III/2: 377—403; III/3: 423—430.
— Was ist eine Funktion? In: Boltzmann-Festschrift, Leipzig 1904, 656—666.
— Antwort auf die Ferienplauderei des Herrn Thomae, in: Jahresber. d. Dt. Mathem.-Ver. 15, 1906, 586—590.
— Die Unmöglichkeit der Thomaeschen formalen Arithmetik aufs Neue nachgewiesen. Ebda. 17, 1908, 52—55.
— Schlußbemerkung. Ebda. S. 56.
— Über Logik und Mathematik. (Hs. Frühling 1914). Abschr. im Inst. f. math. Log. u. Grundlagenforschung in Münster i. W.
— Logische Untersuchungen. Dritter Teil: Gedankengefüge, in: Beitr. z. Philos. d. Dt. Idealismus 3, 1923, 36—51.
— Ein unbekannter Brief von Gottlob Frege über Hilberts erste Vorlesung über die Grundlagen der Geometrie. Hrsg. v. Max Steck, in: Sitz.-Ber. Heidelb. Akad. d. Wiss., Math.-naturw. Kl. 1940, 6; 1940.
— Unbekannte Briefe Freges über die Grundlagen der Geometrie und Antwortbriefe Hilberts an Frege. Aus dem Nachlaß von Heinrich Liebmann hrsg. und mit Anmerkungen versehen v. Max Steck. Ebda. 1941, 2. Abhdlg. Heidelberg 1941.
— Translations from the philosophical writings of G. F. Ed. P. Geach and M. Black. Oxford, New York 1952.
— The fundamental laws of Arithmetic. Üb. aus Grundgesetze d. Arithmetik v. J. Stachelroth u. P. E. B. Jourdain, in: The Monist 25, 1915, 481 ff.
— Aritmetica e logica. Traduzione e note del Prof. L. Geymonat. Torino 1948. Darin 15—187: I fondamenti dell'aritmetica.
Zahlreiche Notizen von Frege in: Jourdain, The development.
Gentzen, G.: Über die Existenz unabhängiger Axiomensysteme zu unendlichen Satzsystemen, in: Math. Annalen 107, 1932, 329—350.
— Untersuchungen über das logische Schließen, in: Math. Zeitschr. 39, 1934, 176—210 u. 405—431.
Gergonne, J. D.: Essai de dialectique rationnelle, in: Annales de mathém. pures et appl. 7, 1816/17, 189—228.
Gödel, K.: Die Vollständigkeit der Axiome des logischen Funktionenkalküls, in: Monatsh. f. Mathem. u. Phys. 37, 1930, 349—360.
— Über formal unentscheidbare Sätze der Principia Mathematica und verwandter Systeme. Ebda. 38, 1931, 173—198. Engl. Princeton 1934.
Gonseth, F. (Hrsg.): Les entretiens de Zurich. Zürich 1941.
Grassmann, R.: Die Begriffslehre oder Logik. 2. Buch der Formenlehre oder Mathematik. Stettin 1872.
— Die Logik und die andern logischen Wissenschaften. Stettin 1890.

Hadamard, J.; Baire; Lebesgue; Borel, E.: Cinq lettres sur la théorie des ensembles, in: Bull. de la Soc. Mathém. de France 33, 1905, 261—273. Neudr. in: Borel, Lecons sur la théorie des fonctions, Paris, 2. Aufl. 1914, 3. Aufl. 1928, 150—160.

Herbrand, J.: Recherches sur la théorie de la démonstration. (Trav. Soc. d. Sc. et d. Lettres de Varsovie, Cl. III: Sc. mathém. et phys., Nr. 33) 1930.

— Sur la non-contradiction de l'arithmétique, in: Journ. f. d. reine u. ang. Mathem. 166, 1931/32, 1—8.

Heyting, A.: Die formalen Regeln der intuitionistischen Logik, in: Sitz.-Ber. d. Preuß. Akad. d. Wiss., phys.-math. Kl. 1930, 42—57. Sep.: Berlin 1930 (g).

— Die formalen Regeln der intuitionistischen Mathematik. Ebda. 57—71 u. 158—169.

— Mathematische Grundlagenforschung, Intuitionismus, Beweistheorie. Berlin 1934.

Hilbert, D.: Über die Grundlagen der Logik und der Arithmetik, in: Verb. d. 3. Int. Mathem.-Kongr. Leipzig 1905, 174—185. Neudr. in: Hilbert, Grundlagen der Geometrie. Berlin, Leipzig: 3. u. 4. A. 1913, 5. u. 6. A. 1923, 243 bis 258; 7. A. 1930, 247—261. Franz.: Sur les fondements de la logique et de l'arithmétique. Üb. P. Boutroux, in: L'Enseignem. math. 7, 1905, 89—103. Engl.: On the foundations of logic and arithmetic. Üb. G. B. Halsted, in: The Monist 15, 1905, 338—352.

— Axiomatisches Denken, in: Math. Annalen 78, 1918, 405—415. Neudr. in: Ges. Abhandlungen III, Berlin 1935, 146—156. Franz. in: L'Enseignem. math. 20, 1918/19, 122—136. Niederl. in: Wiskundig tijdschr. (Haarlem) 16, 1919/20, 208—222.

— Neubegründung der Mathematik, in: Abh. a. d. Math. Semin. d. Hamb. Univ. 1, 1922, 157—177. Neudr. in: Ges. Abh. III, Berlin 1935, 157—177.

— Die logischen Grundlagen der Mathematik, in: Math. Annalen 88, 1923, 151—165. Sonderdr. Berlin 1922. Neudr. in: Ges. Abh. III, Berlin 1935, 178—191.

— Über das Unendliche, in: Math. Annalen 95, 1926, 161—190. Gekürzt. Neudr. in: Jahresb. d. Dt. Mathem.-Ver. 36, 1927, 201—216; u. in: Hilbert, Grundlagen der Geometrie, 7. A. Leipzig, Berlin 1930, 262—288.

— Die Grundlagen der Mathematik, mit einer Anmerkung von P. Bernays und einer Antwort . . . von H. Weyl, in: Abh. a. d. Math. Semin. d. Hamb. Univ. 6, 1928, 65—85. Sep. Leipzig 1928. Neudr. in: Hilbert, Grundl. d. Geometrie, 7. A. Leipzig, Berlin 1930, 289—312.

— und P. Bernays: Grundlagen der Mathematik. 2 Bde. Berlin 1934—1939. Neudr. Ann Arbor 1944.

— und W. Ackermann: Grundzüge der theoretischen Logik. Berlin 1928. 3. A. 1949.

S. a. Frege, Unbekannte Briefe . . .

Hobbes, Th.: Elementorum philosophiae sectio prima de Corpore. London 1655. Engl. 1656.

— Opera philosophica quae latine scripsit I. Ed. Molesworth. London 1839 (g).

Holland, G. J. v.: Abhandlung über die Mathematik, die allgemeine Zeichen-Kunst und die verschiedenen Rechnungsarten. Tübingen 1764.

— Briefe an J. H. Lambert. In: J. H. Lamberts Deutscher Gelehrter Briefwechsel I. Hrsg. J. Bernoulli. Berlin 1781.

Huntington, E. V.: Sets of independent postulates for the algebra of logic, in: Transact. of the Amer. Math. Soc. 5, 1904, 288—309.

Jaśkowski, St.: On the rules of suppositions in formal logic. Warsaw 1934.

Jevons, W. St.: Elementary lessons in logic. London 1870 (u. viele weitere A.). Deutsch: Leitfaden der Logik. Üb. n. d. 22. A. v. H. Kleinpeter. 1. A. Leipzig 1906. 2., durchges. A. mit einem Anh. üb. neuere Logik: Leipzig 1913.

— Pure logic, or the logic of quality apart from quantity. London, New York 1864. Neudr. in: Pure logic and other minor works. Ed. R. Adamson und H. A. Jevons, London, New York 1890, 1—77 (g).

BIBLIOGRAPHY

— The principles of science. 2 Bde. London 1874. 2 Bde. in einem: New York 1875; 2. A. London, New York 1877; 3. A. London 1879.

Jourdain, P. E. B.: The development of the theories of mathematical logic and the principles of mathematics, in: The quart. journ. of pure and appl. math. 41, 1910, 324—352; 43, 1912, 219—314; 44, 1913, 113—128.

Kleene, S. C.: Proof by cases in formal logic, in: Annals of mathematics, 2. ser., 35, 1934, 529—544.

— A theory of positive integers in formal logic, in: Amer. journ. of math. 57, 1935, 153—173 u. 219—244.

— und J. B. Rosser: The inconsistency of certain formal logics, in: Annals of mathematics, 2. ser., 36, 1935, 630—636.

König, J.: Neue Grundlagen der Logik, Arithmetik und Mengenlehre. Leipzig 1914.

Kotarbiński, T.: Elementy teorii poznania, logiki formalnej i metodologii nauk (Elemente der Erkenntnistheorie, der formalen Logik und der Methodologie der Wissenschaften). Lwów 1929.

Ladd (-Franklin), Chr.: On the algebra of logic. In: Stud. in logic by members of the Johns Hopkins Univ. Boston 1883, 17—71.

Lambert, J. H.: Opera Mathematica. Ed. A. Speiser. Zürich, I: 1946, II: 1948.

— Neues Organon. 2 Bde. (in 4 Vol.). Leipzig 1764.

— De universaliori calculi idea, disquisitio, una cum adnexo specimine, in: Nova acta eruditorum, Leipzig 1765, 441—473.

— Beiträge zum Gebrauche der Mathematik und deren Anwendung. Theile 1, 2 (1 u. 2), 3: Berlin 1765—1772.

— Anlage zur Architectonic, oder Theorie des Ersten und des Einfachen in der philosophischen und mathematischen Erkenntniss. 2 Bde. Riga 1771.

— Sechs Versuche einer Zeichenkunst in der Vernunftlehre, in: J. H. Lamberts log. u. philos. Abhdlgen. I. Zum Druck bef. v. Joh. Bernoulli, Berlin 1782, Nr. 1—6.

— Monatsbuch mit den zugehörigen Kommentaren sowie mit einem Vorwort über den Stand der Lambert-Forschung, hrsg. K. Bopp, in: Abhdlg. d. Kgl. bayer. Akad. d. Wiss., Math.-Phys. Kl., 27, München 1915.

— Über die Methode, die Metaphysik, Theologie und Moral richtiger zu beweisen. Hrsg. K. Bopp. (Kantstudien Ergänzungsh. 42). Berlin 1918.

— Briefwechsel zwischen Leonhard Euler und J. H. Lambert. Berlin 1924.

Leibniz, G. W.: Hs. Bibl. Hannover Phil. VII B IV. Abgedr. in: Cout. Op. 295 ff.

— Die philosophischen Schriften. Hrsg. C. I. Gerhardt. 7 Bde. Berlin 1875 bis 1890 (= GP).

— Mathematische Schriften. Hrsg. C. I. Gerhardt. 7 Bde. Berlin, Halle 1849 bis 1863 (= GM).

— Opuscules et fragments inédits de Leibniz. Ed. L. Couturat. Paris 1903 (= Cout. Op.).

— Lettres et fragments inédits sur les problèmes philosophiques (1669—1704), éd. Schrecker. Paris 1934.

— Selections. Ed. Ph. P. Wiener. New York 1951.

— Abhandlung ohne Überschrift, die Characteristica universalia betreffend, in: GP VII, 184—189.

— Dissertatio de arte combinatoria. Frankfurt a. M. 1690. Neudr. in: GP IV, 27—102 (g).

— Non inelegans specimen demonstrandi in abstractis, in: GP VII, 228—235. Engl. in: Lewis, A survey, 373—379.

— Specimen calculi universalis. Z. T. in: GP VII, 218—221; z. and. Teil in: Cout. Op. 239—243.

— Ad specimen calculi universalis addenda. Z. T. in: GP VII, 221—227; z. and. Teil in: Cout. Op. 249.

— Fragment. In: GP VII, 236—247. Engl. in: Lewis, A survey, 379—387.

— Generales inquisitiones de analysi notionum et veritatum (datiert 1686), in: Cout. Op. 356—399.

506

BIBLIOGRAPHY

Leibniz, G. W.: De formae logicae comprobatione per linearum ductus, in: Cout. Op. 292—321.
— Brief an Galloys (1677), in: GM (1. Abt.) I. London, Berlin 1850, 178—182. Z. T. auch in: GP VII, 21 f.
— an C. Rödeken in Berlin, 1708, in: GP VII, 32 f.
— Brief an den Herzog Johann Friedrich, in: GP I, 57—64. Und z. T. in: Couturat, Log. (5.413.), 83, Fußn. 1.
— Brief an Remond, in: GP III, 618—621. Und z. T. in: Couturat, Log. 39, Fußn. 2.
— Abhandlung ohne Überschrift, Vorarbeit zur allgemeinen Charakteristik (I), in: GP VII, 198—203.
— Abhandlung ohne Überschrift, Vorarbeit zur allgemeinen Charakteristik (II), in: GP VII, 204—207.
— De ortu, progressu et natura algebrae, nonnullisque aliorum et propriis circa eam inventis, in: GM VII (2. Abt., III), 203—216.
— De formis syllogismorum mathematice definiendis, in: Cout. Op. 410—416. Texte auch in: Couturat, Log. (5.413.).
Leśniewski, St.: Grundzüge eines neuen Systems der Grundlagen der Mathematik, in: Fund. math. 14, 1929, 1—81.
— Über die Grundlagen der Ontologie, in: Comptes rend. séances Soc. d. Sciences et d. Lettres de Varsovie, cl. III, 23, 1930, 111—132.
Lewis, C. I.: Implication and the algebra of logic, in: Mind, 21, 1912, 522—531.
— A survey of symbolic logic. Berkeley 1918.
— Strict implication — an emendation, in: The Journ. of Philos., Psychol., and Scient. Meth. 17, 1920, 300—302.
— Notes on the logic of intension, in: Structure method and meaning, essays in honor of H. M. Sheffer. Ed. H. Henke and others. New York 1951, 25—34.
— und C. H. Langford: Symbolic logic. New York, London 1932.
Löwenheim, L.: Ueber Möglichkeiten im Relativkalkul, in: Math. Annalen 76, 1915, 447—470.
Lukasiewicz, J.: O logice trójwartościowej (Über dreiwertige Logik), in: Ruch filoz. (Lwów) 5, 1920, 169—171.
— Logika dwuwartościowa (Zweiwertige Logik), in: Przegl. filoz. 23, 1921, 189—205.
— Elementy logiki matematycznej (Elemente der mathematischen Logik). Warszawa 1929 (lithogr.).
— Philosophische Bemerkungen zu mehrwertigen Systemen des Aussagenkalküls, in: Comptes rend. séances Soc. d. Sciences et d. Lettres de Varsovie, cl. III, 23, 1930, 51—77.
— Bedeutung der logischen Analyse für die Erkenntnis, in: Actes du 8. Congr. Int. de Philos. à Prague. (Prag) 1936, 75—84.
— A system of modal logic, in: The Journal of Comp. Syst. (St. Paul, Minn.) 1, 1953, 111—149.
— Arithmetic and modal logic. Ebda. 1, 1954, 213—219.
— und A. Tarski: Untersuchungen über den Aussagenkalkül, in: Comptes rend. séances Soc. d. Sciences et d. Lettres de Varsovie, cl. III, 23, 1930, 30—50.
Lullus, Raymundus: S. Raymundus Lullus.
Maimon, S.: Versuch einer neuen Logik oder Theorie des Denkens. Berlin 1794. Neudr.: Berlin 1912.
McColl, H.: The calculus of equivalent statements and integration limits, in: Proc. of the London Math. Soc. 9, 1877/78, 9—20 u. 177—186; 10, 1878/79, 16—28; 11, 1879/80, 113—121.
— Symbolic reasoning (VI), in: Mind 14, 1905, 74—81.
— Symbolic logic and its applications. London 1906.
Meinong, A.: Über Gegenstandstheorie, in: Untersuchungen zur Gegenstandstheorie und Psychologie. Leipzig 1904, 1—50.
— Über Annahmen. 2., umgearb. A. Leipzig 1910.
Mitchell, O. H.: On a new algebra of logic, in: Stud. in logic by membres of the Johns Hopkins Univ. Boston 1883, 72 ff.

BIBLIOGRAPHY

Morris, C. W.: Foundation of the theory of signs. Chicago 1938.
— Signs, language, and behavior. New York 1946.
Nicod, J. G. P.: A reduction in the number of the primitive propositions of logic, in: Proc. Cambr. Philos. Soc. 19, 1917—1920, 32—41.
Peano, G.: Arithmetices principia, novo methodo exposita. Augustae Taurinorum (Turin) 1889.
— Sul concetto di numero, in: Riv. di mat. (Turin) 1, 1891, 87—102 u. 256—267.
— Notations de logique mathématique. Introduction au Formulaire de Mathématique. Turin 1894.
— Studii di logica matematica, in: Atti d. R. Accad. d. Scienze di Torino 32, 1897, 565—583.
— Formulaire de mathématiques 2, § 1: Logique mathématique. Turin 1897.
— Formulaire de mathématiques 2, § 2: Arithmétique. Turin 1898.
— Formulaire de mathématiques 2, § 3: Logique mathématique — Arithmétique — Limites — Nombres complexes — Vecteurs — Dérivées — Intégrales. Turin 1899.
— Formulaire mathématique 4. Turin 1902.
— Formulario mathematico 5. Torino 1905—1908.
Peirce, C. S.: Collected Papers. Ed. C. Hartshorne und P. Weiß. III—V: Cambridge (Mass.) 1933—1934 (= CP).
— On an improvement in Boole's calculus of logic, in: Proc. of the Amer. Acad. of Arts and Sciences 7, 1867, 250—261. Neudr. in: CP III, 3—15 (g).
— Grounds of validity of the laws of logic: Further consequences of four incapacities, in: The journal of spec. philos. 2, 1868/69, 193—208. Neudr. mit Korr. in: CP V, 190—222 (g).
— Description of a notation for the logic of relatives, resulting from an amplification of the conceptions of Boole's calculus of logic, in: Memoirs of the Amer. Acad. 9, 1870, 317—378. Sep.: Cambridge (Mass.) 1870. Neudr. in: CP III, 27—98 (g).
— A Boolian algebra with one constant (ca. 1880), in: CP IV, 13—18.
— On the algebra of logic. Chapter I: Syllogistic. Chapter II: The logic of non-relative terms. Chapter III: The logic of relatives, in: The Amer. Journal of Math. 3, 1880, 15—57. Verb. Neudr. in: CP III, 104—157.
— On the logic of number. Ebda. 4, 1881, 85—95. Verb. Neudr. in: CP III, 158 bis 170.
— A theory of probable inference. Note B: The logic of relatives, in: Stud. in logic by members of the Johns Hopkins Univ. Boston 1883, 187—203. Neudr. in: CP III, 195—206 (g).
— On the algebra of logic. A contribution to the philosophy of notation, in: The Amer. Journal of Math. 7, 1885, 180—202. Und sep.. Neudr. in: CP III, 210—249 (mit vorher unveröffentlichter „Note": 239—249) (g).
— The critic of arguments, in: The Open Court 6, 1892, 3391—3394 u. 3416 bis 3418. Neudr. in: CP III, 250—265 (g).
— The regenerated logic, in: The Monist 7, 1896, 19—40. Neudr. in: CP III, 266—287 (g).
— The logic of relatives, in: The Monist 7, 1897, 161—217. Neudr. in: CP III, 288—345 (g).
— The simplest mathematics (1902), in: CP IV, 189—262.
Ploucquet, G.: Sammlung der Schriften, welche den logischen Calcul des Herrn Professor Ploucquet betreffen, mit neuen Zusätzen hrsg. v. Fr. A. Bök. Frankfurt, Leipzig 1766, Tübingen 1773.
— Methodus tam demonstrandi directe omnes syllogismorum species, quam vitia formae detegendi ope unius regulae. 1763. Neudr. in: Sammlung der Schriften, hrsg. Bök.
— Methodus calculandi in logicis, praemissa commentatione de arte characteristica. (Frankfurt, Leipzig) 1763. Neudr. in: Godofredi Ploucquet Principia de substantiis et phaenomenis, 2. A. (Frankfurt, Leipzig) 1764. Auch in: Sammlung der Schriften, hrsg. Bök.

BIBLIOGRAPHY

Plouquet, G.: Untersuchung und Abänderung der logicalischen Constructionen des Herrn Professors Lambert. Tübingen 1765. Neudr. in: Sammlung der Schriften, hrsg. Bök.

Post, E. L.: Introduction to a general theory of elementary propositions, in: The Amer. Journal of Math. 43, 1921, 163—185.

Ramsay, F. P.: The foundations of mathematics, in: Proc. of the London Math. Soc., 2. Ser., 25, 1926, 338—384. Neudr. in: The found. of math. and other log. essays. London 1931; 2. A. 1950, 1—61 (g).

Raymundus Lullus: Ars magna et ultima, in: Raymundi Lulli opera ea quae ad adinventam ab ipso artem universalem . . . pertinent. Argentorati 1617, 218—663.

Reichenbach, H.: Philosophic foundations of quantum mechanics. Berkeley, Los Angeles 1944. 2. A. 1946.

— Nomological statements and admissible operations. Amsterdam 1953.

Richard, J.: Les principes des mathématiques et le problème des ensembles, in: Rev. gén. des sciences pures et appl. 16, 1905, 541 ff.

— Lettre à Monsieur le rédacteur de la Revue générale des sciences pures et appliquées (Teilw. Neudr. d. Vorgenannten), in: Acta Math. 30, 1906, 295 f. (g).

— Sur la logique et la notion de nombre entier, in: L'Enseignem. math. 9, 1907, 39—44.

Rosser, J. B.: A mathematical logic without variables, in: Annals of mathematics, 2. ser., 36, 1935, 127—150; und in: Duke mathematical journal 1, 1935, 328—355.

S. a. Kleene u. Rosser.

Russell, B.: Sur la logique des relations avec des applications à la théorie des séries, in: Rev. de math. (Riv. di mat.) 7, 1900—1901, 115—148.

— Existence and being, in: Mind 10, 1901, 330 f. Abgedr. in: Russell, The principles 449 (g).

— The principles of mathematics. London 1903. 2. A. London 1937 und Neudr. 1942, 1948, 1950.

— On denoting, in: Mind 14, 1905, 479—493 (g). Auch in: Readings in philos. analysis. Sel. and ed. H. Feigl und W. Sellars. New York 1949, 103—115.

— Mathematical logic as based on the theory of types, in: The Amer. Journal of Math. 30, 1908, 222—262.

— Introduction to mathematical philosophy. London 1919; 2. A. 1920. Deutsch: Einführung in die mathematische Philosophie. Üb. E. J. Gumbel und W. Gordon, München 1923; 2. A. München 1930. Franz.: Introduction à la philosophie mathématique. Üb. G. Moreau. Paris 1928.

S. a. Whitehead, A. N. und B. Russell.

Schönfinkel, M.: Über die Bausteine der mathematischen Logik, in: Math. Annalen 92, 1924, 305—316.

Schröder, E.: Der Operationskreis des Logikkalküls. Leipzig 1877.

— Über das Zeichen. Karlsruhe 1890. Engl.: Signs and symbols, in: The Open Court 6, 1892, 3431—3434 u. 3441—3444 u. 3463—3466.

— Vorlesungen über die Algebra der Logik (Exakte Logik). Leipzig, I: 1890, II/1: 1891, III: 1895, II/2: 1905.

Sheffer, H. M.: A set of five independent postulates for Boolean algebras, with application to logical constants, in: Transact. Amer. Math. Soc. 14, 1913, 481—488.

— Notational relativity, in: Proc. of the Sixth Int. Congr. of Philos., New York 1927, 348—351.

— The general theory of notational relativity. 1921 (Nicht im Buchhandel).

Skolem, Th.: Einige Bemerkungen zur axiomatischen Begründung der Mengenlehre, in: Wissenschaftl. Vorträge, geh. a. d. 5.¹ Kongr. d. Skandinav. Math. in Helsingfors 1922, Helsingfors 1923, 217—232.

— Über einige Grundlagenfragen der Mathematik. Skrifter utgitt av Det Norske Videnskaps-Akademi i Oslo, I. Matematisk-naturvidenskapelig klasse, 4, 1929.

BIBLIOGRAPHY

Solbrig, D.: De scripturae oecumenicae, quam omnes gentes . . . etc., in: Miscell.
Berol. ad increm. scient. Contin. I, 1723.
Solly, T.: A syllabus of logic. Cambridge 1839.
Tarski, A.: Über einige fundamentale Begriffe der Metamathematik, in: Comptes rend. séances Soc. d. Sciences et d. Lettres de Varsovie, cl. III, 23, 1930, 22—29.
— Fundamentale Begriffe der Methodologie der deduktiven Wissenschaften I, in: Monatsh. f. Math. u. Physik 37, 1930, 361—404.
— Pojęcie prawdy w językach nauk dedukcyjnaych. Warszawa 1933. Deutsch: Der Wahrheitsbegriff in den formalisierten Sprachen. Üb. L. Blaustein. Verm. um ein Vorwort v. Verf. in: Studia philos. (Leopoli) 1, 1936, 261—405. (Sep. 1935).
— Einführung in die mathematische Logik und in die Methodologie der Mathematik. Wien 1937.
— The semantic conception of truth, in: Philos. and Phenomenol. Research 4, 1944, 341—375.
S. a. Lukasiewicz u. Tarski.
Thomas, I.: The logical square and modes of categorical syllogism. In: Contemplations presented to the Dominican Tertiaries, Oxford 1949, 10—23.
— CS(n): An extension of CS, in: Dom. Stud. 2, 1949, 145—160.
— Some laws of the calculus of quantifiers. Ebda. 2, 1949, 285.
— Existence and coherence, in: Methodos 2, 1950, 76—80.
— A new decision procedure for Aristotle's syllogistic, in: Mind 61, 1952, 564 bis 566.
Venn, J.: The logic of chance. London, Cambridge 1866.
— On the diagrammatic and mechanical representation of propositions and reasoning, in: The London, Edinburgh and Dublin Philos. Mag. and Journ. of Science, 5. Ser., 10, 1880, 1—18.
— On the forms of logical propositions, in: Mind 5, 1880, 336.
— Symbolic logic. London 1881; 2. verm. A. 1894.
Wajsberg, M.: Aksjomatyzacja trójwartościowego rachunku zdań (Axiomatisierung des dreiwertigen Aussagenkalküls). (Mit deutsch. Zusammenfassung) in: Comptes rend. Séances Soc. d. Sciences et d. Lettres de Varsovie, cl. III, 24, 1931, 126—148.
Weyl, H.: Das Kontinuum. Kritische Untersuchungen über die Grundlagen der Analysis. Leipzig 1918. Neudr.: Leipzig 1932.
— Über die neue Grundlagenkrise der Mathematik, in: Math. Zeitschr. 10, 1921, 39—79.
Whitehead, A. N.: Mathematics. In: The Encyclopedia Britannica, 14. A., XV. London, New York 1929, 85—89. (Auch schon in d. A. seit 1911 und in d. späteren.) Neudr. in: Essays in science and philosophy. New York 1947, London 1948. Deutsch: Mathematik, in: Philosophie und Mathemathik (Vorträge u. Essays v. A. N. W.), Wien 1949, 125—150.
— Indication, classes, numbers, validation, in: Mind 43, 1934, 281—297 u. 543. Neudr. in: Essays . . .
— Remarks, in: The philos. review 46, 1937, 178—186. Neudr. als „Analysis of meaning" in: Essays . . .
— Mathematics and the good. In: The philosophy of A. N. W. Ed. P. A. Schilpp. Evanston, Chicago 1941, 666—681. Neudr. in: Essays . . . Deutsch: Die Mathematik und das Gute, in: Philosophie und Mathematik (Vorträge und Essays v. A. N. W.), Wien 1949, 69—90.
— und B. Russell: Principia Mathematica. Cambridge (= PM). I: 1910; 2. verm. A. 1925 (Neudr. 1935, 1950) (g). II: 1912; 2. A. 1927 (Neudr. 1950)(g). III: 1913; 2. A. 1927 (Neudr. 1950). Einleit. deutsch als: Einführung in die math. Logik. Üb. H. Mokre. München, Berlin 1932.
Wittgenstein, L.: Logisch-philosophische Abhandlung. Einleitung v. Bertrand Russell, in: Annalen der Nat.-philosophie 14, 1921, 185—262. Neudr. m. engl. Übers.:

510

Wittgenstein, L.: Tractatus logico-philosophicus. New York, London 1922 (u. mehrere spätere A.) (ɡ). Neudr. mit ital. Übers. v. G. C. M. Colombo: (Mailand, Rom) 1954.

Zermelo, E.: Beweis, daß jede Menge wohlgeordnet werden kann, in: Math. Annalen 59, 1904, 514—516.

— Untersuchungen über die Grundlagen der Mengenlehre I. Ebda. 65, 1908, 261—281.

5.3. General history of mathematical logic
5.31. Works on the whole period or large parts (up to 20th century), encyclopedic articles

Bell, E. T.: Men of mathematics. New York 1937, 2. A. 1946. Franz.: Les grands mathématiciens. Üb. A. Gandillon. Paris 1939.

Beth, E. W.: Kanttekeningen op de geschiedenis der wijsbegeerte (Bemerkungen zur Geschichte der Philosophie), in: Alg. Nederl. Tijdschr. v. Wijsb. en Psych. 36, 1942/43, 80—83.

— Logica, in: Eerste Nederlandse systematisch ingerichte encyclopaedie, Bd. I, Amsterdam 1946, 113—119.

— Hundred years of symbolic logic (engl., mit Zusammenfassungen in engl., franz. und deutsch.), in: Dialectica (Neuchâtel), 1, 1947, 311—346.

— The origin and growth of symbolic logic. Paper, zusammengefaßt in: JSL 13, 1948, 62 f.

— Aufsatz mit demselben Titel in: Synthese 6, 1947/48, 268—274.

— Critical epochs in the development of the theory of science, in: The British Journ. of Philos. of Science 1, 1950.

Couturat, L.: IIme Congrès de Philosophie. — Genève. Comptes rendus critiques. II: Logique et philosophie des sciences. Séances de sect. et séances générales, in: Rev. de metaph. et de mor. 12, 1904, 1037—1077.

Daan, A.: Logistiek, in: Encyclopaed. handboek van het moderne denken, 2. A., Arnhem 1942, 420—425.

Enriques, E.: Per la storia della logica. Bologna 1922. Deutsch: Zur Geschichte der Logik. Üb. L. Bieberbach. Leipzig, Berlin 1927. Franz.: L'évolution de la logique. Üb. G.-E. Monod-Herzen. Paris 1926.

— Il significato della storia del pensiero scientifico. Bologna 1938.

— Compendio di storia del pensiero scientifico. Bologna 1937.

— und G. de Santillana: Storia del pensiero scientifico I. Milano, Roma 1932.

García Bacca, J. D.: Simbólica (lógica). In: Enciclopedia Espasa IX, Barcelona 1934, Anh., 1329—1339.

Huntington, E. V. und Ch. Ladd-Franklin: Logic, symbolic. In: The encyclopedia Americana, IX, New York 1905; und: Ausg. 1941, Bd. 17, New York, Chicago 1941, 568—573.

Ito, M.: Kagaku ronrigaku no tenbo (Ein Überblick über die wissenschaftliche Logik), in: Kisokagaku 3, 3, 1949, 294—299.

Jørgensen, J.: Einige Hauptpunkte der Entwicklung der formalen Logik seit Boole, in: Erkenntnis 5, 1935/36, 131—142.

S. a. Jørgensen 1.22.

Jourdain, P. E. B.: S. Jourdain (5.2.).

Kaczorowski, St.: Logika matematyczna. Cz. I: Algebra logiki (Math. Logik. Teil I: Die Algebra der Logik.). Lwów 1938. 2. A. Łódź 1946.

— Logika matematyczna. Cz. II: Logika nowożytna. (Math. Logik. Teil II: Die neue Logik.) Lwów 1938.

Levi, B.: Logica matematica. In: Enciclopedia italiana di scienze, lettere ed arti, Bd. 21, Roma 1934, 398—401.

Liard, L.: Les logiciens anglais contemporains. Paris 1878, 2. A. 1883, 3. A. 1890, 5. A. 1907. Deutsch: Die neuere englische Logik. Üb. J. Imelmann. Leipzig 1883. Russisch: Anglijskié réformatory logiki. Üb. N. Davydov. St. Petersburg 1897.

BIBLIOGRAPHY

Loria, G.: La logique mathématique avant Leibniz, in: Bull. des sciences math. (Paris), 2. Serie, 18, 1894, 107—112.

Nicod, J.: Mathematical logic and the foundations of mathematics. In: The encyclopaedia Britannica, 12. A., Bd. 31; London, New York 1922, 874 ff.'

Peano, G.: Origine du signe ⊃, in: L'intermédiaire des mathématiciens 10, 1903, 70. S. dazu auch den Aufsatz von H. Brocard, ebda. 13, 1906, 18.

Pieri, M.: Un sguardo al nuovo indirizzo logico-matematico delle scienze deduttive. Catania 1907.

Ramsey, F. P.: Mathematical logic. In: The encyclopaedia Britannica, 13. A., 2. Zusatzband; London, New York 1926, 830—832.

Reichenbach, H.: The rise of scientific philosophy. Berkeley, Los Angeles 1951.

Reyes y Prósper, V.: Proyecto de clasificación de los escritos lógico-simbólicos especialmente de los post-Booleianos, in: El progreso matemático 2, 1892, 229—232.

— La logica simbolica en Italia. Ebda. 3, 1893, 41 ff.

Scholz, H.: Natürliche Sprachen und Kunstsprachen, in: Semester-Ber. (Münster i. W.), 11. Semester, Winter 1937/38, 48—85. Auch in: Blätter f. dt. Philos. 12, 1938/39, 253—281 (um ein Vorwort vermehrt).

Shearman, A. T.: The development of symbolic logic. London 1906.

Stebbing, L. S.: Logistic. In: The encyclopaedia Britannica, 14. A., Bd. 14, London 1929, 330—334. Neudr. in: Encycl. Brit., Ausg. v. 1944; Chicago, London, Toronto 1944, Bd. 14, 330—334. Und: 1950.

Vacca, G.: Sui precursori della logica matematica, in: Rev. de math. (Riv. di mat.) 6, 1896—1899, 121—125.

— Sui precursori della logica matematica II: J. D. Gergonne. Ebda. 183 ff.

Vailati, G.: Pragmatismo e logica matematica, in: Leonardo 4, 1906. Neudr. in: Scritti di G. Vailati (1863—1909), Leipzig und Florenz 1911, 689—694. Engl.: Pragmatism and mathematical logic, ub. H. D. Austin, in: The Monist 16, 1906, 481—491.

5.32. Mathematical logic in 20th century
5.321. General

Beth, E. W.: Fundamental features of contemporary theory of science, in: The British Journ. of Philos. of Science 1, 1950.

Blanché, R.: Logique 1900—1950, in: Rev. philos. de la France et de l'Etranger 143, 1953, 570—598.

Carruccio, E.: Recenti sviluppi della logica matematica, in: Atti del Convegno di Pisa 23—27 sett. 1948, Città di Castello 1949.

— Matematica e logica nella storia e nel pensiero contemporaneo. Torino 1951.

dal Pra, M.: L'empirismo logico dal 1930 ad oggi, in: Riv. crit. di storia d. filos. 7, 1952, 62—67.

Feys, R.: Les logiques nouvelles des modalités, in: Rev. néoscol. de philos. 40, 1937, 517—553.

— Logique formalisée et philosophie, in: Synthese 4, 1947/48, 283—289.

— Logistique. Chronique des années 1939—1945. Paris 1950.

Fraenkel, A. und J. Bar-Hillel: Le problème des antinomies et ses développements récents, in: Rev. de metaph. et de mor. 4, 1939, 225—242.

Geymonat, L.: La crisi della logica formale. In: N. Abbagnano und Persico, Fondamenti logici della scienza, Torino 1947, 111—135.

— Logica matematica. Sviluppi recenti. In: Enciclopedia ital. di scienze, lettere ed arti, 1938—1948, 2. Zusatzbd. (I—Z), Roma 1949, 226 f.

Grelling, K.: Der Einfluß der Antinomien auf die Entwicklung der Logik im 20. Jahrhundert. In: Trav. du IXe congr. int. de philos.; VI: Logique et mathématiques. Paris 1937, 8—17.

Jørgensen, J.: Hovedstrømninger i nutidens filosofi (Hauptströmungen der

BIBLIOGRAPHY

Philosophie der Gegenwart), in: Ajatus (Helsinki) 15, 1948 (ersch. 1949), 67—89.
— Traek af deduktionsteoriens udvikling i den nyere tid (Abriß der neueren Entwicklung der Theorie der Deduktion). Kopenhagen 1937.
Reymond, A.: Les principes de la logique et la critique contemporaine. Paris 1932.
Scholz, H.: Was will die formalisierte Grundlagenforschung? in: Deutsche Mathematik 7, 1943, 206—248.
Stegmüller, W.: Hauptströmungen der Gegenwartsphilosophie. Wien, Stuttgart 1952.
Thomas, I.: Farrago logica, in: Dom. Stud. 4, 1951, 69—79.
— Introductory notes to modern logic, in: Blackfriars 33, 1952, 299—305.

5.322. Germany

Dubislav, W.: Les recherches sur la philosophie des mathématiques en Allemagne. Üb. E. Levinas, in: Recherches philos. 1, 1931/32, 299—311.
Grelling, K.: Philosophy of the exact sciences: its present status in Germany. Üb. E. L. Schaub, in: The Monist 38, 1928, 97—119.

5.323. France

Boll, M. und J. Reinhart: Logic in France in the twentieth century. In: Philosophic thought in France and the United States. Ed. M. Farber. Buffalo 1950, 181—201.
Destouches, P.: La logique symbolique en France et les récentes Journées de Logique, in: Rev. philos. de la France et de l'Etranger 136, 1946, 221—225.

5.324. Great Britain

Metz, R.: Die mathematische Logik. In: Die philos. Strömungen der Gegenwart in Großbritannien, von R. Metz, Bd. 2, Leipzig 1935, 247—264. Engl.: Mathematical logic. In: A hundred years of British philosophy, by R. Metz; New York, London 1938, 705—726.

5.325. Italy

S. 5.918. u. 5.919.

5.326. Netherlands

Beth, E. W.: Exact-wetenschappelijke wijsbegeerte in Nederland (Philosophie der exakten Wissenschaften in den Niederlanden), in: Nieuw tijdschr. v. wiskunde 35, 1947, 100—104.

5.327. Poland

Ajdukiewicz, K.: Logistyczny antyirracjonalizm w Polsce (Logistischer Antiirrationalismus in Polen), in: Przegl. Filoz. (Warszawa), 37, 1934, 399—408.
— Der logistische Antiirrationalismus in Polen, in: Erkenntnis 5, 1935/36, 151—161.
Bocheński, I. M.: Philosophie. In: Pologne 1919—1939, Neuchâtel 1947, III, 229—260.
Grégoire, F.: La philosophie polonaise contemporaine, in: Rev. philos. de la France et de l'Etranger 142, 1952, 53—71.
Gromska, D.: Philosophes polonais morts entre 1938 et 1945, in: Stud. philos. (Posen) 3, 1939—1946 (ersch. 1948), 40—91 (?).
Jordan, Z.: The development of mathematical logic and of logical positivism in Poland between the two wars. London, New York, Toronto 1945.
Vaccarino, G.: La scuola polacca di logica, in: Sigma 2, 1948, 527—546.

Zawirski, Z.: Les tendances actuelles de la philosophie polonaise, in: Revue de synthèse 10, Sciences de la nature et synthèse générale, 1935, 129—143.
Zich, V. O.: Logistika v Polsku (Logistic in Poland), in: Česká mysl 33, 1937, 23—36.

5.328. United States of America

Benjamin, A. C.: Philosophy in America between the two wars. In: Philosophic thought in France and the United States. Ed. M. Farber. Buffalo 1950, 365—388.
Feys, R.: Directions nouvelles de la logistique aux Etats-Unis, in: Rev. néoscol. de philos. 40, 1937, 398—411.
Hiż, H.: Logika. In: Filozofia w Stanach Zjednoczonych 1939—1947 (Philos. in d. Ver. Staaten 1939—1947), 241—249. Dies in: Przegl. filoz. 44, 1948, 234—282.
Lenzen, V. F.: Philosophy of science in America. In: Philosophic thought in France and the United States. Ed. M. Farber, Buffalo 1950, 505—524.
Quine, W. V.: Os Estados Unidos e o ressurgimento de logica. In: Vida intelectual nos Estados Unidos, Sao Paulo, 2, 1946, 267—286.

5.33. Old and new logic

Bendiek, J.: Scholastische und mathematische Logik. (2.3.).
Beth, E. W.: De logistiek als voortzetting van de traditionele formele logica (Logistik als Fortsetzung der traditionellen formalen Logik.), in: Alg. Nederl. Tijdschr. v. Wijsb. en Psych. 34, 1940/41, 53—68; auch in: Annalen v. h. Genootschap v. wetenschappelijke philos. 11, 1941, 1—16.
Bocheński, I. M.: O „relatywizmie" logistycznym (Über den logischen „Relativismus".) In: Myśl katolicka . . . 87—111 (Franz. Zus.fassg.: 180 ff.).
— Tradycja myśli katolickiej a ścisłość (Die Tradition des katholischen Denkens und die Exaktheit.) Ebda. 27—34 (Franz. Zus.fassg.: 165 ff.).
Carnap, R.: Die alte und die neue Logik, in: Erkenntnis 1, 1930/31, 12—26. Franz.: L'ancienne et la nouvelle logique. Üb. E. Vouillemin, m. einer Einf. v. M. Boll. Paris 1933.
Clark, J. T.: Conventional logic and modern logic. Woodstock (Md.) 1952.
Czeżowski, T.: Quelques problèmes anciens sous la forme moderne, in: Stud. philos. (Posen) 3, 1939—1946 (ersch. 1948), 101—113.
Drewnowski, J. F.: Neoscholastyka wobec nowoczesnych wymagań nauki (Die Neuscholastik und die heutigen Erfordernisse der Wissenschaft). In: Myśl katolicka . . . 49—57 (und franz. Zus.fassg.: 169 ff.).
Freitag gen. Löringhoff, Bruno: Logik, ihr System und ihr Verhältnis zur Logistik. Stuttgart und Köln 1955.
Greenwood, Th.: Les fondements de la logique symbolique. Bd. 1: Critique du nominalisme logistique. Bd. 2: Justification des calculs logiques. Paris 1938.
— A classical approach to mathematical logic, in: The Australasian journ. of psychol. and philos. 17, 1939, 1—10.
— The unity of logic, in: The Thomist 8, 1945, 457—470.
Günther, G.: Logistik und Transzendentallogik, in: Die Tatwelt 16, 1940 (ersch. 1941), 135—147.
Hoenen, P.: De logica nova et antiqua, in: Gregorianum 20, 1939, 273—280.
Kraft, V.: Die moderne und die traditionelle Logik, in: Wissenschaft u. Weltbild (Wien) 3, 1950, 28—34.
Lukasiewicz, J.: W ohronie logistyki (Zur Rechtfertigung der Logistik). In: Myśl katolicka . . . 12—26 (Franz. Zus.fassg.: 159—164).
Myśl katolicka wobec logiki współczesnej (La pensée catholique et la logique moderne). Poznań 1937. (Mit franz. Zus.fassg. 155—196. Diese sep.: Cracovie 1937.)
Quine, W. V.: O sentido da nova logica. Sao Paulo 1944.
Ritchie, A. D.: A defense of Aristotle's logic, in: Mind 55, 1946, 256—262.

Salamucha, J.: O „mechanizacji" myślenia (Über die „Mechanisierung' des Denkens). In: Myśl katolicka . . . 112—121 (u. franz. Zus.fassg.: 182—186).
— O możliwościach ścisłego formalizowania dziedziny pojęć analogicznych (Über Möglichkeiten genauer Formalisierung im Bereich analoger Begriffe.) Ebda. 122—155 (u. franz. Zus.fassg.: 186—193).
— Zestawienie . . . (3.3.).
Scholz, H.: Die mathematische Logik und die Metaphysik, in: Philos. Jahrb. d. Görres-Ges. 51, 1938, 257—291.
Thomas, I.: Logica moderna y logica clasica, in: Estudios filos. 3, 1953, 467 bis 471.

5.4. Leibniz and other logicians before Boole
5.41. Leibniz
5.411. Bibliography

S. Ropohl 5.412.
Bodemann, E.: Der Briefwechsel des G. W. Leibniz in der Kgl. Bibliothek zu Hannover, beschr. v. E. B. Hannover 1889.
— Die Leibnizhandschriften der Kgl. Bibliothek zu Hannover. Hannover, Leipzig 1895.
Gehlen, A.: Bericht über neue Leibniz-Forschungen, in: Blätter f. dt. Philos. 9, 1935, 313—321.
Hartmann, H.: Die Leibniz-Ausgabe der Berliner Akademie. Ebda. 13, 1939, 408—421.
Ravier, E.: Bibliographie de la philosophie de Leibniz. (Diss. Clermond-Ferrand). Caen 1927.
Ritter, P.: Neue Leibniz-Funde, in: Abhdlgen. d. Berliner Akademie d. Wiss. 1904.
Rix, H.: Report on Leibnitz-Newton manuscripts in the possession of the Royal Society of London. London 1880.
Schrecker, P.: Une bibliographie de Leibniz, in: Rev. philos. de la France et de l'Etranger 126, 1938, 324—346.
Trendelenburg, A.: Die im Nachlasse Leibnizens auf der Bibliothek zu Hannover aufbewahrte Tafel der Definitionen, in: Monatsber. d. Berliner Akad. d. Wiss. 1861, 170 ff.

5.412. General accounts

Brunner, F.: Etudes sur la signification historique de la philosophie de Leibniz. Paris 1951.
Cassirer, E.: Leibniz' System in seinen wissenschaftlichen Grundlagen. Marburg 1902.
Fischer, K.: Gottfried Wilhelm Leibniz. Leben, Werke und Lehre. 4. A. Heidelberg 1902.
Halbwachs, M.: Leibniz. (Nouv. éd. rev. et augm.) Paris o. J.
Iwanicki, (J.): Leibniz et les démonstrations mathématiques de l'existence de Dieu. Paris 1934.
Jasper, J.: Leibniz und die Scholastik. (Diss. Leipzig.) Münster i. W. 1898—99.
Kuhn, F.: Die historischen Beziehungen zwischen der stoischen und der Leibnizschen Philosophie. (Diss.) Leipzig 1913.
Mahnke, D.: Leibnizens Synthese von Universalmathematik und Individualmetaphysik I, in: Jahrb. f. Philos. u. phänomenolog. Forschg. 7. Sep.: Halle 1925.
Matzat, H. L.: Untersuchungen über die metaphysischen Grundlagen der Leibnizschen Zeichenkunst. Berlin 1938.
Merz, J. Th.: Leibniz. London 1884 u. 1907. Deutsch, üb. C. Schaarschmidt: Heidelberg 1886.
Nason, J. W.: Leibniz and the logical argument for individual substances, in: Mind 51, 1942, 201—222.

BIBLIOGRAPHY

Nostiz-Rieneck, R. von: Leibniz und die Scholastik, in: Philos. Jahrb. d. Görres-Ges. 7, 1894, 54 ff.
Piat, C.: Leibniz. Paris 1915.
Ropohl, H.: Das Eine und die Welt. Versuch zur Interpretation der Leibnizschen Metaphysik. Mit einem Verzeichnis der Leibniz-Bibliographien. Leipzig 1936.
Russell, B.: A critical exposition of the philosophy of Leibniz. Cambridge 1900. 4. A. 1951. Franz.: La philosophie de Leibniz. Üb. J. u. R.-J. Ray. Paris 1908.
Saw, R. L.: Leibniz. Baltimore 1954.
Schmalenbach, H.: Leibniz. München 1921.

5.413. His logic

Britzelmayr, W.: Über die älteste formale Logik in deutscher Sprache, in: Zeitschr. f. philos. Forschung 2, 1947, 46—68.
Brunstäd, F.: Die mathematische Logik. In: Brunstäd, Logik (Handb. d. Philos., Abt. I, Beitrag A); München, Berlin 1933, 79—84.
Carruccio, E.: I fini del „calculus ratiocinator" di Leibniz, e la logica matematica del nostro tempo, in: Boll. d. Unione Mat. Ital., Ser. 3, 3, 1948, 148—161.
Cohen, J.: On the project of a universal character, in: Mind 64, 1954, 49—63.
Couturat, L.: La Logique de Leibniz d'après des documents inédits. Paris 1901.
Dalbiez, R.: L'idée fondamentale de la combinatoire leibnizienne, in: Trav. du IXième Congr. Int. de Philos.; VI: Logique et mathématiques, Paris 1937, 3—7.
Diels, H.: Über Leibniz und das Problem der Universalsprache, in: Sitz.-Ber. Berliner Akad. d. Wiss. 1899, 579 ff. (oder: 32, 1889, 1—24?).
di Rosa, L.: Il principio degli indiscernibili. Leibniz e Kant, in: Studi Francescani 8, 1936, 336—361.
Dürr, K.: Neue Beleuchtung einer Theorie von Leibniz. Grundzüge des Logikkalküls. Darmstadt 1930.
— Die mathematische Logik von Leibniz, in: Stud. philos. (Basel) 7, 1947, 87—102.
— Leibniz' Forschungen im Gebiet der Syllogistik. Berlin 1949.
Frege, G.: Über den Briefwechsel Leibnizens und Huygens mit Papin, in: Jenaische Zeitschr. f. Nat.-wiss. 15, 1882, 15. Suppl.-Heft, 29—32.
Jourdain, P. E. B.: The logical work of Leibniz, in: The Monist 26, 1916, 504—523.
Kern, H.: De Leibnitii scientia generali commentatio, Progr.. Halle 1847.
Květ, F. B.: Leibnitz'ens Logik. Prag 1857.
Lindemann, H. A.: Leibniz y la lógica moderna, in: Anales d. l. Soc. Cient. Argentina 142, 1946, 164—176.
Mahnke, D.: Die Indexbezeichnung bei Leibniz als Beispiel seiner kombinatorischen Charakteristik. 1913 (Bibl. Math., 3. Folge, Bd. 13).
— Leibniz als Begründer der symbolischen Mathematik, in: Isis 9, 1927, 279 bis 283.
Quesada, F. M.: Sintesis de la conferencia sobre la „Lógica de Leibniz", in: Actas d. l. Acad. Nac. d. Cienc. Exact., Fís. y Nat. de Lima 10, 1947, 79—83.
Rescher, N.: Leibniz's interpretation of his logical calculi, in: JSL 19, 1954, 1—13.
Sanchez-Mazas, M.: Sobre un pasaje de Aristóteles y el cálculo lógico de Leibniz, in: Riv. di filos. (Madrid) 10, 1951, 529—534.
— La lógica matemática en Leibniz, in: Theoria (Madrid) 2, 1954, Heft 7/8.
— Notas sobre la combinatoria de Leibniz. Ebda. 133—145.
Sauer, H.: Über die logischen Forschungen von Leibniz, in: Gottfr. Wilh. Leibniz (Vorträge . . .), Hamburg 1946, 46—78.
Schischkoff, G.: Die gegenwärtige Logistik und Leibniz, in: Beiträge z. Leibniz-Forschung I, Reutlingen 1947, 224—240.
Scholz, H.: Leibniz und die mathematische Grundlagenforschung, in: Jahresber. d. dt. Mathem.-Ver. 52, 1942, 217—244.
Schrecker, P.: Leibniz et le principe du tiers exclu, in: Actes d. Congr. Int. de Philos. Scient.; VI: Philos. des mathématiques, Paris 1936, 75—84.

BIBLIOGRAPHY

Schrecker, P.: Leibniz and the art of inventing algorisms, in: Journ. of the hist. of ideas 8, 1947, 107—116.
Servien, P.: Le progrès de la métaphysique selon Leibniz et le langage des sciences, in: Rev. philos. de la France et de l'Etranger 124, 1937, 140—154.
Tönnies, F.: Leibniz und Hobbes, in: Philos. Monatsh. 23, 1887, 557 ff.
Tramer, M.: Die Entdeckung und Begründung der Differential- und Integralrechnung durch Leibniz im Zusammenhang mit seinen Anschauungen in Logik und Erkenntnistheorie . . . Bern 1906.
Trendelenburg, A.: Über das Element der Definition in Leibnizens Philosophie, in: Monatsber. d. Berliner Akad. d. Wiss. 1860, 374 ff. Auch in: Trendelenburg, Hist. Beiträge zur Philos. III, 1867, 48—62.
— Über Leibnizens Entwurf einer allgemeinen Charakteristik. Abhdlgen. d. Berliner Akad. d. Wiss. 1856. Auch in: Trendelenburg, Hist. Beiträge zur Philos. III (od. II), 1867, 1—47.
Vacca, G.: La logica di Leibniz, in: Rev. de math. (Riv. di mat.) 8, 1902—1906, 64—74.
Vailati, G.: Sul carattere del contributo apportato dal Leibniz allo sviluppo della logica formale, in: Riv. di filos. e scienze affini 12, 1905, 338—344. Neudr. in: Scritti di G. Vailati (1863—1909); (Leipzig, Florenz) 1911, 619 bis 624.
Wiener, Ph. P.: Notes on Leibniz' conception of logic and its historical context, in: The philos. review 48, 1949, 567—586.
Yost, R. M., Jr.: Leibniz and philosophical analysis. Berkeley, Los Angeles 1954.

5.42. Bolzano

Bar-Hillel, Y.: Bolzano's definition of analytic propositions, in: Methodos 2, 1950, 32—55. Auch in: Theoria 16, 1950, 91—117.
Dubislav, W.: Bolzano als Vorläufer der mathematischen Logik, in: Philos. Jahrb. d. Görres-Ges. 44, 1931, 448—456.
Heesch, E.: Grundzüge der Bolzanoschen Wissenschaftslehre. Ebda. 48, 1935, 313—341.
McGill, V. J.: Notes on the logic of grammar, in: The philos. review 39, 1930, 459—478.
Scholz, H.: Die Wissenschaftslehre Bolzanos, in: Semesterber. (Münster i. W.), 9. Sem., Winter 1936/37, 1—53. Erweit. in: Abhdlg. d. Fries'schen Schule, N. S. 6, 399—472.
Smart, H. R.: Bolzano's logic, in: The philos. review 53, 1944, 513—533.
Theobald, S.: Die Bedeutung der Mathematik für die logischen Untersuchungen Bernard Bolzanos (Diss. Bonn 1929). Koblenz 1928.

5.43. Other mathematical logicians before Boole

Aner, K.: Gottfried Ploucquets Leben und Lehren. Halle 1909.
Bergmann, H.: Maimons logischer Kalkül, in: Philosophia 3, 1938, 252—265.
Bornstein, P.: Gottfried Ploucquets Erkenntnistheorie und Metaphysik (Diss. Erlangen). Potsdam 1898.
Brulez, L.: Delboeufs Bedeutung für die Logik, in: Kant-Studien 24, 1919/20, 52—106.
Czeżowski, T.: Przyczynek do sylogistyki Arystotelesa (Brentanowska teoria wniosków kategorycznych). (Beitrag zur aristotelischen Syllogistik [Die Theorie der kategorischen Schlüsse bei Brentano].) (Mit franz. Auszug.) In: Stud. Soc. Scient. Torunensis, Sect. A, 2, 1950, 65—76.
Dürr, K.: Die mathematische Logik des Arnold Geulincx, in: The journ. of. unif. science (Erkenntnis) 8, 1939/40, 361—368. Zusammenfassung in: JSL 4, 1939, 177.
— Die Logistik Johann Heinrich Lamberts, in: Festschr. 60. Geburtst. Prof. Dr. A. Speiser, Zürich 1945, 47—65.

BIBLIOGRAPHY

Eisenring, M. E.: Johann Heinrich Lambert und die wissenschaftliche Philosophie der Gegenwart. Diss. Zürich 1944.
Hillebrand, F.: Die neuen Theorien der kategorischen Schlüsse. Wien 1891.
Krienelke, K.: J. H. Lamberts Philosophie der Mathematik. Diss. Halle 1909.
Lambert, J. H.: In algebram philosophicam Cl. Richeri breves adnotationes, in: Nova acta eruditorum, Leipzig 1767, 334—344.
Land, J. P. N.: Brentano's logical innovations, in: Mind 1, 1876, 289—292.
Peano, G.: Un precursore della logica matematica, in: Riv. di mat. 4, 1894, 120.
Venn, J.: Notice of Castillon's Sur un nouvel algorithme logique, in: Mind 6, 1881, 447 f.
Wisdom, J.: Interpretation and analysis in relation to Bentham's theory of definition. London 1931.

5.5. Boole; English and American logicians before Russell
5.51. Boole

Anonymer Verfasser: George Boole, in: Proc. of the Royal Soc. of London 15, 1867; Obituary notices of fellows deceased, VI—XI.
Bobynin, V. V.: Opyty matématičeskago izložénia logiki. Vypusk 1: Raboty Boolea, Sočinenie Roberta Grassmanna (Teil I: Arbeiten von Boole und Robert Grassmann). (Moskau) 1886. Vypusk 2: Sočinenia Ernesta Schrödera (Teil II: Arbeiten von Ernst Schröder). (Moskau) 1894.
Halsted, G. B.: Boole's logical method, in: The journ. of spec. philos. (St. Louis, Mo.), 12, 1878, 81—91.
— Professor Jevons' criticism of Boole's logical system, in: Mind 3, 1878, 134—137.
Harley, R.: George Boole, F. R. S., in: The Brit. quart. review 44, 1866, 141 bis 181.
— Remarks on Boole's „Mathematical Analysis of Logic', in: Report of the 36th meeting of the Brit. Ass. for the Advancem. of Science; London 1867, Notices and abstracts, 3—6.
— On Boole's „Laws of Thought", in: Report of the 40th meeting of the Brit. Ass. for the Advancem. of Science; London 1871, Notices and abstracts, 14 f.
— A contribution to the history of the algebra of logic. In: Report of the 50th meeting of the Brit. Ass. for the Advancem. of Science, London 1881.
Hesse, M. B.: Boole's philosophy of logic, in: Annals of science (London), 8, 1952, 61—81.
Jevons, W. S.: Artikel über George Boole in: Encyclopaedia Britannica, Ausg. v. 1955, Bd. 3; Chicago, London, Toronto; 882 f.
Kneale, W.: Boole and the revival of logic, in: Mind 57, 1948, 149—175.
Nagel, E.: „Impossible numbers": a chapter in the history of modern logic, in: Stud. in the hist. of ideas (New York), 3, 1935, 427—474.
Prior, A. N.: Categoricals and hypotheticals in George Boole and his successors, in: The Australasian journ. of philos. 27, 1949, 171—196.
Venn, J.: Boole, George. In: Dictionary of National Biography, vol.5; London, New York 1886, 369 f.

5.52. De Morgan

Halsted, G. B.: De Morgan as logician, in: The journ. of spec. philos. (St. Louis, Mo.), 18, 1884, 1—9.

5.53. Jevons

Keynes, J. N.: Über W. S. Jevons. In: Encyclopaedia Britannica, 10. A., London 1902.
Liard, L.: Un nouveau système de logique formelle. M. Stanley Jevons. In: Rev. philos. de la France et de l'Etranger 3, 1877, 277—293.

Mays, W.: Mechanized reasoning, in: Electronic engineering 23, 1951, 278. (Bezieht sich auf: McCallum und Smith, Mechanized reasoning. . . .).
Mays, W., C. E. M. Hansel, D. P. Henry: Note on the exhibition of logical machines at the joint session, July 1950, in: Mind 60, 1951, 262 ff.
Mays, W. und D. P. Henry: Logical machines. New light on W. Stanley Jevons, in: The Manchester guardian, Nr. 32677 (14. Juli 1951), B, S. 4.
— Exhibition of the works of W. Stanley Jevons, in: Nature 170, 1952, 696 f.
McCallum, D. B. und J. B. Smith: Mechanized reasoning — logical computors and their design, in: Electronic engineering 23, 1951, 126—133.
— The authors reply. Ebda. 278. (Bezieht sich auf: Mays, Mechanized reasoning.)
Riehl, A.: Die englische Logik der Gegenwart, in: Vierteljahresschr. f. wissenschaftl. Philos. 1, 1877, 50—80.
Schlötel, W.: Eine Berichtigung zu dem Aufsatz von A. Riehl: „Die englische Logik der Gegenwart". Ebda. 455—457.
— Eine Selbstberichtigung. Ebda. 614 f.
S. a. Shearman, A. T. (5.31.), Halsted (5.5.).

5.54. Peirce

Buchler, J.: Peirce's theory of logic, in: The journ. of philos. 36, 1939, 197—215·
Burks, A. W.: Peirce's conception of logic as a normative science, in: The philos. review 52, 1943, 187—193.
Dewey, J.: Peirce's theory of linguistic signs, thought, and meaning, in: The journ. of philos. 43, 1946, 85—95. (S. dazu: Morris, Ch.: Note thereon. Ebda. 196. Dewey, J.: Reply thereto. Ebda. 280). Auch in: Dewey, J. und A. F. Bentley, Knowing and the known, Boston 1949.
Kempski, J. v.: C. S. Peirce und die ἀπαγωγή des Aristoteles. (2.3.)
Keyser, C. J.: A glance of some of the ideas of Charles Sanders Peirce, in: Scripta math. 3, 1935, 11—37. Neudr. in: Mathematics as a culture clue and other essays, by C. J. K.; New York 1947, 155—188.
— Charles Sanders Peirce as a pioneer. In: Galois lectures; New York 1941, 87—112.
Reyes y Prosper, V.: Charles Santiago Peirce y Oscar Howard Mitchell, in: El progr. mat. 2, 1892, 170—173.
Russell, F. C.: Hints for the elucidation of Mr. Peirce's logical work, in: The Monist 18, 1908, 406—415.
Ueyama, S.: Development of Peirce's theory of logic, in: The science of thought (Tokio) 1, 1954, 25—32.
Weiss, P.: Peirce, Charles Sanders, in: Dictionary of American biography 14, New York 1934, 398—403.
Young, F. H.: Charles Sanders Peirce. America's greatest logician and most original philosopher. (Vorgetr. am 15. Oktober 1945 der Pike County Hist. Soc. in Milford, Penn.) Privatdr. 1946.

5.55. Other English and American mathematical logicians before Russell

Halsted, G. B.: The modern logic, in: The journ. of spec. philos. 17, 1883, 210—213.
Ladd-Franklin, Chr.: On some characteristics of symbolic logic, in: The Amer. journ. of psychol. 2, 1889, 543—567.
— Dr. Hillebrand's syllogistic scheme, in: Mind 1, 1892, 527—530.
Reyes y Prosper, V.: Cristina Ladd Franklin. Matematica americana y su influencia en la logica simbolica, in: El progr. mat. 1, 1891, 297—300.
— Charles Santiago Peirce y Oscar Howard Mitchell (5.54.).
Shearman, A. T.: Some controverted points in symbolic logic, in: Proc. of the Arist. Soc., n. s. 5, 1905, 74—105.

5.6. Frege, Peano, Schröder
5.61. Frege

Bachmann, F.: Untersuchungen zur Grundlegung der Arithmetik mit besonderer Beziehung auf Dedekind, Frege und Russell. (Diss.) Münster i. W. 1934.

Beth, E. W.: Naschrift (Nachschrift) (zu: Beumer, En historische bijzonderheid . . .), in: Simon Stevin 25, 1946/47, 150 f.

Beumer, M. G.: En historische bijzonderheid uit het leven van Gottlob Frege (1848—1925). (Eine Einzelheit aus dem Leben Gottlob Freges [1848—1925]). Ebda. 146—149.

Black, M.: A translation of Frege's Über Sinn und Bedeutung. Introductory note, in: The philos. review 57, 1948, 207 f.

Husserl, E. G.: Frege's Versuch. In: Philosophie der Arithmetik, Leipzig 1891, 129—134.

Jourdain, P. E. B.: Introductory note, zu: Frege, The fundamental laws of arithmetic. Üb. aus ,,Grundges. d. Arith." v. J. Stachelroth und P. E. B. Jourdain, in: The Monist 25, 1915, 481—484.

— The function of symbolism in mathematical logic, in: Scientia 21, 1917, 1—12. Franz.: La fonction du symbolisme dans la logique mathématique. Üb. E. Philippi. Ebda. Supplément, 3—15.

Korcik, A.: Gottlob Frege jako twórca pierwszego systemu aksjomatycznego współczesnej logiki zdań (Gottlob Frege, Urheber des ersten axiomatischen Systems der zeitgenössischen Aussagenlogik), in: Roczn. fíloz. 1, 1948, 138 bis 164. Franz. Zusammenfassung: ebda. 332.

Linke, P. F.: Gottlob Frege als Philosoph, in: Zeitschr. f. philos. Forschung 1, 1946/47, 75—99.

Lukasiewicz, J.: Zur Geschichte . . . (1.23.).

Myhill, J.: Two ways of ontology in modern logic, in: The review of metaph. 3, 1950, 367—384.

Papst, W.: Gottlob Frege als Philosoph. (Diss.) Berlin 1932.

Peano, G.: Risposta, in: Rev. de math. (Riv. di mat.) 6, 1896—1899, 60 f.

— Studii di logica matematica, in: Atti d. Reale Accad. d. Scienze di Torino 32, 1897, 565—583. Deutsch: Über mathematische Logik; in: Genocchi, Differentialrechnung und Grundzüge der Intregralrechnung, hrsg. G. Peano, üb. G. Bohlmann u. A. Schlepp, Leipzig 1899, 336—352.

Perelman, Ch.: Metafizyka Fregego (Freges Metaphysik). (Poln. m. franz. Zusammenfassung.) In: Kwart. fíloz. 14, 1938, 119—142.

— Etude sur Gottlob Frege, in: Rev. de l'Univ. de Bruxelles 44, 1938/39, 224—227.

Russell, B.: The logical and arithmetical doctrines of Frege. Als ,,Appendix A" in: The principles of mathematics, 501—522.

Scholz, H.: Was ist ein Kalkül und was hat Frege für eine pünktliche Beantwortung dieser Frage geleistet? In: Semester-Berichte (Münster i. W.), 7. Sem., Sommer 1935, 16—47.

— Die klassische deutsche Philosophie und die neue Logik, in: Actes du Congr. Int. de philos. scient.; VIII: Hist. de la log. et de la philos. scient., Paris 1936, 1—8.

— und F. Bachmann: Der wissenschaftliche Nachlaß von Gottlob Frege. Ebda. 24—30.

Smart, H. R.: Frege's logic, in: The philos. review 54, 1945, 489—505.

Thomae, J.: Bemerkung zum Aufsatze des Herrn Frege, in: Jahresber. d. dt. Mathem.-Ver. 15, 1906, 56.

— Gedankenlose Denker, eine Ferienplauderei. Ebda. 434—438.

— Erklärung. Ebda. 590 ff.

Wells, R. S.: Frege's ontology, in: The review of metaph. 4, 1951, 537—573.

Whitehead, A. N.: Remarks, in: The philos. review 46, 1937, 178—186. Neudr. als ,,Analysis of meaning" in: Essays in science and philos., New York 1947, 122—131 u. London 1948, 93—99.

Wienpahl, P. D.: Frege's Sinn und Bedeutung, in: Mind 59, 1950, 483—494.

5.62. Peano

Cassina, U.: Vita et opera di Giuseppe Peano, in: Schola et vita 7, 1932, 117 bis 148. (Peano-Bibliographie: 133—148).

— L'œuvre philosophique de G. Peano, in: Rev. de métaph. et de mor. 40, 1933, 481—491.

— L'opera scientifica di Giuseppe Peano, in: Rendiconti d. Semin. Mat. e Fis. di Milano 7, 1933, 323—389.

— Su la logica matematica di G. Peano, in: Boll. d. Unione Mat. Ital. 12, 1933, 57—65.

— Parallelo fra la logica teoretica di Hilbert a quella di Peano, in: Period. di mat., Ser. 4, 17, 1937, 129—138.

— L'idéographie de Peano du point de vue de la théorie du langage, in: Riv. di mat. d. Univ. di Parma 4, 1953, 195—205.

Collectione de scripto in honore de Prof. G. Peano in occasione de suo 70° anno ... Suppl. ad „Schola et vita", Mailand 1928.

Couturat, L.: La logique mathématique de M. Peano, in: Rev. de métaph. et de mor. 7, 1899, 616—646.

di Dia, G.: Formulario Mathematico et latina sine-flexione de G. Peano. In: Collectione ..., 53—69.

Feys, R.: Peano et Burali-Forti précurseurs de la logique combinatoire, In: Actes du XIème Congr. Int. de Philos.; V: Log., analyse philos., philos. d. math.; Amsterdam, Louvain 1953, 70—72.

Frege, G.: Lettera del sig. G. Frege all'Editore (datiert: 29. Sept. 1896), in: Rev. de math. (Riv. di mat.) 6, 1896—1899, 53—59.

— Über die Begriffsschrift des Herrn Peano ... (5.2.).

Levi, B.: L'opera matematica di Giuseppe Peano, in: Boll. d. Unione Mat. Ital. 11, 1932, 253—262.

— Intorno alle vedute di G. Peano circa la logica matematica. (A prop. del preced. art. del prof. U. Cassina). Ebda. 12, 1933, 65—68.

Natucci, A.: Fundamentos de arithmetica secundo G. Peano. In: Collectione ..., 70—75.

Padoa, A.: Ce que la logique doit à Peano. In: Actes du Congr. Int. de philos. scient.; VIII: Hist. de la log. et de la philos. scient.; Paris 1936, 31—37.

Stamm, E.: Logica matematico de Peano. In: Collectione ..., 33 ff.

— Józef Peano (Poln.), in: Wiadom. mat. 36, 1934, 1—56.

Vacca, G.: Logica matematica. L'indirizzo di Peano. In: Enciclop. ital. di scienze, lettere ed arti, 1938—1948, Seconda append. (I—Z); Roma 1949, 226.

Vailati, G.: La logique mathématique et sa nouvelle phase de développement dans les écrits de M. J. Peano, in: Rev. de métaph. et de mor. 7, 1899, 86—102. Neudr. in: Scritti di G. Vailati (1863—1909); Leipzig, Florenz 1911, 229—242.

5.63. Schröder

Church, A.: Schröder's anticipation of the simple theory of types, in: The journ. of univ. science (Erkenntnis) 9, 1939, 149—152.

Löwenheim, L.: Einkleidung der Mathematik in Schröderschen Relativkalkül, in: JSL 5, 1940, 1—15.

Lüroth, J.: Ernst Schröder †, in: Jahresber. d. dt. Mathem.-Ver. 12, 1903, 249—265.

Reyes y Prosper, V.: Ernesto Schroeder. Sus merecimientos ante la Logica, su propaganda logico-matematica, sus obras, in: El progr. mat. 2, 1892, 33—36.

S. a. Bobynin (5.5.).

5.7. Russell and Whitehead

Bernstein, B. A.: Relation of Whitehead and Russell's theory of deduction to the Boolean logic of propositions, in: Bull. of the Amer. Math. Soc. 38, 1932, 589—593.

BIBLIOGRAPHY

Broad, C. D.: Alfred North Whitehead (1861—1947), in: Mind 57, 1948, 139—145.
Copleston, F. C.: Bertrand Russell, in: Rev. de filos. (Madrid) 9, 1950, 261—278.
del Pando, J. E.: La logica de Bertrand Russell, in: Univ. de Antioquia 37, 1940, 85—104.
Feibleman, J.: A reply to Bertrand Russell's introduction to the second edition of The principles of mathematics. In: The philos. of B. Russell. Ed. P. A. Schilpp; Evanston, Chicago 1944, 155—174.
Ghyka, M.: Bertrand Russell and scientific philosophy, in: The personalist 28, 1947, 129—139.
Gödel, K.: Russell's mathematical logic. In: The philos. of B. Russell. Ed. P. A. Schilpp; Evanston, Chicago 1944, 123—153.
Hammerschmidt, W. W.: Alfred North Whitehead, in: Scripta Math. 14, 1948, 17—23.
Jourdain, P. E. B.: The philosophy of Mr. B*rtr*nd R*ss*ll, in: The Monist 21, 1911, 481—508; 26, 1916, 24—62. Verm. Neudr.: The philosophy of Mr. B*rtr*nd R*ss*ll, with an appendix of leading passages from certain other works, London 1918.
— Mr. Bertrand Russell's first work on the principles of mathematics, in: The Monist 22, 1912, 149—158.
Leggett, H. W.: Bertrand Russell, O. M. A pictorial biography. New York 1950.
Nagel, E.: Russell's philosophy of science. In: The philos. of B. Russell. Ed. P. A. Schilpp; Evanston, Chicago 1944, 317—349.
Pereira, R. C.: Alfred North Whitehead, in: Rev. mat. hispano-americana, Ser. 4, 9, 1949, 49—52.
Quine, W. V.: Whitehead and the rise of modern logic. In: The philos. of A. N. Whitehead. Ed. P. A. Schilpp; Evanston, Chicago 1941, 127—163.
Ramsey, F. P.: Russell, Bertrand Arthur William Russell, 3rd Earl. In: The encyclopaedia Britannica, 14. A., Bd. 19; London, New York 1929, 678 f.; neue A. Chicago, London, Toronto 1944.
Reichenbach, H.: Bertrand Russell's logic. In: The philos. of B. Russell. Ed. P. A. Schilpp; Evanston, Chicago 1944, 21—54.
Russell, B.: My mental development. Ebda. 1—20.
— Reply to criticisms. Ebda. 679—741.
— Whitehead and Principia Mathematica, in: Mind 57, 1948, 137 f.
— Alfred North Whitehead, O. M., in: Riv. crit. di storia d. filos. 8, 1953, 101—104.
Sanger, Ch. P. und anonym. Verf.: Russell, Bertrand Arthur William Russell, 3rd Earl. In: Encyclopaedia Britannica, Bd. 19; Chicago, London, Toronto 1950; 678.
Strachey, O.: Mr. Russell and some recent criticisms of his views, in: Mind 24, 1915, 16—28.
Tallon, H. J.: Russell's doctrine of the logical proposition, in: The New Scholasticism 13, 1939, 31—48.
Ushenko, A.: The logics of Hegel and Russell, in: Philos. and phenomenol. research 10, 1949, 107—114.
Whittaker, E. T.: Alfred North Whitehead 1861—1947, in: Obit. not. of fellows of the Royal Soc. 6 (17), 1948, 281—296.
Wiener, P. P.: Method in Russell's work on Leibniz. In: The philos. of B. Russell. Ed. P. A. Schilpp; Evanston, Chicago 1944, 257—276.
S. a. *5.11.*

5.8. Foundations
5.81. General

Ambrose, A.: A controversy in the logic of mathematics, in: The philos. review 42, 1933, 594—611.
Baldus, R.: Formalismus und Intuitionismus in der Mathematik. Karlsruhe 1924.
Bense, M.: Geist der Mathematik. München, Berlin 1939.

Beth, E. W.: L'évidence intuitive dans les mathématiques modernes. In: Trav. du IXe Congr. Int. de Philos.; VI: Log. et math.; Paris 1937, 161—165.
— Inleiding tot de wijsbegeerte der wiskunde (Einführung in die Philosophie der Mathematik). Antwerpen und Brussels, Nijmegen und Utrecht 1940, 2. A. 1942.
— Wijsbegeerte der wiskunde (Philosophie der Mathematik), in: Euclides 17, 1940/41, 141—158.
—‘Les fondements logiques des mathématiques. 2. éd. rev. et augm. Paris, Louvain 1955.
Black, M.: The nature of mathematics. A critical survey. London 1933, New York 1934. 2. A. London 1950, New York 1950.
Cavaillès, J.: Méthode axiomatique et formalisme. I: Le problème du fondement des mathématiques. II: Axiomatique et système formel. III: La non-contradiction de l'arithmétique. Paris 1938.
— Sur la logique et la théorie de la science (postum). Paris 1947.
Church, A.: The present situation in the foundation of mathematics. In: Gonseth, Philos. math. 67—72.
d'Abro, A.: The controversies on the nature of mathematics. In: The decline of mechanism (in modern physics), New York 1939, 186—213.
Davis, H. T.: A survey of the problem of mathematical truth. Als Einl. in: Counting and measuring, by H. von Helmholtz, trans. by Ch. L. Bryan, New York 1930, V—XXXIV.
Dingler, H.: Der Zusammenbruch der Wissenschaft und der Primat der Philosophie. München 1926, 2. A. 1931. (Bes. 75—97, in d. 2. A. auch 414 f.).
Dubislav, W.: Die sog. Grundlagenkrise der Mathematik, in: Unterrichtsbl f. Math. u. Nat.-wiss. 37, 1931, 146—152.
— Die Philosophie der Mathematik in der Gegenwart. Berlin 1932.
Feys, R.: Fondements et méthodes des mathématiques. Notes sur la réunion d'études de Zurich, in: Rev. philos. de Louvain 42, 1939, 78—88.
Fraenkel, A. A.: The recent controversies about the foundations of mathematics, in: Scripta math. 13, 1947, 17—36.
Fraenkel, A.: Über die gegenwärtige Grundlagenkrise der Mathematik, in: Sitz.-ber. d. Ges. zur Förd. d. ges. Nat.-wiss. zu Marburg 1924, 117—132.
— Die neueren Ideen zur Grundlegung der Analysis und Mengenlehre, in Jahresber. d. dt. Mathem.-Ver. 33, 1924, 97—103.
— Über die gegenwärtige Krise in den Grundlagen der Mathematik, in: Unterrichtsbl. f. Math. u. Nat.-wiss. 31, 1925, 249—254 u. 270—274.
— On modern problems in the foundations of mathematics. Üb. S. Neumark in: Scripta math. 1, 1932/33, 222—227.
Garcia Bacca, J. D.: Assaigs moderns per a la fonamentació de les matemàtiques, in: Soc. Cat. de Ciènc. Fis., Quím. i Mat., Publ. 1, 225—275.
Gentzen, G.: Die gegenwärtige Lage in der mathematischen Grundlagenforschung, in: Forschungen z. Log. u. z. Grundl. d. exakt. Wiss., neue Folge 4, Leipzig 1938, 1—18; auch in: Deutsche Math. 3, 1938, 255—268.
Gonseth, F.: Les fondements des mathématiques. Paris 1926.
— (Hrsg.): Philosophie mathématique. Paris 1939.
Larguier, E. H.: The schools of thought in modern mathematics, in: Thought (New York) 12, 1937, 225—240.
— Concerning some views on the structure of mathematics, in: The Thomist 4, 1942, 431—444.
Lietzmann, W.: Formalismus und Intuitionismus in der Mathematik, in: Zeitschr. f. math. u. nat.-wiss. Unterr. . . . 56, 1925, 355—358.
Mannoury, G.: Methodologisches und Philosophisches zur Elementar-Mathematik. Haarlem 1909. Neuausg.: Assen (ca. 1947).
Poincaré, H.: Les mathématiques et la logique, in: Rev. de métaph. et de mor. 13, 1905, 815—835; 14, 1906, 17—34 u. 294—317. Veränd. u. verm. Neudr. in: Science et méthode, Paris 1908. Russ.: (St. Petersburg) 1910, (Odessa) 1910. Poln.: Nauka i metoda, üb. v. M. H. Horwitz, 1911. Z. T. engl. als: The new

logics, üb. G. B. Halsted, in : The Monist 22, 1912, 243—256; und als: The latest effort of the logisticians, üb. G. B. Halsted, ebda. 524—539. Ganz engl. in: Poincaré, The foundations of science, üb. G. B. Halsted, bes. Vorw. v. Poincaré u. Einl. v. J. Royce; New York 1913. Auch als: Science and method, üb. F. Maitland, Vorw. v. B. Russell; London, Edinburgh, Dublin, New York o. J.

Ramsey, F. P.: The foundations of mathematics, in: Proc. of the London Math. Soc., 2. Ser., 25, 1926, 338—384. Neudr. in: The found. of math. and other log. essays, ed. R. B. Braithwaite; New York, London 1931 (Neudruck: New York 1950), 1—61.

— Mathematics, foundations of. In: The encyclopaedia Britannica, 14. A., Bd. 15; London, New York 1929, 82 ff. Neudr. Chicago, London, Toronto 1944.

Schmeidler, W.: Neuere Grundlagenforschungen in der Mathematik, in: Unterrichtsbl. f. Math. u. Nat.-wiss. 35, 1929, 193—198.

Skolem, Th.: Litt om de vigtigste diskussioner i den senere tid angaaende matematikkens grundlag (Einiges über die wichtigsten Auseinandersetzungen der jüngsten Zeit betreffend die Grundlagen der Mathematik), in: Norsk mat. tidsskr. 8, 1926, 1—13.

— Über die Grundlagendiskussionen in der Mathematik. In: Den Syvende Skandinav. Matematikerkongr., Oslo 1930, 3—21.

Stabler, E. R.: An interpretation and comparison of three schools of thought in the foundations of mathematics, in: The math. teacher 28, 1935, 5—35.

Weyl, H.: Über die neue Grundlagenkrise der Mathematik, in: Math. Zeitschr. 10, 1921, 39—79.

— Die heutige Erkenntnislage in der Mathematik, in: Symposion (Berlin) 1, 1925—1927, 1—32. Sonderdr. Erlangen 1926.

— Philosophie der Mathematik und der Naturwissenschaft I. München, Berlin 1926. Hebräisch: Jerusalem 1945. Engl. (durchges. u. verm.): Philosophy of mathematics and natural sciences, Princeton 1949.

Zawirski, Z.: Stosunek logiki do matematyki w świetle badań współczesnych (Die Beziehung der Logik zur Mathematik im Lichte neuer Forschungen). In: Księga pamiątkowa ku czci prof. Władysława Heinricha, Kraków 1927, 171—206.

5.82. Brouwer and intuitionism

Bernays, P.: Sur le platonisme dans les mathématiques, in: L'Enseignem. math. 34, 1935/36, 52—69.

Bockstaele, P.: Het intuitionisme bij de Franse wiskundigen (Intuitionismus bei den französischen Mathematikern), Brussels 1949.

Brouwer, L. E. J.: Historical background, principles and methods of intuitionism, in: South African journ. of science 49, 1952/53, 139—146.

Dresden, A.: Brouwer's contributions to the foundations of mathematics, in: The Bull. of the Amer. Math. Soc. 30, 1924, 31—40.

Heyting, A.: Formal logic and mathematics, in: Synthese (Amsterdam) 6, 1947/48, 275—282.

Larguier, E. H.: Brouwerian philosophy of mathematics, in: Scripta math. 7, 1940 (ersch. 1941), 69—78.

Menger, K.: Der Intuitionismus, in: Blätter f. deutsche Philos. 4, 1930, 311—325.

Zawirski, Z.: Geneza i rozwoj logiki intuicjonistycznej (Entstehung und Entwicklung der intuitionistischen Logik), in: Kwart. filoz. 16, 1946, 165—222.

5.83. Hilbert and formalism

Anonymer Verfasser: Le professeur David Hilbert, in: Le mois 70 (Oktober 1936), 263—267.

Bachiller, T. R.: David Hilbert, in: Rev. mat. hispano-americana, Ser. 4, 3, 1943, 77—81.

Bernays, P.: Die Bedeutung Hilberts für die Philosophie der Mathematik, in: Die Naturwissenschaften 10, 1922, 93—99.
— Über Hilberts Gedanken zur Grundlegung der Arithmetik, in: Jahresber. d. dt. Mathem.-Ver. 31, 1922, 10—19.
— Die Philosophie der Mathematik und die Hilbertsche Beweistheorie, in: Blätter f. dt. Philos. 4, 1930, 326—367.
— Hilberts Untersuchungen über die Grundlagen der Arithmetik. In: David Hilbert, Gesammelte Abhandlungen III, Berlin 1935, 196—216.
— Sur les questions méthodologiques actuelles de la théorie Hilbertienne de la démonstration. In: Gonseth (Hrsg.), Les entretiens . . . (5.2.), 144—161.
Chevalley, C., und A. Dandieu: Logique hilbertienne et psychologie, in: Rev. philos. de la France et de l'Etranger 113, 1932, 99—111.
Cipolla, M.: Sui fondamenti logici della matematica secondo le recenti vedute di Hilbert, in: Annali di mat. pura e appl., 4. Ser., 1, 1923/24, 19—29.
MacLane, S.: Hilbert-Bernays on proof-theory, in: Bull. of the Amer. Math. Soc. 41, 1935, 162—165.
Mahnke, D.: Von Hilbert zu Husserl, in: Unterrichtsbl. f. Math. u. Nat.-wiss. 29, 1923, 34—37.
van Veen, S. C.: In memoriam David Hilbert (1862—1943). (Holländ.) In: Mathematica B (Zutphen) 11, 1943, 159—169.
Weyl, H.: David Hilbert 1862—1943, in: Obit. not. of fellows of the Royal Soc. 4 (13), 1944, 547—553.
— David Hilbert and his mathematical work, in: Bull. of the Amer. Math. Soc. 50, 1944, 612—654.

5.9. Other logicians

S. a. Bobynin (5.5.).

5.901. Bornstein

Wąsik, W.: Benedykt Bornstein (1880—1948), in: Przegl. filoz. 44, 1948, 444 bis 451.

5.902. Cantor

Bernstein, F.: Die Mengenlehre Georg Cantors und der Finitismus, in: Jabresber. d. dt. Mathem.-Ver. 28, 1919, 63—78.
Fraenkel, A.: (Biographie Georg Cantors). In: Cantor, Gesammelte Abbandlungen mathematischen und philosophischen Inhalts, hrsg. E. Zermelo, Berlin 1932.

5.903. Cavaillès

Dubarle, D.: Le dernier écrit philosophique de Jean Cavaillès, in: Rev. de métaph. et de mor. 53, 1948, 225—247 u. 350—378. (Betr.: Sur la logique et . . . [5.81.]).
Dubarle, R. P.: Jean Cavaillès et la philosophie, in: Les études philos. (Paris), n. s. 3, 1948, 82.
Ferrières, G.: Jean Cavaillès philosophe et combattant (1903—1944). Paris 1950.
Granger, G. G.: Jean Cavaillès ou la montée vers Spinoza, in: Les études philos. (Paris), n. s. 2, 1947, 271—279.

5.904. Couturat

Dassen, C. C.: Luis Couturat, in: Anales de la Soc. Cient. Argentina 118, 1934, 136—143.
— Vida y obra de Luis Couturat, in: Anales de la Acad. Nac. de Cienc. Exact., Fis. y Nat. de Buenos Aires 4, 1939, 73—204.
Schnippenkötter, J.: Die Bedeutung der mathematischen Untersuchungen Couturats für die Logik, in: Philos. Jahrb. d. Görres-Ges. 23, 1910, 447—468.

5.905. Herbrand

Chevalley, C.: Sur la pensée de J. Herbrand, in: L'Enseignem. math. 34, 1935 bis 1936, 97—102.

5.906. Keyser

Bell, E. T.: Cassius Jackson Keyser, in: Scripta math. 14, 1948, 27—33.

5.907. Kotarbiński

Rand, R.: Kotarbińskis Philosophie auf Grund seines Hauptwerkes: „Elemente der Erkenntnistheorie, der Logik und der Methodologie der Wissenschaften" (= Elementy teorji poznania . . .: *5.2.*), in: Erkenntnis 7, 1938, 92—120.

5.908. Leśniewski

Ajdukiewicz, K.: Die syntaktische Konnexität (*5.2.*).
Słupecki, J.: St. Leśniewski's protothetics, in: Stud. Log. (Warszawa) 1, 1953, 44—112.
Sobociński, B.: An investigation of protothetic. Bruxelles 1949.
— L'analyse de l'antinomie russellienne par Leśniewski, in: Methodos 1, 1949, 94—107 u. 220—228 u. 308—316.

5.909. Meinong

Russell, B.: Arbeiten über Meinong in: Mind 8, 1899, 251—256; 13, 1904, 204 bis 219 u. 336—354; 14, 1905, 530—538; 15, 1906, 412—415; 16, 1907, 436 bis 439.

5.910. Nagy

Padoa, A.: Albino Nagy, in: Riv. filos. 4, 1901, 427—432.

5.911. Nelson

Bernays, P.: Über Nelsons Stellungnahme in der Philosophie der Mathematik, in: Die Naturwissenschaften 16, 1928, 142—145.
Kraft, J.: Introduction. In: Socratic method and critical philosophy. Selected essays by Leonard Nelson. New Haven 1949, IX—XXII.

5.912. Neupositivismus

Feys, R.: Neo-positivisme en symbolische logica (Neu-Positivismus und symbolische Logik), in: Annalen v. het Thijmgenootschap 37, 1949, 150—159.
Hess, M. V.: Mathematical logic in modern positivism, in: The journ. of philos. 30, 1933, 242—245.
von Wright, G. H.: Logistisk filosofi (Logistische Philosophie), in: Nya Argus (Helsinki) 31, 1938, 175—177.
S. a. *5.11.*

5.913. Poreckij

Dubágo, D.: P. S. Porěckij (russ.), in: Bull. de la Soc. Phys.-Math. de Kasan, 2. Ser., 16, 1908, 3—7.
Sleszyński, J. (I. Slěšinskij): Památi Platona Sérgééviča Porěckago (In memoriam Platon Poretsky), in: Věstnik opytnoj fiziki i eléméntarnoj matématiki (Odessa) 487, 1909.

BIBLIOGRAPHY

5.914. Reichenbach

Clay, J.: Obituary. Hans Reichenbach, in: Synthese 9, 1953, 10 ff.

5.915. Sheffer

Korcik, A.: Geneza pomysłu Sheffera dotyczacego redukcji pięciu stałych logicznych do pewnej stałej różnej od nich (Die Entstehung von Sheffers Idee einer Reduktion von fünf logischen Konstanten auf eine von ihnen verschiedene Konstante), in: Rocz. filoz. (Lublin) 2/3, 1949/50 (ersch. 1951), 423—428.
S. a. 5.11.

5.916. Sleszyński

Hoborski, A.: Jan Sleszyński (Wspomnienie pośmiertne). (Jan Sleszyński [Nachruf]), in: Wiadomości mat. 36, 1934, 71—75.

5.917. Stebbing

Keeling, S. V.: Prof. Susan Stebbing, in: Nature 152, 1943, 377.
Magg, P.: Homage to Susan Stebbing, in: The personalist 27, 1946, 165—172.
Wisdom, J.: L. Susan Stebbing, 1885—1943, in: Mind 53, 1944, 283 ff. Und in: Philosophical studies, essays in memory of L. S. Stebbing, London 1948, 1—4.

5.918. Vacca

Carruccio, E.: Giovanni Vacca matematico, storico e filosofo della scienza, in: Boll. d. Unione Mat. Ital., Ser. 3, 8, 1953, 448—456.
Frajese, A.: Ricordo di Giovanni Vacca, in: Archimede 5, 1953, 86 f.

5.919. Vailati

Facchi, P.: I contributi di G. Vailati alla metodologia ed all' analisi del linguaggio, in: Riv. crit. di storia d. filos. 7, 1952, 41—48.

5.920. Wittgenstein

D. A. T. G. und A. C. J.: Ludwig Wittgenstein, in: The Australasian journ. of philos. 29, 1951, 73—80.
Ferrater Mora, J.: Wittgenstein, símbolo de una época angustiada, in: Theoria (Madrid) 2, 1954, 7/8, 33—38.
Gabriel, L.: Logische Magie. Ein Nachwort zum Thema Wittgenstein, in: Wissensch. u. Weltbild (Wien) 1954, 288—293.
Gasking, D. A. T.: Anderson and the Tractatus logico-philosophicus, in: The Australasian journ. of philos. 27, 1949, 1—26.
Russell, B.: Ludwig Wittgenstein, in: Mind 60, 1951, 297 f.
Ryle, G.: Ludwig Wittgenstein, in: Analysis (Oxford) 12, 1951, 1—9. Ital. (üb. F. Rossi Landi), in: Riv. di filos. 43, 1952, 186—193.
Wisdom, J.: Ludwig Wittgenstein, in: Mind 61, 1952, 258—260.

5.921. Zawirski

Gawecki, B. J.: Zygmunt Zawirski (1882—1948), in: Przegl. filoz. 44, 1948, 436 bis 443.

6. THE INDIAN VARIETY OF LOGIC

6.1. History of Indian philosophy
6.11. Bibliography

Annual Bibliography of Oriental Studies for 1946—1950. Kyoto University. June 1952.
Annual Bibliography of Oriental Studies for 1951—1952. Kyoto University. March 1954.
A Union List of Printed Indic Texts and Translations in American Libraries ... by M. B. Emenau ... New Haven (Conn.). 1935.
Bibliographie bouddhique, hrsg. Lalou u. Przyluski. Paris 1928 ff.
Regamey, C.: Buddhistische Philosophie. BESP 20/21. Bern 1950.
S. a. Dasgupta u. Winternitz (*6.121.*).

6.12. General accounts, works of reference
6.121. General

Dasgupta, S. N.: A history of Indian Philosophy. 4 Bde. Cambridge 1922—49.
Deussen, P.: Allgemeine Geschichte der Philosophie. Leipzig I/1: 1915; İ/2: 1899, 2. A. 1907 (engl.: Edinburgh 1906); I/3: 1908.
Frauwallner, E.: Geschichte der indischen Philosophie. Salzburg I 1953, II 1956.
Glasenapp, H. v.: Entwicklungsstufen des indischen Denkens. Halle 1940.
— Die Philosophie der Inder. Stuttgart 1949.
Grousset, R.: Les philosophies indiennes, les systèmes. 2 Bde. Paris 1931.
Hiriyanna, M.: The essentials of Indian philosophy. London 1949.
Radhakrishnan, S.: Indian Philosophy. 2 Bde. London 1927.
Strauß, O.: Indische Philosophie. München 1925.
Suali, L.: Introduzione allo studio della filosofia indiana. Pavia 1913.
Tarn, W. W.: The Greeks in Bactria and India. Cambridge 1938.
Winternitz, M.: Geschichte der indischen Literatur. 3 Bde. Leipzig 1907/20.

6.122. Buddhism and Jinism

Bu-ston: History of buddhism. Üb. E. Obermiller. 2 Bde. Heidelberg 1931/32.
Conze, E.: Buddhism, its essence and development. Oxford 1951.
Glasenapp, H. v.: Der Jainismus. Eine indische Erlösungsreligion. Berlin 1925.
Hôbôgirin: Dictionnaire encyclopédique du bouddhisme d'après les sources chinoises et japonaises. Hrsg. Lévi u. Takakusu, red. Demiéville. Tokio 1929 ff.
Keith, A. B.: Buddhist philosophy in India and Ceylon. Oxford 1923.
Kern, H.: Geschiedenis van het Buddhisme. Haarlem 1882. Deutsch: Der Buddhismus und seine Geschichte in Indien. Üb. Jacobi. 2 Bde. Leipzig 1882 bis 1884. Franz.: Histoire du bouddhisme dans l'Inde. Üb. Huet. 2. Bde. Paris 1901—1903.
Kitayama, J.: Metaphysik des Buddhismus. Versuch einer philos. Interpret. der Lehre Vasubandhus u. seiner Schule. Stuttgart, Berlin 1934.
La Vallée Poussin, L. de: Le bouddhisme d'après les sources brahmaniques, in: Le Muséon 2, 1901.
— Bouddhisme, opinions sur l'histoire de la dogmatique. Paris 1909.
— Le dogme et la philosophie du bouddhisme. Paris 1930.
Oldenberg, H.: Buddha, sein Leben, seine Lehre, seine Gemeinde. 1. A. Stuttgart, Berlin 1881; 10.—12. A. Berlin 1923.
Rhys Davids. C. A. F.: Manual of buddhism for advanced students. London 1932.

BIBLIOGRAPHY

Rhys Davids, T. W.: Buddhism. London 1880 u. später. Deutsch (üb. Pfungst): Leipzig 1899.
Rosenberg, O.: Die Probleme der buddhistischen Philosophie. A. d. Russ. üb. v. E. Rosenberg. Heidelberg 1924.
Ščerbatskoy: s. Stcherbatsky.
Schubring, W.: Die Lehre der Jainas nach den alten Quellen dargestellt. Berlin, Leipzig 1907.
Stcherbatsky, Th.: The central conception of buddhism and the meaning of the word dharma. (Royal Asiatic Soc. Prize Publ.) 1923.
Takakusu, J.: The essentials of buddhist philosophy. Honolulu 1947.
Thomas, E. J.: The history of buddhistic thought. London 1933.
Tucci, G.: On some aspects of the doctrines of Maitreyanātha and Asaṅga. Calcutta 1930.

6.2. Editions of texts, translations *

Abhidhamma-piṭaka: s. Kathā-vatthu.
Ālambanaparīkṣā (von Dignāga). Hrsg., üb. u. erl. v. E. Frauwallner, in: WZKM 37, 1930, 174—194.
Annambhaṭṭa: s. Tarkasaṃgraha, Tarka-saṅgraha.
Anvīkṣānayatattvabodha: s. Nyāya-Sūtras.
Bhāradvāja: s. Nyāyavārttika.
Bhāṣāparicheda (von Viśvanātha Nyāyapañcānana Bhaṭṭa). Deutsche Üb. v. O. Strauß. Leipzig 1922.
Bhāṣya (von Praśastapāda): s. Praśastapāda.
Bhāṣyacandra: s. Nyāya-Sūtras.
Bhaṣyatātparyya: s. Kālīpada.
Bodhasiddhi: s. Nyāya-Sūtras.
Dharmakīrti: s. Sambandhaparīkṣā.
Dharmottara: „Das Werk über die Sonderung." Hrsg. u. üb. v. E. Frauwallner unt. d. Titel: „Beiträge zur Apohalehre", in: WZKM 44, 1937, 233—254 (Text) u. 255—278 (Übers.) u. 278—287 (Zus.-fssg.).
     S. a. Nyāyabinduṭīkā.
Dignāga (= Diṅnāga): Fragments from Diṅnāga. Ed. H. Randle. London 1926. Ergänzt v. G. Tucci. In: JRAS (GB), April 1928, 377—390.
     S. a. Ālambanaparīkṣā, Nyāyamukha, Nyāyapraveśa.
Dīpikā: s. Tarkasaṃgraha.
Divākara, Siddhasena: s. Nyāyāvatāra.
Gaṅgeśa: s. Tattva-cintāmaṇi.
Gautama: s. Nyāya-Sūtras.
Govardhana: s. Tarkabhasa.
Haribhadra: s. Nyāyapraveśa.
Jagadīśa: s. Kālīpada.
Janakī Nāth Bhattāchārya: s. Nyāya-siddhānta-mañjarī.
Jayanārāyaṇa: s. Vaiśeṣika-Sūtras.
Kālīpada: MM. Śri Kālīpada Tarkāchārya's edition of the Praśastapādabhāṣyam. Sanskrit Parishat Series 15. (Enthält auch Jagadīśas Sūktidīpikā und Kālīpadas Bhaṣyatātparyya, dies letzte in Bengali.)
Kaṇāda: s. Vaiśeṣika(-Sūtras).
Kārikāvalī (von Viśvanātha Nyāyapañcānana Bhaṭṭa). Ins Engl. üb. u. hrsg. v. E. Röer unt. d. Titel „Divisions of the Categories of the Nyaya Philosophy." (Bibliotheca Indica) Calcutta 1850.

* Die Werke sind hier, von wenigen Ausnahmen abgesehen, nach den Anfangsbuchstaben der Titel geordnet, nicht nach jenen der Namen der Verfasser. Diese Namen werden aber auch aufgeführt, und dabei wird auf die zugehörigen Titel verwiesen. — Uneinheitlichkeiten und Fehler in den Transkriptionen mag der Leser entschuldigen. Die Schwierigkeiten, die sich ergaben, waren für einen Nicht-Indologen wohl nicht ganz zu überwinden.

BIBLIOGRAPHY

— (von Viśvanātha Pañcānana Bhaṭṭācārya) mit des Verfassers eigenem Kommentar Siddhāntamuktāvalī aus dem Sanskr. üb. v. O. Strauß. Leipzig 1922.

(Kathā-vatthu). Points of Controversy or Subjects of Discourse being a translation of the Kathā-vatthu from the Abhidhamma-piṭaka, by Shwe Zan Aung and Mrs. Rhys Davids. London 1915.

Keśavamiśra: s. Tarkabhāṣā.

Kumārila Bhaṭṭa: s. Ślokavārttika.

Kunst, A.: Probleme der buddhistischen Logik in der Darstellung des Tattvasaṅgraha. Krakau 1939.

Laugākṣi Bhāskara: s. Tarkakaumudī.

Mathurānātha: s. Tattva-cintāmaṇi.

Mathurā Nātha Tarkavāgīśa: s. Vyāptipañcakarahasyam.

Milinda-pañha: The questions of King Milinda. Trans. from the Pāli by T. W. Rhys Davids. Oxford I: 1890, II: 1894.

— Die Fragen des Königs Menandros. Aus d. Pāli z. ersten Male ins Deutsche üb. v. Dr. F. O. Schrader. 1. Teil: Berlin, o. J. (1905).

— Die Fragen des Milindo. Aus d. Pāli zum 1. Mal vollständig ins Deutsche üb. v. Nyānatiloka. München-Neubiberg o. J. (1919?). (Nicht vollständig.) (g)

— Les questions de Milinda. Franz. Üb. d. ersten 3 Bücher des Milinda-pañha v. L. Finot. Paris 1923.

Mitabhāṣiṇī: s. Saptapadārthī.

Nyāyabhāṣya (von Vātsyāyana). Ins Engl. üb. v. G. Jhā, in: Indian Thought, Allahabad 1910—1920.

Nyāyabinduṭīkā (von Dharmottara). Zit. nach BL.

Nyāyadarśana (Gautama Sūtra) Bhāṣya (von Vātsyāyana). Sanskrit Text trans. and expl. in Bengali by P. Tarkavāgīśā. 5 Bde. Calcutta 1924.

Nyāyadīpa: s. Tarka Tāṇḍava.

Nyāyakandalī: s. Padārthadharmasaṅgraha, Praśastapāda.

Nyāyamukha of Dignāga. Cur. G. Tucci. Heidelberg 1930. (g)

Nyāyanibandhaprakāśa: s. Nyāya-Sūtras.

Nyāyapraveśa of Diṅnāga (?) I. Sanskrit Text ed. and rec. by N. D. Mironov, in: T'oung Pao (Leiden) 1931.

— Sanskrit Text with commentaries. Baroda 1930.

— Tibetan Text. Baroda 1927.

— (von Dignāga) and Haribhadra's commentary on it. Hrsg. N. D. Mironov, in: Festgabe f. R. Garbe, Erlangen 1927, 37—46.

Nyāya-siddhānta-mañjarī, by Janakī Nāth Bhattāchārya, in: The Pandit (1907—14).

Nyāya-Sūtras, of Gautama, with Vātsyāyana's Bhāṣya and Uddyotakara's Vārttika. Trans. into Engl. by M. G. Jhā. (g)

    I: Adhyāya I, with notes from Vācaspati Miśra's Tātparyaṭīkā and Udayanācārya's Pariśuddhi. Allahabad 1915.

    II: Adhyāya II, with notes from Vācaspati Miśra's „Nyāya-Vārttika-Tātparya", Udayana's Pariśuddhi and Raghuttama's Bhāṣyacandra. Allahabad 1917.

    III: Adhyāya III, with notes from Vācaspati Miśra's Tātparyaṭīkā, Udayanācārya's Pariśuddhi, Vardhamāna's Nyāyanibandhaprakāśa and Raghuttama's Bhāṣyacandra. Allahabad 1919.

    IV: Adhyāyas IV and V, with notes from Vācaspati Miśra's Tātparyaṭīkā, Udayanācārya's Pariśuddhi and Bodhasiddhi, Vardhamāna's Anvīkṣānayatattvabodha and Raghuttama's Bhāṣyacandra. Allahabad 1919.

— Üb. (engl.) v. Ballantyne. Allahabad 1850—1854.

— Text, Übers., Erl. und Glossar v. W. Ruben. Leipzig 1929. (g)

Nyāyavārttika (von Uddyotakara [Bhāradvāja]). Engl. Üb. v. G. Jhā, in: Indian Thought. Allahabad 1910—1920.

S. a. Nyāya-Sūtras.

Nyāya-Vārttika-Tātparya: s. Nyāya-Sūtras.

Nyāyāvatāra, the earliest Jaina work on pure logic, by Siddhasena Divākara,

BIBLIOGRAPHY

with Sanskrit Text and Comm. ed. with notes and engl. transl. by S. C. Vidyābhūṣana. Calcutta 1908.
Padārthacandrikā: s. Saptapadārthī.
Padārthadharmasaṅgraha of Praśastapāda, with the Nyāyakandalī of Śrī-
dhara. Trans. into Engl. by M. M. G. Jhā, in : The Pandit 25, 1903, 1—16; 26,
1904, 17—104; 27, 1905, 105—184; 28, 1906, 185—232; 29, 1907, 233 ff.;
30, 1908, 281 ff.; 31, 1909, 345 ff.; 32, 1910, 401 ff.; 35, 1913, 501 ff.; 36,
1914, 609 ff.; 37, 1915, 668 ff.
Padārtha-tattva-nirūpaṇa of Raghunātha Śiromaṇi, with the commentaries of
Raghudeva and Rāmabhadra Sārvabhauma, in: The Pandit (1903—05).
Parameśvara, Ṛṣiputra: s. Ṛṣiputra Parameśvara.
Pariśuddhi: s. Nyāya-Sūtras.
Praśastapāda: The Bhāṣya of Praśastapāda together with the Nyāyakandalī
of Śrīdhara, ed. by Vindhyeśvarīprasāda Dvivedin. Benares 1895.
S. a. Kālīpada, Padārthadharmasaṅgraha.
Rāghavendratīrtha: s. Tarka Tāṇḍava.
Raghudeva : s. Padārtha-tattva-nirūpaṇa.
Raghunātha Śiromaṇi: s. Padārtha-tattva-nirūpaṇa.
Raghuttama: s. Nyāya-Sūtras.
Rāmabhadra Sārvabhauma : s. Padārtha-tattva-nirūpaṇa.
Ṛṣiputra Parameśvara: s. Tattvavibhāvanā.
Sambandhaparīkṣā (von Dharmakīrti), hrsg. u. üb. v. E. Frauwallner, in: WZKM
41, 1934, 261—300.
Sāṃkhyakārikā: s. Sāṃkhyatattvakaumudī.
Sāṃkhyatattvakaumudī, ein Kommentar zur Sāṃkhyakārikā (von Vācaspati
Miśra). Hrsg. u. ins Engl. üb. v. G. Jhā. Bombay 1896.
— In deutscher Üb. nebst einer Einl. über das Alter und die Herkunft der
Sāṃkhya-Philosophie v. R. Garbe. München 1891. Auch: Abhdlg. d. kgl.
Bayer. Akad. d. Wiss., I. Cl., XIX. Bd., III. A.
Sandarbha: s. Saptapadārthī.
Śaṅkara Miśra: s. Vaiśeṣika-Sūtras.
Saptapadārthī of Śivāditya, with translation, Mitabhāṣiṇī, Padārthacandrikā,
and Sandarbha. Calcutta Sanskrit Series 8.
Sārvabhauma: s. Padārtha-tattva-nirūpaṇa.
Sarvadarśanasaṃgraha. Das vom Buddhismus handelnde Kapitel ist üb. in:
La Vallée Poussin, L. de, Le bouddhisme ... (6.122.).
Siddhāntamuktāvalī: s. Kārikāvalī.
Siddhasena Divākara: s. Nyāyāvatāra.
Śiromaṇi: s. Padārtha-tattva-nirūpaṇa.
Śivadatta Miśra: s. Vyāptipañcakarahasyam.
Śivāditya: s. Saptapadārthī.
Ślokavārttika (von Kumārila Bhaṭṭa). Engl. Üb. v. G. Jhā, in: Bibliotheca In-
dica. Calcutta 1900—1908.
Śrīdhara: s. Padārthadharmasaṅgraha, Praśastapāda.
Sūktidīpikā: s. Kālīpada.
Tarkabhāṣā (von Keśavamiśra). Oxford, Bodleian Library, Sanskrit-Hs. 170 d.
(Winternitz 1307). 1613.
— with the commentary of Govardhana, hrsg. v. Sh. M. Paranjape. Poona
1894, 2. A. 1909.
— or Exposition of Reasoning. Trans. into Engl. by M. G. Jhā, in: Indian
Thought. Allahabad 1910.
(—) An Indian primer of philosophy or The Tarkabhāṣā of Keśavamiśra. Trans.
with an intr. and notes by Poul Tuxen. Kopenhagen 1914.
Tarkācārya: s. Kālīpada.
Tarkakaumudī (von Laugākṣi Bhāskara). Aus d. Sanskr. üb. v. E. Hultzsch,
in: Zeitschr. d. dt. morgenld. Ges. 61, 763.
Tarka-saṅgraha (von Annambhaṭṭa). Ed. with notes by M. R. Bodâs. (Bombay
Sanskrit Series.) 1918.

BIBLIOGRAPHY

(—) A primer of Indian logic according to Annambhaṭṭa's Tarkasaṃgraha. Hrsg. M. S. Kuppuswami Sastri. Madras 1932. 2. A. o. J.

(—) Le compendium des Topiques (Tarka-Saṃgraha). Texte, trad., comm. par A. Foucher. Paris 1949. (g)

Tarkasaṃgraha (von Annambhaṭṭa) mit des Verfassers Dīpikā. Aus d. Sanskr. üb. v. E. Hultzsch. Abhdlg. d. kgl. Ges. d. Wiss. zu Göttingen, phil.-hist. Kl., Neue Folge, Bd. IX, 1907, Berlin 1907. (g)

Tarka Tāṇḍava of Śrī Vyāsatīrtha with the comm., Nyāyadīpa of Śrī Rāghavendratīrtha. Ed. by D. Srinivasachar, V. V. Madhwachar, and V. A. Vyasachar. Mysore 1932.

Tātparyaṭīkā: s. Nyāya-Sūtras.

Tattvabindu by Vācaspatimiśra with Tattvavibhāvanā by Ṛṣiputra Parameśvara, ed. by V. A. Ramaswami Śastri. (Annamalai Univ. Sanskrit Series 3) Chidambaram 1936.

Tattva-cintāmaṇi of Gaṅgeśa, with the commentary of Mathurānātha: Tattvacintāmaṇi-rahasya. Bibliotheca Indica 1892—1900.

Tattva-cintāmaṇi-rahasya: s. Tattva-cintāmaṇi.

Tattvasaṅgraha: s. Kunst, A.: Probleme ...

Tattvavibhāvanā: s. Tattvabindu.

Tucci, G.: Pre-Diṅnāga Buddhist texts on logic from Chinese sources. (Gaekwad Oriëntal Series) Baroda 1926.

Udayana: s. Nyāya-Sūtras.

Udayanācārya: s. Nyāya-Sūtras.

Uddyotakara: s. Nyāya-Sūtras, Nyāyavārttika.

Vācaspatimiśra: s. Nyāya-Sūtras, Sāṃkhyatattvakaumudī, Tattvabindu.

Vaiśeṣika. Die Lehrsprüche der Vaiśeṣika-Philosophie von Kaṇāda. Aus d. Sanskr. üb. u. erl. v. Dr. E. Röer, in: Zeitschr. d. dt. morgenländ. Ges. 21, 1867, 309—420; 22, 1868, 383—442. (g)

— -Sūtras of Kaṇāda, with the comm. of Śaṅkara Miśra and extraits from the texts of Jayanārāyaṇa. Transl. by Nandalal Sinma. Allahabad 1911.

Vardhamāna: s. Nyāya-Sūtras.

Vātsyāyana: s. Nyāyabhāṣya, Nyāyadarśana Bhāṣya, Nyāya-Sūtras.

Viśvanātha Nyāyapañcānana Bhaṭṭa: s. Bhāṣāparriccheda, Kārikāvalī.

Viśvanātha Pañcānana Bhaṭṭācārya: s. Kārikāvalī.

Vyāptipañcakarahasyam of Mathurā Nātha Tarkavāgīśa with supercommentary of Śivadatta Miśra. Kashi Sanskrit Series 64.

Vyāsatīrtha: s. Tarka Tāṇḍava.

6.3. Works on the whole of Indian logic, or on large periods

Gupta, S. N.: The nature of inference in Indian logic, in: Mind 6, 1895, 159 bis 175.

Ingalls, D. H. H.: Materials for the study of Navya-Nyāya logic. Cambridge (Mass.), London 1951 (= MNN).

— The comparison of Indian and Western philosophy, in: The journ. of Oriental research (Madras) 22 (Sept. 1952—June 1953), Parts I—IV, Madras 1954, 1—11.

Jacobi, H.: Die indische Logik, in: Nachr. d. kgl. Ges. d. Wiss. zu Göttingen aus dem Jahre 1901, phil.-hist. Kl., 458—482.

Jhā, G.: Sadho Lal Lectures on Nyāya, in: Indian Thought, Allahabad 1910 bis 1920.

Keith, A. B.: Indian logic and atomism; an exposition of Nyāya and Vaiśeṣika systems. Oxford 1921.

Randle, H. N.: Indian logic in the early schools. Oxford 1930.

— A note on the Indian syllogism, in: Mind 33, 1924, 398—414.

Ščerbatskoy: s. Stcherbatsky.

Schayer, St.: Studien zur indischen Logik I: Der indische und der aristotelische

BIBLIOGRAPHY

Syllogismus, in: Bull. int. de l'Ac. Pol. des Sciences et des Lettres, Cl. de philol., Cl. d' hist. et de philos., année 1932 (ersch. 1933), 98—102.
— Studien zur indischen Logik II: Altindische Antizipationen der Aussagenlogik. Ebda., année 1933 (ersch. 1934), 90—96.
— Über die Methode der Nyāya-Forschung, in: Festschr. M. Winternitz, Leipzig 1933, 247—257.
— Staroindyjskie antycypacje logiki współczesnej (Altindische Antizipationen der modernen Logik), in: Ruch fiioz. 13, 1935, 4.
Stasiak, St.: Fallacies and their classification according to the early hindu logicians, in: Rocz. Orient. (Lemberg) 6, 1929, 191—198.
Stcherbatsky, Th.: Buddhist logic. 2 Bde. Leningrad 1932. (Bd. I = BL)
Sugiura, S.: Hindu logic as preserved in China and Japan. Philadelphia 1900.
Ui, H.: Der Ursprung der Trairūpya-Liṅga-Theorie in der indischen Logik, in: Commemoration volume, the 25th ann. of the found. of the professorship of science of religion in Tokyo Imp. Univ., ed. by the Celebration Committee, Tokyo 1934, 343—345.
Vidyābhūṣaṇa, S. C.: A history of Indian logic, ancient, mediaeval and modern schools. Calcutta 1921.
— Indian logic. Mediaeval school. Calcutta 1909.

6.4. Detailed questions

Athalye-Bodas: The Tarka-Saṃgraha of Annambhaṭṭa. Bombay 1897.
Bhattacaryya, Dineścandra: Baṅgalir Sarasvat Avadān, pratham bhāg. Baṅge Navyanyāyacarccā. Calcutta 1358 (= A. D. 1951).
Bhattacharya, V.: Einleitung zu: (Dignāgas) Nyāyapraveśa. Tibetan Text. Baroda 1927.
— The Nyāyapraveśa of Dinnāga, in: The Ind. Hist. Quart. (Calcutta) 3, 1927, 152—160.
Bhīmāccārya, Jhalakīkar: Nyāyakośa or Dictionary of the technical terms of the Nyāya philosophy. Poona 3. A. 1928.
Chatterjee, S. C.: The Nyāya theory of knowledge: a critical study of some problems of logic and metaphysics. Calcutta 2. A. 1950.
— The theory of Pakṣatā in Indian logic, in: The philos. quart. 14, 1938, 52—59.
Dhruva, A. B.: Einleitung zu: (Dignāgas) Nyāyapraveśa, Sanskrit Text with commentaries. Baroda 1930.
Faddegon, B.: The Vaiçeṣika-system, described with the help of the oldest texts. Amsterdam 1918.
Frauwallner, E.: Dignāga und anderes, in: Festschr. M. Winternitz, Leipzig 1933, 237—242.
— Zu den Fragmenten buddhistischer Logiker in Nyāyavārttikam, in: WZKM 40, 1933, 281—304.
Hacker, P.: Jayantabhaṭṭa und Vācaspatimiśra, ihre Zeit und ihre Bedeutung für die Chronologie des Vedānta, in: Beitr. z. ind. Philos. u. Altertumskunde, W. Schubring z. 70. Geburtstag dargebr., Hamburg 1951, 162 ff.
Ingalls, D. H. H.: Śaṅkara on the question: Whose is avidyā?, in: Philosophy East and West (Honolulu) 3, April 1953, 69—72.
Iyengar, H. R. R.: Kumārila and Diṅnāga, in: The Ind. Hist. Quart. (Calcutta) 3, 1927, 603—606.
— Vasubandhu and the Vadavidhi. Ebda. 5, 1929, 81—86.
Keith, A. B.: The authorship of the Nyāyapraveśa. Ebda. 4, 1928, 14—22.
— Vasubandhu and the Vadavidhi. Ebda. 221—227.
La Vallée Poussin, L. de: L'Abhidharmakośa de Vasubandhu. 6 Bde. Paris 1923—1931.
Naik, B. S.: The theory of predication in Vedānta, in: The philos. quart. 14, 1938, 214—220.
Raju, P. T.: The principle of four-corned negation in Indian Philosophy, in: The Review of Metaphysics 7, 1953, 114—125.

Regamey, C.: Die Religionen Indiens, in: Christus und die Religionen der Erde, hrsg. v. F. König, Bd. III, Wien 1951, 73—227.
Ščerbatskoy: s. Stcherbatsky.
Sen, S.: A study on Mathurānātha's Tattva-Cintāmaṇi-Rahasya. (Diss. Amsterdam) 1924.
Stcherbatsky, Th.: Erkenntnistheorie und Logik nach der Lehre der späteren Buddhisten. Üb. O. Strauß. München-Neubiberg 1924.
Tubianski, M.: On the authorship of Nyāyapraveśa, in: Bull. de l'Acad. d. Sciences de l'URSS 1926.
Tucci, G.: Is the Nyāyapraveśa by Diṅnāga?, in: JRAS (GB?), January 1928, 7—13.
— On the fragments from Diṅnāga. Ebda. April 1928, 377—390.
— Buddhist logic before Diṅnāga. Ebda. July 1929, 451—488.
— Notes on the Nyāyapraveśa by Śaṅkarasvāmin. Ebda. 1931, 381—413.
Ui, H.: Seshiu no inmyosetsu (Die Logik des Vasubandhu), in: Journ. of the Taisho Univ. 1930.
Vidyābhūṣaṇa, S. C.: The Nyāyasūtras of Gotama. Allahabad 1909.
Windisch, E.: Über das Nyāyabhāṣya. Leipzig 1889.

6.5. Chinese sophistic and methods of discussion

Francke, H.: Sinologie. Bern 1953.
Hu Shish (Suh Hu): The development of the logical method in ancient China. Shanghai 1. A. 1922, 2. A. 1928.
Kou Pao-Koh, J.: Deux sophistes chinois: Houei Che et Kong-Souen Long. Paris 1953.
Maspero, M. H.: Notes sur la logique de Mo-tseu et son école, in: T'oung Pao I927.
Masson-Oursel, P.: La démonstration confucienne, in: Rev. de l'hist. des religions 67, 1913, 49—54.
S. a. BL I 52—55.

Additions to Bibliography see p. 567

III. INDICES

2. INDEX OF LOGICAL SYMBOLS

References containing decimal points are to texts or commentaries on them; others are to pages

3. INDEX OF MNEMONICS

References are given as in Index 2

4. SUBJECT INDEX

References are given as in Index 2

INDICES

c., 53.05; c. sufficient to cause illation, 52.03; verbal c., 52.03

Combination: 10.33, 11.19, 11.22, 21.18, 32.34, 38.17, 42.22, 279; c. of relatives, 47.15

Combinatorial: c. method, 38.07, 258, cf. 315; c. arguments, see argument(s), combinatorial

Combinatory logic: see logic combinatorial

Combined in: 52.03

Commentaries: syncretizing tendency of c., 134

Commutative (process): see addition, logical, is c.

Comparative (the): 31.01

Comparison: 52.05, 52.14, 431

Completion: need for c., 42.03, 42.09

Complex: c. of ideas, 41.11; of signs, 41.11; c. signifiable, 29.17

Composite and divided sense: 29.10 ff., 224–231

Composite modal proposition: see proposition, modal, composite

Composition: fallacies of division and c., 29.10

Comprehension: 36.10, 40.13, 258; c. and extension, 36.09 ff.

Computation: 38.04

Concept: 1.07, 27.01, 35.40, 36.08 f., 36.17, 42.09, 48.21, 48.24, 48.32; c. and class, 45.02; c. and predicate, 48.21; c. as function, 45.02; existence as note of a c., 39.12; formed (constructed) c., 39.03; fundamental, ultimate, indefinable c., 46.19; mental c., 35.40; number and c., 39.10; c. of second order, 39.12; primitive c., see idea, primitive; relation and c., 48.21; term and c., 48.21; the c. Φ (ξ), 46.13; universal c., 36.10

Conception(s): 16.20 f., 19.07

Conceptus objectivus, subjectivus: 110 to 111

Conclusion: 14.02 f., 21.01, 31.40, 43.30, 51.07, 52.06, 53.09, 53.23, 53.26, 69, 431; c. from possible premisses, 33.21; c. potentially among premisses, 22.15 ff.; truth of the c., 38.25; universal c., 24.08

Conclusive argument, see argument, conclusive

Concomitance: 1.15–1.17, 53.21, 53.23

Condition: 20.07, 24.09, 30.04; c. in X, 46.22; c.s of the 4th figure, 32.26; c.s of truth and falsity, 42.25, 42.29 f.

Conditional: c. connective, see connective, c.; c. proposition, see proposition, c.; c. syllogism, see syllogism, conditional; truth of c., 30.17

Conjunction: 1.13, 19.10. 26.09, 122; see also connection

Conjunctive (the): 121

Conjuncts: number of c., 35.39

Connection: 19.09, 19.15, 20.19, 30.11, 42.20, 53.09, 432; c. between terms, 30.07; causal c. between two contents, 41.12; inseparable c., 53.09; necessary c., 15, 18; c. of two essences in an individual, 440; principle of c. of terms, 34.06

Connective(s): 19.15; conditional c., 30.10; c. expressing a reason, 30.10; disjunctive c., 1.14; implicative, separative, conjunctive c., 19.15; propositional c., xiii, 1.14; rational c., 39.10; term. c., xiii, 1.14; c. which shows, 19.15

"Connexive": 20.09

Consequences: 15.01, 20.20, 21.18, 26.12, 27.13, 29.14, 30.01 ff., 31.15, 31.20, 35.55, 41.20, 150, 152, 156, 161 ff., 257; a .c. is a proposition, 30.10; accidental c., 30.07; active, passive c., 35.12; c. based on term-logic relationships, 30.07; complete c., 20.211; c. conceived as proposition in accord with Stoic definition. 30.10; essential c., 30.07; formal c., 30.12 ff., 30.16, 31.22, 31.39, 35.09, 159; material c., 30.12 ff.; natural c., 30.07, 31.02, 31.10; necessity of c., 29.11; non-syllogistic c., 30.11; c.s of the set x, 38.30; permissive c., 30.16; c. pertaining to propositional-logic and to term-logic; 30.07, 198; rule of c., 30.13, 31.14 ff.; simple c., 30.15, 31.40; simply true c., 30.12; theory of c.s, xii; c. *ut nunc,* 30.10, 30.15 f., 31.40, 32.42, 198

Consequent: 1.05, 1.07, 11.24, 20.05, 29.11, 30.04, 30.07, 30.10, 30.17, 31.02, 31.05, 31.09, 31.11, 31.13 ff., 31.18 ff., 31.34 f., 31.39, 41.12, 42.36, 43.21; accidental and natural conditional c.s, 24.10; fallacy of c., 11.24; c. incompatible with antecedent, 20.09 f., 30.17; necessity of the c., 29.11; possible c., 31.19; c. potentially contained in antecedent, 20.13; c. understood in the antecedent, 30.17; refutation which de-

p., 227; possible and compossible p., 33.21; p. potentially containing three terms, 17.07; reversal of p.s, 13.21; *see also* premiss(es), transposition of; single p., 21.17, 21.19; singular p., 256; p. taken in the composite and in the divided sense; 227; transposition of p.s, 32.14; *see also* premiss(es), reversal of; truth of p.s, 10.06; universal negative p., 17.09, 24.07; *see also* proposition; sentence
Preposition(s): 1.13
Present: 27.14, 28.01, 28.07 ff., 28.17, 29.01, 30.12
Presupposition: all p.s formulated expressly and without gaps, 283
Prime: the even p. other than 2, 46.21; p. number, *see* number, prime
Principle: p. inexpressible symbolically, 43.25; p. of association, 43.29; p. of addition, 43.27; p. of assertion, 43.36; p. of contradiction, 12.19 ff., 31.17, 40.06, 43.38, 46.17; p. of exportation, 43.36; p. of factors, 43.36; p. of indiscernibles, 16.14, 357; *cf.* 16.20 ff.; p. of permutation, 43.28; p. of summation, 43.30; p. of syllogism, 43.33; p. of tautology, 43.26; p. of *tertium exclusum*, 12.30 ff., 39.17, 293; p. of transposition, 43.33
Privation: 12.02
Privative: p. axiom, *see* axiom, p.; p. qualification, *see* qualification, p.
'Probable': 10.03, 44
Probability: 42.01; calculus of p., 49.08; degrees of p., 49.08
Probandum: 52.10 f., 53.10, 53.17, 53.18, 54.05
Probans: 52.12
Procedure: 'hypothetical' p., 88
Process of criticism: 11.01; *see also pons Asinorum*
Product: 42.03, 42.36, 43.35 f., 44.03, 49.03, 21, 442; middle term as a p., 12.281; p. of classes, 45.10; p. of propositions, 30.11, 45.10; relative p., 47.04, 47.14, 47.24, 384
Progression: 38.14
Pronoun: 27.01
Proof: 21.01, 49.12, 52.03; *see also* demonstration; p. by setting out (terms), 13.13, 68; complete p., 477; direct p., 14.10 ff.; formalized p., 43.45; formalized methods of p., 49.12; indirect p., 16.33, 77 ff.; theory of p., 38.28
Proper name, *see* name, proper

Property: 1.19, 11.08, 11.13, 14.03, 27.01, 44.26, 46.15, 46.28, 134; all p.s, 48.26; hereditary p., 47.31 ff.; imposed p., 443; nth order p.s, 48.24; p.s of terms, 149, 152, 156, 163 f.; *see also proprietates terminorum;* predicative p.s, 48.24; second-order p., 48.24; specific p., 443
Proportion: 28.18, 38.14, 179
Proportionality: 28.18, 179
Proposition: 19.06, 19.12, 31.35, 35.39, 36.08, 41.11, 41.20, 42.07, 42.12, 43.16, 43.18, 45.01, 51.07, 52.03, 52.06, 53.09, 53.26, 20, 47; *see also* premiss; sentence; p. about propositions, 48.11; all p., 48.22; p. alone is true or false, 10.34; analysis of p.s, 11.13, 16.261, 27.20, 29.02 ff., 17, 42, 43, 80, 322; extensional a. of p.s, 29.02, 29.03; p. and denotation, 46.17; p. and meaning, 46.19; p.s and objects, 41.01; p. and problem, 11.02 f.; p. and proposition (Satz), 44.14; p. and propositional function, 46.19; p. and sentence, 10.34; p. and terms, *see* term(s), and propositions; p. as true, 19.12, 20.09 f.; assertoric, p., 29.01; atomic or elementary p., 41.01, 43.25, 48.21; bad p., 20.09; categorical p., 29.01; 31.22 f.; c.p. and conditional p., 44.11; causal p., 31.01, 122; *see also* axiom, causal; class-propositions, 47.15, 432–433; comparative, p., 31.01; complete p., 42.08; composite p., 30.10, 224; compound p., 41.06; p.s concerning the *dictum* and concerning the thing, 29.09; conditional p., 11.24, 20.07, 21.02, 21.06, 30.10, 31.01, 41.14, 44.11; definition of c.p., 20.14, 31.19, 43.24; truth of a c. p., 30.17; connected p., 20.05, 20.07 f., 20.09 f., 20.13, 21.02, 22.21; contingent p., 30.12; conversion of p.s, 32.08; *see also* sentences, conversion of; c. of modal p.s, 15.17, 17.12 ff., 33.13 ff.; c. of necessary p., 15.163, 33.18 f.; copulative p., 20.19, 30.01, 31.22, 31.27 f., 31.30; affirmative c. p., 31.25 f., 31.29, 31.35 f.; negative c.p., 31.35, 43.35 ff.; definite p., 44.10; disjunctive p., 20.14 ff., 20.17 f., 30.19 f., 31.01, 31.10, 31.22, 31.32 ff., 31.39, 34.07; affirmative d. p., 31.31, 31.35; negative d. p., 31.36; quasi-d. p., 20.18; sub- d.p., 20.18; divided sense of p.,

BIBLIOGRAPHY

ADDITIONS TO BIBLIOGRAPHY

1.22
Church, A.: Introduction to mathematical logic, I. Princeton 1956.
2.3
Meredith, C. A.: The figures and moods of the *n*-term Aristotelian syllogism, in: Dominican Studies 6, 1953, 42–47.
3.92
Brettle, S.: San Vicente Ferrer und sein literarischer Nachlaß. Münster i. W. 1924.
Gorce, M.: Les bases de l'étude historique de Saint Vicente Ferrer. Paris 1935.
Henry, D. P.: Numerically definite reasoning in the *Cur Deus Homo*, in: Dominican Studies 6, 1953, 48–55.
Miralles, M. G.: Escritos filosoficos de San Vicente Ferrer, in: Estudios Filosoficos (Santander) 4, 1955, 279–284.
Prior, A. N.: The *Parva Logicalia* in modern dress, in: Dominican Studies 5, 1952, 78–87.
— On some *consequentiae* in Walter Burleigh, in: The New Scholasticism 27, 1953, 433–446.
Wyclif, Johannes: Tractatus de Logica. Ed. M. H. Dziewicki, London, 1893–9.
4.2
Hocking, W. E.: Two extensions of the use of graphs in elementary logic, in: University of California Publications in Philosophy, 2, 1909, no. 2, 31–44.
Johnson, W. E.: Logic, Part I 1921, Part II 1922, Part III 1924, Cambridge.
Łuszczewska-Romahnowa, S.: An analysis and generalization of Venn's diagrammatic decision procedure, in: Studia Logica (Warsaw) 1, 1953, 245–6. English summary of Polish, 185–213, and Russian, 214–244.
Reid, Th.: The item listed originally appeared in Home's History of Man (Edinburgh 1774) as an appendix to vol. 2, books 3, sketch 1, 168–241, the extract 2.04 occurring on p. 193.
Sturmius, J. C.: Universalia euclidea, Haag 1661.
5.2
Church, A.: A note on the Entscheidungsproblem, in: JSL 1, 1936, 40–41, 101–102.
— The calculi of lambda conversion, Princeton 1941.
Curry, H. B.: A simplification of the theory of combinators, in: Synthèse (Bussum) 7, 1948/49, 391–399.
Feys, R.: Logistiek I, Antwerp 1944.
— La technique de la logique combinatoire, in: Rev. Phil. de Louvain 44, 1946, 74–103, 237–270.
Peirce, C. S.: Collected Papers etc. This item should comprise also vol. II.
Rosenbloom, P.: The elements of mathematical logic, New York 1950.
Rosser, J. B.: New sets of postulates for combinatory logic, in: JSL 7, 1942, 18–27.
5.327
Anon.: Jan Lukasiewicz (1878–1956), in: Studia Logica (Poznań) 5, 1957, 7–11.
Sobociński, B.: In memoriam Jan Lukasiewicz, in: Philosophical Studies (Maynooth) 6, 1956, 3–49.
5.51
Celebration of the Centenary of The Laws of Thought by George Boole, in: Proceedings of the Royal Irish Academy, 57, A, 6, 1955, comprising the following:
Taylor, G.: George Boole, 1815–1864, 66
Rhees, R.: George Boole as student and teacher, 74.
Hackett, F. E.: The method of George Boole, 79.
Thomas, I.: Boole's concept of science, 88.
Feys, R.: Boole as a logician, 97.
— Boolean methods of development and interpretation, 107.
Brouwer, L. E. J.: The effect of intuitionism on classical algebra of logic, 113
Rosser, J. B.: Boole and the concept of a function, 117.
Craven, T. L.: An engineering application of Boolean algebra, 121.

CPSIA information can be obtained
at www.ICGtesting.com
Printed in the USA
BVOW08s1718171117
500588BV00012B/368/P